"Adam Smith's work revolves around the contradiction between the assumption of an impartial spectator and self-interest as the primary motivation for human action. *The Individual and the Other in Economic Thought* examines the tension between moral and rational agency, by considering the historical development of economic theory and its ethical background and implications."

Vangelis Chiotis, Anglia Ruskin University, UK

The Individual and the Other in Economic Thought

The Philosophy of Economics primarily considers the economic agent as a moral subject. Economics, however, has long overlooked the agent's moral – that is to say, reasonable – dimension, to focus instead on the strictly rational. This volume seeks to address this neglected topic through exploring the Individual and the Other.

The economic agent refers to "himself" (herself) in terms of his desire and passions, yet also refers to others besides himself. For the rational economic agent, what is the nature of this relationship with the Other? Should it not be understood as undergoing a transformation once we come to consider the economic agent as a *reasonable* being? Through what process does the Other pass from being an instrument at the disposal of a rational agent to being an end in itself for a moral subject? In other words, how does another become "an Other"? These questions are behind the re-examination of certain fundamental notions which takes place in this book, an examination which involves a re-reading of certain great authors. With contributions from authors around the world, this work is divided into three main parts. The first deals with individuals from the history of economic thought such as Adam Smith, Karl Marx and Hannah Arendt; this is then followed by a thematic section in which the concepts of recognition and subjectivity are questioned in a market context. Finally, the third part offers an analysis of the issue of "the Individual and the Other" in different fields of the recent economic analysis including game theory, decision theory or social choice.

The Individual and the Other in Economic Thought aims to help the reader better understand how the relationship between the Individual and the Other has been conceived, conceptualized and framed in economic analysis. It will be of great use to graduate students, scholars and any reader interested in this crucial issue.

Ragip Ege is Emeritus Professor in Economics at the University of Strasbourg, France, and a member of the Bureau d'Economie Théorique et Appliquée (BETA). His recent research activities focus on the problems of ethics and justice and he is particularly interested in Hegelian political and economic thought.

Herrade Igersheim is a CNRS Research Associate Professor at the University of Strasbourg, France, and Deputy Director of the Bureau d'Economie Théorique et Appliquée (BETA). Her research focuses on economics and philosophy, welfare economics and experimental economics devoted to voting methods.

Routledge INEM Advances in Economic Methodology
Series Edited by Esther-Mirjam Sent, the University of Nijmegen, the Netherlands.

The field of economic methodology has expanded rapidly during the last few decades. This expansion has occurred in part because of changes within the discipline of economics, in part because of changes in the prevailing philosophical conception of scientific knowledge, and also because of various transformations within the wider society. Research in economic methodology now reflects not only developments in contemporary economic theory, the history of economic thought, and the philosophy of science; but it also reflects developments in science studies, historical epistemology, and social theorizing more generally. The field of economic methodology still includes the search for rules for the proper conduct of economic science, but it also covers a vast array of other subjects and accommodates a variety of different approaches to those subjects.

The objective of this series is to provide a forum for the publication of significant works in the growing field of economic methodology. Since the series defines methodology quite broadly, it will publish books on a wide range of different methodological subjects. The series is also open to a variety of different types of works: original research monographs, edited collections, as well as republication of significant earlier contributions to the methodological literature. The International Network for Economic Methodology (INEM) is proud to sponsor this important series of contributions to the methodological literature.

Philosophy of Mathematics and Economics
Image, Context and Perspective
Thomas A. Boylan and Paschal F. O'Gorman

The Individual and the Other in Economic Thought
Edited by Ragip Ege and Herrade Igersheim

Economics and Performativity
Exploring Limits, Theories and Cases
Nicolas Brisset

For a list of titles please visit: www.routledge.com/Routledge-INEM-Advances-in-Economic-Methodology/book-series/SE0630

The Individual and the Other in Economic Thought

Edited by Ragip Ege and Herrade Igersheim

Routledge
Taylor & Francis Group
LONDON AND NEW YORK

First published 2019
by Routledge
2 Park Square, Milton Park, Abingdon, Oxon OX14 4RN

and by Routledge
52 Vanderbilt Avenue, New York, NY 10017, USA

First issued in paperback 2020

Routledge is an imprint of the Taylor & Francis Group, an informa business

British Library Cataloguing-in-Publication Data
A catalogue record for this book is available from the British Library

Library of Congress Cataloging-in-Publication Data
Names: Ege, Ragip, editor. | Igersheim, Herrade, editor.
Title: The individual and the other in economic thought : an introduction / edited by Ragip Ege and Herrade Igersheim.
Description: Abingdon, Oxon ; New York, NY : Routledge, 2018. | Series: Routledge INEM advances in economic methodology | Includes bibliographical references and index.
Identifiers: LCCN 2018009648 (print) | LCCN 2018011359 (ebook) | ISBN 9781315113258 (Ebook) | ISBN 9781138080706 (hardback : alk. paper)
Subjects: LCSH: Economics—Philosophy.
Classification: LCC HB72 (ebook) | LCC HB72 .I525 2018 (print) | DDC 330.01—dc23
LC record available at https://lccn.loc.gov/2018009648

ISBN 13: 978-0-367-58822-9 (pbk)
ISBN 13: 978-1-138-08070-6 (hbk)

Typeset in Times New Roman
by Apex CoVantage, LLC

Contents

Contributors

Catherine Audard, London School of Economics, UK.

Edgardo Bucciarelli, Università degli Studi G.D'Annunzio Chieti Pescara, Italy.

Daniel Diatkine, Université d'Evry-Val-d'Essonne, France.

Jean-Pierre Dupuy, Stanford University, USA.

Ragip Ege, Université de Strasbourg, France.

Ghislain Fourny, ETH Zürich, Switzerland.

Robert Gallagher, Eudemian Institute, Lebanon; Honorary Research Associate, Institute for Philosophy and Social Theory, University of Belgrade, Serbia.

Nizar Hariri, Université Saint-Joseph de Beyrouth, Lebanon.

Herrade Igersheim, CNRS, France.

Gilles Jacoud, University of Saint-Etienne, France.

André Lapidus, Université Paris 1 Panthéon-Sorbonne, France.

Lauren Larrouy, Université Côte d'Azur, France.

Nicola Mattoscio, Università degli Studi G.D'Annunzio Chieti Pescara, Italy.

Francis Munier, Université de Strasbourg, France.

Jonathan Perraton, University of Sheffield, UK.

Tony Ernesto Persico, Ministry of Economy and Finance, Italy.

Thi Kim Cuong Pham, Université de Strasbourg, France.

Cyrielle Poiraud, Université de Strasbourg, France.

Marlyse Pouchol, Université de Reims, France.

Stéphane Reiche, MINES ParisTech, France.

Sylvie Rivot, Université de Strasbourg, France.

Stefano Solari, University of Padua, Italy.

Riccardo Soliani, Università di Genova, Italy.

Iona Tarrant was a lecturer at the University of Sheffield, UK.

Fabrice Tricou, Université Paris Nanterre, France.

Eleonora Viganò, Institute of Biomedical Ethics and History of Medicine, University of Zurich, Switzerland.

Benoît Walraevens, Université de Caen Normandie, France.

Jean Mercier Ythier, Sorbonne Universités Panthéon-Assas, France.

The Individual and the Other in economic thought

An introduction

Ragip Ege and Herrade Igersheim

Today, one of the main concerns of economics is to deal both with the economic aspect of the Individual, traditionally seen as *rational*, and with her moral dimension, which focuses instead on the *reasonable*. We mean by 'rational' a behaviour exclusively motivated by the self-regarding preferences of the subject, while 'reasonable' refers to the relationships she has with the others. Many economists are now expressly determined to question the nature of these relationships and to attempt to articulate the rational and reasonable dimensions of an individual, both on a conceptual level as well as on an analytical one. The contributions of this collective book aim at examining in what conditions one comes to consider the others as ends and not as means and how the self- and other-regarding attitudes can be conciliated.[1] They thus join the efforts of a long theoretical and philosophical tradition from Smith to Hegel aiming at reconciliating the particular and the universal.

Such questioning led us to consider the philosophical dimension of economics – it led us, in other words, towards a re-examination of certain fundamental notions, and to a re-reading of certain great authors. The chapters are gathered into three parts. The first part is textual and deals with several great authors who made history of economic thought in relation with the issue 'The Individual and the Other' (Smith, Saint-Simon, Mill, Fourier, Marx, Proudhon, Arendt, Sen). The second part is thematic and gathers chapters which especially question the concepts of recognition and subjectivity in a market context. The third part of the book is analytic and examines the issue 'The Individual and the Other' in different fields of the recent economic analysis as game theory, decision theory or social choice.

The first part of our book "The Individual and the Other in the History of Thought" starts with a chapter entitled "From Vanity to the Love of Systems, from Luxury to the Accumulation of Capital, from the Gaze of Others to the Endless Process". Daniel Diatkine and Benoît Walraevens deal with the parable of the 'poor man's son' which is one of the most commented passages of the *Theory of Moral Sentiments*. The authors claim that the real motivation of his action is a passion Smith coined 'the love of systems'. But this passion is not specific to the poor man's son and is also shared by the merchant and the politician who both love "the perfection of police, the extension of trade and manufacture", i.e., "noble and magnificent objects". In 1759, Smith explicitly exposes the meeting between two lovers of systems: the merchant and the politician. Their complicity is founded on this common love. A few years later, Smith discovers through Quesnay and Mirabeau the mercantilism which will become his main target in the *Wealth of Nations* on the very basis of this complicity. However he does not speak any more about it. According to the authors, this is a new *Das Adam Smith Problem*, which does not rely on an alleged contradiction between the two main works of Smith, but on an overlooked complementarity.

In the second chapter, "Charles Fourier: A 'Non-Scientistic' Conception of Justice", Ragip Ege and Sylvie Rivot attempt to demonstrate that the way one perceives the others as well as one's attitude towards them determine the form of the social structure a thinker wishes to realize. The investigation of the authors aims to bring into light that the *otherness* is a matter of deep concern for Fourier. His generous tolerance towards what is *different* leads him to follow the route initiated by the ancient Greeks for whom justice is "displayed towards others", to borrow Aristotle's word in *The Nicomachean Ethics*. To this extent, the social conception of Fourier appears as profoundly non-paternalistic, i.e., 'non-scientistic': in his world, what is just is the good *of* others.

Nizar Hariri in the third chapter "Mill's Qualitative Hedonism as an Ethics of Desire: Towards an Intersubjective Concept of Pleasure" aims to address the polemic related to the qualitative evaluation of pleasure (the quality vs. quantity debate). By suggesting an alternative explanation to Mill's higher pleasures doctrine, the author argues that the only acceptable interpretation of Mill's qualitative distinction of pleasures considers that all judgements on the quality of pleasure are grounded in an intersubjective understanding. Exploring this specific aspect of Mill's work shows that higher pleasures are those that we judge as being capable of increasing the level of concordance among individuals while matching individual self-development with that of all the others. Therefore, the qualitative distinction of pleasures can be reconstructed as an ethics of desire, showing that we can reach a better political organization of our desires and pleasures by decreasing non-necessary sufferings.

The object of the fourth chapter "The Worker at the Heart of the Analysis: the Saint-Simonian Approach to Political Economy" by Gilles Jacoud is based on the principal Saint-Simonian writings printed between 1825 and 1832 and demonstrates how their approach to political economy is new and what status they confer upon the worker. The worker is seen here as the Individual who is the real producer in modern societies, while the idler corresponds to the Other; the aim of the Saint-Simonian doctrine being to reduce the initial dependency in which the worker finds himself with the idler. The first part of the chapter explains why it is indispensable to put the worker at the heart of the analysis in the Saint-Simonian approach. The second part shows further that the Saint-Simonians attempt to include the figure of the worker into the research programme of political economy.

The fifth chapter "Economics and Humanity: Theory of Development in A. Sen and the Concept of Human Integral Development" by Tony E. Persico, Nicola Mattoscio and Edgardo Bucciarelli puts into light the relationships between the Catholic ethics regarding economic development and Amartya Sen's theory of human development. The aim of the work is to find a common field that allows a dialogue between the two frameworks. According to the Catholic social teaching, the development must be integral, which implies the involvement of the whole man to reach its full realization. It means ensuring the highest degree of opportunity for all men. For Sen, development is the expansion of human possibilities for all the individuals. It involves the expansion of instrumental freedoms, in a design in which freedom is at the same time the mean and the aim of development. Linking the two approaches, it is thus possible to reach a complete and unified vision of the human development by considering the relational nature of human beings.

Marlyse Pouchol in the sixth chapter "The Disappearance of a Moral Attitude. An Analysis Comparing H. Arendt and F. von Hayek" puts into light that both Friedrich Hayek and Hannah Arendt evoke a disappearance of a moral attitude with the transformation of economics and the rise of totalitarian regimes in the 20th century, without, though, developing the same type of analysis. The first part of this chapter returns to the source of their disagreement by presenting their different approaches to economics, and consequently to politics as well. The second part aims to support Arendt's position that gives back a positive sense to politics against that of Hayek who considered it a harmful practice which gave rise to Soviet and Nazi totalitarianism. She notably associated a moral attitude reflected in a respectful relation with the 'other' to a mental practice exercised in solitude, demanding free time and physical inactivity. However it turns out that such conditions tend to disappear once the maintenance of an economic dynamic has become the alpha and omega of politics.

The seventh chapter "Karl Marx and Charles Fourier: Criticism of Contemporary Society and New Philosophical Anthropology" by Riccardo Soliani aims at comparing the dialectic between philosophical anthropology and transformation of society in Marx and Fourier. According to Marx, the liberation of Man can happen only in the classless society, established by the proletarian revolution. According to Fourier, people must begin to live in communities ruled by the 'law of attraction', and the example of these happy men, living their passions, will move the entire humanity. The dialectic between philosophical anthropology and social transformation in these two authors develops in an opposite way. Another topic considered is the respective vision of the freed Individual in the future society. Indeed, Marx's scope is the analysis of the present time and its possible development, not prophecy. However, his critical analysis on capitalist mode of production involves some hints about the emancipation of the Individual which can be fruitfully merged with Fourier's original vision of man, to suggest a possible way of transformation to our age of anxiety.

Catherine Audard's contribution opens the thematic part of our work "The Individual and the Other as Recognition and Subjectivity". Her chapter entitled "Self-Development and Social Justice" focuses on the left-liberalism and the apparently insurmountable task of reconciling Individual rights and freedoms with the demands of social justice. The author argues that both the cases for social justice and for liberal individualism would be strengthened with a better conception of the Self and of her needs as a developing being. Whereas classical economics has its starting point in the Self as a given being and tends to take "men's propensities and inclinations as given, whatever they are and then seek the best way to fulfil them" as stressed by Rawls in his *Theory of Justice*, it would be important to understand the human individual as a self-developing being that nevertheless relies on her relationships to others to fulfil her potential. This is why the 'container-like' view of the Self that is shared by both utilitarianism and libertarianism should be rejected as it treats individuals as given things, not as developing persons, making it impossible to make sense of the demands of justice. Instead, the author argues, solidarity and social justice should be understood as necessary conditions of human self-development. However this all depends on a proper understanding of self-development for which a detour through Kant's transcendental argument will be necessary.

The ninth chapter "Aristotle on Reciprocity and Social Health" by Robert Gallagher supports that Aristotle's notion of 'reciprocity' unites his considerations of the just in economic affairs, of the passions of the economic agent and of exchange as gift and counter-gift, and includes citizens treating their economic partners ('sharers') as ends in themselves rather than means. Reciprocity, Aristotle says, is necessary to preserve states because communities are "composed of people who differ in kind", for "it is not from two doctors that a community arises, but from a doctor and a farmer, and in general from those who are different and not equal". If the sharers did not differ from each other, they would have nothing to offer each other; they come together into community so that the needs that the Individual cannot satisfy on his/her own can be satisfied by another. Exchange, then, is defined by the parties involved, not just by the goods.

Francis Munier in the tenth chapter "The Self and the Others. Recognition and Subjective Well-Being: Some Empirical Evidences" deals with the links between interpersonal relations, economic behaviour and subjective well-being. His thesis is that happiness is the outcome of an interactive process between individuals on the one hand, and favourable micro- and macro-social conditions on the other hand. Besides, the author considers that recognition is an ontological basis of the individual's happiness. A more fruitful connection between economics and social philosophy and an alternative understanding of the individual in economics are exposed. The chapter ends with an empirical analysis based on the assumption that recognition affects subjective well-being: the three spheres of recognition provided by Honneth and some proxies' variables based on the OECD database of Better Life Index are used.

The eleventh chapter "On Levinas's Political 'Theory': A Two-Dimensional Conception of Justice from the Perspective of Equality" focuses on Emmanuel Levinas's conception of justice as based on his original account of the being, which suggests that the 'responsibility for the Other' is the principle of individual subjectivity and freedom. The specific concepts of the 'Self', and the 'Other', prove to be crucial regarding political issues and their analysis leads to understand the notion of justice according to two different views in Levinas. Cyrielle Poiraud argues that the 'same' involves a political idea of justice, based on the principle of equality, whereas the 'Other' refers to an 'ethical' form of justice that involves inequality. The chapter thus aims at shedding light on Levinas's conception of justice which is rather scattered in his works and essentially revealed through the critique of institutional justice he undertakes, as a "tyranny of totality" (see Chapter 11). Now, this type of justice, and modern theories in general, are based on the demand for equality, so as Sen notably showed in 2009. But Levinas precisely calls into question this principle of equality: it denies, according to him, the true essence of the being, whose freedom must be found in heteronomy. The question of the justification of the norm of equality of social justice theories is then at stake.

The aim of the twelfth chapter "The 'Recognition' of the Other as a Pre-requisite for Fair Market Prices" is to further develop the application of the philosophical grounds of recognition to economic exchanges through the theorization of the legal elements behind economic processes. Therefore, the proposed perspective includes a definition of the legal elements that enter economic interactions, which are conceived here as being framed by the identities of the interacting parties and by their reciprocal recognition of rights. According to Stefano Solari, liberty is thus seen as being juridically framed as it is in ethical liberalism. The corresponding economic theory is inspired by Institutionalism. The author notably attempts to examine the economic processes going on in the civil society as institutionalized processes by not simply incorporating an ethical dimension, but rather by using a complete set of variable context elements understood through a unitary view of action; and to avoid an abstract theory of ethics and justice in favour of a practical theory inspired by an ideal-realistic approach in order to highlight the social and economic role of legal rights.

Eleonora Viganò in the thirteenth paper "The Agent as an End in Itself in the Economic Domain from a Biological and Smithian Perspective" analyzes the process by which the other becomes an end in itself in the evolution of human beings from a self-interested basis. Second, she identifies the hindrances to that process in the marketplace and tries to explain why they occur. Third, she suggests how to remove these obstacles, by using a principle of conduct which includes treating the other as an end in itself and which is equally valid in both the moral and the economic spheres: the moral and economic virtue of prudence, as described by Adam Smith. Finally, while Smith emphasizes the economic usefulness of the moral virtue of prudence, the author points out the 'moral usefulness' of prudence for economics.

The fourteenth chapter marks the beginning of the analytical part of our book "The Individual and the Other in Modern Economic Analysis". "Perfect Prediction Equilibrium" by Ghislain Fourny, Stéphane Reiche and Jean-Pierre Dupuy introduces in the framework of finite games in extensive form with perfect information and strict preferences a new equilibrium concept: The Perfect Prediction Equilibrium (PPE). In the Nash paradigm, rational players consider that the opponent's strategy is fixed while maximizing their payoff. The PPE, on the other hand, models the behaviour of agents with an alternate form of rationality that involves a Stackelberg competition with the past. Agents with this form of rationality integrate in their reasoning that they have such accurate logical and predictive skills, that the world is fully transparent: all players share the same knowledge and know as much as an omniscient external observer. In particular, there is common knowledge of the solution of the game including the reached outcome and the thought process leading to it. The PPE is stable given each player's knowledge of its actual outcome and uses no assumptions at unreached nodes. The chapter gives the general definition and construction of the PPE as a fixpoint problem, proves its existence, uniqueness and Pareto optimality, and presents two algorithms to compute it. Finally, the PPE is put in perspective with existing literature (Newcomb's problem, Superrationality, Nash Equilibrium, Subgame Perfect Equilibrium, Backward Induction Paradox, Forward Induction).

The purpose of the fifteenth chapter "Consumption Externality and Pigovian Taxation. A Comparison between Rawls and Bentham" is to apply two distinct conceptions of justice – the Rawlsian maximin conception of justice and the Benthamian utilitarianism – to a simple model with consumption externality. Herrade Igersheim and Thi Kim Cuong Pham first remind the normative values of these two traditions, in particular the fact that they correspond to radically opposite theories: respectively, a deontological theory which conceives human beings as ends and a teleological one which sees them as means. Then, the second step of this investigation consists in applying these two doctrines to a simple model with consumption externality: two corrective policies are thus analyzed, discussed and compared.

In the sixteenth chapter "David Hume and Rationality in Decision-Making: A Case Study on the Economic Reading of a Philosopher" by André Lapidus, it is shown that Hume's theory of passion, such as elaborated mainly in Book II of the *Treatise of Human Nature* (1739–40) and in the *Dissertation on the Passions* (1757), gives rise to a conception of the decision process which challenges the canonical approach to the rationality of decision, as rationality of preferences and rationality of choice. The paper states that when adopting a Humean perspective, rationality is not embodied as consistency requirements of individual behaviour, but may emerge as a possible outcome of some dispositions of our mind, which make the world inhabited by our emotions.

The seventeenth chapter entitled "The Ontology of Schelling's 'Theory of Interdependent Decisions'" by Lauren Larrouy offers a methodological contribution on Schelling's insight into game theory drawing both on his proposition for a "reorientation of game theory" and his dynamic models of residential segregation. It aims to show how these respective works exhibit coherences in Schelling's thinking. It is often claimed that Schelling criticizes standard game theory without proposing any analytical solutions. To the contrary, the author asserts that some of the methodological constraints Schelling identifies in standard game theory support the proposition of a new type of modelling in the dynamic models of residential segregation: the first agent-based modelling. It is argued that the agent-based models provide a theoretic ground to formalize most of the methodological innovations proposed in his "reorientation of game theory". To understand such a claim, the author stresses the social ontology underlined in Schelling's conception of a "theory of interdependent decisions".

According to Jean Mercier Ythier in the eighteenth chapter "Instrumental Rationality, Prudence and Communicative Action: Deliberation in, and Communication through, Individual Rational Decision-Making", communicative action flourishes from valid intersubjective communication through and about the choice of courses of action. The author distinguishes two variants of rational preferential choice: a) instrumental rationality, construed as rational preferential choice of means, from given, singular preferences over generic circumstances of choice; and b) prudence, conceived as deliberated choice of ends in given, singular circumstances of action. Then, the author argues that each variant supports a distinct set of norms and practices of communicative action, namely: a) contracts, and notably the contracts of market exchange, which perform the integration of the singular ends of instrumentally rational individual agents into efficient interaction; and b) forms of prudential decision-making, such as jurisprudence, or the clinical practice of medicine, which perform the integration of the singular cases confronting 'prudent' individual agents, under common rules for contextual action. Finally, it is claimed that the full flourishing of communicative action calls for the development of both types of norms and practices, and supposes that an appropriate balance be struck between them.

The nineteenth chapter "Conflicts between Liberty and Social Welfare in Historical Perspective" by Iona Tarrant and Jonathan Perraton seeks to shed further light on the idea of conflict between liberty and social welfare, formalized by Amartya Sen in 1970, by setting this in historical context. In particular it draws upon the political philosophy of Jean-Jacques Rousseau. Given Sen's result, it could be claimed that some analytical device could be used, albeit implicitly, to resolve the conflict between liberty and social welfare in Rousseau's thought. The paper uses the methodology of microeconomics to interpret Rousseau's *Social Contract* and identify what that analytical device could be. Most social choice theorists accept a conventional mono-utility approach; given this there are a very limited number of ways out of the conflict, and most theorists who claim to resolve the conflict effectively choose either social welfare over liberty or vice versa. Here the authors propose a dual utility device as offering a potential additional route out of the paradox, one that can be seen as making sense of Rousseau's conception of the social contract.

The twentieth and final chapter of our book, "Oneself, the Other and Both in Bargaining Models", first points out that the bargaining situation represents a challenge for players equipped with mechanical rationality and for the theorist depicting their interaction: the achievement of a good solution is essentially unjustified if each player sticks to maximizing rationality. Fabrice Tricou then stresses that the construction of a game *à la* Rubinstein, generating an agreement as a strategic equilibrium, is quite remarkable; but this accomplishment is essentially due to the brightness of the model maker, the rationality of the *independent* agents being a component of the story built on rules given to them. On the contrary, the author argues that in axiomatic models such as the Nash solution, postulates picked by the theorist reflect principles chosen by *autonomous* persons, each synthetic solution expressing the social choice of a specific kind of contractual association. Such a view may lead to a critical appraisal of the Nash programme.

Note

1 This collective book is the proceedings of the 2nd International Conference "Economic Philosophy", which was held at the University of Strasbourg from 9th to 10th October 2014, on the theme "Oneself and the Other".

Part I

Textual part

The Individual and the Other in the history of thought

1 From vanity to the love of systems, from luxury to the accumulation of capital, from the gaze of others to the endless process

Daniel Diatkine and Benoît Walraevens

Introduction: three passions

It is well known that Book II of the *Wealth of Nations*[1] insists on a passion common to all of us, the "desire to better our condition":

> a desire which, though generally calm and dispassionate, comes with us from the womb, and never leaves us till we go into the grave. In the whole interval which separates those two moments, there is scarce perhaps a single instant in which any man is so perfectly and completely satisfied with his situation, as to be without any wish of alteration or improvement, of any kind.
>
> (WON, II.iii.28, p. 341)

Therefore, this desire is universal. Today, we are satisfied with noting that Smith had already formulated what now seems obvious to us: the idea that the maximisation of intertemporal utility is the mainspring of human action. It is perhaps an essential motivation. But the form that it can take within Smith's work varies and is contradictory at times. Firstly, we also know that this passion is stressed in Book II because this volume is dedicated to capital and its accumulation as a result of parsimony, which is itself one of the main effects of this desire. Smith therefore insists on what will later be referred to as the propensity to save, a faculty which is deployed in different ways according to the type of income that it is applied to. The propensity to save of employees and independent workers, who spend almost all of their income on wage-earners' consumer goods ("necessaries" or "conveniencies") or on manufactured luxury goods ("luxuries" or "amusements"), is inevitably much weaker than that of the commercial industrialists who save their profits to accumulate capital. If the independently wealthy do not save at all, or very little, it is because they devote the greater part of their income to purchasing luxury goods in order to gratify another passion: *vanity*.

This passion is first and mainly discussed in the *Theory of Moral Sentiments*.[2] We know that this book places the gaze of others at the heart of its analysis, since that gaze is the foundation of the impartial spectator, Smith's concept for explaining the formation of the sense of moral obligation which for Hume remained as mysterious as it was vital for all forms of social life. While the impartial spectator is the result of the gaze of others, it is not its only possible outcome: vanity also stems from it. And satisfying vanity is clearly the aim of the acquisition of luxuries.

At a first glance, Smith's position on vanity and luxuries in TMS seems ambiguous. On the one hand, vanity corrupts our moral sentiments and luxuries are seen as "baubles" and "trinkets of frivolous utility". On the other hand, the desire for luxuries seems to be the cause that changed the face of the world. Several commentators have dealt with this difficult issue (Hont and Ignatieff 1983; Brown 1994; Fleischacker 2004; Griswold 1999). We will argue that a key for understanding Smith's seemingly ambiguous position on luxuries in TMS is to take into account the role of the love of systems, which is another motivation for action, distinct from vanity and independent of the social gaze. We will show that the love of systems, explicitly opposed by Smith to Humean utility, is an aesthetic principle which is generally unknown of the people who experience it.

Our paper is structured as follows: "Vanity and the division of commodities in TMS" focuses on the links between vanity and luxuries in TMS, studying three chapters in which they play a prominent role. Then "Vanity, the love of system and the desire for luxury: aesthetics and accumulation of wealth" returns to the famous parable of the poor man's son. It discusses the usual interpretation, which explains the poor man's son behaviour by vanity only. According to us, it is the "love of systems" rather than vanity that moves him, for vanity is only a teaser for the poor man's son. The fourth and conclusive part of the paper attempts to show how the love of systems seems to create a bridge between TMS and WON,[3] that is, between luxuries and capital.

Vanity and the division of commodities in TMS

Satisfying vanity is undoubtedly for Smith the aim of the acquisition of luxuries. More precisely, vanity generates the distinction between luxuries and other goods (necessaries and conveniencies). One of the purposes of this section is to highlight the fact that this distinction is peculiar to the TMS. This point is important because it prefigures the distinction between wage goods and other goods, and finally between basic and non-basic commodities, which is typical of classical economics. We strive for luxuries not for the superior pleasure and comfort they can give us but primarily for being looked at, loved and admired. It is a social motive, the desire for the approval of others, which first drives people towards luxury goods.

At first sight, though, Smith's position on luxury in TMS seems ambiguous.[4] On the one hand, vanity is nothing but a negative form of the relation to others that is the core of the TMS. We know that the first issue Smith wants to solve is the issue of understanding the sentiment of obligation: how can a sign – a promise – generate a sentiment, the sentiment of obligation?

In other words, how are "speech acts" (Austin 1962) possible? We also know Smith's response: the impartial spectator, constructed through the inversion of the standard relation of sympathy – the actor, and not only the spectator, judges him- or herself by adopting the point of view of both a real spectator and an imaginary spectator, the impartial spectator, the "man within". Vanity is the cause (or the effect) of perversion of this process.

On the other hand, vanity generates a dividing or subgrouping within the set of goods. Luxuries are the objects of vanity. Other goods (wages goods) are not. However, the latter are divided into two subsets: necessaries (or necessities) and conveniencies. The latter used to be luxuries. The transformation of luxuries into conveniencies characterises the progress of society. While several commentators (Hont and Ignatieff 1983; Brown 1994; Fleischacker 2004; Griswold 1999) have focused on the relationship between vanity and the parable of the "Poor Man's Son", this ambiguous relationship between vanity and social progress did not receive much attention in Smith's scholarship. Smith combines a critique of the superficiality, pointlessness and deceitfulness of individuals' consumption of luxury goods with a defence (*à la* Mandeville [1714]) of the economic and social benefits of people's relentless desire for luxury.

Ambition, vanity and luxury

The first part of TMS in which Smith deals with the concepts of vanity and luxury is the famous chapter called "Of the Origin of Ambition, and of the Distinction of Ranks" (TMS, I.iii.2). Smith had claimed before that people are more disposed to sympathise with joy than with sorrow. The consequence of this, as he argues in this chapter, is a natural tendency of men to sympathise with the rich and to despise the poor because, *in our imagination*, we think that the condition of the former is much more enjoyable than that of the latter. That is why "we make parade of our riches, and conceal our poverty" (TMS, I.iii.2.1, p. 50). The enjoyment of wealth and luxury is based, first and foremost, on ostentation and display, i.e. on *visibility*. What is, Smith asks, "the end of avarice and ambition, of the pursuit of wealth, of power, and preheminence?" (ibid.). It is not to get the "necessities of nature": food, clothing and shelter, of which even the meanest labourer is easily supplied with. Indeed, he spends "a great part" of his revenue in "conveniencies, which may be regarded as superfluities, and . . . upon extraordinary occasions, he can give something even to vanity and distinction" (ibid.). This excerpt is highly illuminating about Smith's conception of luxury. First, it exhibits Smith's tri-partition of consumption goods between necessities, conveniences and luxuries, whose definitions are given in WON (V.ii.k.2–3, p. 870). Second, it shows that for Smith luxury is not a definitive privilege of the rich, even if it is mainly so, because what is luxury today can become a conveniency tomorrow.[5] Third, "vanity and distinction" are the strongest motives of the desire for luxuries in Smith's works. The final cause of the "great purpose of human life", the desire to better our condition, is not only to get wealth, luxury and power *per se*, it is also, and above all, to be looked upon, loved and admired by our fellows. It is not the intrinsic pleasure of refined, luxury goods that interests us, Smith claims. It is first and foremost our desire for others' sympathy and admiration that prompts us to want these goods. In Smith's words, it is "vanity, *not the ease, or the pleasure*, which interests us" (ibid., our italics). And vanity is based on being the object of sympathy and approbation. Man lives in the eyes of others. The man of "rank and distinction" is "observed by all the world" and "every body is eager to look at him, and to conceive, at least by sympathy, that joy and exultation with which his circumstances naturally inspire him" (ibid.). Importantly, the desire for wealth and luxury is prompted by a deception of our imagination leading us to believe that the "condition of the great" is "a perfect and happy state" (ibid., p. 51). But it is only in our "waking dreams and idle reveries" that it is so. The happiness and pleasures we ascribe to the condition of the rich and powerful from being the constant objects of observation and sympathy more than compensate, "in the opinion of mankind", the "loss of liberty with which it is attended" and "all that toil, all that anxiety, all those mortifications which must be undergone in the pursuit of it" (ibid., p. 51). We should not be worried about this, however. This deception of our imagination has positive consequences for society. Among them is the fact that men's proclivity "to go along with all the passions of the rich and powerful" is the foundation of the "distinction of ranks, and the order of society" (ibid., p. 52), therefore preserving the peace and stability of society. Obviously, Smith's purpose here is not that of a moralist. As Hume did before him, he wants above all to describe and explain human behaviour. Significantly, humour is not absent from his text. The tone is quite different when Smith discusses the corruption of moral sentiments.

The corruption of moral sentiments and the "parade of riches"

The next chapter of TMS (I.iii.3) about the corruption of the moral sentiments by which we admire the rich and despise the poor, added to the last edition of TMS, both confirms and completes Smith's previous reasoning on vanity and luxury. Everyone wants "to deserve, to acquire and to enjoy the respect and admiration of mankind", Smith writes (TMS, I.iii.3.2, p. 62). One way to get this, as we now know, is to follow the "road" of wealth and power. There is another path, however: the one leading to virtue and wisdom (ibid.). Most people are and always will be admirers of wealth and greatness. Why is it so? Wealth and greatness are more visible than virtue and wisdom. The former present to us a "picture" which is "more gaudy and glittering in its colouring . . . forcing itself upon the notice of every wandering eye", while the latter attract "the attention of scarce any body but the most studious and careful observer" (ibid.). Therefore, it is easier for people to identify the rich and powerful and, more importantly, to identify with them. The characters of those who choose this road are made of "ambition and *ostentatious* avidity" (ibid.), of "presumption and *vanity*" (TMS, I.iii.3.3, p. 62). The novelty of this late addition is a negative side to the admiration for and indulgent approbation of the behaviour of the rich and powerful. There are, Smith claims, "hypocrites of wealth and greatness" like the coxcombs[6] (TMS, I.iii.2.5, p. 55), trying to assume "the equipage and splendid way of living of his superiors, without considering that whatever may be praiseworthy in any of these, derives its whole merit and propriety from its suitableness to that situation and fortune which both require and can easily support that expence" (TMS, I.iii.3.7, p. 64). Here Smith suggests that luxury spending *per se* should not be morally reprehensible. Buying luxuries can be proper and praiseworthy, depending on your social rank and fortune. It is not, however, once you try to assume a condition that is not yours and, by this fact, "must soon reduce [you] to beggary", an argument we can find in Hume too. Luxury seems excessive and blameworthy to Smith once it goes against the interest of the individual, or against "prudence". The argument will be used in WON (II.iv) when he pleads for a low legal rate of interest to exclude "prodigals" from loan markets. Wealth and greatness impose on the rich and powerful some specific "duties" toward others (TMS, I.iii.3.7, p. 64). They must distinguish themselves from the mob in terms of behaviour, manners and consumption patterns, leading "what is called the fashion" (ibid.).

Fashion, custom and luxury

Smith studies this topic in a chapter called "Of the Influence of Custom and Fashion upon Our Notions of Beauty and Deformity". It introduces an essential element of the demand for luxuries (and conveniences): beauty, broadly defined here as the aesthetic quality of the object that gratifies our natural sense of taste.[7] Several elements can give some "beauty" to consumer goods. In this part of TMS, Smith is interested in revealing how the standards of taste are, like moral standards, the immanent products of social interactions. In other words, the beauty people ascribe to "productions of the arts" is under the dominion of "custom" and "fashion" (TMS, V.1.2, p. 194).[8] The latter is "a peculiar species of it" (ibid.). It refers to the taste, preferences and sense of beauty commonly held in the higher ranks of society[9] whose "graceful . . . easy and commanding manners . . . joined to the usual *richness* and *magnificence* of their dress, give a *grace* to the very form which they happen to bestow upon it" (TMS, V.1.3, pp. 194–5).[10] In other words, fashion defines what the luxuries are in a specific time and place. There is no fixed and external standard of beauty and hence of luxury. Proof is that once the rich cease to use this form of dress, "it loses all the grace, which it had appeared to possess before, and being now used only by the inferior ranks of people, seems to have something of their meanness and awkwardness" (TMS, V.1.3, p. 195). People of high rank love to distinguish themselves in consuming scarce, refined and beautiful goods. As soon as they see their inferiors consuming them, they no longer desire these goods.[11] They then fall into another category: custom. It is no coincidence that Smith uses this word, typical of his moral enquiry, in an economic context. Custom is "founded on habit and prejudice" rather than "upon reason and nature" (TMS, V.1.4, p. 195). It represents the general point of view about what is proper to own and consume to live a decent and dignified life. For example, "a man would be ridiculous who should appear in public with a suit of clothes quite different from those which are commonly worn, though the new dress should in itself be ever so graceful or convenient" (TMS,V.1.5, p. 196). This clearly anticipates Smith's broad, social and moral definition of "necessities" (WN, V.ii.k.2–3, p. 869–70), also called "conveniencies", in WON (see I.v.1, p. 47; I.xi.c.7, p. 181; II.ii.45, p. 299), where they are seen as what "custom" and "decency" prescribe to wear and own.[12] With modes which are "continually changing", the demand for dress and furniture is constantly renewed and what were luxuries in the past can become the necessities and "conveniencies" of the present. The desire for luxury seems to be prompted only by others' regard, approbation and admiration. But it is not.

Vanity, the love of system and the desire for luxury: aesthetics and accumulation of wealth

One of the major problems posed by the TMS is therefore that of the role played by *vanity* in the formation of moral judgement and in the action of individuals. In the first chapter of the fourth section, Smith seems to see the vanity of the rich and the admiration that they give rise to among the poor as one of the great motivations behind the increase in the wealth of society. This raises a question already posed by I. Hont and M. Ignatieff (1981–2005, 1983, p. 298): how can we render compatible Smith's apparent disdain of the accumulation of wealth in the TMS, in which the desire for luxuries is seen merely as a taste for "baubles and trinkets" satisfying our childish vanity, with his emphasis on the *widespread* accumulation of wealth in WON?

I. Hont and M. Ignatieff (1981–2005, 1983, p. 298) acknowledge that the task is not easy. V. Brown (1994, p. 86 and sqq.) devoted a large part of her book to try to answer this question. Smith apparently assimilates wealth and greatness with "baubles and trinkets" within a Stoic discourse that forms a hierarchy of virtues and vices under the control of the "impartial spectator". However, Smith considers that the vast majority of humanity does not share this hierarchy of virtues and does not always obey, or is ignorant of, the injunctions of the impartial spectator. It is in this way that Smith insists on the fact that only a minority chooses justice over greed. After having identified these positions in Smith's work, V. Brown then bases her analysis on Chapter 1 of Book IV of TMS "Of the Beauty . . ." containing the parable of the "poor man's son", to complete her demonstration. She sees in this chapter the expression by Smith of his Stoic conception whereby material wealth that satisfies vanity does not contribute to moral good (*summum bonum*).

This analysis by V. Brown, although it deepens our knowledge of the problem, does not appear to solve it, except by suggesting that Smith had passed from an elitist Stoic position in the TMS to another, anti-Stoic position in the WON. It raised a great deal of interest. C. L. Griswold (1999, p. 222) was inspired by it to support the idea that Smith was apparently defending the following theses: a) the search to accumulate wealth by certain agents does not generally procure them happiness; b) this unhappiness of certain agents contributes nonetheless to the happiness of humanity. However, more recently, S. Fleischacker (2004) returned to the question posed by I. Hont and M. Ignatieff by highlighting the fact that this position leads to a dramatic contradiction: how is it possible to support both the notion that the desire for wealth not only makes those who strive for it unhappy and that it implies the moral corruption of these agents, while, at the same time, approving of an economic system that encourages the accumulation of wealth?[13] In more general terms, how can we render the Stoic discourse expressed in the

TMS compatible with the constant affirmation of the WON whereby the "desire to improve one's fate" (interpreted here as the insatiable desire for wealth) is *universal and permanent* for everyone? S. Fleischacker asks these questions, but unfortunately does not answer them. In this, we thus find a variant of *Das Adam Smith Problem*, opposing Smith's moral philosophy to his political economy.

As we will show, this difficulty is only apparent. To understand this point we must first ask: what exactly is the issue of this chapter of the TMS? The title is unambiguous: "*Of the Beauty Which the Appearance of Utility Bestows upon All the Productions of Art, and of the Extensive Influence of This Species of Beauty*." Consequently, the issue of this chapter is *aesthetic*. How are our judgements about beauty formed? Here, these judgements do not depend on customs, "habit or prejudices". They are independent of the gaze of others. The issue now is to understand *how* they depend on the utility of the object. From the outset Smith writes:

> That utility is one of the principal sources of beauty has been observed by everybody who has considered with any attention what constitutes the nature of beauty. . . . That the fitness of any system or machine to produce the end for which it was intended, bestows a certain propriety and beauty upon the whole, and renders the very thought and contemplation of it agreeable, is so very obvious that nobody has overlooked it.
>
> (TMS, IV.1.1, p. 179)

So *everybody* agrees with what we could (perhaps) now call a sort of "functionalism", i.e. beauty defined as the fitness of a system to produce the end for which it was intended. Notice that utility as *a source of beauty* is defined in a different way from today. In this context, utility presupposes an *intention*. Since Bentham, intention presupposes utility.

The issue is: why and how this "fitness" generates an aesthetic feeling? Hume gave a first answer:

> The cause too, why utility pleases, has of late been assigned by an ingenious and agreeable philosopher. . . . The utility of any object, according to him, pleases the master by perpetually suggesting to him the pleasure or conveniency which it is fitted to promote. . . . The spectator enters by sympathy into the sentiments of the master, and necessarily views the object under the same agreeable aspect.
>
> (TMS, IV.1.2. p. 179)

According to Smith, this explanation of the aesthetic pleasure provoked by utility is incomplete. It is not the utility of the object that always gives this pleasure to its owner:

> But that this fitness, this happy contrivance of any production of art, should often be more valued than the very end for which it was intended; and that the exact adjustment of the means for attaining any conveniency or pleasure,

> should frequently be more regarded than that very conveniency or pleasure, in the attainment of which their whole merit would seem to consist, has not, so far as I know, been yet taken notice of by anybody. That this however is very frequently the case, may be observed in a thousand instances, both in the most frivolous and in the most important concerns of human life.
>
> (TMS, IV.1.3, p. 179)

So it is not the utility (the fitness to the *end*) of the object which gives rise to the aesthetic pleasure, it is something else: the fitness of the *means* (used to produce the object, carrier of the utility). Commentators generally perceive this "something else" as a criticism of utility as an aesthetic principle. Smith wants to explain why the "appearance" of utility pleases and most readers suppose that Smith makes a distinction between an "apparent", a "false" utility as it is perceived by the vulgar (snobs, conceited people) and a sort of "true" utility perceived by the sage (stoic philosopher).

However, Smith is clear: what is frequently "more valued" than "pleasure" (i.e., the utility) is "the means for attaining any conveniency or pleasure". If Smith writes *any* pleasure, it seems evident that his purpose is not to make any discrimination between useful objects. Some may be trifling, as are trinkets and toys, others may be very important as are wealth and greatness, others, as "great systems of public policy", are obviously useful (even when they are false!). The difficulty in this text lies in the meaning of the words "appearance of utility". Toys and trinkets, greatness and wealth, systems of public policy have the "appearance of utility". They have the appearance of utility, but from what point of view? From a cynical point of view, all seem trifling, since they don't contribute to "real happiness":

> In what constitutes the real happiness of human life, they [those who seemed to have been left out in the partition] are in no respect inferior to those who would seem so much above them. In ease of body and peace of mind, all the different ranks of life are nearly upon a level, and the beggar, who suns himself by the side of the highway, possesses that security which kings are fighting for.
>
> (TMS, IV.1.10, p. 185)

This famous proposition concludes the no less famous "invisible hand" metaphor in TMS. This one says that inequalities of wealth do not imply the impoverishment of the poor, since the expenditures of the rich ensure the employment of the former. So the poor is not "left out of the partition", for the natural wage is always sufficient, in any stage of the society, to afford him the "ease of body". Besides, even the "beggar, who suns himself by the side of the highway" and *chooses* to be left out of the partition[14] enjoys "the security". Diogenes, the cynic, may approve of this beggar. It seems difficult to suppose that the impartial spectator follows suit. The choice of dependence upon benevolence is difficult to defend.

Actually, from Diogenes's point of view, systems of public policy, or wealth and greatness, are nothing but trinkets. Not for Smith, as we shall see. But if this is the case, where is the "appearance of utility"? Smith gives a striking answer to this question. If we think that an object is *beautiful*, we have the idea that this object is *useful* (for us, or for the people who enjoy it or for the public) but what attracts us first is not that utility, but the "exact adjustment of the means" to their end (their utility).

This idea is twofold: first; it is this "exact adjustment of the means" which arouses the aesthetic sentiment; secondly, subjects generally *do not know* this origin of their aesthetic sentiment. Often (though not always), they believe that they are interested in the finality of the object and are unaware of the real motive behind their interest or admiration. Maybe they think that they are maximising (final) utility; however, they are in fact maximising an *unknown argument* of their utility function. This argument is the exact adjustment of the means to the ends. Since they ignore this argument, they are the victims of a *deception*:

> And it is well that nature imposes upon us in this manner. It is this *deception* which rouses and keeps in continual motion the industry of mankind. It is this which first prompted them to cultivate the ground, to build houses, to found cities and commonwealths, and to invent and improve all the sciences and arts, which ennoble and embellish human life; which have entirely changed the whole face of the globe, have turned the rude forests of nature into agreeable and fertile plains.
>
> (our emphasis) (TMS, IV.1.10, p. 183)

If this deception was the one that Diogenes despises, it would be strange (if not absurd) to congratulate it so warmly! We may conclude that Smith is not Diogenes. Smith describes three kinds of aesthetic objects. The first, and perhaps the most misleading, concerns trinkets. For example a precise watch may be bought not because its owner needs to be *precisely* on time, but because the individual admires the *precision* of the machine (TMS, IV.1.5, p. 180).

This distinction between the arguments of a utility function seems pointless today ("*De gustibus non disputandum*"), because we are economists, and economists are not concerned with aesthetics. Unfortunately for us, Smith, in this chapter, is concerned with aesthetics. And, according to him, somebody may buy a watch for aesthetic motives and Smith wants to know why. Of course we cannot exclude vanity as another motive (a rather frivolous one) to buy a luxury watch. However, we must emphasise that this is not what Smith affirms.

> Nor is it only with regard to such frivolous objects that our conduct is influenced by this principle; it is often the secret motive of the most serious and important pursuits of both private and public life.
>
> (TMS, IV.1.7, p. 181)

Yet what is the "secret motive of the most serious and important pursuits of both private and public life"? We must wait for four pages to know the name of this motive: it is the love of systems. Before this unveiling, Smith exposes the famous parable of the "poor man's son". Here vanity and luxuries act as teasers to the poor man's son. He admires the wealth exposed by conceited rich people. Yet:

> If we examine, however, why the spectator distinguishes with such admiration the condition of the rich and the great, we shall find that it is not so much upon account of the superior ease or pleasure which they are supposed to enjoy, as of the numberless artificial and elegant contrivances for promoting this ease or pleasure. He does not even imagine that they are really happier than other people: but he imagines that they possess more means of happiness. And it is the ingenious and artful adjustment of those means to the end for which they were intended, that is the principal source of his admiration.
>
> (TMS, IV.1.8, p. 182)

Everybody (except a cynical philosopher) may admire "the condition of the rich and the great". Yet everybody doesn't become rich and great. Paradoxically, it is precisely because the poor man's son actually does not desire the happiness of the rich and the great, and because he is motivated by another motive, a "secret motive", that he comes to accumulate wealth. Surprisingly, the accumulation of wealth is explained by aesthetic considerations.[15] It is because he thinks that wealth and greatness are beautiful that the poor man's son can accumulate wealth and acquire greatness! But the "secret motive" may disappear:

> In the languor of disease and the weariness of old age, the pleasures of the vain and empty distinctions of greatness disappear. . . . In his heart he curses ambition, and vainly regrets the ease and the indolence of youth. . . . In this miserable aspect does greatness appear to every man when reduced either by *spleen or disease* to observe with attention his own situation, and to consider what it is that is *really* wanting to his happiness. Power and riches appear then to be, what they are, enormous and operose machines contrived to produce a few trifling conveniencies to the body, consisting of springs the most nice and delicate, which must be kept in order with the most anxious attention, and which in spite of all our care are ready every moment to burst into pieces, and to crush in their ruins their unfortunate possessor. They are immense fabrics, which it requires the labour of a life to raise, which threaten every moment to overwhelm the person that dwells in them, and which while they stand, though they may save him from some smaller inconveniencies, can protect him from none of the severer inclemencies of the season. They keep off the summer shower, not the winter storm, but leave him always as much, and sometimes more exposed than before, to anxiety, to fear, and to sorrow; to diseases, to danger, and to death.
>
> (TMS, IV.1.8, p. 182, emphasis added)

We may now understand what happens when the "deception" disappears and what exactly this deception is. The poor man's son is not interested in happiness but in the means of obtaining happiness. He mistakes the end for which an object was intended and the means used to make this object. When the poor man's son is ill, this deception disappears, and he adopts Diogenes's depressive point of view. However, this breakdown does not last long:

> But though this splenetic philosophy, which in time of sickness or low spirits is familiar to every man, thus entirely depreciates those great objects of human desire, when in better health and in better humour, we never fail to regard them under a more agreeable aspect. . . . We are then charmed with the beauty of that accommodation which reigns in the palaces and oeconomy of the great; and admire how everything is adapted to promote their ease, to prevent their wants, to gratify their wishes, and to amuse and entertain their most frivolous desires. If we consider the real satisfaction which all these things are capable of affording, by itself and separated from the beauty of that arrangement which is fitted to promote it, it will always appear in the highest degree contemptible and trifling. But we rarely view it in this abstract and philosophical light. We naturally confound it in our imagination with the order, the regular and harmonious movement of the system, the machine or oeconomy by means of which it is produced.
>
> (TMS, IV.1.9, p. 183)

Smith's thesis is surprising: we need to be sick to adopt a splenetic philosophy, a philosophy that nevertheless allows us to measure the "real satisfaction" afforded by wealth and greatness. When he escapes to his breakdown, then the poor man's son becomes again a lover of systems. Moreover, the lover of trinkets and the self-made man are not the only lovers of systems:

> The same principle, the same love of system, the same regard to the beauty of order, of art and contrivance, frequently serve to recommend those institutions which tend to promote the public welfare. When a patriot exerts himself for the improvement of any part of the public police, his conduct does not always arise from pure sympathy with the happiness of those who are to reap the benefit of it. It is not commonly from a fellow-feeling with carriers and waggoners that a public-spirited man encourages the mending of high roads. When the legislature establishes premiums and other encouragements to advance the linen or woollen manufactures, its conduct seldom proceeds from pure sympathy with the wearer of cheap or fine cloth, and much less from that with the manufacturer or merchant. The perfection of police, the extension of trade and manufactures, are noble and magnificent objects. The contemplation of them pleases us, and we are interested in whatever can tend to advance them.
>
> (TMS, IV.1.11, p. 185)

Now we understand what is the origin of the collusion between merchants and legislators. As we know this collusion is what defines the mercantile system (Smith's target in the WON). Great merchants (and not only the poor man's son) and great legislators are lovers of systems. However, they are not alone: political economy system makers are also system lovers. Smith was a system lover, and his readers are system lovers too (Diatkine 2010, 2013; Tegos 2013).

We may conclude this point. We do not find the difficulty underlined by Hont and Ignatieff (1981), Brown (1994), Fleischacker (2004) and Griswold (1999). Luxuries are not the poor man's son's *real* target. Luxuries are important, because they are *teasers* for the self-made man. However, if vanity was his exclusive passion, he could not achieve his task. He needs to be a system lover (albeit unconsciously) in order to accumulate wealth. The deception of the lover of systems lies not in confusing "false" utility and "real" utility; his deception lies in confusing "the very end for which [an object] was intended" and "the exact adjustment of the means for attaining any conveniency or pleasure". In other words, Smith was not Diogenes; he was Smith.

Conclusion

Luxury and vanity play a considerable role in the TMS: expenditure on luxury goods enables the endogenising of the preferences of those who contemplate the enjoyment of riches. Smith thus breaks away from the moral debate characterising the "luxury quarrel" and situates it within the psychological register of the TMS. In the WON, the accumulation of wealth is no longer characterised by sumptuous spending, but by parsimony and the accumulation of capital by the "employers" of productive labour (the merchants and industrialists). As Retat writes (1994, p. 83), "the movement that passes from luxury as a proponent of economic growth to luxury as a proponent of economic restraint, and from 'expenditure' to 'accumulation', finds its outcome in Smith".

Naturally, this substitution of capitalists for the rich is by no means anodyne. This is what a comparison between the "invisible hands" present in both books would demonstrate. The first ensures the compatibility of the interests of the rich and the poor, since the rich exchange the wheat that they cannot consume for luxury goods produced by the poor. However, the "invisible hand" of the WON is supposed to ensure the compatibility between the interest of the capitalists and the general interest provided that the capitalists content themselves with pursuing their private interest and are prevented from claiming to pursue the general interest. We have sought to demonstrate that the poor man's son is not prompted by vanity, but by another passion whose very existence is unknown to him. The spectacle of the vanity of the rich excites him, but he does not share their passion for luxury. The passion that animates him is that of the means that would enable him to acquire these luxury goods, the acquisition of which he indefinitely postpones. This passion is therefore insatiable and it characterises capitalism. The gaze of others becomes secondary. The capitalist accumulates within the secret workshop of production.

Notes

1 Then WON.
2 Then TMS.
3 Using a more strictly economic perspective, Brewer (1998) tries to explain the different treatments of luxury in the *Lectures on Jurisprudence* and in WON.
4 Marshall (2000, p. 637) underlines this ambiguity of Smith with regard to the morality of luxury and finds its cause in the general influence of Hutcheson on his thinking.
5 This is confirmed in WON (V.ii.k.5, p. 871; V.ii.e.6, p. 842).
6 On the character of the "coxcomb" in Smith, see Tegos (2013).
7 Luxury is seen as a natural gratification of taste and refinement in LJ. See in particular LJ(A), vi.12–13; LJ(B), 208, p. 488.
8 For more details on Smith's analysis of fashion see Smith (2012).
9 "That is not the fashion which every body wears, but which those wear who are of a high rank, or character" (TMS, V.1.3, p. 194).
10 Thus, contrary to Smith (2012, p. 516), we don't think that for Smith custom and fashion differ only with regards to the duration of their cycles, with fashion cycles being necessarily shorter. The distinction, we argue, is also about the social rank of people who follow the one or the other.
11 As Smith rightly noted (2012, p. 509), luxuries "have their fashion value from their scarcity, and when they lose this scarcity as they are copied by others, they lose their value as status symbols".
12

> By necessaries I understand, not only the commodities which are indispensably necessary for the support of life, but whatever the *custom* of the country renders it indecent for creditable people, even of the lowest order, to be without. . . . Under necessaries therefore, I comprehend, not only those things which nature, but those things which the established rules of decency have rendered necessary to the lowest rank of people.
>
> (WN, V.ii.k.3, pp. 869–70)

13 "If Griswold is right, Smith urges us throughout TMS to see the pursuit of wealth as morally corrupting and conducive to unhappiness, but also applauds a social system that depends upon, and encourages, that very pursuit" (Fleischacker, 2004, p. 104).
14 Remember the famous proposition "Nobody but a beggar chooses to depend chiefly upon the benevolence of his fellow-citizens" (WON, I.ii.2, p. 27). Evidently, the situation of the "involuntary" beggar is not discussed here.
15 Remember the importance of the aesthetic argument to explain the preference of merchant and merchants and manufacturers investing at home rather than in foreign trade. We know that this argument is crucial for the "invisible hand" metaphor in the WON.

Bibliography

Aspromourgos, Tony. 2009. *The Science of Wealth*. London: Routledge.

Austin, John. 1962. *How to Do Things with Words*. Cambridge: Cambridge University Press.

Berry, Christopher. 1994. *The Idea of Luxury: An Historical and Conceptual Investigation*. Edinburgh: Edinburgh University Press.

Bloomfield, Arthur. 1975. "Adam Smith and the Theory of International Trade", in A. S. Skinner and T. Wilson (eds.), *Essays on Adam Smith*. Oxford: Clarendon Press.

Bréban, Laurie, and Lapidus, Andre. 2013. "Adam Smith on Lotteries: An Interpretation and Formal Restatement", *PHARE working paper*.

Brewer, Anthony. 1998. "Luxury and Economic Development: David Hume and Adam Smith", *Scottish Journal of Political Economy*, 45(1): 78–98.

Brown, Vivienne. 1994. *Adam Smith's Discourse: Canonicity, Commerce and Conscience*. London and New York: Routledge.

Cunningham, David. 2006. "David Hume's Account of Luxury", *Journal of the History of Economic Thought*, 27(3): 231–50.

Diatkine, Daniel. 2010. "Vanity and the Love of System in *Theory of Moral Sentiments*", *The European Journal of the History of Economic Thought*, 17(3): 383–404.

Diemer, Arnaud. 2013. "Quand le luxe devient une question économique: retour sur la querelle du luxe du 18ème siècle", *Innovations*, 41: 9–27.

Elmslie, Bruce, and Sidgley Norman. 2002. "Vent for Surplus: A Case of Mistaken Identity", *Southern Economic Journal*, 68(3): 712–20.

Epstein, Stephan. 2000. *Freedom and Growth: The Rise of States and Markets in Europe, 1300–1750*. London: Routledge.

Fleischacker, Samuel. 2004. *On Adam Smith's Wealth of Nations. A Philosophical Companion*. Princeton: Princeton University Press.

Garegnani, Pierangelo. 1990. "On Some Supposed Obstacles to the Tendency of Market Prices toward Natural Prices", in G. Caravale (ed.), *Equilibrium and Economic Theory*. London: Routledge.

Griswold, Charles. 1999. *Adam Smith and the Virtues of Enlightenment*. Cambridge: Cambridge University Press.

Hont, Istvan, and Michael Ignatieff. 1983. "Needs and Justice in the Wealth of Nations" in Istvan Hont and Michael Ignatieff (eds.), *Wealth and Virtue: The Shaping of Political Economy in the Scottish Enlightenment*. Cambridge: Cambridge University Press.

Hume, David. 1752 [1777]. "Essay on Refinement in the Arts", in Eugene Miller (ed.), *Essays Moral Political and Literary*. Indianapolis: Liberty Fund.

Jeck, Albert. 1994. "The Macrostructure of Adam Smith's Theoretical System: A Reconstruction", *The European Journal of the History of Economic Thought*, 1(3): 551–76.

Jennings, Jeremy. 2007. "The Debate about Luxury in Eighteenth and Nineteenth Century French Political Thought", *Journal of the History of Ideas*, 68(1): 79–105.

Kurz, Heinz. 1992. "Adam Smith on Foreign Trade: A Note on the 'Vent for Surplus' Argument", *Economica*, 59: 475–81.

Kwass, Michael. 2003. "Ordering the World of Goods: Consumer Revolution and the Classification of Objects in Eighteenth Century France", *Representations*, 82(1): 87–116.

Mandeville, Bernard. 1714. *The Fable of the Bees, or Private Vices Public Benefits*, part 1. London: J. Roberts.

Marshall, Mike. 2000. "Luxury, Economic Development, and Work Motivation: David Hume, Adam Smith, and J. R. McCulloch", *History of Political Economy*, 32(3): 631–48.

Mill, John S. 1848–1965. *Principles of Political Economy with Some of Their Applications to Social Philosophy*. Vols II and III of *The Collected Works of John Stuart Mill*. London: Routledge & Kegan Paul.

Myint, Hla. 1958. "The 'Classical Theory' of International Trade and the Underdeveloped Countries", *Economic Journal*, 68: 317–37.

Negishi, Takashi. 1989. *History of Economic Theory*. Amsterdam: North Holland.

Ravix, Joel. 2013. "Luxe, Innovations et crise: les enseignements des économistes Classiques", *Innovation*, 41: 29–49.

Retat, Pierre. 1994. "Luxe", *Dix Huitième Siècle*, 26: 79–88.

Ricardo, David. 1817–1951. *On the Principles of Political Economy and Taxation*, Vol. I of *The Works and Correspondence of David Ricardo*, eds. P. Sraffa and M. H. Dobb. Cambridge: Cambridge University Press.

Shovlin, John. 2008. "Hume's *Political Discourses* and the French Luxury Debate", in *David Hume's Political Economy*. London: Routledge.

Smith, Adam. 1759–1976. *The Theory of Moral Sentiments*. The Glasgow Edition of the Works and Correspondence of Adam Smith. Oxford: Clarendon Press.

Smith, Adam. 1776–1976. *An Inquiry into the Nature and Causes of the Wealth of Nations*. The Glasgow Edition of the Works and Correspondence of Adam Smith. Oxford: Clarendon Press.

Smith, Craig. 2012. "Adam Smith's Collateral Inquiry: Fashion and Morality in *The Theory of Moral Sentiments* and the *Wealth of Nations*", *History of Political Economy*, 45–3: 505–22.

Tegos, Spiros. 2013. "Adam Smith, Theorist of Corruption", in Christopher Berry, Maria Paganelli, and Craig Smith (eds.), *Oxford Handbook of Adam Smith*. Oxford: Oxford University Press.

Tilly, Charles. 1994. *Cities and the Rise of States in Europe, A.D. 1000 to 1800*. Boulder, San Francisco, and Oxford: Westview Press.

West, Edwin. 1990. *Adam Smith and Modern Economics*. Aldershot: Edward Elgar.

Winch, Donald. 1978. *Adam Smith's Politics: An Essay in Historiographic Revision*. Cambridge: Cambridge University Press.

2 Charles Fourier

A ‘non-scientistic’ conception of justice

Ragip Ege and Sylvie Rivot

In this paper, we attempt to demonstrate that the nature of the representation of the others as well as the attitude towards them determines the form of the social structure a thinker considers just and desirable. The idea of justice and the representation of the otherness are closely tied. We argue that the depth of Fourier’s thought lies in this: not only is he delighted with the differences the human world harbours; he also makes use of all his theoretical and creative forces to achieve the conditions of the endless emancipation of differences. In this issue he follows the route initiated by the ancient Greeks for whom justice is “displayed towards others”, to borrow Aristotle’s word in *The Nicomachean Ethics* (Aristotle 1893, bk V-1). ‘*Differences*’ signify here the irreducible diversity of individuals as particular subjects and their infinite capacity for imagining and creating unexpected new forms of existence. Fourier is one of the great minds who do not fear the diversity. This feature brings him close to Hegel.

Our chapter is organised as follows. The first part is dedicated to Fourier’s conception of mankind. In the second part, we will focus on Fourier’s attitude towards the “negative”, to borrow Hegel’s terminology. The third part will be devoted to Fourier’s genuine appraisal of justice.

What makes a human being?

Fourier has an unwavering faith in the human being’s ability to reach true happiness by himself. For him there exists a natural order, the ‘societary order’ (*ordre sociétaire*) that has been wanted by God, and that has been perverted in ‘Civilisation’ – our modern industrial world – by both philosophers and economists. Fourier sets himself clearly apart from the ‘moralists’ when he claims to have established in a scientific and comprehensive way the universal functioning principles of our world. He even compares himself to Newton when in his *Theory of the Four Movements*, he attempts to extend Newton’s discovery to the social, animal, organic and material world. His basic discovery runs as follows:

> I conjectured that if God had given so much influence to passionate attraction and so little to its enemy, reason, it must be in order to lead us to the order of the progressive Series in which all aspects of attraction would be satisfied.
> (Fourier [1808] 2006, 15)

For Fourier there is a science to be discovered. But this science is based on the principle of the "passionate attraction" and relies accordingly on a study of passions. This leads Marx in his criticism of Berliner speculative intellectuals to praise French authors and especially Fourier, whom he quotes in French: "*L'homme est tout entier dans ses passions*" ("Man is entirely in his passions", Marx's letter to Feuerbach quoted by M. Rubel 1982, 424). This world of passions is the one wished by God and with which we ought to comply. In his world:

> These distributions of series must be organised by attraction; each group must be composed only of sectarians (*sectaires*) passionately engaged, without having recourse to the vehicles of needs, morale, reason, duty and constraint.
> (Fourier [1829] 1966–68, 6:52)

Yet, what is the nature of God according to Fourier? As stated by Schérer, "Fourier builds a non ideologist notion of God, identified to Reason (. . .), able to absorb, beyond its erratic behaviour, all the nature and primarily the passions from which it was previously dissociated" (Schérer 1970, 26). Beyond the five sensitive passions (linked to our five senses) and the four affective ones (i.e. friendship, love, family and ambition) that make us cooperate with others, there are three other passions (i.e. the *Papillonne*, the *Cabaliste* and the *Composite*), all of them critical for the organisation of a 'phalanx'.[1] The *Papillonne*, the "anti-philosophical passion" (Fourier [1822] 1966–68, 5: 533) attracts us towards diversity and leads us accordingly to belong to about forty series in a phalanx. Obviously, this passion is far from bloomed up in a modern, 'civilised' world, which obliges a man to do always the same work: "so many monotonies for the spirit and the body" (Fourier [1822] 1966–68, 5: 533). The *Cabaliste* passion expresses our taste for intrigues; it makes us join groups according to the feelings that other members of the group inspire us. It will lead us to be generous towards people that we love (artists, lovers and so on). The *Composite* passion is the most beautiful one: it expresses our desire for concordance, harmony and the blending of our senses in any activity; it is the combination of pleasure, both physical and spiritual. These three distributive passions are almost unknown in Civilization: "only a few glimmers have appeared on the horizon, just enough to arouse the anger of moralists in their relentless war against pleasure" (Fourier [1808] 2006, 85). In contrast, these passions are at the outset of the 'Association' advocated by Fourier since the love for competition, for diversity and for cooperation will ensure the full blooming of the former nine passions.

It goes without saying that we do not intend to take Fourier's views on the human being too literally. But it still remains that Fourier strikingly appears highly concerned about the necessity to preserve the diversity among human beings. What is more, from these twelve radical passions exactly 810 general human characters can be inferred because of the gradations to be found in each human being. More or less the same number will be found in equal proportion in the global population. It can be noticed that Fourier claims to be realistic and therefore acknowledges statistical error. That is the reason why "Fourier is far from a fanatical arithmetic addict (*arithmomane*) and his series are of a great variety" (Queneau 1963, 47).

Beyond statistical error, his series (*séries*) "describe an evolution and put into words movement, the movement of things themselves" (Queneau 1963, 47). In relation with this non-dogmatic character of Fourier's approach to human fact, the following observation of Engels is highly significant: "Fourier, as we see, uses the dialectic method in the same masterly way (*mit derselben Meisterschaft*) as his contemporary, Hegel" (Engels [1880] 1973). It should also be noticed that in *The German Ideology* Marx and Engels blame Grün for being too critical towards Fourier's concept of series. For them, Grün did not attempt

> to show how Fourier came to deal with *séries*, and how he and his disciples constructed them. . . . It is only possible to criticise such constructions (and this applies also to the Hegelian method) by demonstrating how they are made and thereby proving oneself master of them (*man beweist, dass man Herr über sie ist*).
>
> (Marx and Engels [1845–46] 1969, 499)

In the end, to fully understand Fourier's conception of the individual it must be kept in mind that Fourier seeks to escape definitely our modern world, corrupted by industry and commerce – which he hates – and to come back to the natural world designed by God, in which the prime importance will be given to agriculture. Fourier is buoyed by a new hope, namely to implement an ideal society mainly based on agriculture and divided in small communities (the 'phalanxes') in which everyone knows each other and thus in which cooperation between individuals is possible. Hence, there is room in Fourier's world for a 'natural' man, whose essence is the enhancement of pleasure. But Fourier's natural man is much more sophisticated than Rousseau's *bon sauvage*, "seeking only for food, a female, and rest" (Bell [1968–69] 1992, 200). To this extent, Fourier's standpoint is not backward-looking.

For what interests us here, the main lesson to be drawn is that in the "combined order . . . you will see there is nothing vicious in your passions" (Fourier [1808] 2006, 72). Here, Fourier's psychosocial theory ensues directly from this analysis of the human character. Fourier is highly confident in the autonomy of the individual and in his ability to reach happiness by himself. And this confidence is established in a highly 'scientific' way in the sense that man, if not corrupted by our industrial world, would behave naturally and spontaneously according to these universal laws of attraction, just like the planets and so on obey the Newtonian principles in the inanimate world. In brief, Fourier's society is "the calculus of pleasures" (Fourier [1822] 1966–68, 2: 163). This explains why Fourier has great admiration for Bentham's '*felicific calculus*'. Indeed, he states: "I saw only one civilised writer who came very close to the definition of the real Happiness; it is Mr Bentham who requires realities and not illusions" (Fourier [1829] 1966–68, 6: 348). Yet, Fourier parts company with the utilitarians on the practical issue of the social reform needed if one plans to achieve the greatest happiness. In

Fourier's world, there is simply no room for pain, and by the way no balance to be found between pleasures and pains: "to understand Fourier on this point amounts to understanding how his thought follows on from the 18th century and to understand that he is not the first of the morose socialists but instead the latest of the *libertines*" (Schérer 1970, 119).

Thus, in no way the human being for Fourier needs to be re-educated for behaving according to social welfare. That is the reason why, despite the claim to have discovered a new science, Fourier's utopia cannot be considered as a '*scientism*' in the French sense of the word. 'Scientism' is the belief in the fact that the condition of a good life, the condition of the happiness is the assimilation of a precise knowledge elaborated by a wise theoretician. The 'scientistic' vision of the world is the deep conviction that the individual can only reach what is good for him if he conforms his behaviour to the teachings of a science created for the individual but outside the individual. In other words, the 'scientistic' vision of the world considers the individual as a child who needs necessarily an education, or more precisely a re-education, in order to become an adult, to perform his personality. According to this vision happiness, and even more true life, is a question of knowledge. On the contrary Fourier's new science, the "passionate attraction", is the discovery of a divine mechanism that governs both human beings and the world. If this divine mechanism is not yet fully effective this is not because of the lack of education of individuals but because of the lack of liberty. If the absurd limitations and the constraints that oppress individuals in the present world were deleted, they would spontaneously follow the requirements of the 'passionate' mechanism.

The attitude towards the 'negative'

First of all, let us be precise what we mean by the 'negative'. We use the term 'work of the negative' in reference to Hegel's conception of negativity. Two meanings of the 'negative' must be distinguished in Hegelian philosophy. The first meaning applies to the technical level. Dialectical approach of human reality considers the force of negativity as the essential driving force of History. In this sense negativity means the negation (criticism, reject, refusal, contestation, abolition, withdrawal, struggle, etc.) of what is simply 'given' at a particular moment in the process of the constant transformation of human reality. Thanks to negativity, human reality becomes a dynamic process; it escapes the immobility of the persistence of one single form or figure throughout its existence. Negativity ensures human reality the possibility of its internal transformation, the possibility of moving from one form to another, throughout the destruction of one form by another. In other words, negativity livens up human reality. History as such owes its existence to 'the work of the negative'. The latter introduces the mediation in the immediacy of a static world that refuses the change and the novelty.

But one can consider a more comprehensive meaning of the 'negative'. Still from a dialectical point of view, oppositions such as positive and negative, good and evil, truth and falsehood lack any foundation. With regard to our attempt to grasp the nature of Fourier's thought, we use this general meaning, for Hegel says: "Nor is there such a thing as the false (*Falsches*), any more than there is something evil (*Böses*)" (Hegel [1807] 1973, 40). In human reality nothing can be judged and excluded as purely unessential. The 'unessential', as a constitutive component of a changing reality, is essential as unessential. In other words, as far as human reality is a process of 'becoming' (*das Werden*) under construction, an element judged as wrong or unessential at a particular moment of the becoming will certainly contribute to the formation of reality at another moment of the evolutionary process. But yet the process requires to have at its disposal the conditions of its development. Therefore, a dialectical point of view refuses to proceed to a selection, purge or purification of human reality, through an immediate and brutal intervention with the intent to separate the wheat from the chaff. The Hegelian approach of mankind reality does not fear the negative since the negative is, just like the positive, a force that works through the formation of reality. One can describe such an apparent paradoxical process as the 'positivity of the negative'. Such a theoretical attitude makes sense to the extent that the theoretician pays attention to the becoming, to reality as a changing process. In this context, the 'work of negative' means that if reality is left free and without constraint to its own dynamism, such or such element considered as negative could prove to be as useful and necessary as an element considered as positive. The idea is to let the forces of a reality work freely through their process in becoming.

Let us apply this dialectic to Fourier. Fourier acknowledges the – apparent – insuperable gap between our unlimited desires and our bounded resources. Here, he stands in strong opposition with the moralist vision of the world. Moralists "argue that they are rectifying God's work, tempering or repressing the passions they cannot satisfy and sometimes do not even recognize" (Fourier [1808] 2006, 74). In Fourier's understanding of the human nature, there is no bad instinct to be inhibited. "Here stands Fourier's victory: for him, normality does not exist" (Barthes 1971, 1098). Quite the contrary:

> All the arrangements of the combined order will produce complete contrasts to our own customs, and will make it necessary to protect everything we call vice, such as greed and sexual intrigue; the cantons where these so-called vices will be most in evidence will be those which develop industry to the most complete state and whose shares are most sought after for capital investment.
>
> (Fourier [1808] 2006, 72)

For Fourier, in a state of nature the world is governed by the principle of the "passionate attraction": there are no bad instincts to be repressed but only passions, bad and good, both highly necessary for collective welfare. Such a view on bad instincts and vices might echo Marquis de Sade. Yet, "Sade takes the crime seriously, and grants it an absolute positivity and an absolute finality" (Schérer 1970, 28). By contrast, crime does not exist against God in Fourier's world, in the sense that all our passions are legitimate. These passions were designed by God; we should conform to them. At first sight, some of our passions, like for example greediness, seem to be dangerous, and one might wish to reject and inhibit them accordingly. But for Fourier these outward 'bad' passions necessarily contribute to the right order. The 'negative' should not be excluded but integrated, since it contributes to the 'positive'. In Fourier's words: "our passions become all good, if we develop them in the serial order (*ordre sériaire*) to which God destines them" (Fourier [1829] 1966–68, 6: 314). In other words, "the established crime is at the root of the real crime, that is the perversion of the natural purpose of the repressed passion" (Schérer 1970, 28). That is precisely the reason why "Harmony will decongest passions, sadism will be reduced" (Barthes 1971, 1100). To this extent Fourier can be considered as being part of Hegel's tradition for whom, as reminded above, nothing should be rejected as unessential, false, erroneous or evil.[2] Since our passions were intended by God, their operation and their interactions necessarily contribute to the happiness of the individual. In short, Fourier is not afraid of the negative.

That is the way the 'natural education' given in a phalanx is supposed to develop and bring to perfection all the germs given by nature. That is precisely how the combined order would provide much more wealth than our civilised order, 'surpluses' (*surabondance*) becoming a recurrent scourge, just as the 'shortages' (*disettes*) (Fourier [1808] 2006, 161) experienced in our industrial world. We should prevent ourselves from inhibiting our passions. On the contrary, Fourier compels us to release all our passions, both bad and good, "because true happiness consists in satisfying all one's passions" (Fourier [1808] 2006, 86). For Fourier man is an infinite potentiality of passions: his character is the work of his particular choices regarding his passions, that is to say the work of his liberty and not the result of external circumstances.

The otherness and the issue of justice

From the outset Fourier opposes a paternalistic and 'scientistic' approach to justice. He focuses his attention on the conditions of possibility of justice in a world of infinite diversity – even if Fourier does not address this difficult problem directly. Among the conditions mentioned above, work constitutes one of the most important. Fourier strongly advocates for the preservation of individual property rights. In sharp contrast with certain radical socialist doctrines such as Robert Owen's reform program, Fourier thinks that "the property spirit is the most powerful lever ever known to electrify the Civilised; one can estimate without exaggeration that the product of an owner would be the double of the product of salaried or slavish labour" (Fourier [1822] 1966–68, 4:171). The defence of private ownership goes hand in hand with the abolishment of salary system:[3] incentives would replace authority for ensuring efficiency. That would be done through the replacement of wage earners with owners co-interested and associated. In other words, there are two powerful motives for these individuals: Ownership and Truth.

Fourier himself acknowledges several conditions of feasibility of such an organisation. How is it supposed to work? There is first of all the guarantee of a minimal basic income. Yet, Fourier's minimum income is slightly different from our modern conception (Cunliffe and Erreygers 2001). For what concerns us here, it should be underlined that in Fourier's system the minimum income is paid in kind, if only because there is no money in Fourier's system. Furthermore, this basic income is given without any counterpart in terms of work and it can in no way be reduced to a minimum that would prevent the poor from starving to death. In line with his theory of passions, his conception of minimum revenue necessarily integrates pleasure.

The second condition, which is critical for Fourier's system, is to show respect for individual freedom. That is precisely what undermines one's ability to pursue happiness in an industrial capitalistic world. As a natural right of the human being, individual passions should be allowed to bloom out. As a direct outcome of his non-utilitarian (not to say his anti-utilitarian conception of labour), work ought to be undertaken freely. Industry would then become "an amusement" (Fourier [1808] 1966–68, 292). In Fourier's utopia there is no pain necessarily sustained in order to fulfil oneself; there is no negative to be reduced. The naïve reader might ask what would happen for hard tasks associated with very low attractiveness, such as mining. Fourier's answer is simple: in his "combined order" gold, silver and luxuries would be worthy, since mining is not very attractive, and thus highly expensive (Fourier [1808] 1966–68, 307). Just as in a liberal system, goods would be produced and exchanged according to the value given to them by the individual desires of the society. To the best of our knowledge there are very few occurrences in Fourier's writings of this concern for hard work, for 'repulsive' (*répugnant*) work as distinct from 'attractive' (*attrayant*) work to borrow Marx and Engels's words.[4] Clearly, 'repulsive work' implies a utilitarian relationship with work – a critical point ignored by Fourier. It is a deep matter of conviction for Fourier that "one succeeds in Series only by passion: the serial mechanism rejects anyone who is not strongly passionate for the managed specie by each group to which he belongs" (Fourier [1822] 1966–68, 4: 408).[5]

In Fourier's system both efficiency and fair repartition are obtained through the following principle: in a 'phalanx' everyone belongs to several series. Efficiency requires for Fourier to gather people as unequal as possible according to their endowments in labour, capital and talent. First of all, it should be noticed that division of labour would be implemented just as in a capitalist system. Everyone is most capable in small and repetitive tasks. However, concentrating on this sole principle and forgetting the whole passions of the individual is detrimental for efficiency. Here can be found the main criticism against the manufacture system advocates: tasks are far too repetitive and workers are far too specialised. For Fourier this is far from natural in that the full blooming of the human being's passions is prevented. Hence a "societary industry" should operate through "reunions" as large as possible, sessions as short as possible, subdivisions as detailed as possible, and above all "attraction" and "charm" (Fourier [1822] 1966–68, 2: 37). People voluntarily cooperate inside series they choose to belong to and series compete between themselves.[6] This ensures that the product repartition according to labour, capital and talent is fair: if I bring more capital and less labour than the other in a particular series, I will bring in turn less capital and more talent in another one. A fair repartition would be ensured thanks to greed instincts. Here is a critical outcome of Fourier's lack of fear over the 'negative'. For him there are no bad instincts to be inhibited, but only passions to bloom out. Despite its apparent negativity, greediness possesses its absolute necessity through the positive that it provides. The mechanism of repartition between diverse owners offered by Fourier provides for "*absorbing* the individual greediness in the collective interests of the Series" (Fourier [1822] 1966–68, 5: 533; emphasis added). In a world in which everyone is an owner, the individual becomes in Fourier's view an autonomous body. The individual is deemed responsible. Fourier was highly confident in the individual ability to behave spontaneously in accordance to collective interest, provided that one let him express both his bad and good instincts. The negative has to be integrated and absorbed, rather than inhibited. To this end private property is the true motive of efficiency.

We face here the question of *utilitarianism*. It is possible to observe some utilitarian accents in Fourier's economic analyses. But it is necessary to precise the specific content of his utilitarianism. Fourier's concept of utility concerns fundamentally individual happiness, which involves a vision of labour not merely as means to the benefit of an external finality but as an activity among others, which provides happiness to the individual. Labour and pleasure are mutually exclusive concepts in both the socialist and liberal worlds. Therefore, the condition of the pleasure or of the happiness is the rational and efficient organisation of work, i.e. of the suffering. By contrast Fourier has unwavering confidence in the goodness of passions. Such a confidence allows him to let the individual free to choose his work in following his own passions. As we will develop below, the confidence in others is a determining factor regarding the question of justice.

A 'non-scientistic' conception of justice

In Fourier's system of thought there is a natural order as wished by God that has been perverted in Civilisation and that should be re-established in a 'societary order'. Just as the material world is by itself self-adjusting, we should come back to this natural order, in which there is no bad instincts to be inhibited and good feelings to be encouraged, but only passions to be bloomed out. According to Fourier, we should escape the modern industrial world, as it has been perverted by merchants and speculators and come back accordingly to the natural society as designed by God, in which agriculture would be predominant. However, this scientific view of society does not mean that Fourier's approach is 'scientistic'. Individuals should conform to the natural principle of 'attractive passion', just like particles, planets and so on conform to the Newtonian attraction laws. As Barthes says, the world of Fourier is a

> combination of differences [which] involve that the individuality of every term is respected: one does not try to straighten up, to correct, to remove a taste, whatever it could be (and however 'strange' it is); on the contrary, one asserts, claims with emphasis, recognizes, legalizes it; one strengthens it by associating all those who want to practise it.
>
> (Barthes 1971, 1112)

There is no room in Fourier's system for a class of 'social engineers' who would possess this scientific knowledge and would implement the required technology in accordance. Hence, in Fourier's utopia there is no need to attribute power to some individuals in the political sphere: there is not, on the one hand, the class of the ones who know and, on the other, the class of those who do not know and who ought to obey the formers. To this extent, "the whole tenor of Fourier's thought is anarchistic. . . . The essential characteristics of anarchism, the accentuation of individual differences, the absence of authoritarian control, an organisation of society based entirely upon individual agreement, are all to be found in Fourier" (Mason 1928, 257).

A point to be emphasised is that Fourier's conception of justice ensues from his 'social science' of a natural order. Fourier deals explicitly with "distributive justice" (Fourier [1829] 1966–68, 6: 354), that is the law of repartition in a societary order (*ordre sociétaire*):

> finally we arrive to the main object, to the terrifying problem of implementing a vivid justice, a full harmony in the sharing of benefits and a satisfying reward for everybody according to his three industrial faculties, labour, capital, and talent.
>
> (Fourier [1829] 1966–68, 6: 308)

Fourier proves highly concerned by the "problem of repartition, whose solution is highly critical for the whole societary mechanism (*mécanisme sociétaire*)" (Fourier [1829] 1966–68, 6: 270). Here again, Newtonian principles should apply:

> In the whole system of nature, equilibrium operates through the gathering of opposite forces that are named in physics centripetal and centrifugal; in the same way the equilibrium of repartition has its *centripetal* impulse, the one of greediness, and its *centrifugal* impulse, the one of generosity.
>
> (Fourier [1829] 1966–68, 6:319)

How does it work? As mentioned above the initial condition, which is far from fulfilled in our civilised world, is to guarantee a minimal standard of living to anybody: "the first sign of justice should be to guarantee to the crowd an increasing *minimum* according to the social progress" (Fourier [1829] 1966–68, 6: 354). Second, there is the issue of sharing the global product obtained in a phalanx. Again, as seen above, there are no more wage earners but only co-interested owners. Here, it should be kept in mind that Fourier's basic purpose is to "cause the antagonisms of classes to disappear" (Fourier [1829] 1966–68, 6: 276) in an unequal society. Indeed:

> Far from being an obstacle, these inequalities are on the contrary the essential spirit: one cannot organise series without a great inequality of wealth, character, tastes, and instincts: if this scale of inequalities did not exit, we should create it, establish it in every way before we could associate the passionate.
>
> (Fourier [1829] 1966–68, 6: 6)

For simplicity's sake, the problem of distribution can be seen as a twofold problem: first, there is the sharing between series; second the problem of sharing within each series that constitute the 'phalanx', each individual belonging to several series to which he brings capital, labour and talent. As far as the remuneration of capital is concerned, Fourier argues that "nothing is easier than the repartition in proportion to capital: this is a strictly arithmetic operation, well known by everybody" (Fourier [1829] 1966–68, 6: 303).[7] Things become more complicated concerning labour and talent. Here, the first step in the sharing process is to classify series according to the benefit they provide to the collective. For each series, "its retribution is according to the rank it occupies in the panel of functions divided in three classes, *necessity*, *utility* and *pleasure*" (Fourier [1829] 1966–68, 6: 304). Now, series are classified according to a very different principle from the one enforced in our perverted 'civilised' world: "it is not on the value of the product that we order the ranks (of all the series) but on the influence of a task for the mechanics of attraction and for the harmony" (Fourier [1829] 1966–68, 6: 304). In other words, activities considered as basic and of prime necessity in our perverted world are not necessarily of first order in a societary society: charming activities might be more essential for social harmony than farming. That is also the reason why in such a Fouriers's world "the more a work excites attraction, the less pecuniary value it possesses" (Fourier [1829] 1966–68, 6: 307). The next step is to go downward and to apply the same mechanism of repartition within each series. The key mechanism that ensures that such a law of repartition is effective within a series is the *Papillonne* passion: this principle guarantees the preservation of diversity in the different activities offered in a phalanx: "each individual is obliged for his own interests to speculate in inverse order of the civilised, and to vote in each sense in favour of equity" (Fourier [1822] 1966–68, 5: 529). In contrast to the corrupted world in which we live these days, each individual belongs simultaneously to several series to which he brings capital, labour and talent in different proportions. Both and at the same time my greedy and my generous instincts will lead me to favour labour here but talent there; consequently I will be able to favour harmony between all the series that constitute society.

For Fourier justice does not imply re-shaping mankind. There is no room for individuals that would know better than others and that would take power accordingly. We do not need highly qualified people to govern society and to re-shape the real. Individuals only have to conform to their natural passions. Fourier's basic purpose is to ensure the blooming of each individual, in his diversity. Real diversity can only exist in a world in which individuals enjoy the recognition (*Anerkennung* in Hegelian terminology) of the community that considers them as *free wills*, i.e. as adult individuals able to organise their lives according to their particular choices or *will*. This implies that individuals should be considered as adults.

A world in which prevails real diversity is a world that makes room for the *otherness*, the other corresponding by definition to what is beyond our control. As Aristotle says in the *Nicomachean Ethics* "justice alone of all virtues is thought to be another's good, as implying this relation to others; for it is another's interest that justice aims at" (Aristotle 1893, Book V-1). The 'fear of the negative' we discussed above appears here as the fear of the other. Accordingly, justice in Fourier is the exact opposite to a 'scientific' justice, which would imply a kind of justice founded on science and which would eventually mean the negation of the issue of justice. Being just means making room for the other, that is making room to the 'negative'. In a world in which diversity is promoted to the extreme:

> the need for justice will exist in the details as in the whole of the repartition. The regime of the passionate series is a mechanism that *sweats justice* (*sue la justice*), and that turns into thirst for justice the so-called vice named thirst for gold.
>
> (Fourier [1829] 1966–68, 6: 313)

Fourier's utopia seeks to escape the material conditions of the modern industrial society of his time. Accordingly, he proves rather optimistic regarding the ability of mankind to be spontaneously led to collective happiness. Basically, Fourier is not distrustful towards the world. And he is highly concerned by the otherness. For him, "it is through the extreme inequality of fortunes that we arrive at this beautiful agreement of generosity: it would suffice of a grain of equality, of a proximity of fortunes, to prevent this sort of agreement" (Fourier [1829] 1966–68, 6: 321). Now, to understand such a statement it is necessary to keep in mind that, for him, the diversity that is at stake does not only apply to our wealth in terms of capital, but also to our natural penchant for music, theatre and so on. Everyone has a specific potential to express, and the task attributed to the 'natural education' is precisely to develop each individual talent. Instead of implementing a strict equality and uniformity between individuals, justice stands for the conditions of the diversity and the multiplicity of passions and desires.

Conclusion

The basic concern of our inquiry is theoretical. Our aim is to identify in Fourier a basic conception of mankind that has far-reaching consequences for the social organisation called for – despite the delirious aspects of the world he dreams of. Our interest for Fourier is in no way on a practical level. In our view the matters of concern that drive the whole of the Fourier's scientific and social project are strikingly utopical. All Fourier's efforts aim to imagine a non-paternalistic (what we called a 'non-scientistic') relation to others. Fourier refuses to consider the other as a reality to be redressed, rectified or re-educated by instilling in the other the teachings of true science. Fourier has a firm confidence in the individual capacity to organise one's existence in the most perfect way if he is left free to obey his passions. From this point of view Fourier's ideas on the education of children are extremely significant and deep on an ethical level. In his chapter entitled "Education in the *Harmony*" (*Education harmonienne*) he declares insistently that by the age of two the child should be considered as an adult in the sense that following his passionate nature "he can be exempted from every master (*chef*)" (Fourier [1829] 1966–68, 6: 184).

Fourier is probably the unique social theoretician of the 19th century to have such a confidence in the individual capacity for self-organisation. The real respect for others lies in such an unconditional confidence. Among the systems offered in the 19th century Fourier's is without any doubt the least exposed to the danger of totalitarianism.

Notes

1 Precisely, Fourier argues about the serial [*sériaire*] mechanism:

> "Let us observe that its compass is always UNIQUE: always the rigorous deference to the wish of the three neutral or distributive passions, all three constantly and combinationally developed in the societary order, which satisfies:
>
> 11th: the *Papillonne*, the largest possible diversity in individual functions;
> 10th: the *Cabaliste*, through the ternary classification of intrigues, their methodical contrast. . .
> 12th: the *Composite*, [permanent composed charm] through the combined intervention of the four springs of enthusiasm and equilibrium.
>
> These three passions are thus the oracle that is supposed to be ever consulted, in any problem concerning the Harmony system"
>
> (Fourier [1822] 1966–68, 5: 534–35).

2 On this question of the absence of the pure negativity to simply reject or exclude in Fourier's thought see the luminous text of Italo Calvino (1971), particularly p. XXV.

3 That leads Fourier to argue:

> Thanks to these gradations of societary interests, the inferior is interested in the well-being of the superior; and their union being cemented by the usual meeting in the attractive works and the affairs in the industrial series, one has nothing to dread of the full freedom of the common people who, in its current state of misery and jealousy, would use its independence only in the purpose of spoil and slaughter its superiors.
>
> (Fourier [1822] 1966–68, 3: 175)

4 Marx and Engels make use of this opposition between repulsive and attractive work in their *German Ideology* ([1845–46] 1975) in the section entitled "Fourierism" in the Chapter dedicated to Karl Grün's *True Socialism*. The wording that they use is in French, "*travail répugnant*" and "*travail attrayant*".

5 See also the following quotation: "Serial work charms the senses because each group exercises it on a variety that it has passionately. The one who loves only green pippin refuses to work in the yellow pippin tree, and even less for the other apple-trees" (Fourier [1822] 1966–68, 4: 408).

6 Let us specify the link between Fourier's theory of passions and his efficiency principle. Efficiency and fair repartition are ensured thanks to the enforcement of the three distributive passions almost forgotten in Civilisation. Indeed, everyone enrols in series according to his own ability and character: this is in accordance with the cabalist passion of competition and intrigue. Each 'series' session in a phalanx is very short (at most two hours), in accordance to the 'Papillonne' passion for diversity. Last, the enforcement of the 'composite passion' for cooperation ensures that individuals will be volunteers, and thus motivated in their series.

7 Fourier is not always consistent on this point. Sometimes he calls for a remuneration of capital more than proportionate, probably to attract the wealthy in his phalanx program.

Bibliography

Abensour, M. 1986. Robert Owen. In *Dictionnaire des oeuvres politiques*, edited by F. Chatelet, O. Hatelet and E. Pisier. Paris: Presses Universitaires de France.

Aristotle. 1893. *Nicomachean Ethics*, English trans. by F.H. Peters, M.A. London: Routledge & Kegan Paul, Trench, Truebner & Co. (available on: http://oll.libertyfund.org/index.php?option=com_staticxt&staticfile=show.php%3Ftitle=903&layout=html).

Barthes, R. 1971. *Sade, Fourier, Loyola*. Paris: Editions du Seuil. Reproduced in Barthes, R. 1994. *Oeuvres Complètes, tome 2 (1966–1973)*. Paris: Editions du Seuil, 1039–1177.

Bell, D. [1968–69] 1992. Charles Fourier: Prophet of Eupsychia. *American Scholar* 38(1): 41–58. Reproduced in *Pioneers in Economics, Vol. 31. Dissenters: Charles Fourier (1772–1837), Henri de Saint-Simon (1760–1825), Pierre-Joseph Proudhon (1809–1865), John A. Hobson (1858–1950)*, edited by M. Blaug. Aldershot: Elgar Publishing Limited.

Calvino, I. 1971. « Introduzione » to Charles FOURIER, Teoria dei quattro movimenti. II nuovo mondo amoroso e altri scritti, Turin, Einaudi Editore, VII–XXXVII.

Considérant, V.P. and M. Lechevalier. 1832. Prospectus Général. *Le Phalenstère*.

Cunliffe, J. and G. Erreygers, G. 2001. The Enigmatic Legacy of Charles Fourier: Joseph Charlier and Basic Income. *HOPE* 33(3): 459–84.

Deleuze, G. 1986. *Foucault*. Paris: Editions de Minuit.

Ege, R. 2000. L'Economie politique et les systèmes sociaux pendant la première moitié du XIXè siècle. In *Nouvelle Histoire de la pensée économique*, edited by A. Béraud and G. Faccarello. Paris: La Découverte.

Engels, F. [1880] 1973. *Die Enwicklung des Sozialismus von der Utopie zur Wissenschaft*. In *Karl Marx/Friedrich Engels Werke*. Berlin: Dietz Verlag, Band 19, 1973: 177–228. English trans. by E. Aveling, *Socialism: Utopian and Scientific*. In *Marx/Engels Selected Works*. Moscow: Progress Publishers, 3 (1970): 95–151.

Fourier, Ch. [1808] 1966–68. *Théorie des Quatre Mouvements et des Destinées Générales*. Vol. 1 of *Œuvres completes de Charles Fourier*. Paris: Anthropos.

Fourier, Ch. [1808] 2006. *The Theory of the Four Movements*, edited by G.S. Jones and I. Patterson. Cambridge: Cambridge University Press.

Fourier, Ch. [1822] 1966–68. *Traité de l'association domestique-agricole*. 2 vols. Vols 2–5 of *Œuvres completes de Charles Fourier*. Paris: Anthropos.

Fourier, Ch. [1829] 1966–68. *Le Nouveau Monde Industriel et Sociétaire*. Vol. 6 of *Œuvres completes de Charles Fourier*. Paris: Anthropos.

Halévy, E. [1901] 1995. *La Jeunesse de Bentham 1776–1789*. Paris: Presses Universitaires de France.

Harvey, R.H. 1949. *Robert Owen: Social Idealist*, University of California Publications in History, Vol. 38. Berkeley: University of California Press.

Hayek, F.A. 1983. *Law, Legislation and Liberty: A New Statement of the Liberal Principles of Justice and Political Economy, Rules and Order*. Vol. 1. Chicago: University of Chicago Press.

Hegel, G.W.F. [1807] 1973. *Phänomenologie des Geistes*. Frankfurt am Main: Suhrkamp Taschenbuch Wissenschaft, English trans. by A.V. Miller, *Phenomenology of Spirit*. Oxford: Oxford University Press, 1977.

Marx, K. and F. Engels [1844–45] 1972. *Die heilige Familie oder die Kritik der kritischen Kritik gegn Bruno Bauer und Kunsorten*. In *Karl Marx/Friedrich Engels Werke*. Berlin: Dietz Verlag, Band 2: 3–223. English trans. by R. Dixon and C. Dutts, *The Holy Family a Critique of Critical Criticism: Against Bruno Bauer and Company*. In *Marx/Engels Selected Works*. Moscow: Progress Publishers, 1975, 4: 4–211.

Marx, K. and F. Engels [1845–46] 1969. *Die deutsche Ideologie*. In *Karl Marx/Friedrich Engels Werke*. Berlin: Dietz Verlag, Band 3: 5–530. English translation: *The German Ideology*. In *Marx/Engels Selected Works*. Moscow: Progress Publishers, 5: 19–539.

Marx, K. and F. Engels [1848] 1969. *Manifest der Komunistischen Partei*. In *Karl Marx/ Friedrich Engels Werke*. Berlin: Dietz Verlag, Band 4: 459–93. English trans. S. Moore, *Manifesto of the Communist Party*. In *Marx/Engels Selected Works*. Moscow: Progress Publishers, 1: 98–137.

Mason, E.S. 1928. Fourier and Anarchism. *The Quarterly Journal of Economics* 42 (February): 228–62.

Morton, A.L. 1962. *The Life and Ideas of Robert Owen*. New York: Monthly Review Press.

Owen, R. [1813] 1963. A New View of Society, or Essays, on the Principle of the Formation of the Hunan Character, and the Application of the Principle to Practice. In *A New View of Society and Other Writings*. London and New York: Everyman's Library: 3–90.

Owen, R. [1816] 1963. An Address To The Inhabitants Of New Lanark. In *A New View* . . . : 93–119.

Owen, R. [1817] 1963. A Catechism of the New View of Society and Three Addresses (Letters). In *A New View* . . . : 170–223.

Owen, R. [1818a] 1963. On the Employment of Children in Manufactories. In *A New View* . . . : 130–9.

Owen, R. [1818b] 1963. To the British Master Manufacturers, on the Employment of Children in Manufactories. In *A New View* . . . : 140–7.

Owen, R. [1820] 1963. Report to the County of Lanark. In *A New View* . . . : 245–98.

Owen, R. [1842–1844] 1993. *The Book of the New Moral World*. In *Selected Works of Robert Owen*, edited by G. Claeys. Vol. 3. London: William Pickering.

Queneau, R. 1963. *Bords: Mathématiciens, précurseurs, encyclopédistes*. Paris: Herman Courbevoie.

Rawls, J. 1993. *Political Liberalism*. New York: Columbia University Press.

Rubel, M. 1982. "Notice" to *La Sainte Famille*. In *Oeuvres III Philosophie*, edited by K. Marx. Paris: Gallimard, La Nouvelle Revue Française, Bibliothèque de la Pléiade.

Schérer, R. 1970. *Charles Fourier ou la contestation globale: Présentation, choix de textes, bibliographie par René Schérer*. Paris: Editions Seghers.

Smith, A. [1759] 2000. *The Theory of Moral Sentiments*. New York: Prometheus Books, Great Books in Philosophy.

Smith, A. [1776] 1999. *The Wealth of Nations, Books IV-V*, edited by A. Skinner. London: Penguin Books.

Stein, von L. 1842. *Der Socialismus und Communismus des heutigen Frankreichs: Ein Beitrag zur Zeitgeschichte*. Leipzig: Otto Wigand.

3 Mill's qualitative hedonism as an ethics of desire

Towards an intersubjective concept of pleasure

Nizar Hariri

In line with Jeremy Bentham and James Mill's work, utilitarianism is a hedonistic doctrine that considers pleasure to be the purpose of life, an ultimate end of all our actions, and the highest good. Even the rightness of an action depends entirely on the pleasure that it produces for the greatest number. Accordingly, an action is considered morally good if the sum of pleasures that it generates for the greatest number exceeds the sum of pains.

Therefore, utilitarianism is different from ethical egoism because its normative criterion is the greatest happiness principle: one ought to maximize the greatest happiness for the greatest number and not merely the pleasure of a particular individual. However, one main objection to Bentham's moral principle concerns the quantitative evaluation of pleasures. Bentham assumes that one pleasure is worth just as much as another one if they both produce the same increase in happiness (decrease in unhappiness). Can any action (the most vulgar one for example) be considered truly moral only because it satisfies utilitarian calculus? And what if maximizing utility was to be attained only through pleasures of the belly (or the underbelly)? Could we morally justify pleasures that might compromise human dignity? And what if pleasures of the greatest number were to be achieved through violence, crime or dictatorship?

In his defense of utilitarianism, John Stuart Mill introduced a qualitative analysis, distinguishing lower kinds of pleasures from qualitatively higher ones. By this qualitative distinction, he argues that the quest for pleasure does not necessarily lead to a degrading lifestyle (a debauched animalistic one, for instance). According to Mill, utilitarianism is not a 'doctrine worthy only of swine' (Mill, 1863: 137). Pleasure cannot be reduced to the satisfaction of the most basic appetites or to the pursuit of antisocial lifestyles. Even if he considers pleasure to be the ultimate end, Mill reminds us that not all pleasures are to be chosen, and not any kind of pleasure is necessarily desirable. As I show in this article, Mill's highest pleasures, in their very *nature*, are closely linked to his ideal of self-development and self-perfection.

This qualitative distinction of pleasures has given rise to a lot of controversies. Some critical readings suggest that Mill cannot justify this qualitative distinction of pleasure without relying on non-hedonistic intuitions (Sidgwick, 1902; Riley, 2003; Perricone, 2011; Schaupp, 2013). Therefore, when comparing quality to quantity, the most challenging task is to determine which pleasures are the most desirable for the individual, while also being the most suitable for others. Thus, is the ideal of self-development compatible with a hedonistic ethics, and under which conditions?

This paper aims to address the polemic related to the qualitative evaluation of pleasure (the quality vs. quantity debate). By suggesting an alternative explanation to Mill's higher pleasures doctrine, I argue that the only acceptable interpretation of Mill's qualitative distinction of pleasures considers that all judgments on the quality of pleasure are grounded in an intersubjective understanding. At this condition, the qualitative distinction would not contradict his professed hedonism, as some might object to him (the utilitarian hedonism debate).

According to this reading, judging the quality of pleasures requires a social evaluation founded on a public use of reason that may lead to an intersubjective agreement. Moreover, only an intersubjective understanding of the highest pleasures can provide solid foundations to a hedonistic doctrine claiming that pleasures enable humans to realize their higher potentialities in their own way, while matching them with the development of the whole society. Therefore, Mill's qualitative utilitarianism does not rely on non-hedonistic intuitions. On the contrary, it is the consecration of a hedonism that is conscious of its own limits, the limits of our social judgment on what is higher in terms of pleasure, simply because the 'questions of ultimate ends are not amenable to direct proof' (Mill, 1863: 134).

Exploring this specific aspect of Mill's work shows that the highest pleasures are those that we judge as being capable of increasing the level of concordance among individuals while matching individual self-development with that of all the others. Therefore, the qualitative distinction of pleasures can be reconstructed as an ethics of desire, in the sense of a critical doctrine that aims to liberate human beings from all that prevent them from pursuing the life that they deem worth living.

The first section summarizes the quality vs. quantity debate, by opposing Mill's doctrine of higher pleasures to Bentham's calculus of utility. The second section discusses the hedonistic foundations of Mill's utilitarianism, showing that differences in quality of pleasure cannot be reduced to differences in quantities, and do not contradict hedonistic utilitarianism. The third section explores two properties of pleasure that are needed to reconstruct a hedonistic ethics of desire: a) the quality of pleasures is evaluated through an intersubjective understanding; and b) the highest pleasures are those that we judge as being capable of matching individual self-development with social progress, therefore increasing the level of concordance among individuals. The conclusion draws ethical orientations showing that we can reach a better political organization of our desires and pleasures by decreasing non-necessary sufferings.

Mill's ethics of desire vs. Bentham's utilitarian calculus

Bentham's utilitarianism is based on an arithmetic evaluation of pleasures, with seven quantitative criteria that measure utility: intensity, duration, certainty, propinquity, fecundity, purity and extent. Mill's objection to this quantitative utilitarianism is well-known: 'it would be absurd that while, in estimating all other things, quality is considered as well as quantity, the estimation of pleasures should be supposed to depend on quantity alone' (Mill, 1863: 138). According to Mill, even though any pleasure is considered good, certain types of pleasure are to be preferred to others, regardless of their respective quantities, because 'some *kinds* of pleasures are more desirable and more valuable than others' (Mill, 1863: 138).

Mill's demonstration runs in two steps. First, he starts by showing that two actions producing the same amount of pleasure can be distinguished qualitatively, and one can prefer a pleasure to another for its qualitative superiority. Second, he claims that a pleasure could be preferred to another even if associated with a lower quantity of pleasure (or a greater arduousness): the first one could be 'placed so far above the other' due to its qualitative superiority. Mill concludes that if all those who experienced both pleasures still prefer the first one, in this case 'we are justified in ascribing to the preferred enjoyment a superiority in quality, so far outweighing quantity as to render it, in comparison, of small account' (Mill, 1863: 139).

Even though some people are 'capable of no pleasures except those of which swine are capable' (Mill, 1863: 138), qualitatively higher pleasures are in line with the ideal of the full realization of human potentialities, because they improve self-development and drive social progress. Moreover, Mill suggests that no reasonable human being would accept to barter his highest human faculties for the satisfactions of a pig, and it is 'better to be Socrates dissatisfied than a fool satisfied' (Mill, 1863: 140). Thus, Mill considers that higher pleasures are intrinsically superior, and their qualitative superiority does not succumb to relativism (Dorsey, 2013). Therefore, if one ought to maximize the greatest happiness for the greatest number, one must increase the quality of pleasures and not merely their quantity.

Once admitted, the qualitative dimension of utility raises a number of questions. How can one evaluate pleasures if they are no more reduced to measurable physical quantities? One can assert that the pleasure of reading Shakespeare is qualitatively superior to those of gambling or eating. But how can one conclude that it is more desirable? According to Mill, the former is superior, even if it is associated with greater arduousness (more time consuming and requiring a greater intellectual investment). But how can one guarantee that most men would agree on such an evaluation? Elizabeth Anderson objects to Mill by claiming that no empirical evidence can support his qualitative distinction. She adds that, even if she personally is a fan of Shakespeare, she is not willing to give up on chocolate desserts (Anderson, 1991). Are we all certain to succeed in this challenge of 'books before chocolate' (Schaupp, 2013)? And does this distinction imply that Mill's utilitarianism crosses the strict borders of hedonism?

Regarding this particular aspect, Mill's explanations are scarce and have been extensively commented on, leaving room for diverse interpretations and controversies. The following section discusses two main objections to Mill's qualitative analysis. A first set of objections holds that the qualitative distinction of pleasures is irrelevant or poorly significant, as long as different qualities of pleasures could be amenable to differences in quantities (Quincy, 1980; Klocksiem, 2010; Schaupp, 2013). A second set of critiques tries to demonstrate that Mill is incapable of founding his qualitative distinction of pleasures without referring to a non-hedonistic renunciation of pleasure (Riley, 2003; Tännsjö, 2007; Hauskeller, 2011).

A qualitative and hedonistic utilitarianism

Are differences in qualities amenable to differences in quantities? Concerning this first objection, some textual evidence show that Mill clearly conceived an irreducible distinction, of *nature*, between quantity and quality of pleasure. Indeed, according to Mill, the horizon of ultimate ends is not merely the sum of desires and pleasures, because it is related to an ideal of self-development and cannot be reduced to simple quantification. In Mill's work, the opposition between different kinds of pleasures is related to an irreducible distinction between this ideal of happiness and the simple satisfaction of the lowest desires or pleasures.

Accordingly, some authors try to vindicate Mill's qualitative utilitarianism by claiming that it is grounded in a non-hedonistic renunciation of pleasure. Since Mill has stated that the ideal of 'happiness as self-development' is not compatible with the satisfaction of all pleasures, some critical readings consider that he is turning his back on his professed hedonism. Other authors hold that Mill's distinction could lead to a eudemonistic utilitarianism which is opposed to hedonism (Cowling, 1963; Dilhac, 2012). However, by expanding happiness beyond the strict limits of the satisfaction of all pleasures, Mill is not defending eudemonistic positions nor Aristotelian-inspired conceptions of virtue (Nussbaum, 2004).

The misunderstanding is rooted in Mill's writings which might lead the reader to believe he radically distinguishes between sensible pleasures and intellectual pleasures, in a dualistic fashion. In reference to the mind-body problem, could Mill be considered as a dualist philosopher? According to Mill,

> there is no known Epicurean theory of life which does not assign to the pleasures of the intellect, of the feelings and imagination, and of the moral sentiments, a much higher value as pleasures than to those of mere sensation.
>
> (Mill, 1863: 138)

A misreading of Mill's argument would state from here that qualitatively higher pleasures are indeed pleasures of the mind as opposed to those of the body. And it is through this distinction between body and mind that Mill's detractors interpret his theory of highest pleasures as strictly related to pleasures of the mind. For instance, Michael Hauskeller objects to Mill by asserting that if he were to choose between the pleasure of a Mozart concert and that of a sexual relationship, and even though he is a Mozart fan, he would be entitled to prefer the latter in certain contexts. The author also notes that 'since people only rarely are lucky enough to have sex while attending a public Mozart performance, in most cases they will have to choose between the two' (Hauskeller, 2011). However conceiving qualitative pleasures in a dualistic fashion, as being by nature (ontologically) antithetical to pleasures of the body, is a slip, shared by many readers and commentators.

It is absurd to consider that higher pleasures could be pure intellectual pleasures separated from the body, since the pleasure is by definition a decrease in pain and suffering. And Mill defines the ultimate end as 'an existence exempt as far as possible from pain, and as rich as possible in enjoyments, both in point of quantity and quality' (Mill, 1863: 142). Since pain could never be conceived as purely mental, pleasure is also felt in the body, even when it is related to intellectual activities. Even the greatest conquests of science and culture are considered by Mill to be the promises of decreasing pain and suffering for the greatest number (Mill, 1863: 146).

Mill always claimed that pleasures are heterogeneous, mixing quantities and qualities and involving several human faculties at the same time. Whether qualitative or quantitative, pleasures are always experienced in the body as sensible pleasures, even when they are related to intellectual experiences. By stating that the more a pleasure recedes from 'satisfaction of swine' the higher it is, one is not necessarily rejecting pleasures of food and sex or asserting that poetry is more pleasurable even for the hungers. One may mean that the pleasure related to a sexual act (or a meal) is qualitatively higher when it combines several faculties of body and spirit, and qualitatively lower when it is incapable of bringing into play higher faculties. Similarly, the pleasure related to a poem is qualitatively higher when it combines an intellectual value with sensible pleasures felt in the body. Surely, individuals who only seek the lowest pleasures have a highest probability of being satisfied, whereas individuals who have higher aspirations know that they are pursuing 'an imperfect happiness' (Mill, 1863: 140).

Let us take for example Mill's famous dilemma of the individual who frantically indulges in gambling and alcohol. Mill's utilitarianism faces here the same problem as that of Bentham's: must we tolerate a pleasure (or a lifestyle) that is deemed by some as being contrary to individual perfection and social development? Mill's answer is utilitarian and hedonistic at the same time: as long as the pleasures of drinking and gambling do not harm others, they must be tolerated; forbidding these pleasures is in itself a violation of the harm principle. Therefore, according to Mill, one should not proscribe nor prescribe. And as Alain Ryan suggests, it is only when the behavior of the alcohol abuser begins to harm others that it becomes reprehensible (Ryan, 1991). Brown also agrees with this reading of Mill according to which the only limit to discuss the appropriateness of these behaviors would be the limit of the law (the existence or absence of harm to others) (Brown, 1973).

In this case, Mill's position does not condemn pleasures of the body as opposed to those of the spirit. It rather asserts that the pleasure of drinking heavily is lower than the pleasure associated with a more moderate consumption. It is not the *more* you drink, the happier you are, and there is always a limit to the quantity of alcohol that one may drink. It is rather about *how* you drink.

Accordingly, the distinction between different kinds of pleasures is an ultimate foundation for a hedonistic theory that is perfectly in line with Epicurus to whom pleasure is the ultimate end, but all pleasures need to be evaluated according to another principle, a prudence or a wisdom that Epicurus described as being 'a more precious thing even than philosophy' (Epicurus, 1926: 91). In his 'Letter to Menoeceus', Epicurus stated that 'every pleasure because of its natural kinship to us is good, yet not every pleasure is to be chosen: even as every pain also is an evil, yet not all are always of a nature to be avoided' (Epicurus, 1926: 89). Epicurus himself offered a classification of desires that distinguishes between different kinds of pleasures, and his hedonism is founded on this ethical evaluation of desires and pleasures.

If one agrees with Bentham that pleasure is the principle of any action and the ultimate aim, therefore one must be capable of suggesting orientations in terms of selecting the best pleasures, showing how to evaluate those pleasures by another criterion. And this is specifically the task to which Mill's utilitarianism is devoted. By referring to Epicurus against Bentham, Mill is not turning his back on hedonism; he is showing that it is not enough for a hedonistic doctrine to assert that pleasure is an ultimate end. Stating that we should seek pleasure is one thing and evaluating which pleasure to choose is another one. Therefore, the qualitative distinction of pleasures is the ultimate foundations for a hedonistic doctrine claiming that we should rule our life with pleasures *only because* we are capable of choosing among them.

Going back to the example of the alcohol abuser, the pleasure of drinking remains inferior to the pleasure of reading, regardless of what the alcohol abuser thinks about it. Mill's conception of qualitative pleasure does not admit here any form of relativism. And we all have the right to worry about close persons when we think they are harming themselves. But Mill's liberal view allows individuals to harm themselves while seeking their pleasures (to consume alcohol or drugs to excess), as long as they are not harming others. As a solution to this dilemma, Mill suggests dialogue, persuasion or argumentation, or even scorn and disdain: we can show the alcohol abuser how much we disagree with his behavior and we may try to convince him to change his lifestyle.

Accordingly, the main difference between the Epicurean classification of desires and Mill's qualitative distinction of pleasures is that the latter is less restrictive and does not prescribe some desires and pleasures as being 'natural' or 'necessary' as the former does. According to Mill, even though any pleasure is good, the experienced value of a pleasure depends on its aptitude to realize the highest potentialities and the originality of every individual. Mill refers to these properties of highest pleasures as 'a necessary part of a perfectly just conception of Utility or Happiness, considered as the directive rule of human conduct' (Mill, 1863: 142). The next section tries to discuss these properties, showing the kinds of pleasures that are the most desirable for the individual while being the most legitimate for others.

An intersubjective conception of utility

In a genealogy that goes from Epicurus to Mill, would it be possible to reconstruct a hedonistic ethics according to which pleasures would be 'a little higher' than the underbelly, without necessarily being separated from the body (like pure spiritual or metaphysical ones)? Motivational structures of human behavior have been discussed at length by authors like Spinoza, Nietzsche or Freud; their theories are far beyond the restricted limits of utilitarianism. However, I argue that Mill's philosophy can lead to an ethics of desire which could guide our choices in the quest for happiness and clarify the ends that each individual is legitimately allowed to pursue in his or her attempt to realize what he or she considers to be a good life or a life worth living.

Mill's distinction of the highest pleasures might be the starting point for a practical and critical theory of desires, an ethics of desire that refers to two joint dimensions of pleasure: a) the quality of pleasures is evaluated through intersubjective understanding and an intersubjective agreement may be reached; and, b) the qualitative superiority of a pleasure is attested in its capacity to increase self-development of individuals in a way that concurs with the development of the whole society, generating higher concordance among humans.

The quality of pleasures is evaluated through intersubjective understanding

Concerning the evaluation of the quality of pleasures, Mill insists on two points that might seem contradictory: on one hand, he states that the quality of a pleasure depends on the nature of the object of pleasure; on the other hand, he admits that the judgment on the quality of pleasures is related to the authority of those 'who have experienced' and 'those who are competently acquainted' to judge pleasures. So when it comes to evaluate the quality of pleasures and to determine if one pleasure is more valuable than another, the judgment is established through a confrontation between different points of view of these 'competent judges' (Dorsey, 2013). But does it mean that the quality depends on the preferences showed by these judges? Is it intrinsic or extrinsic to the object of pleasure? Mill states that competent judges 'do give a most marked preference to the manner of existence which employs their higher faculties' (Mill, 1863: 139). But what if the competent judges have different or contradictory opinions regarding some qualities?

The rest of this section will try to show that an intersubjective conception of pleasure is the only possible explanation of Mill's 'authority of competent judges'. An intersubjective understanding of pleasure is needed in order to explain how the quality of a pleasure is inherent to an object of pleasure and, at the same time, the result of a social evaluation involving those who have experimented it.

At first, the quantity of a pleasure can vary depending on the person and the context, whereas the quality of a pleasure is intrinsic to an object or an activity.[1] Thus, quantities of pleasures may vary between two different persons, and they vary for the same person in two different contexts. Such pleasure that seemed strong to me at a certain period of time might seem less intense at another point. But the quality of a pleasure is deemed as such, regardless of one's personal evaluation, 'and there can be no appeal' (Mill, 1863: 141).

Therefore, a Goethe poem would provide a qualitatively higher pleasure than a text written by a seven-year-old child, regardless of what an illiterate person would think about it. Thus, the individual agent is sovereign in his evaluation of pleasures only when they are considered from a quantitative point of view. But the judgment on the quality of pleasures is neither objective nor subjective: it is intersubjective. Therefore, Peter and Paul would be the only one to judge if an apple or a pear gives them more or less pleasure, when this pleasure is conceived only as a physical measure. Indeed, these evaluations are related to purely sensible pleasures, felt in the body without other means of interpersonal comparisons. In that sense, quantitative judgment on pleasure is purely subjective. However, the qualitative appreciation of pleasure relies on an intersubjective understanding, a comparison based on a social evaluation.

The intersubjective understanding lies in the confrontation between different points of view, while taking into account the judgment of those who have experimented these pleasures and who can be designated as being 'competent judges'. The qualitative dimension of utility is the result of an intersubjective understanding because the only authority to consult is the judgment of those who are capable of higher pleasures. And in case they have a disagreement, Mill considers that we should take into account the opinion of 'the majority among them'. Mill notes that 'there needs be the less hesitation to accept this judgment respecting the quality of pleasures, since there is no other tribunal to be referred to even on the question of quantity' (Mill, 1863: 141).

Thus, our only access to the value of pleasures and pains is through the feelings and judgment of the experienced judges. Moreover, qualitative judgments can be described as being 'intersubjective' when they are deduced from the commandments of reason oriented toward the public utility. And this is specifically why qualitative judgments are prone to be disputed, argued and debated. It is also because of their nature of intersubjective goods, mediated by symbols, seen in relation to others, appreciated in the eyes of the others. To target the qualitatively higher pleasures is therefore to make a public use of reason, and to live under the commandment of a reason that is oriented towards others. Whereas quantities of pleasures are appreciated from the position of the solitary and isolated agent, qualities of pleasures are appreciated in a dialogic manner. Learning qualities of pleasure, as well as the development of originality and the blooming of individuality, is mediated by symbols, by language, by an intersubjective understanding and by what Mill designated as being the 'the real morality of public discussion' (Mill, 1859: 61).

Those pleasures attested in a public discussion to have a qualitative superiority would be those who increase the capacity of individuals and groups to experience better pleasures, or to decrease their sufferings. This horizon of ends acquires an intersubjective dimension, because the highest pleasure at stake is specifically one that might be considered higher by and for the greatest number, and 'there can be no doubt that it makes other people happier, and that the world in general is immensely a gainer by it' (Mill, 1863: 142).

Consequently, higher pleasures could be defined as pleasures that help humans overcoming the limitations that might prevent them from realizing their full potentialities. In that sense, a qualitatively higher pleasure will be described as qualitatively superior because of its public, intersubjective nature, being specifically 'good' for everybody. It is not about saying that the pleasure of contemplating a Van Gogh painting is preferable to the pleasure of reading Shakespeare from a qualitative point of view or vice versa; but that being 'literate or educated' is preferable to being 'illiterate or ignorant' because the former would enable the individual to enjoy certain qualities of pleasures that would be otherwise unattainable. These pleasures are said to be qualitatively superior because they are established by a public deliberation, the intersubjective understanding being the basis, the medium and the end of any quality of pleasure.

As a result, there is no superior authority established metaphysically to judge on qualities of pleasures and pains. The tribunal that should be consulted on qualities of pleasures is not the judgment of a particular person. Comparing qualities of pleasures with others, learning from 'those who know and appreciate' higher pleasures, is not surrendering to the diktat of a moral authority in terms of quality of life. Because what defines this quest for pleasure is above all the freedom of each individual to compare and to choose the most suitable pleasures for each situation. And finally, most importantly, it is not about prescribing practices of pleasure, nor stating that this form of life is culturally superior to another. Seeking a qualitatively higher form of life is adhering to a lifestyle that is justified publicly because it is commanded by a public use of reason.

Qualitatively higher pleasures increase the level of concordance among humans

Mill indicates that utilitarianism 'could only attain its end by the general cultivation of nobleness of character even if each individual were only benefited by the nobleness of others' (Mill, 1863: 142). Yet, this interdependence between the personal development on each individual and the social progress was better investigated in his previous essay, 'On Liberty'.

By bridging the two essays, one may conclude that the quest for higher quality of pleasures (and of life) is the quest for one's individuality and originality, rather than the submission to rules prescribed by others. Ultimately, qualitatively higher pleasures match individual pleasures with those of the greatest number. As an ultimate end of human behavior, higher pleasures are mediated by learning qualities of pleasures through sociability. And that is the reason why we need experts in high qualities of pleasure, original people and strong individualities capable of showing us how to improve the quality of our own life.

> There is always need of persons not only to discover new truths, and point out when what were once truths are true no longer, but also to commence new practices, and set the example of more enlightened conduct, and better taste and sense in human life.
>
> (Mill, 1859: 71)

Learning qualities of pleasure is performed through education, then emulation and finally through knowledge and 'mental superiority', in the sense of a capacity to be guided by 'wise or noble things' (Mill, 1859: 74). Mill keeps in mind that few people effectively pursue qualitatively higher pleasures, and that the misery of humankind is the result of the neglect and ignorance of this greater good. However, the quest of originality remains for each one of us the desire to cultivate and develop our higher faculties.

> To a certain extent it is admitted that our understanding should be our own: but there is not the same willingness to admit that our desires and impulses should be our own likewise; or that to possess impulses of our own, and of any strength, is anything but a peril and a snare. Yet desires and impulses are as much a part of a perfect human being as beliefs and restraints.
>
> (Mill, 1859: 66)

This desire drives the development of one's own faculties while converging with social development. Indeed, pleasures that have the most utility (therefore, qualitatively higher pleasures) are in fact pleasures that accord best with their potentialities. Higher pleasures could be defined as the ones that increase the level of concordance among humans. Mill refers to this ideal of self-development in its richest diversity as 'originality' and 'individuality', and the perfection of the individual is considered to be 'the highest and most harmonious development of his powers' (Mill, 1859: 64).

The comparison here with Spinoza or Nietzsche seems obvious, especially when Mill affirms that we actually increase our 'power' by satisfying our desires and tendencies according to our own inclinations, seeking a perfection within our own complexions. But it is in reference to Von Humboldt that Mill analyzes this ideal of the 'individuality of power and development' (Mill, 1859: 64).

What Mill implies by originality and individuality has nothing to do with selfishness or egoistic individualism: originality is the tendency of each singular individual to live according to his own complexions. And this perfection of originality depends on the confrontation with other persons, the social comparison being the only medium: 'the first service which originality has to render them (non-original individuals), is that of opening their eyes: which being once fully done, they would have a chance of being themselves original' (Mill, 1859: 73).

Originality is therefore conceived to be a common tendency among all human beings, although few people succeed in developing this originality to the level of perfection. Each man has different inclinations, but we all seek to attain a greater power. Consequently, the highest pleasures theory defended by Mill is not related to a metaphysical conception of happiness that the philosopher would arbitrarily or abstractly define. Qualities of pleasures must correspond to the aspirations of each one of us, to our personal capacities and singular inclinations. One must see 'what the body can do' according to Spinoza's formula. Therefore, a Shakespeare play between the hands of an illiterate is not necessarily a source of pleasure and inversely a life of debauchery is not suitable for a higher spirit like Socrates's. It is better to be a Socrates dissatisfied than a fool satisfied, but not everyone is meant to live like Socrates. One can judge the pleasure of reading Shakespeare as being qualitatively superior to other pleasures, but this does not imply prescribing

Shakespeare to all human beings, or forbidding more inferior pleasures. The command that would emerge out of this would rather be the necessity to fight illiteracy or any cultural handicap that would prevent the greatest number from enjoying such high qualities of pleasures. It is in that sense that we can denounce illiteracy as an 'economic bad', because we have all the reasons to think that by eradicating it, we can increase the qualities of pleasures for the greatest number. Therefore, activities associated with qualitatively higher pleasures are as legitimate for the individual as they are for the collectivity, and they are associated by definition with a decrease in social sufferings.

Conclusion

In my rereading of Mill, I have identified three dimensions of pleasure that are essential to the foundation of hedonistic utilitarianism as an ethics of desire. First, pleasure is appreciated in its qualitative dimension that trumps the quantitative one, to the point of making the latter superfluous. Second, the qualitative evaluation of pleasure relies on an intersubjective understanding. Finally, the highest qualities of pleasures link the happiness of the individual with the development of the whole society, because the highest pleasure specifically appears in a public discussion as being desirable for all the others. We have insisted on these three dimensions because they refer to a 'perfectly just conception' of pleasure.

Mill's theory of qualitative pleasures could be the foundation for an ethics of desire because it justifies a life entirely oriented towards pleasure without plunging in a degrading lifestyle (that would be despicable for the individual or reprehensible by others). From a critical point of view, this ethics denounces actions or pleasures that would turn away humans from their highest faculties, or make them endure non-necessary sufferings. 'All the grand sources, in short, of human suffering are in a great degree, many of them almost entirely, conquerable by human care and effort' (Mill, 1863: 146). It is therefore possible to reformulate Mill's utilitarianism as an ethics that is close to the intuitions of Amartya Sen (Sen, 1987) and to his capability approach.

Let us consider a last dilemma that was introduced by Sen himself. Donna has discovered that a group of racists are planning to beat Ali and the only way for her to prevent this crime is by breaking into Charles's room, in order to find Ali's phone number. According to Sen, a deontological evaluation limited to Ali's sacred right to preserve his physical integrity will fail to justify Donna's intervention, since she is violating Charles's privacy and property right. And a simple utilitarian calculus may also fail to save Ali, since the pleasure of the racists (and the pain caused to Charles) may outweigh the decrease of pleasure felt by the victim. Should we allow the beating to occur, since it maximizes utility for the greatest number?

Sen's solution refers to what he calls a goal-rights system stipulating that every human being has the right not to be deprived of some 'functioning'. Sen suggests that individuals may rearrange their preferences and priorities according to the context, and in this case it might be claimed that Ali's right to physical integrity is more important than a property right. In line with Mill's qualitative utilitarianism, a qualitative approach of pleasure may reach the same conclusion as Sen's capability approach, and most probably it can better account for this case since it does not need to invocate any 'right' (Donna's right to violate Charles's intimacy, for instance). Indeed, by preventing the beating, Donna is entitled to justify her behavior from an intersubjective point of view: the pleasure of Ali will be considered qualitatively superior to any other concurrent pleasure or pain, in any subsequent discussion. Therefore, no claim is made on the right to violate Charles's property right. As stated by Mill:

> To save a life, it may not only be allowable, but a duty, to steal, or take by force, the necessary food or medicine, or to kidnap, and compel to officiate, the only qualified medical practitioner. In such cases, as we do not call anything justice which is not a virtue, we usually say, not that justice must give way to some other moral principle, but that what is just in ordinary cases is, by reason of that other principle, not just in the particular case. By this useful accommodation of language, the character of indefeasibility attributed to justice is kept up, and we are saved from the necessity of maintaining that there can be laudable injustice.
>
> (Mill, 1863: 200)

In this sense, we may all agree that Donna has a duty towards Ali, but not any duty gives birth to a right (even if our duty is to save a life, we do not have the 'right' to steal, to kidnap, etc.). However, Donna's behavior would be approved in any subsequent discussion, and an agreement on the legitimacy of her behavior could be reached through the public use of reason, because no one can reasonably claim that the pleasure of the racists is to be preferred qualitatively. In this sense, the qualitative distinction of pleasures can be understood as a principle of hope, meaning a critical principle that aims at emancipation, because it is oriented against any form of deprivation or limitation that would hamper a person's liberty and would prevent self-improvement and perfection.

Stating that the happiness for the greatest number is an ultimate end is therefore not the illusory praise of a life full of continuous enjoyments or permanent pleasures. Mill reminds us that increasing pleasures is another way of saying that we are capable of decreasing sufferings. Indeed, believing that the ideal of pleasure is to be found in some state of permanent ecstasy or uninterrupted enjoyments, is asking Nature a lot more than it can offer. Seeking qualitatively higher pleasures is acting to decrease those sufferings, address those handicaps and free the greatest potentialities that would be hampered by our social relations. Therefore, an ethics of desire is understood as a critical doctrine of pleasures formulated against any form of deprivation or limitation that would prevent us from pursuing our life projects.

Defending a qualitative utilitarianism is first of all showing, within the organization of our social relations and existing social institutions, what prevents each one of us from leading the happy life that he tends to. It is also showing that non-necessary sufferings can be decreased and that the means used for this end are desirable for individuals and groups. Finally, qualitatively higher pleasures are pleasures that increase the aptitude of the individuals and groups to experience other pleasures, even better and unsuspected. The main virtue of higher pleasures is probably their ability to liberate new, unexpected potentials, and to awaken sleeping powers by opening new horizons for the individual and for the greatest number.

Note

1 And this is why differences in quality could never be amenable to differences in quantity, since the assessment process is not the same.

Bibliography

Anderson, E. (1991) 'Mill and Experiments in Living', *Ethics*, 102: 4–26.

Audard, C. (2011) 'The Ideal of Self-Development: Personal or Political?' in Gosseries, A. and Vanderborght, Y. (eds.) *Arguing about Justice, Essays for Philippe Van Parijs*, Louvain: Presses Universitaires de Louvain.

Bentham, J. (1789) *An Introduction to the Principles of Moral and Legislation*, London and New York: Methuen, 1982.

Brink, D. (1992) 'Mill's Deliberative Utilitarianism', *Philosophy and Public Affairs*, 21: 67–103.

Brown, D.G. (1973) 'What Is Mill's Principle of Utility', *Canadian Journal of Philosophy*, 3(1): 1–12.

Cowling, M. (1963) *Mill and Liberalism*, Cambridge: Cambridge University Press.

Dilhac, M.-A. (2012) 'Diversité et tolérance dans le libéralisme de John Stuart Mill', *The Tocqueville Review/La revue Tocqueville*, 33(1): 67–100.

Dorsey, D. (2013) 'The Authority of Competence and Quality as Extrinsic', *British Journal for the History of Philosophy*, 21(1): 78–99.

Epicurus. (1926) 'Letter to Menoeceus', in Bailey, C. (ed.) *Epicurus: The Extant Remains*, Oxford: Oxford University Press.

Hauskeller, M. (2011) 'No Philosophy for Swine: John Stuart Mill on the Quality of Pleasures', *Utilitas*, 23(4): 428–46.

Klocksiem, J. (2010) 'The Amenability of Pleasure and Pain to Aggregation', *Ethical Theory and Moral Practice*, 13(3): 293–303.

Mill, J.S. (1859) 'On Liberty', in Gray, J. (ed.) *On Liberty and Other Essays*, 1–128, Oxford: Oxford University Press.

———. (1863) 'Utilitarianism', in Gray, J. (ed.) *On Liberty and Other Essays*, 129–201, Oxford: Oxford University Press.

Nussbaum, M. (2004) 'Mill between Aristotle and Bentham', *Daedalus*, 133(2): 60–8.

Perricone, C. (2011) 'Aesthetic Judgment: It's All about How Much', *Journal of Speculative Philosophy*, 25(4): 323–42.

Quincy, K. (1980) 'The Higher Pleasures and Their Quantification', *Polity*, 12(3): 457–80.

Riley, J. (2003) 'Interpreting Mill's Qualitative Hedonism', *The Philosophical Quarterly*, 53(212): 410–18.

———. (2015) 'Is Mill an Illiberal Utilitarian?' *Ethics*, 125(3): 781–96.

Ryan, A. (1991) 'John Stuart Mill's Art of Living', in Gray, J. and Smith, G.W. (eds.) *On Liberty in Focus*, 162–9. London: Routledge.
Saunders, B. (2010) 'J. S. Mill's Conception of Utility', *Utilitas*, 22(1): 52–69.
Schaupp, K. (2013) 'Books before Chocolate? The Insufficiency of Mill's Evidence for Higher Pleasures', *Utilitas*, 25(2): 266–76.
Sen, A. (1987) *On Ethics and Economics*, Oxford: Basil Blackwell.
Sidgwick, H. (1902) *Outlines of the History of Ethics*, Indianapolis: Hackett Publishing, 1988.
Tännsjö, T. (2007) 'Narrow Hedonism', *Journal of Happiness Studies*, 8: 79–98.

4 The worker at the heart of the analysis

The Saint-Simonian approach to political economy

Gilles Jacoud

Claude Henri de Rouvroy, Count of Saint-Simon[1] (1760–1825), developed for a time thinking close to Jean-Baptiste Say in political economic matters. Say was in effect the most renowned French economist during the first half of the nineteenth century and Saint-Simon considered him as the scholar to have led the most useful work in this discipline.[2] He took from Say the fundamental concepts of industry, production and utility (Saint-Simon 2012, vol. 2: 1774; vol. 4: 3233). However, Saint-Simon did not follow Say in his differentiation between political economy and politics (ibid.: vol. 2: 1496–8, 1783; vol. 3: 2016–17). He also distanced himself from the liberalism advocated by the author of *A Treatise on Political Economy* and developed a conception of well-being which was not reduced to the wealth of nations.

When Saint-Simon died in 1825 after having produced a wealth of literature that caused him to be counted among the philosophers and economists of the period, his disciples immediately endeavoured to spread his work. From 1825 to 1832, a period during which they constituted a relatively unified group, they devoted all of their energy not only to making Saint-Simon's writings known but also to completing them by an impressive editorial production.[3] At Olinde Rodrigues's behest and then those of Saint-Amand Bazard and Prosper Enfantin, they propagated Saint-Simonian thinking in the newspapers they headed, specifically, the *Producteur* (from October 1825 to October 1826), then the *Organisateur* (from August 1829 to August 1831) and then the *Globe* (from November 1830 to April 1832). They also offered a series of conferences that gave rise to the *Exposition* of Saint-Simonian doctrine from 1830 onwards. They moreover made their writings known by putting together different works from their articles already printed in the press.

The Saint-Simonians bore a project that was at once industrial, intellectual and moral for society, and political economy was conceived in relation to this project. They considered, as the preface of *Économie politique et politique* (a work constituting a collection of articles printed in the *Globe*) specifies,

> all questions of *political economy* must be brought back to a common principle, and that, in order to judge the *utility* of a measure or an *economic* idea, one must absolutely examine if this measure or idea is *directly* advantageous

to the WORKERS, or whether it contributes *indirectly* to the improvement of their fate.

(Enfantin 1831: IX–X)

In proceeding in this manner, the Saint-Simonians contributed to the setting up of another approach to political economy. While it traditionally developed from 'a reasoning in which "oneself" is the motivator' (Berns 2014: 1) and never broached the relationship 'in regards to the "other"' (ibid.), the Saint-Simonians put this other who is the worker at the heart of their analysis.

Economists contemporary to the Saint-Simonians such as Jean-Baptiste Say were in effect interested in individuals engaged in economic activity where each was considered in relation to oneself. They were not examined in relation to the other and had that been the case, it would have been within the context of non-conflictual relationships. If forms of dominion existed, political economy placed itself in the dominant's point of view, whether in abandoning the study of the political and social environment that allowed this domination and perpetuated it, or by focusing on the means of reinforcing the situation of those who dominated. These dominators, whether a sovereign for whom one sought to increase the wealth or a landowner in considering how to accrue their revenues are idlers from a Saint-Simonian standpoint.[4] The idlers had dealings with workers, but the Saint-Simonians reproached the economists for having no interest in their fate.

In contrast to the economists ignorant of the relationships between those dominating and those dominated (the latter represented by the workers) or overlooking their fate, the Saint-Simonians sought to place the worker at the heart of the analysis. The worker is the true actor of productive activity, and the idler becomes someone who certainly has ties to the worker, but whose role is to be minimised. An understanding of production mechanisms requires concentration on the worker becoming the economic agent, and an implementation of the objectives of political economy must aim to reduce their dependence on the idler.

The object of this article is, based on the principal Saint-Simonian writings printed between 1825 and 1832, to demonstrate how their approach to political economy was new and what status it conferred upon the worker. A first part will explain why it was indispensable to put the working man at the heart of the analysis of the Saint-Simonian approach. A second part will show how the Saint-Simonians believed political economy should be envisaged to put the worker at the core of the thinking.

Why put the worker at the heart of the analysis?

In the society that the Saint-Simonians observe, the worker is not only a dominated being but also an exploited one. Denouncing this exploitation and explaining the mechanisms is not only necessary in a perspective of the struggle for a better social justice, but also in the context of seeking greater economic efficiency since the existing economic and social order is not the most appropriate for developing economic activity.

The worker is exploited

The history of humankind is a history of 'the exploitation of man by man' (Bazard et al. 1830: 104). The society in which the Saint-Simonians lived did not distinguish itself from this point of view from those that preceded it since this exploitation exerted 'in the past as slavery in its most direct and vulgar form, perpetuates itself at a very high level in the relationships between owners and workers, masters and salaried employees' (ibid.). Societies are class societies in which one is dominant and the other dominated, and contemporary society fell within the extension of societies all characterised by exploitation. Certainly 'they are far, no doubt, from the respective conditions where these classes are placed today, from those that found themselves in the past masters and slaves, patricians and plebeians, lords and serfs' (ibid.) but the exploitation was no less real. The worker working for an employer is no longer a slave who is the property of a master but the transaction that he makes with his employer is not done on equal footing: 'he is obliged to accept it as his life depends upon it, as he is solely reduced to waiting for his daily nourishment gleaned from yesterday's work' (ibid.).

The society in which the Saint-Simonians live is thus a society in 'two classes, the IDLE and the WORKERS' (Enfantin 1831: 57). The first corresponds to a bourgeoisie constituted of capitalists and landowners. The second is often designated as being for industrialists. The term was derived from industry, and best understood in the context of the period, that is to say, productive activity. It was defined as 'the whole of agriculture, manufacturing and trade, by which all classes of society reciprocally meet their needs' (Allier 1826: 574). Industry, therefore, is not limited solely to the manufacturing sector but encompasses the activities in the remit of agriculture or services. The industrialist is he who works and lives off his work in one of these areas. This term covers the worker as it does the entrepreneur who recruits him for doing such and such a task.

The exploitation results from the situation in which the idler and the worker find themselves even before the production is accomplished. The idler, generally by his birth, is an owner whom thanks to his possessions can be dispensed of working. He does not, therefore, play any role in the productive activity unless it is to rent the capital that is needed for production to the industrialist. From there flows exploitation. The inequity of the conditions ensures that certain men '*own* the instrument of work whilst others *borrow* it' (Enfantin 1831: 55). Those who borrow pay a remuneration for this purpose to idle owners. The idlers, therefore, obtain revenues paid by the industrialists in a system where 'the former live off a part of the fruit of the work provided by the latter' (ibid.).

The revenue that the idler receives can take on different forms depending on what he lends to the worker. It could include rent from housing and farming, and other forms of rent or revenue that the Saint-Simonians assimilated in any case to interest. In this society divided into two classes, 'that which OWNS and *does not work*, and that which *works* WITHOUT OWNING' (ibid.: 49), the interest is the revenue of the class that owned, no matter what form the income takes. In regards to the distribution of the revenues, the improvement of the fate of the idlers is accomplished to the workers' detriment. The idlers do not participate directly in the productive activity but ensure that this activity provides them with the highest possible income.

> These *lazy individuals* are, however, very busy, they are active and involved; they are restless, they reason and discuss, they judge all points, and everything seems either good or bad to them, according to whether their farm rent, their annuities and their house rents are paid to them regularly and generously, or, on the contrary, are delayed, reduced or unpaid; in other words, they are highly active to increase or preserve their share of the fruits of the work which they take annually from the *workers* in order to maintain their *idleness*.
>
> (ibid.: 66)

By increasing the portion of production that falls into the hands of the idlers, an increase in interest rates reinforces the exploitation while its decrease reduces it. Whilst 'WORKERS wish for an increase in *wages*, a decrease in *interest, house and farm rents*' (ibid.: 54), the idle, who live due to the revenues of property, 'think the very opposite of the WORKERS' (ibid.).

The level of interest is, therefore, a good indicator of the degree of exploitation in society. At the heart of a class of workers, its increase penalises the entrepreneur as much as it does the labourer. If the entrepreneur has to pay higher interest to the capitalist or landowner providing him with the instrument of work, he is forced to reduce the wages he pays to the labourer. He himself, even if he does not directly pay the interest, is therefore affected by its increase since it has negative repercussions on the wages he earns.

In the perspective of improving workers' situations, there is, therefore, a stake in causing the interest rate to drop. This decrease does not just correspond to social preoccupations but also to economic considerations in a context where the existing economic and social order penalises economic activity.

The economic and social order curbs economic activity

In this society of exploitation where the idlers choose for which industrialists they provide the instruments of work and strive to obtain the highest possible interest, economic activity is penalised on several accounts.

First, the fact that the idlers could secure their subsistence without working does not permit the economy to mobilise all of its potential labour. An economy in which the return on capital dispenses their owners from working 'richly supports a host of lazy individuals' (ibid.: 66). As they dispose of sufficient revenues, the idlers are not incited to work. They represent a potential productive force that is unused, and so the production is situated at a level inferior to what could have been reached if all the available labour had been employed. Deprived of the contribution of 'a large class' (ibid.: 85), the economy realises production that is not optimal in regards to what it could have achieved. As a result, one can consequently understand that idleness can bring about 'the distressing spectacle of the inaction of inert productive forces' (Enfantin 1826: 76).

Second, if the idlers' capital does not remain unused since it is provided to the industrialists, nevertheless there continues to be a problem of allocation of resources. Indeed, nothing ensures that the idle owners have the necessary skills for attributing their capital to those knowing how to use it best. 'The repartition of the instruments of work is done by isolated individuals, unaware of both the needs of industry, of men and of the means capable of satisfying them' (Bazard et al. 1830: 119). Those who receive the capital are not necessarily in a position to make the best usage of it. Inversely, industrialists whose projects are pertinent and who might have the skills to bring them to fruition risked not being able to realise them because they are unable to obtain the instruments of work. The problem of allocation, therefore, comes from the fact that the industrialist is subject to the decision of the owners of these instruments and nothing guarantees that he will be able to obtain them.

> What should he do if the material means of execution, without which his thinking remains sterile, is not at his disposal? How can he procure it? He will have to approach the owners, the capitalists, possessors of *instruments* indispensable to the development of his industry, and to submit himself to their decision; but these men, called in this way to judge these projects, are they competent judges for him? Can they draw from, in their relationships with the workers, sufficient lights to appreciate the borrower's capacity, and the appropriateness of the use of capital that is asked of them? No, no doubt, they are strangers to the work of industry, to the men who conceive, direct and execute this work, they can therefore not estimate the guarantees of morality and intelligence that the entrepreneur presents, and which the business demands.
>
> (ibid.: 120)

More generally, production is lacking an organisation allowing it to determine where and by whom the capital must be used. 'Each is left with his personal knowledge; no overall view presides over the production: it takes place without discernment, without foresight; it lacks on one level, on another, it is excessive' (ibid.: 119).

Finally, the price at which the idlers provide the industrialists with the instruments of work was also a problem. If one has to acknowledge an economic function to the owners, it is that of making the capital pass into the hands of the industrialists.

> Land, capital and all the other objects of property, whatever they are, are INSTRUMENTS OF WORK; owners and capitalists (two classes which are not different in this respect) are the DEPOSITARIES OF THESE INSTRUMENTS; their function is to *distribute* them to the workers.
>
> (ibid.: 118)

And yet not only does nothing guarantee that they lend these instruments to the right people, but they do it by demanding a price that could be problematic.

> Is this function, the only one carried out by these individuals as owners, carried out with intelligence, cheaply, in a way which encourages the growth of industrial products? Seeing the relative abundance in which this large number of men live, evaluating the large part given to them in annual production, we have to admit that their services are not cheap.
>
> (ibid.)

The production cost rose by these expenses that the industrialist has to bear, obliged to pay interest or variants that are house rent, farm rent or any other form of rent. This cost is all the higher since the owner, ignorant of the aptitudes of the industrialist that he lends to, increases this cost with a risk premium more or less high based on how much he trusts him. In short, 'in the name of commission and interest, he makes him pay for an insurance premium proportional to the uncertainties presented by an ability he does not know' (Decourdemanche 1831: 24). This cost is liable to deter productions that would have been realised if the necessary capital to fulfil them had been obtained at a better price.

The Saint-Simonians cannot be satisfied with such an order characterised by conditions of production that are far from being optimal. If it is necessary to improve the worker's situation, it remains unclear how to assign them a new role in the way perceived by political economy.

How to envisage political economy in order to put the worker at the heart of the analysis?

The way in which economists had until then seen political economy, without giving thought to the origin of property or questioning the fact that by their birth, individuals found themselves owners of instruments of work permitting them to live idly was unsatisfactory. The Saint-Simonians wanted to make it evolve towards an industrial policy that took into account the social context in which the production was performed. The economy, which could not be cut off from the other dimensions of society, had to be reorganised for the benefit of the worker.

Political economy must evolve towards an industrial policy

Focusing on the taking into account of the worker's interest, the Saint-Simonians boasted of having introduced a 'new principle in *political economy*' (Enfantin 1831: x). The exploitation of the worker finds its origin in the conditions in which the property of the instruments of work constitute themselves. And yet economists failed to study it.

> Most of them and especially he whom epitomises just about all of them, Mr. Say, regard property as an existing fact, which they have not examined

> the origin of nor the progress, of which they do not even seek the social *utility*.
>
> (Bazard et al. 1830: 145)

The absence of reflection on the part of economists on the origins of property and the validity of a life of idleness ensured by the holding of capital gave a certain legitimacy to the selfsame holders.

> All economists, and Say in particular, taught them that one produced in two ways, by one's labour and by one's capital; they find the first method too awkward; they limit themselves to the second, which is in effect more commodious and want their capital to produce the most possible in order to produce the least possible themselves.
>
> (Enfantin 1831: 100)

The capitalists had from thereupon every latitude to justify their situation and their behaviour by relying on the contributions of the economists.

> These esteemed citizens can, therefore, ease their conscience with all the force of the arguments of economic science, such as it is taught today. 'We are *resting*, they can say, but our capital *works*; we doze, but they are watching; *therefore* . . . it is right that we consume the fruit of *their* labour and *their* watch.'
>
> (ibid.)

David Ricardo and Thomas Robert Malthus went further by showing

> *that the difference in the quality of exploited land allowed use of, without inconvenience, a portion of the social products for something other than the upkeep of the farmers*; but from this truth they concluded, quite simply even if it had not been clearly expressed yet, that this available part of products was and *should be* used to feed, *in idleness*, noble landowners. In a word, they legitimised, as much as they were able, the political organisation, in which a part of the population lives at the expense of the other.
>
> (Bazard et al. 1830: 147)

The physiocrats of the previous century themselves also contributed to such a legitimisation since they 'based their political system on the interest of owners' (ibid.: 148), even if they did not defend their idleness.[5] By applying the principle of utility to property, Jeremy Bentham was also induced to legitimise it (Bazard et al. 1830: 163–6). One had to wait for Sismondi for an author to start pointing out an antagonism between the owners of capital and the workers. By placing himself 'in opposition, on capital points, with the principal organs of economic science, Mr. de Sismondi noticed that a different interest had to necessarily drive the idle *owners*, and the *workers* who make use of the property' (ibid.: 145–6).

The inadequacies of the economists' approach and the arguments that they provided for owners did not as such signify their studies were discredited in the eyes of the Saint-Simonians. They did not hesitate to emphasise that 'economists have rendered a great service by being the first to consider the material interest' (Enfantin 1831: 55) which had been previously left aside. They did not hesitate to sing their 'praises to Quesnay, to Smith, and even to Mr. Say who popularised them' (ibid.) or to proclaim themselves as being 'admirers of Bentham' (Bazard et al. 1830: 163). However, it remained true that the economists

> have the pretension of showing how this wealth is *formed*, *distributed* and *consumed*; but it is of little importance to them to discover if this wealth, *formed* BY LABOUR, will always be *distributed* according to birth and *consumed* in large part by idleness.
>
> (ibid.: 150)

The major criticism directed towards them was having 'considered the *current constitution of property* as being an unchanging fact' (Enfantin 1831: 55).

The restrictive approach of authors such as Say, who glossed over the political context in which the economy functioned, had to be rethought.

> Economists . . . have claimed that they are not involved in *politics*, that their science made little account of the forms of government and that they were merely examining how wealth is *produced*, *distributed* and *consumed*, independently of the social organisation to which the *producers*, *distributors* and *consumers* are subjected. The result of this position is that their works are a perpetual *mystical* abstraction outside any form of *reality*, intellectual gymnastics which have given rise to precious thinking mechanisms, rigorous logicians, stunningly erudite statisticians, out-and-out calculators who treat men as if they were x and y, manipulating them like lowly matter, moving them around in their minds and in their books like machines.
>
> (ibid.: 114)

They failed to make practitioners emerge who push humanity onto the path of progress. The 'LAISSEZ FAIRE LAISSEZ PASSER' (ibid.) hardly incited action; it was, therefore, necessary for the Saint-Simonians to follow another approach.

> So for us, political economy is transformed into INDUSTRIAL POLICY, meaning the science whose object is to determine the SOCIAL CONDITIONS in which the *work instruments*, the *products of work* and the *workers* themselves would best be *combined* and *divided*, in a word, ORGANISED.
>
> (ibid.)

The economy must be reorganised for the benefit of the worker

The Saint-Simonian vision of the new organisation to be put into place was not limited to the economic area. 'The *common* aim of the city is MORAL, *physical* and *intellectual* progress of citizens' (ibid.: 127). The industrial policy that the Saint-Simonians wished to substitute the political economy for had to be, therefore, focused on the different dimensions of society. Instead of only being interested in its material dimension as the economists were, they also focused their attention on its intellectual and moral dimension. Thinking about social life was reflecting on what the industrial organisation should be but also its scientific and the religious organisations.[6] Three actors play a significant role in these three forms of organisation. He who is at the heart of the religious organisation and contributes to moral progress is the artist or the priest in the Saint-Simonian sense.[7] The achievement of intellectual and scientific progress rests on the scholar. As for the improvement of the material situation of individuals, it falls under the responsibility of the industrialist.

The transition to the new order advocated by the Saint-Simonians, even if it brings about a radical transformation of society, should not be done in a brutal manner.[8] It must result from an evolution and not a revolution from which the workers would have nothing to gain.[9] Change must correspond with social justice preoccupations and economic efficiency.

In matters of social justice, there must no longer be '*privilege of birth*' (Enfantin 1831: 59). It is because they are well-born that many owners can allow themselves, contrary to workers, to live while doing nothing.[10] One must, therefore, act at the moment when they receive the property that allows them to remain idle, by draining the capital that was passed down to them (Jacoud 2014: 309–12). The abolition of collateral estates, which would end situations in which the heirs received the property of the deceased they hardly had any ties with, and the increase of inheritance taxes in a direct line is hence to be implemented to reduce the transmission of property and dry up the source of idleness. Socially just, such measures moreover present the advantage of obtaining resources for the state to facilitate the achievement of other parts of the Saint-Simonian project.

In matters of economic efficiency, it is necessary to favour the decrease of the interest rate. It is compatible with social justice concerns as it amounted 'to reduce the rent given by the *worker* to the *idle* owner' (Enfantin 1831: 61). It is 'favourable to the WORKERS' (ibid.: 63) and, in reducing the cost of obtaining capital, it stimulates economic activity. This drop in the interest rate falls within a progression where the Saint-Simonians attribute an essential role to credit.

> The purpose of credit is to transfer work instruments from the hands of the *idle* to *labouring* hands, and consequently to put capital *at the disposal of each worker* more easily, that is to say, land, houses, factories and all the instruments required for the development of his *ability*.
>
> (ibid.: 45)

One strives towards such a result in a Saint-Simonian thought that considered that 'when wealth, which is always either an *instrument of work* or a *mainstay of idleness*, comes into labouring hands, the measure leading to this is good' (ibid.: 77).

To achieve this result, the Saint-Simonians rely on a new banking organisation. The banks are in effect 'INTERMEDIARIES between *owners of capital* and *workers*' (ibid.: 98) likely to allow the latter to acquire the instruments of work necessary to them cheaply for producing. The supplying of bank capital by the state, notably permitted by the use of resources obtained by taxing estates, guarantees that they will act in favour of workers (ibid.: 101). The public ownership of capital rules out in effect the risk of seeing banks maintaining a high interest rate and not distributing the capital in the most favourable manner for production. Called to function within the framework of a hierarchical banking system combining centralisation and specialisation (Jacoud 2010: 16–24), directed by managers acquainted with industrial realities, they become able to pilot the productive activity for the benefit of all.

> If credit is refused to *a branch* of industry, it is because, in the interest of *all*, the capital has been judged capable of being better used; if a man does not receive the instruments of work he requested, it is because *competent* managers consider him more suited to another function.
>
> (Bazard et al. 1830: 135)

To give the worker his rightful place, the economic organisation the Saint-Simonians aimed for must not rest on the competition between the economic actors[11] but on their cooperation at the heart of a society that gives itself the means to recognise everyone's merits and to put each worker in the situation that best demonstrates his skills.[12]

Conclusion

For the Saint-Simonians, a society in which the idler lived thanks to resources procured for him by the worker he exploited was not acceptable. It is socially unjust and lacking efficiency on an economic level. Due to his birthright, the idler finds himself an owner of capital that he rents to the worker, which allows him to perceive an interest that dispenses him from working. The higher the interest rate is, the more his situation becomes comfortable. Inversely, the high level of interest, which accounts for the degree of exploitation of the worker by the idler, draining the revenues of the worker and the high price that he has to pay to obtain the instruments of work is dissuasive and penalises economic activity. As a part of a global project for society, whose economy is a critical dimension without being the only one to be taken into consideration, it was advisable to put the worker at the heart of the analysis. Once the reality of the exploitation is recognised and the wish to end it asserted, the mode of action remained to be determined. Social justice demands the suppression of the automatic transmission of property by fiscal measures that target estates. Economic efficiency necessitates a reorganisation of productive activity that allows, thanks to an effective banking system, an allocation of capital at a lesser cost and to the users most capable of using it efficiently. Society could in this way evolve towards the new world desired by the Saint-Simonians where '*everyone would be classified according to his ability and remunerated according to his works*' (Enfantin 1831: 39).

Therefore, from this analysis of the Saint-Simonians it would appear that in a conception of political economy based on the existence of relationships between oneself and the other, oneself is the worker, a real producer likely to correspond to different concrete situations, while the other becomes the idler whose role should be minimised. This role is not only to be minimised in the understanding of the mechanisms involved in production, but also must be due to political economic measures destined to reducing the initial dependency in which the worker finds himself with the idler.

Whereas, in the words of Berns, the previous political economy favoured oneself and scarcely addressed its relationship to the other, Saint-Simonian political economy constructed an analysis based on the link to the other, the latter becoming the idler from whom the worker must emancipate himself. The success of the Saint-Simonian project leads however to such a reduction of the space devoted to the idler, and indeed to their decline that their vision of political economy utterly centred on the worker might lead to abandoning the study of the relationships to the other, having lost his *raison d'être*.

Notes

1 This title, which is still conferred on Saint-Simon, serves to distinguish him from his illustrious relative, the Duke of Saint-Simon, who was a memorialist at Louis XIV's court and during the Regency. But in 1790 he gave up his title, and he eventually abandoned it in his publications, which led his publishers to edit his *Œuvres complètes* under the name of Henri Saint-Simon in 2012.

2

> Of all those who have had a hand in the work, the scholars who wrote on political economy seem to me to have made the most useful works, and the *Traité d'économie politique* of Mr. Say seems to me the book where the largest number of coordinated positive ideas are. His work has been influential. His work contains all that the political economy has discovered and demonstrated up to now. It is, at present, at the forefront of this science in Europe (Saint-Simon 2012, vol. 2: 1496–7).

Saint-Simon regretted that Say, whose work was well received abroad, hardly benefited from public recognition in France (ibid.: 1678).

3 As early as 1833, one of Saint-Simon's followers, Henri Fournel, produced the first catalogue of Saint-Simonians's writings in a work which ran to no less than 130 pages (Fournel 1833).

4 From a Saint-Simonian point of view, the consolidation of existing institutions could, therefore, only reinforce the situation of those who dominated. This is the case for banks, for example, since 'the existing banks are founded by and for the idlers' (Enfantin 1831: 98).

5

> Placed at a lofty viewpoint by their master, they had sensed that their system would only have value so long as the *owners* played a role other than that of the *lazy*, and that they would render to society services that would largely compensate the sacrifice that it imposed upon them in their favour; but here their efforts were vain.

> They could very well preach to the rich idlers, have them commit to living on their properties, head the farm skillfully, to become, in a word, the first labourers of the state, opening *model furrows*, as did the emperor of China, their voices not getting past the antechamber of the palace of our lords, the owners. It would not bother them in their splendid banquets, it would not suddenly awaken them in their sleep (Bazard et al. 1830:148–9).

6 These three forms of organisation were the object of distinct articles in the *Globe* and reprinted in *Économie politique et politique*.

7

> By ARTISTS, we mean the men who by their thoughts and their acts, by the MORALITY of their whole lives inspire FEELINGS of generosity and LIKING, men who unite, who ordain, who LINK other men; the ARTIST, as we see him, he is above all the RELIGIOUS man, the PRIEST of the Saint-Simonian order (Enfantin 1831: 123).

8

> Saint-Simon's doctrine, like all new general doctrines, certainly does not suggest keeping or superficially changing what exists: its purpose is to profoundly and radically change the system of *feelings*, *ideas* and *interests*; and yet it does not call for an upheaval of society. The word upheaval is always linked to an idea of blind, brutal force, whose aim is destruction; such characteristics are far from those of Saint-Simon's doctrine. This doctrine does not possess or recognise other forces to lead men than those of *persuasion*, *conviction*; its objective is to *build* and not to *destroy*; it is always placed with a view to order, harmony and construction, either producing an idea in its purely *speculative* worth, or calling for the material *edification* which this idea determines. Saint-Simon's doctrine does not wish to cause an upheaval or a revolution; it comes to predict and accomplish a *transformation*, an *evolution* (Bazard et al. 1830: 137).

9 'Any idea of *violence* to put an end to such a situation would be absurd on the part of the *workers*' (Enfantin 1831: 67–8). They must 'pacifically and little by little escape from their exploitation by the *idle*' (ibid.: 76).

10 'The former are IDLE, or can be so, whilst the others WORK and cannot rest for a year, a month or a day without starving to death' (Enfantin 1831: 60).

11

> We have pointed out that these principles of freedom and *unlimited competition* which always constitute the dogma of periods of transition, the beliefs of moments of crises in social life, have only a *negative* value; and as long as the reign of these principles is extended, no overall vision oversees material activity, no balance, no proportion, no harmony can exist between the different types of work and finally that these endeavours are as badly planned and badly carried out as can be expected from a partnership in which the choice of directors is left to chance.
>
> Let us look at society around us. Numerous crises and deplorable catastrophes smite industry daily; a few people have started to notice, but they do not realise the cause of such great disorder, they do not see that this disorder is the result of the implementation of the principle of *unlimited competition.*
>
> What does competition achieve other than a deadly war which is perpetuated, in a new shape, from one individual to another, from one nation to another? (Bazard et al. 1830: 127).

12

> Let us imagine ourselves in a new world. Here it is no longer owners, isolated capitalists, strangers by their habits to industrial tasks, who regulate the choice of enterprises and the destiny of the workers. A *social* institution is in charge of these functions which are so badly carried out today; it is the *depositary* of all the

> production instruments; it manages all the material exploitation; it thus has an overall view which allows it to see all the parts of the industrial *workshop* at the same time; by its branches it is in contact with all the regions, with all kinds of industry, with all the workers; it can thus evaluate the general needs and individual needs, provide labour and tools where they are needed, in a word, manage production, harmonising it with consumption, and giving the working instruments to the most deserving industrialists, as it is constantly striving to assess their abilities, and it is in the best position to develop them (Bazard et al. 1830: 121).

Bibliography

Allier, J. (1826) 'Crédit, discrédit, banquiers, industriels, industrie, producteurs', *Le Producteur*, 2: 566–76.

Bazard, S-A. et al. (1830) *Doctrine de Saint-Simon: Première année. Exposition. 1829*, Paris: Mesnier.

Berns, E. (2014) 'Temps et altérité en économie', 2nd International Conference "Economic Philosophy", University of Strasbourg, 9–10 October.

Decourdemanche, A. (1831) *Aux industriels: Lettres sur la législation dans ses rapports avec l'industrie et la propriété*, Paris: Imprimerie de Guiraudet.

Enfantin, P. (1826) 'Considérations sur l'organisation féodale et l'organisation industrielle', *Le Producteur*, 3: 66–85.

———. (1831) *Économie politique et politique*, Paris: Imprimerie de Guiraudet.

Fournel, H. (1833) *Bibliographie saint-simonienne*, Paris: Alexandre Johanneau.

Jacoud, G. (2010) *Political Economy and Industrialism. Banks in Saint-Simonian Economic Thought*, London: Routledge.

———. (2014) 'Droit de propriété et économie politique dans l'analyse saint-simonienne', *Revue économique*, 65(2): 299–316.

Saint-Simon, H. (2012) *Œuvres Complètes*. 4 vols., Paris: Presses universitaires de France.

5 Economics and humanity

Theory of development in A. Sen and the concept of human integral development

Tony Ernesto Persico, Nicola Mattoscio and Edgardo Bucciarelli

Introduction

The economy, as a science, finds methodologies and solutions, while the ethics answers the question of the meaning of human, and therefore also of economic, actions. The economy is not ethically neutral, because it cannot alienate to answer about dignity and human needs. Instead, it is precisely in comparison with the human needs that the economy exceeds the mere search for a quantitative result and is realized as a social science: fully human and fully science. The relationship between religion and economics is one of the first points of analysis of the broader relationship between ethics and economics. Economic theory has started a slow analysis route of the connection between religion and economics. Some authors acknowledged an important role to Catholicism in the beginning of the bank system and in the birth of the first economic concepts, like the role that they attributed to the works of Dominicans, Benedictines and Franciscans theologians. This is not surprising if we consider that the first approaches to economic problems were born within the medieval moral thought and if we think about the role of Benedictine and Franciscan authors. We can think of Schumpeter, who describes the religious St. Antonino from Florence (1389–1459), as "perhaps the first man to whom it is possible to ascribe a comprehensive vision of the economic process in all its major aspects" (Schumpeter, 1954, p. 91).

Our study is positioned between religion[1] and economics. The study focuses on the contribution of Catholic teaching about development and its relationship with the theory of human development proposed by the Nobel Prize economist Amartya Sen. The study cannot be exhaustive at all and it will even make an extreme synthesis of the reasoning, focusing on the elements considered more relevant. The theory of human development proposed by Sen is well structured for those who read it and it is formalized by numerous contributions of economic science. We cannot say the same for the concept of Integral Human Development (IHD) proposed by the Catholic Social Teaching (CST) of the Church. The Compendium of the CST of the Church states that "Church's social doctrine was not initially thought of as an organic system, but was formed over the course of time through the numerous interventions of the Magisterium on social issues" (CST 72). In fact, "it develops through different reflections applied to the changing situations of this world, under the driving force of the Gospel as the source of renewal" (OA 42).

In the next section, we will analyze the idea of development as it presents in Catholic social thought. In this way, we can verify how the assumptions of Christian morals allow a juxtaposition with Sen's work, to find an effective opportunity of dialogue between the two contributions. It's also necessary to specify the nature of IHD proposed by the Catholic teaching to explore the possibilities of comparison with the economic theory. Benedict XVI affirms that economics isn't ethically neutral and for this reason it must be structured and institutionalized in an ethical way: "economics needs ethics in order to function correctly – not any ethics, but an ethics which is people-centered" (CV 45). Similarly, Sen adopts an ethics that depends on the position of the person and, displaying the influence of ethics on human behavior, he rejects the individualistic motivation as a guide for human action, in favor of the concepts of well-being and ability to act. Before Sen, Myrdal posed the problem about the non-neutrality of economic theory, about the fact it was easily influenced and about its need of a major transparency of the orientation given by the decision makers (Myrdal, 1969).

In the third section, we enter into the heart of the study, focusing on the dialogue between the two paradigms: IHD and the theory of human development proposed by Sen. To do this, we initially identify a common background because both Sen and the social doctrine are placed on a normative/ethical level. The common background includes several assumptions like: the agreement of Sen with the idea – proposed first by the CST – that humanity has a common destiny, the relationship between freedom and responsibility, the recognition of the complexity of the phenomenon of socio-economic development and the relational nature of the person. In addition, we will demonstrate how the concept of development, present in Sen, reflects the character of wholeness suggested by the Catholic teaching. To do this, we will first focus on the concept of freedom and its central role in the development process for the ethical and economic disciplines.

The study conducted is placed in a double frame of reference: on the one hand, we find the work of economists, above all several contributions of Sen, which were compared with the issue of ethics and economics; while, on the other hand, we find the work of theologians who have focused on the analysis of the social teaching and have built pieces of common field between the two disciplines, starting from the religious side of the problem. According with our purpose, we try to reach a possible central location between the two points of view. What we can find with this analysis is not two perfectly complementary halves. Instead, we can find some points of similarity, which come from the same origin. Finally, we individuated Aristotle's theory of origin and the special anthropological attention as a base for a vision of development that is common to the two areas.

Origin and ethics of integral human development

The context of the relationship religion/economics

The study of the thought of an economist cannot exclude the mentioning of the authors he refers to. This is more than ever real for the study of the thought of a pontiff. In this chapter, we will investigate on the formation of the concept of development in CST. At the end of the chapter we will check how the assumptions of Christian ethics allow not only the juxtaposition with the work of Sen, but also an effective opportunity for dialogue between the two contributions. After a long debate in the Catholic world, Pope John Paul II (SRS 41) confirmed that the social thought must be considered part of the moral theology, the same that in philosophical terms we are accustomed to call Christian ethics (Grillo, 2010). This has a crucial importance for our study. If the social thought was considered merely as an indication of a pastoral nature, it would lack the ethical character of the two concepts we are considering. If the understanding of the historical economic development makes an extensive use of economic positive science, an indication of the future choices and judgment on economic policy is an area reserved for the science of economics ethic, as in Sen works. CST in the same way tries to conjugate evangelical views with historical context and to pursue a moral guidance. Pope Pius XI, after the Great Recession, directly addresses the relationship between ethics and economics: "it is an error to say that the economic and moral orders are distinct and alien and that the former doesn't depend in any way on the latter" (QA 42).

The IHD is constituted by three main elements: a contingent data, that is the position of the Church about historical development problems; a personal data that is the moral imperative of human development; and a relational data that is the realization of development "of all man and of all men" (PP 13). On this purpose, the lexical closeness of Sen and the CST is emblematic: we can take as example the terms "integral development" introduced by Paulus VI and Maritain (Maritain, 1936) and the Senian "integrated approach" and his "development in comprehensive sense".[2] The linkage between the Christian view of development and Sacred Scriptures is one of the implicit premises. Becchetti proposed an interesting comparison between the concepts of sympathy and commitment already present in Sen (Sen, 1997) and the concept of conversion presented by Saint Paulus (Becchetti, 2009). The man who observes the precepts without understanding them is like the man who obeys a moral commitment. Instead, the converted man follows the "love commandment", adhering so completely to it he modifies his structure of preferences, as it happens in the case of sympathy described by Sen.

The construction of the idea of integral human development

Following, we recall the essential tools to our analysis because it is impossible to trace the centuries-old history of the Church's Magisterium.[3]Until the revolutions of the XVIII century, it would have been unthinkable for Christians to engage in any social action outside of a society founded on Christianity (Ruggeri, 2009).

In this period the Church found itself in a minority condition and it often had defensive behavior and attitudes of closure, but from 1900 it started comparing itself with the external world. At the beginning of the XX century CST considered development as a reflection in an international dimension of the principles of justice, truth and love, to which national communities are subjected. These principles derive from Thomistic and natural philosophy. Unlike what happens in the Protestant world, it is only in the XX century that the Catholic Church abandoned the idea of a "Christian economy", i.e. a proper economic model, and joined the recognition and the utilization of economic science in its analysis (Duchini, 1989).

The dialogue with the contemporary world has intensified after the Second Vatican Council of 1962–1965. Inside the Gaudium et spes we can find a section dedicated to the theme of economic development, in which a human central position is directly related to economics: "man is the source, the center, and the purpose of all economic and social life" (GS 63). Useful for incoming comparison is the definition of the common good as "the sum of those conditions of social life which allow to groups as to individuals, to reach their fulfillment" (GS 26). This definition is inserted into the duality of the person and of society according with Maritain thought, that is that society is person of people (Maritain, 1947). The document proposes a series of reliefs on world conditions among which the observation of social disparities between nations stands out. The consideration of the consequences of this situation is extremely modern: "while a few enjoy very great power of choice, the majority are deprived of almost all possibility of acting on their own initiative and responsibility" (GS 63). The possibility of acting can be posed in relation with the Sen definition of capabilities in the theory of human development (Sen, 1987). We will also analyze the concept of freedom contained in the conciliar document: "only in freedom man can direct himself toward goodness" (GS 17).

Paulus VI too gave his contribution on the issue of possibilities:

> the developing and the highly-developed economies there is a great disparity in their overall situation and in their freedom of action. In order that international trade be human and moral, social justice requires that it restore to the participants a certain equality of opportunity.
>
> (PP 61)

The concept was further focused through the definition of development with the encyclical Populorum progression: development is authentic if it "must foster the development of each man and of the whole man" (PP 14). The concept of integrity is central in the thought of Jacques Maritain, who – with other personalist philosophers (Mounier, 1938) – influenced the Council documents (Maritain, 1936).

IHD is also related to the idea of the "universal destination of goods",[4] the same that allows the limitation of "private property" (PP 24). At this regard, it should be noted how the same Sen, while appreciating the universalist position of Rawls's theory of justice (Rawls, 1971), doesn't consider applicable the idea of an institutional base that can be common to the whole planet (Sen, 2002b). In addition, the encyclical gave a negative opinion of international liberalism, guilty of having created a competitive market that accentuated the difference between countries rather than heal them (Barucci and Magliulo, 1996). Once again, we can find similarities with the thought of Sen on the gap between rich and poor countries (Sen, 1999c).

The reflection on IHD according with the contribution of John Paul II passes from an economic approach to a politic one. Behind political causes there are the moral causes of underdevelopment as called by the Pope. These latter bring to reverse the values' scale in the relation between ethics and economics (Musu, 1991). The violation of the basilar human rights always leave from the violation of human freedom in its different forms: economic, social, cultural and spiritual. The Pope asks: "the denial or the limitation of human rights . . . do these not impoverish the human person as much as, if not more than, the deprivation of material goods?" (SRS 15). Freedom becomes in his view the measure of development in full accord with Sen (Sen, 1999c).

Pope Benedict XVI's social encyclical Caritas in veritate makes a Christological foundation of IHD (Grillo, 2010): the assumption of "charity in truth" is indicated as the main propulsive force for a real development. The principle of freedom is updated by Benedict XVI, who posed it in relation with responsibility: "this freedom concerns the type of development we are considering, but it also affects situations of underdevelopment which are not due to chance or historical necessity, but are attributable to human responsibility" (CV 17). At the basis of the argument of Benedict XVI there is the consideration of non-neutrality of globalization. He affirms that "this freedom concerns the type of development we are considering, but it also affects situations of underdevelopment which are not due to chance or historical necessity, but are attributable to human responsibility" (CV 42). At this stage, we can observe the full maturity of the concept of IHD and at its updating inside the global context. During this period, we retrieve the direct contact between social teaching and scripture, the "Primacy of the Word". Next to the role of Bibliology in the development of the social doctrine, it emerges the participation of "civil economists" as Zamagni (Feix, 2015). We may terminate this brief excursus underlining how the proposals of the social teaching meet in several occasions the thought of Sen. He escapes from attitudes that reject globalization, calling for a better use of its benefits in favor of the most disadvantaged (Sen, 2002a). He also agrees with the CST (SRS 14) that the geography of poverty needs to be rewritten including large areas of rich countries afflicted by "new poverties" (Sen, 2003).

Which compatibility?

For the Catholic social teaching, development should be integral in referring to person, to material necessities and spiritual aspirations, and referring to the individual and the whole of humanity. Development so intended is ethical, and so realizable towards personal choices. It occurs an integral epistemology, referring to Maritain's words, that would be capable of dealing with empiric knowledge, modern thought but also wisdom and classical thought (Fornero and Tassinari, 2002). This address can be found in Sen's pages where we can read some references to Asian tradition and Aristotle philosophy. In addition, Sen deepened the relation of ethics and economics in his *On Ethics and Economics* (Sen, 1987): the positive economics has come to elude a series of ethical issues that, years later, would have shown the weaknesses of the neoclassical reconstruction of human behavior.

Sen refuses the individualism of those theoretical approaches that, excluding interpersonal usefulness, don't take care about social effects in economic choices (Sen, 1987). He refuses the idea of individual utility as an evaluation measure and he introduces the concepts of well-being and of faculty to act (Sen, 1985). The result of this innovation is that we can consider the choices made by a person not to improve his own well-being but to support important causes or the common good (Sen, 1990b). This means that non-evaluative economics, left outside of any ethics point of view, is usually inadequate to a scientific comprehension of economic acting (Zamagni, 1990). Benedictus XVI affirms in effect that economics isn't neutral and for this reason it should be structured and institutionalized in an ethical way (CV, n. 36). Both the Pope and Sen note that if business ethics is sufficient for the market, it is not sufficient for the full realization of human development that also includes social and political aspects. According to Sen we can find the main limits in the problems of inequality, the environment and cooperation external to the market (Sen, 1999c). We can now draw a profile of the first "ethical demands" proposed by Sen:

1 Role of personal ethics
2 Existence of an objective ethics
3 Subjective character of objectivity.

Christian ethic founds itself on the personalist principle, which is the full recognition of dignity of man and of his relational nature that made of him a "naturae rationalis individua substantia".[5] Pope Benedict XVI says: "the economy needs ethics to function correctly – not any ethics whatsoever, but an ethics which is people-centered". The main role of economics in the promotion of the person, his freedom and human rights finds the first motivation in the Church intervention: the concern for the good of mankind. Christian thought studies the constitutive dimension of a person as a bearer of relations, from Augustine and Boethius to Mounier and Ricoeur. The second demand could be: can a religious ethic support a theory of freedom like Sen's one? The economist affirms that an objective conception of ethic can coexist with a normative ethic but it must recognize the value of people capacity in choosing what they think has value (Sen, 1987). It cannot be different, because religious confession and morals are meaningless without freedom of choice. Even if indirectly, one of the consequences of the first two assumptions, the personal and objective character, allows the construction of an objective ethic model mediated by beliefs and information of the person. Thus, Sen adopts an ethic which depends on the position of the person (Sen, 2002c). Then, the last question is: can this "positional objective ethics" coexist with Catholic ethics? The answer is traced within the so-called Conciliar morals, i.e. an ethics of the first person: an ethic approach based on subjectivity, in a way that we can speak about a subjective objectivity. We can use a phenomenological reading in which the ethical limit is passed through a process of inter-subjective knowledge[6] (Casazza, 2007).

Dialogue between paradigms

The shared background

The analysis of the formation of the concept of human development led us to anticipate some of the aspects of closeness between Sen and CST. These common points are not delegated to secondary aspects, but they represent the conceptual structure which support the two visions of development. We have already discussed the recognition of the encyclicals inside the moral theology. Now let Sen justify a normative economic theory as "people themselves have responsibility for the development and change of the world in which they live" (Sen, 1999, p. 282). This attitude is not limited to the negative effects but is extended to all the positive intervention (Sen, 1990a). With this assertion, Sen is lined up with the idea of the common destination of humanity, proper of CST, but especially in measure with the relationship with freedom and responsibility that we have seen in Benedict XVI's thought (CV 17).

Another common point is the shared recognition of the complexity of the phenomenon of socio-economic development. This means to consider the outcome of the development process as a composite, a qualitative and a quantitative one. This is possible by recognizing the relational nature of the person. This allows us to identify a second basis of sharing. This one is a prerequisite for any choice both in economics – which considers reactions and externalities – and in the ethical field, bearing in mind that in the context of the legislation the two planes coincide. The social teaching, on the other hand, takes the concept of the relationship directly from the Trinitarian theology of Catholicism, according to which there is no love without relationship. As Berdyaev said "our social doctrine is the Trinity" (Bello, 1989, p. 148).

Following in our study, we will try to explain how the concept of development present in Sen's work reflects the character of integrality proposed by social teaching. Which is the position of the person in the economic system for the CST and Sen? The answer is contained in the idea of centrality and human purpose. If Sen believes that the new phase of development theory goes for the increase of human capital, on the other hand, he fears a possible exploitation of man (Gentilucci, 2008). He emphasizes that human beings are not the medium of goods' production, but they are the purpose (Sen and Anand, 1994). The comparison with the aforementioned document Gaudium et spes is immediately visible (GS 63). Sen recognizes two possible visions of development: the first is defined as "fierce" and it sees a series of social and democratic guarantees as luxuries that should be avoided; the second, "sweet", is comprehensive of these guarantees

(Sen, 1997). Both Sen and the CST approach to development refer to the second view. For Sen, this model combines both human rights and economic growth, and it is one of the best systems for the processes of development (Sen, 1997). The refusal of considering human development as a luxury reserved to rich nations – or a temptation for developing countries – has important empiric evidences, observed in the investment in human capital made by nations (Ishi, 1995). This type of consideration isn't only coherent with the idea of horizontal integrality of development – real development is for all men – but it constitutes also a concrete demonstration of his empiric validity.

Inside Sen's theory we can find the concept of functioning, that is what a person desires to be or to do, and the concept of capability, the alternative ensemble of functioning that a person is able to choose (Sen, 1999a). These last represent a form of substantial freedom, and for this reason Sen describes development as the removal of several forms of un-freedoms and the increase of the capabilities of people (Sen, 1999c). This fact marks a return to an "integrate approach" to socio-economic development on the track of Adam Smith's teaching. According to Sen, capabilities are the possibility of an individual to realize his own objective and human development to "contribute directly to the quality of life and to its flourishing" (Sen, 1999c, p. 144). It does not surprise that, years before, personalist philosophers, faced with the problem of the creation of categories, talked about conditionings and attitudes of person.[7] The sharing of the binomial complexity-person by Sen and CTS is underlined by the respect that both have for the originality of each person, implied in Christian religion, and that is translated in Sen's work in the attention for the heterogeneity of people and their different possibilities of realization (Sen, 1992).

Freedom and development

In our comparison freedom has a relevant role both as a standalone element and in the form of instrumental freedoms for something else. We can mark four profiles of confrontation:

1 Constitutive profile: fundamental role of freedom
2 Evaluative profile: freedom as evaluation key of development
3 Instrumental profile: acknowledgment of instrumental freedom
4 Humanitarian profile: derivation of human rights from freedoms.

According to Sen, freedom has a central role in the theory of "development as freedom". Freedom has a proper direct value: first there is the elementary freedom of survival for which it is not necessary to find indirect justifications invoking his economic effects (Sen, 1999c). For Sen, freedom is the necessary condition for which men can choose between capabilities and it has a constitutive role for the enrichment of human life (Sen, 1999c). In the same way, for religious thinking, freedom has a key role because it is a condition of the conversion and so of the truth: human freedom undertakes its obedience to truth and then to the duty of respecting the rights of other men (CA 17). Paulus VI posed the relation between development, freedom and possibility (PP 61) in the same way that for Sen development is expressed by the increase of freedoms and then of capabilities.

Freedom takes an evaluative role for economics and ethics. In fact, if capabilities can replace the indicators based on income, without hiding the obvious correlations between the two elements, this means that freedom can have an evaluative role of the results and of the guidance of economic politics (Sen, 1999c). Paul VI had severely criticized the unique use of economic indicators, suggesting a more careful approach to the quality of social life. The Pope said that "the quality and the truth of human relations, the degree of participation and of responsibility, are no less significant and important for the future of society than the quantity and variety of the goods produced and consumed" (OA 41).

We often think about an idea as freedom as it is made absolute by religious morals until it becomes an ontological category unusable in the solution of real problems. On the contrary, CST posed freedom in concrete situations, arriving to the formulation of a plural structure composed by several freedoms. John Paul II in his encyclicals Sollecitudo rei socialis and Centesimus annus proposes a series of "instrumental" freedoms: economic freedom, politic freedom, social freedom, cultural and spiritual freedom. The underlying logic can be easily traced already in the Council document Gaudium et spes (GS 26). The contents are recalled also in the encyclical Caritas in veritate by Benedict XVI and they can be easily related to the five "instrumental" freedoms proposed by Sen as freedom in development: a) political freedom; b) economic infrastructures; c) social occasions; d) transparency guarantees; e) social security. Instrumental freedoms constitute a big unique theoretical corpus shared between Sen and social teaching. Thus, for example, the reading of the collapse of the Soviet bloc by Sen coincides with the one proposed by John Paul II: the negation of the market was accompanied by the privation of indispensable freedoms that changed into a lack of capabilities, and from a last analysis into a negation of possibilities of the realization of man.

The protection of instrumental freedom can be translated into the protection of human rights both in Sen and in CST. Pontiffs greet with benevolence the developments of international humanitarian development not only in relation with religious freedom but also referring to the whole set of "instrumental freedoms". We had to underline that Sen opposites himself to those who criticize the legitimacy of human rights, understood as pre-institutional, protecting in this way also the Christian ethics that affirms the idea of universal human rights. On the contrary, he says that it is the ethical claim that vouches for the institutional recognition of the rights that men consider important (Sen, 1999c). Sen shares the concern expressed by John Paul II (SRS 38) about the danger that the declarations of rights may fail to an operational implementation: the reference to these rights presses anyone who can do it to make them effective (Casazza, 2007).

Democracy and development paradigms

The identity of views about the democratic character of development descends from Sen's freedom-based discussion. Per Sen, the solution of development issues passes through a democratic discussion, the affirmation of the transparency and the broadening of economic freedom. Comparing the two fronts, the request to put the markets in conditions of better functioning, with more equity and with adequate integrations, is unequivocal (Sen, 1999c). For both fronts, in fact, development is participative and it aligns itself with the democratic participation: if real development is contradistinguished by horizontal integrity, that is comprehensive of all men, then the "developing and strengthening a democratic system is an essential component of the process of development" (Sen, 1999c, p.157). Sen "relates the idea of subsidiarity to that of democracy in general and democratic evaluation in particular" (Sen, 2011, p. 15). The two areas of analysis have in common the possibility to universalize the value of democracy, not in the sense that all cultures share it, but because every nation can appreciate its value after having experienced it (Bazzichi, 2004). The importance from a "constitutive" point of view and from an instrumental point of view of political freedom depends also on the dynamism of the ethical discussion about the formation of values (Sen, 2004).

Sen fears that a major attention to the dynamics of the economic growth can overshadow the role of freedoms and democratic debate (Sen, 1999b). We recall here that one of the elements of the social teaching critique of the economic system is that a higher level of well-being cannot replace freedom and human dignity (SRS 33). We must highlight that Sen uses the concept of ability to resolve the conflict between human rights and collective purpose: if on the one hand the search for the common good limits individual choices, on the other hand the pursuit of this search allows the person more choice and possibilities otherwise impossible (Sen, 2000). In this way, we introduce the last step of our analysis: the consideration of the aim of rights in relation to common good.

CST defines the common good in an extensive way: opened to all those functions which respect the normative provision (GS 26). It is more than an ahistorical approach to the problem: it is centered on the adherence to the historicity and to the evolution of human needs, so that morality can deal with the social dynamics of the moment. This setting is like Sen's one, who – faced to set the operations required by his theory – prefers to avoid a limited list (Sen, 1999d). This derives from the common Aristotelic root of the conception of property and richness as instruments "useful for anything else". This orientation was made proper by Thomism thought and then CST. Nonetheless we had to deal with two levels: from one side the common good superior to the sum of individual interests and the common good available to everyone according to their needs (Zamagni, 2010). Sen argues similarly that the sense of creating wealth is to be more human (Sen, 1997). Sen's position, in the middle of natural and positive law, is nearer to the first position than the second. This last can be seen also overlapped with the character of integrality of development. The question of the work of Sen is in fact devoted to the understanding of how man should live. He recognizes also that a partial movement in the direction of an ethical acceptance of rights can shake from the bottom traditional economic theory (Sen, 1987). The removal of disparities and the protection of human rights can be easily read in the double path of extension of capabilities and realization of the integrality of human development proposed by social teaching.

Concluding remark

The study permitted the comparison of the views of development present in Sen's work and in social teaching. The purpose of the first step was dedicated to identify the most important elements of development vision from the Church's point of view. This view was summarized in the concept of integral human development. The definition and analysis of this concept has shown how the common space between the two subjects examined were not limited to side elements, but concern the main bases of the two ideas of socio-economic development. Both move from a ethical/normative setting with a marked emphasis on the vocation/responsibility faced with the persistence of the conditions of inequality. Inequality is reinterpreted in a qualitative way and it includes the real possibilities of realization of the human person and his freedoms.

The key element of the coexistence between religious ethic and economic theory stays for Sen in the guarantee of freedom of men. So, it doesn't amaze that freedom posed itself as a basis of sharing, with the view of human development as freedom by Sen or with the view of IHD. Both views recognize the moral nature of the choices inherent to development processes moving from the complexity and the relationality of development. Freedom is understood as a constitutive and instrumental value for the promotion and verification of human development. This represents the realization of the possibilities of man and the protection of his rights. Anyway, such rights must be exercised in a right equilibrium in reason for common good (and for not becoming an occasion of un-freedom for the others). In this sense, Sen and the pontiffs have in common an integrate view of development, representing all men and all the dimension of the whole human being.

There are some differences between the two points of view. For social teaching, the right to live – Sen speaks about reproductive freedom – cannot be submitted to other purpose, the human person should not be at the service of the economic system but its aim. However, it should be noted that Sen's position about the "terrorism" of the Club of Rome and the phenomenon of "missing women" sounds like a proof of the Church position, always in contrast with any form of birth control, especially in developing countries (Sen, 2002c) (Sen, 1999c). In conclusion, this dialogue's exercise gives some suggestions for both subjects. Economics is enriched by the comprehension of behaviors, deducing important indications of normative character. Social teaching gains in accuracy of analysis and in concreteness, and it often find the empirical proof of the rightness of its positions. So, we conclude our study remembering the indication of Sen, who sees in the dialogue the best way to face development economic and politics problems.

Notes

1 In the following, words and expressions as religion, theology, teaching, doctrine, Church, Christian and social teaching are related to the Catholic Church and Catholic Social Teaching unless otherwise indicated. This is not to deny the precious contribution of other religions, but simply to avoid constant repetitions in the text.
2 This happens through the words of Wolfensohn J. D., *A Proposal for Comprehensive Development Framework*, World Bank, 1999, in Sen (1999c).
3 For more details see Bucciarelli et al. (2011).
4 The idea was introduced by John XXIII in 1963.
5 Boethius, De persona et duabus naturis, cap. 3, P.L. 64, 1343.
6 As in the work of E. Stein (1917) who takes the concept from Husserl (1859).
7 See Mounier (1961); Ricoeur (1983).

Bibliography

The documents of the Holy See were published by Libreria Editrice Vaticana, Rome, Italy.

QA Pius XI, Quadragesimo anno, (1931).

GS Conc. Vat. II, Gaudium et spes, (1965).

PP Paul VI, Populorum progressio, (1967).

OA Paul VI, Octagesima adveniens, (1971).

SRS John Paul II, Sollecitudo rei socialis, (1987).

CA John Paul II, Centesimus annus, (1991).

CST Compendium of the Catholic Social Teaching, (2004).

CV Benedict XVI, Caritas in veritate, (2009).

Barucci, P. and Magliulo, A. 1996. *L'insegnamento economico sociale della Chiesa (1981–1991)*. Milano: Mondadori Ed.

Bazzichi, O. 2004. Dottrina sociale della Chiesa e democrazia. *La Società*, pp. 711–24.

Becchetti, L. 2009. *Oltre l'homo oeconomicus*. Roma: Città Nuova Editrice.

Bello, T. 1989. *Sui sentieri di Isaia*. Bari: Ed. la meridiana.

Boethius, A. M. S. 1847. *Liber de persona et duabus naturis contra Eutychen et Nestorium*. PL, 64, 1337–1354.

Bucciarelli, E. Mattoscio, N. and Persico, T.E. 2011. The Christian ethics of socio-economic development promoted by the Catholic Social Teaching. *The Journal of Philosophical Economics*, 1, pp. 90–119.

Casazza, F. 2007. *Sviluppo e libertà in Amartya Sen: Provocazioni per la teologia morale*. Roma: Editrice Pontifica Università Gregoriana.

Cremona, D. 1991. *Carità e interesse in San Antonino da Firenze*. s.l.: Aleph.

Duchini, F. 1989. Insegnamento sociale della Chiesa, scienza economica, attività economica. In *Alcune considerazioni sulle radici storiche del problema*. Il magistero sociale di Paolo VI. Milano: Vita e Pensiero.

Feix, M. 2015. Vers une nouvelle économie ? À propos de l'exhortation apostolique du pape François. La joie de l'Évangile. *Revue d'éthique et de théologie morale*, pp. 3/89–110.

Fornero, G. and Tassinari, S. 2002. *Le filosofie del Novecento*. Milano: Mondadori.

Gentilucci, C.E. 2008. Il concetto di sviluppo in Amartya Sen e nella Dottrina sociale della Chiesa. *Studi economici e sociali*, pp. 47–58.

Grillo, G. 2010. *Sommario della Dottrina sociale della Chiesa*. Genova: Ed. Marietti 1820.

Husserl, E. 1859. *Husserliana*. Vol. 13–15. Springer. (ed. used 1966).

Ishi, H. 1995. *Trends in the allocation of public expenditure in light of human resource development- Overview in Japan*. Manila: Asian Development Bank.

Maritain, J. 1936. *Humanisme intégral*. s.l.: s.n.

Maritain, J. 1947. *Da Bergson a Tommaso d'Aquino*. Milano: Mondadori.

Mounier, E. 1938. *A personalist manifesto*. s.l.: Longmans Green.

Mounier, E. 1961. *Traitè du caractère*, in Oeuvres, Seuil, Paris.

Musu, I. 1991. La Centesimus Annus e l'economia. *La Società*, n°1.

Myrdal, G. 1969. *Objectivity in social research*. New York: Pantheon Book.

Nozick, R. 1974. *Anarchy, state and utopia*. s.l.: Harper Collins Publishers.

Rawls, J. 1971. *A theory of justice*. Cambridge, MA: Belknap Press of Harvard University Press.

Ricoeur, P. 1983. *Meurt le personalisme, revient la personne*, in Esprit, n°1, pp. 113–119.

Ruggeri, G. 2009. Riforma politica, Riforma ecclesiale. In *Quando i cristiani non erano moderati*. Bologna: Il mulino.

Schumpeter, J. A. 1954. *History of economic analysis*. Routledge (ed. used 1986).

Sen, A., 1933. *Development As Freedom*. New York. Anchor Books, (ed. used 2000)

Sen, A. 1985. Well-being, agency and freedom: The Dewey Lectures 1984. *Journal of Philosophy*, p. 82.

Sen, A. 1987. *On ethics and economics*. Oxford: Basil Blackwell Publishing.

Sen, A. 1990a. *Individual freedom as a social commitment*. New York: New York Review of books.

Sen, A. 1990b. Rational fools: A critique of the behavioural foundations of economic theory. In *Beyond self-interest*. Chicago: s.n., pp. 29–37.

Sen, A. 1992. *Inequality reexamined*. Oxford: Oxford University Press.

Sen, A. 1997. Development thinking on the beginning of XXIst century. In *Economic and social development into XXIst century*. Washington, DC: Johns Hopkins University Press.

Sen, A. 1999a. *Commodities and capabilities*. s.l.: Oxford University Press.

Sen, A. 1999b. La crisi ecologica? Una sifda per l'economia etica. *Etica per le professioni*, n° 1, pp. 69–71.

Sen, A. 1999c. *Lo sviluppo è libertà*. Milano: Arnoldo Mondadori Editore.

Sen, A. 1999d. *Uguali e diversi davanti alla salute*. Keiron, pp. giugno 8–16.

Sen, A. 2000. Human rights and human development. In *Human development report 2000*. New York: s.n., pp. 19–26.

Sen, A. 2002a. Globalization, inequality and global Protest. *DEV 45*, n° 2, pp. 11–16.

Sen, A. 2002b. *Globalizzazione e libertà*. Milano: Mondadori.

Sen, A. 2002c. *Rationality and freedom*. s.l.: Harvard University Press.

Sen, A. 2003. *The local and the global*. Turin Workshop "Globalization and Local Development". Turin. 27–28 November.

Sen, A. 2004. *La democrazia degli altri: Perchè la libertà non è una invenzione*. Milano: Mondadori.

Sen, A. 2011. *Justice: Subsidiarity and capabilities*. Milan: Eupolis. Lectio Magistrali 11th May.

Sen, A. and Anand, S. 1994. *Sustainable human development: Concepts and priorities*. New York: United Nation Development Program.

Smith, A. 1776. *The wealth of nations. 2000 a cura di*. s.l.: Modern Library.

Stein, E. 1917. *On the problem of empathy*. Springer. (Ed. used 1964–2013).

Zamagni, S. 1990. Sulla cooperazione tra scienza economica e etica: ragione, problemi, prospettive. *Atti della Accademia delle Scienze dell'Istituto di Bologna, Rendiconti*. Vol. 78. Bologna: Bononia University Press.

Zamagni, S. 2010. Catholic social thought, civil economy, and the spirit of capitalism. In *The true wealth of nations*. s.l.: Oxford University Press, pp. 63–93.

6 The disappearance of a moral attitude

An analysis comparing H. Arendt and F. Hayek*

Marlyse Pouchol

Relations with the 'other' were profoundly changed with the transformation of economics. Two authors, Friedrich Hayek (1899–1992) and Hannah Arendt (1906–1975) evoke a disappearance of a moral attitude, without, however, placing it in the same era nor assigning it the same origins. Similarly, the two established a link between this disappearance and the rise of totalitarian regimes in the 20th century, without, though, developing the same type of analysis. In both cases one finds a sort of responsibility of intellectuals in the course of those dramatic events, but for diametrically opposite reasons. While Hayek accuses a "constructivist" undertaking of presumptuous intellectuals who believe themselves endowed with the ability to judge what is good for society, Arendt deplores the absence of the custom of a faculty of judgement among "professional thinkers", a custom which could have triggered an opposition before it was too late.

Superficial similarities between the two mask radical divergences. The first part of this text returns to the source of their disagreement by presenting their different approaches to economics, and consequently to politics as well. Hayek follows Adam Smith in his understanding of economics, which is through an exchange of things, making the 'other' a "partner" with whom one "exchanges, shares and lends".[1] Given this, economics is understood as commerce, a word which, in the larger 18th-century sense, refers back to communication between people, supposing a "speaking together" and mutual respect. Arendt considers more production than exchange, in such a way that economics is, on the contrary, associated with violence. Manufacturing itself already contains a principle of violence against nature in as much as it is true that it is "impossible to make a table without chopping down a tree". It therefore follows that production activities require being restrained within acceptable limits. She thus placed herself in opposition to an entire tradition of thinking which, by making the economy the path to pacifying human relations, led to reducing politics to a means to serve the economic process. Arendt sought to present a concept of politics different from one arising from economics which had gained general acceptance in modern times. However, she had difficulty in making herself heard in a century of specialists in resolving the problems of society, as hers is a conception that provides no precise practical propositions nor recommendations for institutional structures. She postulated simply a regime that trusts in everyone's ability to think about anything.

This latter point aims to support Arendt's position that gives back a positive sense to politics against that of Hayek who considered it a harmful practice which gave rise to Soviet and Nazi totalitarianism. Arendt has another vision of history. The programmed extermination of people in the course of the 20th century under totalitarian regimes reveals a collapse which must, in her view, be linked to a sort of extinction of the life of the mind due to the eviction of the activity of thinking. In her later writings, following the publication in 1963 of *Eichmann in Jerusalem: A Report on the Banality of Evil*,[2] Hannah Arendt defined and developed her way of seeing moral phenomena. During a lecture given in 1970 – published under the title *Thinking and Moral Considerations*[3] – she sought to present the tenets of what she decided to call "her concept" of the banality of evil. She admits that "thinking" – that mental activity consisting of questioning oneself consists of immunising oneself against the fact of doing evil. She then associated a moral attitude reflected in a respectful relation with the 'other' to a mental practice exercised in solitude, demanding free time and physical inactivity. However it turns out that such conditions tend to disappear once the maintenance of an economic dynamic has become the alpha and omega of politics.

Economic violence or political violence

Arendt did not convince committed intellectuals of either wing because she did not take up the causes they espoused: defence of the underdog or defence of laisser-faire. She defended political liberty founded on another idea of humanity than that which had gained acceptance among economists, one which linked progress solely to human productivity and reduced the activities of the mind – thinking, wanting or judging – to secondary activities whose sole reason for being was to serve human productivity. Before presenting the importance Arendt accorded to mental life and more precisely to the activity of thinking, it is of course useful to mention that she was not ignorant of the problems which an expansion of the economy posed.

Economy, violence and transformation of politics

If the governments which appeared from the 1930s in the Soviet Union and in 1938 in Germany and which made terror a principle of government show quite clearly a collapse of morals, this does not signify that Arendt took it as a cause of Fascism.

She places *The Origins of Totalitarianism* (1951) above all in an expansion of production which, with no other aim than to increase the value of capital, as an endless process demanding an ever-increasing expropriation of the population. Arendt agrees with Marx, "who is the only one to have dared think analytically about this new process of production"[4] which spread progressively throughout Europe from the end of the 17th century by linking it to a primitive accumulation of capital. This he had associated, in reference to the enclosure movement in England, to a private appropriation of things once communal and accessible to all.

She also shared the view of Rosa Luxemburg, who felt, unlike Marx, that expropriation is not only a phenomenon original to capitalism but co-substantial to it, recurring anytime the logic of capital demanded. Thus, for her, it is not exactly the exploitation of labour in factories which characterises capitalism, but much more an expropriation: "the deprivation for certain groups of their place in the world and their naked exposure to the exigencies of life".[5] In this analysis, one cannot hope that capitalism collapses of itself, undermined by its own contradictions. The accumulation of capital, which feeds itself on factors exterior to it, pushes ever farther its conquest of territories and constantly enlarges its sphere of influence by expanding into domains until then outside the field of economy.

Arendt also follows the analysis of Hilferding who, in his work of 1910, *Finance Capital*,[6] painted a picture of a conflictual international situation by drawing on the consequences of the phenomenon of the exportation of capital by European countries towards unexploited countries, particularly in Africa. She presented the three decades of 1884–1914 – which correspond to an "Age of Imperialism" – as a period "of an almost complete break in the uninterrupted flow of Western history which man had experienced for more than two thousand years".[7] This imperialism, completely unlike the ambitions to construct an empire and impose a civilisation along the traditions of ancient Rome, was a phenomenon of purely economic origin. Protecting the interests of a few who had decided to transform foreign territories into areas to invest their capital, became from this period, a guideline for sitting governments. Hilferding highlights a major change in attitude on the part of the capital-holding bourgeoisie towards the state. When they established and took charge of workshops and factories, capital holders began to oppose political absolutism, the rules of corporations, and struggle against mercantile policies which imposed taxes on their imports. British entrepreneurs could be quite in favour of free trade because they had no need of the state to manage those activities well. "At least in principle, economic life was to be excluded entirely from the sphere of state regulation, and politically the state was to confine itself to the maintenance of public order and the establishment of civil equality".[8] In the age of finance capital, everything changed. Finance capital "detests the anarchy of competition and wants organization, though of course only in order to resume competition on a still higher level". It does not want "liberty, it wants domination". It needs "a state which can intervene in every corner of the globe and transform the whole world into a sphere of investment for its own finance capital . . . a state which is strong enough to pursue an expansionist policy and the annexation of new colonies".[9] In adhering to the demands of finance capital claiming an expansionist policy, "the whole world view of the bourgeoisie" was revolutionised. It ceased to be "peace-loving", although it had used harmony of interests and peace as one argument in favour of its ideal in the age of individual industrial enterprises. The idea of humanity founded on the equality of peoples no longer suited them. It was replaced by "a glorification of the greatness and power". "The national idea which . . . recognized the right of all nations to independent existence as states . . . is now transformed into the notion of elevating one's own nation above all others". The goal had in the meantime become to "secure for one's own nation the domination of the world, an aspiration which is as unbounded as the capitalist lust for profit from which it springs".[10] Hilferding considers it an "extraordinary perversion" of the national ideal, which no longer arose from a democratic principle of equality of man but from "the privileged position claimed for one's own nation". In no longer being solely industrial but also financial, it had become a conqueror and thus had to construct a new justification.

> [I]t appears to the ruling nation that this domination is due to some special natural qualities, in short to its racial characteristics. Thus there emerges in racist ideology, cloaked in the garb of natural science, a justification for finance capital's lust for power.[11]

For Arendt, as for Hilferding, imperialism reflected a real mutation of the state, transformed into an organ to constrain the population in the service of special interests and as such, should be considered as something new. Both refuse to interpret it as a characteristic of the state which, by its nature, cannot be anything else but an instrument in the service of the powerful. Here, it should be recalled that in the 16th century Jean Bodin, theoretician of the modern state, foresaw the unity of the realm and a principle of government able to overcome the religious wars between Catholics and Protestants, widespread at the time. Hilferding reminds us that "the modern state arose as a realization of the aspiration of nations for unity"[12] and not to oppress the population and to make them obey, as was the case with colonial administrations which support the necessity of enhancing capital "and uses [the power of the state] for forcible expropriation in order to create the required free wage proletariat".[13] It was not the "highest stage of capitalism", as Lenin interpreted it, but the beginning of a new era of capitalism, one which modified the sense and raison d'être of political institutions.

The structures remained but their functions were transformed. Politics disappeared, to be replaced by administration. The state became an organ to direct a social complex whose aim was to produce, and to enrich the country. The nation was viewed as a vast enterprise whose members, interdependent, necessarily form a whole, to be administered and guided in the direction of progress. Unity was no longer an objective to be achieved, but an obvious fact to the extent that those who did not adhere to the new construct who were not interested would be treated as deviants and enemies of the nation.

Understand or explain history

If Arendt reveals the economic origins of totalitarianism, she resists making economics the principle explanation for historical events. The economic circumstances which allowed these regimes to appear do not suffice to explain the fact that the totalitarian dictators, Stalin or Hitler, were able to take command of a state and impose a logic of ideas as principles of government, a logic which led to the elimination of all those not consistent with it. Arendt supplied no answers to common questions like: How does one explain the appearance of totalitarianism? She raises other questions: What happened? Why was there no opposition before the terror was put in place? Why did moral rules collapse so quickly? She broke with the intellectual approach of "professional thinking" – which sees its task in providing explanations – and thus refused to adopt a position of a scientific observer of phenomena, drawing conclusions in the form of general laws like that of the universal attraction of planets. Even more, she rejected the relevance of such a position. In other words, she sought to provide a response to the questions she was concerned with, ones which did not interest professional thinkers at all, while not providing a response to what was the sole pertinent question in their eyes. There was a double source of misunderstanding which necessitates, on the one hand, justifying Arendt's refusal to take up the task of explanation – characteristic of the function attributed to intellectuals in the modern era – and, on the other, defending the pertinence of her questions.

An explanation implies a coherent chain of cause and effect as inexorable as 2 and 2 making 4. Seeking to explain historical events translates thus as seeking to place history in a causal chain arising from a logic of coherent ideas, which implies eliminating facts that do not fit in the chain, thus leading those thinkers who focus too scrupulously on the task they think is theirs to deny reality. Negating evidence could well be a characteristic symptom of the professional disease of thinkers too preoccupied with a task they can never really accomplish.

Instead of explaining totalitarianism, Arendt proposed understanding it, which implied confronting reality and admitting facts that did not enter into preconceived explanative schemes, something which assumes a willingness to question oneself. Understanding, unlike explaining – which is based on the scientific method – regards history as in the phrase of the poet René Char, a phrase Arendt drew on: "our heritage was not preceded by any testament". Nothing is written in advance. The past contains the seeds of what is to come, but there were other seeds which could have led to other events. Admitting that what came to pass might not have happened is in the end a way of reintroducing the unpredictable nature of history as well as recognising the existence of political liberty, which Arendt defined as the collective liberty to start anew. While understanding preserves this collective liberty, explanation, linked "to the modern concept of history"[14] introduced by Hegel, leads to eliminating this liberty as every tragic event would always be interpreted as the result of an action that man should never have undertaken. On the contrary, for Arendt, who denounced an explicative approach, the Terror did not constitute an inevitable product of the French Revolution and Hegel was mistaken to make a link which led to recommending reducing liberty. Equally, Stalinism was not the logical result of the Russian Revolution and Marx could not be held responsible for the liquidation of the kulaks.

The criticism she aims at Marx was certainly not due to his having envisaged the possibility of creating a new society. This is, on the contrary, was a point in favour for the 19th-century thinker and critic of an economic thinking which based its hopes for progress on the capitalist mode of production. The problem arose from the fact that he had modelled political action on the fabrication of things, thus creating a link between political liberty and violence done to nature along the lines of the well-known cliché "You can't make an omelette without breaking eggs". Arendt fought the "innermost belief"[15] of the modern era wherein history is "made" by man in the sense that they manufacture it. She insisted on a difference between action and fabrication. Fabrication corresponds to an activity taken up in knowledge of the reason; the results aimed for are present in the mind before becoming tangible in a process of fabrication. It has a beginning and an end. On the other hand, "human action", in distinction from fabrication and production, hardly ever achieves precisely what it intends as it acts in a framework of "many wills operating in different directions".[16] In the larger sense, acting means taking an initiative and the consequences of that action in the concert of human affairs are as unexpected as they are incalculable. They also have no detectable end. 'True' history, composed of a multitude of histories of diverse relations between individuals different from one another, remains ever elusive as it has no beginning and no end. Thinkers cannot believe that they are capable of anything else than making a narrative of events, implying that they chose a beginning leading to an end, itself meant as a beginning for later generations.

The problem with explicative theories of history is not exactly that they are false; they often contain elements related to real events. Rather it is related to the role theoreticians attribute to them, just as declaring a theory is false is to suppose that there exists a true one yet to be discovered. Far from breaking with this approach, she on the contrary renews it. It is the quest for the true explicative theory which is the source of difficulty. Whatever the chain of logic presented, adopting one or another theory leads to denying the existence of political liberty and losing interest in political action, something which would not really be of consequence if it did not lead to discouragement when faced with events which demand opposition. At the beginning of the 1930s in Germany, Arendt was troubled by the behaviour, not of her enemies, but of her friends

> who had done nothing to bring this situation about. They were not responsible for the Nazis, they were only impressed by the Nazi success and unable to pit their own judgment against the verdict of History, as they read it.[17]

The case of Heidegger – who did not protest against the banning of Jews from the universities although he was a brilliant philosopher who had learned a lot from them – is a slap in the face, raising questions about the collapse of personal judgment and its link with the attitudes of those who have taken up the job of thinker.

Since Arendt's death in 1975, 'professional thinkers' preoccupations have not changed much; the desire to explain has remained dominant and the negation of political liberty still more accentuated. The recommendation to 'laisser-faire', arising from economic thinking of the last third of the 18th century, has been transformed, taking on a very anti-political twist. While in Smith's view it was only a recommendation addressed to governments, advising them to let individuals manage their economic activity, it attained a new level with Hayek, becoming an injunction addressed to everyone. Hayek commands us to not intervene in the course of a process of historical evolution and explains that we must "laisser-faire" the "laisser-faire", arguing that any intervention leads to catastrophe.

Hayekian explanation of totalitarianism

Friedrich Hayek was born in Austria in 1899. He was awarded the Nobel Prize in Economics in 1974 and crowned a very extensive oeuvre by writing a work in three volumes, *Law, Legislation and Liberty* with the last volume, published in 1979, entitled *The Political Order of a Free People*. He died in 1992 having defended the economic principle of laisser-faire all his life, but with his own particular arguments quite different from those of economists. While economic liberalism had up to then been defended by pointing out the benefits of a system of markets and private property, Hayek took a completely different path.[18]

He was quite critical of liberal economists who, like Walras, sought to demonstrate that prices set in conditions of free competition corresponded to a just remuneration for the efforts made by its participants. Hayek contested this approach by highlighting its non-scientific aspect. In his view, it is not possible to determine what exactly a just price is and it would ill-serve the cause of liberalism to pretend to be able to do so. He contrasted the position of "social science scientist" of excessive pretention with an ancestral humility which shows itself to have been in the end quite beneficial for human progress. Thus he writes,

> Indeed, these ancestors of ours thought and "acted under a strong impression of the ignorance and fallibility of mankind", and, for instance, argued that the precise "mathematical price" at *which* a commodity could be justly sold was only known to God, because it depended on more circumstances than any man could know, and that therefore the determination of the "just price" must be left to the market.[19]

Hayek felt that the superiority of the market system could not be demonstrated using positive arguments and remarked that liberal economists' efforts at such demonstration did not prevent the Russian Revolution of 1917 from taking place. Quite the contrary, by bringing the criteria of justice to the foreground, they allowed debates on the theme to develop and legitimised the complaints of those who did not gain from the game of exchanges. Equally, in emphasising that one benefit of a market system was to assure a balance of supply and demand, they led people to believe that a state-planned economy could, without problem, replace a market economy.

Hayek established a line of reasoning which allowed him to deduce that relations of economic exchange had a much more important function than that previously envisaged by economists. He felt able to state that economic relations assured "political order", arguing that the disorder and inter-individual violence characteristic of totalitarian societies directed by a state should be seen as the logical result of a desire to replace them. In his analysis, the root of the problem lay in the 18th century, the Age of Enlightenment, when men began to believe that their intellectual ability to reason constituted a means of conceiving an organisation for society. Hayek condemned what he called "constructivism" of which were guilty those philosophers who, like Rousseau, encouraged the French Revolution. The large number of those who developed and spread ideas critical of the established order were the main culprits.

In other words, the political liberty which Arendt sought to defend – a collective liberty to make a new start – appears to him as the most pernicious superstition in the mind of humans and should be seen as the cause of 20th century totalitarianism. It should be mentioned that Hayek's condemnation of political liberty comes from his adopting in entirety views put forward by Marx who, as seen above, associated it with violence and saw the new community as something a professional thinker could be the inventor of. The difference lay in that instead of supporting political liberty, he fought against it.

The logic of his view led him to advocate a reduction of the role of politics. He condemned above all legislative power – the power to "make" laws – that men unduly attributed to themselves. Law, true law, could not be made by any person in particular, nor by philosophers or other social thinkers giving voice to the people, without being freedom-destroying and negating human plurality. History showed that all other laws conceived of by human minds lead to "the road to serfdom",[20] which led in turn to totalitarianism. True law could only be those drawn from the functioning of economic exchange because they were the only ones emanating from the whole of the active population and thus the only ones able to respect individual and economic liberty.

Hayek urged a return to the law of the market, meaning that it was necessary to get rid of all laws giving rights to certain social categories at the expense of others, laws which had been introduced since the 19th century in all Western democracies. Having denounced the excessive pretentions of social thinkers, he found himself forced to justify his recommendation – which ran contrary to all forms of human intervention during the course of history – by emphasising that it was based on scientific truth. In *Law, Legislation and Liberty*, the law of the market takes on the contours of a law explaining the evolution of the human species, something which could contribute complementary elements to Darwin's theories. Hayek felt able to state that it was economic exchange relations which allowed man to progress and to become more and more intelligent over the course of the centuries.

He denounced "the fatal presumption" which consisted of imagining that man was naturally gifted with reason. In his view, one must, on the contrary, admit that "man is not born wise, rational and good, but has to be taught to become so".[21] Those qualities could not be acquired through education, which is nothing but a transmission of knowledge, but through relevant training – like experimental physical training allowing trial and error similar to an athletic apprenticeship in the field, a solitary process during the course of which each draws his own personal lessons which are not really communicable to others in words. This would create a well-functioning mind capable of adapting to any new situation. Hayek extended this model of an experimental apprenticeship into a theory of evolution with the idea that action, or rather physical activity, forged man's intellectual faculties. He also stated that: "Man acted before he thought and did not understand before acting".[22] Improving the performance of the human mind originated in man's submission to the necessity of engaging in economic activities. Returning to the law of the market was thus imperative for all those "whose main interest is the growth of the human mind".[23]

From where does a moral attitude arise?

While for Hayek totalitarianism resulted from abandoning laisser-faire economics – sapped by human interventionism – during the course of an evolution which would necessarily lead to the perfecting of the human mind, for Arendt things were exactly the opposite. Totalitarianism resulted from laisser-faire economics, the absence of human intervention which could have prevented the process of appropriation of the world by the few and exploitation of the rest from continuing unchecked. The former developed his analysis by researching the causes of abandoning laisser-faire, which led him to accuse the "social philosopher" who believes in political liberty and propagates his ideas among the rest of the people. Arendt, for her part, questioned the absence of intervention, which also led to a critique of the philosopher once he succumbs to that professional illness of thinkers which breaks out when they lose sight of the raison d'être of the activity of thinking. That raison d'être cannot be but this: Asking what we are doing. The philosopher cannot exempt himself from this questioning. Arendt argued that a moral attitude is linked to the fact of questioning oneself, which implies that ready-made answers and the assurance with which they are put forward leads, whatever the content, to the disappearance of a moral attitude. In this point of view, it is clear that Hayek, who complained about the disappearance of morality, only puts down a new explanation of the origin of evil, one that promotes the extinction of a moral attitude.

Hayek and the responsibility of philosophy in the disappearance of morality

Generally a moral attitude, that is to decide not to do an evil act, is most often linked to an obligation to follow the rules of behaviour, rules whose content can be approximately summed up by the Ten Commandments – of Jewish origin but taken up again by Jesus and which form the base for all religions. Arendt's position explains that if the content of the rules constitutes what one could call morality, a moral attitude – in other words the fact of conforming to its commandments – cannot arise from obedience to an authority or submission to rules. An authentic moral attitude can only arise from the need to accept them. Hayek, on the other hand, adopted the common concept in supposing that morality is linked to a respect for the rules, innovating, however, in supposing that morality does not arise from divine law but from laws of the market.

He thus supports the idea that the relation with others via the media of economic exchange imposes "rules of just conduct" on every participant, making them beings both inventive and moral. This would then constitute an explanation of economic development associated with technical progress and, at the same time, an explanation for the violence unleashed when the rules are replaced by positivist laws invented by the human mind. The appearance of 'exchange' explains the passage from primitive unproductive societies to an economic order of continual progress. His condemnation of man-made law implies that the mode of relations between individuals was not conceived deliberately by the human mind but arose "spontaneously". Hayek feels able to propose a "conjectural history" which supposes that such exchanges were implemented from an experimental act made by a person who sought to free himself from his original community and enter into contact with the outside world, one which bore fruit and thus perpetuated. He made the following supposition:

> Perhaps one might even say that the development of universal laws did not begin within the organized community of the tribe but rather with the first instance of silent barter when a savage placed some offering at the boundary of his territory of his tribe in the expectation that a return gift would be made in a similar manner, thus beginning a new custom.[24]

Relations mediated by an exchange of things, instituted incidentally, allowed a transformation of enemies into friends and established a sort of peaceful competition between individuals, each of whom sought to be a winner by being ever more inventive. The relation functioned as a neural stimulant, which explains technical inventions, but also as a sort of hormonal tranquiliser, reducing the warlike impulses of primitive man. Reasonable and wise man was born of this type of relation to the other which has no need to be written down and proclaimed but rather functions invisibly. The fact that Hayek evoked a silent barter is significant of his lack of consideration for the spoken word and his suspicion in respect of human relations established directly by language.

His theory of human evolution was not unconnected with a conception of a good education suitable to prepare a child for adulthood. A child becomes a responsible being not by listening, but by being required to make an effort. The 'social philosopher' who challenges the established order in 'exchange', listens to the complaints of the least well-off and proposes the means of organising human relations in a more egalitarian manner should be considered responsible for a degeneration of the human mind. State intervention, which began with 19th-century social laws, was leading to a regression of the human being to an infantile state where he becomes demanding and idealistic, challenging the old order, questioning authority and the values of traditional morality. In helping the losers in the game of exchange, in giving them rights, the system of prices is upset, introducing misinformation which are the origins of overcapacity of production, crises and unemployment which in turn lead to a political economy, aggravating still more the situation. In wishing to establish social justice, the philosopher is the origin of such economic failure by adding a perversion of rights in that not everyone is subject to the same law. Worse still, ill thought-out interventions have a consequence on prices, which otherwise allow people to know the value of their actions and to adapt their activities to the needs of society as a whole. Humankind thus loses the instrument which up to then had allowed them to direct their action well, to take up good conduct in both senses of the term: a conduct conforming to scientific truth and one conforming to morality.

For him, the social philosopher who imagines being able to replace the law of laisser-faire economics by an invented law greatly overestimates man's intellectual capabilities. Contrary to the hopes propagated by such philosophers, Hayek sought to establish that relations of economic exchange were indispensable for beings whose reasoning could not be an instrument capable of determining what was just and what not. Man does not have the capacity of judgement – this was the scientific truth that Hayek sought to deliver. Beyond this illusion about man, philosophers deceive themselves concerning their own intellectual capabilities in imagining that their reason is an instrument to discover truth. Concerning this point, social philosophers were only following an old illusion which dates back to the birth of philosophy in Ancient Greece. In the myth of the cave, Plato contrasted two types of being: those who remain governed by their senses and have only a distorted view of reality and the philosopher, a being of reason who leaves the cave and comes out into the light. Hayek denounced this characteristic presumption of philosophers, explaining that philosophers, no more than others, can accede to the truth by using reason. Drawing on Popper's *The Logic of Scientific Discovery* (1935), he agreed that authentic knowledge can only come from the result of experiments with ideas and not from pure intellectual speculation. This argues for, once again, exchange relations which could be considered as a means of experimenting with ideas and thus constitutes a process of scientific discovery open to everybody.

In taking Arendt's argument, it becomes clear that Hayek's reasoning always contains the same error; believing that imposing rules of just conduct is the way to preserve morality – something which leads the Austrian author to argue that the true task of executive power is to submit all people, rulers and rules, to the just law of the market, provided that it was liberated from the legislative power which humans unduly grant themselves when they 'fabricate' laws.

Arendt's position: support political liberty against conceptualisation

To put it succinctly, the contrast between the two authors can be summed up by saying that Hayek promotes a return to laisser-faire economics because the human mind does not have the capability of judging the value of what they do – totalitarianism having furnished the proof of this lack of reason – while Arendt experienced the rise of Nazism as a revelation that the ability to judge could be abandoned, including by the most intelligent, under the guise of letting run its course a historical necessity which does not in fact exist.

The desire to explain historical development and produce a theory leads to one taking on the role of observer of what is happening and to see in the events only a confirmation or refutation of existing theories while forgetting the possibility of acting. Taking an overview means adopting the position of an entomologist observing a society of bees to explain how it works and to see oneself as an insect with predictable behaviour, the secrets of which need to be unlocked. This position transforms the existential question 'Who am I?', which can only be answered in relation to the 'other', into a scientific question 'What am I?' or even 'What is a human being?' with the response supposing a reduction of human plurality to a unique genre. While the first question leads to a moral attitude in making the other an indispensable interlocutor, the second eliminates all possibilities of understanding the raison d'être of politics. Arendt demonstrates that it is denying "plurality, . . . the fact that men, not Man, live on the earth and inhabit the world"[25] which closes the path to an authentic sense of politics. "For all scientific thought, in biology as well as psychology, in philosophy as well as theology, only man exists, just as in zoology there is only the lion".[26] It is only when starting from plurality that one is able to distinguish a function of politics, that is to create a "common world" among beings that are different from each other but who need to communicate with one another to become someone, a human – a unique being that is never "the same as anyone else who has ever lived, lives, or will live",[27] a being about whom one can tell stories and write a biography. And if one admits this plurality and the sense of politics associated with it, it becomes clear that communication among beings by word is an essential element in maintaining the existence of a common world. The "sciences today have been forced to adopt a 'language' of mathematical symbols which, though it was originally meant only as an abbreviation for spoken statements, now contains statements that in no way can be translated into speech"[28] increases even more the difficulty in capturing the sense of politics by offering supplementary motives, implying that they can be ignored. The demands of logical coherence to which professional thinkers are subject eliminate the three elements of authentic politics which are "action", transformed into behaviour in the view of the entomologist, "plurality", reduced to a uniqueness of the human genre and "the word" where the words are not taken as ideas but as concepts, useful instruments for explanation and not for communication. Authentic politics cannot be captured by professional thinkers to the extent that it is collective action which gives existence to a common world while the theoretician, especially the economist, is forced to postulate the existence of a whole, as if they were dealing with a beehive, in order to find a response to the question which they see as fundamental: How do bees behave? They could just as well ask what the queen is good for, what is the effect of the division of labour between her and the 'workers' and how is honey produced. All the questions raised by economists are based on a conception of humanity as a whole formed by beings of human genre, while humanity designates the quality of the beings which emerge when speaking among themselves of things which concern everyone.

In contrast to a concept of humanity seen as a whole, Arendt employs an idea of humanity which dates back to the birth of philosophy. While Hayek turned back to Plato to detect the errors of philosophers who did not have a scientific understanding of man, Arendt begins with the idea of humanity as was developed by the philosophers in their writings. This is not to say that she follows the entirety of their works.

Arendt takes up the Plato of the *Dialogues* and the one who wrote the *Apology of Socrates*, but not the Plato of the *Republic* and the *Laws* who invented the myths such as the one of the cave opposing two categories of persons. Her critique of the myths takes an opposite sense than that of Hayek. Where, for the latter, philosophers are no more able than the average person to discover the truth using their intellectual capabilities, for Arendt the average person has the same capability to judge as philosophers.

For her, Plato errs in not admitting this and when he invents "the concept of government" charged with bringing into line the greatest number and in imagining that fear of hell could be a means to obtain this obedience. His republic conceived by a philosopher king inaugurated "a common place" which we have inherited whose aim is that "a political community (is) made of those who govern and those who are governed" and which supposes that the former give the orders and the latter obey. He was the first to have provided "a blueprint for the making of political bodies"[29] which shows a profound incomprehension of the nature of political power. Arendt shows that Plato's endeavours had elsewhere ended in "a complete fiasco". The real power associated with the liberty to found something new cannot arise from the "consent" of the largest number because "no man, however strong, can ever do anything, good or bad, without the help of others".[30] "Consent" is not quite the same thing as "obedience", which is what is demanded of a slave or a child or which religions demand when they say that one must obey the voice of God.

The Plato which interests Arendt is that of the *Dialogues*, the one who brings to the fore the humanity of speaking together, the one interested in mental life and who transmits the teachings of Socrates, that well-known person in Athens who wrote nothing, who thought about all subjects and who spoke to everybody. Socrates, who "cannot have believed that only the few are capable of thought",[31] embodies the common man who interrogates and questions others, but does not offer a definitive response. He does not start down the path leading to fixing words in concepts although they were, originally, expressions of ideas arising from experiences. The activity of thinking Arendt talks about designates the activity of questioning that Socrates dedicated himself to which she distinguishes from that of Plato and Aristotle when they sought to provide answers and began to produce concepts. The admiring surprise, for example, one experiences when witnessing acts of considerable nerve or great generosity leads one to speak of courageous or just acts, leading in turn to questions such as "What is courage? What is justice?",[32] but such questions cannot produce definitive answers. The words "courage" or "justice" remain ideas as long as they are associated with an experience. On the other hand, they become concepts which fix the meaning when professional thinkers find a response to them. Theory becomes the reference for what is a courageous or just act at the expense of the opinions expressed by the viewers of a remarkable act. Experiencing the same admiration and speaking about it allows one to perceive the existence of shared values which are the manifestations of a community of minds, while conceptualisation eliminates the conditions of the existence of mental life.

Activity of thinking, capability of judging and moral attitude

The activity of thinking developed by Socrates is what "Plato translated into conceptual language as the soundless dialogue . . . between me and myself".[33] In the activity of thinking, one is at the same time oneself and another oneself to whom one asks questions, a sort of 'two in one' which reflect on the events and experiences which cross our lives. This is nothing more than "the habit of examining whatever happens to come to pass or to attract attention".[34] It arises from an everyday experience and one should expect to see it done by "every sane person no matter how erudite or ignorant, how intelligent or stupid he may prove to be".[35] Unlike the activity of production by a professional thinker, it does not depend on intellectual potential, it is not linked to acquired skills and is not evaluated by performance. It is an activity characteristic of a being of intermediate (interventionist?) nature, who is not an animal because he poses questions, but who is not a god because he doesn't have the answers. The activity does not produce any knowledge which could be transformed into rules of conduct applicable in every circumstance. It is, on the contrary, the manifestation of an embarrassment when faced with an unexpected situation or event. Far from resulting in certitudes, the activity renews doubts. "the business of thinking is like the veil of Penelope: it undoes every morning what it had finished the night before".[36] It produces nothing concrete and tangible which could last and be transmitted. Simultaneous with the state of surprise which sets it off, the activity is inseparable from the person doing it and thus cannot be done by proxy. "Each new generation, every new human being . . . must discover and ploddingly pave anew the path of thought"[37] which leaves nothing behind it.

However, one shouldn't see this activity as a sort of training of the mind that could lead to wisdom. Socrates knows that he is not wise. Thinking does not only imply "thinking by yourself" but also "thinking for yourself". Arendt explains that with Socrates the activity gains its impulse from a need to be in harmony with himself. He knew that once he returned home to his solitude, he was no longer the person who addressed others and could say "I" but a stranger to himself, unable to pass a judgement on the public person that he was for the others. Knowing that he would be confronted by the judge who would not leave him be, he avoided making enemies. Socrates offered only two positive propositions: "Both occur in the Gorgias . . . it was written shortly before Plato became head of the Academy"[38] which could seem to be rules for life leading to wisdom or a guide to moral conduct should be interpreted as a consequence of that need. His first positive proposition "It is better to be wronged than to do wrong" could be taken for cheap moralising, but it means the same thing as the second – "It would be better . . . that multitudes of men should disagree with me rather than I, being one, should be out of harmony with myself and contradict me".[39] The idea thus put is a process of adjustment aiming at a coherence between the public being who presents himself to others as being someone and a private being who questions the values of the actions taken by the other himself. The absence of thought plunges one, on the contrary, into incoherence, forcing a sort of schizophrenia, a doubling of personalities which has become essential to ensure that the public being and the private being never meet to discuss among themselves. While forming an inseparable whole, the two beings are necessarily distinct because they take up alternatively two types of incompatible occupations: "Sometimes I think and sometimes I am" as Arendt sums it up in quoting Paul Valéry (Discours aux chirurgiens, in *Variétés Paris*, 1957, volume I, p.916), in *The Life of the Mind* (French publication / "La vie de l'esprit", Paris PUF, 1992, p. 96). She then contrasts his conception of the activity of thinking with Heidegger who considers it to be a process of unifying the being. Unity is not the product of thought. It destroys, on the contrary, authentic thought based on the irreducible character of the duality of a being, alternatively unique when he is in communication with others in the public sphere and plural while he is alone and he thinks in the private sphere.

The habit of questioning one's own acts, born of a need to be in harmony with oneself, proves to be extremely precious. It brings out "the ability to judge", that is "the ability to tell right from wrong, beautiful from ugly"[40] which "we could call the most political of mental abilities" in the moments when that proves necessary. In researching an adjustment between particular experiences from the present and general opinions accepted in the past, the need to be in harmony with oneself leads to attacking prejudices, just as the activity of thinking proves dangerous for all beliefs.

> It is in its nature to undo, unfreeze as it were, what language, the medium of thinking, has frozen into thought – words (concepts, sentences, definitions, doctrines). . . . The consequence of this peculiarity is that thinking inevitably has a destructive, undermining effect on all established criteria, values, measurements for good and evil, in short on those customs and rules of conduct we treat of in morals and ethics.[41]

The challenging effect of the ability to judge is to be considered as beneficial. As a by-product of the activity of thinking, the ability to judge is matched with its antidote as this activity, constantly renewed, leads to no new certitude able to replace the values called into question. Thus "thinking is equally dangerous to all creeds and, by itself, does not bring forth any new creed".[42]

Contrary to Hayek's deductions, it is not the ability to judge which leads to the disappearance of morality, because it is not contained in the moral precepts or other rules of good conduct to be imposed on individuals. The appearance of totalitarian regimes reveals that the rules can be easily replaced, with the moral commandment "You shall not kill" transformed into its opposite: An order to kill which was followed without a guilty conscience, not because the individuals are evil and violent but because they consider that their duty was to submit themselves to the orders coming from above.

The case of Eichmann was exemplary in this point. Attending Eichmann's trial in Jerusalem, she noticed that nothing in the words of this director of organising the transport of Jews to extermination camps indicated that he was an anti-Semite. He was someone satisfied for having done well what was asked of him. In other words, denouncing anti-Semitism, stigmatising racist comments does not constitute an approach able to change his position of submitting to orders, which is the deepest problem. This analysis does not mean, obviously, that racism and anti-Semitism are not reprehensible doctrines, but the question which arises is to understand how such an inept ideology, born of deranged minds, could have been installed as a principle of government to which almost the entire population consented. Arendt considers that the problem arose from the disappearance of the activity of thinking, which is the disappearance of the need to be in harmony with oneself which is, in her view, the true cause of the collapse of morality. However, one must specify that she does not conceive of morality as behaviour consistent with doing good deeds. This is a religious acceptance of a morality which transforms Socrates's mental dialogue "of two in one" into listening to the voice of god which the faithful conscientiously obey. Questioning oneself leads, on the contrary, to what one could call a moral attitude which consists of abstaining from doing evil. This is doubtless the same as conforming to the Ten Commandments but with one difference, which is their acceptance – not because they are imposed but because an ever-questioning thinking being constantly updates them.

While for Hayek, the troubles of the 20th century are the result of abandoning the economic principle of free exchange, Arendt establishes that it is much more the abandoning of an idea of humanity born in the days of Athenian democracy even before the philosophers appeared and monotheist religions established themselves. In other words, morality has a political origin. Under such conditions, all those who wish a return to morality can only hope for a change in politics able to favour the activity of thinking and to revive confidence in our ability to judge.

Notes

* Translated from the French by Dr. David Higgins.

1 See the call for papers of the 2nd International Colloquium "Economic Philosophy", Strasbourg, 9 and 10 Oct., 2014.

2 Arendt, Hannah, *Eichmann in Jerusalem: A Report on the Banality of Evil*, New York: The Viking Press, 1963.

3 Arendt, Hannah, 'Thinking and Moral Considerations', *Social Research* 38, 1971, 417–46.

4 Arendt, Hannah, *Édifier un monde*. Paris: Éditions du Seuil, 2007, p. 126 (into English by translator).

5 Arendt, Hannah, *The Human Condition*, Chicago: University of Chicago Press, 1958, p. 255.

6 Rudolf Hilferding, *Finance Capital: A Study in the Latest Phase of Capitalist Development*, London: Routledge & Kegan Paul, 1981, available at www.marxist.org (no pagination).

7 Arendt, Hannah, *Imperialism*, Boston: Houghton, Mifflin, Harcourt, 1968, p. 3.
8 Hilferding, *Finance Capital*, chap. 22.
9 Ibid.
10 Ibid.
11 Ibid.
12 Ibid.
13 Ibid.
14 Arendt, Hannah, *On Revolution*, New York: Viking Press, 1963, p. 51.
15 Arendt, *The Human Condition*, p. 228.
16 Arendt, Hannah, 'Religion and Politics', in *Essays in Understanding 1930–1954*, New York: Schocken Books, 1954, p. 376.
17 Arendt, Hannah, 'Personal Responsibility under Dictatorship', in *Responsibility and Judgement*, New York: Schocken Books, 2003, p. 53.
18 See for a presentation of Hayek's position: Marlyse Pouchol 'Contre une philosophie post-hayékienne', *Cahiers d'Économie politique*, no. 65, Paris: L'Harmattan, 2013.
19 Hayek, Friedrich, *Law, Legislation and Liberty, Vol. 1, Rules and Order*, London: Routledge, 1973, p. 21.
20 Hayek, Friedrich, *The Road to Serfdom*, London: Routledge, 1944.
21 Hayek, Friedrich, *The Fatal Conceit: The Errors of Socialism*, London: Routledge, 1988, p. 21.
22 Hayek, *Law*, p. 18.
23 Hayek, Friedrich, *Scientism and the Study of Society*, New York: The Free Press, 1952, p. 102.
24 Hayek, *Law*, p. 82.
25 Arendt, *The Human Condition*, p. 7.
26 Arendt, Hannah, *The Promise of Politics*, New York: Schocken Books, 2005, p. 93.
27 Arendt, *The Human Condition*, p. 8.
28 Ibid., p. 4.
29 Ibid., p. 227.
30 Arendt, 'Personal Responsibility under Dictatorship', p. 47.
31 Arendt, Hannah, *The Life of the Mind*, Boston: Harcourt, 1978, p. 180.
32 Ibid., p. 166.
33 Ibid., p. 185.
34 Ibid., p. 5.
35 Arendt, 'Thinking', p. 422.
36 Ibid., p. 425.
37 Arendt, Hannah, 'The Crisis in Culture: Its Social and Its Political Significance', in *Between Past and Future: Six Exercises in Political Thought*, New York: Meridian, 1961, p. 210.
38 Arendt, 'Thinking', p. 438.
39 Ibid., p. 439.
40 Ibid., p. 446.
41 Ibid., p. 434.
42 Ibid., p. 435.

7 Karl Marx and Charles Fourier

Criticism of contemporary society and new philosophical anthropology

Riccardo Soliani

Introduction

Several great economists enriched their reflection with an anthropological vision, which engaged in a critical dialogue with the economy and society of their time. Karl Marx devoted to his vision of the human being the *Manuscripts of 1844* and other works of the same period, some of which written with Engels. The individual in his relationship with the others, his liberty and the mode to express his whole potentiality in a historically determined environment are the issues dealt with in those writings. According to Marx, the fundamental historical determination is the mode of production. The scientific analysis of capitalism allows him to single out the historical pathway to trespass it. In the new classless society, the relationship between people will be rational and authentic: then human potentiality will be fully developed. Even though the fundamental vision of the "young Marx" would not significantly change later, Marx's philosophical anthropology remained in the backstage with regard to his political and economic reflection.

Charles Fourier has a revolutionary philosophical anthropology, which suggests a radical transformation of many aspects of society. However, his criticism, appreciated by Marx and, particularly, Engels for its biting sarcasm,[1] does not involve the mode of production, where waged labour (albeit radically reorganized) and private ownership of the means of production remain. Indeed Fourier is convinced that capitalists should support the "New World", which would allow them huge profits.[2]

Both criticism and praxis of Fourier begin from his anthropology: by releasing people's "passions", the repressive and inhuman society will be dismantled, and will blossom the New World, which Fourier describes with the utmost accuracy. The play of the passions and the strength of the example will transform human relations and the entire society: starting from his vision of the subject, Fourier is able to criticize the present world and draw the future.

The aim of the present paper is twofold: first, to compare the dialectic between philosophical anthropology and transformation of society in both authors; second, to highlight their respective criticism to human relations in the contemporary society, and the nature of the new "association" between men and women in the society they fight for and forecast.

According to Marx, the liberation of Man can happen only in the classless society, established thanks to the proletarian revolution. According to Fourier, people must begin to live in communities ruled by the newly discovered "law of attraction", and the example of these happy men, who live according to their passions and enjoy them, will move the entire humanity. The dialectic between philosophical anthropology and social transformation in our two authors develops in opposite way: from revolution to liberation, complete human development and new social links, in Marx; from few spontaneous communities where men and women live and work according to the "attraction", to the transformation of the whole human society: a revolution pushed by the strength of example, rather than by weapons.

The respective vision of the freed individuals and the new form of links among them is another topic I consider. Marx doesn't offer a complete portrait, apparently leaving this task to future authors: his scope is the analysis of the present time and its possible development, not foretelling. However, some hints about this can be found in Marx's work. Comparing these clues with the pages of Fourier about Man and his passions, interesting analogies emerge.

Finally, my work puts forward some reflections about the importance that utopian philosophical anthropology has in our advanced capitalist society. The critical analysis of Marx can be fruitfully merged with Fourier's original vision of Man, to suggest a possible way of transformation from our age of anxiety.

Some reflections on young Marx's philosophical anthropology

Introduction

To single out the fundamental outlines of Marx's vision of Man, one can usefully read his early works, when he starts to reflect on political economy from his peculiar materialistic approach. As is well known, Marx began his studies from the ancient Greek materialism (Democritus and Epicurus) and the critical assimilation of Hegelian Idealism. In the forties Marx establishes the basis of his interpretation of the history of human civilization and evolution, moving from Feuerbach and Hegel. The study of political economy is the quite natural consequence of his materialistic approach. The continuity between the initial phase of his work and the maturity, i.e. the *Capital*, is witnessed by the *Grundrisse*, written in 1857–58, but published only in 1938: here we can see that the ideas elaborated in the forties are present in his mind more than ten years later. Then I maintain that there is a substantial continuity in his thought, also when he is working on *Capital*.[3]

The starting point of Marx is Man and his primary needs. The core of Marx's materialism is that we can understand history and give it sense only if we move from material needs, which men satisfy in new ways through time.[4] Needs are common both to men and animals; but animals adapt to Nature, whilst men modify it according to their projects, as described in the well-known passage of *Capital* about the bee and the architect.[5] Labour is just the act of modifying nature in order to satisfy human needs; it has an inner "teleology", since Man sets up in his mind the scheme, means and goals of labour before implementing it, and in such a way he can dominate Nature.

From the very birth of humanity, the action of transforming Nature is actually a social action, as Aristotle had already noted, and this fact might be the real source of language and cultural transmission over generations. Here one could find the legacy of Vico, whose works Marx knew, although the textual evidence is quite scarce.[6] Human relations are born because men have been living and working together, in order to survive, from the dawn of humanity. Then, the material necessity gives birth to social organizations and all types of social relations, among which family. Presumably in 1881–82,[7] Marx had been studying the work of the anthropologist Morgan, published in 1877.[8] Marx praises the historical sense of Morgan and his view of the monogamist family and private property as the result of a very long evolution, where the material elements of social development and their effects are on the foreground. Following Morgan, he observes that the contemporary family is created by society and gradually develops at the same pace of it. In the future, the monogamist family could be not equal to the tasks set by society, taking for granted the social progress; but it is impossible to forecast the structure that the new family, like each other institution, will assume.[9]

On these themes, in the *Postfazione* to the Italian edition Iacono quotes the correspondence between Marx and Engels and the *Grundrisse*, where the very complex relation between blood links and the evolution of the mode of production is discussed. It appears that the core issue is the impossibility of a general theory of history: similar events have different consequences in different historical conditions, and in primitive communities based on kinship, the mode of production may be different and is not crucial for their development.[10]

Since "[t]he original conditions of production . . . cannot themselves originally be products",[11] the real historical process to expound is the separation between the "inorganic" conditions of human existence and the human activity: "a separation which is completely posited only in the relation of wage labour and capital",[12] that is, the birth of capitalism. Indeed, in antiquity there was no inquiry into which form of landed property is the most productive: the question was always which mode of property creates the best citizens.[13] Marx cites approvingly Fourier, who links civilization with monogamy and private property of land, and adds that the modern family contains the seeds of *servitus* (slavery), particularly serfdom and domestic servanthood.[14]

The anthropological notes, written almost twenty-five years after *Grundrisse*, show the persistent interest of Marx towards the historical forms of human production and reproduction. The historical evolution of the relationships between the Subject and the Other, where the Other can be the different types of families, or the entire society, is constantly merged with Marx's research on the modes of production and, then, on the paths to trespass capitalism. The forms of the future, perhaps non-monogamist family, and, generally speaking, of the entire future society, are unpredictable: but the relation between the Subject and the Other will be more "human".

Engels based his essay on the origin of the family, private property and the state, written one year after his friend's death,[15] on his research and also on the Marx's notes on Morgan. Engels wrote that his book was "in a sense, the execution of a bequest".[16] Indeed, here several intuitions of Marx appear developed. The transformation of the relations between men from the primitive and pre-capitalistic society to the rise of modern capitalism is described with many references to history and anthropology. In the Ch. ix "Barbarism and Civilisation" the origin of slavery, then the cleavage into exploiters and exploited, is traced back in the first great social division of labour, when productivity and wealth increased dramatically. This influenced heavily the family and the social role of the woman. With trade expansion, inequality soared and the capitalist State, a power apparently standing above society, was born, to moderate the social antagonism. In Engels's words,

> the great "truth" was discovered that man also can be a commodity; that human energy can be exchanged and put to use by making a man into a slave. . . . The active became the passive, whether the men liked it or not.[17]

The Subject is before the Other, again: but their respective condition of active human beings depends on their social role. Now greed is the steering force of civilization, whose final aim is wealth, not of society, but of the single individual, involved in an endless conflict.

Marx's thought was called "philosophy of the *praxis*", that is philosophy of labour and, more generally, of material and cultural forms of human action. Humanism and historicism are the roots of the anthropology of Marx, as underlined by Italian philosophers like Antonio Labriola and Antonio Gramsci; and also by Karl Löwith, who states the close continuity between Hegel and Marx.

We can see here a sort of negation for trespassing (*aufhebung*); indeed, Marx, *à la* Hegel, trespasses Hegel himself, without coming back to the materialism of the 18th century. The Hegelian totality is, in Marx, the connection between social Man and Nature: there Man is active subject of transformation and natural object at the same time. The historical forms of Marxian totality are the "socio-economic formations", defined according to the prevailing relation of production: slavery, feudalism, capitalism. The transformation of the mode of production brings about the transformation of the way of thinking, and perceiving and understanding reality. Therefore, the forms of social conscience, like family, religion, ethics, nation, are not given once for all, nor do they exist *per se*; they are historically determined. This is the reversal of the Hegelian dialectic: the starting point of Marx is just Man in his historical context, that is, more precisely, in the current mode of production: capitalism.[18]

Marx is influenced and stimulated by Feuerbach and his materialist humanism. Indeed, following an ancient stream, which goes back to Epicurus, Feuerbach has a vision of the Christian God as creation on men. One must come back from Heaven to Earth: God is a duplicate of human characteristics, particularly of love. According to Feuerbach, the initial push comes from human senses. Man is sensibility, like in Condillac and other Enlightenment philosophers.

We can observe here an indirect link between Marx and Fourier. Indeed, the French author focuses his analysis, and his pathway to liberation, on human passions, which should be unchained: only in this way humanity will be free and social and economic life will blossom. Feuerbach, approvingly expounded by Marx, puts love at the centre of his criticism to religion, in a Sensist *tournure*.

In his *Manuscripts*, Marx founds on labour the relation between the human beings. Also passions are important, but we must consider and interpret them in their historical dimension. Man is primarily hinged upon his biological characteristics, but he is continually evolving. Also the five senses evolve.[19]

Man transforms Nature and, in this way and thanks to this process, also his institutions and then himself. This is the core point of the philosophical anthropology of Marx. The object, says Marx in his *First Thesis on Feuerbach*, must be conceived as human activity (*praxis*), that is subjectively.[20] Indeed, *praxis* originates from the necessity of satisfying needs, and, in historically determined ways, it modifies and shapes reality. Then Nature is always human and Man is always natural, just because both Nature and Man evolve on the basis of human activity. Here the Subject meets Nature. Now, not only is Nature the Object, but it is also a form of Other, being shaped by the Subject himself: this is the Marxian solution to the dualism Subject/Object.

This has an important consequence, because, according to the materialism of Feuerbach (and, before, of the early materialists of the 18th century), men are the result of their respective environment and education; but he forgets that men themselves modify the environment, and the "educator" is to be "educated" in his turn. Thus, such a primitive, deterministic and dualistic materialism ends to divide society in two parts: the upper one, who rules, and the lower one, who must obey, as Marx remarks in the *Third Thesis on Feuerbach*. Education and environmental constraints are important, but must be grasped in their whole complexity, viz. the dynamism of the relation Man–environment and the link between educators, educated people and principles transmitted, which is really composite and changing.

Interestingly, Fourier also considers the different setting up of labour as the main way to the human emancipation. Indeed, it should follow passions, in particular *Cabaliste*, *Composite* and *Papillon*. The real education process is: to recognize passions and to live according to the rules fixed in *Armonia*. The core difference is the historical dimension, because, apparently, Fourier deems in passions as the original, non-historical basis of human nature.[21] Once recognized, admitted and organized, the society would achieve his goals, and the path of its further evolution would be fixed in the system of the *Series*. The Marxian *praxis* here becomes pre-ordered *routine*, although full of happiness.[22]

The constitution of labour and labourers in capitalism

In Marx's humanism, as expressed in his *Manuscripts* of 1844, knowledge, sociality and culture are founded on labour. This is the profound reason for which he is interested in political economy. His analysis of labour takes into consideration specifically how it is performed in capitalism; that is, the category of waged labour. Not is the entity of salary at stake here, but rather the social relation itself, where the means of production are property of a social class, and another social class owns nothing but his capacity to work. Therefore capital is accumulated labour, but, at the same time, it is social power exerted by men on men.[23] Marx sets in the wake of Classical British political economy; but he singles out the historical dimension of capitalism, marked by the conflict between capitalist and labourer already seen by Smith.

"Alienation" (*Entfremdung*) is the specific mode of the process of objectivation of labour in capitalism, which completely permeates the relation between the Subject and the Other. The labourer does not own the fruit of his labour, nor can he decide the organization of his activity. The proprietor of the means of production indeed rules also the conditions of labour. Men cannot express their personality in their activity.[24]

Although very few people notice it (because they are "submerged" into this historical formation), under capitalism all connections between human beings and between men and Nature are really "inhuman", since they derive from the fundamental relation that is the alienated labour. For example, the apparently "natural" private property is the result of alienated labour; not *vice versa,* as we read in the first Notebook of the *Manuscripts*.[25] Freedom, emancipation, authentic human relations will be possible only after the revolutionary trespassing of capitalism; i.e., after the abolition of waged labour and alienation.[26] Then the idea of democracy expressed by the young Marx in 1843 will be realized: law will exist for Man, it will be real human existence and self-determination of people.[27] The Subject and the Other will be reconciled: the State will be administration and labour will be the higher expression of Man.

Such trespassing will be Communism. But the very idea of communism has been born into capitalism; namely, it has been set against it, like atheism, which rises against religion. Therefore, it is not sufficiently detached from capitalism yet; indeed, it is determined in juxtaposition to capitalism. Only when the "fully developed" communism fights no more against capitalism (viz., after its suppression), then Man will be finally free and the process of humanization of Nature and naturalization of Man will be able to start. Not only utility, but also beauty will be characters of human *praxis*. This is the top point of Marx's *ethos*.[28]

We can argue, but there is no direct and clear textual evidence that "humanization" and "naturalization" will bear the hallmarks of passion's liberation: once alienation cancelled, the authenticity should rule, and harmony, no more conflict, should be the atmosphere of the fully developed communism.[29] A Fourierist society? We cannot say it, albeit several characteristics would be similar. However, we must hold that, on its turn, also such the future society, coherently with Marx's historical materialistic approach, will evolve, transforming dialectically in something other and different, which nobody can guess now. This perspective seems far from Fourier, who fancies extraordinary future stages of development for Earth and mankind once and for all, and other early Socialists.

After *Manuscripts*, Marx goes on with his reflections upon "alienation". Starting from the focal point of labour, alienation arrives to involve also politics, religion and art, which are to be set into their economic and social formation, in order to be fully understood.[30]

Capitalism has internal contradictions, but also internal rationality, that is productive rationality that dominates religion, art, passions and so on. Therefore, one's human potentiality remains external to him, and cannot be really realized. This is the very sense of "estrangement", which literally means "coming out from oneself". Estrangement is a specification of alienation that refers to human capabilities.[31] The historical lack of human development, due to alienation and estrangement, engenders an empty space, which is occupied by "fetishes" and idols, that is by commodities. The commodity is the ultimate goal of capitalism; it is the fetish behind which human relations conceal themselves. Market economy and market prices are not transparent and we cannot easily see the social connection from which the value of each commodity derives in the conflictual market society.[32] Human labour disappears, it is embedded into its product, the commodity, and it is not evident that, when one buys a commodity, he is really buying labour of other people. This is "reification": the Other considered as a thing. The Subject is surrounded by the universe of commodities and can reach the Other only through the market relation. According to the well-known passage of the First Book of *Capital*, "the social relations between persons in their work" appear as "material relations between persons and social relations between things". A few lines below, Marx cites Galiani's *Della Moneta*: "value is a relation between persons" and comments: "he ought to have added: a relation concealed beneath a material shell".[33]

These four key words (alienation, estrangement, fetishism and reification) depict the anthropology of Marx. Everything that impoverishes Man, alienates him, puts him in the position of worshipping "fetishes" is inhuman. When social awareness of such an alienation rises, revolution will burn out and a major change-over (a new dialectical synthesis) will take place. This is a historical process of self-liberation and emancipation for everybody, even for the capitalists that hinder it. On this point, in Marx's thought not only is Hegel present, but also Saint-Simon.

Labour and alienation: what does the liberation of labour mean?

When labour is no more alienated, free creativity springs up. Now labour expresses a social need satisfied by labour itself, that is, free human activity. We pass from the kingdom of necessity to the kingdom of liberty, as Marx writes in the third book of *Capital*.[34] In the new society, labour itself is no more a mean to satisfy needs; it itself becomes the first human need. In a well-known passage of *German Ideology* we can read that Man should be at the same time and over the same day hunter, fisherman and philosopher.[35]

But, at least partly, the "rationally regulated" kingdom of necessity must survive. One can think of solving the puzzle by the reduction of the working time, or its intensity. At the same time, the new society should go beyond the division of labour, very useful to overcome Nature, but intrinsically contradictory and likely to give birth to relations of power and dominance, especially in the division between intellectual and manual work. We can find here another point of contact with Fourier, who faced the same problem through job rotation, and the thorough and rigorous channelling of passions.

Marx's thought is a philosophy of labour, by which he wants to build the collective subject, that is social Man and his history, along the path broken by Vico and German historicism. The core point is the interaction Man–Nature, Man–Man, Man–society. The civil improving of men cannot happen simply thanks to their individual amelioration, or noble ideals. It must go through the change of the mode of production, as it results from the historical evidence. Even Robinson Crusoe succeeded in surviving thanks to his cultural heritage (a collective, not individual endowment), not just thanks to his individual effort.

Revolution, transformation of the mode of production, reduction of the working time, have the same scope: the effectual application of values like universal brotherhood and equality. For this reason Bloch singled out the "concrete utopia" of Marx,[36] whose hope urges to the discovery of the collective subject able to transform the productive relations.[37] Since this collective subject endures alienation and reification, it wants to subvert the oppressive social order. Finally, the current "economic society" will have to give way to the authentic human society, dominated by extra-economic relations.

Marx tries to establish a "New Science" of capitalism. He wants to go beyond both the mere yearning for a better world, and the absolute pragmatic attachment to what already exists. His project is total, and founded not on psychology, ethics or religion, but rather on the historical analysis of the original elements of human existence, that is labour, transformation of Nature, self-transformation through Nature.

Institutions and, generally speaking, culture are superstructure, in mediate, dialectical connection with the productive relations. For example, in the *Introduction to the Critique of Political Economy* Marx proposes to analyze the pieces of art in their historical context, to check their criticism to contemporary society, or, on the contrary, their support to the dominant class. Then one can distinguish between valuable art and ideology.[38]

On this point we can couple Marx and Freud as scholars who intend to look beyond social mask and ideology, their common problem being the connection between reality and appearance. Fetishism, on the one side, and lapses and dreams, on the other, convey information about reality that must be decrypted and rationalized. Both Marx and Freud underline the continuity between the social and the natural essence of Man. The *gnosis* is not the knowledge of the external world, of the object; it is rather the comprehension of the subject, i. e. Man himself and his connection with the Other (society) and Nature.

The different modes of knowledge are not "objective": in the historical materialist approach, they depend on the period and the mode of production. The acknowledgement of the natural, material essence of Man and his passions can open the way to the re-definition of the utterly different from the bourgeois system of values.[39]

The biting wit of Fourier

Fourier's criticism: passions, not modes of production, are the roots of social relations

Fourier's criticism begins with the *doute absolu* and the *écart absolu* as the methodological approach to consider *Civilisation.*[40] Examining his thought, we should be interested in his criticism of the external and internal constraints that tame human passions and should look for what is feasible, putting aside the fantastic aspects. Fourier has an almost instinctual abhorrence of cities, their pollution, their labyrinthine alleys: they are his nightmare. On the other hand, the big corpus of his work is really a labyrinth, which, however, raised the admiration of Marx and Engels, who invite to go beyond the "systematic form" of Fourier and grasp the authentic content of his system. His suggestions are almost totally utopian, even though we must remember that this "utopian" reformer had an important group of followers, who established Fourierist communities, which, in some cases, lasted for several years. Obviously, Fourier's utopian suggestions cannot be fully realized, but they are the necessary benchmark and reference for all great projects of social reform.

The bold criticism of *Civilisation* can be found also in Marx, who praised the sharp wit of Fourier, which offered relevant hints to better understand capitalism. Moreover, we can observe that also for Marx the free springing up of passions will be a hallmark of the new society, when alienation and fetishism fade out. The Fourierist organization of labour, although presented in odd ways, contains very modern elements, such as job rotation and job satisfaction, which are relevant also for the emancipation of labourers in the future communist society of Marx.

One real great divide with respect to Marx lays in the historical development of the social change. Also Fourier recognizes the core role of labour; but he does not offer any explanation about the constitution of society starting from labour, as Marx does. The constitution of society, according to Fourier, derives from passions, and its organization must be rationally decided and projected according to the eternal laws that Fourier himself describes.[41] The fundamental historical discontinuity is "before" and "after" Fourier, who discovered, like a demiurge, the almost mathematical formula to free passions and set up institutions, thanks to which people are happy and productivity and profits soar. Capitalism and market economy are not in question: Fourier does accept them, and the distribution between profit and salary is favourable to the former.[42]

Liberation in Fourier begins with the passions;[43] the end of the individual selfishness and the different organization of labour are consequences of it. The analysis of the modes of production is extraneous to Fourier, and he does not elaborate any theory about the rise of social hierarchy and the repression of passions. Interestingly, in his system social hierarchy remains, both in social rites, and in more practical issues, like the apartments where people live in the *Phalanstère*: all of them are comfortable, but they are different for the different roles people play in the group. The examples he provides concern mainly farming, gardening and *ateliers* that look like craftman's workshops, rather than big factories: Fourier does not discuss waged labour.

Here another great divide from Marx emerges. We can say that the two major obstacles to freedom are, according to Marx: a) the cooperation between individuals must pass through the market, that is through an institution that is a sort of apparently natural, blind, strong and impersonal agent; b) labourers are not the owners of the means of production. Only the suppression of market and the collective property of the means of production will allow the full sociability of individuals.

Now, we can ask ourselves whether in contemporary societies market is the only impersonal institution that causes alienation. If we believe that in our complex world this is not the case, we should apply the theory of alienation not only to market, but also to the complexity itself, as Petrucciani and Texier propose.[44] Then the perfect correspondence between market and alienation disappears, and the role of the State and legal system emerges, as elements that can create alienation or help to fight against it. This renews the importance of Fourier: indeed, if alienation and its consequences have a genesis wider and more diversified with respect to Marx's idea, then all great social institutions that bind passions are to be investigated and criticized. Not only are the causes of alienation to be caught in the moment of production, but they are present in many situations of the collective life.

Labyrinths and passions: Fourier from the nightmare to the rational dream

While Marx, as we have seen, can be compared with Freud with reference to the "unmasking" of contemporary society, Fourier, as Freudian *ante litteram*, can be put next to him just with reference to the pleasure principle. We could say that Fourier is more daring than Freud, because in the future society he excludes both repression and sublimation. The three fundamental passions he discovers, *Cabaliste*, *Composite* and *Papillonne*, regard the intrigue, the strong enthusiasm and the passion for what is new.[45] The current *Civilisation* represses these passions, and, at the same time, is badly influenced by them. The *Société festive*[46] will liberate them, transforming the passions in socially positive forces: e.g., the *Papillonne* brings about the job rotation and the enhancement of individual capabilities (the dream of the young Marx and Engels: philosopher in the morning, fisherman in the afternoon); the *Composite* and the *Cabaliste* converts to emulation and strategies by which the different teams try to win the several, thoroughly regulated competitions that take place in *Armonie*. Once recognized as a part of human nature, these irrational and potentially disruptive forces become well balanced in the future society, where they are positive energies and source of social links. Everything is established in advance; but the realization of the social mathematics is spontaneous, because Fourier is really convinced that the *Phalange* of around 1,600 people does contain the number and variety of Passions necessary to reach an equilibrium.[47]

In the social philosophy of Fourier, the "passionate attraction" is primarily seen as a biological and vital mechanism, with no room for transcendence. It is a law common to humans, animals and even inanimate beings. The Deity of Fourier, in fact, has little to do with the God of the revealed religions. It is not the consequence of alienation, nor is it part of the system of dominance, since social dominance should not exist in *Armonia*. There, religion and liturgy are festive moments of collective rituals, almost theatrical events, which strengthen the social links: the Subject and the Other meet and almost mingle.[48]

Sade is a not recognized source of the ideas of Fourier: but the "sadism" of *Eros*, its destructive and selfish part, fades out in the Fourierist social mechanism of "distribution" of passions, which satisfies everybody. And this happens for all negative forces that could jeopardize *Armonie*. They will be tamed, or diverted, or converted in a positive dash, thanks to the meticulous rules that Fourier proposes, including a "horoscope" that should allow to prevent crime and, on the other side, boost individual endowment: and here the dream looks like a nightmare.[49] Fourier discovers even the most intimate passions, irrational by definition, and offers several schemes, tables, formulas, to rule them in the future society, to achieve the top happiness for the entire humanity. This is, at the same time, the core of his genius and his greatest limitation. But we can put it near the description of communism that we find in the *Manuscripts of 1844*, particularly in the pages where the humanity's relish for sensuality, after ridding of the current social order, is depicted. Also in those pages we have the seeds of a treatment of passions.[50] But it is an "euphoric vision of a human body benignly restored to itself [, which] would seem free of desire".[51] I would prefer "free of negative drive, which could destroy the social order". In Eagleton's analysis, it is up to Freud to cast doubt on this vision.

I think that we can add Fourier to the group of anti-philosophers who emancipate senses and include passions in the social order.[52] The relation between the Subject and the Other is seen by him in its profound nature as socially determined and, at the same time, involving the deepest parts of one's character, which are almost impossible to explain. For this reason, the equilibrium of passions cannot be reached at the individual level; we have seen that only on, let's say, stochastic basis, the equilibrium is achieved in the 1,600 people of the *Phalanstère*.

Very interestingly, Fourier's reflections about the roots of his theory can be found in his comment to Owen.[53] Owen, only one year older than Fourier, was a well-known British socialist, who trusted in the great power of education and well-being on men. In the twenties of the 19th century his experiment of New Lanark and his writings were frequently discussed also in France. Fourier remarks five errors in Owen: New Lanark is too big (3,000 people); agriculture is quite neglected; its members have nearly the same wealth; there are too strict rules, so that the atmosphere is austere; the distribution of income is unfair and not well established. Fourier thinks that every community must include no more than two thousand people: his world is characterized by relatively small, independent and competing groups of production. Competition is really important and goes together with the birth of the social link. This is witnessed by the role played by agriculture; indeed, industrial work is not able to create such a link, whereas agriculture is more attractive and stimulates competition and *intrigues industriels*.

Also the rules' sternness is hardly attractive. Then there are a couple of criticisms that shed light on Fourier's idea of equality/inequality. He notes that all dwellers of New Lanark share the same social condition and wealth. This is negative, he says, because there the stimulus of *contraste* lacks and such equality hindrances the creation of *séries complexes*. At the same time, distribution of income should proportionate to capital, labour and *talents*; but Owen does not recognize it and misses the spur of *intérêt*, which is necessary to enhance the performance of the system and get people better.

Now we should guess whether, in the new society of *Armonie*, individual self-interest might play also a destructive role, leading to the evils of contemporary society. Fourier believes that in *Armonie* the composition of interests, not mediated by the market, but meticulously reckoned, can have only a positive result. Indeed, the personal *intérêt* is a part of human nature, and the future happy society must allow all passions to fully develop. Then in the organization of social labour both cooperation *and* competition are relevant. Fourier singles out also the phases of decline: he is not at all optimistic about the future of humanity in the very long run ("fall and milky dissipation"), even after the application of his system and the new foundation of ethics on what would be called later the pleasure principle.

According to Marx, the revolutionary process that defeats capitalism is the *cause* of the release of passions, not the *effect* of it. The change in the mode of production engenders also an evolution in the human passions and their hierarchy, through the dialectical process by which the way to get subsistence and "all the necessaries and conveniences of life"[54] is the very basis of society. On its turn, the new social organization modifies human behaviour even in the intimate sphere, as witnessed, for instance, by the different types of family and conjugal relationship over time and in different communities. Finally, Fourier looks at passions as the original, immutable keystones of Man and society. Marx looks at passions as a part of human nature that is historically determined, and determines history: they shape history, but the historical evolution changes them, in a complex dialectical relation, so that one can hardly imagine the role and structure of freed passions after the trespassing of capitalism. This is another relevant divergence between Fourier and Marx.

Materialism and final asset of property: Fourier between innovation and conservation

The liberation of (and from) labour is perhaps the core point of Fourier's project, and the main issue that brings him near to Marx. In addition to the redistribution of capital through the specific calculation for the allocation of dividends to shares, there is a redistribution operated through a guaranteed income for all, without any obligation to work or actively seek a job. The basic income is a satisfying supply of goods and services, also including leisure and entertainment. In the world of Fourier this is possible and appropriate because the liberated labour is really a pleasure, so the relief from poverty does not encourage laziness, and the pressure of firing is not necessary to force people to work. Furthermore, life in the phalanstery can be pleasant (or even possible) only if nobody is in state of poverty and envy; at the same time, the rich benefit from the fact that the poor have a satisfying moral and intellectual status.[55] The argument of Fourier deserves attention today; when cooperation in the working process, and in networks where knowledge spreads, is more and more important, the distinction between working time and leisure time fades out, and also in advanced countries inequality is increasing.

In Marxian language, alienation and fetishism do not exist in *Armonia*, because human relations and, in general, relations between human beings, animals and things are really authentic and coherent with passions. I guess that here a field of research opens, about the view of human passions in Fourier and in authors like Vico (that Fourier had hardly read) or, more recently, Jung, born 38 years after Fourier's death. The treatment of religion and tradition in Vico suggests an original interpretation of their evolution in different eras, which compares the ages of Man and of humanity and offers a peculiar vision of the progress and fall of civilization. On the other hand, the theory of the collective unconscious of Jung offers an important key to fathom the role played by human passions in the evolution of myth, religion and art. Indeed, if the collective unconscious is the psychical structure of humanity, it should give room to passions: and Fourier believes that just the liberation of passions can determine the rise and setting up of institutions that will lead to an age of joy and happiness, followed, as we have seen, by decline and fall ("milky dissipation").[56] In this perspective, the change of the mode of production could be the future result of such a liberation, albeit not foreseen by Fourier; the point of view is opposite to Marx's.

Fourier argues that in the future society people will have new behaviours and new values, which will get humanity wealthier and happier. This will not be the final achievement of a complex and difficult historical evolution, as it happens in historical materialism. On the contrary, this will be the result of the action of the freed passions according to the law of attraction, which is a simple, objective truth that could have been discovered earlier; but that did not happen due to dull-minded intellectuals and moralists.

However, one cannot help remarking that Fourier, *naïvement*, does not take into account the existence of negative passions, which can break up society. In truth, Fourier seems to assume that even they can benefit the society, provided they are properly directed; then they will turn out to be really positive. It seems to be an *ad hoc* argument; but it is the consequence of the audacious intellectual choice of the idea of a society where all aspects of Man are freely expressed.

A striking example of such lack of observation of reality is the question of the attractive work. It is certainly true that gardening and cultivation of vegetables, as well as other activities appreciated by Fourier, can be pleasant, but when one needs to achieve high levels of productivity, as it is necessary to feed a large city, then those jobs become as tiresome as any other, perhaps even more. As evidence of this, in the thirties Charles Gide presented a detailed study on the working conditions in the agricultural region surrounding Paris, just to criticize Fourier's argument.[57] Here the classical difference emerges between the work done to produce use value and the work done to create surplus in capitalist economy, which pushes workers to increase their efforts to paroxysm to get a salary or, in the case of small independent producers, to get the maximum profit and defeat competitors. With steadfast faith, Fourier sees the future world covered by a network of independent associations that directly produce and exchange the product of their work without intermediaries. He pursues a project of radical subversion of society, but he intends to keep private property, capital and waged labour, without realizing the contradictions that arise when accumulation begins to widen the gap between the rich and the poor and capitalist economy crashes against the organization of labour based on the law of attraction.

Together with Fourier's appeal to free passions and rejection of the coercive state, we must not fail to look at the conservative aspects of his thought. In the future society, where *civilisation* gives way to *attraction*, property and inheritance rights, interest on capital and inequality remain. In order to realize that society, Fourier calls for the help of the upper class, promising an extraordinary increase in production and wealth.[58] In short, the relevant economic reforms invoked by Fourier regard: eliminating brokerage between production and consumption, organizing consumption and production on a large scale, balancing the disproportion between the industrial and the agricultural sectors (the latter considered penalized), and switching from extensive to intensive agriculture.[59] He believes that industrial production will have to decrease, since better quality of products and simplicity of life will cause the demand to drop. He intends to maintain the private ownership of the means of production and to establish the common ownership of several consumption goods, in the name of rationalization and against waste. The *comptoirs communaux*, very similar to consumption cooperatives, which should operate during the transition to the *Phalanstères*, are the starting point for the introduction and success of the principle of association. The distribution of income among labour, capital and "talent" is fixed in advance, but according to rates not much different from those of capitalist market economy and labour does not play a *léonin* role.[60]

Marx and Fourier: an impossible dialogue?

What does it remain of Fourier? Can we say that he is alive and relevant today? Maybe the sole approach to him is to take his thought as a way to improve both our ability to think of freedom and look at it; and our ability to cope with the human boundless desire. His rational dream is just a reference point, an enchanted city we will never reach (like the "Invisible cities" of Italo Calvino, great admirer of Fourier): but what really matters is the path to get there.

Fourier tells us the story of a new social organization, where even the potentially disruptive passions can be properly set in the social framework and become positive for the social order. Production is intended to satisfy human needs, without luxury. Emulation and ambition have their space in social rites and events; they exist also in the economic sphere, but according to specific rules, are different from the free market competition. The natural law of attraction plays the pivotal role in all fields of social life. The relation between the Subject and the Other is authentic, fully human. There is a sound, regulated emulation between the *sociétaires*, no greed, no scarcity. The realm of necessity appears defeated.

Here we can see the great analogy *and* difference from Marx. Their common aim is to free labour: it becomes the way by which Man can realize himself, and the Subject can go towards the Other, after the end of alienation. According to Marx, the way to the full liberation of labour and human passions is the historical passage to the socialist mode of production. According to Fourier, the liberation of labour is the consequence of the new social organization, ruled by the natural law of attraction. Then the liberation of labour and human passions are the core point for both of them, but the path to achieve it is different: a historical, revolutionary process for Marx; the discovery and voluntary application of a natural law for Fourier. We must note that Fourier does not ignore history, and the decline and the end of the world are described in his imaginative prose; but history follows a sort of natural Fate, and human activity can scarcely influence it. Fourier and Marx are poles apart in the vision of the forces that rule historical evolution.

In the future society, labour will become what it is in its real essence; that is, the core of human life, which allows men to develop their creativity. Both Marx and Fourier are aware that the isolated Man cannot survive, and in reality he does not exist; then individual creativity must realize in social form. Fourier provides detailed information about such a social form, viz. the future organization of labour. Marx does not, whilst he expounds the characteristics of labour in capitalistic economy.

Here another difference between them emerges. Marx notes that waged labour is oriented towards the production of exchange value and surplus value: labourers are compelled to create surplus value, in order to obtain their subsistence. Then the abolition of waged labour is the *conditio sine qua non* to achieve the liberation of labour. This means that the capitalist mode of production is not compatible with such a liberation, and, in general, with the liberation of passions. On the contrary, in capitalism also passions become commodities. Fourier does not consider the specificity of the waged labour. In his theory, it is the reform of consumption that modifies production. This change, together with the new organization that assigns the primary role to passions, frees labour. Then waged labour remains, but composition of output and job organization are different. Labourers are happy because they have a strong sense of belonging to their *Phalanstère* and do pleasant activities even performing their jobs, oriented to produce use value, that is goods that satisfy "real", not induced, needs. Furthermore, no conflict will rise about income distribution, which is fixed *a priori*.

The separation between labourers and their products, and the class struggle, should be overcome by the free play of the passions of 1,600 individuals, which will combine harmoniously. To combine harmoniously Marx and Fourier is more difficult, but to find a *fil rouge* between Marx's description of the concrete historical *praxis*, and Fourier's imaginative prose does remain a fascinating challenge. However, if we look in depth into Fourier's pages, the latter is not less concrete that the former, as demonstrated, several years later, by the modern research in social psychology. Marx foresaw the great capitalistic crisis; we could add that Fourier, a few years before, had foreseen the awful consequence of the political repression of passions.

Notes

1 See for example: Marx (1976): 44, letter to Kugelmann dated October 9, 1866, where Marx recognizes Fourier's intuition and description of a new world; Marx (2009): 192, 194, letters to Annenkov, dated December 28, 1846, where Marx praises the ability of Fourier to imagine the "socialist sentimentality", and to Schweitzer, dated January 24, 1865, where Marx maintains that the relation between Proudhon and, on the other hand, Saint-Simon and Fourier, "is about the same as that of Feuerbach to Hegel"; Engels (1947) [1878]: part III, par. I., where Engels finds in Fourier "a criticism of the existing conditions of society, genuinely French and witty", and "at his greatest in his conception of the history of society", since

> [h]e proves . . . that civilisation moves in a "vicious circle", in contradictions which it constantly reproduces without being able to solve them; hence it constantly arrives at the very opposite to that which it wants to attain, or pretends to want to attain, so that, e.g., '"under civilisation poverty is born of superabundance itself". Fourier, as we see, uses the dialectic method in the same masterly way as his contemporary, Hegel.

2 Fourier (2005) [1829[1], 1845[2]], Prefazione – Articolo secondo "Sovrabbondanza del prodotto societario"; Schumpeter (2003) [1954]: 555, n. 11, where Schumpeter observes that in Fourier's scheme the share of income assigned to profit and interest is larger than in the capitalistic system of his time; Beecher (2008) [1986]: cap. 10, par. 1 and cap. 12, par. 2, where Beecher underlines the large increase of production foreseen by Fourier and his non-egalitarian attitude.

3 On the continuity of Marx's thought, see Musto (2016): Appendice, where the program of the French socialist labourers' party (1880), which Marx gave an important contribution to, is reported: it appears that, in a concrete document, the emancipation of the productive class is at the first place, followed by practical proposals in that sense; Musto (2011): cap. 8, par. 7; Dussel (2001) [1988]: chapt. 12, especially par. 5.

4 For a quite recent, synthetic and dense analysis of the evolution of Marx's materialism, see Cingoli (2005). 119–32, esp. 119–28 focalised on the "young" Marx.

5 Marx (1990) [1867]: Ch. 7, par. 1.

6 See for example Marx (1990) [1867], Ch. 15, par. 1, n. 4, where Vico is cited because he noted that human history differs from natural history in that we make the former, not the latter.

7 See Foraboschi (2009): 23.

8 Lewis Henry Morgan, *Ancient society or researches in the lines of human progress from savagery through barbarism to civilization*, Chicago, Kerr, 1877. Marx's personal notes on Morgan and Maine were published by Lawrence Krader: *The ethnological notebooks of Karl Marx*, Assen, Van Gorcum & Co., 1972. A different edition was published in Italy in 2009 (see bibliography).

9 Marx (2009) [1881–82]: 69 and 71. See also Capogrossi Colognesi (2009): 12–13.

10 Iacono (2009): 306.

11 Marx (1973) [1857–58]: 489, italics in the original.

12 *Ivi.*

13 *Ibidem*: 487.

14 Marx (2009) [1881–82]: 62–3.

15 Engels (1942) [1884].

16 Engels (1942) [1884]: Preface to the first edition.

17 Engels (1942) [1884]: Ch. ix.

18 The birth of conscience and ideology in Marx is clearly depicted, among others, by Balibar (1994) [1993]: Ch. 3, particularly pp. 59 ff., where the analysis is focused on the *Thesis on Feuerbach* and *The German Ideology*.

19 See Eagleton (2016): Ch. 3 "Emancipating the senses", where Marx is called "a somatic materialist whose starting point is active, sensuous, practical human life". Marx, like Nietzsche and Wittgenstein, "was a philosopher with a deep-seated scorn for philosophising" (61).

20 "The chief defect of all hitherto existing materialism (that of Feuerbach included) is that the thing, reality, sensuousness, is conceived only in the form of the object or of contemplation, but not as sensuous human activity, practice, not subjectively" (Marx 1992 [1845]: 421).

21 Fourier speaks about his criticism of civilization and the *Series of Passions*, which are the fundamental constituents of human nature. The Series must continue, are not given once for all; and human activity transforms Nature. But the apparent historical evolution is predetermined in the complex mechanism of the *Series*. See, for example, Fourier (1971) [1808]: 10 and 17, and Ch. 1, part b) "I Destini generali", par. "Le 32 Fasi sociali" and par. "Le 18 Creazioni", from the *Theory of Four Movements*.

22 Marx in fact believed that certain aspects of humanity remain more or less constant. "Marx is . . . a storicist, but not a full-blooded one. . . . [He] believes in immutable realities, one of which is the need of labour" (Eagleton (2016): 70).

23 See, for example: Marx (1993) [1857–58], Notebook IV, where we find this passage: "Thus capital creates the bourgeois society, and the universal appropriation of nature as well as of the social bond itself by the members of society" (409); Marx (1990) [1867], Ch. 14, par. 5, where we find this passage: "In manufacture, as well as in simple co-operation, the collective working organism is a form of existence of capital" (481).

24 On the exact meaning on the word "alienation" in Marx, see Schacht (1970): 111–14, where the definition "separation through surrender" appears the most fitting, even though, according to Schacht, the word has a too large meaning in Marx's reflection, and may result in confusion.

25 Marx (1992) [1844]: 331–32. See Musto (2005b): 169–70.

26 Marx (1980) [1844]: 69 ff. See Lordon (2015) [2010]: espec. 15–19, 27–33, who adopts a "Spinozian" approach.

27 Marx (2008) [1843]: 70–1. See Cacciatore (2005): 152–53.

28 See for example Marx (1980) [1844]: 107–11.

29 Lordon observes that the achievement of high productivity through free creativity is the great promise of contemporary cognitive capitalism; but neither is it currently fulfilled, nor in the capitalistic mode of production is its fulfilment possible. This is a new dialectical contradiction of capitalism (Lordon (2015) [2010]: 160–1). We can add that this issue, singled out in a Spinozian approach to Marx, represents a point of contact between Marx and Fourier. See also the stimulating reflections of Tosel about the Other, which would be the empty space without domination and violence, where the newly born institution creates new social links without exploitation. Then the Other would be the being-in-common of all individualities, essentially "human" against the inhumanity of the liquid capitalism (Tosel (2005): 333).

30 The reflections in Catephores (1987): 45–9; Spinella (1996): 44–54; Petrucciani (1996): xx, are still very interesting. Catephores notes that "alienation undermines both solidarity and the capacity for purposeful interaction with the environment . . . giving rise to feelings of loneliness, powerlessness and aimlessness that afflict human lives" (46–7). It is founded "on strictly economic grounds, without necessarily referring to concepts imported from ethics, psychology or philosophy" (47). Spinella, and also Petrucciani in his *Introduction* to Spinella's book, emphasize Marx's critique to the productive rationality as an end in itself, which restrains human empowerment and opportunity of creating social relations that does not involve economic activity. Then "Critique of Political Economy" means freeing humanity from the dominance of political economy and needs: this is the profound meaning of Marx's work and the link between political economy and philosophical anthropology.

31 Marx (1980) [1844]: 69–86; Marx (1993) [1857–58]: 831–3; Marx (1990) [1867]: Ch. 1, par. 7; Ch. 7.

32 Shaikh observes that the capitalist social organization creates a general climate of conflict, which the bourgeois notion of perfect competition conceals (Shaikh (1990): 75). In the competitive market (and, generally speaking, in capitalist society) there is the general dependence of individuals on each other, even though they are indifferent one another. The Subject cannot reach the Other. Thus the general social relationship has, on its other side, the individual loneliness, and sociability and loneliness are reciprocally involved. See Basso (2008): 29–30, who analyzes the *Grundrisse* on this point. Tomba (2011) remarks that, in Marx's theory, the trespassing of capitalism and the full and free development of individuals are, at the same time, the fall of the previous modes of production. Then development and decadence are strictly joint (141).

33 Marx (1990) [1867]: Ch. 1, par. 4: 166–67 and n. 29.

34 Marx (1991) [1894]: Ch. 48, part III:

> Freedom, in this sphere, can consist only in this, that socialized Man, the associated producers, govern the human metabolism with nature in a rational way, bringing it under their collective control instead of being dominated by it as a blind power; accomplishing it with the least expenditure of energy and in conditions worthiest and appropriate for their human nature. But this always remains a realm of necessity. The true realm of freedom, the development of human powers as an end in itself, begins beyond it, though it can only flourish with this realm of necessity as its basis. The reduction of the working day is the basic prerequisite.
>
> (959)

35 "[I]n communist society, where nobody has one exclusive sphere of activity but each can become accomplished in any branch he wishes, society regulates the general production and thus makes it possible for me . . . to hunt in the morning, fish in the afternoon, rear cattle in the evening, criticise after dinner, . . . without ever becoming hunter, fisherman, herdsman or critic" (Marx, Engels 1845–46).

36 Bloch speaks about the *bons sens*, synonymous of an open-minded and active attitude, as the character of an authentic Marxian political *praxis*, which eliminates the antithesis between sobriety and enthusiasm. They converge in something new, and cooperate to the concrete utopia. See Bloch (1972) [1968]: 61–2; the passage is from *Das prinzip Hoffnung*, 1959.

37 Fusaro (2005) discusses the different interpretation of Marx offered by Bloch and Löwith about the relation among philosophy, utopia and hope, underlining the gap between the first (according to Bloch, hope would be a strong point of Marx's theory) and the second (according to Löwith, hope would be a weak point of Marx's thought). About Bloch, see Toscani (2009).

38 Marx (1993) [1857–58]: 110–11. In various *loci*, the relationship between structure (mode of production) and superstructure (art, religion, aesthetics. . .) appears to be depicted, even by Marx himself (for intimate persuasion or, in some case, for the sake of argument), in a deterministic way. See, among others, Petrucciani (2009): 122–6, where the author demonstrates also the theoretical necessity, in Marx's vision, that men not only are recognized as holders of material needs, but also as holders of instances of truth, which is an active historical force; and holders of profound psychical needs, as, among others, Castoriadis (who is cited) states (125–6). We can call "passions" such psychical needs, thus establishing a link with Fourier. Interestingly, in his "spinozian" interpretation of Marx, Lordon defines institutions as "combined affective devices" (Lordon 2015: 176): the reference to passions is evident.

39 Petrucciani (2012): 42–3.

40 Fourier (1971) [1808]: 7–13.

41 Fourier is an offspring of the same tree of French materialists Lamettrie or Helvétius, although he is critical against the previous century. See Fourier (1971) [1808]: 7–10,

where he states that, after the Revolution, the impossibility of effective social reforms has become evident, together with the necessity of a new social science (9). See also Calvino (1971): xix.

42 Fourier (1971) [1808]: 152 ff., where the distribution of product between labour, capital and skills is described. See also *supra*, n. 2.

43 Fourier (1971) [1808]: 25–37.

44 Petrucciani (2012): 52–62; Texier (1991): 97–122.

45 Fourier (1971) [1808]: 25–33, esp. 32.

46 This expression by Fourier was used by Henri Desroche in the title of his book: see References.

47 Beecher (2008) [1986]: 210.

48 Fourier (1971) [1808]: 111–34.

49 Here we find a further striking difference with the materialism of Marx. Eagleton treats this point brilliantly. With reference to the "pre-history" (as called by Marx), when the social constraints were considered natural, Eagleton, interpreting Marx, writes that the truly historic act is to break with the past and construct a more open-ended narrative. "It is because such a saga would not be predictable, unlike the behaviour of a caterpillar, that Marx has strikingly little to say about the future" (Eagleton (2016): 75).

50 Marx (1992) [1844]: 348–52.

51 Eagleton (2016): 81.

52 Balibar (1994) [1993]: 7–13; see also Eagleton (2016): 93.

53 Fourier (1966–68) [1822]: vol. III (it includes the *Traité de l'Association domestique agricole*, later inserted in the *Théorie de l'Unité Universelle*, posth. 1842, in four volumes): 3–8; Fourier (2005) [1829[1], 1845[2]]: 422–25. See on this point: Beecher (2008) [1986]: Parte Terza, cap. 18, par. 3.

54 As is known, those words open the *Wealth of Nations*. See Smith (1981) [1776]: vol. I, 10.

55 Fourier (1966–68) [1822]: vol. III, 15–16.

56 Fourier (1971) [1808]: 54–5; Calvino (1971): xv.

57 Gide (2001): vol. IV, 56. Emulation, rotation and free development of passions should solve the problem; in Fourier's world: one can think of children who collect garbage, or of competition between communities and *Phalanstères*, inspired by the Cabalistic passion (Fourier (2005) [1829[1], 1845[2]]: Sezione Prima "Analisi dell'attrazione appassionata, Seconda Avvertenza"; Sezione Terza "Educazione armoniana", Sesta Avvertenza "Educazione della seconda e terza fase dell'infanzia"). A couple of striking sentences of *Grundrisse* summarize Marx's appreciation of Fourier and criticism of him: when "labour becomes attractive work, the individual's self-realization, . . . in no way means that it becomes mere fun, mere amusement, as Fourier, with *grisette*-like naïveté, conceives it. . . . Labour cannot become a play, as Fourier would like, although it remains his great contribution to have expressed the suspension not of distribution, but of the mode of production itself, in a higher form, as the ultimate object" (Marx (1993) [1857–58]: 611 and 712). Here Marx apparently thinks that the radical change of the organization of labour would involve also the trespassing of capitalism.

58 Fourier (2005) [1829[1], 1845[2]]: 101–20.

59 Marx notes this point in the third *Manuscript*, singling out the link between Fourier and Physiocracy. See Marx (1980) [1844]: 107.

60 Fourier (2005) [1829[1], 1845[2]]: cap xxxiv. See *supra*, n. 2.

Bibliography

Balibar, Etienne (1994) *La filosofia di Marx*, trad. it. di Andrea Catone, Roma, Manifestolibri. Orig. ed. *La philosophie de Marx*, Paris, La Découverte, 1993.

Basso, Luca (2008) *Socialità e isolamento: la singolarità in Marx*, Roma, Carocci.

Beecher, Jonathan (2008) *Fourier: Il visionario e il suo mondo*, trad. it. di Roberto Cruciani, Bolsena, VT, Massari. Orig. ed. *Charles Fourier: The visionary and his world*, Berkeley, Los Angeles, London, University of California Press, 1986.

Bellofiore, Riccardo (2008) "Dai 'Manoscritti del 1844' al 'Capitale', e ritorno. Storia e natura, universalità e lavoro, crisi e lotta di classe nei 'Grundrisse'", in: *La lunga accumulazione originaria: politica e lavoro nel mercato mondiale*, a cura di Devi Sacchetto e Massimiliano Tomba, Verona, Ombre Corte.

Bloch, Ernst (1972) [1968] *Karl Marx*, trad. it. di Luciano Tosti, Bologna, Il Mulino. Orig. ed. *Über Karl Marx*, Frankfurt am Main, Suhrkamp Verlag, 1968.

Cacciatore, Giuseppe (2005) "Il Marx 'democratico'", in: Musto (ed.) (2005a), 145–60.

Calvino, Italo (1971) "Introduzione", in: Fourier (ed.) (1971), vii–xxxvii.

Capogrossi Colognesi, Luigi (2009) "Presentazione", in: Marx (ed.) (2009), 7–17.

Catephores, George (1987) "Alienation", in: *The new Palgrave – Marxian economics*, edited by John Eatwell, Murray Milgate and Peter Newman, New York and London, W. W. Norton & Co, 45–9.

Cingoli, Mario (2005) "Marx e il materialismo", in: Musto (ed.) (2005a), 119–32.

Desroche, Henri (1975) *La Société festive: du fouriérisme écrit aux fouriérismes pratiqués*, Paris, Le Seuil.

Dussel, Enrique (2001) *Towards an unknown Marx: A commentary on the 'Manuscripts of 1861–63'*, edited by Fred Moseley, transl. by Yolanda Angulo, London and New York, Routledge. Orig. ed. *Hacia un Marx descondido*, Mexico, Siglo XXI, 1988.

Eagleton, Terry (2016) *Materialism*, New Haven and London, Yale University Press.

Engels, Frederick (1942) *The origin of the family, private property and the state [1884]*, transl. by Alick West, now available in www.marxists.org.

Engels, Frederick (1947) *Anti-Düring: Herr Eugen Dühring's revolution in science [1877–78]*, transl. by Emil Burns, Moscow, Progress Publishers, now available at www.marxists.org.

Foraboschi, Politta (2009) "Introduzione", in Marx (ed.) (2009), 19–26.

Fourier, Charles (1966–68) *Oeuvres complètes de Charles Fourier*, Paris, Anthropos.

Fourier, Charles (1971) *Teoria dei Quattro Movimenti: Il Nuovo Mondo Amoroso*, a cura di Italo Calvino, trad. it. di Enrica Basevi, Torino, Einaudi.

Fourier, Charles (2005) *Il nuovo mondo industriale e societario*, trad. it. di Maria Alberta Sarti, Milano, Rizzoli. Orig. ed. *Le nouveau monde industriel et sociétaire, ou invention du procédé d'industrie attrayante et naturelle distribuée en séries passionées*, 1 ed. 1829, 2° ed. 1845, Paris, Librairie sociétaire.

Fusaro, Diego (2005) *Filosofia e speranza: Ernst Bloch e Karl Löwith interpreti di Marx*, Padova, Il Prato.

Gide, Charles (2001) *Coopération et économie sociale 1886–1904*, Texte présenté et annoté par Patrice Devillers, dans *Les oeuvres de Charles Gide*, collection dirigée par Marc Pénin, vol. 4, Paris, L'Harmattan.

Iacono, Alfonso M. (2009) "Postfazione", in Marx (ed.) (2009), 305–10.

Lordon, Frédéric (2015) *Capitalismo, desiderio e servitù. Antropologia delle passioni nel lavoro contemporaneo*, trad. it. di Ilaria Bussoni, Roma, DeriveApprodi. Orig. ed. *Capitalisme, désir et servitude: Marx et Spinoza*, Paris, La Fabrique, 2010.

Marx, Karl (1976) *Lettere a Kugelmann*, trad. it. di Carlo Jülg, Roma, Editori Riuniti.

Marx, Karl (1980) *Manoscritti economico-filosofici del 1844*, trad. it di Norberto Bobbio, Torino, Einaudi. Orig. ed. *Oekonomisch-philosophische Manuskripte aus dem Jahre 1844*.

Marx, Karl (1990) *Capital: Critique of political economy. Volume 1*, transl. by Ben Fowkes, London, Penguin Books. Orig. ed. *Das Kapital: Kritik der politischen Oekonomie, I*, 1867.

Marx, Karl (1991) *Capital: Critique of political economy. Volume III*, transl. by David Fernbach, London, Penguin Books. Orig. ed. *Das Kapital: Kritik des politischen Oeconomie, III*, edited by Frederick Engels, 1894.

Marx, Karl (1992) *Early writings*, transl. by Rodney Livingstone and Gregor Benton, London, Penguin Books.

Marx, Karl (1973) *Grundrisse: Foundations of the critique of political economy (Rough Draft)*, transl. by Martin Nicolaus, London, Penguin Books. Orig. ed. *Grundrisse der Kritik der Politischen Oekonomie*, 1857–58, first published 1939.

Marx, Karl (2008) *Critica della filosofia hegeliana del diritto pubblico [1843]*, trad. it. di Galvano della Volpe, Macerata, Quodlibet.

Marx, Karl (2009) *Quaderni antropologici* [1881–82], Milano, Unicopli.

Marx, Karl and Engels, Frederick (1845–46) *The German ideology*, [1846] now available in www. marxists.org.

Musto, Marcello (ed.) (2005a) *Sulle tracce di un fantasma: L'opera di Karl Marx tra filologia e filosofia*, Roma, Manifestolibri.

Musto, Marcello (2005b) "Marx a Parigi: la critica del 1844", in Musto (ed.) (2005a), 161–78.

Musto, Marcello (2011) *Ripensare Marx e i marxismi*, Roma, Carocci.

Musto, Marcello (2016) *L'ultimo Marx 1881–1883. Saggio di biografia intellettuale*, Roma, Donzelli.

Petrucciani, Stefano (1996) "Introduzione" Spinella (ed.) (1996), xvii–xxii.

Petrucciani, Stefano (2009) *Marx*, Roma, Carocci.

Petrucciani, Stefano (2012) *A lezione da Marx*, Roma, Manifestolibri.

Schacht, Richard (1970) *Alienation*, London, Allen and Unwin.

Schumpeter, Joseph A. (2003) Storia dell'analisi economica, 3 voll., trad. it. di Paolo Sylos Labini e Luigi Occhionero, Torino, Bollati Boringhieri. Orig. ed. *History of Economic Analysis*, 1954, New York, Oxford University Press, and London, George Allen and Unwin.

Shaikh, Anwar (1990) "Capital as a social relation", in: *The new Palgrave – Marxian economics*, edited by John Eatwell, Murray Milgate and Peter Newman, New York and London, W. W. Norton & Co, 45–9.

Smith, Adam (1981) *An inquiry into the nature and causes of the wealth of nations [1776]*, 2 vol., Indianapolis, Liberty Fund. Reprint of the "Glasgow edition", 1976.

Spinella, Mario (1996) *Lineamenti di antropologia marxiana*, Roma, Editori Riuniti.

Texier, Jacques (1991) "Le concept de *Naturwüchsigkeit* dans l' 'Ideologie allemande'", *Actuel Marx*, 9: 97–122.

Tomba, Massimiliano (2011) *Strati di tempo. Karl Marx materialista storico*, Milano, Jaca Book.

Toscani, Franco (2009) "Speranza e utopia nel pensiero di Ernst Bloch", *Koinè*, XVI: 3–21.

Tosel, André (2005) "Perché la proposta del comunismo della finitudine?" in Musto (ed.) (2005a), 325–33.

Part II

Thematic part

The Individual and the Other as recognition and subjectivity

8 Self-development and social justice[1]

Catherine Audard

The 'container-like' conception of the Self: a liberal view?

One major difficulty any left-liberal or social liberal is faced with is the conflict between individual rights and freedom and the demands of social justice. If liberal individualism is understood, following Macpherson famous expression, as "possessive individualism", absolute property rights strongly oppose any form of redistribution.[2] Both libertarianism and utilitarianism share this vision of the individual as a "container" that is defined *quantitatively* as the result of an accumulative process of as many possessions and resources as possible, even at the expense of the similar rights and demands of others.

Hobbes's vision of human life in the state of nature as "solitary, poor, nasty, brutish and short" is typical of this territorial view of the Self. This is the result of his quantitative Galilean method that dissolves political society into its basic components: individual human beings and the mechanical forces that animate them: passions, appetites and desires. Human beings are understood as elementary particles or atoms, the interaction among which results in society. As in any mechanical apparatus, they are motivated by one unique force or "power", the desire to live and the fear of death, and one unique principle, "the right of nature or the liberty to use his own power as he wills himself for the preservation of his own nature" and property or "his natural right to everything; even to one another's body".[3] Acquisitive appetites cannot be restrained without alienating this initial natural liberty, which is Hobbes's version of the liberal ideal of individual sovereignty. The peaceful coordination of individual passions and interests is thus impossible in the absence of an absolute superior authority or sovereign: the Leviathan.

Classical liberalism's answer to Hobbes claims to reconcile the sovereignty of the individual with social peace and cooperation. Individuals are not motivated by one single force, the fear of death and the will to dominate, but by a *plurality* of conflicting desires and motives, compensating and neutralizing each other. For instance, David Hume observes that, in reality, individuals are not totally amoral, but are motivated by limited egoism and limited altruism as shown in their natural sympathy for their fellow human beings' pains or pleasures. Self-love and self-interest are not necessarily the enemies of society but as famously expressed by Adam Smith, the search for profit can be the basis of useful social enterprises, as shown by the rise of capitalism in the eighteenth century. Destructive passions such as greed and the thirst for domination and power can be compensated by positive passions; and, according to Montesquieu, the "doux commerce" will pacify human nature. Economic growth and prosperity will create the bonds that absolute authority, be it that of the Church or the State can no longer guarantee.

However, for Bentham, the diverse passions and interests as well as Hobbes's acquisitive appetites are only facets of one fundamental force: the *greatest happiness principle*. Cooperation among possessive individuals is not impossible, but contrary to Montesquieu and the liberal illusion, it is far from natural or spontaneous. It is the result of artifices or "sanctions" as Bentham calls them that constrain asocial passions and maximize public happiness, thanks to the "interest-and-duty junction principle". Bentham is possibly not a classical liberal in the sense that he appeals to sanctions and coercions, the State having a part to play in implementing these sanctions, but he is still a liberal in the sense that he sees social cooperation as the com-possibility of individual liberties, based on the common psychological and moral bond provided by the utility principle.

Still, liberals limit themselves to justifying the possibility of social *cooperation* among "possessive" and selfish individuals on the basis of "l'intérêt bien entendu".[4] Social justice is not mentioned, as it would impose unacceptable demands on the individual search for happiness and fulfilment. But what if individuals could not satisfy themselves and their appetites without contributions from others, connected through an invisible but powerful social network of past generations as well as contemporaries? What if social cooperation needed "justice as reciprocity"?[5] For Rawls, for instance, lasting cooperation needs an agreement on a political conception of justice because all who are engaged and do their part in cooperation expect a fair return for their contribution that, in turn, should be assessed against an agreed and shared benchmark. Without justice, cooperation collapses as neither the fear of the Leviathan nor the passions and the interests or the happiness principle are enough to bind together free individuals each with their own conflicting interests. It is of the utmost importance, then, to be able to derive social justice from individual interests as Rawls endeavours to do in his *Theory of Justice*.

The Self as a developing being

I would like to suggest that the answer to the liberal predicament can be found in a conception of the Self as a developing being, opposed to the atomistic Cartesian conception of the Self as a 'container'.[6] This would provide an argument against the reduction of individualism to egoism. As Tocqueville famously says, "Whereas our ancestors spoke of egoism, we now speak of individualism".[7]

Rawls on 'plans of life' and 'self-realization'

One distinctive feature of Rawls's analysis of rationality and "thin theory of the good" is that it uses a *developmental* view of the Self, referring to plans of life, not to instant satisfaction.[8] "A person's good is determined by what is for him the most rational *long-term plan of life* given reasonably favourable circumstances". This is what makes her a unified moral person and "a person may be regarded as a human life lived according to a plan", not simply as a thing.[9] I will come back to the moral dimension later.

Three ideas are of note here. To be rational is, first, to be able to plan and to schedule activities and resources for the *long term*, envisaging the consequences of so doing: a temporal horizon is a necessary condition for rationality. Instead, to take "men's propensities and inclinations as given, whatever they are and then seek the best way to fulfil them" is a mistake concerning the very nature of rationality.[10] Second, to be rational is to be capable of using the means necessary to promote one's ends and thus, to project oneself in the future within a temporal horizon. "Rational individuals, whatever else they want, desire certain things as prerequisites for carrying out their plans of life".[11] Taking interests as given without any consideration for the *ends* pursued is also a mistake in that second sense. Thirdly and as a consequence, a degree of freedom to choose and rank satisfactions is necessary for rationality. To ignore that is another mistake leading to the familiar dilemmas of interpersonal comparisons of welfare. Defining the good in developmental terms or plans of life allows interpersonal comparisons not of satisfaction – which is impossible – but of the *means* to promote satisfaction. What is compared are not subjective states of mind or satisfactions, but "things which it is assumed they all normally need to carry out their plans".[12] A conception of the Self as a developing being, capable of choosing, planning and adapting resources for its own ends is implied here.

This conception is reinforced when Rawls analyzes the temporal sequence in which our activities are carried out and the role of deliberative rationality to organize properly this sequence of activities.[13] For long-term plans, the principle of inclusiveness is added to the familiar principles of rational choice: "Human beings have a higher-order interest to follow the principle of inclusiveness". This means that "the more inclusive plan is to be preferred . . . rationality means preferring, other things equal, the greater means for realizing our aims and the development of wider and more varied interests". This is where Rawls introduces the notion of self-development as self-realization: "human beings enjoy the exercise of their realized capacities (their innate or trained abilities), and this enjoyment increases the more the capacity is realized or the greater the complexity".[14] This leads to rejecting the view that our interests are fixed. As a consequence, the principles of rational choice, in particular that of maximization, are not sufficient for ranking our plans of life. Instead, Rawls moves towards a fuller description of rationality in the face of long-term decisions. The principle of responsibility to self is derived naturally from the idea of a plan of life: "a rational individual is always to act so that he need never blame himself no matter how his plans finally work out". "Acting with deliberative rationality, we are responsible to ourselves as *one person over time* . . . for *our future self and the interests of others*. . . . The principle of responsibility to self resembles a principle of right".[15]

From the idea of long-term planning, Rawls now moves to the idea of a developing Self, striving to implement its plans and getting pleasure from their realization. As he puts it, according to the Aristotelian principle,[16] "human beings enjoy the exercise of their realized capacities (their innate or trained abilities) . . . and are led to expect even greater satisfaction once we acquire a greater repertoire of skills". The more complex activities give even more pleasure over time. A companion principle is that " as we witness the exercise of well-trained abilities by others, these displays arouse a desire that we should be able to do the same things ourselves". This explains the *social interdependency* of rational plans of life, which are good if "they are likely to enhance the good of others" and if "others confirm and take pleasure in what we do". Our nature as self-developing beings and the type of satisfaction we gain from that development are dependent on others' validation and reciprocity and on fair and just social conditions. My conclusion, at this stage, is not that Rawls has a fully developed notion of the Self, but that the shift to a *long-term* conception of our ends combined with the Aristotelian principle yields a better understanding of the connection between self-development and social justice.

Sen on capabilities

Amartya Sen's critique of rational choice theory is another source of inspiration for a similar understanding of the Self as a developing being. In *Rationality and Freedom* as in *The Idea of Justice*, he rejects the "extremely limited understanding of reason and rationality" in favour of a distinction between "having reasons to choose something" and a capacity to project ends in a temporal horizon, and "what would be rational for us to choose" at a certain point in time. The main point here is the ability to sustain the choice after scrutiny, that is, the *time-relevant* conception of rationality. But it is mostly in Sen's interpretation of *freedom* as a component of human well-being that we find the link with *self-development*. "The process of choice itself is significant" and "individual advantage is judged in terms of the person's capability to do things she has reason to value". "The capability approach focuses on human life, and not just on some detached objects of conveniences, such as incomes or commodities that a person may possess".[17] Like Rawls and against resource-based or utility-based conceptions of the good, Sen is looking for a freedom-based approach, a way of understanding social justice in terms of the treatment of persons, not solely the distribution of goods. The developmental conception of persons is the answer to this concern for justice, which is perfectly expressed by Elizabeth Anderson: justice should be considered "as a relationship among people rather than merely as a pattern in the distribution of divisible goods . . . injustices may be better remedied by changing social norms and the structure of public goods than by redistributing resources".[18]

Mill, Humboldt and Marx on self-development

In their critique of the 'container-like' view of the Self, Rawls and Sen each in their different ways refer to an older tradition, which emerged with Humboldt, Mill, and also Karl Marx in the middle of the 19th century: the turn from an atomistic view of the Self to a *developmental* and historical one. It finds its fullest expression in John Stuart Mill's conception of "the free development of individuality as one of the leading essentials of well-being" and as "the chief ingredient of individual and social progress" (*On Liberty*, 1859, p. 73). It is also present, of course, in the young Marx's *1844 Manuscripts* and in his *German Ideology* (1845–6) where it appears as a collective as well as a personal task in a way that is still deeply influential.

John Stuart Mill is responsible for initiating this new view and transforming the liberal understanding of the individual. One is not born an individual, one becomes one. "Become what you are" said Goethe's Faust. Quoting Humboldt as one of his main sources with Coleridge, Mill summarizes his ambitions at the start of *On Liberty* (1859):[19] "The grand leading principle towards which each argument unfolded in these pages directly converges, is the absolute and essential importance of human development in its richest diversity". In the famous Chapter III he claims that "the end of man is the highest and most harmonious development of his powers to a complete and consistent whole . . . therefore the object towards which every human being must ceaselessly direct his efforts is the individuality of power and development" (*On Liberty*, 1859, p. 73). There are at least four important benefits to be drawn from this understanding of the Self as a progressive being.

First, individuality needs freedom and equal rights for all, as individuals can only flourish through personal free choices and deliberative rationality. "Though our character is formed by circumstances, our own desires can do much to shape those circumstances. . . . We have real power over the formation of our own character".[20] That process of individuation is most likely to be successful if we are allowed to make our own choices and to develop capacities, which would have been left dormant if society or public opinion were our only source of direction.

> The human faculties of perception, judgment, discriminative feeling, mental activity, and even moral preference, are exercised only in making a choice. . . . The mental and moral, like the muscular powers, are improved only by being used. . . . He who chooses his plan for himself employs all his faculties.[21]

Secondly, in order to develop their potentialities, each individual necessarily relies on the cooperation of the others over time. "Experiments in living" as Mill says, and an exposure to a variety of contexts, cultures, experiences and values that individuals on their own could not access are hugely beneficial to this process. Against classical liberalism, Mill stresses the social dimensions of self-development. Society is *instrumental* for personal self-development in as much as it provides individuals with necessary public goods: education, health, employment, housing, security and safety, etc. But it is also *constitutive* as it provides us with new ends and values, directions and models, which we could not discover on our own or within our own culture. What is distinctive and new in Mill's view is that this is not simply an instrumental relation, but a constitutive one and the reason why individual development cannot be separated from social development. For both the young Marx and John Stuart Mill, self-development, the fulfilment of individual aspirations and potentialities, was impossible without social development and, in turns, contributes to it. The *Solidarist* movement in France and the 'new' liberalism in Britain are good examples of how to combine respect for individual development and social solidarity.[22] Individuals can only develop their potential and 'become themselves' if they meet favourable social conditions and opportunities in education, family structures, housing, health, etc. but if they also are confronted with values and ends transmitted through cultural institutions, universities, courts, etc. The role of the State is to provide these essential public goods without which individuals cannot flourish. Social liberalism is based on such an assumption.

Thirdly, social and intellectual *progress* is the expected result of freedom to develop and individual creativity. Freedom as absence of arbitrary interference will open up new directions and new interests that will benefit all and nurture rationality through discussion and comparisons, as Mill explains in Chapter 2. "We can never be sure," he wrote, "that the opinion we are endeavouring to stifle is a false opinion, and if we were sure, stifling it would be an evil still".[23] Only through free debate can such critical skills be developed and maintained. Our self-development as reasonable persons, capable of critically assessing our beliefs and actions depends on it. And if our beliefs and actions emerge intact from the critical assessment such debate involves, if they survive the struggle in the "marketplace of ideas", then, and only then, will one be entitled to accept them as justified. Even so, though this is the best guarantee that there is sufficient reason to justify accepting a belief as true or an action as right, fallibility means, of course, that the debate must be ongoing.

Finally, freedom to develop is an essential constituent of *happiness*. Mill is thus able to reformulate the classical utilitarian definition: "I regard utility as the ultimate appeal on all ethical questions; but it must be utility in the largest sense, grounded on the permanent interests of man as *a progressive being*".[24] This should be understood in the context of his indirect utilitarianism: "I never, indeed, wavered in the conviction that happiness is the test of all rules of conduct, and the end of life. But I now thought that this end was only to be attained by not making it the direct end ".[25] Individuality, in other words, becomes with Mill one of the main ingredients of human happiness, individually and collectively and it is for that reason that it should be cultivated. As John Skorupski writes, "the liberal ideal of self-culture is perfectly compatible with the greatest happiness principle as only the fullest self-development of one's potential gives access to the highest forms of human happiness. Rawls called this the Aristotelian Principle".[26]

Three interpretations of self-development

So far, we have avoided a central question, which is: why should self-development be a good thing? What about the 'free' development of criminal anti-social impulses? What about the selfishness of self-development? Is self-development a good thing in itself, or only with respect to external values: social progress, general utility or human excellence? How should we argue for the morality of self-development? How do we guarantee the fit between individual development and the principles of justice?

It all depends on our understanding of the idea of self-development. Is it a purely *natural* process, developing innate capacities without external interventions? In that case, the weight of the 'social debt' seems minimal and the role of social justice limited. Is it a purely *adaptive* process to external social conditions, for instance the conditions of the labour market, without any room for personal choice? It is not a surprise if self-development in that case has limited selfish aims, developing only sellable skills at the expense of personal fulfilment, especially in a competitive context. Finally, is self-development a *creative* process, where personal choices and responsibility overrule social input and external contributions? The 'social debt' can be legitimately ignored in that case and the individual can see herself as the mistress of her own destiny, ignoring the demands of social justice. As we can see, the main problem is that of assessing the share of the social input in the process itself, both in the aims and means of personal development. This is indeed a very difficult question and there is no way an exact balance sheet of the cost/benefits for society and for individuals can be provided. Instead of providing a calculus, we can only expect the developmental outlook to support a growing awareness of individual achievements as a joint-result, of success as a social product and of social justice as an essential condition for it.

First, we have to deconstruct the productivist model of self-development as a simply *adaptive* process. In that case, the Self's talents, abilities and qualities and their development are valued uniquely for their utility, their results both for society and the individual, as means to an end, as potential 'goods' in order to achieve certain aims, in the way a tool is shaped to produce certain results. The aims are given independently from any long-term project or plan of life; the talents are only valued as goods or resources and self-development is shaped according to external aims and demands. This obviously does not represent an improvement on the 'container-like' view of the Self, which remains passive in the process. The 'productivist' model does not treat individual potentialities as part of a personal or a collective project. It represents self-development as detached from the individual's own aims, from the deliberative rationality necessary for ranking ends and means, without a true self-projection in time. It is right then to talk of a dehumanizing effect, of 'reification': human beings and their capacities are seen as means without ends. Unfortunately, this is the most common understanding of self-development, for example, in education or training where talents are simply selected and developed according to specific given managerial or economic aims and needs.

At the other end of the spectrum, we should equally reject the illusions of the Romantic's claims that 'authentic' or 'true' self-development is a creation similar to the *creative* process that produces a work of art. This is a model of self-development, which is pregnant in the young Marx as well as in Humboldt and Mill. Innovation, originality and singularity are the main values, signalling the ability of the Self to free itself from external conventions and pressures. This can lead to ignoring the role played by the 'good' of justice for individuals and the importance of the 'social debt', of the underlying immanent interdependency between members of society. As well as being an unachievable goal, except for a minority, the Romantic vision implies that only the 'hyperself', the superior being, is capable of creating herself without any outside help. In Nietzschean terms, to shape oneself freely like a work of art, ignoring the pressures of reality and of material constraints, the demands of society and of moral norms, to be the creator of one's own means of development as well as one's aims, is claimed to be the 'true' meaning of freedom. In contrast a majority of sub-human beings remain the mere recipients of means for survival. Self-affirmation is the privilege of the strong against the herd. This is an ideal that cannot be realized unless the needs and rights of others are trampled upon. If it is understood in this sense, it does not make space for social responsibility and the role played by others in one's own achievements. It is a-moral and a-political in a dangerous way.

Finally, there is the 'naturalistic' model of self-development understood as a '*natural*' and spontaneous process. The question is how autonomous this is. Some will insist that self-development is a process that should not be interfered with. The Self is defined as possessing both actual and potential properties. These potential properties are innate and apparently dormant, but develop according to a natural process that is, as Mill puts it, comparable to "the growth of a tree":

> Human nature is not a machine to be built after a model, and set to do exactly the work prescribed for it, but a tree, which requires to grow and develop itself on all sides, according to the tendency of the inward forces which make it a living thing.
>
> (Mill, *On Liberty*, 1859, p. 75)

Unfortunately, the metaphor is ambiguous. If the process demands only minimal interference, it is not a good description of *human* development. For instance, if abilities and talents are seen as naturally or genetically distributed among human beings, then, the resulting inequalities will be seen as justified as in the case of 'natural liberty' (Rawls, TJ, p. 57) and only an authoritarian arbitrary power would be able to redress the natural distribution. This is why the privileged always claim to have been successful on their own merits: talents, character, courage, etc., whereas social justice is a necessary support for the less privileged. However, if the metaphor is that of a natural process, which human interventions can support and enhance in yielding better results, then, we should understand self-development according to the ecological model, a result of the collaborative efforts of mankind and nature. Let us conclude with Rawls that

> It is important not to confuse the idea of social union with the high value put upon human diversity and individuality as found in Mill's *On Liberty* . . . and in German Romanticism . . . or with the conception of the good as the harmonious fulfillment of natural powers by (complete) individuals; nor, finally, with gifted individuals, artists, and statesmen, and so on, achieving this for the rest of mankind.
>
> (Rawls, TJ, p. 460, note 4)

If we want self-development to be relevant for social justice in the sense suggested by Mill, Rawls and Sen, we need to embed its morality into its meaning without any ambiguity. This is what I will now try to show with the help of Kant's transcendental argument.

The Kantian argument

Here we need a detour through Kant's *Critique of Pure Reason*, to overcome the conceptual confusions between self-development and mere change, creation or adaptation.

The Self as a developing being appears to us in a paradoxical form, both the same and different. This leads to the *Non-Identity problem*: how can we say that the self-developing individual remains the same person? We are witnessing the changes, the results, but, as we have seen, we cannot properly assess the intervening external or internal factors. This is essential for matters of social justice where we need to make sure that people claiming justice are the same as those who have suffered injustices, in spite of the role of all these intervening factors, personal responsibility, chance, contingencies of birth, social environment, etc. If what is allocated modifies identity, the recipient cannot say that he would have been better or worse off under a different distribution. However, following Kant, I suggest that we can overcome this paradox in the following way. The individual as a *phenomenon* is an empirical entity, conditioned by space and time: it is constantly changing. But it is also aware of these changes, and free from these spatio-temporal conditions, free to move backwards and forwards instead of being fixed at a certain point in space and time. It can then be described as a *noumenon*, a mental entity. If the Self is represented as *both* in time and space and outside, we can solve the Non-Identity problem, which stems from an instantaneous point of view on the Self. This is Kant's Transcendental Argument.

I would insist that, contrary to many interpretations, Kant is not saying that we have a dual ontological nature, which would be nonsense, a metaphysical claim condemned to contradiction. He is only saying that *the Self can be correctly described from this dual standpoint, as both empirical and noumenal.* As a result, we can understand how the Self can develop, remaining the same while changing because it can synthetize and make sense of external inputs and internal changes into a continuous development. We should note here that self-development has no perfectionist connotation, only that changes can be organized into a meaningful and goal-directed series of events, instead of a set of chaotic experiences, what David Hume called "a bundle of perceptions". When Kant writes that "it must be possible for the 'I think' to accompany all my representations", he only underlines a truism, that "otherwise something would be represented to me which could not be thought at all".[27] This is not an ontological claim as there is no possibility of knowing the 'I think', but an epistemological claim, as the 'I think' is the presupposition, or as Kant says, "the original apperception" which is presupposed by any representation but cannot itself "be accompanied by any further representation" (p. 153). This is why the unity of self-consciousness, or self-identity through time, is "transcendental": it is a condition of possibility for any representation through space and time, which cannot itself be represented or intuited. The emphasis in Kant is on something, which is essential for Mill and for Rawls: the capacity to synthetize the various experiences through time into a meaningful goal-directed whole, 'my' experiences. Contrary to the 'container-like' view of the Self, Kant saw human beings as capable of self-development not simply as living beings, but as end-setting beings, setting themselves goals and orientations through time. "The analytic unity of apperception is possible only under the presupposition of a certain synthetic unity".[28] If we now turn to practical reason and morality, we can say with Kant that *what makes us "persons or ends in themselves", and not solely means, is the capacity to set ourselves ends and aims, to construct plans of life*. Such an analysis should allow for a better sense of what self-development really means, as the American philosopher Christine Korsgaard shows:

> So, Kant asserts, the unconditionally valuable thing must be "humanity" or "rational nature", which he defines as the capacity to set an end. . . . We must regard ourselves as capable of conferring value upon the objects of our choice, the ends that we set, because we must regard our ends as good. But since "every other rational being thinks of his existence by the same rational ground which holds also for myself", we must regard others as capable of conferring value by reason of their rational choices and so also as ends in themselves. Treating another as an end in itself thus involves making that person's ends as far as possible your own. . . . For this reason, it is our duty to promote the happiness of others – the ends they choose. . . . The goodness of rationally chosen ends is a matter of the demands of practical reason rather than a matter of ontology.
>
> (Korsgaard, *Creating the Kingdom of Ends*, 1996, pp. 260–1)

Self-development as a social process

Let us summarize that far from being an autonomous natural process or an individual creation or a mere adaptation to the context, self-development is a *social* process in the sense that as developing beings, we stand together with each other, we need each other, even if we are not fully aware of it. This is what Durkheim and Bourgeois called the "fact of solidarity".[29] Self-development is a social process, not in the sense that it is fully conditioned by external socio-economic factors, but that it needs external as well as individual inputs. This is why Rawls uses the expression "social union" to describe the social structure that is at work in the development of the Self and its capacities, to distance himself from any social determinism as well as from the illusions of the purely individualistic view of society as 'private society'.

> We need one another as partners in ways of life that are engaged in for their own sake and the successes and enjoyments of others are necessary for and

> complementary to our own good. . . . Rational plans of life normally provide for the development of at least some of a person's powers. The Aristotelian Principle points in this direction. Yet one basic characteristic of human beings is that no one person can do everything that he might do. . . .
>
> Thus we may say following Humboldt that it is through social union founded upon the needs and potentialities of its members that each person can participate in the total sum of the realized natural assets of the others. We are led to the notion of the community of humankind.
>
> (Rawls, TJ, pp. 458–9)

> Persons need one another since it is only in active cooperation that one's powers reach fruition. Only in a social union is an individual complete.
>
> (ibid. note 4, p. 460)

My first conclusion is then that the conception of the Self as a developing being and of this process as a *social* process defeats selfishness and opens the way for a different view of liberal individualism that is compatible with, and even needs social justice. However, at this stage, we have only a general framework, not a specific one. In order for desires to be desires *of* the Self, whatever that is, and not *for* the Self, we need other factors such as education, social and political emotions, etc. The capacity to anticipate others' needs and desires is a necessary, but not a sufficient condition. We must have a higher-order desire for social institutions that will include others' needs and choices in our reasoning. This desire is itself fashioned by education and a conception of justice in a circular way. As Rawls famously said, "those who can give justice are owed justice" (TJ, p. 446). It would be an illusion to believe that self-development includes an immanent sense of justice whereas the latter is dependent on the interplay between institutions and personal choices.

The second conclusion is that social justice itself should be understood differently in view of this reinterpretation of the Self as a progressive and developing being. In particular, *the demand for freedom and responsibility for one's own ends should come to the forefront of social justice*, avoiding as much as possible the "undue reliance on assistance".[30] Such a view has important consequences for the Welfare State and leads Rawls to a critique of its emphasis on assistance rather than on fighting the causes of inequality. Only a concerted effort of redistribution of "the ownership of wealth and capital" can overcome natural as well as social inequalities and give reality to *equality of opportunities* and its fair value.[31] Following James Meade (1964)[32] Rawls is thus in favour of a "property-owning democracy" which considerably changes the scope and institutions of social justice.

> The idea is not simply to assist those who lose out through accidents and misfortunes (although this must be done) but instead to put all citizens in a position to manage their own affairs and to take part in social cooperation on a footing of mutual respect under appropriately equal conditions.
>
> (TJ, p. xv)

But I would like to add that a main condition remains, that the institutions of social justice leave open a *temporal horizon* of choices and opportunities against which the Self can project itself and develop as freely as possible. Financial security and property ownership are certainly necessary conditions, but without a sense of the future and a trust in it, development remains an illusion. The point I would like to conclude with is that the *temporality of self-development* needs to be properly understood. In order to understand social justice as grounded in individual freedom to develop, we need a much more complex understanding of what it means to develop one's potential within a free and democratic context. We need a re-humanization or a 'de-naturalization' of temporality and opportunities. We have seen that self-development cannot be understood simply in terms of a natural gradual process. Nor can opportunities be understood simply as 'chances'. They are very often events or 'turning points' because of existing conditions that will change the process. Opportunities only become such if there exists prior to them a temporal horizon to which the individual can relate and on which she can base her hopes. The central notion here is very close to Sen's *capabilities*. The capacity to transform resources and opportunities into welfare relies on the capacity of the individual to project onto an open horizon. External interventions such as social measures can only be successful if there exists prior to them a horizon that allows the individual person to project onto.

Let me conclude and illustrate the importance of this horizon with an example drawn from a recent book by the French sociologist Eric Maurin, *La peur du déclassement* (2009).[33] The book is a brilliant analysis of a widespread social attitude, fear in the face of losing one's social status and security through unemployment, generated by high levels of joblessness in France (around 20% of the 18–24-year-olds). However, there is a stark contrast between perception and reality. For 40% of the French population, fear of joblessness is real whereas the chances of losing one's job are minimal, given the high level of job protection for those in work. Among the sources of this insecurity are the strong inequalities between jobless and employed people, those who have a status and those who have none. The horizon is closed at a very young age with no second chance in a society still shaped by status and expectations of 'jobs for life'. There is no place for self-development in either the educational system or the jobseekers' outlook. Such an ideology produces high levels of anxiety and depression, not simply injustices that remain incomprehensible in a rich and prosperous democracy. As Maurin says, it is not the loss of status, which is problematic; it is the fear of the loss and the absence of projects and alternative solutions. This shows how important the perception of temporality, of self-development as a fair opportunity throughout all their lives is for promoting a just and democratic society.

Notes

1 This paper is based on a lecture I gave at the University of Luxembourg, 5 December 2011 and on another I gave at the Strasbourg Conference 9 October 2014.

2 C.B. Macpherson, *The Political Theory of Possessive Individualism, Hobbes to Locke,* Oxford, Oxford University Press, 1962. See also Richard Tawney (2004), *The*

Acquisitive Society (1920), New York, Dover Publications. For a critique of Macpherson, see James Tully, *Locke in Context*, Cambridge, Cambridge University Press, 1993, chapter 2.

3 T. Hobbes, *Leviathan* (1651), C.B.Macpherson ed., London, Penguin, 1985.

4 A. de Tocqueville, *Democracy in America II* (1840), A. Goldhammer tr., New York, The Library of America, 2004, Part II, Chapter VIII.

5 J. Rawls, *Political Liberalism*, New York, Columbia University Press, 1993 and 1996, p. 16: "Fair terms of cooperation specify an idea of reciprocity . . . and a conception of political justice".

6 For a critique of self-interest maximization, see A. Sen, *Rationality and Freedom*, Cambridge, MA, Harvard University Press, 2002, and 'Rational Fools', *Philosophy and Public Affairs* 11, 317–44, 1977.

7 de Tocqueville, *Democracy in America* (1840), II, II, p. ii.

8 On plans of life, see J. Rawls, *A Theory of Justice* (TJ afterwards), Cambridge, MA, Harvard University Press, 1971 and 1999, §15 and §§63–5.

9 Ibid. §15, p. 79, (my emphasis), §60 and §63, p. 358.

10 Ibid. §6, p. 27.

11 Ibid. §60, p. 348.

12 Ibid., p. 81.

13 Rawls, TJ §63, p. 360 and §64.

14 Ibid. §65, pp. 364–5 and 374.

15 Ibid., p. 371 (my emphasis).

16 Ibid., p. 374, n.20, p. 376 and p. 387.

17 A. Sen, *The Idea of Justice: The Idea of Justice*, London, Allen Lane, 2009, p. 231 and 233.

18 Elizabeth Anderson, 'What is the Point of Equality', *Ethics* 109/2 (January 1999), p. 336.

19 J.S. Mill (1838) *Essay on Bentham and* (1840) *Essay on Coleridge*, in *Dissertations and Discussions*, M. Warnock (ed.), London, Fontana, 1966.

20 J.S. Mill, *Autobiography*, ed. J.M. Robson, London, Penguin Books, 1989, p. 135, and *Logic*, Book VI.

21 Mill, *On Liberty* (1859), chapter 3, pp. 74–5.

22 On 'Solidarism' and 'New Liberalism', see J.T. Kloppenberg, *Uncertain Victory*, Oxford, Oxford University Press, 1986.

23 Mill, *On Liberty* op.cit., chapter 2, p. 37.

24 Mill, *On Liberty*, op.cit., chapter 1, p. 31 (my emphasis).

25 Mill, *Autobiography*, op.cit., p. 117.

26 J. Skorupski, *Why Read Mill Today?* London, Routledge, 2006, p. 27.

27 I. Kant, *Critique of Pure Reason* (1787), tr. N. Kemp –Smith, London, Palgrave MacMillan, 1990, pp. 152–3.

28 Ibid., p. 154.

29 On Léon Bourgeois's 'solidarism', see J.T. Kloppenberg, *Uncertain Victory*, Oxford, Oxford University Press, 1986, S. Lukes, *Emile Durkheim*, London, Penguin Books, 1973.

30 J.S. Mill, *Principles of Political Economy* (1848) in *The Collected Works of John Stuart Mill*, vol. II and III, J.M. Robson (ed.), London and Toronto, Toronto University Press, 1963–1979: "The problem to be solved is therefore one of peculiar subtlety as well as importance; how to give the greatest amount of needful help, with the smallest encouragement to undue reliance on it".

31 Rawls, TJ, p. xiv, and *Justice as Fairness: A Restatement*, Cambridge, MA, Harvard University Press, 2001, §§41–2 and §49. For similar views, see T. Piketty, *Capital in the XXIst Century*, Cambridge, MA, Harvard University Press, 2014, chapter 15.

32 J.E. Meade, *Efficiency, Equality and Property-Owning Democracy*, London, G. Allen & Unwin, 1964, and M. O'Neill and T. Williamson (dir.), *Property-Owning Democracy: Rawls and Beyond*, Oxford, Wiley-Blackwell, 2014.

33 Eric Maurin, *La peur du déclassement*, Paris, Le Seuil, 2009.

Bibliography

Anderson, E. (1999), 'What is the Point of Equality', *Ethics* 109/2, pp. 287–337.
de Tocqueville, A. (1840), *Democracy in America II*, A. Goldhammer (tr.), New York, The Library of America, 2004.
Hobbes, T. (1651), *Leviathan*, C.B.Macpherson (ed.), London, Penguin, 1985.
Kant, I. (1787), *Critique of Pure Reason*, N. Kemp –Smith (tr.), London, Palgrave MacMillan, 1990.
Kloppenberg, J.T. (1986), *Uncertain Victory*, Oxford, Oxford University Press.
Korsgaard, C.M. (1996), *Creating the Kingdom of Ends*, Cambridge: Cambridge University Press.
Lukes, S. (1973), *Emile Durkheim*, London, Penguin Books.
Macpherson, C.B. (1962), *The Political Theory of Possessive Individualism, Hobbes to Locke*, Oxford, Oxford University Press.
Maurin, E. (2009), *La peur du déclassement*, Paris, Le Seuil, 2009.
Meade, J.E. (1964), *Efficiency, Equality and Property-Owning Democracy*, London, G. Allen & Unwin.
Mill, J.S., (1838), *Essay on Bentham* and (1840) *Essay on Coleridge*, in *Dissertations and Discussions*, M. Warnock (ed.), London, Fontana, 1966.
Mill, J.S. (1843), *A System of Logic* in T*he Collected Works of John Stuart Mill*, vol. VII and VIII, J.M. Robson (ed.), London and Toronto, Toronto University Press, 1963–1979.
Mill, J.S. (1848), *Principles of Political Economy* in *The Collected Works of John Stuart Mill*, vol. II and III, J.M. Robson (ed.), London and Toronto, Toronto University Press, 1963–1979.
Mill, J.S. (1859), *On Liberty*, eds. J. Gray and G. W. Smith, London, Routledge, 1991.
Mill, J.S. (1873), *Autobiography*, J.M. Robson (ed.), London, Penguin Books, 1989.
O'Neill, M. and Williamson, T. (dir.) (2014), *Property-Owning Democracy: Rawls and Beyond*, Oxford, Wiley-Blackwell.
Piketty, T. (2014), *Capital in the XXIst Century*, Cambridge, MA, Harvard University Press.
Rawls, J. (1971 and 1999), *A Theory of Justice* (TJ afterwards), Cambridge, MA, Harvard University Press.
Rawls, J. (1993 and 1996), *Political Liberalism*, New York, Columbia University Press.
Rawls, J. (2001), *Justice as Fairness: A Restatement*, Cambridge, MA, Harvard University Press.
Sen, A. (1977), "Rational Fools", *Philosophy and Public Affairs* 11, 317–44.
Sen, A. (2002), *Rationality and Freedom*, Cambridge, MA, Harvard University Press.
Sen, A. (2009), *The Idea of Justice: The Idea of Justice*, London, Allen Lane.
Skorupski, J. (2006), *Why Read Mill Today?* London, Routledge.
Tawney, R. (2004), *The Acquisitive Society* (1920), New York, Dover Publications.
Tully, J. (1993), *Locke in Context*, Cambridge, Cambridge University Press.

9 Aristotle on reciprocity and social health[1]

Robert Gallagher

Introduction: the problem

Modern economic theories obscure social relations between human beings, that is, between oneself and the other.[2] They fail to include human beings in their representations of exchange, which is one of the most significant acts through which human beings relate to one another in societies, apart from their relations with families and loved ones. In place of the living social relations between human beings they substitute imaginary social relations between things. As Marx writes, "The mutual relations of the producers, within which the social character of their work affirms itself, take the form of a social relation between the products," that is, "The work of the individual asserts itself as a part of the work of society, only by means of the relations which the act of exchange establishes directly between the products" (Marx 1967: 76–87).[3] Consequently, all social relations are dissolved and extinguished under the power of exchange value, for "The dissolution of all products and activities into exchange values presupposes the dissolution of all fixed personal (historic) relations of dependence in production, as well as the all-sided dependence of the producers on one another." Under exchange value, "all individuality and peculiarity are negated," and the individual, who formerly was recognized through the function that she performed in her community now is reduced to possessing her social power as well as her bond with society, only in her pocket as cash (Marx 1973: 156, 157). Oneself and the other are dissolved in exchange value, for under modern economic theory, price relations are the only relations, rather than simply a mediation. As a result, classical and neo-classical political economists such as Smith, Marx, Mill and Jevons consider it unnecessary to include the persons involved, in their representations of exchange, such as this first algebraic formula of classical exchange set down by Marx (Marx 1962: 63):

$$x\,\text{commodity A} = y\ \text{commodity B}, \qquad (C)$$

where x, y are the respective quantities of the commodities A, B.[4] Formula C simply states that "The value of a thing means the quantity of some other thing, or of things in general, for which it exchanges" (Mill 1929: iii.6).[5]

This was not always the way matters were understood, for from ancient Greece through the mediaeval period, exchange was modelled – following Aristotle's theory – not only as a relation between two commodities, but more importantly as a relation between two persons. The persons were later dropped from the representation upon questionable assumptions. Gilpin suggests why: "In the abstract world of the economist, all individual consumers are assumed to be alike, that is, homogeneous. All individual producers are assumed to be alike also . . . individuals everywhere are still believed to be essentially the same" (Gilpin 2001: 52). If all exchangers, producers, and consumers are "essentially the same," then the persons involved in production or in an exchange become a common factor that can be dropped from the economist's model and formulae, for, then, oneself and the other are "essentially the same," and neither represents anything variable or incommensurable. In other words, as Gilpin says, "in the abstract world of the economists," differences between human beings and the mutual relations between them are definitely not taken into account. If people are the same, then their mutual relations can be ignored. Bentham justified that view with his claim that all humans are motivated only to maximize pleasure and minimize pain (i.e., maximize utility) (Bentham 1948). If we are all so motivated, then we are "essentially the same."

I propose that if we are to represent the relation between oneself and the other in economic activity, we need put aside theories that place the human being qua moral subject outside the representations of economic activity, for the relation between oneself and the other is not even *representable* by theories that accept formula C as a sufficient model of exchange, for such models exclude the relation between oneself and the other that we seek to capture. This requires that we put aside Enlightenment-inspired theories, based as they are on the assumption that all are the same in nature, and instead look towards those who have challenged the status quo of economic deliberation in the past two centuries. Such a survey can result in a list of thinkers who, for various reasons, turned to Aristotle for ideas and inspiration in constructing alternative theories of justice or economy: To cite just a few, Marx drew his distinction between use-value and exchange value from Aristotle's *Politics* and developed his theory of the contradictions in capitalism, in part, from that work (cf. Marx 1904: 19, 1962: 49ff, 100n39, 167n6).[6] Polanyi found in Aristotle a theory of exchange as a "mutual sharing," in Greek, *metadosis* (Polanyi 1968a). Rawls in part bases his *Theory of Justice* on an Aristotelian principle of human motivation which he constructs from *Nicomachean Ethics* books vii and x and calls "the Aristotelian principle" (Rawls 1999: 374–9).[7] Finally, Nussbaum, following Aristotle, criticizes the social contract tradition for its assumption that "contracting parties are rough equals" (Nussbaum 2006: 69, 71). The work of all those writers suggests that examining the writings of Aristotle may be a way out of our present difficulties.

Self and other in Aristotle's theory of political economy

It is striking that Aristotle formulates his theory of political economy as a representation of the relationship between oneself and the other in the everyday life of a community (*koinōnia*). He refers to members of a community as *koinōnoi*, "sharers" (*EN* 1133b3).[8] The relationships between sharers in which they exchange goods with each other Aristotle terms civic friendship (*politikē*) (*EN* 1163b34). Aristotle says that the human being first experiences friendship in relations with siblings and parents within the household (*EE* 1242a40-b1, *EN* 1161b27–31). Civic friendship is the generalization of that familial friendship first to kin outside one's immediate household and ultimately to other members of one's community. For a city-state originates from households that develop into villages as the children of an original household establish their own (*Pol.* 1252b16–18).[9] As sons and daughters of a patriarch establish their own households and exchange necessary items with each other, those households come to constitute a village of related kin based on familial friendship. Several such villages, insofar as they collectively achieve nearly complete self-sufficiency, form a city-state (*Pol.* 1252b27–30).[10]

For Aristotle the basis of civic friendship is the sharers' need for each other: "need holds a community together as if it were a single entity" (*EN* 1133b7). Only because we each need different things and fulfil different functions in our communities and provide different products, only for those reasons, is there reason for us to associate with each other and exchange (*EN* 1133a16–19). For if our needs were the same (as modern economists, following Bentham, claim), we would not be functionally different individuals and thus would have no reason to exchange, for how could I exchange with someone who has the same needs as I? (*Pol.* 1261a23–4). Rather, in the market we would compete in seeking the same goods. Only if we differ from each other, are reciprocity and equality between us possible (*Pol.* 1261a29–31). For out of our difference, we have need of each other, and consequently respect each other and are moved to treat each other with dignity. For I have need of the other, and the other has need of me, at the very least, insofar as we each need the functions that each fulfils and the products that each produces. That is why Aristotle designates civic friendship a friendship in accordance with usefulness (*chrēsimon*) (*EN* 1155b19), though not only with respect to advantage (*to sumpheron*) (*EN* 1160a11), for like all forms of friendship it concerns moral action, i.e. are we behaving justly towards our friend? (*EN* 1160a2). The friendship is useful if one's civic friend acts justly, i.e. does not exploit you or use you as a means. In this way, civic friendship contains the kernel of friendship in accordance with virtue.[11] Accordingly, Aristotle is concerned to preserve civic friendship and communities based on it.

Metadosis

Aristotle asks: What preserves such "communities of exchange"? His answer is "proportional reciprocity" in the exchange relations between the sharers (*EN* 1132b31–3). He explains that if the sharers do not benefit each other in their exchanges, then

1 Giving-of-a-share (*metadosis*) does not occur, but it is by giving-of-a-share that they remain together. That is the reason they established a sanctuary of the Graces (*Charitōn*), so that there would be giving-back-in-turn (*antapodosis*).

> For the following is peculiar to grace (*charis*): that we must serve-in-turn the one who has shown kindness (*charisamenos*) to us, and take the lead in showing kindness (*charizomenos*) in the future ourselves. And that which brings about a giving-in-return (*antidosis*) that is proportional in diagonal pairing (*EN* 1133a2–7).

The very word by which Aristotle refers to the act of exchange – *metadosis* – which Polanyi translates as "mutual sharing" – already brings persons into the representation of exchange, for only persons can "give a share," or "share mutually," and the very point of that sharing is for the community to "remain together." So, both the activity and its purpose are social and relate oneself and the other. Moreover, and to the annoyance of some contemporary thinkers (e.g., Meikle 1997: 154; Judson 1997; Miller 1998),[12] Aristotle advances grace and kindness as underpinnings of *metadosis* and community economic activity. He says that the Greeks established sanctuaries to the Graces so that citizens would be motivated by grace to practise reciprocity in exchanges, that my partner in exchange, my other, would "give back in turn" (*antapodosis*) to me, after I had "given a share" of my goods to her.[13] Furthermore, grace is socially transformative: Not only must we "serve in turn the one who has shown kindness to us" in an exchange, but that experience will educate us to "take the lead in showing kindness in the future ourselves," to others, in other exchanges.

In his text, Aristotle then immediately begins to construct proportions to represent *metadosis*. He assigns the symbols α, β to the persons involved, and γ, δ to their *erga* (*EN* 1133a7–8, b4–5). He explains that it is necessary for party α to receive from party β her *ergon* (i.e., product or result of her work), and that party α must "give a share" of his to her (*EN* 1133a8–10). If that is done in accordance with reciprocal equality, then there will be reciprocity and the community will stay together. If not, then the transaction is not fair and the community will dissolve (*EN* 1133a12).

It becomes apparent from examination of Aristotle's text that *metadosis* is a "status transaction" (Polanyi 1968a: 152).[14] Aristotle begins to study *metadosis* in the *Nicomachean Ethics* by examining the following proportion:

2 As farmer is to shoemaker, so the *ergon* of the shoemaker is to that of the farmer (*EN* 1133a32–3).

With the algebraic symbols that he assigns to the persons and the goods, we can restate that proportion as follows:

$$\frac{\alpha}{\beta}=\frac{\delta}{\gamma} \qquad (A).$$

The inclusion of a ratio of the persons confirms that *metadosis* is a status transaction, for the parameters representing the two exchangers have different values: The exchangers have different, unequal "worth."

Distributive, corrective and reciprocal justice

Aristotle introduces the ratio $\frac{\alpha}{\beta}$ in *EN* v.3 when he is presenting a general introduction to his treatment of distributive (*nemōntai* at *EN* 1131a24), and corrective justice (*to diorthōtikon*) (*EN* 1131b24) and within corrective, reciprocal justice (*to antipeponthos*) (*EN* 1132b21). He says that justice is a mean between "the more" (profit) and "the less" (loss) with respect to two persons and two objects of interest (*pragmata*), i.e. goods (*EN* 1131a10–18). Because of that, justice must be represented by four terms, two for the persons involved and two for the objects (*EN* 1131a18–20). The parties to a transaction are represented with respect to their worth or merit (*ek toû kat' axian*), the determination of which usually depends on the socio-political faction that is judging worth – oligarchs, aristocrats and democrats each judging worth according to different standards, oligarchs by wealth, democrats by whether one is free (a binary function) and aristocrats by "virtue" (*EN* 1131a24–9). Aristotle evaluates worth with respect to the function (*ergon*) that a sharer fulfils in a community (*Pol.* 1253a23; *EN* 1137a16), as discussed below. Parties to a transaction are usually "unequal" (*anisou, mē isoi*) (*EN* 1131a11, 24); in the language of the *Eudemian Ethics* one party is "superior" (*huperechōn*) (*EE* 1242b7), the other "lesser" (*elattō*) (*EE* 1242b8) or "outdone" (*huperechomenos*) (*EE* 1242b15). Aristotle concludes his introductory remarks in *EN* iii by saying that "justice is something proportional" in at least four terms (*EN* 1131a29), as in Proportion A, above. Aristotle then develops proportions to represent distribution of contributions to a common fund. In an example, what one can withdraw depends on how much one paid into the fund (*EN* 1131b3–12). But Aristotle also promotes redistribution of wealth within the *polis* to assist the poor. He recommends: a) That the poor be exempt from having to contribute for the common meals of the city (*Pol.* 1130a3–13); b) That the state provide block grants to the poor for the establishment of homesteads or for starting a trade or farming (*Pol.* 1320a35-b2, 7–9); and c) That the wealthy pay for the attendance of the poor at obligatory meetings of the assembly (*Pol.* 1320b2–4). It is as if Aristotle believes that out of the loins of the poor may come the next general, and therefore the community must join together to help the poor man raise and provide for his family and involve them in public affairs. Therefore, distributive justice, at least on the level of the *polis*, can result in the poor receiving "unearned" distributions. The spirit of such distributions is expressed in Aristotle's theory of reciprocal justice, discussed below.

In the next chapter of *EN* v, Aristotle discusses corrective justice, and presents his defining treatment of profit and loss. This chapter states the reasons behind his formulation in *EN* v.3 that justice is a mean between the more (profit) and the less (loss) with respect to two persons and two objects of interest (*pragmata*) (*EN* 1131a10–18). Profit (*kerdos*) and loss occur when one party receives an excess (*to pleon*) beyond half the value of "the good" (*to agathon*) subject to the transaction (*EN* 1132a14–19). Aristotle represents the situation with a line segment that has been unequally divided between the two parties; the imbalance must be corrected (*EN* 1132a24–9). Aristotle concludes:

> 3 These names, both loss and gain, have come from voluntary exchange; for to have more than one's own is called gaining, and to have less than one's original share is called losing, e.g. in buying and selling and in all other matters in which the law has left people free to make their own terms; but when they get neither more nor less but just what belongs to themselves, they say that they have their own and that they neither lose nor gain. Therefore, the just is intermediate between a sort of gain and a sort of loss (*EN* 1132b11–19).[15]

Clearly, reciprocal justice, which Aristotle says pertains to "communities of exchange" (*EN* 1132b31–3), is a species of corrective justice, for after Aristotle discusses distributive justice, he says that corrective justice is the only "remaining" type of justice (*EN* 113b25) and then discusses corrective and reciprocal justice. Moreover, the principal example he gives of injustices requiring correction are those that arise as a result of voluntary exchange (*EN* 1132b11). So, reciprocal justice is part of corrective justice (Danzig 2000). Polanyi argues that reciprocal justice employs both redistribution and exchange as "subordinate methods" (Polanyi 1968b). Polanyi means that the distribution to the poor of land, of corn or of payments for the performance of citizens' duties, "all are a very real tribute to the strength of the *redistributive factor in classical communities*. The basic economic organization of the *polis* was redistribution of the proceeds of common activity" (Polanyi 2014: 157–8). Just how this appears in Aristotle's treatment of exchange, we will now investigate.

"Worth" in Aristotle's theory of justice

Aristotle says that the ratio $\frac{\alpha}{\beta}$ signifies the relative worth or merit of the parties to a transaction (τὸ κατ' ἀξίαν) (*EN* v.3.1131a24, viii.14.1163b11–12), that is, $\frac{\alpha}{\beta}$ represents the initial social conditions prior to an exchange, e.g. in an oligarchy the relative wealth of the parties (*EN* v.3.1131a25–9), for as noted above, Aristotle says that parties to many transactions are unequal. By including the ratio $\frac{\alpha}{\beta}$ in formula A, Aristotle makes possible a certain social criticism. When α, β represent conventional notions of worth, matters external to the production of the *erga* determine the exchange. Such estimations of worth amount to *social status* or *relative power*. For Aristotle, this seems simply to be an explanation for how things really are, rather than a proposal for how they should be. That is, Aristotle teaches us to interpret such a relation as C, above, as a simplification of formula A, where the effect of $\frac{\alpha}{\beta}$ is *concealed* in the exchange proportion.

In contrast, Aristotle himself evaluates worth in terms of the function that one has in one's community. Providing an illustration of this in *EN* v.9, Aristotle says that a doctor *is* the *ergon* he actualizes: it is easy, he says, to know about the various remedies for illness, but how one should dispense them and to whom and when, "that much a function (*ergon*) is what it is to be a doctor" (*EN* 1137a16). In general, *ergon* signifies not only a product or service provided but also the artisan who provides it, for providing that product (*ergon*) is his function (*ergon*) in the community, a function he performs by applying his art, for the *function* of a house builder in the community is to build houses for other sharers, and this is his *work* (*ergon*).

Returning to our discussion of social status, the result of an exchange governed by formula A is that the party with higher status or more power exploits the one with less. Notice that the ratio of the products $\left(\frac{\delta}{\gamma}\right)$ inverts the relationship of the sharers: Passage 2 (and formula A) take the ratio of β's *ergon* to α's, which is the inverse of the ratio of the sharers $\left(\frac{\alpha}{\beta}\right)$. Indeed, in the *Eudemian Ethics* Aristotle calls the proportion described in passage 2 "inverted" (*EE* 1242b7).[16] The import of that inversion is that under formula A party β turns over more of his *ergon* to party α than is the worth of the *ergon* of party α. A simple transformation of A shows that, i.e.:

$$\delta = \frac{\alpha}{\beta}\gamma \qquad (A_1)$$

which states that the product δ that Party β has to hand over to party α must be greater in value than the product γ that party α hands over to her/him, by the factor $\frac{\alpha}{\beta}$, which is their relative social status.[17] As Aristotle warns, "nothing prevents the *ergon* of one [β] from being more valuable than that of the other [α]" (*EN* 1133a12–13), for when $\frac{\alpha}{\beta} > 1$, e.g., when party α is wealthier than party β, then $\delta > \gamma$ and the *ergon* of β is more valuable than that of α. Such an exchange is not "fair." Party α is materially rewarded through the transaction due to possessing a higher status. Theoretically, that means that *exchange value is a function not only of the value of the goods exchanged, but also of the social status of the exchangers*. With that theorem, Aristotle overturns modern economic theories by showing that the exclusion of persons, of oneself and the other, invalidates their exchange models.

Aristotle's representation of inequality in exchange contradicts modernity's dogma that everyone is equal and treated equally. Aristotle describes the experience of the poor. Aristotle's point is that inequality in exchange relations is a reality we need face. Indeed, there are grounds for holding that in exchange in contemporary market economies in the advanced sector, economic power determines the terms, as Wolff has argued and is also shown by this author's case studies on domestic and international transactions (Wolff 1982; Gallagher 2018). The exchange model of classical political economy – represented in formula C, above (or in the prose of Smith, Jevons and Mill quoted in the corresponding endnote) – is a reduction of Aristotle's model to the case of α = β, i.e. $\frac{\alpha}{\beta} = 1$. That case is unrealistic since, as Aristotle argues, people who have the same talents have nothing to exchange with each other. In assuming that exchangers are "rough equals," as Nussbaum charges, classical political economists and modern contract theorists eliminate anything variable or incommensurable with the unfounded assumption that all humans are "essentially the same" (Nussbaum 2006: 69, 71).

Corrective reciprocal justice

At least one classical political economist, however, acknowledges difference, while he nonetheless advances formula C. In a passage that seems to be commenting on Aristotle, Marx says:

> 4 If individual α had the same need as individual β, and if both had realized their work in the same object [of production], then no relation whatever would be present between them; considering only their production they would not be different individuals at all. . . . Only differences between their needs and between their production gives rise to exchange and to their social equation in exchange . . . their natural difference puts them reciprocally into the relation of equality. In this respect, however, they are not indifferent to one another, but integrate with one another, have need for one another; so that individual β, as objectified in [her] commodity, is a need of individual α, and vice-versa . . . that each confronts the other as owner of the object of the other's need, proves that each of them reaches beyond his own particular need etc., as a *human being*, and that they relate to one another as human beings (Marx 1973: 242–3).[18]

Marx admits that it is our difference that not only brings us to exchange, but also brings us to become interested in one another, to acknowledge our "need for one another," as Aristotle also says. That interdependent need is the heart of our humanity, says Marx, because it "proves that each of them reaches beyond his own particular need" to the other, "as a *human being*, and that they relate to one another as human beings." Though Marx succumbed to the ideology of classical political economy in his theory of exchange (as in his formula C), passage 4 above reflects a more nuanced understanding. Aristotle, by contrast, did not abandon human beings to the status of being "essentially the same," but incorporated difference between exchangers into his model of exchange. Furthermore, Aristotle, out of his profound grasp of the humanity of sharing, calls upon sharers in a community to be gracious and kind in their exchanges with one another, and not exploit one another, as formula A_1 would have it. His solution to the problem of the more powerful citizen exploiting the weaker, is to re-invert formula A with the procedure he calls "diagonal pairing," so that the exchange benefits the weaker party, "the one who is [usually] outdone" (Gallagher 2012: 685–9). In *Eudemian Ethics*, he puts his proposal into the mouth of that party:

> 5 But the one who is outdone reverses the proportion [A] and pairs the terms diagonally (*EE* 1242b15–16).

If we "reverse" ratio $\frac{\delta}{\gamma}$ in Proportion A, we produce a new proportion, which is not "inverted"[19]

$$\frac{\alpha}{\beta}=\frac{\gamma}{\delta} \qquad \text{(B).}$$

In contrast to the use of Proportion A, the result of applying Proportion B is different: the two parties do not remain in the same relative material positions as before, but the position of the weaker is improved at the expense of the superior. For when $\frac{\alpha}{\beta}>1$ in exchanges governed by Proportion B, the one who draws the most from the transaction is the one who receives γ, and that is party β, for now the converse of A_1 is operative, that is,

$$\gamma=\frac{\alpha}{\beta}\delta \qquad (B_1)$$

and party α hands over more of his *ergon* than the *ergon* of party β is worth. The lesser party receives from the superior in proportion to the latter's superiority, that is, he hands over much less of his own product in exchange for the goods of the superior one, to settle the transaction. So, in this exchange, party β receives γ in accordance with his need.[20] Here we see a formula which demonstrates that reciprocal justice is a species of corrective justice, for formula B ensures that injustices suffered by the poor in the past are corrected through its application.

For the stronger, however, this operation changes the transaction from a money-making one to a loss and now the community and his friendship with the lesser becomes a "liturgy" (*leitourgia*) (1242b16–18), i.e. a public service to the community. On the superficial level, in order to equalize the transaction, Aristotle proposes to compensate the superior party for her loss by awarding public honour (*timē*) (18–21), which amounts to social influence and protection from law suits (Gallagher 2014b: 155–7). But his real message appears a few pages later and is of a different sort: For a relationship through which superior members of a community benefit more needy ones – such as that under consideration – characterizes for Aristotle a special sort of civic friendship (*philia*), the aim of which is to maintain the existence, the being, of the lesser party (*EE* 1244a24, 27–8). "For the superior one who benefits another wills, by his *ergon*, existence for the other, and to the one who has given existence the other must give back in turn" (ἀνταποδιδόναι) (*EE* 1244a28–30).[21] Here again we see *antapodosis* at work. It is a function of superior members of the community to support the existence, the being, of weaker ones. In this way, such a superior sharer uses wealth the best (*EN* 1120a6–7), and in doing so, he fulfils a communal function, for wealth is one of the qualities of the community (*Pol.* 1296b18), and its use consists in spending and giving (*EN* 1120a8). The beneficiaries give honour back in turn (*EE* 1242b19).

Aristotle's proposal encourages superior parties to practise the virtue of generosity towards their other, the "lesser" or "outdone" members of their community. In so relating to the other, the superior ones move towards the good life as a life of virtue. Moreover, the superior party's practice of grace (*charis*) inspires the practice of grace in his other, the beneficiaries (*EN* 1133a3–5), for, as Aristotle says, we are moved to serve in turn the one who has been kind to us, and in the future to take the initiative in acting kindly ourselves (*EN* 1133a4–5). The person who experiences kindness (*charis*), expresses gratitude (*charis*) and is moved to be kind (*charizomenos*) in the future.[22] So, the grateful person becomes the kind person. By giving a material benefit to the lesser, the superior gives the lesser the material sufficiency (*autarkia*) to practise the good life, for the good life requires that (*Pol.* 1253b25). Due to the beneficence of the superior party, his other – the weaker – obtains respite from the material want that makes it difficult to experience the good life, and thus to express the virtue of generosity towards her others. In this way, the lesser is enabled to rise from passivity, as a receiver, to activity, as a giver, for "we exist in activity, since we exist by living and doing" (*EN* ix.7). So, "the giver has more being than the receiver" (Hunt 1975: 243). Thus, the superior one supports not just the mere existence of the lesser, but also his existence as a virtuous individual.

Reciprocal justice in the 21st century?

Let us now look towards a contemporary application of Aristotle's ideas. Suppose that Aristotle's proposal, that the stronger aid the weaker, became the norm throughout a society: What would be the result? For one, the average value of $\frac{\alpha}{\beta}$ in exchanges would decline towards 1, or, making that into a positive function, the average value of $\frac{\beta}{\alpha}$ would increase. Such increase in the average value of $\frac{\beta}{\alpha}$, I propose, would represent an increase in reciprocity, which Aristotle argues is the key to social health. Under that circumstance, I argue, there would be less alienation of person from person. Oneself and one's other would be more closely bound. Accordingly, I have attempted to construct an Aristotelian Social Welfare Function (SWF) based on this analysis, that maximizes social welfare as reciprocity (Gallagher 2018). I define social welfare as a function of the average relative social status at work in an economy. In quantitative studies, I approximate that by the ratio of the income shares of lower quintiles of the population to higher ones, e.g., $\frac{Q_5}{Q_1}$ is the ratio of the lowest income quintile to the first. Figures 9.1 and 9.2 show $\frac{Q_5}{Q_1}$ per capita for the U.S. and Germany for recent decades.

Figure 9.1 indicates that social welfare has been steadily on the decline in the U.S. since 1976. The figure shows the effect, upon those in lower quintiles, of the concentration of U.S. national income into the top decile reported by Piketty and Saez (Piketty and Saez 2013). Recent work argues that social mobility is low in the U.S. in recent decades, making it difficult for offspring to escape from the deterioration in living conditions represented by Figure 9.1 (Chetty et al. 2014). Figure 9.2 shows that Germany has not produced the gross inequities that have

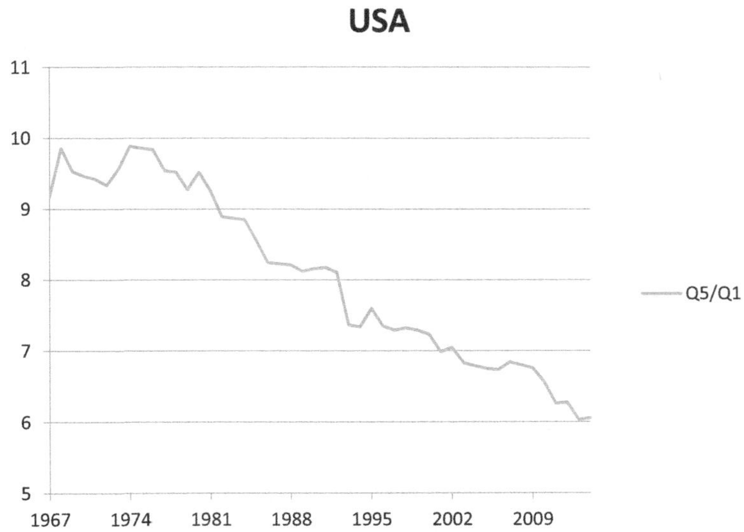

Figure 9.1 Ratio of income share of lowest quintile to highest in percentages in U.S.

Source: Data from U.S. Census Bureau (2016)

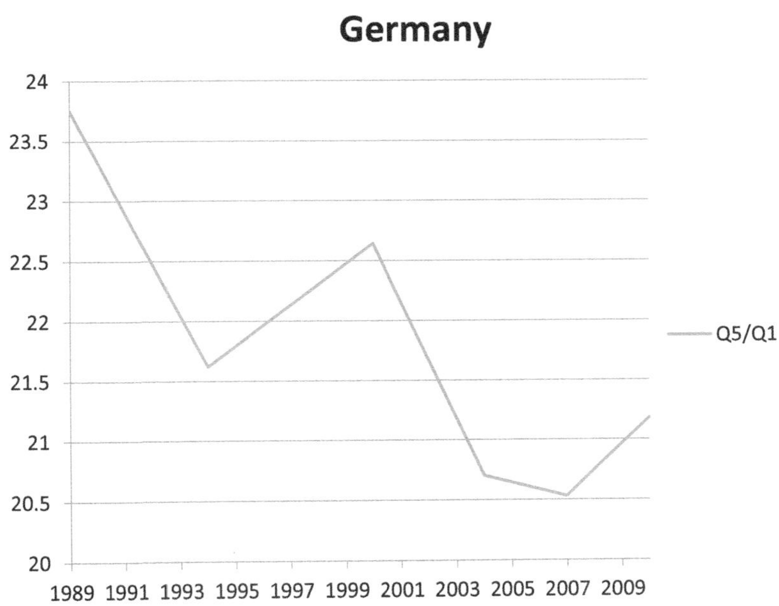

Figure 9.2 Ratio of income share of lowest quintile to highest in percentages in Germany

Source: Data from World Bank (2016)

developed in the U.S.A. In 2009 reciprocal social welfare in the U.S. was 6.5%, but 21% in Germany, more than 3 times the U.S. value. In the same year, France's value was over 23%, Italy almost 19%, Spain 16.5% and Greece 17.5%.[23] It is clear that Europeans defend the social welfare of their peoples better than Americans. Europeans enjoy values of reciprocal social welfare 2 ½ to 3 ½ times greater than Americans. All that indicates that there is a stronger community bond in at least continental European countries, mediated through tax-funded social welfare programs, as one conference participant suggested. Oneself and the other are more closely bound in Europe. By contrast, the U.S. has largely abandoned FDR's graduated income tax under the initiatives of Reagan and the Bushes (Piketty and Saez 2003).

This difference in social welfare between Europe and America may have its roots in the circumstance that American capitalism "did not develop on the foundation of a feudal system, but developed rather from itself . . . not as the result of a centuries-old movement, but rather as the starting-point of a new movement" (Marx 1973: 884; cf. Marx 1997: 463). As a result, the mediaeval traditions of community and of a complex nexus of social ties among individuals and classes do not exist in America.

Notes

1 An earlier version of this paper was presented at the 2nd International Conference "Economic Philosophy," at the University of Strasbourg, 9–10 Oct 2014, organized by Bureau d'Economie Théorique et Appliquée (BETA) of CNRS.

2 Possible exceptions include the theories of Rawls and Sen. With his "difference principle" Rawls (1999) attempts to represent difference between the expectations of persons, and proposes to aide those less well-off in some small respect, and in this limited sense he represents relations between oneself and the other. In "Equality of What?" Sen (1980: 202) says that we must recognize "the fundamental diversity of human beings." Sen asserts that "people seem to have very different needs" and that we need attend to their differences by supporting basic capabilities. In so representing and attending to difference, Sen makes progress in representing and attending to relations between oneself and the other. See Gallagher (2018) for more detailed discussion of Rawls and Sen.

3 In these remarks, Marx expresses a view consistent with the classical political economy of Smith and Ricardo. Cf. also endnote 4 below.

4 This model is that of Smith, Mill, Jevons and Marx. In *Wealth*, Smith says that "value in exchange" is "the power of purchasing other goods which the possession of that object conveys" (Smith 1976: i.4.13), i.e., from formula C, $A = (y/x)\ B$. Mill (1929): see the main text. B. Jevons: "the value of the ton of iron is equal to the value of the ounce of gold" (Jevons 1924: 78), which statement is equivalent to formula C; again, $A = (y/x)\ B$. Formula C is taken from Marx (1962: 63), but Marx's innovation here is only to state in a formula what the others say in prose.

5 Cited in Jevons (1924: 77).

6 On use-value and exchange value, see also Aristotle (*Pol.* i, chapters 8 and 9); Meikle (1995: 52n7); Gallagher (2018, chapter1). In *Capital*, Volume I, Part II, "The Transformation of Money into Capital," Marx (1962) presents "The General Formula of Capital" and "Contradictions in the General Formula" (Widersprüche der allgemeinen Formel). In a long footnote Marx shows that he draws this analysis of exchange and circulation from Aristotle (*Pol.* i.9). Meikle also notes that Marx develops his models of circulation from Aristotle; see Meikle (1995: ch. 3, esp. 52n7).

7 In addition, I argue in Gallagher (2018) that Rawls develops from Aristotle's theory of the role of social status in exchange, his "difference principle" that the well-off should not be permitted to benefit from an economic activity unless the less well-off also benefit to some degree.
8 In the case of Aristotle, we follow standard scholarly practice of citing his works by their abbreviation, in this case "EN" for *Nicomachean Ethics*, followed by the Bekker page number. Abbreviations are defined by work in the bibliography.
9 Such may be the origin of the original tribal structure of the city-state.
10 In contrast to Plato, for Aristotle, "Household becomes to city not stumbling-block, but building-brick" (Price 1990: 193).
11 This is no space here to discuss the other type of friendship, that in accordance with the pleasant.
12 Meikle (1997: 154) has gone so far as to say that to the principal issues of EN v.5 "koinônia and the spirit of the Graces and of gift and counter-gift, have no application," which seems odd in the light of passage 1. Even Thomas d'Aquino (1964) in his *Commentary on Aristotle's Nicomachean Ethics* passed over the issue of grace in Aristotle's economic thought, as though it had no significance.
13 The Graces are minor deities in the pantheon that represent for Aristotle, the virtues of graciousness, kindness and generosity. The shrine on the Acropolis was sculpted by none other than Socrates. See Pausanias (1918: 9.35.1).
14 On status transactions and on transactions of a multilateral character, see Polanyi (1968a). In *metadosis*, the transaction at least begins as a bilateral one, between two individuals or households, and is not mediated through a nexus of kinship relationships.
15 Ross's translation from Aristotle 1908.
16 Following MS Π which reads *anestrammenōs*.
17 For the long form of this analysis, see Gallagher (2012).
18 Translation revised by this author. Italics in original, underscore added.
19 In formula A each *ergon* is diagonally opposed to its producer/sharer. Now, in the new proportion, each *ergon* is paired with its producer/sharer. The procedure pairs the terms that had been diagonally opposed.
20 So, contrary to Scaltsas (1995: 258), the transaction is determined by the lesser party's individual need for the *erga* of the superior one, not by some generalized need for them "in society."
21 Reading αὐτοῦ, as in the manuscript.
22 So, this study confirms that Konstan is right to say that the primary affect associated with χάρις is gratitude.
23 Figures from calculations of $\frac{Q_5}{Q_1}$ based on U.S. Census Bureau (2016) and OECD (2014) data.

Bibliography

Aristotle. 1957. *Aristotelis Politica (Pol.)*. Ed. by W. D. Ross. Oxford: Clarendon Press.

Aristotle. 1975. *Aristotelis Ethica Nicomachea (EN)*. Ed. by I. Bywater. Oxford: Clarendon Press.

Aristotle. 1981. *The Athenian Constitution, the Eudemian Ethics, On Virtues and Vices*. Ed. & trans. by H. Rackham. London: Heinemann.

Aristotle. 1984. *The Complete Works of Aristotle*. Ed. by J. Barnes. Princeton, NJ: Princeton University Press.

Aristotle. 1991. *Aristotelis Ethica Eudemia (EE)*. Ed. by R. R. Walzer and J. M. Mingay. Oxford: Clarendon Press.

Aristotle. 1908. *Nicomachean Ethics*. Trans. by W. D. Ross. Oxford: Clarendon Press. Available at http://classics.mit.edu/Aristotle/nicomachaen.html

Bentham, J. 1948. *A Fragment of Government* and *An Introduction to the Principles of Morals and Legislation*. Oxford: Basil Blackwell. Originally published 1789.
Chetty, R., Hendren, N., Kline, P., Saez, E., and Turner, N. 2014. "Is the United States Still a Land of Opportunity? Recent Trends in Intergenerational Mobility." *American Economic Review, Papers and Proceedings*, 104(5): 141–7.
Danzig, G. 2000. "The Political Character of Aristotelian Reciprocity." *Classical Philology*, 95: 399–424.
Gallagher, R. 2011a. "Aristotle on *eidei diapherontes*." *British Journal for the History of Philosophy*, 19(3): 363–84.
Gallagher, R. 2011b. "Aristotle's *peirastic* Treatment of the *Republic*." *Arch. für Geschichte der Philosophie*, 939(1) (March): 1–23.
Gallagher, R. 2012. "Incommensurability in Aristotle's Theory of Reciprocal Justice." *British Journal for the History of Philosophy*, 20(4): 667–701.
Gallagher, R. 2014a. "In Defense of Moral Economy: Marx's Criticisms of Aristotle's Theory of Value." *Archiv für Rechts- und Sozialphilosophie*, 100(1): 112–29.
Gallagher, R. 2014b. "The Role of Grace in Aristotle's Theory of Exchange." *Methexis*, 26: 145–62.
Gallagher, R. 2018. *Aristotle's Critique of Political Economy*. London: Routledge.
Gilpin, R. 2001. *Global Political Economy*. Princeton, NJ: Princeton University Press.
Hunt, L. 1975. "Generosity." *American Philosophical Quarterly*, 12: 235–44.
Jevons, W. 1924. *The Theory of Political Economy*. London: Macmillan & Company.
Judson, L. 1997. "Aristotle on Fair Exchange." *Oxford Studies in Ancient Philosophy*, 15: 147–75.
Konstan, D. 2006. *The Emotions of the Ancient Greek: Studies in Aristotle and Classical Literature*. Toronto: Toronto University Press.
Marx, K. 1904. *A Contribution to the Critique of Political Economy*. Chicago: Kerr.
Marx, K. 1962. *Das Kapital. Band I*. In K. Marx and F. Engels, *Werke*, Band 23, S. 11–802. Berlin, DDR: Dietz Verlag. Available at <www.mlwerke.de/me/me23/me23_000.htm>
Marx, K. 1967. *Capital. Vol. 1*. Ed. by F. Engels & trans. by Moore & Aveling. New York: International Publishers.
Marx, K. 1969. *Die deutsche Ideologie*. In *Werke*, Band 3, S. 5–530. Berlin, DDR: Dietz Verlag.
Marx, K. 1973. *Grundrisse*. London: Penguin Books.
Marx, K. 1976. *Capital. Volume 1*, trans. by B. Fowkes & Intro. by E. Mandel. London: Penguin Books.
Marx, K. 1997. *The German Ideology, Part I*. In *Writings of the Young Marx on Philosophy and Society*, pp. 403–73. Ed. & trans. by L. Easton and K. Guddat. Indianapolis: Hackett Publishing.
Meikle, S. 1991a. "Aristotle and Exchange Value." In *A Companion to Aristotle's Politics*. Ed. by D. Keyt and F. Miller. Oxford: Oxford University Press.
Meikle, S. 1991b. "Aristotle on Equality and Market Exchange." *Journal of Hellenic Studies*, 11: 193–6.
Meikle, S. 1997. *Aristotle's Economic Thought*. Oxford: Clarendon Press.
Mill, J.S. 1929. *Principles of Political Economy*. London: Longmans, Green & Co.
Miller, F. 1998. "Was Aristotle the First Economist?" *Apeiron*, 31: 387–98.
Nussbaum, M. 1988. "Nature, Function, and Capability: Aristotle on Political Distribution." *Oxford Studies in Ancient Philosophy*, Supplementary Volume: 145–84.
Nussbaum, M. 1990. "Aristotelian Social Democracy." In *Liberalism and the Good*, pp. 203–52. Ed. by R. B. Douglass, G. Mara, and H. Richardson. New York: Routledge.

Nussbaum, M. 2000. *Women and Human Development: The Capabilities Approach*. Cambridge: Cambridge University Press.

Nussbaum, M. 2006. "Poverty and Human Functioning: Capabilities as Fundamental Entitlements." In *Poverty and Inequality*. Ed. by D. Grusky and R. Kanbur. Stanford: Stanford University Press.

OECD. 2014. "Income Distribution and Poverty." *OECD.StatExtracts*. <http://stats.oecd.org/Index.aspx?DataSetCode=IDD>

Pausanias. 1918. *Description of Greece*. Ed. & trans. by W. Jones. London: Heinemann.

Piketty, T. and Saez, E. 2003. "Income Inequality in the United States, 1913–1998." *Quarterly Journal of Economics*, 118(1): 1–39.

Piketty, T. and Saez, E. 2013. "Top Incomes and the Great Recession." *IMF Economic Review*, 61(1): 456–78.

Polanyi, K. 1968a. "Aristotle Discovers the Economy." In *Primitive, Archaic, and Modern Economies*, pp. 78–115. Ed. by G. Dalton. Garden City, NY: Anchor Books.

Polanyi, K. 1968b. "The Economy as Instituted Process." In *Primitive, Archaic, and Modern Economies*, pp. 139–74. Ed. by G. Dalton. Garden City, NY: Anchor Books.

Polanyi, K. 2014. "Market Elements and Economic Planning in Antiquity." In Polanyi, K. *For a New West*. Cambridge UK: Polity Press, 2014.

Price, A. W. 1990. *Love and Friendship in Plato and Aristotle*. Oxford: Oxford University Press.

Rawls, J. 1999. *A Theory of Justice*. 2nd ed. Cambridge, MA: Harvard University Press.

Scaltsas, T. 1995. "Reciprocal Justice in Aristotle's *Nicomachean Ethics*." *Archiv für Geschichte der Philosophie*, 77: 248–62.

Sen, A. 1980. "Equality of What?" In *Tanner Lectures on Human Values*. Vol. I. Ed. by S. McMurrin. Cambridge: Cambridge University Press; reprinted in John Rawls et al., *Liberty, Equality and Law*. Cambridge: Cambridge University Press, 1987.

Sen, A. 1984. *Resources, Values and Development*. Cambridge, MA: Harvard University Press.

Sen, A. 1985. "Well-Being, Agency and Freedom: The Dewey Lectures 1984." *Journal of Philosophy*, 82.

Sen, A. 1986. "The Standard of Living." In *Tanner Lectures on Human Values*. Vol. VII, Ed. by S. McMurrin. Cambridge: Cambridge University Press.

Smith, A. 1976. *An Inquiry into the Nature and Causes of the Wealth of Nations*. Oxford: Oxford University Press.

Thomas d'Aquino [Aquinas]. 1964. *Commentary on Aristotle's Nicomachean Ethics*. Vol. 1, trans. by C. I. Litzinger. Chicago: H. Regnery.

U.S. Census Bureau. 2016. "Selected Measures of Household Income Dispersion: 1967–2014." Available at <www.census.gov/hhes/www/income/data/historical/inequality/Table%20IE-1.pdf>

Winship, S. 2015. "Has Rising Income Inequality Worsened Inequality of Opportunity in the United States?" *Social Philosophy and Policy*, 31(2): 28–47.

Wolff, R. P. 1982. "Reply to Roemer." *Philosophy & Public Affairs*, 12(1): 84–8.

World Bank. 2016. "For Income Share Held by Highest 20%." <http://data.worldbank.org/indicator/SI.DST.05TH.20/countries>; for income share held by lowest 20% <http://data.worldbank.org/indicator/SI.DST.FRST.20>; Data downloaded 3 April 2016.

10 The self and the others

Recognition and subjective well-being: some empirical evidences

Francis Munier

Introduction

Friedman and Friedman (1990, p. 5) assert that the free market works "without requiring that people talk or love each other". This statement, devoid of the possibility of affecting others, translates with an emphasis on self-love, selfishness and lack of social interaction in the neoclassical approach. Based on rational choice theory, this behavior of the selfish, lonely and hedonistic economic man (Laval, 2007) has been criticized by contemporary philosophers and sociologists notably from the movement MAUSS.

Only recently has economic analysis begun to explore individual interactions by studying the links between interpersonal relations, economic behavior and subjective well-being. Empirical studies show that frequent and good relationships with friends, relatives and colleagues are positively correlated with economic performance and happiness of the individual (Aslam and Corrado, 2007; Winkelmann, 2004; Haller and Hadler, 2006).

These results led to a new interpretation of the Easterlin paradox (Easterlin, 1974) in the sense that lower inter-subjectivity in quantity and quality compensates, or even negates, the positive effect of additional income on subjective well-being, notably in the long term. In this, it seems interesting to add a relational treadmill with a similar logic as a hedonic one, and aspiration and social comparisons. Thus, following Diwan (2000), when society becomes more abundant, the positive effect of improving economic conditions on subjective well-being is offset by a lower frequency and quality of interpersonal relationships, with less consumption of relational goods in favor of positional goods.

Based on these results, our thesis is that happiness is the outcome of an interactive process between individuals on the one side, and favorable micro- and macrosocial conditions on the other side. The second assumption is to consider that recognition is one ontological basement of the individual's interactions.

We retain then a philosophical approach, specifically one that examines the concept of recognition as an ontological dimension of the individual to give him/her greater interpersonal skills. Recognition provides an original analytical framework of human being and his inter-subjectivities to enrich the relational dimension between self and others. Furthermore, theories of recognition motivate important debates in philosophy but the dissemination of these ideas remains marginal in the field of economics (Hoevel, 2013). Our approach tries to provide some elementary blocks for this analytical framework.

The aim of this article is to clarify the concept of the relation of self with others providing openings for "I" and "You" (Buber, 1992). The purpose is two-fold, and original, in that our work seeks to match the philosophical approach of recognition along with the economics of happiness, and to provide some empirical findings of the impact of recognition on subjective well-being, using the OECD database of the Better Life Index (OECD, 2015).

The first part is devoted to a synthesis of the concept of recognition of contemporary approaches (Honneth, 1992, 2006; Taylor, 1991, 1992; Fraser, 2011 or Ricoeur, 1996, 2005) to overcome the dilemma of subjectivity that could be (for a first stage) a difficulty for relationships of a deeply social person. The second part is devoted to the search for a more fruitful dialogue between economics and social philosophy as well as renewal of what could be the understanding of the individual in economics. After showing that the approach based on recognition enriched the economy of esteem (Brennan and Pettit, 2004), our analysis will use recent developments in economics of happiness to show the importance of recognition in understanding the relational need of economic man in his quest for the "good life" (as eudemonism). The third and last part will present our empirical analysis based on the assumption that recognition affects subjective well-being. More precisely, we consider the three spheres of recognition provided by Honneth and propose some proxies variables based on the OECD database of the Better Life Index.

Theories of recognition: a short overview

The purpose of this section is to provide an overview of recent theories of recognition in the field of social philosophy to highlight the ontological dimension of inter-subjectivity of the individual as a vital need for relationship. This philosophical basement seems promising to establish a link between self and other.

The philosophy of Hegel (1807) is often considered the origin of the concept, although ancient philosophers such as Aristotle and Plato also compared the individual to a social animal through the prism of recognition (without conceptualizing the term as such). Other scholars underline this idea of recognition, such as Jean-Jacques Rousseau (1762) who stressed that man has a vital need to be recognized by others, or Smith (1759) who discusses the concept of "sympathy" (Russ, 2014).

According to Hegel (1807), the individual aspires to be perpetually recognized by the other. This form of recognition, however, can lead to unprecedented violence since it can result in a real "struggle of death" (based on the dialectic of servitude) for recognition in areas such as justice, love and the State. But beyond this fight, for Hegel, recognition is ontological. Honneth (2013) and Neuhouser (1986) confirm this ontology and suggest, using some psychological texture, the individual can access self-awareness only by engaging in a relationship based on recognition when the egocentric desire is limited by the benefit of the other.

Coming from the Frankfurt School, Honneth (1992, 2006) also takes on the question of the struggle, inspired both by Hegel (1807) and Mead (1934). Our empirical strategy will be based on Honneth's approach. He develops an operative and normative social theory of recognition as a moral relationship between individuals who are in the context of a moral grammar of social conflicts (Ferrarese, 2013). For this philosopher, society cannot be defined as a simple sum of selfish and rational individuals. On the contrary, individuals are moral and the quest for recognition appears as an essential vector of individual interactions (*Sittlichkeit* in Hegel).

In this, the individual does not only search for materialistic maximization but also and above all, recognition of others. This view is in opposition to the atomistic vision of the neoclassical individual. This leads to the idea that well-being is not solely based on the utility function but more based on a relationship with others, consideration and respect. The regard of the other becomes the epicenter of individual fulfillment. This inter-subjectivity is within three spheres of recognition: intimacy on the principle of love, community on the principle of solidarity and legal relations on the principle of equality.

The approach proposed by Taylor (1991, 1992) is somewhat different though the concept of recognition remains at the heart of his analysis. The author mainly analyzes the recognition of minorities in a multicultural logic and advocates communitarianism. He posits lack of recognition as the cause of injustice and violence. His analysis of modernity is remarkable. He highlights the crisis of identity as a corollary source of perversion coming from the notion of authenticity. Authenticity is a moral ideal stemming from the work of Rousseau and Herder. In modern society, this ideal has deteriorated because it is too based on a form of flourishing where relativism is a destructive part of human relations. The principle is that everyone has the right to organize his life as he wants and that no one else can dictate anything to him. The danger can be a retreat, an exclusion, an unconsciousness even of the great problems that transcend the self (political, religious, historical) and thus a shrinking of life. In other words, the exacerbated search for authenticity in ordinary life leads to an alteration of the self with others in a favor of a purely instrumental relationship.

Fraser (2011) evaluates this approach based only on symbols and identity of recognition. By focusing too much on recognition, the risk, according to the author, is obscuring the question of material redistribution. This dichotomy of two forms of intangible and material recognition is eminently important for economists, but at this stage and in view of our subject, we maintain that recognition provides a promising conceptual element to renew the sense of economic man between self and others.

As part of his three studies, Ricoeur (1996, 2005) attempts to clarify the philosophical definition of recognition. Based on a lexicographical study, he categorizes recognition at three levels: self, the one related to identification and the one linked to mutual recognition. The latter seems interesting in that it does not consider recognition as a struggle but as a form of pacification.

At this stage, our main purpose is to highlight the ontological dimension of recognition as a vector of a "good life". Now, we must examine the relationship between happiness and recognition to advance our demonstration.

Happiness and recognition

In this section, we match some findings of economics of happiness with fundamental traits of theories of recognition. We consider that this theoretical fertilization will provide evidence that relationships are the soil of happiness.

It is important to clarify that our approach is different than that of the economy of esteem proposed by Brennan and Pettit (2004). Indeed, some would be tempted to consider that there is already an economy of esteem, so why then try to build an economy of recognition? Brennan and Pettit (2000, p. 78) define esteem as

> Assume that we each care about whether others think well of us in certain ways, even if they say or do nothing to express this: we each cherish the esteem, and shrink from, the disesteem, of our fellows. Assume that even if they do or say nothing it is often obvious - often indeed a matter of shared awareness between an agent and observers - that some others see and think well, or see and think badly, of what one of us does. Or that there is a risk that they may do so. And assume, finally, that depending on how we act, we may each increase or decrease the expected esteem that we enjoy.

In other words, esteem is just a force/incentive to adopt a good behavior according to the others. In this approach, esteem is not ontological.

As the authors stress, the economy of esteem is a hidden economy. By this way, they assume that supply and demand of esteem exists. They also consider that there exists at least three different ways in which people can compete for esteem:

> One will be by competing in regard to performance. Another will be by competing for the sort of publicity that will maximize the esteem their performance earns. And a third will be by competing to frame their publicly observed behaviour in such a way as to maximize esteem.
>
> (Brennan and Pettit, 2000, p. 94)

This approach is interesting because it clarifies that behind the market of goods and services, people also seek esteem and search for recognition. The economy of esteem is a relevant proposal, but our purpose based on the philosophical concept of recognition is different. Certainly, a hidden economy exists, but beside that, we think that we need to further explore the ontology of the individual thanks to the recognition prism.

The approach based on the esteem considers that the individual seeks the esteem of the other. Meanwhile, in the recognition-based approach, the individual seeks recognition but mainly because it provides self-esteem, self-confidence and self-respect. It is these particular aspects that help us link recognition and happiness, and thus provide a richer analytical framework for the argument of our purpose.

We assume that recognition is the foundation of the happiness of individuals. Like work in positive psychology, we believe that happiness is the others

> the human being is made to live in relationship with others. What makes us happy is to value others and to be valued, to listen and be heard; in short, to love and be loved, simply. The self-interest and interest in the other are not only compatible, but even more mutually beneficial.
>
> (Lyubomirsky, 2014, p. 16)

Clearly, this concept is very far from Friedman and Friedman's quote (1990, p. 5) highlighted in the introduction. Scientific research from the field of positive psychology should, in our view, further feed the economic analysis to bring in more humanity (Di Tella *et al.*, 2003; Oswald, 1997).

In this regard, we consider that the concept of relational goods brings some key elements to the relational view of the economic individual (Nussbaum, 1986; Gui, 1987). Relational goods are defined as non-material goods ensuring interpersonal relationships. Nussbaum (1986) states that these properties are based on friendship, mutual love and commitment. Relational goods are outside market transactions but have a strong influence on the happiness of individuals (Bruni, 2013) by incorporating other aspects such as generosity, altruism, gratitude and compassion.

Interpersonal relationships arise from different feelings, including the fundamental factor of recognition for our identity (self) (Taylor, 1991). We need others to understand who we are and what we want to become.

The main findings in psychology (Layard, 2007) and economics of happiness (Frey and Stutzer, 2002) also show a positive correlation between certain personality traits and happiness. These include empathy (Rifkin, 2009) and self-esteem. Empathy is based on the search and understanding of social relations, a form of ultimate recognition of the other.

These social emotions (Lordon, 2013) have a positive impact on the happiness of individuals. Self-esteem is defined by four factors: self-acceptance, evaluation, comparison and efficiency. We find here the self in relationships with others and so again recognition as identification according to the definition of Ricoeur (2005).

Moreover, comparison with others is also a determining factor in explaining human behavior. By nature, people compare themselves to others (Franck, 2010). This character is found in a form of a gregarious selfishness (Dufour, 2007) and explains the Easterlin paradox (1974) that relative income seems more relevant than absolute income in explaining the gap between changes in GDP per capita and the evolution of subjective well-being. As shown by Bartolini (2013), highlighting the concept of "Negative Economic Growth" (Bartolini and Bonatti, 2003), it is precisely the poverty of relations that induces the paradox of happiness. Again, comparison in human behavior is akin to forms of seeking recognition.

Similarly, the employed are happier than the unemployed, and then work, in a broad definition, is considered as a potential source of happiness (Oswald, 1997). This result is contrary to the standard approach that considers the hypothesis of an economic agent, who chooses between leisure time and consumption. Working time is accepted only because higher consumption is not by itself. Work is rather a possible form of self-fulfillment because it induces and involves social relations. This explains why the unemployed are significantly less happy than people who work (Di Tella *et al.*, 2001). Leisure is also a source of happiness in that it responds to social and relational needs (Lu and Hu, 2005).

It seems important at this stage to point out the correlation between inter-subjectivity and individual happiness. The examination of the characteristics of relational goods shows some acquaintance with the philosophical concept of recognition in the sense of a moral grammar of inter-subjectivity. The identity of the individuals involved in the relationship is crucial. Self-identity is built through the relationship with the other. Reciprocity, therefore, is crucial for a positive relationship. We find here the issue of mutual recognition. The motivations of individuals are essential and different from optimization of satisfaction. Motivations are created through relationships and are free because these goods are designed without any economic return otherwise they would not exist. In other words, the hedonistic individual cannot find happiness in the neoclassical sense. As Konow and Earley (2008) said the one who seeks happiness for himself will not find it because of the hedonistic paradox. This eudemonistic view, as Aristotle suggests, is a promising way to analyze the metamorphosis of the homo economicus within the dialectic of "happiness – recognition".

We are now proposing to move on to our empirical analysis to try to validate our hypothesis that recognition positively affects well-being. To do so, we will mainly use the approach of Honneth.

Empirical findings

The empirical analysis will be done in three stages. Stage one will present the methodology. The second stage will provide information on the database, and the third and final stage will present results and interpretations.

Methodology

The variables we build are based on the Honneth proposal of three spheres of recognition. At this point, it seems reasonable to give more details about these spheres of recognition linked to features of happiness.

Honneth (1992, 2006) of the Frankfurt School becomes inspired by Mead (1934) and takes over the question of the struggle for recognition. He develops a working social theory and a normative context of recognition as a moral relationship between two individuals, which lie within the framework of well-being in the sense that recognition leads to esteem, confidence and respect as mediators of happiness.

For this philosopher, society cannot be defined as merely a sum of selfish and rational individuals. On the contrary, individuals are moral and the search for recognition seems to be an essential component of individual interactions. Honneth explores a more human-based model of socialization that frames the three spheres of recognition: love, rights and solidarity. Based on this aim, Honneth explains and claims the importance of social relationships to the development and upkeep of a person's identity. Honneth argues that without the three forms of recognition, personal identity cannot be established and mediates unhappiness for the individual.

When recognition is successfully achieved, the three spheres become significant in the development of well-being. This positive self-realization is subordinated to the corresponding spheres of love, rights and solidarity as, respectively, self-confidence, self-respect and self-esteem, as vectors of happiness.

Love relationships describe those where there are stout emotional links between few people. These are primary relationships such as intimate relationships, friendships and the relationship between parent and child. Honneth's work stresses that it is only through the successful adaptation of love as form of recognition that subsequent forms of rights and solidarity can be properly established: "for it is only this symbiotically nourished bond, which emerges through mutually desired demarcation, that produces the degree of basic individual self-confidence indispensable for autonomous participation in public life" (Honneth, 1995, p. 107).

The recognition of rights differs from love recognition. While love is distinguished by emotional and affective considerations, recognition of rights is historically rooted and mainly cognitive. The recognition of rights refers to the moral responsibility of individuals within a community to face justice equally. Perception, and obviously existence, of equal law is positive in terms of recognition and self-respect.

The third principle of recognition, solidarity, indicates that individuals always need a form of social esteem, linked positively to their personal characters and aptitudes. The principle of solidarity is related to self-realization, based on achievement of the identification of different forms of personal fulfillment. The status of a person could be measured by honor, or today, by recognition of his own abilities, talents and achievements. Nowadays, esteem in postmodern societies is also conceived by the work we do and how it is done. Recognition comes from the society as a mediator of self-esteem and well-being.

Database

OECD decided to implement a new framework with better indicators of what could be a "good life". We use 34.000 data observations from the OECD Better Life Index. The data are based on official surveys such as OECD or National Accounts, United Nations Statistics, National Statistics Offices, Gallup World Poll. Using both objective and subjective indicators, The Better Life Index covers 11 topics that reflect what could be essential to well-being in terms of material living conditions (housing, income, jobs) and quality of life (community, education, environment, governance, health, life satisfaction, safety and work-life balance). Each topic is built on one to four specific indicators. For straightforwardness, weights have been set equal to the grade of 1 for all topics. The Index covers 35 OECD member countries. We use definitions of OECD for each indicator.

The dependent variable Life satisfaction measures SUBJECTIVE WELL-BEING (SWB) and shows how people evaluate their life rather than their current feelings. Respondents were asked to rate their general life satisfaction on a scale from 0 to 10, using the Cantril Ladder (known also as the "Self-Anchoring Striving Scale").

The independent variables are the three spheres of recognition: SOLIDARITY, LOVE, and RIGHTS.

For our empirical strategy, we retain these indicators from the OECD database: Jobs, Civil engagement, Community, and Safety, to propose new variables that appear as suitable proxies for the three spheres of recognition. For each sphere, we calculate the arithmetic mean of the sub-indicator without any weight, to not give more importance to one of them. The choice is based on more similarities between OECD data and definition of the three spheres of recognition from Honneth.

We consider that SOLIDARITY is based on Jobs, which includes Job security, Employment rate, Personal earnings, and Civic engagement. Basically, employment rate is the number of employed persons aged 15 to 64 over the population of the same age, as defined by the International Labor Organization. This framework of solidarity highlights social esteem of society as a form of recognition.

With more solidarity as social esteem, it seems that people are more involved in social life and engagement. Recognition as social esteem is, for instance, an incentive to participate in civil society and civic engagement. Civic engagement shows how individual engagement is built in the development of laws and regulations. Voter turnout is defined as the ratio between the number of individuals that cast a ballot during an election (whether this vote is valid or not) to the population registered to vote.

Using this construct of the sphere of recognition of solidarity, we have this first hypothesis.

Hypothesis 1: SOLIDARITY positively affects Subjective well-being.

LOVE is defined as community, based on the indicators of quality of one's social network. The measure is founded on perceived social network and the question "If you were in trouble, do you have relatives or friends you can count on to help you whenever you need them, or not?" and it considers the respondents who answer positively.

Hypothesis 2: LOVE positively affects Subjective well-being.

RIGHTS could be measured by safety using indicators such as lower homicide rate and assault rate. The indicator includes deaths due to assault and the question: "Do you feel safe walking alone at night in the city or area where you live?"

Using these two indicators, a mitigated impact is possible on subjective well-being. The result will depend on the salience effect on happiness between these indicators.

> Hypothesis 3: RIGHTS positively affect Subjective well-being when the moderator is feeling safe.
>
> Hypothesis 4: RIGHTS negatively affect Subjective well-being when the moderator is homicide rate.

Results and interpretations

Our empirical strategy is done in three stages. Stage one is to determine correlations. The second step is to conduct cluster analysis, and the final step will present the results of a regression model.

The correlation (Table 10.1) shows a strong correlation between the sphere of SOLIDARITY (.66) and LOVE (.52) with the SWB, while the correlation with RIGHTS is not significant. The last result shows possible mitigation.

The first correlation analysis confirms our hypothesis 1 and 2. SOLIDARITY and LOVE have a positive impact on well-being as mediator of recognition.

The next step conducts two classification classes (Table 10.2). The QCL_2 introduces only the recognition variables and thus leads to three groups of countries.

What is interesting to observe is that by conducting another analysis (QCL_1) with the four variables (including the variable SWB), we get the same groups of countries.

The cluster analysis shows that the three spheres of recognition, SOLIDARITY, LOVE and RIGHTS, are independent variables of the dependent variable SWB. It is not a question of interpreting the cardinal results for each country, but rather to

Table 10.1 Correlations

		SOLIDARITY	*LOVE*	*RIGHTS*	*SWB*
SOLIDARITY	Pearson Correlation	1	.294	.268	.666**
	Sig. (Bilateral)		.091	.126	.000
	N	34	34	34	34
LOVE	Pearson Correlation	.294	1	.439**	.521**
	Sig. (Bilateral)	.091		.009	.002
	N	34	34	34	34
RIGHTS	Pearson Correlation	.268	.439**	1	.039
	Sig. (Bilateral)	.126	.009		.828
	N	34	34	34	34
SWB	Pearson Correlation	.666**	.521**	.039	1
	Sig. (Bilateral)	.000	.002	.828	
	N	34	34	34	34

** Correlation is significant for level 0.01 (Bilateral)

Source: OECD (2015)

Table 10.2 Cluster analysis

Countries	*SOLIDARITY*	*LOVE*	*RIGHTS*	*SWB*	*QCL_2*	*QCL_1*
Australia	17,80	92,00	9,60	7,30	1	3
Austria	13,80	89,00	9,10	6,90	1	3
Belgium	12,90	94,00	7,50	6,90	1	3
Canada	13,70	92,00	9,80	7,30	1	3
Denmark	15,00	95,00	8,90	7,50	1	3
Finland	12,60	95,00	9,30	7,40	1	3
Germany	12,00	94,00	9,00	7,00	1	3
Iceland	14,80	96,00	9,40	7,50	1	3
Ireland	12,30	96,00	9,30	7,00	1	3
Luxembourg	15,10	87,00	8,70	6,90	1	3
Netherlands	13,30	90,00	8,30	7,30	1	3
New Zealand	15,00	94,00	9,40	7,30	1	3
Norway	15,50	94,00	9,10	7,40	1	3
Poland	10,20	91,00	9,80	5,80	1	3
Spain	7,40	95,00	8,70	6,50	1	3
Sweden	16,40	92,00	8,30	7,20	1	3
Switzerland	12,80	96,00	8,70	7,50	1	3
United Kingdom	14,30	91,00	9,70	6,80	1	3
United States	13,50	90,00	8,90	7,20	1	3
Korea	14,70	72,00	9,50	5,80	2	2
Mexico	10,80	77,00	0,40	6,70	2	2
Chile	5,80	86,00	6,80	6,70	3	1
Czech Republic	9,70	85,00	9,20	6,50	3	1
Estonia	8,00	89,00	7,30	5,60	3	1
France	10,70	87,00	8,40	6,50	3	1
Greece	5,50	83,00	8,70	4,80	3	1
Hungary	9,30	87,00	8,80	4,90	3	1
Israel	9,00	87,00	7,40	7,40	3	1
Italy	9,70	90,00	8,40	6,00	3	1
Japan	10,90	89,00	10,00	5,90	3	1
Portugal	7,50	86,00	7,90	5,10	3	1
Slovak Republic	7,90	90,00	9,10	6,10	3	1
Slovenia	10,50	90,00	8,80	5,70	3	1
Turkey	10,00	86,00	8,20	5,60	3	1

QCL_2: CLASSIFICATION CLASSES with 3 VARIABLES

QCL_1: CLASSIFICATION CLASSES with 4 VARIABLES (we add SWB)

Source: OECD (2015)

determine a possible form of causality effect between the supposed independent variables and dependent variable.

We now run a regression and get the following results (without standard errors and for non-standardized coefficients):

SWB = 0,075 LOVE +0,158 SOLIDARITY-0,168 RIGHTS

Both LOVE and SOLIDARITY positively affect SWB, and we find that RIGHTS negatively affect SWB because individuals place more importance on the homicide rate than on a feeling of security. The impact of the first indicator, homicide rate, overtakes the impact of the second indicator, feeling safe. Hypothesis 4 is validated.

For SOLIDARITY, contrary to the standard approach to the economy, it is important to consider that labor does not only offer a salary and that it is not only a source of disutility. On the contrary, labor could be a source of relationships and could induce satisfaction (job satisfaction). The link between job satisfaction and well-being is well known in the literature.

Work has obvious economic and social benefits. Having a job helps individuals stay in touch with society, build self-esteem, build social esteem and develop new skills and a sense of accomplishment. Happiness is not only judged by basic material conditions (work, money, house, car, etc.). It is also a construction built from favorable psychological abilities and morality. It is therefore also about

Table 10.3 Coefficients[a]

Model		*Non-standardized coefficients*		*Standardized factors coefficients*	*t*	*Sig.*
		A	*Standard error*	*Bêta*		
1	(Constant)	–.556	1.499		–.371	.714
	Love	.075	.019	.491	3.998	.000
	Solidarity	.158	.030	.612	5.352	.000
	Rights	–.168	.060	–.341	–2.799	.009

a Dependent variable: SWB

Source: OECD (2015)

Table 10.4 R and Standard Error

Model	*R*	*R-two*	*R-two adjusted*	*Standard error of the estimate*
1	.807[a]	.650	.616	.49786

a Predicted values: (constants). RIGHTS. SOLIDARITY. LOVE.

Source: OECD (2015)

Table 10.5 ANOVA[a]

Model		*Sum of squares*	*ddl*	*Average of squares*	*D*	*Sig.*
1	Regression	13.839	3	4.613	18.611	.000[b]
	Residue	7.436	30	.248		
	Total	21.275	33			

a Dependent variable: SWB. b Predicted values: (constants). RIGHTS. SOLIDARITY. LOVE.

Source: OECD (2015)

being and not just *having*. Being quiet, serene and stable are elements of social recognition.

High-employment countries are also richer, more stable and healthier politically. That is why trust in the government is crucial for social cohesion and well-being. Greater transparency is not only essential to maintaining integrity in the public sector; it also contributes to better governance. These features enhance and incentivize voter participation and civic engagement related to well-being. Since Helliwell and Putman (2005), we know that the capital social of a society is based principally on trust, and that trust positively affects SWB.

As for LOVE, humans are social animals (as Aristotle stressed), and the frequency of our contact with others and the quality of our personal relationships are therefore crucial determinants of our well-being. Studies show that time spent with friends is associated with a higher average level of positive feelings (Vaillant, 2012).

Considering RIGHTS, personal safety is an essential element for the well-being of individuals. One of the greatest impacts of crime on people's well-being seems to be due to the sense of vulnerability it causes. In this way, recognition can also be understood as a form of social resilience, compassion and as a source of relational wealth and well-being. In difficult situations, emotional resilience (Ryan *et al.*, 2005) is a form of recognition that allows people to turn to others for emotional support. Misrecognition and invisibility are the ills of our modern societies, as Honneth says, and it is in this that recognition takes on its full scale for individual and societal well-being.

Conclusion

The purpose of this article was to show the importance of human relations as a factor of happiness. Based on this observation, we felt it was essential to conceptualize the notion of the relationship between individuals based on the concept of recognition. We thus resume the hypothesis that recognition is a vital need for the human being, following the seminal thinking of Hegel and recent developments of Honneth.

A first step was therefore to establish the link between recognition and relations, and recognition and subjective well-being. A second step was to empirically validate the hypothesis that recognition positively affects happiness.

Starting from the OECD database on the Better Life Index, we conducted an empirical strategy in different phases: cluster analysis, correlation and regression model. We defined proxies for describing the three spheres of recognition of Honneth: LOVE, SOLIDARITY and RIGHTS.

The results show a strong and significant impact of LOVE and SOLIDARITY on subjective well-being, while RIGHTS is less significant.

The limits to this work lie, in our view, on too much proxy nature of the variables defining the three spheres of recognition. Although the results are positive, it seems to us that it would be beneficial to explore more appropriate data to study the relationship between recognition and subjective well-being.

Bibliography

Aslam, A. and Corrado, L. (2007), "No Man Is an Island: The Inter-Personal Determinants of Regional Well-Being in Europe", Cambridge Working Papers in Economics, n° 717.

Bartolini, S. (2013), *Manifeste pour le bonheur*, Les Liens qui Libèrent, Paris.

Bartolini, S. and Bonatti, L. (2003), "Endogenous Growth and Negative Externalities", *Journal of Economics*, 79, pp. 123–44.

Brennan, G. and Pettit, P. (2000), "The Hidden Economy of Esteem", *Economics and Philosophy*, 16, pp. 77–98.

Brennan, G. and Pettit, P. (2004), *The Economy of Esteem: An Essay on Civil and Political Society*, Oxford University Press, Oxford.

Bruni, L. (2004), "The Happiness Transformation Problem in the Cambridge Tradition", *The European Journal of the History of Economic Thought*, 11(3), pp. 433–51.

Bruni, L. (2013), "Relational Goods: A New Tool for an Old Issue", *Estudos Contemporâneos da Subjetividade, ECOS*, 3(2), pp. 173–78.

Buber, M. (1992), *Je et Tu*, Editions Aubier, Collection: Bibliothèque philosophique.

Diwan, R. (2000), "Relational Wealth and the Quality of Life", *Journal of Socio-Economics*, 28, pp. 305–40.

Dufour, D.-R. (2007), *Le Divin Marché, la révolution culturelle libérale*, Denoël, Paris.

Easterlin, R. (1974), "Does Economic Growth Improve the Human Lot? Some Empirical Evidence", in Paul A. David and Melvin W. Reder, eds., *Nations and Households in Economic Growth: Essays in Honor of Moses Abramovitz*, Academic Press Inc., New York.

Ferrarese, E. (2013), *Qu'est-ce que lutter pour la reconnaissance ?* Editions Le Bord de l'eau Collection: Diagnostics, Lormont.

Franck, R.H. (2010), *La course au luxe. L'économie de la cupidité et la psychologie du bonheur*, Editions Markus Haller, Paris.

Fraser, N. (2011), *Qu'est-ce que la justice sociale ? Reconnaissance et redistribution*, La Découverte, Paris.

Frey, B. and Stutzer, A. (2002), *Happiness and Economic: How the Economy and Institutions Affect Human Well-Being*, Princeton University Press, Princeton.

Friedman, M. and Friedman, R. (1990), *Free to Choose: A Personal Statement*, Harvest Book-Harcourt Inc., San Diego, New York and London.

Gui, B. (1987), "Eléments pour une définition d'économie communautaire", *Notes et documents*, 19–20, pp. 32–42.

Haller, M. and Hadler, M. (2006), "How Social Relations and Structures Can Produce Happiness and Unhappiness: An International Comparative Analysis", *Social Indicators Research*, 75, pp. 106–216.

Hegel, G.W.F. (1807), *Phénoménologie de l'esprit*, Ellipse, Paris.

Helliwell, J.F. and Putman, R.D. (2005), "The Social Context of Well-Being", in F.A. Huppert, N. Baylis and B. Keverne, eds., Oxford University Press, Oxford.

Hoevel, C. (2013), *The Economy of Recognition, Person, Market and Society in Antonio Rosmini*, Springer, Dordrecht, Heildeberg, New York and London.

Honneth, A. (1992), *Kampf um Anerkennung*, Suhrkamp Verlag. Ed. Frankfurt am Main. *La lutte pour la reconnaissance*, Les éditions du Cerf, Paris.

Honneth, A. (1995), *The Struggle for Recognition: The Moral Grammar of Social Conflicts*, Polity Press Cambridge, MA.

Honneth, A. (2006), *La société du mépris. Vers une nouvelle théorie critique*, La Découverte, Paris.

Honneth, A. (2013), *Ce que social veut dire*, tome 1 *Le déchirement du social*, Gallimard, Paris.

Konow, J. and Earley, J. (2008), "The Hedonistic Paradox: Is Homo Economicus Happier?" *Journal of Public Economics*, 92, pp. 1–33.
Laval, C. (2007), *L'homme économique: Essai sur les racines du néolibéralisme*, Gallimard, Paris.
Layard, R. (2007), *Le prix du bonheur: Leçons d'une science nouvelle*, Armand Collin, Paris.
Lordon, F. (2013), *La société des Affects : Pour un structuralisme des passions*, Seuil, L'ordre philosophique, Paris.
Lu, L. and Hu, C.-H. (2005), "Leisure Experiences and Happiness", *Journal of Happiness Studies*, 6(3), pp. 325–42.
Lyubomirsky, S. (2014), *Qu'est-ce qui nous rend vraiment heureux ?* Arènes Editions, Paris.
Mead, G.H. (1934), *Mind, Self, and Society*. Ed. by C.W. Morris, University of Chicago Press, Chicago, 1967.
Neuhouser, F. (1986), "Deducing Desire and Recognition in the Phenomenology of Spirit", *Journal of the History of Philosophy*, 24(2), pp. 243–62.
Nussbaum, M. (1986), *The Fragility of Goodness: Luck and Ethics in Greek Tragedy and Philosophy*, Part 2, 2nd ed., Cambridge University Press, Cambridge.
OECD (2015), http://www.oecdbetterlifeindex.org/
Oswald, A.J. (1997), "Happiness and Economic Performance", *The Economic Journal*, 107(445) (November), pp. 1815–31.
Ricoeur, P. (1996), *Soi-même comme un autre*, Seuil, Collection: Points Essais, Paris.
Ricoeur, P. (2005), *Parcours de la Reconnaissance – Trois Etudes*, Folio essais, Paris.
Rifkin, J. (2009), *The Empathic Civilization: The Race to Global Consciousness in a World in Crisis*, 1st ed., Tarcher, New York, Boston.
Rousseau, J.-J. (1762), *Du contrat social*, GF, Flammarion, Paris, 2011.
Russ, R. (2014), *How Adam Smith Can Change Your Life: An Unexpected Guide to Human Nature and Happiness*, Portfolio, Penguin Books, New-York.
Ryan, R.M., Laguardia, J., Solky-Butzel, J., Chirkov, V. and Youngmee, K. (2005), "On the Interpersonal Regulation of Emotions", *Personal Relationships*, 12, pp. 145–63.
Smith, A. (1759), *Théorie des sentiments moraux*, PUF Quadrige, Paris, 2014.
Taylor, C. (1991), *The Malaise of Modernity*, House of Anansi Press, Toronto.
Taylor, C. (1992), *Sources of the Self – The Making of the Modern Identity*, Harvard University Press, Boston.
Tella, R. Di, MacCulloch, R.J. and Oswald, A.J. (2001), "Preferences over Inflation and Unemployment: Evidence from Surveys of Happiness", *The American Economic Review*, 91(1) (March), pp. 335–41.
Tella, R.Di., MacCulloch, R.J. and Oswald, A.J. (2003), "The Macroeconomics of Happiness", *The Review of Economics and Statistics*, 85(4), pp. 809–27.
Vaillant, G.E. (2012), *Triumphs of Experience: The Men of the Harvard Grant Study*, The Belknap Press, Boston.
Winkelmann, R. (2004), "Subjective Well-Being and the Family: Results from an Ordered Probit Model with Multiple Random Effects", Institute for the Study of Labor, Bonn, IZA DP N° 1016.

11 On Levinas's political 'theory'

A two-dimensional conception of justice from the perspective of equality

Cyrielle Poiraud

Introduction

Modern theories of justice are generally based on an imperative of equality whose necessity is usually justified as being the condition of impartiality (Sen, 2009). Thus, a large number of social justice theories includes nowadays an egalitarian perspective, as seeking for the right "space" of equality (Sen, 1880, 1992), but assuming at the same time the necessity of a general frame of equality, notably regarding the moral and political faculties of people considered as citizens. The promotion and justification of this norm of equality appears explicitly since Rawls (1971), who puts impartiality as the necessary condition of possibility of justice, so that it appears as an asserted principle of justice for modern normative theories. Even Sen (2009) showed that those who reject equality as an object of justice still rely on it as a basic imperative of justice that ensures at least non-discrimination within the frame of the considered society and theory. However, this kind of egalitarian conception has been the target of some philosophical analysis, notably the one of Levinas, who did not seem to agree with this justification of the norm of equality and rather criticized it, as related to a totalitarian conception of social life. Indeed, he refuses the foundations of what he calls "Western philosophy" and so of the tradition of modern political theory[1] that considers, according to him, the being as an ego enclosed on itself: he asserts that subjectivity and freedom are really born in the encounter with the Other, offering a reversal in the structure of the being's subjectivity, that calls into question the traditional modern conceptions of justice.

The work of Emmanuel Levinas indeed provides an original conception of the being in that the principle of its subjectivity and freedom lies in its relationship with the Other: it is in this "ethical" relationship that the "primary truth" can be found. Now, the ethical relationship, in the sense of Levinas, has a specific meaning in that it is based on the "responsibility for the other", from which the subject cannot escape. This responsibility arises from an encounter, with the Other, who manifests itself through his "face". "The access to the face is straightaway ethical" (Levinas, 1982, p. 79), so that the structure of subjectivity of the "Ego" gets reversed and here lies the main originality of Levinas's thought: before the Other, I am no longer a self dominated by my own will, but my essence is *commanded* by the responsibility I hold toward this Other, and this determines the conditions of my liberty, as freed from the closure of the ego who alienates everything by identifying it to its essence. According to Levinas, subjectivity is "initially for an other" (ibid., p. 93): the responsibility for the Other is the "essential, primary, fundamental structure of subjectivity" (ibid., p. 91).

The notion of Ego also appears under the term of "Same" in Levinas and refers to a process of self-identification where the being only reports to itself: the will exists in itself and for itself and thus represents a "Totality", determining a being enclosed on itself, "allergic" to alterity. However, the key notion in Levinas's thought is the one of Other, as a presence which is absolutely exterior to the Ego, impossible to alienate. The Other relies on transcendence and invokes the idea of "Infinity" as opposed to totality: it prevents the ego from completing its totality, as it resists any process of identification by a particular will. It involves a relationship based on asymmetry – the ethical relationship – and defines the moment of the for-the-other. Now according to Levinas, the encounter with the face of the Other is what reveals the truth of the being and is thus the foundation of justice, as the justification of his right to be. This conception of justice is to be understood in an "ethical" perspective, that is to say, a form of justice which is not institutional.

Considering that the true essence and freedom of the being is to be actualized through this ethical form of justice, Levinas undertakes a critique of institutional justice, that he qualifies as "impersonal" and says that it carries in itself a "tyranny" – the one of Totality, as related to "universal rules". The scheme he implicitly designs corresponds to a structure of strict equality which negates the responsibility for the Other (through which only the being can be truly free) as it prevents social relationships from being asymmetrical, and is thus based on the conception of the being as an Ego. Nevertheless his critique, from *Totality and Infinity* (1961) to *Otherwise Than Being* (1974) will move towards the acknowledgment of the necessity of this form of justice, of a political device that allows equality in social relationships, so that we eventually find some form of justification of the norm of equality even in Levinas's works. One difficulty with Levinas's thought is that it relies on many concepts of his own, sometimes convoluted but whose clarification and understanding are necessary in that they take part in the reasoning leading to his approach of justice – which is precisely based on his conception of the being that involves specific concepts such as Totality, Infinity or else the Responsibility for the Other.

The aim of this paper is twofold: first, it tends to shed light on Levinas's political theory which is rather implicit and scattered throughout his writings, by showing its two-dimensional aspect as based on his dialectics of the same and the Other, so that we get two sides of justice – political and ethical. Second, this issue is to be integrated within the one of the justification of the norm of equality that rules modern theories of justice: Levinas first seems to reject equality and with it political justice which is based, according to him on the totality of the Ego, in favor of the principle of alterity, the ethical principle which founds ethical justice – so that Levinas seems to plead for inequality as the condition of freedom. Nevertheless, in his later works, Levinas admits the utility and even the necessity of equality, so that this inquiry into his political thought provides elements to both, calling into question this norm of equality as the condition of justice, and justifying it.

The idea of a two-dimensional conception of justice in Levinas has already been suggested, mainly separating the political/ontological from the metaphysical/ethical aspects (Thomas, 2004, p. XV). However, our investigation seeks to specifically shed light on the principles involved by each perspective, namely equality (based on sameness) and inequality (based on alterity) and their justification. Levinas's "political theory"[2] has also been the target of some studies, notably through the examination of his critique of the tyranny of totality and of the liberal individualism paradigm of "Western philosophy" (Kyongsuk Min, 1998; Kirkpatrick, 2011). We tend to further these analyses in order to include them within a larger reflection that integrates a focus on the notion of equality and its role regarding the conditions of possibility of justice. The question of impartiality is nearly absent from Levinas's work (or as for being criticized as the realm of impersonal reason), so that the justification of equality is to be found this time in the nature of the being, which is torn, in Levinas, between absolute sameness through identification and strict inequality in the relation with the Other.

The question at stake is then to determine what this relation between the Same and the Other involves, notably in terms of freedom, recognition and justice, in Levinas, following the issue of the justification of the norm of equality in modern social justice theories. First, the analysis of the duality of the Same and the Other shows the movement of subjectivity in the being, from the moment of the for-itself towards the for-the-Other. Second, the idea of responsibility for the Other appears as the foundation of subjectivity and freedom, revealing the principles of ethical justice. Finally, Levinas's critique of the "tyranny" of totality is what allows understanding his implicit conception of political justice, based on a principle of equality: the justification of this norm is here called into question but finally acknowledged as necessary for practical reasons.

From the same to the other

This section aims at precising the nature of these central concepts in Levinas's thought as they constitute the basis of his two-dimensional conception of justice. First, the Ego, or the Same, is in Levinas a being completely enclosed on itself so that it refers to totality and admits equality as its principle. Second, the Other, that refers to infinity and involves a structure of inequality, appears as absolute exteriority and as the new point of view that philosophy should take to understand subjectivity and freedom, as it is the encounter with the Other that frees the self.

The ego or the same

The ego refers to the concept of identity as sameness and to a constant process of identification: its essence lies in the will that can alienate all things to itself, thus generating a unified being, a totality – a "same". It appears as a negative modality of being in Levinas, which cannot meet the conditions of true liberty, as determined as a will enclosed on itself: "the freedom that establishes itself in the same ends up prisoner of the same" (Levinas, 1994, p. 62). As exclusively particular, the ego's will recalls the nature of the person as described by G.W.F. Hegel in his *Elements of the Philosophy of Right*,[3] in the moment of the civil society, moment of the for-itself, which describes the subject as determined by the will to follow his own interest, the will that tends to itself. The agent can there appropriate things that are exterior to himself. And as a "person", he is a subject of rights, free, whose will is first immediately infinite – spontaneously, as empty – and can thus particularize itself in all things, as it is firstly pure indetermination (Hegel, [1820] 2003, pp. 153–4). This type of freedom is thus limited to the only free-will: it is the power of the will to choose between all of its possibilities. This way, the object of right in the moment of property in Hegel, is the realization of the liberty of the abstract will in general, of a singular person who only reports to herself (ibid.). The will then exists in itself and for itself, and produces itself in sight of itself, whereas the thing has a substance only in sight of something else. And by appropriating a thing, the individual gives it his own will as determination and essence, thus identifying it to himself and producing a unified totality. However, in Hegel, the for-itself refers to one specific step of the ethical life, to a step of emancipation for the spirit, whereas in Levinas, the modality of being of the ego ends up in solitude, as related to "the dogmatism and the spontaneity of the same" (Derrida, 1964, p. 343).

Indeed, for Levinas, this mode of being as identification, as a process of alienation of things that is obstruction of the being with a surplus of materiality, negates liberty: "the relation of identification is the overload of the ego by the self, the interest that the ego has for itself, or the materiality" (1983, p. 51). That is how Levinas comes to describe this mode of being as a *Totality*: "The individuality of the ego is distinguished from any given individuality by the fact that its identity is not constituted by what distinguishes it from others, but by its self-reference" (1987a, p. 28). Now totality is opposed to the idea of infinity in Levinas, which designates exteriority, what is fundamentally other, different from the ego. The consistence of the ego's being lies in its "essence" which "rubs off on as an invincible persistence in the essence, filling any interval of void which would come and interrupt its exercise" (1978, p. 15). Levinas adds that "the essence is *intéressement*" (ibid.), and as an "invincible persistence" of persevering in its own being, the ego seems to have war as its only way out, in that it does not have any possibility of return on itself, regarding its inability to open onto exteriority. It thus tends only towards the realization of his own will, of his self-interest, that is achieved in the exercise of its right on anything – in Hegel's sense of the person. Now, as this totality finds its consistence in *intéressement*, it is egoism, and every ego being determined as such gets into conflict with every other. This is how "the *intéressement* of the being dramatizes in the egoisms in struggle with one another, all against all, in the multiplicity of allergic egoisms which are at war against each other, and thus, together" (ibid.).

The nature of the ego refers to a war of all against all, recalling the Hobbesian state of nature (1651). Indeed, as "allergic" to exteriority, the ego repels the other ceaselessly, seeing it as an opponent, as the incarnation of the limitation of his essence's sovereignty. Now, Hobbes, starting from this rational fiction of the state of nature in which man is a wolf for man, determines the conditions of peace as a reciprocal limitation of this total being, in the sense of a negative freedom which involves the absence of obstacles in the realization of self-interest. Levinas makes several references to Hobbes's thought, especially as embodying the core of modern "Western philosophy" that conceives the being, but also social issues, under the paradigm of totality – that is, reason is the principle of social life so that social justice is ruled by "universal" and "impersonal" laws that negate the uniqueness of people. This "tyranny of totality", which characterizes modern political theory according to Levinas is what he tends to reverse, by inverting the sense of subjectivity through the introduction of exteriority and transcendence in the subject's nature. Indeed, his conception is at the opposite of Hobbes's one: the justification of society, of institutionalized politics is precisely to be found in the need for limiting, not the will's arbitrary and infinite power, but the infinite responsibility one has initially towards the Other.

The Other: the encounter

There is a presence which is absolutely exterior from the ego, that the same cannot identify to him and alienate – the one of the Other, which determines pure alterity: "human alterity, is not thought from the purely formal and logical alterity by which the terms of a multiplicity are distinguished" (1978, p. 14); as alterity is to be found beyond the simple distinction that is made between several individualities, it is the very exteriority, exteriority in itself. The "alterity of the Other", "is not a particular case – a sort – of alterity, but its original ex-ception" (1978, p. 279): it is transcendence, the Infinite, so that the ego cannot, in any way, grasp, appropriate or study the Other as if it were its object.

The Other then appears as what prevents the ego from completing its totality: it disrupts its mode of being and inverts the structure of its subjectivity which was then determined only as a particular will tending to itself. As fundamentally exterior, transcendental, the Other is the one that the ego cannot reduce to itself, to its own identity. It cannot include it in its totality as it resists the process of identification: the Other cannot be the ego's object as "the alterity of the Other is not determined, not grasped nor comprehended, by the I; alterity weighs on the I with the force, the disturbance, of its passing, its infinite and unrepresentable withdrawal" (1987a, p. XIX). Now, the ego comes in relation with the Other through a specific event: the encounter, through the Other's *face*, that settles the "ethical relationship". This encounter provokes a distance between the ego and the same, as the Other imposes itself as a necessity, a demand in front of which the ego cannot retreat and which comes limiting its arbitrary and spontaneous liberty.

The "face" is central in Levinas's ethics: it is through it that the reversion of subjectivity happens, as it is through it that the Other commands the ego and calls him to his responsibility. Indeed, as the Other is not merely another juxtaposed ego, who would thus be the same, the encounter reveals Alterity, breaking the totality, thus opening the structure of social life. As ethical, the Other's face is *meaning*; it is speech, ordering its duty to the ego. Thus, whereas the ego is the uncontested sovereign in its relation to the same, to what he can alienate by identification, when meeting the Other, the face as the expression of alterity, its vulnerability becomes the master. The meaning of the face is commandment, and its first word asserts the interdiction of murder (Levinas, 1963, p. 22).

Whereas the Ego is the emblematic figure of the moment of the for-itself, the Other introduces exteriority as a principle in the subject's mode of being, which is then determined by the moment of the for-the-other – the authentic modality of the being in Levinas. This is why what he refuses to call ontology is for him ethics: it is not the Ego, as identity, as the same, who is the basis of the being's truth, but the Other, from the responsibility he orders to the subject. This encounter with exteriority, the ethical relationship,

> consists in approaching an absolutely exterior being. The infinity of this being, which one cannot therefore contain, guarantees and constitutes this exteriority. It is not equivalent to the distance between a subject and an object. . . . The exteriority of the infinite being is manifested in the absolute resistance which by its apparition, its epiphany, it opposes to all my powers
>
> (Levinas, 1987a, pp. 54–5)

so that the Other, from its transcendence, disrupts the structure of the ego's will. Indeed, "transcendence is what faces us. A face breaks up the system" (ibid., p. 43), namely the system of totality, the imperial power of the same on all things.

However, Levinas argues that it is precisely this interruption of totality that frees the ego:

> The face, the countenance, is the fact that a reality is opposed to me, opposed not its manifestations, but as it were in its way of being, ontologically opposed. It is what resists me by its opposition and not what is opposed to me by its resistance. This means that this opposition is not revealed by its coming up against my freedom; it is an opposition prior to my freedom, which puts my freedom into action. It is not that to which I oppose myself, but what is opposed to me.
>
> (ibid., p. 19)

He thus offers a conception for which freedom is no longer based on an individual conception of the subject and the will, including notions such as autonomy in the traditional sense: "the structure of my freedom is . . . completely reversed" (ibid., p. 55), that is, freedom is to be found in ethics, and thus starts with the responsibility for the Other. From the "tyranny of totality" of the being which identifies everything to itself, that determines the totality of social life and political justice with a State that identifies all its members to one overall reason, Levinas tends to move towards a social theory that makes room for alterity, that is to say according to him, that makes room for justice.

Responsibility for the Other, freedom and justice

In this section, we further explore the idea of a reversal in the being's subjectivity through the understanding of Levinas's radical conception of the responsibility for the Other. First, it appears as the principle of freedom: the paradigm of autonomy changes for heteronomy, in that the being becomes truly free only as its will is invested by alterity. Second, this reversal has several implications, notably in terms of recognition: identity and alterity provide categories for understanding Levinas's bivalent conception of justice.

Responsibility as freedom: the reversal of subjectivity

The principle of responsibility for the Other is asserted as the "essential, primary, fundamental structure of subjectivity" by Levinas. Now, responsibility is according to him "responsibility of what is not my fact, or even not my business" (1983, p. 91). This responsibility is not the one of the subject regarding the actions that result from his own will, but really the responsibility *for* the Other, so that subjectivity "is not a for-itself; it is, again, initially for another" (ibid., p. 93). The responsibility for the Other arises from the encounter with the face that reveals the Other's extreme vulnerability, as a commandment. Now, the Other, as pure exteriority – Alterity – then becomes the content of my will (though not the object), so that the being's principle moves from autonomy to heteronomy in this encounter. Indeed, "the presence of the other – privileged heteronomy – does not collide with freedom but invests it" ((Levinas [1961]1971, p. 84): as an ego, a same, my will is in a sense empty, as it can alienate all things without restriction, thus defining the reign of spontaneous arbitrariness. Freedom is then meaningless, without content, and Levinas asserts that "freedom is not naked" ([1961]1971, p. 83): authentic freedom must be "invested" by responsibility so that only the presence of the Other, and the responsibility towards him as its result, dresses freedom up and makes it meaningful.

The Other thus gives the being an ethical content, but without depriving it from its freedom. On the contrary, Levinas suggests the truth of liberty lies in alterity: "the other, absolutely other – *Autrui* – does not limit the freedom of the Same. By calling him to his responsibility, *it establishes and justifies it*. The relation with the other . . . heals the allergy" ([1961]1971, p. 215, my emphasis). The ethical dimension of alterity brings justice to the being, in the sense of justification and thus frees it from the tyranny of totality: we saw how the ego refers to a negative type of freedom as mutual limitation of the arbitrary will, for which "allergy" is an image. This is how freedom lies in heteronomy, in the command of the Other that invests me and that is responsibility.

Levinas goes even further on the idea of heteronomy, considering subjectivity is "sacred in its alterity, regarding which, in an undeniable responsibility, I settle myself with my sovereignty removed. Paradoxically, *it is as alienus – stranger and other – that man is not alienated*" (1978, p. 99, my emphasis): here is the most demonstrative occurrence of the reversal Levinas operates regarding subjectivity.

The idea is really to consider the individual from a new point of view, no longer from within himself and his own will and autonomy but from his ethical relation to the Other, to alterity, understanding how one does or should welcome it.

Now, this reversal takes part of Levinas's critique of the individualistic paradigm of modern Western philosophy, for which autonomy as free will and reason represents the absolute value – as he conceives it – where everything starts from the for-itself. For Moses (2006), Levinas pointing to ethics as the absolute priority reveals his critique of autonomy as the original principle of subjectivity (p. 384). Now, Levinas questioning autonomy refers to his critique of modern political theories[4] as based on the principle of totality. And establishing alterity, and thus infinity, as the principle of subjectivity and freedom has several implications, notably in terms of recognition regarding society and its principles of organization.

Indeed, while criticizing the ego's nature as a relation to totality, Levinas develops a binary conception which only oscillates between Totality and Infinity, so that it appears radical and involves a fundamentally inegalitarian structure of the being in its relation to the Other: the ethical relationship is asymmetrical and reflects the impossibility for any process of mutual recognition to be effective, as the Other is perceived through his transcendence and commands responsibility:

> In the relation with the other, the other appears to me as the one to whom I owe something, for whom I have a responsibility. From there, the asymmetry of the relationship I-you, and the radical inequality between the I and the you, because all relation with the other is a relation with a being towards whom I have obligations.
>
> (1995, p. 111)

Now, to be effective, recognition needs equality between the parties, as Kojève shows (1981):[5] the responsibility for the Other is unequivocal, and the donation of oneself that it involves determines a system in which rights and duties are not reciprocal, and which seem to exclude the right to follow one's own interest, as it refers to the arbitrary and spontaneous freedom of the ego: it only takes form in the selfish realization of the will by and for itself. It then appears that there is a gap between pure identity and radical alterity: the ego and the Other determine two different modalities of being and it seems that they are each to be related to a different social system.

The ambiguity of recognition: from equality to inequality

The principle of responsibility for the Other involves a specific, even radical, conception of recognition, which is in Levinas torn between the ideas of identity and alterity, and is then completely exclusive of one another. Indeed, on the one hand, the ego which assimilates things in order to identify them to its own being, acknowledges them as identical to itself. On the other hand, the subject who has encountered the Other recognizes him as transcendental, absolutely exterior, and is obliged before his commandment. There is no intermediary form of recognition, between radical sameness and otherness. Subjectivity is deeply linked to the principle of responsibility for the Other, as the ego cannot access the truth of its being without completing his duty towards the Other. This relies on the fact that "the other is in no way another ego, taking part with me in a shared existence" (1983, p. 63). This conception of the Other, as pure exteriority, excludes the possibility of a symmetrical relationship, of mutual recognition between the same and the Other.

The Other imposes its transcendence onto the Ego's being so that Levinas's conception involves two extreme forms of recognition: one that expresses in terms of equality, in the recognition of identity, and the other one, based on a strict inequality, in the recognition of Alterity, involves a relation without reciprocity. It is then in this sense that the principle of responsibility for the Other implies a form of justice that rejects the principle of equality, which however has been established as a norm for modern political theories and is usually considered as a fundamental demand for any theory of justice in that impartiality is its necessary condition (Sen, 2009).

Thus, it seems that we never have in Levinas the possibility of a double recognition, of both the same and the other, of identity and alterity, that is however to be found in each subject. Justice itself seems missing in the sense that the ego is everywhere dominated by the Other, and that the asymmetry of their relationship prevents equality from rising. More than asymmetry, it is sometimes subordination that characterizes this relationship, and that determines the modalities of recognition, as considered by Levinas. Indeed, "to recognize the other – is to give. But it is giving to the master, to the lord, to the one we approach as a 'thou' [*vous*] in a dimension of height" ([1961]1971, p. 73). Now, this reject of equality in the intersubjective relationship leads us to distinguish justice according to two different perspectives regarding Levinas's conception, although this differentiation is not explicit in his work. The inequality of the ethical, asymmetric relationship actually does determine the conditions of justice, but as "*ethical*", that he separates from the type of justice that we shall call "*political*", as based on the principle of equality and framed by a legal structure, as institutional. Now, it seems that according to Levinas, recognition is properly a political issue:

> The distance that separates happiness and desire, separates politics and religion. Politics tends to reciprocal recognition, that is to say, equality; it ensures happiness. And political law achieves and consecrates the struggle for recognition. Religion is desire and not struggle for recognition.
>
> (Levinas [1961]1971, p. 35)

Reciprocity is at the heart of politics and it is in that that ethical justice, based on the relation with alterity, is distinct from institutional justice: if reciprocity were to happen between an ego and an Other, this relation would be the one of an I and sameness, subsumed under totality. Thus, totality is the result of political justice, and that is why Levinas argues in favor for a pure asymmetry in the ethical relationship, as its principle: there is a "radical inequality" between the I and the you, regarding the obligations the ego has towards the other (Levinas, 1995, p. 111). However, equality and reciprocity allow comparison, namely what is needed for political justice. Although Levinas criticizes its totalitarian nature, especially in *Totalité et Infini* (1961), the evolution of his thought makes him later admit, notably in *Autrement qu'être ou au-delà de l'essence* (1974) and *Altérité et transcendance* (1995) some form of necessity of political justice, suggesting that there is a need for passing "from a relation without reciprocity to a relation where, between the members of society, there is a reciprocity, an equality" (1995, p. 112). This sentence is quite revealing of the fact that Levinas does put the issue of political and social organization on the table, even though he essentially displays it as a critique of totality. It also shows that the justification of political justice and so of equality relies on the need for limiting the infinite responsibility for the Other, that is to say on the nature of ethical justice.

A two-dimensional approach of justice

The conception of the being in Levinas's thought is two-dimensional: from the same to the Other, he defines two distinct principles, namely identity and alterity. Now, those principles involve two perspectives of justice: on the one hand the political dimension of justice relies on identity and totality and deals with the social and economic structure of society. On the other hand, the ethical dimension of justice relies on alterity and infinity, aiming at justifying the being and its freedom. In this section, we first tend to clarify Levinas's political conception of justice, notably through the exploration of the critique he makes of it. Second, we deepen the ethical dimension of justice by showing how the two approaches are finally complementary, even in Levinas's thought, regarding the justification of equality.

Political justice: the rejection and justification of equality

Political justice would therefore be the one framed by institutions. It is based on the requirement of equality and thus refers to a system of rights which aims at recognizing the equal nature of the various members of a community as moral subjects. This type of justice allows symmetry in the relationship of the ego and the other, so that equality is guaranteed. However, although Levinas himself puts forward the possibility and even the necessity of such a form of justice, he denounces it as the instrument of Totality. This critique of political theory takes part of a larger problem according to him, which is the ego-focused perspective of Western philosophy whose rationality is completely oriented towards the same as a totality and its free arbitrary will:

> That the free will is arbitrary, and that one must leave this elementary stage, is an old certainty of philosophers. But for all of them this arbitrariness refers to a rational foundation, a justification of freedom by itself. The rational foundation of freedom is still preeminence of the same.

> Moreover, the necessity of justifying the arbitrary is due only to the failure suffered by an arbitrary power. *The very spontaneity of freedom is not into question* – such seems to be the dominant tradition of Western philosophy. Only the limitation of freedom would be tragic or scandalous. . . . In particular, modern political theories since Hobbes deduce the social order from the legitimacy, the incontestable right, of freedom.
>
> (1987a, p. 57)

Levinas's critique of political justice essentially targets the assertion that the egalitarian law promoted by such a form of justice does not recognize alterity, the fundamental difference between the exteriority of the subjects, and thus evacuates the responsibility that falls onto each. This way, "politics, abandoned to itself, carries in itself a tyranny. It deforms the self and the Other that triggered it, because it judges them according to universal rules", determining an "impersonal justice" ([1961] 1971, p. 335): it is impersonal in that it makes all subjects interchangeable, thus negating the principle of alterity – so that equality is contrary to the authentic subject's nature and cannot achieve liberty according to Levinas's conception.

Eventually, Levinas questions the totalitarian nature of political justice which aims at encompassing the plurality of distinct subjects under one same unity, targeting specifically Europe as led by a kind of egocentric rationality:

> The problem of Europe and of peace, is precisely the one of the contradiction of our conscience of Europeans. That is the problem of humanity in us. . . . Peace from the truth, from the truth of a knowledge for which the diverse, instead of getting opposed, accorded or unified; for which the stranger is assimilated; from which the other gets conciliated with the identity of the identical in each. Peace as the return of the multiple to unity. . . . Peace from the State that would gather men who participate to the same ideal truths.
>
> (1995, pp. 136–7)

The notion of Ego is the basis of modern political thought and through the critique of its structure, it is also a critique of individual liberalism and of the contractarian tradition that appears in Levinas. He suggests that these philosophies are based on a logics of subsumption, of appropriation and assimilation, as "looking for the whole universe in the self-consciousness" (1995, p. 138). Now, political justice establishes equality between subjects of rights, so that they are to be seen as egos in Levinas's terms. It thus recognizes them as strictly equal, as legal selves, baring them of their subjectivity. But if the content of subjectivity is the responsibility for the Other, in which the truth of the being is to be found, and thus determines its true modality of being as based on exteriority, we understand why Levinas rejects political justice as the relevant structure for society, in that the State represents "the interiorization of external relations" (1987a, p. 23), encompassing the absolute singularity of each individual under the same totality, thus negating infinity and the responsibility for the Other. This results from the "philosophy of the same" (1987a, p. 50) that Levinas points out as the "Western thought", from which results a totalitarian way of thinking and social organization according to him.

He moreover states that "autonomy, the philosophy which aims to ensure the freedom, or the identity, of beings, presupposes that freedom itself is sure of its right, is justified without recourse to anything further, is complacent in itself, like Narcissus" (1987a, p. 49). Now, justification is precisely what the being needs to be free, so that Levinas develops a conception of justice in those terms, as ethical, as based on the responsibility for the Other, the inverted movement of subjectivity. It is questionable to base justice on the privilege granted to the Other. Then, as soon as "in justice, there is comparison and the other does not have any privilege comparing to me" (1995, p. 139), political justice is "limitation" of the responsibility for the Other. Justice, as comparison, negates alterity and thus the responsibility for the Other, so that the ego's focus is the basis of political theory and seems to tolerate only a negative form of freedom. However, this limitation of the responsibility for the Other also appears as the condition for the organization of social life, so that Levinas eventually acknowledges political justice and equality:

> But in the real world there are many others. When others enter, each of them is external to myself, problems arise. Who is closest to me? Who is the Other? Perhaps something has already occurred between them. We must investigate carefully. Legal justice is required. There is need for a State.
>
> (1989, p. 247)

The issue of the third party there arises: social life counts many Others so that there is a need for mediating all those asymmetrical relations that one has with all others: legal, or political justice is justified by the need for limiting the infinite responsibility, as the condition of possibility of social life then, so that equality is finally required, but in a formal, artificial sense.

Levinas nevertheless still asserts the insufficient nature of political justice: it must be exceeded by another form of justice in that "justice [as political] which is unavoidable, needs another 'authority' than the one of proportions established between wills that are straightaway opposed and opposable" (1987b, p. 168).

Ethical justice: exceeding political justice

This superior "authority" that must control, in a sense, and disrupt the totality of political justice is ethical justice, in the sense of justification – what gives the being its true meaning and freedom; the "justice of the for-the-other" (1998, p. 108). As justification, ethical justice is associated to the responsibility for the Other, the one that determines the duty of the same towards the Other, and prevents the same from identifying the Other to himself. It thus relies on the social structure of the ethical relationship, that is a relation with absolute alterity, transcendence, so that its principle is inequality and mutual recognition or equality is nowhere to be found.

It is questionable for the subject to "answer to his right to be, not as related to the abstraction of some anonymous law, to some juridical entity, but in the fear of the for-the-Other" (1998, p. 108). One then has to *answer* to his rights, as if they were duties: it is not under the act of a legal reason that people are granted with rights in the ethical sphere but only through the encounter with the face of the Other and the way they hold their responsibility. Thus, we understand ethical justice as the fundamental *demand* for justice, without which institutional justice cannot exist. Levinas indeed suggests that morality is prior to any established social or cultural structure: "Before culture and aesthetics, meaning is situated in the ethical, presupposed by all culture and all meaning. Morality does not belong to culture: it enables one to judge it; it discovers the dimension of height. Height ordains being" (1987a, p. 100). Levinas conceives ethics as being at the roots of any sociality and thus of justice. There seems to be no such thing, no human activity, that can preexist, logically, ethics, that can have a reality before the encounter with the face of the Other.

Now, although this ethical sense of justice appears as rather metaphysical, it has concrete implications, notably regarding its role towards political justice. Indeed, and this is why we argue in the sense of the complementarity of the ethical and the political dimensions of justice, "nothing could replace the control of the responsibility of the 'one for the other' that determines the limits of the State" (1995, p. 147). There appears a form of mutual limitation: political justice arises from the need for limiting the ethical responsibility, while as based on it, its universal and impersonal rationality must be limited by ethical justice, so that it seems necessary to maintain the tension between the two kinds of justice: ethical justice as the justification of politics and as its safeguard from the tyranny of totality.

Indeed, ethical justice is established as a protection against the tyranny of political justice:

> We must impose commands on ourselves in order to be free. But it must be an exterior command, not simply a rational law, not a categorical imperative, which is defenseless against tyranny; it must be an exterior law, a written law, armed with force against tyranny. Such are commands as the political condition for freedom.
>
> (1987a, p. 17)

Exteriority is still at the heart of his conception of liberty: there can be no freedom and thus no justice without the encounter with infinity as the ego would then still be enclosed on its own totality and this mode of being refers to tyranny, namely the negation of liberty.

Nevertheless, it does seem, especially regarding Levinas's resilience towards the practical necessity of political justice, that both principles, equality and alterity, must be considered as coexisting in order to fully understand the nature of the being, who is, in reality, determined by both totality and infinity, as both a for-itself and a for-the-other. Pierre Hayat in his preface to *Freedom and Command* explains that

> here lies the whole of the tension of the social on which Levinas invites to think: with the necessity of equality around the impersonal law, the value of the ethical relation that we do not reach through reciprocity and symmetry must be acknowledged
>
> (Levinas, 1994, p. 29):

this tension, between the same and the Other must be maintained to grasp the whole of sociality and of justice.

Concluding remarks

Levinas's conception of the being, and more specifically of ethics as the first philosophy, is the basis to this analysis of his idea of justice. The tension between the same and the Other determines the principles of his social theory: from sameness that leads to equality, to alterity, that leads to inequality, he draws a two-dimensional conception of justice that includes a political perspective on the one side, and an ethical one on the other. Based on his rather explicit but evolving critique of the former, it appears that he rejects the principle of equality as unfair. But fairness is rather to be understood, in Levinas, as justification, and more specifically as justification of the being, of his right to be and freedom. That is the role of ethical justice, in the responsibility for the Other that involves transcendence – transcendence of the Other that the ego can never alienate – as the ego is rather the Other's alienness, so that his being is justified and freed in heteronomy. That reverse in the structure of subjectivity constitutes an original turn in the way of thinking about the condition of possibility of freedom, and thus puts equality rather as a device, as a practical means to organize social life, than an end in itself.

Notes

1 Levinas uses the very large and ambiguous term "Western philosophy" to refer to a system of thought based on a conception of the being as enclosed in a relation to sameness. He strongly criticizes this vision and includes the modern tradition of political theory in it, starting with Thomas Hobbes, and then Heidegger's ontology. Some authors have nevertheless showed that his conception of Heidegger's work is sometimes misguided (for instance Raffoul, 2006) and we also call to vigilance regarding his lack of precision about which authors he includes under the vast term of "Western Philosophy", especially when speaking of the contractarian tradition.

2 The term of "theory" might seem misused in that Levinas's political thought appears more as political considerations than as a structured theory. However, we argue that put together, these considerations form an argumentation about the conditions of possibility of justice that we aim at clarifying.

3 Hegel has a specific place in Levinas's work: although barely quoted, his conception of social life and the "Hegelian totality" is targeted by Levinas. See for instance Rey (2006), Simhon (2006) and Balbontin-Gallo (2015).

4 Levinas's critique of the contractarian tradition is ambiguous in that he only calls into question Thomas Hobbes's positions, but does not refer explicitly to other authors who could be affiliated to this tradition.
5 His account of the master and the slave dialectics shows how ineffective recognition is when happening in an asymmetrical relationship: it ends with only one being recognized by the other and even the master receives unauthentic acknowledgment in that the slave is not considered as human enough to be able to operate an act of recognition.
6 Quotations from Levinas's French original works have been translated in English by the author.

Bibliography[6]

Alford, C.F., 2004, "Levinas and Political Theory", *Political Theory*, 32(2): 146–71.

Balbontin-Gallo, C., 2015, "Hegel/Levinas et le problème de la reconnaissance", Thèse de Doctorat en Philosophie, sous la direction de Catherine Chalier et Axel Honneth, Nanterre, Université Paris-Nanterre.

Bergo, B., 2002, "Remarks on Emmanuel Levinas's Contribution to Classical and 'Situated' Justice", *Theori: A Journal of Social and Political Theory*, 100: 38–63.

Chalier, C., 2006, "Révélation et totalité", *Revue internationale de philosophie*, 1(235): 5–14.

Ciaramelli, F., 2006, "Le refus de l'immédiat Remarques sur Levinas et la question de la Justice", *Revue Internationale de Philosophie*, 60(235): 61–74.

Critchley, S., 2004, "Five Problems in Levinas's View of Politics and the Sketch of a Solution to Them", *Political Theory*, 32(2): 172–85.

Derrida, J. 1964, "Violence et Métaphysique: Essai sur la pensée de Levinas", *Revue de Métaphysique et de Morale*, 3: 322–54.

Hayat, P., 2009, "Emmanuel Levinas: une intuition du social", *Le Philosophoire*, 2(32): 127–37.

Hegel, G.W.F., 2003 [1820], *Principes de la Philosophie du Droit*, Paris, PUF.

Herzog, A., 2002, "Is Liberalism 'All We Need'? Lévinas' Politics of Surplus", *Political Theory*, 30(2): 204–27.

Hobbes, T., 2000 [1651], *Léviathan*, Paris, Gallimard.

Kojève, A., 1981, *Esquisse d'une phénoménologie du droit*, Paris, Gallimard.

Kirkpatrick, K., 2011, "Levinas' Challenge to Abstract Law: Politics as Totality and Religion as Motivation for the Truly Just", *Ars Disputandi Supplement Series*, 5: 225, 235.

Kyongsuk Min, A., 1998, "Toward a Dialectic of Totality and Infinity: Reflections on Emmanuel Levinas", *The Journal of Religion*, 78(4): 571–92.

Larochelle, G., 2004, "Liberté et justice chez Levinas: L'expérience de l'impossible", *Revue Philosophique de Louvain*, 4(102): 583–609.

Levinas, E., 1963, *Difficile liberté: Essais sur le Judaïsme*, Paris, Albin Michel.

Levinas, E., 1971 [1961], *Totalité et Infini: Essai sur l'extériorité*, Paris, Martinus Nijhoff.

Levinas, E., 1978 [1974], *Autrement qu'être ou au-delà de l'essence*, La Haye, Martinus Nijhoff.

Levinas, E., 1982, *Éthique et Infini, Dialogues avec Philippe Nemo*, Paris, Fayard.

Levinas, E., 1983 [1979], *Le Temps et l'autre*, Paris, PUF.

Levinas, E., 1987a, *Collected Philosophical Papers*, Translated by Alphonso Linguis, Dordrecht, Martinus Nijhoff.

Levinas, E., 1987b, *Hors sujet*, Montpellier, Fata Morgana.

Levinas, E., 1989, "Ideology and Idealism", in *The Levinas Reader*, Oxford, Wiley-Blackwell.

Levinas, E., 1994, *Liberté et commandement*, Fata Morgana, Saint-Clément-la-Rivière.
Levinas, E., 1995, *Altérité et transcendance*, Fata Morgana, Saint-Clément-la-Rivière.
Levinas, E., 1998, *Éthique comme philosophie première*, Paris, Payot et Rivages.
Moses, S., 2006, "L'idée de justice dans la philosophie d'Emmanuel Levinas", *Revista Portuguesa de Filosofia*, 62: 379–98.
Raffoul, F., 2006, "Being and the Other: Ethics and Ontology in Levinas and Heidegger", in *Addressing Levinas*, Evanston, Northwestern University Press, 138–51.
Rawls, J., 1999 [1971], *A Theory of Justice*, Cambridge, MA, Harvard University Press.
Rey, J.F., 2006, "Le maître absolu: Hegel et Hobbes dans la pensée d'Emmanuel Levinas", *Revue Internationale de Philosophie*, 235: 75–89.
Sen, A.K., 1980, "Equality of What?", in McMurrin, S., *Tanner Lectures on Human Values*, Vol 1, Cambridge, Cambridge University Press.
Sen, A.K., 1992, *Inequality Reexamined*, Oxford, Clarendon Press.
Sen, A.K., 2009, *The Idea of Justice*, Cambridge, MA, Harvard University Press.
Simhon, A., 2006, *Levinas critique de Hegel*, Paris, Vrin.
Thomas, E.L., 2004, *Emmanuel Levinas: Ethics, Justice, and the Human beyond Being*, New York and London, Routledge.

12 The *recognition* of the other as a pre-requisite for fair market prices

Stefano Solari

The relational approach to economic processes, recognition and justice

Sociality shapes cognition, values, rights and, definitively, action. The self develops in relation to others; therefore, a proper understanding of the genesis and development of social phenomena is usefully based on a cognitive and relational perspective. Actually, many of the theoretical elements that economics usually considers to be static can be better understood as relational and, definitely, subject to change and, sometimes, to a certain degree of control. Economics has emphasized the aspect of *choice* and has either downplayed *interaction* or framed it in a way that is functional to individual choice in a static setting. Even game theory has always minimized the cognitive issues involved in games and exalted unrealistic mechanisms, as backward induction, oriented at reducing the political dimension of human interaction.[1] On the other hand, a cognitive relational approach can supply a relevant perspective to frame a variety of issues that are relevant in exchanges. In particular, it can actively bring juridical variables into the study of economics.

Economic justice is one of the fields of inquiry that can benefit from a relational approach. There is a formal justice that is grounded in the state, where 'to be just' means to conform to rules; and there is another kind of justice, informal and grounded in morality, meaning the respect of others' humanity, which is often understood as being based on the principle of equality.[2] Economic processes are characterized by a complex interplay of morals, ethics and justice (Jürgen Habermas, 2015). In this paper, there is no intention to deny the relevance of redistribution or to criticize the logics of arguments in favour of redistribution that are the foundation of social democracy – from Rawls to van Parijs or Kolm. However, this set-up of the problem has eclipsed the problem of *primary distribution* and *fair market prices*. That problem is normally hidden by the relevance that we attribute to the interplay between demand and supply, which is studied at given preferences. Nonetheless, there is a complex social and legal interaction behind demand and supply that has an impact on prices; precisely, it affects the definition of reservation prices defined in transactions and how the net value of exchanges is divided between buyers and sellers. A specific case concerns how the prices of factors are shaped in the market, which represents a major political economy issue.

A specific relational approach joining legal and political economy issues (with a social market economy perspective) was developed at the end of eighteenth century and in the first half of the nineteenth century by Hegel with his concept of *recognition*. Actually, this notion was first developed by Rousseau and Fichte, but it was organized into a scientific framework in Hegel's "Naturphilosophie und Philosophie des Geistes" (1805–06) and in his *Philosophy of Right* (1820) as part of *Sittlichkeit*. Later, it was also re-developed by Antonio Rosmini (1865) to support the foundation of his conception of rights. Today, the notion of recognition has been re-proposed by scholars, such as Taylor (1979, 1992) and Honneth (1995, 2000, 2010), who have rediscovered Hegel in alternative to contemporary *proceduralism*. This approach supplies a micro-interpretation about how the roots of social bonds and sources of solidarity are generated. It connects relational socio-cultural dynamics to the development of institutions and also allows for connecting rights to the distribution of income.[3] In particular, Honneth has argued that there is a connection between how social groups "strive for recognition" and redistribution.

The aim of this paper is to further develop the application of the philosophical grounds of recognition to economic exchanges through the theorization of the legal elements behind economic processes. Therefore, the proposed perspective includes a definition of the legal elements that enter economic interactions, which are conceived here as being framed by the identities of the interacting parties and by their reciprocal recognition of rights.

The problem of recognition, as framed by Honneth, is presented in the next section. In the third section, Hegel and Antonio Rosmini's framework of recognition is addressed in relation to its use in a transaction economics framework and in relation to identity economics (Davis, 2011). In the fourth section, the complex definition of rights in cognitive interactions is presented, and in the subsequent section, the idea of property rights is criticized and placed in the context of the recognition framework. In the fifth section, transaction economics is analyzed and developed in conjunction with the recognition of legal elements. Finally, the pathologies of recognition are examined in light of the primary distribution issue.

The primacy of inclusion in Honneth

Axel Honneth has explicitly connected the problem of recognition to political economy. He (2010, p. 9) laments that contemporary theories of social justice focus on procedural logics and distributive justice performed by the state. Proceduralism, and the emphasis on the state, cannot provide satisfactory solutions to the contemporary distributive problems caused by deregulated markets. Redistribution is certainly necessary, but, at the same time, it is undesirable that free and self-determined individuals are in a state of constant dependence and guardianship (which is not the spirit of Justice). Moreover, if market outcomes are perceived as 'natural' or 'fair', as there is an insufficient perception of the unequal conditions in which exchanges take place, this kind of redistribution is considered to be a reduction of liberty for those who have to pay for it. Therefore, the fundamental problem is that contemporary theories based on 'market fundamentalism' privilege ex post redistribution and downplay the opportunities to set up institutions that could help create a more horizontal distribution of income within markets. The view of 'market fundamentalism cum redistribution' lacks the fundamental idea of reciprocity as a foundation of market interactions, and it interprets rights as a 'given stock' that cannot be discussed or modified. Contrary to this vision, rights depend on a continuous reciprocal recognition between individuals, which is often addressed as the broad problem of social inclusion.

Like Hegel and the Aristotelian tradition, Honneth assumes that a *good-life*, and not 'justice', is the end goal of the political community. He aims, first of all, to substitute the theme of redistribution for the problem of inclusion. He seeks to study the moral norms that lie at the ground of the recognition processes on a normative plan (Honneth, 2010, p. 28). This allows him to analyze the problems of social and political exclusion applying a 'practical ethics of everyday actions', in order to work out the normative principles of justice for modern societies in which all the necessary (pre)conditions for the self-realization of individuals are subsumed.

Honneth takes, from Hegel, the principle of intersubjective and reciprocal recognition as shaping the moral identity of modern societies. He also criticizes the insufficient conceptual toolkit of liberalism, as the notion of 'free will', because the simple coupling of abstract rights and morality leads to indeterminacy. The foreseen perspective follows the approach of Hegel, shifting the focus from individual morality to an *ethical life*. That implies developing social conditions wherein subjects would be able to regard one another's freedom to be a precondition of their own individual self-realization. Moreover, Honneth adheres to the Aristotelian conception that avoids anchoring normative principles to external codes of conduct (compulsory laws). That presupposes *communicative relations* to be the 'basic good' in which all humans should be interested in while striving to actualize their freedom. This good is not a good in the narrow sense, as in Rawls (Ege and Igersheim, 2010); rather, it is a common good (Mastromatteo and Solari, 2014). Nonetheless, it is worth discussing in more depth the theoretical origins of the notion of recognition.

The source of rights in recognition

There are two main original sources for the philosophy of recognition: Hegel and Rosmini.[4] The latter found inspiration from the former about this specific issue, but developed his philosophical system in a different direction. The concept of recognition was originally developed by Hegel in "Naturphilosophie und Philosophie des Geistes" (1805–06). Hegel starts from the theorization of Kant and Fichte who assumed that rights and duties as well as the essence of the cognizing and willing individual are parts of the same unity. Kant developed his supreme law of morality – the categorical imperative – that we should consider others as ends and not as means; moreover, he also assumed the principle of non-contradiction as the universal criterion of moral rightfulness. Hegel refuses Kantian dualism between the ideal and the real. He departs from the Kantian approach by asserting that lawfullness and morality cannot be separated. The law represents the external life of man and morality his internal condition. Their unity is expressed as ethicity (*Sittlichkeit*). This implies also a radical epistemological shift, leading to Hegelian historicism.

In his *Philosophy of Right* (1820), Hegel developed the concept of recognition in his legal-economic framework. The individual is seen as bearer of legal rights and a subject contributing to shaping those rights via an intersubjective cognitive process. The laws arise out of this interaction, and the juridical system is defined as the place of actualized liberties (Hegel, 1820, §4). Here, Hegel also formulates his juridical formal imperative, "be a person and respect the others as persons" (Hegel, 1820, §36). Consequently, the social structure of the historical world in which individual agents and institutions find their domain is constituted through recognition (*Anerkennung*), that is to say, through cognitive processes of reciprocal interaction (Testa, 2012, p. 176).

Civil society, in Hegel's view, embodies the essence of economics (Ege and Walraevens, 2011). It is seen as a bond between the single autonomous members in a formal universality (Hegel, 1820, §157). Nonetheless, civil society alone cannot resolve all the tensions between the 'universal' and the 'particular'. That means that markets are not self-reproducing the context they need to perform the desired results. Therefore, collective action is needed to produce merit goods and institutions to sustain market fairness (Ver Eecke, 2008; Mastromatteo and Solari, 2014).

Herrmann-Pillath and Boldyrev (2014) emphasize how Hegel's approach to the market and civil society, which is assimilated to Smith's market, is in line with the idea of *social and distributed cognition* that was later proposed by Friedrich von Hayek. Cognizing (*Erkennen*) is the first form of individual identifiability; recognizing (*Anerkennen*) is a form of cognitive social interaction. The former indicates an identification of an individual and the latter indicates an expressive act of affirmation with a positive meaning.[5] Herrmann-Pillath and Boldyrev (2014) interpret the socio-economic ontology of Hegel as based on *continuity*, *performativity* and *recognition*. Continuity identifies the emergent social phenomena with nature. Performativity means that theories (mental models) affect action. Finally, recognition means that human action is impossible without the mutual recognition of agency as having meaning and intentions in groups of interacting human individuals (Herrmann-Pillath and Boldyrev, 2014, p. 46).[6] Recognition represents a social bond that underlies the sociality of human action and it is of two main kinds: the mutual recognition between individuals, and that between individuals and institutions.

Recognition binds institutions into the system of ethical life (*Sittlichkeit*), which, in Hegel, leads to an organic and ethical state. The 'self' cannot be established separately from the communities of action in which he/she participates. Freedom of choice emerges from human reflexivity mediated by distributed cognition; therefore, it is a cultural and institutional phenomenon. It is not necessarily based on a rational reflection on reasons of actions; it also includes habitual and culturally – and historically –conditioned choices. Thus, the perspective is on action and not so much on choice – as in the case of standard economics.[7] In the identity of universal and particular will, right and duty coincide or, better, are two sides of the same set of relationships. Due to the interdependency of the ethical system, man has rights in as much he acknowledges having duties, and he has duties in as much he has rights (Hegel, 1820, §155).

Rosmini (1845, 1865) developed a philosophy of law that was inspired by Hegel while remaining attached to the Thomistic framework of natural law. Differently from Hegel, Rosmini's analysis of civil society does not end in the synthesis of the organic ethical state. Differently from Hegel, morality remains a subjective force that is orienting recognition, but not leading to a self-dissolution into the ethical life. In Rosmini's work, recognition is a natural attitude that does not lead to a transcendent "we", as it does in Hegel. Nonetheless, Rosmini does not deny the social dimension of human cognition and action. In fact, in Rosmini, the right to property is simultaneously personal, interpersonal and social[8] because rights emerge from social interaction, and this contributes to seeing property as natural and as part of the social law that is the effective legal framework of civil economy. A further way in which Rosmini's philosophical approach differs from Hegel's is that, for Rosmini, the ethical life is not historically determined; instead, it has some reference to Christian principles of the good life.

In the work of both of these philosophers, the processes of reciprocal recognition are the foundations of rights and of the law. Liberty is, therefore, seen as being juridically defined because legal elements are constitutive aspects of freedom and not limits to it. Rights (and duties) are related to the necessary conditions for the realization of 'free will' in the market. According to Rosmini, a right is a moral force that emerges in the relationship between personal freedom and moral law. It is a force that binds the self to others. Therefore, in this view, duty logically allows rights. The rights that we recognize for others are obviously obligations that we are, directly or indirectly, willing to fulfil. Therefore, in both philosophers, genuine law has social foundations. This aspect makes the juridical relationship fundamentally reciprocal and grounded in history, even if that history has a different logic in the two scholars.

In this way, recognition is a cognitive process that has therefore a fundamental juridical dimension, reciprocally defining the entitlements of individuals and the rules of the game. In Hegel, formal law is the final step in the process of developing an ethical society and it loops back to the process of recognition. The state is fundamental in this process, but has a subsidiary role for both Hegel and Rosmini. The latter is somewhat suspect of formal law, which is often an instrument of domination. Therefore, Rosmini holds a realistic perspective predicting the possible non-alignment between social law and the state.

Standard economic theory is based on an impoverished view of the subject as a closed monological entity, and of the social bond as a superficial and interest-driven collection of individuals (Costas Douzinas, 2002). In contrast, the recognition approach is a way of theorizing rights as relational and evolving, not a static stock attributed to the self.

For this current analysis, we stay at the micro-level, where the ethical life is the good living practiced and experienced by each citizen. If, in Hegel, autonomy becomes effective only when it is embodied in political institutions and universal laws,[9] it is, nonetheless, important to focus on the rights and rules that are perceived as effective and that are applied in everyday interactions by members of civil society.[10] Thus, the issue is not only how much the law shapes individual personality, but how we reciprocally construct our personality in a structured environment so that our interactions contribute to modifying the environment. As Douzinas (2002, p. 391), noted:

> Right as a relation between persons who recognize each other in some attribute or characteristic is created in the process of recognition. Private rights, in particular, lead to the recognition of the other as another person, someone carrying weight in his or her abstract capacity for freedom.

Therefore, we start from the process of legal socialization; that is to say, we address the rights, duties and rules we perceive as valid in our process of interaction. In Hegel's work, the term, *right*, is both a *necessary condition* and a *justified claim*.

The concept of identity (Davis, 2011) is relevant for understanding the final outcome of this process. Identity has a dynamic nature because it is a kind of dialogue with others in which a shared meaning is generated. In this process, the legal dimension is a precondition to economic interaction. Legal personality is both defined by the recognition of institutions and by the ongoing recognition of the other (Costas Douzinas, 2002). Formal law contributes to defining a commonality between people (the universal), but it is both the product of past processes of social interaction and the present constraint on the process of recognition of actual institutions. Therefore, when we study the legal elements relevant in an exchange, we should consider both the environment and the actual process of reciprocal recognition between the interacting parties.

Rights claims are often the result of inadequate or defective recognition. However, following Rosmini (1865), the lack of definition of a right is often due to someone being unwilling to bear some duty. That is a sign that the reciprocal dimension of recognition lacks some contribution from the person or institution that is willing to recognize some duty towards others, specified by some category of people.

The unuseful distinction between real and personal rights

Economists emphasize the concept of property right as the object of exchanges. Unquestionably, property rights are central in the process of recognition as they have a social dimension and are produced by mutual recognition (Ege and Walraevens, 2011). Over the last two centuries, this notion has undergone a process of simplification and objectivization that was functional to the development of the economic theory of the market. Today economists as Barzel (1997) consider property rights as "the ability to control or to use assets". Similarly, Allen (2015) defines them more broadly as the "ability to freely exercise a choice" (Allen, 2015, p. 712).[11] This definition sanctions a detachment of the economic perspective from the usual meaning of this term in the legal language, but it captures some important socially 'enabling' characteristics of recognized rights and entitlements in line with the classics. What is missing from these definition of property is that it systematically depends on others' acceptance and that makes it contextual to the political community (Hodgson, 2015).

The idea of *property right*, from Grotius to Pufendorf and Locke, has been defined as an extension of the notion of occupation functional to the 'protective' definition of one's personality (Buckle, 1991; Schlatter, 1951; Pennington, 1998). Therefore, the *suum* has been seen as a pre-legal idea of a personality needing essential possession in order to assure his life. Possession of goods is not factually problematic. It becomes a legal concept when a political community acknowledges a specific sphere of control to the individuals – in which possession is a specific case. Therefore, classical liberal scholars defined property as the right to a variety of personal entitlements needed to protect the *suum*. The right to self-protection results in the right to exclude others from affecting this sphere of the *suum*, but it inevitably depends on others' acceptance. Therefore, property was theorized as something related to personality and not as a simple *dominium* on things. This is why property is also a necessary condition to the effective participation in civil society for Hegel, who adheres to liberalism.

In this context, Hegel's (1820, §40) argument against the dichotomy between *personal* and *real rights* of the Roman law tradition is relevant. In fact, Hegel as well as Rosmini accepts property as a natural right, but this right is conceived as a *personal and actual right*, which is the consequence of the subjectivity of the recognition process, the latter representing the source of rights (Ikäheimo, 2009). Therefore, while there are many kinds of rights, it makes no sense to sharply distinguish between property and personal, civil and human rights in the concept of recognition, as it did for old-liberals.

Actually, the rights entering economic interactions are far more complex than the simple rights on material goods. Our economy is mainly comprised of services that are best defined by the right to access to certain activities. We often exchange bonds as tickets, certificates that define what we will get. In these interactions, the personality of interacting subjects is more and more relevant to defining the prices involved in the transactions. Moreover, marketing techniques teach us that the same good is a social construction, and its appreciation is a complex process that is related to the recognition of the immaterial properties of the others.

The fundamental result is that rights and entitlements have a graduation and a qualitative dimension that is the relevant element of recognition. The space of qualitative right recognition and evaluation is fundamental in the process of evaluation oriented to set prices of exchanges. Honneth (2010) supposes that this process of recognition does not always work well because of: a) physical violence;

b) exclusion and rights deprivation; and c) the degradation of the social value of some forms of self-realization. This paper will focus on the second type of lack of recognition or mis-recognition.

Transactions and the rights-duties framework

According to Honneth and Hartmann (2004), distribution rules are institutionalized forms of production relations, but, firstly, they are institutional forms of the socio-cultural relationships founded in shared beliefs. Honneth mainly looks at redistribution as perversely affected by the lack of recognition of some category of people. That view addresses Honneth's ideas to strive for the recognition of social groups. However, Honneth only sporadically touches on the issue of primary distribution, which is certainly more directly affected by processes of recognition.

Honneth and Hartmann (2004) argue that, in the market, individuals recognize themselves reciprocally as autonomous beings, each acting for the interest of the others. Following Hegel, the market is conceived as ethically framed.[12] The social order of the market includes a dimension of rights and duties, unwritten evaluation rules and the accepted practices of extinguishing obligations. Hegel's notion of "civil honour" as decent remuneration, safety, certainty and respect, is just this aspect of recognition that affects primary distribution. Moreover, in Hegel, the solidarity needed for social integration should spring out of the economy; it should not arise from separated religious morals. Obviously, in Rosmini, religious morals foster natural law and tend to assure healthy recognition processes. However, since Rosmini's dialectics have no synthesis, the process of recognition is more open-ended.

In order to analyze the impact of the more or less virtuous process of recognition, the main economic framework that is able to understand relationality in the allocation of resources is the "transaction" model developed by John R. Commons.[13] In his *Legal Foundations of Capitalism*, Commons developed a legal framework to study transactions under the hypothesis that economic outcomes are fundamentally shaped by the institutional set-up, and he adopted and slightly modified the relational legal theory of Hohfeld (1919). In this perspective, the allocation of goods takes place in a juridical environment, where individuals act in a space defined by a set of symmetric entitlements and working rules.

Hohfeld (1919) pointed out the following symmetrical juridical variables framing transactions: *Right* of A, corresponding to *duty* of B; *Privilege* of A, corresponding to *no-right* of B; *Power* of A, corresponding to *liability* of B; *Immunity* of A, corresponding to *no-power* of B. Therefore, this set of entitlements is always defined in a relationship, where the most fundamental cognitive act is the reciprocal recognition of A and B specific endowments.

In comparison to the cognitive approach of Hegel, the elements of this scheme suffer from a tendency to standardize and simplify rights, tending toward objectivation. However, they can be read as personal entitlements, as in our framework, and they can be declined in various qualities. In particular, they can include

(Kantian) *universal obligations* when the position of B is intended as whoever gets in relationship with A.

Commons (1893, 1924) modified this relational scheme emphasizing transactions taking place within organizations (managerial transactions) and the role of the political administrative authority in allocating resources (rationing transactions). Actually, in Commons, transactions always involve at least five actors: the two interacting individuals A and B, two non-transacting individuals representing the opportunities not taken (opportunity costs, individuals C and D) and the administrative authority in charge of regulating economic processes. Actually, Commons did not introduce the notion of preferences but, rather, the simple classical difference between *use value* and *exchange value*, which determines the opportunities of a transaction. Commons's objective was to describe property as a social creation, as a legal construct that can be adapted and modified. Thus, property is embedded in social and legal relations, where power and authority are also relevant. Consequently, he included some element of administrative control in his legal positions. The resulting framework is basically conflict-ridden and based on imperfect opposites (never coinciding perfectly), such as right-duty, exposure-liberty, power-liability and immunity-disability.

To each legal attribute of A, some corresponding position of B determines a relationship of limits and reciprocation. To this reciprocal interaction, Commons adds the state and the two respective opportunity costs of supply and demand of respectively individual C and individual D (next best alternatives to A and B). This relational environment assures that the underlying processes of recognition are never bi-univocal; rather, they are always socially organized thanks to the comparison of and adaptation to habits and customs. Therefore, a transaction is a multilateral form of relationship. It involves the decision to reciprocally modify rights, often compensated by money (which is a specific right on a symbolic accounting unit). It consists of a consensual modification of the juridical spheres of the parts under the framework of customs, rules and institutions.

The law and the working rules, constituted by practices and customs, integrate this framework. Actually, rules and institutions contribute to defining the legal position, and, at the same time, govern the dynamics of the transaction: rules affect rights. Therefore, rules and rights both define the legal environment, i.e. the state. Commons specifically focusses on institutions and laws that are under the control of the government because he is interested in how society is politically steered by modifying the legal positions of actors. However, he includes working rules resulting from social interaction as customs and habits in the institutions affecting trades, leaving room for our analysis (Commons [1932–33] talks of legal, moral and economic sanctions).

However, our focus in not in allocation (exchange); rather, we emphasize the evaluation process and, before that, the recognition of the rights-duties that come into play. The transaction, in fact, is also the framework in which the *process of evaluation* takes place, a process 'oriented' by institutions and, precisely, by the working rules defining the respective entitlements. Before or concurrently to the evaluation process, the recognition process determines the real objects of transactions: rights that are modified by transacting. That is the reason why institutionalism stresses the role of *social evaluation* instead of basing evaluation on the simple scarcity discovered by the market interaction. Moreover, *social evaluation* underlines the role of individual positions, particularly wealth, in affecting outcomes. Here, we would like to broaden the study to include the definition of reciprocal recognition of rights.

Recognition, social evaluation and unfair prices

Failures in formal laws can result in badly functioning markets. The law, despite being universal, is often unfit to specific situations, thereby assuring excess privileges to somebody or assigning some excess duty to someone else. The state can also be dysfunctional to the recognition of some category of people by weakly enforcing some rights. Similarly, as underscored by institutionalism, unfit institutions can magnify the force of some individuals at the expense of someone else. On the other hand, unfit laws or institutions are the result of an unbalanced process of recognition, which reproduces unfit rights, powers and immunities, blocking the natural evolution of formal rights and rules. Often this is due to bad political systems or to bad political education. Here, we adopt a bottom-up perspective and emphasize the fundamental defects in the reciprocal recognition of rights among interacting parties. Using the same perspective, Rössler (2007) discusses the example of domestic family work, which, in our society, is unrecognized labour. Some examples of immigrant and female labour have been discussed in Solari (2015a). Other less macroscopic phenomena concern manual work depreciation and the falling wages in traditional services. All of this is due to a change in social evaluation, where scarcity is not the evident source of the changing prices.

In general, we can use the cost-benefit language and say that mis-recognition leads to a reduction in reservation prices, both in the maximum price of buyers and the minimum price of sellers. Recognition takes place at the same time as the process of individual evaluation, and it is part of it. Contemporary economics, by logically isolating the identification of rights from the subjective evaluation of 'the good', takes rights as a given; however, they are not. Moreover, economics distinguishes the subjective evaluation of individual parties from the social evaluation due to market interaction. Actually, the approach to recognition does not distinguish these steps, at least not logically, because individual evaluation is always taking place in a social interaction. When we consider issues as disrespect, discrimination and disregard, we deal with problems of recognition that can be studied in their specificity. However, they cannot be separated using processes of economic evaluation as both are part of a unique social process of general evaluation. Individual subjective evaluation emerges in a reciprocal process of communication. Therefore, subjective reservation prices also have a social dimension and they cannot emerge in isolation in a relationship between the individual and the good.

Following the legal interpretation of Hohfeld (1919), different pathologies emerge. *Rights* of A can find little correspondence to *duties* of B, or *duties* of B can be magnified relative to rights of A. The privilege of A can be unrecognized by

B, who does not guarantee his respect. A very frequent case is the excess of power of A, when interacting with B; or a renouncing of A of his/her power because of a lack of recognition of B's liability. Finally, in our society, we often fail to assure immunities to some subject or we assure excess of it. In any case, the pathologies are often qualitative rather than quantitative: we do not often appreciate people's competences, or we overlook the moral or practical personal consequences that the services we demand have on other people (e.g. prostitution).

In Aristotle, the problem of commutative justice finds a solution in the harmonic average between the bids of the transacting parties. This solution is not viable if we admit that contracting parties announce their bids strategically. Therefore, economists tend to apply harmonic mean to reservation prices (which makes the story even less concretely observable). However, here, the issue is also that reservation prices can be distorted by 'mis-recognition'. Buyers or sellers can evaluate reservation prices in a distorted way due to their lack of recognition of the quality of partner's entitlements. That can be voluntary or involuntary, strategic or unconscious. This inability to recognize value or quality arises in a way that is not separable from movements in prices due to relative scarcity or to fraud and force. Nonetheless, it can be logically distinguished, and it can be a source of concern when we design rules for specific markets, as the labour market, or when we implement policies to improve the efficiency of the economy.

Economic evaluation and recognition are interdependent. Recognition can affect prices, and prices can have an impact on recognition. In the former case, let's say an illegal immigrant, suffers from earning lower pay compared to a regular labourer. In the latter case, a person earning high pay can improve his/her social status and advance into a better social position by a re-evaluation of his/her entitlements. Thus, a good process of reciprocal recognition can make market prices fair. On the other hand, the increased effectiveness with which market prices respond to changes in relative scarcity can worsen the problems of recognition. Prices should oscillate by responding to scarcity, as this is good feedback for the economy. It is questionable as to whether or not it is good that prices magnify changes induced by changes in relative scarcity. As prices feed back on structural elements as personal rights, a change that is too intense can have negative effects.

Two problems emerge. What rights should be recognized and how can we distinguish a fair process of recognition from an unfair one? Here, Hegel and Rosmini do not diverge, mainly because what is at stake is a sense of common humanity, which can be found in the idea of *liberty* posited by both scholars, and which, today, tends to assume the shape of the capability theory. The latter becomes an operational framework only if we can define a shared view of human progress. Today, only a politically defined project of amelioration of civil life can be a viable measure of human fulfilment.

Conclusion: just prices and recognition

In this paper the 'market fundamentalist' vision of social democracy is rejected in favour of a more critical view of how markets work. In order to accomplish that change, the simplistic vision of human preferences and property rights must be abandoned in favour of a philosophical background focussing on social cognition, recognition and the ends of economic processes. In present day economics, the concept of property rights is a simplistic notion that should be the object of deeper study integrating insights from the philosophy of law. Moreover, the concept of right can be understood only in relation to duty and in a relational view of the interacting individuals. That means endogenizing the definition of rights in the analysis of economic processes, and in particular of market forms. In this perspective, the simplistic idea of efficiency loses its strengths in favour of a political economy vision of the ends of economic processes where recognition is an important presupposition to a fair result of exchanges. That also means that, when making public choices, the only available reference point is a view of social progress, or the progress of civilization. In any transaction, there is not just one price; rather, there is a set of prices that allow the transaction to correctly respond to relative scarcity and to assure the fulfilment of the transacting parties' capabilities relative to a shared political project. Social policy and education can do much to achieve a fair price mechanism.

Notes

1 With the exception of Aoki (2001) and Herrmann-Pillath and Boldyrev (2014) who developed the cognitive dimension of institutions using a game approach.
2 That is the case of Proudhon and various other theories. See Solari (2015b).
3 Honneth has provided some political economy applications of this idea (1995, 2008; with Hartmann, 2004).
4 Rosmini (1797–1855) belongs to the liberal stream of Catholic thinking. Similarly to Hegel, he reacted to Kantian subjectivism and that helped him develop similar trajectories in the philosophy of law.
5 Ikäheimo and Laitinen (2007) distinguish three kinds of cognitive interactions: identification, acknowledgement and recognition.
6 The relation of recognition is often performative (Testa, 2011).
7 Therefore, according to this philosophy, individuals follow a rule not because they react to incentives, but because they recognize those incentives as part of the institutionalized pattern of action (Herrmann-Pillath and Boldyrev, 2014, p. 65). See also Pippin (2007).
8 See Hoevel's *The Economy of Recognition* (2013).
9 This aspect is less emphasized in Rosmini, where the person is seen as more autonomous relative to institutions.
10 That assures that Rosmini's framework is also applicable.
11 These definitions have the curious effect of attributing an abstract status to the legal concept, which is rather pragmatic, and a factual status to a rationalistic concept. Economic property rights are also wrongly equated with possession, which is not an a-juridical notion.
12 This ethical foundation of markets is a fundamental point of ethical liberalism. On the other hand, it is contrary to the definition of markets developed by Karl Polanyi, which is purely based on scarcity and interest.
13 Contemporary Transaction Cost Economics, while integrating legal elements, allows no opportunity to study the recognition of rights. Actually, it supplies notions as pre- and post-contractual opportunism or information asymmetry, which either shift the attention to other sources of uncertainty or re-orders the elements into different boxes.

Bibliography

Allen, Douglas W. 2015. "On Hodgson on Property Rights." *Journal of Institutional Economics*, 11(4): 711–17.

Aoki, Masahiko. 2001. *Toward a Comparative Institutional Analysis*. Cambridge, MA: MIT Press.

Barzel, Yoram. 1997. *Economic Analysis of Property Rights*. Cambridge and New York: Cambridge University Press.

Buckle, Stephen. 1991. *Natural Law and the Theory of Property: Grotius to Hume*. Oxford: Clarendon Press.

Commons, John R. 1893. *The Distribution of Wealth*. New York: Palgrave Macmillan.

Commons, John R. 1924. *Legal Foundations of Capitalism*. New York: Palgrave MacMillan.

Commons, John R. 1932–33. "The Problems of Correlating Law, Economics and Ethics." *Wisconsin Law Review*, 8: 3–26.

Davis, John B. 2011. *Individuals and Identity in Economics*. Cambridge: Cambridge University Press.

Douzinas, Costas. 2002. "Identity, Recognition, Rights or What Can Hegel Teach Us about Rights?" *Journal of Law and Society*, 29(3): 379–405.

Ege, Ragip. 2005. "L'Agent Économique dans la Philosophie du Droit Hégélienne." *Cahiers d'Économie Politique*, 49: 87–102.

Ege, Ragip, and Herrade Igersheim. 2010. "Rawls' Justice Theory and Its Relations to the Concept of 'Merit Goods'." *European Journal of History of Economic Thought*, 17(4): 1001–30.

Ege, Ragip, and Benoit Walraevens. 2011."G.W.F. Hegel: Toward a Reconciliation." In *Freedom and Happiness in Economic Thought and Philosophy*, eds. Ragip Ege and Herrade Igersheim, 183–97. London: Routledge.

Habermas, Jürgen. 2015. *The Lure of Technocracy*. Cambridge: Polity Press.

Hanfling, Oswald. 2006. "Rights and Human Rights." *Royal Institute of Philosophy Supplement*, 58 (May): 57–94.

Hegel, Georg W. Friedrich. 1805–1806. "Naturphilosophie und Philosophie des Geistes." In *Jenaer Realphilosophie, Vorlesungsmanuskripte zur Philosophie der Natur und des Geistes von 1805–1806*, ed. J. Hoffmeister, Hamburg: F. Meiner, 1969.

Hegel, G.W.F. 1820. *Philosophy of Right*. Kitchener: Batoche Books, 2001.

Herrmann-Pillath, Carstens, and Ivan Boldyrev. 2014. *Hegel, Institutions and Economics*. London: Routledge.

Hodgson, Geoffrey M. 2015. "Much of the 'Economics of Property Rights' Devalues Property and Legal Rights." *Journal of Institutional Economics*, 11(4) (August): 683–709.

Hoevel, Carlos. 2013. *The Economy of Recognition: Person, Market and Society in Antonio Rosmini*. Dordrecht: Springer.

Hohfeld, Wesley Newcomb. 1919. *Fundamental Legal Conceptions as Applied in Judicial Reasoning, and Other Legal Essays*, ed. David Campbell and Phillip Thomas. Aldershot: Ashgate, 2001.

Honneth, Axel. 1995. *The Struggle for Recognition: The Moral Grammar of Social Conflicts*. Cambridge: Polity Press.

Honneth, Axel. 2000. *Suffering from Indeterminacy: An Attempt to Reactualization of Hegel's Philosophy of Right*. Amsterdam: Van Gorcum.

Honneth, Axel. 2008. "Arbeit und Anerkennung: Versuch einer Neubestimmung." *Deutsche Zeitschrift für Philosophie*, 56(3): 327–41, Ital. transl. *Capitalismo e Riconoscimento*, ed. Marco Solinas. Florence: Firenze University Press, 2010.

Honneth, Axel. 2010. "Qual è la Stoffa della Giustizia? Sui Limiti del Proceduralismo Contemporaneo." In *La Stoffa della Giustizia. I Limiti del Proceduralismo*, ed. Axel Honneth. Turin: Trauben, original 2009. "*Das Gewerbe der Gerechtigkeit. Über die Grenzen des zeitgenössischen Prozeduralismus.*" *Zeitschrift für Sozialforschung*, 6: 3–22.

Honneth, Axel, and Martin Hartmann. 2004. "Paradoxien des Kapitalismus. Ein Untersuchungsprogramm." *Berliner Debatte Initial*, 15(1): 4–17. Ital. transl. *Capitalismo e Riconoscimento*, ed. Marco Solinas. Florence: Firenze University Press, 2010.

Ikäheimo, Heikki. 2009. "A Vital Human Need: Recognition as Inclusion in Personhood." *European Journal of Political Theory*, 8(1): 31–45.

Ikäheimo, Heikki, and Arto Laitinen. 2007. "Analyzing Recognition: Identification, Acknowledgement, and Recognitive Attitudes Towards Persons." In *Recognition and Power. Axel Honneth and the Tradition of Critical Social Theory*, eds. Bert van der Brink and David Owen, 33–56. Cambridge: Cambridge University Press.

Mastromatteo, Giuseppe, and Stefano Solari. 2014. "The Idea of 'Common Good' and the Role of the State in Present-Day Social Economics." *Rivista Internazionale di Scienze Sociali*, 1: 85–102.

Pennington, Kenneth. 1998. "The History of Rights in Western Thought." *Emory Law Journal*, 47: 237–52.

Pippin, Robert. 2007. "Recognition and Reconciliation: Actualized Agency in Hegel." In *Recognition and Power: Axel Honneth and the Tradition of Critical Social Theory*, eds. Bert van der Brink and David Owen, 57–78. Cambridge: Cambridge University Press.

Rosmini, Antonio. 1845. *Principles of Ethics*. Transl. by Denis Cleary and Terence Watson from *Principi della Scienza Morale*. Durham: Rosmini House, 1988.

Rosmini, Antonio. 1865. *The Philosophy of Right*, vol. 1: *The Essence of Right*; vol.2: *Rights of the Individual*. Transl. by Denis Cleary and Terence Watson. Durham: Rosmini House, 1993.

Rössler, Beate. 2007. "Work, Recognition, Emancipation." In *Recognition and Power: Axel Honneth and the Tradition of Critical Social Theory*, eds. Bert van der Brink and David Owen. Cambridge: Cambridge University Press, 135–63.

Schlatter, Richard. 1951. *Private Property, the History of an Idea*. London: Allen & Unwin.

Solari, Stefano. 2015a. "Individual Rights, Economic Transactions and Recognition: A Legal Approach to Social Economics." In *Law and Social Economics: Essays in Ethical Values for Theory, Practice, and Policy*, ed. Mark White, 41–59. New York: Palgrave Macmillan.

Solari, Stefano. 2015b. "Social Justice: The Relationship between Economy and the Law in Proudhon." In *Pensiero Critico ed Economia Politica nel XIX Secolo: da Saint-Simon a Proudhon*, eds. Vitantonio Gioia, Sergio Noto, and Alfonso Sanchez Hormigo, 371–81. Bologne: Il Mulino.

Taylor, Charles. 1979. *Hegel and Modern Society*. Cambridge: Cambridge University Press.

Taylor, Charles. 1992. "The Politics of Recognition." In *Multiculturalism: Examining the Politics of Recognition*, ed. Amy Guttman, 25–73. Princeton, NJ: Princeton University Press.

Testa, Italo. 2011. "Social Space and the Ontology of Recognition." In *Recognition and Social Ontology*, eds. Heikki Ikäheimo and Arto Laitinen, 287–308. Leiden: Brill.

Testa, Italo. 2012. "How Does Recognition Emerge from Nature? The Genesis of Consciousness in Hegel's Jena Writings." *Critical Horizons*, 13(2): 176–96.

Ver Eecke, Wilfried. 2008. *Ethical Dimensions of the Economy*. Berlin: Springer.

13 The agent as an end in itself in the economic domain from a biological and Smithian perspective

Eleonora Viganò

Introduction

When the agent meets other agents, she asks herself the fundamental moral question: "How should I treat them?". In the marketplace, the agent meets and interacts with many people; therefore, even the market is a place of morality, but of a very particular kind. It is a particular place of morality for two reasons: firstly, the main aim of economic agents meeting each other in the market is to pursue their personal interests (Herzog 2017); secondly, in our contemporary world, the majority of people encountered in the economic sphere are strangers. In economic relationships, these two characteristics of the market represent a threat to morality because they may induce the agent to treat other economic agents as means to her own ends, and in all moral theories – with the exception of utilitarianism – moral beings cannot use others as means to attain their own goals. Therefore, it seems that the market is a place of morality in which morality continually risks being excluded, with the result that the economic agent cannot be at the same time a moral agent.

However, from a biological and neurobiological perspective, the relationship between the economic actor and the moral agent is closer than commonly believed. Hence, in this chapter, firstly, I will explain the process by which the other becomes an end in itself in the evolution of human beings from a self-interested basis. Secondly, I will identify the hindrances to that process in the marketplace and attempt to explain why they are present. Thirdly, I will suggest how to remove these obstacles, by using a principle of conduct that includes treating the other as an end in itself and that is equally valid in both the moral and the economic sphere: the virtue of prudence described by Adam Smith. Finally, while Smith focuses on the economic usefulness of the moral virtue of prudence, I will point out the "moral usefulness" of prudence for economics, namely the worth of prudence in orienting the economic agent's actions.

The origin of the care for others from the care for oneself

The brains of animals are set to maintain the individual's self-preservation. The process by which the internal conditions of animals are kept within parameters that guarantee their survival is called *homeostasis*. At a very elementary level, the care for oneself includes every action that guarantees one's own survival and well-being (Damasio 2005: 48). Here I define every action aiming at one's own survival and well-being as *self-interested*, in the sense that the only objective of these actions is the individual's preservation. By "taking care of" I mean having an interest, even implicit and non-conscious, in the receiver of the care; this interest results in trying to preserve the receiver of the care and can be attributed to human beings as well as animals.

The origin of care-taking of others goes back to the appearance of mammals on the Earth. Their neural organization adapted to include their offspring in their homeostatic space (Bell 2001) through various changes in the endocrine system, stress regulation, and in the reward-punishment system, which is connected with the learning of the other's emotions and intentions (Carter et al. 2009; Keverne 2004; Moll and Krueger 2006). These changes became affirmed because they were advantageous from an evolutionary point of view: taking care of the offspring resulted in more offspring surviving. The introduction in a mammal's homeostatic space of its offspring – and in some cases of the mate and other individuals of its species – caused the other's survival and well-being to be an interest that the individual had a disposition to promote. Thus, as Patricia Churchland affirmed, the other's survival and well-being are values for the first individual in a very implicit and primitive form (Churchland 2011: 12–14). Therefore, the care for others, which is a substantial part of morality, derives from the extension of the individuals the animal takes care of. Furthermore, the care of others originates from the care of oneself, namely from behavior focused on oneself, which is the basis of the self-interested conduct that is characteristic of the economic sphere (Herzog 2017).

In the history of mankind, the extension of the homeostatic space to non-kin individuals was subsequently favored by three elements that I only sketch here. The first element is the condition in which human beings lived for 99.5% of their evolutionary history: small groups (Baschetti 2007b); the latter are highly positive for the selection of altruistic traits, which are useful for the individual and her community (Baschetti 2007a).[1] The second element is the advent of agriculture, at about 10,000 years ago (representing 0.5% of our history), which brought about bigger groups and less competition for resources (Boyd and Richerson 2005: 225). The third element that promoted the enlargement of the individual's homeostatic space is the spread of commerce, which spurred cooperation not only within the community, but also among groups, as Joseph Heinrich and his colleagues showed. In their cross-cultural behavioral experiments, people from societies that were well integrated in the market donated the most in an anonymous Dictator Game.[2] Market integration was measured by the percentage of calories consumed by a family and obtained through market exchanges.[3]

If one of the main sides of morality comes from self-interested mechanisms, which are typical of the economic agent, and if commerce stimulates cooperation, why does the individual use others as means to her purposes in many occasions in the economic sphere?[4] I will try to answer this question by starting from the biological framework that I have just provided and then delving into two factors that contributed to the enlargement of the individual's homeostatic space: *empathy* and *mentalizing*.

The concealed social nature of the market

The market is a social sphere because the economic agent meets many people and relates to them in different roles, as a producer, consumer, supplier, and so on. In the marketplace, the agent depends on other people because the satisfaction of her personal interests always requires other people's abilities, work, and talents. As Thomas Nagel put in evidence, moral demands arise because others exist and do not want to be treated in certain ways (Nagel 1986: 165). Thus, even in economics, the question concerning that which the agent owes to others or how she should treat them becomes concrete.

According to the process of the natural extension of homeostasis that I have described, the individual should gradually include her customers or sellers in her homeostatic space. In reality, this does not happen; the reason is two particular features of social relationships in the marketplace. The first characteristic consists in the fact that the meetings between the economic agents are driven by self-interest, which is commonly conceived in economics as the maximization of one's utility expressed by one's own preferences (Briggs 2017). In addition, the economic agent sometimes maximizes her utility by taking advantage of others, that is to say, using them as means to her own aims (Sandel 2012). The second feature is the fact that the majority of people encountered in the economic sphere are strangers, especially in our contemporary world: we have often never met the other agents before the transaction, we do not deepen their acquaintance during the process, and we will never meet them again after its conclusion. Moreover, as in our globalized economy transactions are often anonymous and indirect, we do not really encounter people and know their needs. These two characteristics of the market have one thing in common: they make it more difficult to empathize and mentalize with the other, which are two mechanisms enabling the agent to identify herself with the other.

Mentalizing or theory of mind is the capacity to attribute mental states to other people, by representing their intentions, beliefs, and aims. Empathy is the capacity to perceive the emotions of others by sharing these emotions; it can be stimulated even by the perception of unknown people's feelings and it is automatic in the sense that it does not require efforts to activate but it can be inhibited by the individual (Singer and Tusche 2014: 516–17; Singer and Lamm 2009: 81, 83).

From a biological and evolutionary perspective, empathy and mentalizing were pivotal in the enlargement of our homeostatic space. In fact, taking care of others means primarily understanding how others are, i.e. recognizing their needs, intentions, and aims in order to foresee their conduct, and distinguishing that which causes them pain from that which releases it and the different types of suffering that involve different corrective actions (Preston and de Waal 2001). Moreover, if an individual, e.g. a mate or a baby, is part of another individual's homeostatic space, empathy strengthens the closeness of the two individuals because it enables the latter individual to feel emotions very similar to those that the former individual is directly experiencing. Empathy has made mammals quicker and more efficient in the care of their offspring. For instance, if a baby is in a painful situation, first of all, its mother is strongly motivated to cease its pain, because she feels a similar sensation for herself (Churchland 2011: 152–3) through basic mechanisms of empathy and emotional contagion;[5] secondly, the mother is able to discern the baby's type of pain and she takes a suitable corrective action.

At the most abstract level, which is only possessed by humans, mentalizing and empathy are used to adopt the other's point of view and to imagine what the other thinks, feels, and wants (Decety and Lamm 2006: 1151). Imagination extends the reach of empathy and mentalizing, because it enables the individual to adopt the perspective of unknown people. However, the sharing of emotions is easier when people are closer to us, because of an affective proximity (for instance, they are our relatives) or because of a spatial nearness (for instance, we are looking at them) (Singer and Tusche 2014).

In the marketplace, the majority of people the economic agent encounters are not close to her because of kin relations or direct perception. It is only when the economic agent puts herself deliberately in the other's shoes that she realizes that the other is similar to her. In fact, once the other's perspective is taken, the economic agent sees that the other is in the marketplace for the same reason – pursuing her own interests – and that if cheated or mistreated, the other would react in the same way as the economic agent would, if the latter were cheated or mistreated. In other words, the economic agent realizes that the other is another herself.

According to Kant, being an end in itself means having a value that cannot be derived from another source. Being an end in itself is the opposite of being a means, namely having a value for other purposes because some other value has conferred to this means a value for other purposes (Kant 1785: 56–7). The philosophical concept of being an end in itself can be linked with the biological notion of homeostasis: the agent's entire brain and body are set to self-preservation, so being an end in itself is self-evident to her and she has a natural tendency towards preserving herself.[6] Differently, the other becomes an end in itself for the agent, when the agent identifies herself with the other and discovers that the other is similar to her. Therefore, mentalizing and empathy are fundamental starting points in making the agent aware that others are another herself. These two mechanisms – especially the abstract forms of empathy and mentalizing which are based on imagination – are the means of including distant individuals into one's own homeostatic space.

Certainly, the care of the other, once the agent realizes that the other is another herself, assumes different tones, depending on the relationship between the other and the agent. The homeostatic space is not homogeneous: from the agent's perspective, the care of herself and of the people closest to her is always more urgent. However, the identification with unknown individuals makes the agent aware that these strangers are ends in themselves; this acknowledgment prevents her from using others as means, and this is a form of care-taking.

In the economic sphere, the anonymous and indirect transactions with strangers and the predominant motive of self-interest hinder the process by which the economic agent identifies herself with the other, because they conceal the social nature of the market. In fact, in a context of anonymous and indirect transactions with strangers, we do not see the other and her needs, because in reality we do not encounter her. Hence, the mechanisms of empathy and mentalizing are more difficult to activate, and these people cannot be included in our homeostatic space. Concerning the predominant motive of self-interest in the economic sphere, if the agent is completely absorbed by her interests and gives the fulfillment of them the absolute priority, then the care of herself overrides the care of others, so that the agent does not open herself to the perspective of others. Hence, in this case too, the agent does not really encounter others, because if she does not put herself in their shoes, there is no mechanism of identification with others that prevents her from treating them as means to her ends. Following the Kantian definition, in this latter case, the other has no intrinsic value for the economic agent; the only value that the other possesses is conferred by the economic agent and is serving the economic agent's aims.

The main elements of Smith's moral psychology

So far I have shown that in our evolution the care of others comes from the care of oneself and that empathy and mentalizing help the individual to take care of others because they indicate how others are, their feelings, needs, and thoughts. In addition, empathy strengthens the link between the empathizer and the other because it is a sharing of emotions. This biological framework that I have applied to the relationships in the marketplace is very similar to the moral psychology described by Smith in the "Theory of Moral Sentiments". Smith's descriptions of the common principles of human nature, i.e. the characteristics that are common to all humans, is perfectly consistent with the processes of empathy, mentalizing, and the enlargement of the sphere which the individual takes care of.[7] Also, Smith had already determined that it is easier to empathize with people close to us, such as relatives and friends, and for this reason he affirms that the market is not the place where relations are based on benevolence.[8]

I propose the adoption of the Smithian concept of prudence as a norm of conduct that could reduce the concealed social nature of the market. Smith does not use prudence for this purpose. However, prudence is a good candidate to reconcile the economic agent and the moral agent in the economic domain because prudence guarantees that others are ends in themselves and prevents that they are treated as means in both the moral and the economic sphere. Smith never uses the expression "end in itself", but he conveys the same idea when he says that "in the great chess-board of human society, every single piece has a principle of motion of its own"[9] and nobody can interfere with this motion. In addition, he states that when an individual thinks that other people may be sacrificed at any time at her convenience, her conduct is a form of unreasonable and absurd self-love and a gross injustice.[10]

In order to understand the worth and usefulness of prudence with regards to the relationship between the economic agent and the other, I will outline the Smithian moral psychology, which also clarifies the similarity with the biological framework of the origin of the care of others. According to Smith, human beings are multidimensional agents, that is to say they are driven by various natural principles that motivate their actions.[11] Among these principles, there is the care of oneself and the care of others. The care of oneself is morally inferior to the care of others because it is easier for the agent to look after her own interests,[12] since her sensations are more intense than the emotions of others and directly felt. *Sympathy*, which is the Smithian antecedent of empathy, is the mechanism that prevents individuals from being doomed to the neat separation one from another and from being insensible to one another's feelings.[13] Sympathy is "our fellow-feeling with any passion whatever";[14] in other words, it is the feeling of participation for the passion felt by the agent observed by another individual, through an imaginary change of place between the observer and the agent.[15] The first individual approves of the other, only if, once she has put herself in the other's place, she imagines what she herself would feel in that situation and finds that her emotions are similar to the agent's. If sympathy occurs, the agent's conduct is justified. By contrast, if the observer does not manage to sympathize with the agent, she does not approve the latter's behavior, which is not therefore correct or justified.[16]

When the agent assesses her own conduct, the mechanism is similar but another device is introduced: the *impartial spectator*.[17] The individual divides herself into the I-agent that has to be examined, and the I-examiner or judge.[18] The I-examiner is an imaginary spectator who has to be impartial, even though it is difficult for the agent not to be influenced by her passions and involvement in the situation. The impartial spectator is based on the introjection of the real observers whom the individual has encountered during her life, and of her reflection upon how a spectator is ideally impartial. The agent considers her behavior justified only if, by putting herself in the impartial spectator's place, she feels that her emotions as an agent are similar to those of the ideal observer.[19]

Smithian prudence and its role in respecting the other's being an end in itself in the economic domain

The Smithian virtue of prudence is "[t]he care of the health, of the fortune, of the rank and reputation of the individual, the objects upon which his comfort and happiness in this life are supposed principally to depend".[20] Prudence is self-centered because it is about individual interest, but not every goal deriving from self-interest is an expression of the virtue of prudence. Self-interest cannot be a norm or principle of conduct not because it is always immoral, but because human beings pursue their own interests by nature. The normative constituent of prudence that makes it a norm of conduct and a moral virtue is *self-command*. Self-command is the ability to be master of oneself, namely to be able to control or regulate one's own passions to a level that can be approved of by other people and/or the impartial spectator.[21] In Smith's moral system, all virtues are founded on self-command because the latter enables the individual to do her duty by restraining the passions that may mislead her. The perfect knowledge of the moral rules is not sufficient to undertake a moral action because passions often divert the agent's attention from her duties or even make her act against her duties.[22] Smithian prudence is tightly connected with the impartial spectator and sympathy via self-command. In fact, when the agent values her conduct and adopts the other's perspective through imagination, she realizes that her interests are not so overriding compared to those of the other.[23] When the individual enters into the impartial spectator's perspective, again through imagination, she comprehends she is one among many, whose projects and interests are as important as those of the others.[24] So she concludes that she is not justified to follow her passions and to pursue her aims without considering others and their feelings. This does not mean that the agent should suppress her self-interested passions, rather she should control them to a level which can be shared by hypothetical and/or real observers. This level consists in satisfying her own interests without using others for her purposes.[25] In order to not use others for her purposes, when pursuing self-interested aims, the agent should consider the perspective and feelings of the impartial spectator and that of the people she meets in the marketplace and can mistreat.[26] Hence, prudence restores the social nature of the market that is threatened by the anonymous transactions among strangers and the predominance of self-interest by stimulating the identification of the economic agent with other individuals.

In the case of anonymous transactions, if the economic agent follows the norm of prudence in her economic exchanges, then the adoption of the other party's perspective makes her realize that behind that anonymous transaction there is another economic agent with her own aims and interests. Imagination compensates for the impossibility to directly perceive the other, and when the agent manages to carry out the change of place, the transaction becomes less anonymous and more social. Even though the encounter between the two parties is imaginative, it is enough to awaken in the economic agent the awareness that the other is an end in itself. This is possible because the change of perspective is an abstract form of sympathy, in the sense that the economic agent perceives herself to be similar to the other agent in the change of perspective. The similarity does not consist in sharing the same interests and aims – in fact an economic exchange is usually made of contrasting interests among competing participants – but in the fact that for both agents, one's own survival and well-being are interests that each of them wants to pursue and they are in the market just for this purpose. In addition, both parties are similar because each one's actions can affect and hinder the other party's interests. These elements are what the economic agent and the other share with each other in the abstract form of sympathy.

In the case of the predominance of self-interest that renders the individual only devoted to its pursuit, if the economic agent adopts the norm of prudence, then when she puts herself in the other's place, from this position she cannot approve of a behavior that uses the other as a means to her own aims. This is because from this new perspective the economic agent assumes the other's interests and goals and acknowledges that the other is an end in itself. Even in this case, this is due to an abstract form of sympathy, namely the economic agent's acknowledgment to be similar to the other.

In both the cases of anonymous transactions and prevalence of self-interest, the economic agent introduces moral considerations, i.e. treating others as ends in themselves, into her economic decisions driven by self-interest. Therefore, prudence shows that the economic agent can be at the same time a moral agent: on the one hand, prudence is a norm that respects the care of herself and guarantees the pursuit of her personal interests; on the other hand, it opens the economic agent to the care of others.

Certainly, it could be objected that Smithian prudence can be used for motives of self-interest: in order to reach one's own aim, sympathy, empathy, and mentalizing can be devices to predict others' actions and to gain advantage from the prediction. However, when the agent identifies herself with other agents or the impartial spectator, she cannot approve of a behavior that treats others as means. In Smith's words:

> [i]n the race for wealth, and honours, and preferments, [the agent] may run as hard as he can, and strain every nerve and every muscle, in order to outstrip all his competitors. But if he should justle, or throw down any of them, the indulgence of the spectators is entirely at an end.[27]
>
> (TMS II.ii.2.1: 83)

In addition, if the economic agent considers what she would feel if she were in the other's place and would be treated as a means, she undoubtedly would not approve of such a treatment.

The similarity between the extension of the individual's homeostatic space and Smith's moral psychology resides in the fact that Smithian prudence is the starting point of a system based on an enlargement of spheres that the agent looks after, through different virtues. This system starts with the care of oneself, which is pursued through prudence; then, by means of an extension of prudence and by means of beneficence, the care extends to closer people, such as relatives, friends, and also partners in trade;[28] society follows, again through beneficence and also justice;[29] finally, the care-taking extends to all human beings by means of benevolence.[30]

The moral usefulness of prudence in the economic sphere: guiding the agent's economic action by balancing personal interests and the interests of others

The consideration of the feelings of other people and of the impartial spectator restrains the economic agent's self-interest, and only within this limit is self-interest a proper care of oneself, namely it is prudence. According to Smith, as proper care of oneself, prudence is justified in ethics, as well as in economics. In the latter sphere, prudence is not only justified but also highly regarded because it stirs a capitalist economy; Smith states that prudence is "of all the virtues that which is most useful to the individual".[31] Thus, the effort to adopt prudence as a norm of conduct in economic transactions is compensated by the economic advantages that prudence brings about. According to Smith, prudence is economically profitable because, since it is focused on the agent's well-being and possessions, it tends to preserve this condition, and thus it gives priority to the increase of savings over risky economic ventures. Moreover, self-command – which is the normative part of prudence – enables the agent to sacrifice a present pleasure for a likely greater satisfaction in the future.[32] This is a very useful conduct in the economic sphere because it enables the storage of capitals not for present consumption, but as an investment in the economic cycle,[33] which will, in turn, increase savings. Finally, by avoiding the use of others for one's own purposes, prudence promotes a pacific society, which is always favorable in economic exchanges.[34]

While Smith points out the economic value of prudence for the agent, I want to stress the moral worth of prudence for economics. Prudence has shown to restore the social nature of the market. Beyond this, prudence is a fundamental resource in guiding transactions and encounters in the marketplace in the frequent case in which one's own personal interests conflict with demands deriving from others. The economic agent's acknowledgment that the market is a place of morality inhabited by ends in themselves, is only the first step towards the reconciliation of her economic side with her moral side. The next step concerns how to balance personal interests and the interests of others. In fact, on the one hand, if the economic agent extends her personal interests and demands too far, the doubt that she is not doing her duty could arise and this, in turn, brings about a feeling of guilt and inadequacy. On the other hand, if she often sacrifices her interests in favor of others, then she becomes alienated from herself and considers her own existence as less life-worthy. In both cases, the conflicting nature of personal interests and the interests of others makes the agent think that a moral life is rarely a good life, because in the first case the sense of inadequacy and the doubts regarding to which extent she should care about others generate negative feelings, such as guilt or regret; in the second case others' interests frustrate one's own plans.[35]

The capacity of prudence to guide the economic agent in case of conflict between personal interests and the interests of others is based on the degree of development of one's own impartial spectator and on the ability to sympathize with other people. This means that in the same context, with the same people, two different agents could be demanded different duties, that is, different levels of taking care of others, which correspond to their own different impartial spectators and ability to sympathize. The impartial spectator is a creation of the agent, based on her experiences with real spectators and on her reflection on her personal actions and those of others. Therefore, the impartial spectator corresponds to the agent's degree of moral maturation and he *tends* towards impartiality, he is not perfectly impartial. In fact, Smith likens the impartial spectator to a demigod, because

> [w]hen his judgments are steadily and firmly directed by the sense of praise-worthiness and blame-worthiness, he seems to act suitably to his divine extraction, but when he suffers himself to be astonished and confounded by the judgments of ignorant and weak man, he discovers his connexion with mortality, and appears to act suitably, rather to the human, than to the divine, part of his origin.
>
> (TMS III.2.32: 131)

The impartial spectator enables the agent to balance her personal interests together with those of the others in a very personal way: what a given individual owes to another depends on the former individual's ability to identify herself with the other and with a spectator tending to be impartial, and on the ability to enter into their feelings and thoughts. An example regarding one of the most difficult contexts in which one should sympathize may clarify the usefulness of prudence in guiding one's own behavior: the allocation of scarce resources between contemporary people and posterity. In this case, the identification with the other is not easy because future generations are not directly perceptible. In addition, when judging her own actions towards posterity, the individual should have elaborated an inner spectator who is rather impartial and acknowledges that the posterity is an end in itself. If some individuals cannot put themselves into posterity's shoes and sympathize with their feelings of discomfort in living in a polluted environment, prudence does not require them to reduce their energy consumption or choose renewable energies. This is because the moral development of these individuals is so immature that they do not empathize and mentalize with posterity and thus they owe nothing to posterity. Similarly, the impartial spectator of these individuals is not enough impartial to acknowledge the demand to be respected as ends in themselves coming from future generations. Therefore, prudence is a norm of conduct whose content coevolves with the individual's moral maturation.

The adoption of prudence as a normative principle of action has the positive effect of limiting the agent's fragmentation between the care for others and the care for herself, her interests, projects, and desires. When the agent takes a self-interested decision, prudence always suggests to her to justify her personal interests by verifying if the impartial spectator sympathizes with her, a process that is equal to setting a deontological burden on her personal interests. Similarly, when the agent takes a decision involving the interests of others, she does not neglect her personal interests, because prudence is first of all a care of oneself, since "every man is certainly, in every respect, fitter and abler to take care of himself than of any other person. Every man knows his own pleasures and his own pains more sensibly than those of other people".[36]

Conclusion

Human beings are biologically equipped with the tendency to take care of others, which results in an enlargement of the individual's homeostatic space. This homeostatic space has its center in the individual's care of herself, but in mammals it has extended far beyond the individual.

However, in the marketplace, the natural tendency to take care of others is curbed. Smithian prudence can compensate for the lack of this tendency in the market because it represents the enforcement of two processes that are the biological bases of the care of others: empathy and mentalizing. Prudence induces the agent to adopt the other's perspective and to mentalize and sympathize with the other at a very abstract level, through imagination, even though this process is not simple and requires effort and many attempts.

Prudence is a useful norm of conduct in the economic sphere because it supports the agent in recognizing that the other is another herself and thus an end in itself. Furthermore, prudence is worthy in economics because it guides the economic agent in balancing personal interest and the interests of others, which often conflict. In this way, prudence preserves the agent's integrity, since it puts her care for others into contact and not into opposition with the care for herself. The result is that the individual who follows the norm of prudence can be at the same time an economic agent and a moral agent.

Notes

1 By "altruistic traits" I mean the individual's costly behavior that increases another individual's well-being and that thus represents a form of care of others.
2 In the Dictator Game there are two players, A and B. Player A receives an amount of money and has to decide how to divide it between herself and player B, then player B receives player A's offer.
3 See for example Henrich and Boyd (2005) and Henrich et al. 2010 (corrected 2011).
4 Sandel (2012) described many examples of treating the other as a means in the market.
5 Emotional contagion is the tendency to be influenced by another individual's emotional state without awareness of this influence. See Singer and Lamm (2009: 83).
6 In the relation between homeostasis, self-preservation, and being an end in itself, the boundary between the descriptive level that explains how humans are and the normative level that states how they should be, cannot be clearly distinguished. In other words, being an end in itself is something that the individual could respect or, if she accepts to be treated as a means, could not. Thus, being an end in itself is more linked to the normative level, but in humans there is an inclination towards respecting their being ends in themselves that is prompted by their natural tendency to self-preservation. Self-preservation is nearer to the descriptive level than being an end in itself, but, even if it is more difficult, the agent can refuse to follow this tendency, as well (for instance, committing suicide or letting herself die). Self-preservation is the aim of homeostasis which is the element more linked to the descriptive level, since the agent cannot alter this setting of her body and brain.
7 Smith, "The Theory of Moral Sentiments" (from hence TMS), 1759–1790, I.i.1.1–6: 9–11; II.i.5.10: 77–8. VI.ii.1–3: 219–37.
8 Smith, "An Inquiry into the Nature and Causes of the Wealth of Nations" (from hence WN), 1776–1789, I. ii.2: 26–7 and TMS VI.ii.1.1–2: 219.
9 TSM VI.ii.2.17, quot.: 234.
10 TSM II.iii.1.5: 96.
11 TMS VII.ii.3.18: 305.
12 TMS VI.ii.1.1: 219.
13 TMS I.i.1.2: 9. For a detailed account of the concept of sympathy, see Broadie (2006: 163–79; 2009: 200–13); Carrasco (2012b); Griswold (1999, ch. 2); Otteson (2013: 424–9); Raphael (2007, ch. 2); and Heath (1995).
14 TMS I.i.5, quot.: 10.
15 TMS VII.iii.1.4: 317.
16 TMS I.i.3.1: 16–17.
17 For a detailed account of the concept of the impartial spectator, see Broadie (2006: 179–86; 2009: 213–17); Griswold (1999: 129–46); Macfie (1967, ch. 5); and Raphael (2007, chs. 5, 6).
18 TMS III.1.6: 113.
19 TMS III.1.2: 109–10.
20 TMS VI.i.5, quot.: 213.
21 For a detailed study of self-command in Smith's system, see Carrasco (2012a); Montes (2004: 76–86, 110–13); and Vivenza (2001: 57–61).
22 TMS VI.iii.1–3, 11: 237–38, 241.
23 TMS II.ii.2.1: 82–3.
24 TMS III.3.4: 137.
25 TMS II.iii.1.5: 96; III.3.4: 136–7.
26 TMS VI.concl.1: 262.

27 See also WN IV.ix.51: 687 and Calkins and Werhane (1998: 56).
28 TMS VI.ii.1.2–22: 219–27.
29 TMS VI.ii.2.1–18: 227–34; II.ii.3.3–4: 86.
30 TMS VI.ii.3.1–6: 235–7.
31 TMS IV.2.6 quot.: 189.
32 TMS VI.i.11: 215.
33 WN II.iii.14–18: 337–38.
34 See Den Uyl (1991: 131–2).
35 See Williams (1976) and Nagel (1986, ch. 9).
36 TMS VI.ii.1.1, quot.: 219.

Bibliography

Baschetti, R. (2007a) 'The dawn of science-based moral reasoning', *Medical Hypotheses*, 68 (1): 4–8.

Baschetti, R. (2007b) 'Evolutionary, neurobiological, gene-based solution of the ideological "puzzle" of human altruism and cooperation medical hypotheses', *Medical Hypotheses*, 69 (2): 241–49.

Bell, D.C. (2001) 'Evolution of parental caregiving', *Personality & Social Psychology Review*, 3 (5): 216–29.

Boyd, R. and Richerson, P.J. (2005) *Not by Genes Alone: How Culture Transformed Human Evolution*, Chicago: University of Chicago Press.

Briggs, R. (2017) 'Normative theories of rational choice: Expected utility', in E.N. Zalta (ed.) *The Stanford Encyclopedia of Philosophy*. Available HTTP: <https://plato.stanford.edu/archives/spr2017/entries/rationality-normative-utility/> (accessed 10 September 2017).

Broadie, A. (2006) 'Sympathy and the impartial spectator', in K. Haakonsen (ed.) *The Cambridge Companion to Adam Smith*, New York: Cambridge University Press.

Broadie, A. (2009) *A History of Scottish Philosophy*. Edinburgh: Edinburgh University Press.

Calkins, M.J. and Werhane, P.H. (1998) 'Adam Smith, Aristotle, and the virtues of commerce', *The Journal of Value Inquiry*, 32 (1): 43–60.

Carrasco, M.A. (2012a) 'Adam Smith: Self-command, practical reason and deontological insights', *British Journal for the History of Philosophy*, 20 (2): 391–414.

Carrasco, M.A. (2012b) 'From psychology to moral normativity', *The Adam Smith Review*, 6: 9–29.

Carter, C.S., Harri, J. and Porges, S.W. (2009) 'Neural and evolutionary perspectives on empathy', in J. Decety and W. Ickes (eds.) *The Social Neuroscience of Empathy*, Cambridge and London: MIT Press, ch. 13.

Churchland, P.S. (2011) *Braintrust: What Neuroscience Tells Us about Morality*, Princeton, NJ: Princeton University Press.

Damasio, A.R. (2005) 'The neurobiological grounding of human values', in J.P. Changeaux, A.R. Damasio, W. Singer, and Y. Christen (eds.) *Neurobiology of Human Values*, Berlin and New York: Springer.

Decety, J. and Lamm, C. (2006) 'Human empathy through the lens of social neuroscience', *The Scientific World Journal*, 6: 1146–63.

Den Uyl, D.J. (1991) *The Virtue of Prudence*, New York: Peter Lang.

Griswold, C.L. Jr. (1999) *Adam Smith and the Virtues of Enlightenment*, Cambridge: Cambridge University Press.

Heath, E. (1995) 'The commerce of sympathy: Adam Smith on the emergence of morals', *Journal of the History of Philosophy*, 33 (3): 447–66.

Henrich, J. and Boyd, R. (2005) '"Economic Man" in cross-cultural perspective: Behavioral experiments in 15 small-scale societies', *Behavioral and Brain Sciences*, 28: 795–855.

Henrich, J., Ensminger, J., McElreath, R., Barr, A., Barrett, C., Bolyanatz, A., Cardenas, J.C., Gurven, M., Gwako, E., Henrich, N., Lesorogol, C., Marlowe, F., Tracer, D. and Ziker, J., (2010; corrected 2011) 'Market, religion, community size, and the evolution of fairness and punishment', *Science*, 327: 480–84.

Herzog, L. (2017) 'Markets', in E.N. Zalta (ed.) *The Stanford Encyclopedia of Philosophy*. Available HTTP: <https://plato.stanford.edu/entries/markets/> (accessed 10 September 2017).

Kant, I. (1785; 2002) 'Groundwork of the metaphysic of morals', in L. Pasternack (ed.) *Immanuel Kant: Groundwork of the Metaphysic of Morals in Focus*, London and New York: Routledge.

Keverne, E.B. (2004) 'Understanding well-being in the evolutionary context of brain development', *Philosophical Transaction of the Royal Society of London B: Biological Science*, 359: 1349–58.

Macfie, A.L. (1967) *The Individual in Society: Papers on Adam Smith*, London: George Allen & Unwin Ltd.

Moll, J. and Krueger, F. (2006) 'Human fronto-mesolimbic networks guide decisions about charitable donation', *Proceedings of the National Academy of Sciences of the United States of America*, 42 (103): 15623–28.

Montes, L. (2004) *Adam Smith in Context: A Critical Reassessment of Some Central Components of His Thought*, New York: Palgrave Macmillan.

Nagel, T. (1986) *The View from Nowhere*, Oxford: Oxford University, Press, chs 9, 10.

Otteson, J.R. (2013) 'Adam Smith', in R. Crisp (ed.) *The Oxford Handbook of the History of Ethics*, Oxford: Oxford University Press.

Preston, S.D. and de Waal, F.B.M. (2001) 'Empathy: Its ultimate and proximate bases', *Behavioral and Brain Sciences*, 25 (1): 1–20.

Raphael, D.D. (2007) *The Impartial Spectator: Adam Smith's Moral Philosophy*, New York: Oxford University Press.

Sandel, M. (2012) *What Money Can't Buy: The Moral Limits of Markets*, London: Allen Lane.

Singer, T. and Lamm, C. (2009) 'The social neuroscience of empathy', *Annals of the New York Academy of Sciences*, 1156: 81–96.

Singer, T. and Tusche, A. (2014) 'Understanding others: Brain mechanisms of theory of mind and empathy', in P.W. Glimcher and E. Fehr (eds.) *Neuroeconomics: Decision Making and the Brain: Second Edition*, London: Academic Press.

Smith, A. (1776–1789; 1976a) 'An inquiry into the nature and causes of the wealth of nations', in R.H. Campbell and A.S. Skinner (eds.) *The Glasgow Edition of the Works and Correspondence of Adam Smith*, vol. II, Oxford: Clarendon Press.

Smith, A. (1759–1790; 1976b) 'The theory of moral sentiments', in D.D. Raphael and A.L. Macfie (eds.) *The Glasgow Edition of the Works and Correspondence of Adam Smith*, vol. I, Oxford: Clarendon Press.

Vivenza, G. (2001) *Adam Smith and the Classics: The Classical Heritage in Adam Smith's Thought*, New York: Oxford University Press.

Williams, B. (1976) 'Persons, character, and morality', in A. Rorty (ed.) *The Identities of Persons*, Berkeley and Los Angeles: University of California Press.

Part III

Analytical part

The Individual and the Other in modern economic analysis

14 Perfect Prediction Equilibrium

Ghislain Fourny, Stéphane Reiche and Jean-Pierre Dupuy

Introduction

In non-cooperative game theory, one of the most common equilibrium concepts is the Subgame Perfect Equilibrium (SPE) (Selten 1965), a refinement of the Nash Equilibrium (Nash 1951). The SPE is defined for dynamic games with perfect information, which are mostly represented in their extensive form.

The extensive form represents the game as a tree where each node corresponds to the choice of a player, and each leaf to a possible outcome of the game associated with a payoff distribution. This embodies a Leibnizian account of rational choice in a possible-worlds system. The SPE is obtained by backward induction, i.e. by first choosing at the leaves (in the future) and going backward to the root.

While the Nash equilibrium is widely accepted by the game theory community, there is also a large consensus that it does not account for all real-life scenarios. This is because people do not always act rationally in situations where their emotions impact their decisions, but also because different people may have different forms of rationality, Nash describing one of them. The Perfect Prediction Equilibrium (PPE), presented in this paper, is based on a different form of rationality that straightforwardly solves the classical problem of the time-inconsistency of a Pareto-optimal plan, such as arises in the case of keeping a commitment.

Two forms of rationality

A crucial assumption made by the Nash equilibrium in general and the SPE in particular is that each player considers the other player's strategy to be independent of their own strategy. Concretely, this means that the other player's strategy is held fixed while optimizing one's strategy. In the extensive form, it means that, at each node, the player whose turn it is to play considers that former moves (especially the other player's former moves) and her own current choice are independent of each other. Consequently, the past can be taken out of the picture and only the remaining subtree is used to decide on the current move. This motivates Backward Induction reasoning.

This line of reasoning is intuitive to many, because the past is causally independent of the future – which is supported by the fact that nothing has been observed in nature so far that would contradict it.

However, concluding that a rational player *must* make this assumption would be fallacious, as this relies on a confusion commonly made between causal dependency on one side, and counterfactual dependency on the other side. There are concrete examples of situations where two causally independent events are counterfactually dependent on each other. This is often referred to as a statistical dependency in physics (consider quantum measurements done on two entangled photons), and which is of a nature fundamentally different than that of causality.

The relationship between a move and its anticipation has been at the core of numerous discussions in game theory. There is an apparent conflict between a player's freedom to make any choice on the one hand, and the other player's skills at anticipating the moves of his opponent on the other hand.

The Nash equilibrium addresses this tension with the approach described a few paragraphs above. Though, having a different model on the relationship between the past moves and the current move can lead to a different form of rationality that is no less meaningful than the Nash equilibrium approach. A rational player could consider that her decisions are transparent to, and anticipated by former players, and, hence, that she might want to integrate into her reasoning the past's reaction to her anticipated current move. Concretely, this means that a player reasoning that way would think of her relationship with the past not through a Cournot-like competition (that would be the Nash reasoning), but rather through a Stackelberg-like competition (that would be the reasoning in this paper).[1]

Newcomb's problem (see Section "Newcomb's Problem") illustrates that both approaches (Cournot-like, Stackelberg-like) are commonly taken by people in the real world, and that people can feel very strong taking one side or the other. This problem sets up a very simple situation with an action in the past (predicting and filling boxes) and a move in the present (picking one or two boxes), and on purpose leaves open how they depend on each other. Newcomb's problem demonstrates that some people (the *two-boxers*) make the assumption that past actions are counterfactually independent of their own moves and use a dominant strategy, which corresponds to what could be called perfect rationality in its classical game-theoretical sense, or Nash-Perfect rationality (NPR) in this paper. It is based on a Cournot competition with the predictor. Maybe this explains why most game theoreticians are in this category. However, many other people (the *one-boxers*) consider that past actions and their own moves are counterfactually dependent – entangled. Making this assumption is no less rational, as their line of reasoning then comes down to optimizing their utility as well, with a Stackelberg view of the relationship with the predictor's action.

This Stackelberg competition with the past by no means takes away the agents' freedom to make decisions, nor does it break the laws of physics: the dependency with the past is purely based on counterfactual reasoning such as "If I were to make this move, the other player would have predicted it and acted in this other way." There is no such thing as a causal impact on the past or as changing the past.

We call this alternate form of rationality Perfect Prediction rationality (PPR).

Most equilibria in game theory are refinements of the Nash equilibrium. They account for the behavior of players that are Nash-Perfect-rational, while little work has been done for Perfect-Prediction-rational players. This paper introduces the solution concept corresponding to the equilibrium reached by Perfect-Prediction-rational players: The Perfect Prediction Equilibrium (PPE).

The assumptions

This paper defines a solution concept for games that are:

- In extensive form, i.e., the game is represented by an explicit tree, rather than by a flat set of strategies for each player; the game structure is Common Knowledge.
- With perfect information, meaning that for each choice they make, players know at which node they are in the tree.
- With strict preferences,[2] meaning that given two outcomes, players are never indifferent between those.
- Played by rational players, in its widely accepted meaning in game theory, i.e., they are logically smart and play to the best of their interests, preferences and knowledge with the goal of maximizing their utility. The player's rationality is Common Knowledge.
- Played by agents with Perfect Prediction rationality – that is, with a Stackelberg account of the past's reaction, which is the novelty of this paper. The Perfect Prediction rationality (PPR) of the players is Common Knowledge as well.

We are interested in games exclusively played by Perfect-Prediction-rational agents. Past moves are considered to be counterfactually dependent on the current player's move: Would a player play differently than he actually does, then it would be the rational thing to do, and the other player would have anticipated it. This leads to a form of Stackelberg competition where the current player considers the past's reaction function. The reaction function can be seen as literally reading each other's minds (or at least, as believing that the other player does so, which is sufficient). These players consider that there is Common Knowledge (CK) of the solution of the game: CK of the outcome of the game and of each other's thought processes. Hence, PPR can also be seen as the belief that the world is totally transparent, and that the players have as much knowledge as an omniscient external observer (Perfect Prediction).

Outline of the paper

In the remainder of this paper, and for the sake of a smooth read, we will consider, like the Perfect-Prediction-rational players, that it holds that the world is totally transparent and that there is CK of the solution (i.e., of all actual moves) of the game, embracing their account of the world. Our starting point is the question: *if there were an equilibrium which is totally transparent to itself, what would it be?*

Starting with the Perfect Prediction abilities (assumed by the players), two principles are postulated: a) Preemption, b) Rational Choice. Using these two principles, we can show that the equilibrium reached by Perfect-Prediction-rational players, and which we call Perfect Prediction Equilibrium (PPE), exists and is unique. Hence, this answers the question asked above: *assuming that there is an equilibrium totally transparent to itself, then it is necessarily the Perfect Prediction Equilibrium*. Furthermore, because of its uniqueness, the players, aware of the assumptions, are able to unambiguously calculate the PPE and react accordingly, which leads them to this very equilibrium and makes their prediction correct (self-fulfilling prophecy). This closes the loop: the PPE is totally transparent to itself.

In addition, the Perfect Prediction Equilibrium happens to have the property of Pareto optimality: there is no other outcome giving a better payoff to both players.

Hence, all conjectures (existence, uniqueness, Pareto optimality) made by Dupuy (2000) are proven in this paper for the PPE.

In Section "Perfect Prediction", we introduce Newcomb's problem as an illustration of the importance of assuming (or not) counterfactual independence. We then explain the relationship between total transparency and Perfect Prediction. We posit two principles, which we apply to some examples. In Section "Construction of the Perfect Prediction Equilibrium", we give the general definition of the PPE as well as its construction, and prove its existence, uniqueness and Pareto optimality. Finally, Section "Related work" gives links to existing literature on Superrationality, the Backward Induction Paradox, and Forward Induction.[3] In the annex, we provide more technical background for readers interested in deeper details, such as the analysis of the underlying preemption structure of the PPE, from which two algorithms can be derived to compute it. The annex also gives complementary material such as proofs of the lemmas and theorems, a complete analysis of biped games, and the equations behind the PPE.

Perfect prediction

Before giving the formal definition of the PPE and proving its properties, we focus on a few examples, explain the general semantics of Perfect Prediction and of the PPE, and show how it applies to these examples.

Examples used throughout this paper

There are three games used repeatedly as examples in this paper.

Take-or-leave game

The take-or-leave game is represented on Figure 14.1 and goes as follows: "A referee places dollars on a table one by one. He has only *n* dollars. There are two players who play in turn. Each player can either take the dollars that have accumulated so far, thereby ending the game, or leave the pot on the table, in which case the referee adds one dollar to it, and it's the other player's turn to move."

The original TOL game does not satisfy the strict preference assumption,[4] so that this example was slightly modified in such a way that the loser of the game still gets increasing payoffs. This does not modify its (inefficient as we will see) Subgame Perfect Equilibrium.

This type of game has often been used to describe the Backwards Induction Paradox in literature (see Section "The Backward Induction Paradox").

Assurance game

The assurance game (see Figure 14.2) models a basic, asynchronous, Pareto-improving exchange in economics (payoffs are utilities). The rule is as follows. First, Peter has the choice between deviating (D – both players get 0) and cooperating (C). If Peter cooperates, then Mary has the choice between cooperating as well (C), in which case both players get 1, and deviating (D), in which case Mary gets 2 and Peter gets −1.

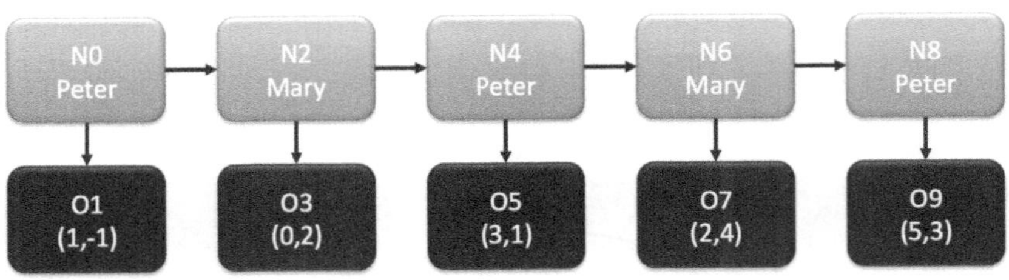

Figure 14.1 The take-or-leave game (n is odd)

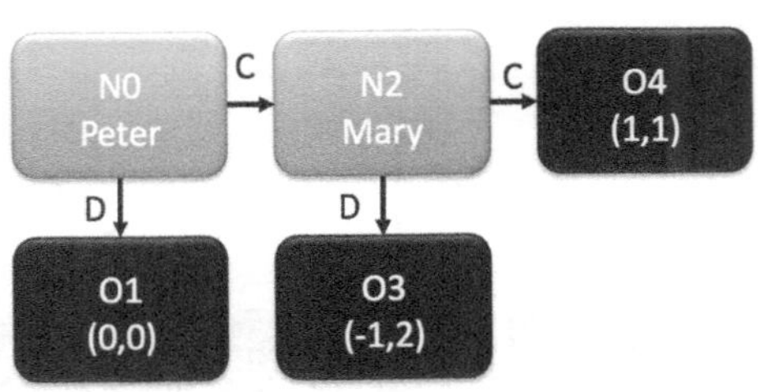

Figure 14.2 The assurance game

This can be interpreted as the possibility for Peter to trust Mary or not, and if he does trust her, Mary can choose to cooperate or not.

Γ-game

The *Γ*-game (see Figure 14.3) aims at demonstrating how the PPE is computed on a slightly more complex game. First, Peter has the choice between two nodes.

If he chooses n_1, then Mary chooses between two outcomes; if he chooses n_2, Mary chooses between two nodes and it is Peter's turn again. This game does not have a particular interpretation – it was simply designed for the reasoning to be interesting and to help the reader understand how the Perfect Prediction Equilibrium works on general trees.

Newcomb's problem

Newcomb's problem (Gardner 1973) is an illustration of how the concepts of prediction and decision interact, and a good starting point to introduce Perfect Prediction. In particular, it is a very good test for distinguishing between agents with two kinds of rationalities that differ by the correlation, or absence thereof, between prediction and decision. Historically, Newcomb's problem, through the research and literature around it, is actually at the origin of the discovery of these two kinds of rationalities, which is why, in this paper, we decided to call them Perfect Prediction rationality (PPR) and Nash-Perfect rationality (NPR), the latter being the one commonly accepted as game-theoretical perfect rationality.

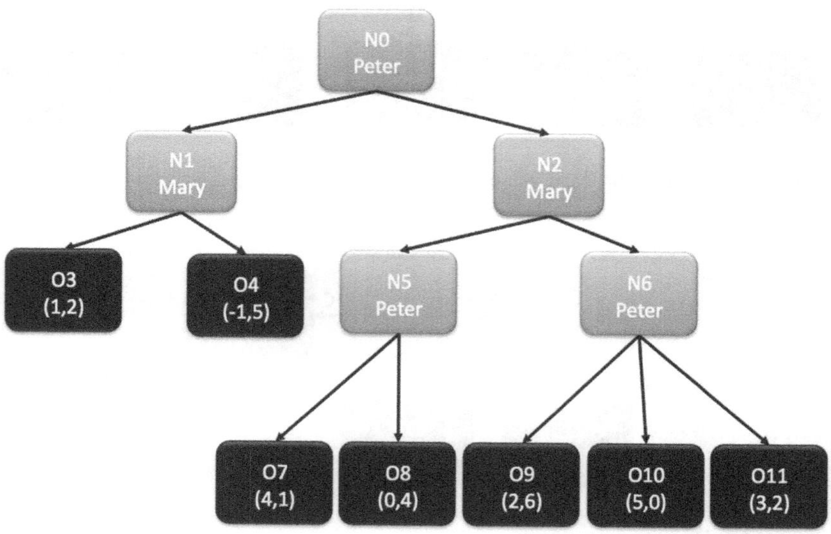

Figure 14.3 The Γ -game

Imagine two boxes. One, B, is transparent and contains a thousand dollars; the other, A, is opaque and contains either a million dollars or nothing at all. The choice of the agent is either C1: to take only what is in the opaque box, or C2: to take what is in both boxes. At the time that the agent is presented with this problem, a Predictor has already placed a million dollars in the opaque box if and only if he foresaw that the agent would choose C1. The agent knows all this, and he has very high confidence in the predictive powers of the Predictor. What should he do?

A first line of reasoning leads to the conclusion that the agent should choose C1. The Predictor will have foreseen it and the agent will have a million dollars. If he chose C2, the opaque box would have been empty and he would only have a thousand. The paradox is that a second line of reasoning (taken by most game theorists as it is consistent with Nash) appears to lead just as surely to the opposite conclusion. When the agent makes his choice, there is or there is not a million dollars in the opaque box: by taking both boxes, he will obviously get a thousand dollars more in either case. This second line of reasoning applies dominance reasoning to the problem, whereas the first line applies to it the principle of maximization of expected utility.

The paradox can be solved as follows (although, to be fair, there is to date no established consensus about it). Two-boxers assume that the choice and the prediction are *counterfactually* independent of each other. In other words, once the prediction is made, the choice is made independently and the prediction, which lies in the past, is held for fixed. Even if the prediction is correct (the player gets \$1,000), it *could have been made wrong* (she would have gotten \$0). One-boxers assume on the contrary that the prediction and the choice are *counterfactually* dependent. In other words, the prediction is correct (player gets \$1,000,000), and if the player had made the other choice, the predictor would have correctly anticipated this other choice as well (she would have gotten \$1,000).

One-boxers and two-boxers are both rational: they merely make different, not to say opposite, assumptions. This illustrates that there are at least two ways of being rational.

A probabilistic illustration along the same lines as this solution has recently been given by Wolpert and Benford (2013). Technically, counterfactual dependence means statistical dependence if events and decisions are seen as random variables. It is a symmetrical relation and ignores the arrow of time (unlike causal dependence).

The Subgame Perfect Equilibrium makes the ("two-boxer") assumption that decisions are counterfactually independent of the past. More generally, Nash Equilibria make the ("two-boxer") assumption that the other players' strategies are held fixed while a single player optimizes her strategy. Perfect Prediction Equilibria, on the other hand, relies on the "one-boxer" assumption of counterfactual dependency. In both cases, players are rational and maximize their utility to the best of their logical abilities. They are, however, rational in two different ways.

Transparency and perfect prediction

In classical game theory (Nash equilibrium), Nash-Perfect-rational agents know that they are rational, know that they know, etc. This is called common knowledge (CK) of rationality in literature. Common knowledge is a form of transparency. In the case of SPE, the possible futures are each considered by, and are transparent to, the current player, for him to decide on his next move.

However, this transparency does not hold the other way round. The player being *simulated* or *anticipated* in a possible future – first and foremost, in a subgame that is not actually on the path to the SPE – cannot be fully aware of the rest of the game (that is, of the overall SPE), as this knowledge would be in conflict with the fact of being playing in the subgame at hand. The past is opaque to her, meaning that she cannot be fully aware of the past thought processes. She simply assumes that the past leading to her subgame is fixed, and the other player knows that she does (CK of *NPR*). This is one-way transparency. A later section goes into more detail on what is known as the Backward Induction Paradox.

It goes otherwise for Perfect-Prediction-rational agents. In a game played by Perfect-Prediction-rational agents, there is common knowledge of rationality as well, in that players know (and know that they know, etc.) that they both react to their knowledge in their best interest. But there is more importantly CK of *PPR*, which means that a) each player considers themselves to be transparent to the *past*, in that they integrate this very CK of PPR in their reasoning and consider themselves to be predictable, and b) each player P considers themselves to be transparent to the *future* as well, in that they know that a future player F considers player P's moves to correlate (counterfactually) with their (F's) decision, whichever way F decides.

This more stringent form of transparency drastically changes the reasoning: since transparency goes both ways, the entire solution of the game (all thought processes, the equilibrium, etc.) is CK. In such a perfectly transparent world, each agent would have the same knowledge of the world as an external omniscient spectator, this fact being CK among the agents.[5] The players (profactually) predict the solution correctly, and would also have (counterfactually) predicted it correctly if it had been different. This is what we call Perfect Prediction. This different relation to time was called Projected Time (and the widespread relation to time Occurring Time) by Dupuy (2000).

Rather than considering all possible futures, the Perfect-Prediction-rational agents assume that there is one solution of the game that is CK, and based on this assumption, compute and find that very solution of the game that is CK. The players react to their CK of the outcome of the game, play accordingly and reach an outcome which is indeed the predicted outcome. This is nothing else than a fixpoint problem, which can be solved and which has a unique solution, as demonstrated in this paper.

A side effect of assuming CK of the game solution is that the construction of the equilibrium in this paper is supported by reasoning only on the equilibrium path. There is one timeline, and it is completely transparent to itself, by its definition as a fixpoint.

Two principles behind the computation of the Perfect Prediction Equilibrium

A Perfect Prediction Equilibrium is a path on the tree which can be reached under the assumption of total transparency, or, in other words, by Perfect-Prediction-rational players that genuinely believe that there is total transparency.

The computation of PPEs by the players or an external game theorist, which is the same, is done by eliminating outcomes of the game which lead to a contradiction (Grandfather Paradox),[6] i.e., which cannot possibly be commonly known as the equilibrium.

At each step of the reasoning, there is CK of the outcomes which are logically impossible (this is part of the thought process). Using this knowledge, it is possible to discard additional outcomes which cannot be commonly known as the equilibrium reached by the game, thanks to the two principles.

First principle

The CK of the outcomes which have been proven logically impossible as well as the assumed CK of the outcome o reached by the game give the players a power of preemption; a player will deviate from the path connecting the root too (we call this path *causal bridge*) if the deviation guarantees to him a better payoff than *o* (whatever the continuation of the game after the deviation can be, and taking into account that some outcomes have been proven logically impossible).

If such is the case, then *o*, which is not a fixpoint, cannot be commonly known as the solution and is logically impossible; it is said to be preempted.[7]

We call preemption this process of breaking the causal bridge in reaction to the anticipation of an outcome (see Figure 14.4).

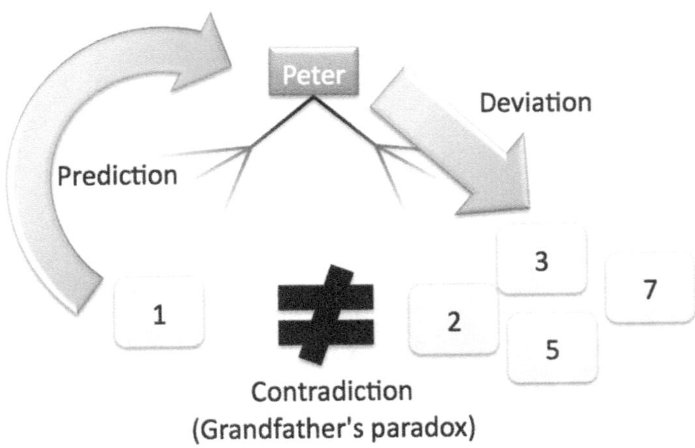

Figure 14.4 Illustration of the first principle

EXAMPLE 1

Let us take o_3 in the assurance game (Figure 14.2). There are no outcomes proven impossible yet. We assume that o_3 is the outcome eventually reached by the game, which is known to the players. For Peter playing at the root, a deviation from n_2 (which is on the path leading to o_3) to o_1 guarantees him a better payoff (0) than what he gets with o_3 (−1). This means that anticipating o_3, Peter deviates and breaks the causal bridge leading to o_3. Hence, o_3 cannot be the solution: it is not possible for Peter to predict o_3 *and* to play towards o_3. o_3 is preempted and is logically impossible. It can be ignored from now on.

EXAMPLE 2

In the Γ-game example, o_4 can also be discarded this way: For Peter playing at the root, a deviation from n_1 (which is on the path leading to o_4) guarantees him a better payoff (4, 0, 2, 5 or 3) than what he gets with o_4 (−1). o_4 is preempted and can also be ignored from now on.

Principle 1 *Let I be the set of the outcomes that have not been discarded yet. The discarded outcomes are ignored. Let n be a given node which is reached by the game and where player p is playing. Let o ∈ I be an outcome among the descendants of n. o is said to be preempted if all outcomes in one of the non-empty*[8] *subtrees at n, give to p a greater payoff than o. A preempted outcome is logically impossible, is hence discarded and must be ignored in the remainder of the reasoning.*

Second principle In the assurance game (Figure 14.2), given the knowledge that o_3 is logically impossible, Peter is faced with the choice between o_1, which gives him 0, and n_2, which gives him eventually for sure 1 since o_3 cannot be chosen. Because he is rational, he chooses n_2. This is the second principle (see Figure 14.5).

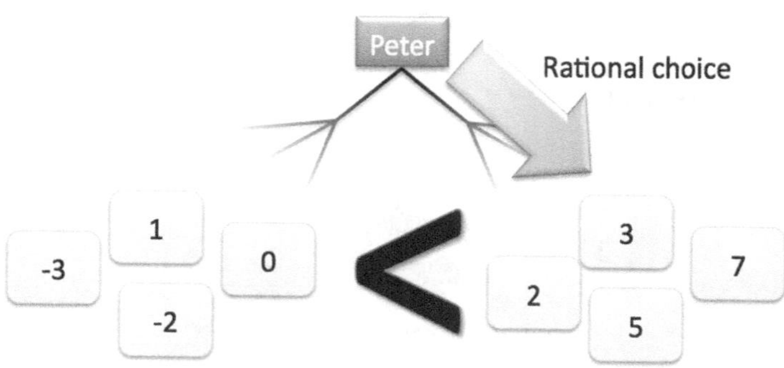

Figure 14.5 Illustration of the second principle

Principle 2 *Let I be the set of the outcomes that have not been discarded yet. The discarded outcomes are ignored. Let n be a given node which is reached by the game and where player p is playing. If all outcomes in one of the non-empty subtrees at n, of root r, are better than any other outcome in the other subtrees, then p chooses r. As a consequence, r is also reached by the game, and all remaining outcomes in other subtrees than the one at r are discarded.*

The second principle is only applicable if all outcomes on the one side are better than all outcomes on the other side. If the payoffs are "interlaced", it does not apply – but in this case, the first principle can be used instead.

Also, the second principle applies in the degenerate case where there is only one unique non-empty subtree. Then the player chooses this subtree.

The reasoning to the equilibrium

Based on the two principles, it is possible to build a system of first-order-logic equations for each game, as described in the annex (Section "Annex - the PPE as the solution of a first-order-logic equation system"). By definition, a PPE is a solution to this system. The equations are divided into three groups:

1 Application of the first principle
2 Application of the second principle
3 Causal bridge enforcement (i.e. an equilibrium must be a consistent path starting from the root).

This system can be solved with a technique which turns out to be a forward induction: one starts at the root, discards all outcomes preempted at this step with the first principle, then moves on to the next node – there is always exactly one – with the second principle (this node is now known to be reached by the game), discards all outcomes preempted at this step with the first principle, moves on to the next node with the second principle, etc., until an outcome is reached.

In the reasoning, the list of logically impossible outcomes is initially empty and grows until no more outcomes can be discarded. In fact, as will be proven in Section "Construction of the Perfect Prediction Equilibrium", under the assumption of strict preferences, exactly one outcome remains. The Perfect-Prediction-rational players have no interest in deviating from the path leading to it and will play towards it: it is the Perfect Prediction Equilibrium, which always exists and is unique.

This system of equations can be described formally, however for pedagogical reasons, from now on, we will reason directly by performing outcome eliminations.

The reasoning is totally transparent and can be performed, ahead of the game or without even playing, by a game theorist or any player, always leading to the same result. Actually, as the structure of the reasoning is a forward induction, it would even be possible to perform the reasoning *as you go* during the game.

Computation of the Perfect Prediction Equilibrium for the three examples

We now show how the forward induction reasoning described above can be applied to the examples.

Assurance game (Figure 14.2)

We begin at the root.

Being Perfect Predictors, the players at the root cannot predict o_3 as the final outcome because of the first principle: the prediction of o_3 would lead Peter to deviate at the root towards o_1, which invalidates this very prediction. We say that outcome o_3 has been preempted by the o_1 move. Therefore, outcome o_3 has been identified as not being part of the solution: it cannot be commonly known as the outcome reached by the equilibrium and is ignored from now on.

This can also be formulated as a reasoning in Mary's mind. She is Perfect-Prediction-rational. Mary includes Peter's past move as a reaction function to her choice between o_3 and o_4. Were she to pick o_3, Peter would have anticipated it as the rational thing for her to do – and he would have picked o_1. But this would be inconsistent with her playing at n_2. Since picking o_3 is correlated with a past reaction (to the anticipation of o_3) that is incompatible with o_3 (Grandfather Paradox), she cannot Perfect-Prediction-rationally pick o_3.

Now that o_3 is (identified as being) impossible, we are left with o_1 and o_4, and we can apply the second principle: Peter knows that Mary is Perfect-Prediction-rational and will not pick o_3. He can either move to o_1 and win 0, or move to n_2 and win 1. He chooses the latter[9] and n_2 is known to be reached by the game.

At n_2, Mary, according to a trivial application of the second principle (she can only choose o_4), moves to o_4, which is known to be reached by the game: it is the only remaining outcome. If there is an equilibrium, it is o_4.

Conversely, it is possible to check that this outcome corresponds to an equilibrium. Predicting o_4, Peter will not deviate: according to the second principle, he moves to n_2, i.e., towards o_4. Mary will not deviate either, since she cannot choose o_3, which is preempted. More precisely, she forbids to herself to pick o_3 because her reasoning as a Perfect-Prediction-rational player stamped it as an illogical move. Like a self-fulfilling prophecy, o_4 is reached by the game: it is the equilibrium (Figure 14.6).

Take-or-leave game (Figure 14.1)

The previous reasoning can easily be generalized to the take-or-leave game (Figure 14.1).

One begins at the root. The application of the first principle here leads to the preemption of o_3 because it would be in the interest of Peter to deviate at node n_0 towards o_1.

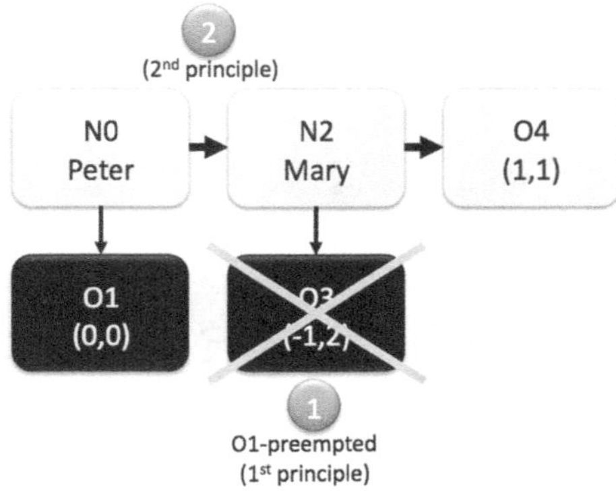

Figure 14.6 The Perfect Prediction Equilibrium in the assurance game

Then, knowing this, according to the second principle, Peter chooses n_2, since all remaining outcomes in this subtree are better (3, 2, 5) than o_1 (1), which is discarded.

At n_2, Mary has to take n_4 since o_3 was proven logically impossible (again, her line of reasoning as a Perfect-Prediction-rational player tells her that it would not be a rational choice).

Then the application of the first principle here leads to the preemption of o_7 because it would be in the interest of Peter to deviate at node n_4 towards o_5.

Then, knowing this, according to the second principle, Peter chooses n_6, since all remaining outcomes in this subtree are better (5) than o_5 (3), which is discarded.

At n_6, Mary has to take n_8 since o_7 was proven logically impossible.

At n_8, Peter chooses the remaining outcome o_9, which is the Perfect Prediction Equilibrium (Figure 14.7).

Γ-game (Figure 14.3)

In this game, the general technique for computing the Perfect Prediction Equilibrium becomes visible.

We start at the root, where the first principle leads to the preemption of o_4 (Peter would deviate to n_2 where all payoffs are higher than −1) and then to the preemption of o_8 (Peter would deviate to n_1 where all remaining payoffs are now higher than 0).

Since the payoffs are no longer interlaced, we can now apply the second principle. Peter chooses n_2 (remaining payoffs: 2, 3, 4, 5) over n_1 (1): n_2 is now known to be reached by the game, o_3 is discarded (see Figure 14.8).

At n_2 (where the only remaining outcomes are o_7, o_9, o_{10} and o_{11}), we apply the first principle with Mary: o_{10} is preempted (Mary would deviate to n_5). Then the

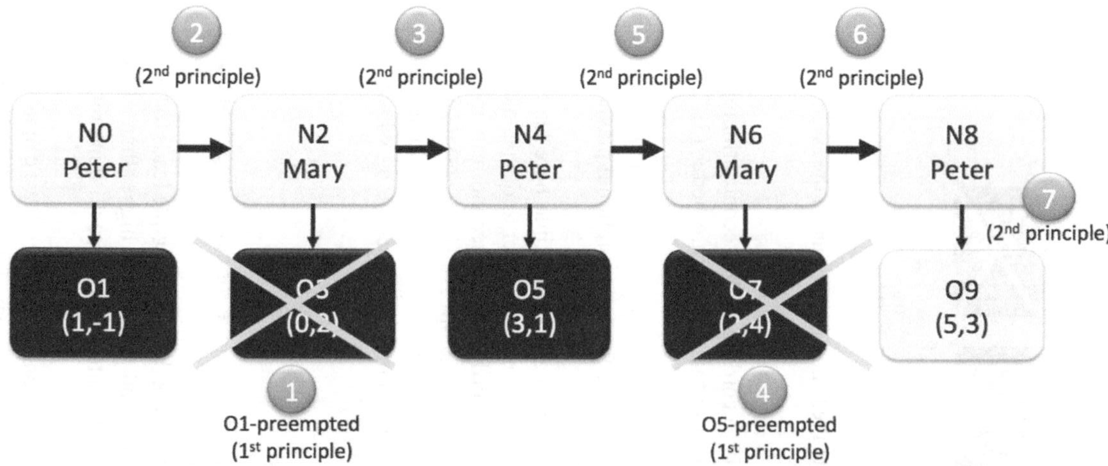

Figure 14.7 The Perfect Prediction Equilibrium in the take-or-leave game (n is odd)

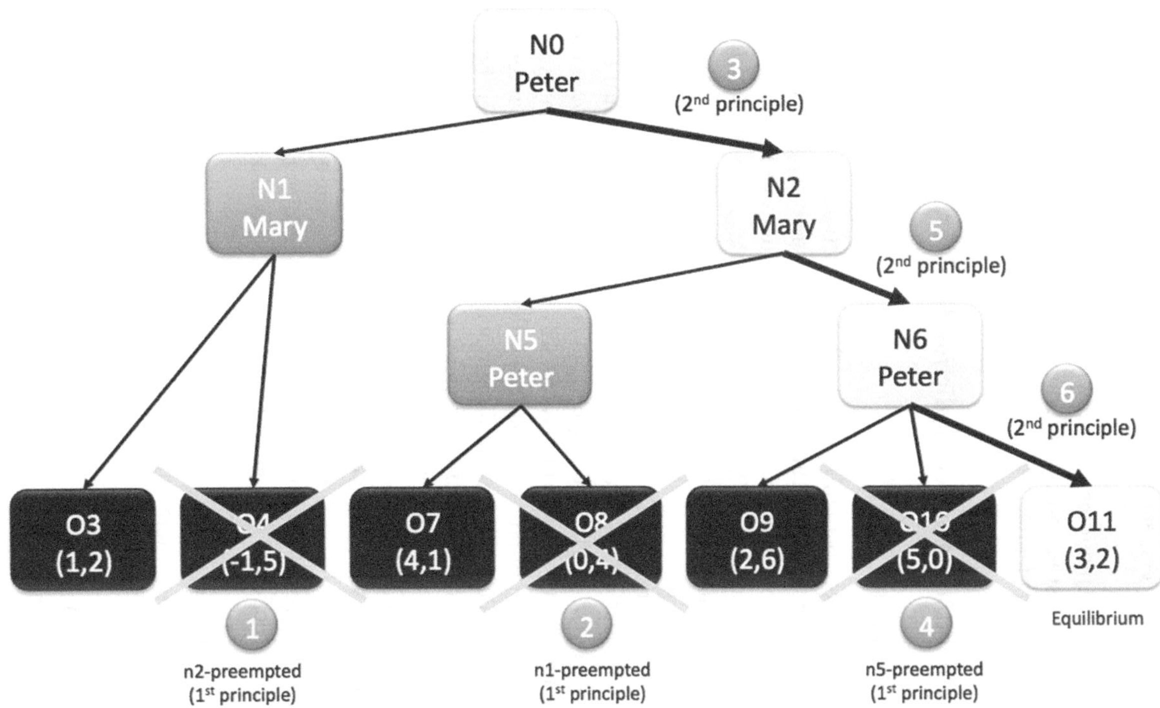

Figure 14.8 The Perfect Prediction Equilibrium in the Γ -game

second principle applies: Mary chooses n_6 (2, 3) over n_5 (1). n_6 is known to be reached by the game, o_7 is discarded.

At n_6 (where the only remaining outcomes are o_9 and o_{11}), we apply directly the second principle: Peter chooses o_{11} (3) over o_9 (2). The game reaches o_{11}. Conversely, the players, anticipating this outcome, will play towards it: it is the equilibrium.

In fact, the algorithmic procedure will always be the same: identify the subgame with the worst payoff and preempt its worst outcomes by making use of other subgames as potential deviations.

Construction of the Perfect Prediction Equilibrium

A general definition

In the former section, we introduced Perfect Prediction, the idea of preemption and two principles, and constructed the PPE for some examples. We now define the Perfect Prediction Equilibrium for all games in extensive form, without chance moves and strict preferences. We assume that both players are Perfect-Prediction-rational. They consider that the solution to the game is CK.

The application of the two principles detailed in Section "Perfect Prediction" allows the elimination of all outcomes but one. The remaining, non-discarded outcome is the Perfect Prediction Equilibrium. It is immune against the CK that the players have of it. The two players, having anticipated it, have no interest in modifying their choices and will play towards this outcome: it is a fixpoint.

Note that the definition of the Subgame Perfect Equilibrium in terms of stability is very similar: it is an equilibrium which is reached when both players have no interest in modifying their strategy, knowing the other player's strategy, *including what he would do at unreached nodes*. In our definition however, we never consider unreached nodes: The Perfect Prediction Equilibrium is stable with respect to the knowledge of itself as a path, and only of itself. This implies that, as opposed to the Nash equilibrium, there is no sense in talking of "equilibria in each subgame". Actually, the different subgames of the tree disappear along the construction of the equilibrium: they are just used as temporary possible deviations.

We believe that the Perfect Prediction Equilibrium fulfills a stability condition which is simpler, more natural and more compact (self-contained) than the Subgame Perfect Equilibrium. It may be regarded as both normative (because the Pareto optimality is an incentive to adopt it in the sense that it never reaches sub-optimal outcomes) and positive (it describes game outcomes encountered in real life, like the assurance game).

The construction of the Perfect Prediction Equilibrium

We consider two-player[10] finite games with perfect information, without chance moves and with strict preferences.

Definition 1 (labeled tree)

A labeled tree is a tree whose root is n_0, and such that:

- each node n, labeled by a player p_n, has a set $F(n)$ of offsprings (nodes or outcomes).
- each leaf is an outcome o labeled by a couple of integers $(a_o^{Peter}, a_o^{Mary})$.
- all $(a_o^{Peter})_o$ are distinct and all $(a_o^{Mary})_o$ are distinct.

The label p_n at node n indicates whose turn it is to play. The offsprings $F(n)$ of node n are player p_n's possible choices.

The label $(a_o^{Peter}, a_o^{Mary})$ at outcome o indicates how much Peter and Mary get.

For convenience, nodes and outcomes are numbered (n_0, n_1 or o_1, n_2 or o_2, . . .) so that it is possible to easily refer to them in the examples.

The last part of the definition corresponds to the assumption that each player has a strict preference between any two outcomes.

We define $D(n)$ as the set of all descendants (nodes and outcomes) of node n; it is the transitive and reflexive closure of the offspring-relation.

To compare outcomes, we write that $o_1 <_p o_2$ whenever $a^p_{o1} < a^p_{o2}$. When the player is clear from the context, we will also say that an outcome is better or worse than another one (meaning for the current player).

EXAMPLE 3

In the assurance game, we have two nodes, n_0 (the root) and n_2, and three outcomes o_1, o_3 and o_4. The players are p_{n_0} = Peter and p_{n_2} = Mary. F is defined as $F(n_0) = \{o_1, n_2\}$ and $F(n_2) = \{o_3, o_4\}$. The payoffs are $(a_{o_1}^{Peter}, a_{o_1}^{Mary}) = (0, 0)$, $(a_{o_3}^{Peter}, a_{o_3}^{Mary}) = (-1, 2)$, and $(a_{o_4}^{Peter}, a_{o_4}^{Mary}) = (1, 1)$. Peter's payoffs are all distinct, as well as Mary's payoffs. D is defined as $D(n_0) = \{o_1, n_2, o_3, o_4\}$ and $D(n_2) = \{o_3, o_4\}$.

A very short summary of the construction of the Perfect Prediction Equilibrium is the following: the reasoning is done by discarding all outcomes which cannot be CK. We start at the root. The outcomes in all direct subtrees but one are discarded, as well as some outcomes in the remaining subtree. The next move has to be the root of the only subtree where at least one outcome remains. Hence, the next move exists and is unique (Lemma 1). We continue with the next move and so on, until an outcome is reached, which is the outcome of the Perfect Prediction Equilibrium.

Initialization, notations: c_i and I_i

An equilibrium is a path[11] $(c_i)_{i=1..d}$ such that the first player starts at $c_1 = n_0$, and at each step i, given c_{i-1}, the next move is $c_i \in F(c_{i-1})$.

Formally:

- $c_1 = n_0$ (the root)
- $\forall i = 1..d - 1$, c_i is a node

- $\forall i = 2..d, c_i \in F(c_{i-1})$
- c_d is an outcome

EXAMPLE 4

In the Γ-game, the equilibrium is (c_1, c_2, c_3, c_4) where $c_1 = n_0$, $c_2 = n_2$, $c_3 = n_6$, $c_4 = o_{11}$.

At each step i we are also given I_{i-1}, a subset of the set $D(c_{i-1})$ of the outcomes descending from the previous move c_{i-1}. This set I_{i-1} is the set of all outcomes that are immune against their knowledge up to c_{i-1} (technically speaking, they have not been discarded yet: the second principle has only been applied up to c_{i-1}, their common ancestor, and they could not be preempted with the first principle at any node earlier on the path).

EXAMPLE 5

In the Γ-game, the sequence would be $I_1 = \{$**all outcomes**$\}$, $I_2 = \{o_7, o_9, o_{10}, o_{11}\}$, $I_3 = \{o_9, o_{11}\}$, $I_4 = \{o_{11}\}$. o_7 is in I_2 because it is not discarded, meaning that if Peter at $c_1 = n_0$ anticipates o_7, he will not deviate. o_8 does not make it in I_2 because it is preempted by Peter at n_0 according to the first principle. o_3 is not in I_2 either since it is discarded by the second principle, as well as all outcomes not in the n_2 subtree.

A node that is not in I_{i-1} cannot be commonly known to be reached by the game, either because it was discarded by the second principle, or because it would bring about a deviation in the past according to the first principle. Note that sometimes, when the outcomes in two subtrees are not interlaced, it can be ambiguous which principle to apply to discard some outcomes: when the second principle potentially selects a subtree, and discards the other outcomes, then the first principle could also be used instead to preempt the very same outcomes with this subtree. This leaves room for a philosophical interpretation (preemption or rational choice), but does not change what outcomes are discarded. This is why, in this section, we will apply the first principle whenever it applies, and then the second principle, but we will push forward the word "discard" instead of "preempt" to leave open which principle is used in the interpretation.

EXAMPLE 6

In the Γ-game, one could also argue that o_3 is not in I_2 by invoking the first principle: o_3 is preempted by the n_2 move. Even with this interpretation, it changes nothing to the fact that all outcomes not in the n_2 subtree are discarded.

In other words, the outcomes that are not in the set I_{i-1} are not to be taken into account anymore: they have been proven not to fit the definition of the equilibrium. The other partially fit the definition: they are immune against their knowledge at least up to c_{i-1}, which means that players will play towards this outcome at least until c_{i-1} is reached, but could still deviate later.

At the beginning I_1 = {all outcomes}, which means that no outcome has been discarded yet: c_1 is the root and is always reached because the game starts here (the causal bridge is secured).

At each step, we discard outcomes (with the first principle, or possibly the second principle for the very last discarding, which is technically equivalent) until all subtrees but one are completely discarded, and finish with the second principle which allows us to move on to the next node and the next step.

Newcombian States

At step *i*, the last move c_{i-1} and the remaining outcomes I_{i-1} are given. For example, at step 2, the last move is the root ($c_1 = n_0$) and the remaining outcomes are all the outcomes (I_1 = {all outcomes}), and we are looking for c_2 and I_2.

We will now define Newcombian States[12] for the player $p_{c_{i-1}}$ (the current player) so as to recursively determine the outcomes that are not immune against their common knowledge because of a deviation at the node c_{i-1}. These outcomes are discarded at this step.

A Newcombian State has a pure part (corresponding to a possible move) and a discarding part (a Newcombian State which invalidates some outcomes as equilibrium candidates, with one of the two principles). It can be thought of as a bundle containing a move (its "pure part") together with the knowledge and the proof (its "discarding part") that some of its descendant outcomes are impossible. The proof that such an outcome is impossible consists of a witness: the move in the discarding part

- to which the player p_{i-1} would deviate according to the first principle if the outcome were predicted
- or to which the player p_{i-1} actually goes according to the second principle.

Definition 2 (Newcombian State, pure part, discarding part)

At step *i*, a Newcombian State of order *k*, with $k \geq 1$, is an element $\eta = (\eta_1, \ldots, \eta_k) \in (F(c_{i-1}))^k$, constituted by offsprings of the last move, such that any two consecutive elements are different:

$$\eta = (\eta_1, \ldots, \eta_k) \in \left(F\left(c_{i-1}\right)\right)^k : \eta_j \neq \eta_{j+1}, j = 1..k-1 \tag{1}$$

The pure part of a Newcombian State is its first element:

$$\mathbf{pure}(\eta) = \eta_1 \in F\left(c_{i-1}\right)$$

The discarding part of a Newcombian State of order $k > 1$ is the element of $(F(c_{i-1}))^{k-1}$ composed by the $k-1$ last elements of η:

$$\mathbf{discard}(\eta) = (\eta_2, \ldots, \eta_k) \in (F(c_{i-1}))^{k-1}$$

EXAMPLE 7

In the Γ-game, (n_1, n_2) is a Newcombian State of order 2. Its pure part is n_1 and its discarding part is n_2. n_2 is a witness that a descendant (o_4) of n_1 is impossible, because it is discarded by the first principle (o_4 is preempted by n_2).

Likewise, (n_2, n_1, n_2) is a Newcombian State of order 3. Its pure part is n_2 and its discarding part is (n_1, n_2). The latter is a witness that a descendant (o_8) of n_2 is discarded by the first principle (it is preempted by n_1 knowing that o_4 is impossible).

Finally, (n_1, n_2, n_1, n_2) is a Newcombian State of order 4. Its pure part is n_1 and its discarding part is (n_2, n_1, n_2). The latter is a witness that a descendant of n_1 (o_3) is impossible. In this case, it is open whether the second principle (Peter chooses n_2, knowing that o_8 and o_4 are impossible, which discards all outcomes in other subtrees) or the first principle (o_3 is preempted by n_2 knowing that o_8 and o_4 are impossible) is applied, liked we mentioned above. Whichever principle is used, o_3 is discarded.

A Newcombian State of order 1 is a pure Newcombian State: no outcome has been discarded yet (unless it was at a former step, but we said that outcomes invalidated at a former step are out of the race anyway).

EXAMPLE 8

(n_2) is a pure Newcombian State, i.e., in which no outcomes have been discarded yet.

Target function and discarding

Each Newcombian State is associated with the subset of the descendants of its pure part that are not discarded by its discarding part. This is defined recursively by making appeal to the target function T_i in the following way:

Definition 3 (Target function and discarding)

At step *i*,

- if η is a first-order Newcombian State, i.e. $\eta = (\eta_1)$, then $T_i(\eta)$ is the set of outcomes that are among the descendants of η_1 and that were not discarded before step *i*:

  $$T_i(\eta) = I_{i-1} \cap D(\eta_1)$$

- if η is a Newcombian State of order $k > 1$, i.e. $\eta = (\eta_1, p)$, then $T_i(\eta)$ is the set of outcomes that are among the descendants of η_1 and that were not discarded before step *i*, *excluding* outcomes worse than the worst[13] [14] [15]outcome in $T_i(p)$ if $T_i(p)$ is not empty.

Every outcome that is excluded that way is called p**-discarded**. Any outcome in $T_i(\eta)$ is said η**-targeted**. If we denote the set of the p-discarded outcomes with

$$P_i(p) = \{o \in I_{i-1} \setminus D(\mathbf{pure}(p)) \mid T_i(p) \neq \emptyset \wedge \forall o' \in T_i(p), o <_{p_{c_{i-1}}} o'\}$$

then

$$T_i(\eta) = (I_{i-1} \cap D(\eta_1)) \setminus P_i(p)$$

which defines a recursion on k.

Note the terminology: an *outcome* is discarded by a *Newcombian State*. The operation of discarding corresponds to the player's behavior described in the principles:

- With the first principle, if, predicting outcome o will happen, she moves to a subtree with outcomes that are all better than o, then o is discarded and is no longer an equilibrium candidate.
- With the second principle, the player selects a move, which discards any outcome in the other subtrees.

EXAMPLE 9

For example in the Γ-game, at the root, i.e. step 2, the target functions for the pure Newcombian States are $T_2(n_1) = \{o_3, o_4\}$ and $T_2(n_2) = \{o_7, o_8, o_9, o_{10}, o_{11}\}$ (they contain all descendants). The corresponding discarding functions are $P_2(n_1) = \emptyset$ and $P_2(n_2) = \{o_4\}$. Knowing this, it is possible to compute the target functions of the Newcombian States of order 1: $T_2(n_2, n_1) = T_2(n_2) \setminus P_2(n_1) = T_2(n_2)$ and $T_2(n_1, n_2) = T_2(n_1) \setminus P_2(n_2) = \{o_3, o_4\} \setminus \{o_4\} = \{o_3\}$.

There are two extreme cases for discarding:

- If $T_i(p) = \emptyset$, or if there is no η_1-targeted outcome worse than the worst p-targeted outcome, then $T_i(\eta) = T_i(\eta_1)$. Discarding η_1-targeted outcomes by p is ineffective.
- If all η-targeted outcomes are worse than the worst p-targeted outcome, then $T_i(\eta) = \emptyset$. This time, discarding the descendance of η_1 by p is at its highest efficiency, since p discards every η_1-targeted outcome. η is called a degenerate state. A degenerate state cannot discard any outcome.

It is only for a degenerate state η that it is ambiguous which principle is being applied: the first one (the outcomes in $P_i[p]$ are preempted) or the second one (the player moves rationally to the pure part of η). For non-degenerate states, only the first principle makes sense.

EXAMPLE 10

At step 1 of game Γ, we have $c_1 = n_0$ and $I_1 = \{\text{all outcomes}\}$ (initial values).

At step 2, we compute the target functions of the Newcombian States:

$$T_2(n_1) = \{o_3, o_4\}$$
$$T_2(n_2) = \{o_7, o_8, o_9, o_{10}, o_{11}\}$$

$$\begin{aligned}
P_2(n_1) &= \emptyset \\
T_2(n_2, n_1) &= T_2(n_2) \\
P_2(n_2) &= \{o_4\} \\
T_2(n_1, n_2) &= T_2(n_1) \setminus P_2(n_2) = \{o_3, o_4\} \setminus \{o_4\} = \{o_3\} \\
P_2(n_1, n_2) &= \{o_8\} \\
T_2(n_2, n_1, n_2) &= T_2(n_2) \setminus P_2(n_1, n_2) \\
&= \{o_7, o_8, o_9, o_{10}, o_{11}\} \setminus \{o_8\} = \{o_7, o_9, o_{10}, o_{11}\} \\
P_2(n_2, n_1, n_2) &= \{o_3, o_4\} \\
T_2(n_1, n_2, n_1, n_2) &= T_2(n_1) \setminus P_2(n_2, n_1, n_2) = \{o_3, o_4\} \setminus \{o_3, o_4\} = \emptyset .
\end{aligned}$$

The entire reasoning (also at n_2 and n_6) is indicated on Figure 14.9, where the order of the sub-steps is indicated by the numbers in gray circles. Sub-steps 1, 2 and 3 are performed by Peter at n_0. One notices that, by discarding all outcomes we can, we are left with outcomes o_7, o_9, o_{10} and o_{11}, and all of them are descendants of n_2, which is chosen by Peter ($c_2 = n_2$ and $I_2 = \{o_7, o_9, o_{10}, o_{11}\}$). Sub-steps 4 and 5 are then performed by Mary at n_2 and sub-step 6 at n_6 by Peter. Actually, it always works in the same way, at each step and for any game: we can discard the outcomes of all subtrees but one, as demonstrated in the next part.

The current player's move

In the example, we saw that after discarding as many outcomes as possible at the root, only outcomes in exactly one subtree remained – this means that this subtree corresponds to the player's next move. We will now show that at any node reached by the game, the current player's move exists and is unique.

Having constructed all Newcombian States at step *i*, a certain amount of outcomes, having been discarded, are impossible. We consider all the outcomes that are still available after this: these are the outcomes that are immune against their knowledge up to the current step.

The set $I_i \subset I_{i-1}$ of all remaining outcomes is given by:

$$I_i = I_{i-1} \setminus \left(\bigcup_{\eta} P_i(\eta)\right)$$

Note that this infinite union is merely a notation, and represents in fact a finite union, since all the $P_i(\eta)$ are subsets of I_{i-1} (and the set of subsets of a finite set is finite). Nevertheless, despite being practical, this notation does not allow to create

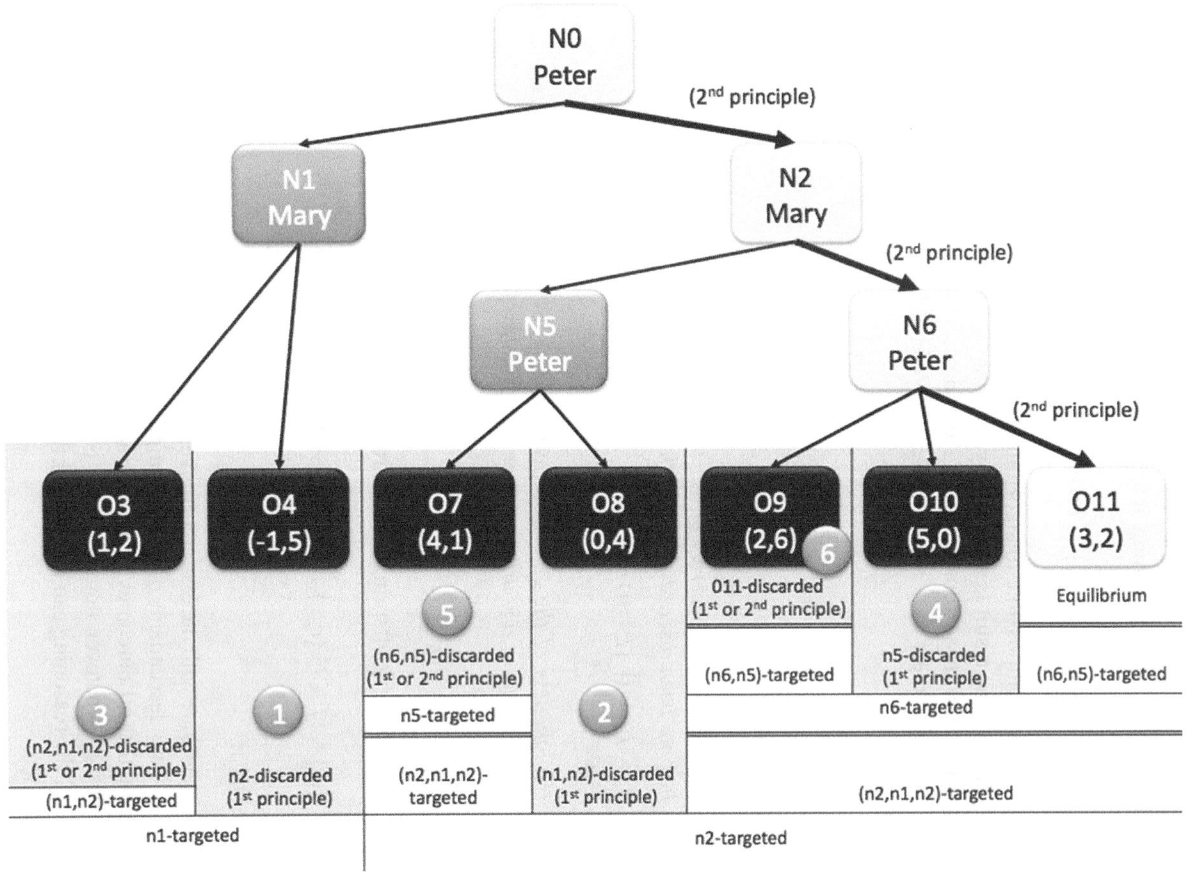

Figure 14.9 The Γ -game with Newcombian States and their targeted/discarded outcomes at the root

any algorithm for computing the equilibrium. We will present another characterization of the current player's move which permits this in Section "General algorithm".

EXAMPLE 11

In the Γ-game, after reasoning at the root, the set of remaining outcomes is

$$I_2 = I_1 \setminus \left(P_2(n_1) \cup P_2(n_2) \cup P_2(n_1, n_2) \cup P_2(n_2, n_1) \cup \ldots\right) = \{o_7, o_9, o_{10}, o_{11}\}$$

Note that it is impossible to algorithmically compute the infinite union with this formula, but the result is obtained by noticing that all other outcomes have been discarded, and these four remaining outcomes cannot be discarded by any of the two principles: they are all better for Peter than any outcome in any other subtree.

Lemma 1

Existence and uniqueness of current player's move

1 *(Existence of the current player's move) There is at least one outcome which has not been discarded during the process:*

$$I_i = I_{i-1} \setminus \left(\bigcup_{\eta} P_i(\eta)\right) \neq \emptyset$$

2 *(Uniqueness of the current player's move) All remaining outcomes are the descendants of one unique offspring of the last player's move c_{i-1}:*

$$\exists! f \in F\left(c_{i-1}\right),\ I_i \cap D(f) \neq \emptyset$$

and this very offspring is the current player's move ci:

$$\{c_i\} \equiv \{f \in F\left(c_{i-1}\right),\ I_i \cap D(f) \neq \emptyset\}$$

EXAMPLE 12

If we continue with the example above, we see that all remaining outcomes (o_7, o_9, o_{10}, o_{11}) are descendants of n_2. This implies that $c_2 = n_2$.

Now that all outcomes in all subtrees but one have been discarded, the game reaches c_i: whatever outcome in I_i is anticipated, the players play towards c_i. Hence, the reasoning can continue at this node, at which further outcomes can be discarded.

End of recursion – definition and theorem

When the path reaches an outcome c_d ($I_d = \{c_d\}$), the induction stops, leaving one non-discarded outcome.

EXAMPLE 12

In the Γ-game, at step 3, the game reaches $c_3 = n_6$ with the remaining outcomes $I_3 = \{o_9, o_{11}\}$. At step 4, it reaches $c_4 = o_{11}$ with $I_4 = \{o_{11}\}$. The induction stops here: o_{11} is reached by the game. (n_0, n_2, n_6, o_{11}) is the equilibrium: under the assumption of total transparency, the players will reach it; even though they know it in advance, they never deviate. Actually, the fact that they know it in advance causes them to reach it.

Definition 4 (Perfect Prediction Equilibrium)

In a game in extensive form represented by a finite tree, with perfect information, without chance moves and with strict preferences between the outcomes, under the assumption of total transparency, a Perfect Prediction Equilibrium is a path leading to a non-discarded outcome, i.e., an outcome which is immune against the CK that the players have of it: the players, anticipating it, have no interest in modifying their choices and do play towards this outcome. It is a fixpoint, in that it follows causally from its prediction.

Theorem 1 (Existence and uniqueness of the Perfect Prediction Equilibrium)

In a game in extensive form represented by a finite tree, with perfect information, without chance moves and with strict preferences between the outcomes, there is one unique Perfect Prediction Equilibrium.

Pareto optimality

The Perfect Prediction Equilibrium has the additional property of always being Pareto-optimal. This concept is of crucial importance in economics. In our case, it means that when the PPE is reached, the payoffs are distributed so that no other equilibrium can make a player better off without making the other player worse off.

Theorem 2

The outcome of the Perfect Prediction Equilibrium is Pareto-optimal among the outcomes of the game.

Note that, although the PPE is always Pareto-optimal, it is not always a Pareto improvement of the SPE (for a counterexample, see the complete analysis of biped games in the Annex, case "1 $\neq$" with $d = 1$ and $f = 0$).

Related work

The Backward Induction Paradox

In the last decades, there has been a debate around the so-called Backward Induction Paradox: CK of rationality is also assumed at nodes that are known to be not reached given this very CK of rationality. This points out that in some way, the SPE is not completely transparent to itself: the players do know their respective strategies, and though cannot be fully – that is, at all nodes in the tree – cognizant of the final equilibrium determined by these two strategies.

One of the motivations behind the Perfect Prediction Equilibrium is to avoid the Backward Induction Paradox (BIP). In this section, we show how literature relates the BIP to the assumption of counterfactual independence and hence, why giving up this assumption circumvents the BIP.

Two kinds of BIPs can be found in literature.

Pettit and Sugden (1989: 169) describe an empirical BIP with the example of the repeated prisoner's dilemma (a game with imperfect information):

> There is a well-known argument – the backward induction argument – to the effect that, in such a sequence, agents who are rational and who share the belief that they are rational will defect in every round. This argument holds however large n may be. And yet, if *n* is a large number, it appears that I might do better to follow a strategy such as tit-for-tat. . . . This is the backward induction paradox.

Baltag et al. (2009: 1) describe a more fundamental, logical BIP as follows:

> in order even to start the reasoning, a player assumes that (common knowledge of, or some form of common belief in) *rationality*' holds at all the last decision nodes (and so the obviously irrational leaves are eliminated); but then, in the next reasoning step (going backward along the tree), some of these (last) decision nodes are eliminated, as being incompatible with (common belief in) *rationality*!

Reny (1992) showed that in the take-or-leave game, CK of rationality is self-contradictory at each node outside of the equilibrium path.

In the last two decades, the Backward Induction Paradox has been the object of an uninterrupted debate. On the one side, Aumann (1995: 647) proved that "common knowledge of rationality (CKR) implies [that players are reasoning by] backward induction" (although he does not "claim that CKR obtains or should obtain"). On the other side, Stalnaker states that "Common knowledge of substantive rationality does not imply the backwards induction solution" (Halpern 2001: 2) and argued (Stalnaker 1998: 43) that Aumann's argument "conflates epistemic and causal independence, implicitly making a strong epistemic independence assumption which it explicitly rejects". The opposition to Aumann's claim was supported by (Binmore 1996) and (Binmore 1997).

Halpern (2001: 1) showed that both sides are right, in that "the key difference between Aumann and Stalnaker lies in how they interpret" the counterfactual' statement "for all vertices *v*, if the player were to reach vertex *v*, then the player would be rational at vertex *v*" (substantive rationality), i.e., whether it is a material[16] or a counterfactual implication.[17]

Baltag et al. (2009: 19) go in another direction by allowing players to have "a moment of temporary irrationality".

We believe that the Backward Induction Paradox is due to the lack of transparency arising from the widespread assumption that present decisions are counterfactually independent of past moves, an assumption also made explicitly by Baltag et al. (2009: 27): "players have no non-trivial "hard" information about the outcomes. . . : they cannot foretell the future, cannot irrevocably know the players' freely chosen future moves (though they do irrevocably know the past, and they may irrevocably know the present)."

Perfection prediction theory aims at giving an alternate game-theoretical solution concept with the exact opposite assumption: there is CK of the outcome of the game, and the past is counterfactually dependent on this outcome. There is also CK of rationality on the equilibrium path, and no need for it outside of this path (no counterfactuals on [un]reached nodes, no substantive rationality).

This happens to lead to cooperative, Pareto-optimal behavior. Hence, the Backward Induction Paradox, in the two formulations given above, does not manifest itself in the PPE theory.

Supporting the possibility of having an alternate theory of rational choice, Kreps (2009) argues that

> when one says "rational choice theory", it sounds as if only one theory or model of choice could qualify. How could two distinct theories or models both be rational? But people behave in different ways, depending on the specific context and the more general social situation, and I see no reason to privilege one universal model of behavior with the adjective rational. To do so is, if not demonstrably silly, at least demonstrably misleading.

Other results in non-Nashian game theory

Hofstadter (1983: 748) introduced the concept of superrationality like so: "Superrational thinkers, by recursive definition, include in their calculations the fact that they are in a group of superrational thinkers." Superrationality is defined for symmetric games. We believe that the Perfect Prediction rationality underlying the PPE is the equivalent of superrationality for games in extensive form, as it shares the core idea of transcending rationality, in that players include the knowledge thereof in their calculations.

More work was done by Halpern and Pass (2013) on normal form games with the concept of translucent players, where information leaks lead to correlations rather than fixed opponent strategies. Halpern and Pass extend the concept of rationalizability to this framework with the concept of Common Counterfactual Belief of Rationality (CCBR), which can be put in perspective with Perfect Prediction rationality. Fourny (2017) showed that CCBR subsumes Hofstadter's work on superrationality in symmetric games. However, known counterexamples show that it does not subsume the Perfect Prediction equilibrium, because the normal form does not catch temporal causality constraints. In general, Halpern's research is also looking at the continuous spectrum between no translucency at all and full transparency, while the PPE focuses on full transparency.

Shiffrin et al. (2009) argue that rationality is "not a normative concept but rather a social consensus of a sufficiently large proportion of humans judged to be sufficiently expert". They point out that normative game theory reaches non-(Pareto)-efficient optima and initiated research to suggest an alternate equilibrium concept that aims at being Pareto-optimal and that differs from the Nash equilibrium. They explicitly point to Hofstadter's superrationality as a starting point. Also, they compare their approach to a single player's playing against himself under the effect of the Midazolam drug, which makes him forget his past decisions while preserving his reasoning abilities. A fundamental difference with the PPE, and point of disagreement in offline discussions, lies in the fact that, unlike the PPE, eliminated outcomes can be reused in the reasoning. Our interpretation is that Shiffrin considers these outcomes to be contingent (similar to the SPE), whereas they are considered impossible by the PPE. Finally, Shiffrin's algorithm faces an exponential explosion of the search space for more than two players. The PPE scales to any number of players with similar algorithms to two players.

Forward Induction

The Perfect Prediction Equilibrium is *de facto* built with a forward induction, since its construction begins at the root and ends at an outcome. Note that, in game theory, the expression "Forward Induction" carries much more meaning than the fact that the reasoning follows a path from the root to an outcome.

Although in the past many Forward Induction Equilibria have been designed, according to Govindan and Wilson (2009: 5), "the literature provides no formal definition of Forward Induction."

We now compare our equilibrium with others found in literature by first looking at differences and then at similarities.

First of all, we limit ourselves to games with *perfect information*, meaning that information sets are all singletons, so that beliefs (as they are defined in the "Sequential Equilibria" of Kreps and Wilson [1982]) are the trivial function 1 on a singleton.

Additionally, Forward Induction is often used with mixed strategies leading to probability distribution over the game outcomes. Usually, Forward Induction seems to select an equilibrium among the Sequential Equilibria as defined by Kreps and Wilson (1982). In our work we only consider pure strategies, with pure game outcomes.

Finally, there is the issue of what happens outside of the path. It has already been addressed, for example in the Weakly Sequential Equilibrium by Kreps and Wilson (1982), where strategies are required to be optimal only on non-excluded information sets (but are defined also on information sets excluded by these very strategies). Cho and Kreps (1987: 180) introduced signaling games, in which they also address this issue: "If one can restrict the out-of-equilibrium beliefs (or hypotheses) of B, one can sometimes eliminate many of the equilibria." We find the same idea in the work of Banks and Sobel (1987: 650): "This section presents an equilibrium concept that refines the set of sequential equilibria in signaling games by placing restrictions on off-the-equilibrium- path beliefs." In our case, pure strategies are simply *not defined at all* outside the equilibrium path. Actually, outside the equilibrium path, it is not even assumed that players are rational.

In spite of these differences (perfect information, pure strategies, no definition outside of the equilibrium path), we can find some interesting similarities with existing Forward Induction Equilibria.

It is commonly assumed that past play was rational, as opposed to Backward Induction, where future play only is supposed to be rational. See for example Govindan and Wilson (2009: 3):

> Kohlberg and Mertens label this result Forward Induction but they and other authors do not define the criterion explicitly. The main idea is the one expressed by Hillas and Kohlberg in their recent survey: "Forward induction involves an assumption that players assume, even if they see something unexpected, that the other players chose rationally in the past", to which one can add that 'and other players will choose rationally in the future.' This is implicit since rationality presumes that prior actions are part of an optimal strategy.

We also assume rationality of other players in the past, but even more than that, we assume that the past has a power of preemption. Technically, in occurring time for example, it could mean that if a player (she) chooses a move towards a preempted outcome, knowing that the other player (he) anticipated this outcome, this contradicts his rationality in the past, hence, she cannot choose such a move.

Preemption has also already been indirectly used in Forward Induction: e.g., by Cho and Kreps (1987: 197):

> Again envisaging the thought process of the players, we have in mind something like Kohlberg and Merten's process of forward induction: will some type of player A, having arrived introspectively at restrictions in B's beliefs (hence B's conceivable actions), see that deviation will lead to a higher payoff than will following the equilibrium?

CK of the equilibrium has already been considered as well: Cho and Kreps (1987: 203):

> An equilibrium is meant to be a candidate for a mode of self-enforcing behavior that is common knowledge among the players. (Most justifications for Nash equilibria come down to something like this. See, for example Aumann [1987] or Kreps [forthcoming]). In testing a particular equilibrium (or equilibrium outcome), one holds to the hypothesis that the equilibrium (outcome) is common knowledge among the players, and one looks for "contradictions".

This is exactly what we do in PPE: it is the only equilibrium stable against its CK. In our case, it is unique and all other paths lead to contradictions.

Note that Govindan and Wilson (2009) also give a proposal for a Forward Induction criterion with mixed strategies and without the perfect information assumption:

> Definition 3.4 (Forward Induction). An outcome satisfies forward induction if it results from a weakly sequential equilibrium in which at every relevant information set the support of the belief of the player acting there is confined to profiles of nature's strategies and other players' relevant strategies.

Although the framework is different, it can be interesting to ask whether the PPE fulfills this criterion, knowing that we are in the special case where we have perfection information and pure strategies which are a special case of mixed strategies, and where the 'knowledge' of each player can be seen as beliefs with probability 1.

The Sequential Equilibrium is close to the Subgame Perfect Equilibrium: in Kreps and Wilson (1982), Proposition 3 says: "if (μ, π) is a Sequential Equilibrium, then π is a Subgame Perfect Nash Equilibrium." Since the PPE is not always an SPE, it is not always a Sequential Equilibrium either.

Now, the Weakly Sequential Equilibrium is more general than the Sequential Equilibrium, in that players' strategies do not need to be optimal at information sets excluded by the equilibrium strategy. Unfortunately, this is not enough: a PPE is not always a WSE either. For example, in the assurance game, the only WSE outcome is (0,0) whereas the PPE leads to its Pareto improvement (1,1). What happens with the WSE is that (1,1), which is the PPE outcome, is already discarded at the beginning of the reasoning by the second player who prefers (−1,2), and the first player then chooses (0,0) by backward induction: there is no notion of preempting (−1,2), which would influence the choice of the second player.

Hence, the Perfect Prediction Equilibrium is not a refinement of any of the above equilibria. While using preemption and CK of the equilibrium outcome, which are not new and have already been addressed in Forward Induction literature, it deviates from the ideas behind the Subgame Perfect Equilibrium.

Although we can find the same intuitions in the Forward Induction literature and in the construction of the PPE, the literature still (implicitly) assumes counterfactual independence of a player's move from the past, whereas we are using the concept of Perfect Prediction.

Starting with the premise that the game is played by agents for whom the world is totally transparent, we established that exactly one equilibrium, the Perfect Prediction Equilibrium, fulfills this requirement.

Conclusion

We introduced an alternate solution concept, the Perfect Prediction Equilibrium, which is reached by players that have a different form of rationality than that used in Subgame Perfect Equilibrium. It accounts for the behavior of players that would

Table 14.1 A summary of the differences between the SPE and PPE paradigms

	Subgame Perfect Equilibrium	*Perfect Prediction Equilibrium*
Form of the game	Extensive	Extensive
Perfect information	Yes	Yes
Number of players	Any	Any
Rationality	Nash-Perfect	Perfect Prediction
Newcomb Choice	Two boxes	One box
Prediction model accounting for counterfactuals	Ad Hoc Prediction ("could have been wrong")	Perfect Prediction ("would also have been right")
Relationship with the past	Cournot-like	Stackelberg-like
Reasoning	Backward Induction	Forward Induction
Indifference between payoffs	Allowed	Not allowed in principle
Existence	Always	Always
Uniqueness	If no indifference	Always
Optimality	–	Pareto
Corresponding normal Form	Nash (subsuming)	Superrationality (not established/ conceptually similar)

pick one box in Newcomb's problem (PPR), as opposed to rational players in the Nash sense (NPR), that would pick two boxes with a dominant strategy argument.

Perfect-Prediction-rational players seem to get a reward over Nash-Perfect-rational players, as the former can only reach Pareto-optimal outcomes.

Table 14.1 summarizes the differences between the SPE paradigm and the PPE paradigm.

As a conclusive remark, it is important to note that, for the equilibrium to be reached, it does not require that Perfect Prediction holds. It suffices that the Perfect-Prediction-rational players believe that it does. Furthermore, the algorithms are simple and efficiently computable. Hence, even if an agent who feels very strong about NPR will not find PPR reasonable, they cannot deny that the PPR reasoning is no less sound that the NPR reasoning and that it has the merit of Pareto optimality.

Acknowledgments

We are thankful to Alexei Grinbaum and Bernard Walliser for their precious advice.

Notes

1 The analogy with Cournot vs. Stackelberg is used to help understand the paradigm shift underlying the PPE. Classically, Stackelberg competition is built on the future's reaction function. In the PPE, we mean Stackelberg competition built on the past's reaction function, which means the reaction function of the past to the anticipation of a move, embedding excellent anticipation skills of the opponent, as opposed to a frozen past in the Nash paradigm.

2 Other formulations found in literature include "in general position" (Aumann 1995), "nondegenerate" (Halpern 2001).
3 In our paper, we use the expression "forward induction" with two meanings. The first one is forward induction by construction: reasoning starts at the root and finishes at an outcome. The second one is the meaning that Forward Induction has accumulated in the history of game theory and which is explained in Section "Related work". For clarity, we refer to the former without capitals "forward induction", and to the latter with capitals "Forward Induction".
4 However, once familiar with the PPE, the reader may notice that this assumption can sometimes be relaxed, and that the original TOL game does have a PPE, too.
5 Some might suggest that this could be considered a Principle Zero, in addition to the two principles described in Section "Two principles behind the computation of the Perfect Prediction Equilibrium". Since we consider this to be part of the fundamentals of the PPE framework though, as opposed to the two principles, which are more algorithmic, we decided not to call it so.
6 The Grandfather Paradox is as follows: a time traveler goes back in time and provokes the death of his grandfather, preventing him from meeting his grandmother. Hence, the time traveler was not born and cannot have traveled back in time. While one might see this as a proof that time travel is impossible, another way to look at it is that the actual timeline is the solution of a fixpoint equation: the past, tampered with by the time traveler, must cause the time traveler's birth for him to be able to go back in time. In terms of game theory, we also encounter a Grandfather Paradox in the following case: an outcome is commonly known to be the outcome of the game; having predicted it, a player deviates from the path leading to it, making the outcome out of reach. Just like for the time traveler, we are looking for the timeline which is immune to the Grandfather Paradox: the outcome which is actually caused by its prediction.
7 With the terminology of the introduction, the Perfect-Prediction-rational agent forbids himself to pick o because it would lead to an inconsistency in his reasoning pattern.
8 I.e. a subtree that only has discarded outcomes cannot be considered.
9 Some might see a paradox here, since outcome o_1 has contributed to the preemption of o_3, but at the same time is impossible because not reached. Actually, there is no paradox. A proposition ("outcome o_3 is part of the solution") which implies a contradiction ("Peter deviates, so o_3 is not part of the solution") is false, but this does not imply that a proposition ("Peter deviates") implied by this proposition is logically true, since false propositions logically imply anything, true or false. In the formalization of the PPE as solution of a first-order-logic equation system, this appears clearly.
10 The formalism can very easily be extended to any number of players. The main difference is that outcomes are labeled by n-tuples of integers instead of couples.
11 We can either consider the equilibrium as the outcome reached by the players, or as the path leading to it, which is equivalent.
12 Newcombian States can be seen as the mathematical counterpart of a player's Perfect Prediction skills. This name has been chosen as a tribute to Newcomb's problem (see Section "Newcomb's problem"). To reach the Perfect Prediction Equilibrium, players reason as one-boxers.
13 An outcome is said *worse* than another outcome if and only if it gives a lower payoff with respect to the current player $p_{c_{i-1}}$.
14 At all vertices in the game. This is the definition used by Halpern (2001).
15 We call this counterfactual independence.
16 I.e., equivalent to "the players do not reach vertex v, or they are rational at vertex v."
17 I.e. "if [the player] were to actually reach v, then what he would do in that case would be rational" (Halpern 2001).
18 It is actually the maximum of a a total order relation. A partial order relation can be defined on all Newcombian States, and Newcombian Classes are defined so as to make this relation a relation of total order on them.

Bibliography

Aumann, Robert J.(1987) Correlated Equilibrium as an Expression of Bayesian Rationality. *Econometrica, LV*: 1–18.

Aumann, R. (1995) Backward induction and common knowledge of rationality. *Games and Economic Behavior* 8: 6–19.

Baltag, A., Smets, S. and Zvesper, J. (2009) Keep "hoping" for rationality: A solution to the backward induction paradox. *Synthese* 169: 301–33, URL: http://dx.doi.org/10.1007/s11229-009–9559-z, 10.1007/s11229–009–9559-z

Banks, J. and Sobel, J. (1987) Equilibrium selection in signaling games. *Econometrica* 55: 647–61.

Binmore, K. (1996) A note on backward induction. *Games and Economic Behavior* 17: 135–7.

Binmore, K. (1997) Rationality and backward induction. *Journal of Economic Methodology* 4: 1: 23–41.

Cho, I.K. and Kreps, D. (1987) Signalling games and stable equilibria. *Econometrica* 76: 117–36.

Dupuy, J.-P. (2000) Philosophical foundations of a new concept of equilibrium in the social sciences: Projected equilibrium. *Philosophical Studies* 100: 323–56.

Fourny, G. (2017) Common counterfactual belief of rationality subsumes superrationality on symmetric games. *arXiv*. URL: https://arxiv.org/abs/1707.01816

Gardner, M. (1973) Free will revisited, with a mind-bending prediction paradox by William Newcomb. *Scientific American* 229: 1.

Govindan, S. and Wilson, R. (2009) On forward induction. *Econometrica* 77: 1: 1–28.

Halpern, J.Y. (2001) Substantive rationality and backward induction. *Games and Economic Behavior* 37(2): 425–35, doi: 10.1006/game.2000.0838, URL: www.sciencedirect.com/science/article/pii/S0899825600908388

Halpern, J.Y. and Pass, R. (2013) Game theory with translucent players. *arXiv*. URL: https://arxiv.org/abs/1308.3778, 1308.3778

Hofstadter, D. (1983) Dilemmas for superrational thinkers, leading up to a luring lottery. *Scientific American*. Reprinted in: Metamagical themas questing for the essence of mind and pattern. 248: 6: 737–55

Kreps, D. (2009) Comments on Dupré, Dupuy, and Bender. *Occasion: Interdisciplinary Studies in the Humanities* 1: 1. URL: http://occasion.stanford.edu/node/15

Kreps, D. and Wilson, R. (1982) Sequential equilibria. *Econometrica* 50: 863–94.

Nash, J. (1951) Non-cooperative games. *Annals of Mathematics* 54: 286–95.

Pettit, P. and Sugden, R. (1989) The backward induction paradox. *The Journal of Philosophy* 86(4): 169–82.

Reny, P. (1992) Rationality in extensive-form games. *Journal of Economic Perspectives* 6(4): 103–18.

Selten, R. (1965) Spieltheoretische Behandlung eines Oligopolmodells mit Nachfragetragheit [An oligopoly model with demand inertia]. *Zeitschrift für die Gesamte Staatswissenschaft* 121: 2: 301–24.

Shiffrin, R., Lee, M. and Zhang, S. (2009) *Rational Games – 'Rational' Stable and Unique Solutions for Multiplayer Sequential Games*. Tech. rep., Indiana University.

Stalnaker, R. (1998) Belief revision in games: Forward and backward induction. *Mathematical Social Sciences* 36(1): 31–56, doi: 10.1016/S0165–4896(98)00007–9, URL: www.sciencedirect.com/science/article/pii/S0165489698000079

Wolpert, D. and Benford, G. (2013) The lesson of Newcomb's paradox. *Synthese* 190(9): 1637–1646, doi: 10.1007/s11229-011-9899-3, URL: http://dx.doi.org/10.1007/s11229-011-9899-3

Annex – preemption structure and algorithms

We proved that the current player's move exists and is unique, but we did not give an explicit way of determining how to compute it. In order to introduce algorithms, we need a further analysis of the preemption structure. After giving an explicit construction of the equilibrium, we derive two algorithms.

Preemption structure analysis – the explicit construction of the PPE

In this part, we first introduce Newcombian Classes for a given step i and then give an explicit characterization of the player's move at the corresponding node.

Newcombian Classes

Two Newcombian States with the same targeting function can be considered equivalent.

DEFINITION 5 (TARGET-EQUIVALENT, NEWCOMBIAN CLASS)

With respect to step i, two Newcombian States η and η' are target-equivalent if they target the same outcomes: $T_i(\eta) = T_i(\eta')$.

This defines an equivalence relation on the set of all Newcombian States relative to the same move: it is reflexive, symmetric and transitive. The equivalence class of a Newcombian State η is denoted $\hat{\eta}$ and is called the Newcombian Class of η.

We naturally extend the target function T_i to Newcombian Classes: $T_i(\hat{\eta}) = T_i(\eta)$, where η is any element of $\hat{\eta}$.

If $T_i(\hat{\eta}) = \emptyset$, then $\hat{\eta}$ is called a degenerate class.

Example 13 In the assurance game, $T_2(o_1) = \{o_1\}$ and $T_2(o_1, n_2) = \{o_1\}$. This means that they belong to the same equivalence class: $\hat{o}_1 = \widehat{(o_1, n_2)}$.

In particular, they can potentially discard the exact same outcomes. Also, in the Γ-game, $T_2(n_2, n_1, n_2, n_1, n_2) = T_2(n_2)$ since (n_1, n_2, n_1, n_2) is degenerate. Hence $\widehat{(n_2, n_1, n_2, n_1, n_2} = \widehat{n_2}$.

Two target-equivalent Newcombian States a) have the same pure part, b) have an order like Newcombian Classes and c) are characterized with their worst payoff.

DEFINITION 6 (PURE PART OF A NON-DEGENERATE NEWCOMBIAN CLASS)

Two non-degenerate target-equivalent Newcombian States always have the same pure part: had they not, then they could not target the same outcomes. Consequently, we can define the pure part of a non-degenerate Newcombian Class

$$\hat{\eta}_1 \equiv \eta_1, \text{ for any } \eta \in \hat{\eta}.$$

DEFINITION 7 (ORDER OF A CLASS)

We call order of a class the minimum of the orders of its elements.

Example 14 In the assurance game, the Newcombian Class $\hat{o}_1 \supset \{o_1, (o_1, n_2)\}$ is of order 1.

DEFINITION 8 (WORST PAYOFF OF A NEWCOMBIAN CLASS)

Let $\hat{\eta}$ be a non-degenerate Newcombian Class. The set of $\hat{\eta}$-targeted outcomes is finite and non-empty. Hence the current player's payoff $\mathbf{payoff}_i = a_i^{pc_{i-1}}$ has a minimum value on this set, which is $\hat{\eta}$'s worst payoff:

$$\mathbf{wp}(\hat{\eta}) = \min_{o \in T_i(\hat{\eta})} \mathbf{payoff}_i(o). \tag{2}$$

PROPOSITION 1

At any step i, a non-degenerate Newcombian Class is characterized by its worst payoff.

Example 15 In the assurance game, at step 2, $\widehat{(n_2,\ o_1)}$ is characterized by payoff 1.

Remark 1 As in Definition 8, we could define the best payoff of a non-degenerate class, but in the general case, we may have different classes with the same best payoff. The best payoff does not characterize a class.

Finally, the combination of Newcombian States (i.e., building a new, higher-order state with a node as the pure part and a Newcombian State as the discarding part) translates naturally to Newcombian Classes.

PROPOSITION 2

Given a move $m \in F(c_{i-1})$ and a Newcombian Class $\hat{\eta}$, the Newcombian Class of (m, η) is the same for all representants η of $\hat{\eta}$. Consequently, one can define for any $\eta \in \hat{\eta}$.

$$(m, \hat{\eta}) = \widehat{(m,\ \eta)}$$

Example 16 In the assurance game, $(n_2, \hat{o}_1) = \widehat{(n_2,\ o_1)}$ (characterized by its worst outcome 1).

The (explicit) current player's move

We now give another formula to compute the next move, which is equivalent to the one given in Definition 1 (the current player's move exists and is unique), with the difference that here the proof gives its explicit construction (the corresponding Newcombian State and the remaining, targeted outcomes). This is necessary for the general algorithm to explicitly compute the Perfect Prediction Equilibrium and also to determine the *minimum level* used in the quick algorithm (Section "Quick algorithm").

PROPOSITION 3

Let $\hat{\eta}^{(i)}$ be the only class that discards any outcome targeted by the brothers of its pure part ($\hat{\eta}^{(i)}$ is also called best Newcombian Class[18] *at step i*):

$$\forall n \in F\left(c_{i-1}\right) \setminus \{\boldsymbol{pure}(\hat{\eta}^{(i)})\}: \quad T_i(n,\ \hat{\eta}^{(i)}) = \emptyset \tag{3}$$

This class $\hat{\eta}^{(i)}$ exists and is unique.

Example 17 In the assurance game, $T_2\,(o_1, n_2, o_1) = \emptyset$ so that $\widehat{(n_2,\ o_1)}$ is the class we are looking for. In the Γ-game, $T_2\,(n_1, n_2, n_1, n_2) = \emptyset$ so that $\widehat{(n_2,\ n_1,\ n_2)}$ is the class that discards any outcome in the other subtrees than that of its pure part.

Now, if we consider any node $n \in F\,(c_{i-1})\backslash\{\mathbf{pure}(\hat{\eta}^{(i)})\}$, i.e. any brother of $\hat{\eta}_1^{(i)}$, then every n-targeted outcome is worse than the worst $\hat{\eta}^{(i)}$ targeted outcome, in other words n's *best payoff* is lower than $\hat{\eta}^{(i)}$'s *worst payoff*.

At this stage, the second principle concludes that the current player moves on to the pure part of $\hat{\eta}^{(i)}$. Later on, a player can only consider outcomes in $T_i(\hat{\eta}^{(i)})$, because had player $P_{C_{i-1}}$ anticipated another outcome, he would have deviated.

It is actually the maximum of a total order relation. A partial order relation can be defined on all Newcombian States, and Newcombian Classes are defined so as to make this relation a relation of total order on them.

PROPOSITION 4

Then:

- *the current player's move is* $c_i = \mathbf{pure}(\hat{\eta}^{(i)})$
- *the remaining outcomes are* $I_i = T_i(\hat{\eta}^{(i)})$

Example 18 In the assurance game, $c_2 = \mathbf{pure}(n_2, o_1) = n_2$ and $I_2 = T_2(n_2, o_1) = \{o_4\}$. In the Γ-game, $c_2 = \mathbf{pure}(n_2, n_1, n_2) = n_2$ and $I_2 = T_2(n_2, n_1, n_2) = \{o_7, o_9, o_{10}, o_{11}\}$.

An illustration of the constructions used in the proofs

The proof of existence in Proposition 3 gives us an explicit algorithm to compute the current player's move. The main idea is to recursively (over k) compute the Newcombian Class $\hat{\eta}_{(k)}^{(i)}$ of order k which has the highest worst payoff.

At some point, one of these Newcombian Classes $\hat{\eta}^{(i)}$ is the one we are looking for.

The following example shows this construction.

EXAMPLE 19

In game Γ, at step 2 (remember that step 1 is directly defined, because the game starts at the root), with respect to Peter (Figure 14.9):

There are two Newcombian Classes of order 1: $\widehat{n_1}$ and $\widehat{n_2}$. Their worst payoffs with respect to Peter are, respectively, −1, and 0. $\widehat{n_2}$ has the highest worst payoff. Hence $\hat{n}^{(2)}_{(1)} = \widehat{n_2}$.

There is only one Newcombian Classes of order 2: $\widehat{(n_1, n_2)}$. $\widehat{(n_2, n_1)}$ is not of order 2, because in fact it is equal to the class $\widehat{n_1}$. Hence we have $\hat{n}^{(2)}_{(2)} = \widehat{(n_1, n_2)}$.

We proceed by iteration:

$\hat{n}^{(2)}_{(1)} = \widehat{n_2}$ and the highest worst payoff is 1 (in n_1's subtree),

$\hat{n}^{(2)}_{(2)} = \widehat{(n_1, n_2)}$ and the highest worst payoff is 2 (in n_2's subtree),

$\hat{n}^{(2)}_{(3)} = \widehat{(n_2, n_1, n_2)}$,

and finally since T1 $(n_1, n_2, n_1, n_2) = \emptyset$, we have $\hat{n}^{(2)}_{(3)} = \widehat{(n_2, n_1, n_2)} = \hat{\eta}^{(2)}$.

Finally, the proof of uniqueness in Proposition 3 provides us with a quick algorithm to determine the current player's move – but by skipping the procedure described in the proof of existence in Proposition 3, we cannot tell the order of the move, only its worst payoff and the targeted outcomes.

Therefore the preemption structure analysis indeed leads to the same results as the original definition, and it is a powerful tool which provides us with two algorithms to compute the equilibrium.

The algorithms

In this part the reader will find two algorithms computing the PPE as presented in Section "Construction of the Perfect Prediction Equilibrium" (see Figure 14.9 and 14.10):

- the general algorithm determines completely the Newcombian structure leading to each current player's move. It has been directly derived from the proof of existence in Proposition 3, so that this proof is a proof of correctness for the algorithm.
- the quick algorithm calculates directly the set of remaining outcomes at each current player's move by choosing the branch with the best outcome and eliminating all outcomes below some minimum level. This algorithm has been directly derived from the proof of uniqueness in Proposition 3, so that this proof is also a proof of correctness for the algorithm.

Both algorithms run in polynomial time with respect to the size of the tree.

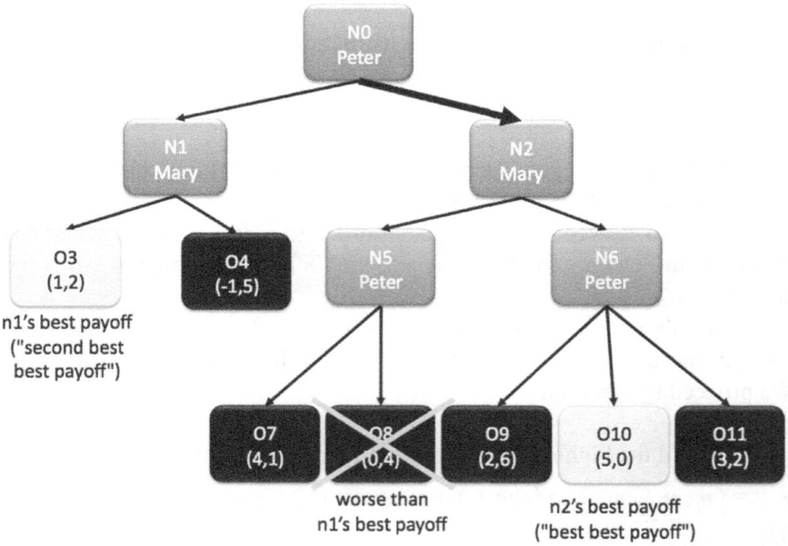

Figure 14.10 Illustration of the quick algorithm to determine step 2 in Game Γ

General algorithm

This algorithm computes explicitly all intermediate discardings. It runs in $O(n^3d)$ where n is the number of nodes and leaves in the tree and d its depth. The equilibrium path is called $(c_i)_{i=1..d}$.

The algorithm is initialized with:

$$c_1 = n_0 \left(\text{the root}\right)$$
$$I_1 = \left\{\text{all outcomes of the game}\right\}$$

Then a finite induction on i gives all $(c_i)_{i=1..d}$ and all $(I_i)_{i=1..d}$:

at each step i, a finite induction on k gives a series of Newcombian States:

$$\{\hat{\eta}^{(i)}_{(1)}\} = \arg \max_{\substack{\hat{\eta} \\ \text{order}(\hat{\eta})=1}} \min_{o \in T_i(\hat{\eta})} \mathbf{payoff}_i(o)$$

$$\{\hat{\eta}^{(i)}_{(k+1)}\} = \arg \max_{\substack{\hat{\eta} \\ \widehat{\eta = (n, \eta^{(i)}_{(k)})} \\ n \in F(c_i - 1) \setminus \{\hat{\eta}^{(i)}_{(k)1}\} \\ T_i(\hat{\eta}) \neq \emptyset}} \min_{o \in T_i(\hat{\eta})} \mathbf{payoff}_i(o)$$

and stops at some k, giving $\hat{\eta}^{(i)}_{(k)} = \hat{\eta}^{(i)}$.

Then

- the current player's move is $c_i = \mathbf{pure}(\hat{\eta}^{(i)})$
- the remaining outcomes are $I_i = T_i(\hat{\eta}^{(i)})$.

The induction ends when the path reaches an outcome:

$$I_d = \{c_d\}.$$

See proof of Proposition 3 for the logic underlying this algorithm.

Quick algorithm

This algorithm calculates the equilibrium path without using the preemption structure. It runs in $O(nd)$ where n is the number of nodes and leaves in the tree and d its depth.

```
o ← the root of the tree
While (o is not an outcome)
    p ← current player at node o
    s ← the subtree starting at an offspring of o
        with the maximum payoff for player p
    If (there are other subtrees than s)
        M ← player p's maximum payoff in the other subtrees than s
        Eliminate all other subtrees than s
        Discard in s all outcomes with a payoff lower than M for player p
        Clean the tree (remove all interrupted paths)
    o ← the root of s
Return o.
```

EXAMPLE 20

An example of application of this algorithm at the root is shown on Figure 14.10. Peter's highest payoff is at the n_2-targeted outcome o_{10}: 5. Among the brothers of n_2, the subtree at n_1 has the highest best payoff: 1. We discard all n_2-targeted outcomes whose payoff with respect to Peter are lower than 1: o_8. We get the same next move $c_2 = n_2$ and the same set $I_2 = \{o_7, o_9, o_{10}, o_{11}\}$ as by doing the full procedure at step 2 (Figure 14.9).

Annex – proofs of lemmas, theorems and propositions

Proof (Lemma 1)

We prove each of the three points:

1 The outcome in I_{i-1} with the highest payoff for the current player $p_{c_{i-1}}$:

$$\arg\max_{o \in I_{i-1}} a_o^{p_{c_{i-1}}}$$

cannot be discarded by a Newcombian State η. Its payoff would namely have to be lower than the worst outcome of a non-empty subset $T_i(\eta)$ of I_{i-1}, which is in contradiction with its definition.

2 Let us suppose that I_i contains at least two outcomes descending from two different offsprings of c_{i-1}.

Let o_m be the worst outcome for $p_{c_{i-1}}$ in I_i and f_m its ancestor among the offsprings of c_{i-1}. We will show that o_m should have been discarded and so cannot be in I_i.

By assumption, there is another offspring $f_p \neq f_m$ of c_{i-1}, with at least one outcome which has not been discarded – let o_p be the worst one of those, and (f_p, η) a Newcombian State. Because o_p is not discarded, $o_p \in T_i(f_p, \eta)$. By definition of o_m and because of the strict preference between two outcomes, om is strictly worse than o_p (which is the worst outcome in $T_i(f_p, \eta)$), thus is preempted by (f_p, η).

This is in contradiction with the fact that $o_m \in I_i$.

Proof (Theorem 1)

The induction presented in Lemma 1 discards all outcomes but one. Furthermore, no other reasoning can discard this last outcome. The two players, having anticipated it, have no interest in modifying their choices and will play towards this outcome. Q.E.D.

Proof (Theorem 2)

Suppose the outcome of the Perfect Prediction Equilibrium o is not Pareto-optimal. Then there must be some outcome o^P, which Pareto-improves o:

$$a_o^{Peter} < a_{o^P}^{Peter}$$
$$a_o^{Mary} < a_{o^P}^{Mary}$$

(Both inequalities are strict because of the strict preferences).

This outcome o^P has been discarded at some move i by a Newcombian State η of order k.

One of two:

- either $o \in T(\eta)$, in which case the current player's payoff at o is greater than (or equal to) η's worst payoff
- or $o \notin T(\eta)$, but since o was not discarded at that stage, the current player's payoff at o is necessarily strictly greater than η's worst payoff.

Since the current player's payoff at o_P is lower than η's worst payoff, in both cases, we have contradicted the above inequalities. Q.E.D.

Proof (Proposition 1)

Given a payoff x, there is only one outcome o that will give x to the current player, in virtue of the assumption that all payoffs are different. If two nodes n and n' in $F(c_{i-1})$ are different, then they cannot target the same outcome: $n \neq n' \Rightarrow T_i(n) \cap T_i(n') = \emptyset$. Hence there is a unique node n in $F(c_{i-1})$ such that outcome o is the descendant of node n.

There is only one Newcombian Class whose pure part is n and whose worst payoff is x. This is because the Newcombian State p discards all outcomes worse than the worst p-targeted outcome, whereas all better outcomes are not discarded. Hence the required Newcombian Class is defined by the set of n-targeted outcomes whose payoffs are greater than or equal to x. Q.E.D.

Proof (Proposition 2)

Discarding only depends on the worst outcome of the discarding Newcombian State. Q.E.D.

Proof (Proposition 3) (Existence and uniqueness of move $\hat{\eta}^{(i)}$)

Uniqueness: The pure part n of the class $\hat{\eta}^{(i)}$ necessarily targets the outcome with the highest payoff with respect to the current player. If not, then $\hat{\eta}^{(i)}$ could not discard precisely this outcome with the highest payoff, which contradicts the definition of $\hat{\eta}^{(i)}$.

Among the brothers of n, we call m the node which has the highest best payoff. Then $\hat{\eta}^{(i)}$'s worst payoff is the minimum of the payoffs of the n-targeted outcomes, which are (strictly) greater than m's best payoff. A reason for it is that it is the minimum level to discard all outcomes targeted by the brothers of n. And it cannot be higher, since there is no other class which could have discarded the outcome relative to this value.

According to Proposition 1, $\hat{\eta}^{(i)}$ is fully determined by its worst payoff.

Existence: let us define a procedure based on several *little steps k*, which are to be distinguished from the *step i*. With respect to step i, we define the **best Newcombian Class of order** k denoted $\hat{\eta}^{(i)}_{(k)}$ by induction on little step k.

Let us begin with $k = 1$. The best Newcombian Class of order 1, $\hat{\eta}^{(i)}_{(1)}$, is the Newcombian Class of order 1 with the highest worst payoff. This class exists, since Newcombian Classes of order 1 are identified with nodes in $F(c_{i-1})$, which are all non-degenerate. Their worst payoffs are all distinct (see Proposition 1), so is $\hat{\eta}^{(i)}_{(1)}$ unique.

$$\{\hat{\eta}^{(i)}_{(1)}\} = \arg \max_{\substack{\hat{\eta} \\ \text{order}(\hat{\eta})=1}} \min_{o \in T_i(\hat{\eta})} \mathbf{payoff}_i(o) \tag{4}$$

Suppose now we have defined $\hat{\eta}^{(i)}_{(k)}$ for some $k \geq 1$. We have to distinguish between two cases:

1. Either $\hat{\eta}^{(i)}_{(k)}$ discards any outcome targeted by the brothers of its pure part $\mathbf{pure}(\hat{\eta}^{(i)}_{(k)})$, so the procedure is over and we have reached $\hat{\eta}^{(i)} = \hat{\eta}^{(i)}_{(k)}$
2. Or there are still some brothers n of $\mathbf{pure}(\hat{\eta}^{(i)}_{(k)})$, such that $(n, \hat{\eta}^{(i)}_{(k)})$ is not degenerate. Then, by definition, the best Newcombian Class $\hat{\eta}^{(i)}_{(k+1)}$ of order $k+1$ will be the non-degenerate class $(n, \hat{\eta}^{(i)}_{(k)})$ with the highest worst payoff.

As for $\hat{\eta}^{(i)}_{(1)}$, this class exists and is unique, because it is the maximum of the injective function $\hat{\eta} \rightarrow \mathbf{wp}(\hat{\eta}) = \min_{0 \in T_i(\hat{\eta})} \mathbf{payoff}_i(o)$ on a finite set:

$$\{\hat{\eta}^{(i)}_{(k+1)}\} = \arg \max_{\substack{\hat{\eta} \\ \hat{\eta}=(n,\hat{\eta}^{(i)}_{(k)}) \\ n \in F(c_{i-1}) \setminus \{\mathbf{pure}(\hat{\eta}^{(i)}_{(k)})\} \\ T_i(\hat{\eta}) \neq \emptyset}} \min_{0 \in T_i(\hat{\eta})} \mathbf{payoff}_i(o) \tag{5}$$

For each $n \in \mathrm{F}(c_{i-1}) \setminus \{\mathbf{pure}(\hat{\eta}^{(i)}_{(k)})\}$, because $(n, \hat{\eta}^{(i)}_{(k)})$ is non-degenerate, there are some n-targeted outcomes which have not been discarded by $\hat{\eta}^{(i)}_{(k)}$, i.e. $\mathbf{wp}((n, \hat{\eta}^{(i)}_{(k)})) > \mathbf{wp}(\hat{\eta}^{(i)}_{(k)})$. Since $\hat{\eta}^{(i)}_{(k+1)}$ is one of these $(n, \hat{\eta}^{(i)}_{(k)})$, $\mathbf{wp}(\hat{\eta}^{(i)}_{(k+1)}) > \mathbf{wp}(\hat{\eta}^{(i)}_{(k)})$.

Since the set of outcomes is finite, the sequence $(\mathbf{wp}(\hat{\eta}^{(i)}_{(k)}))_{k \geq 1}$ cannot increase indefinitely: we will necessarily reach case 1 for some finite k. This shows the existence of $\hat{\eta}^{(i)}$. Q.E.D.

Proof (Proposition 4) (Equivalent definitions of c_i and I_i)

Let us denote c_i and I_i as the current player's move and the set of the not-yet-discarded outcomes as defined in Lemma 1, and let us denote c'_i and I'_i as they are suggested in Proposition 4.

In the uniqueness proof of $\hat{\eta}^{(i)}$ we mentioned that c'_i necessarily targets the outcome o with the highest payoff with respect to the current player. This very outcome cannot be discarded, hence $o \in I_i$. According to Lemma 1, all outcomes in I_i, thus o as well, are the descendants of c_i. Hence $c_i = c'_i$.

I_i is defined as the set of all the outcomes that cannot be discarded at step i. First, we have $I_i \subset I'_i$ since a non-discarded outcome at step i must be a descendant of c_i (Lemma 1) and has to be targeted by the best Newcombian Class (because it is not discarded).

Then, we have $I'_i \subset I_i$: all outcomes in I'_i cannot be discarded by anything, because the worst of them is strictly greater than the best outcome among the descendants of the brothers of c_i (Uniqueness proof of Proposition 3).

Hence, $I_i = I'_i$ as well. Q.E.D.

Annex – biped games: complete analysis

In this section, we perform a complete analysis of biped games and investigate when the Subgame Perfect Equilibrium is the same as the Perfect Prediction Equilibrium and when it is not.

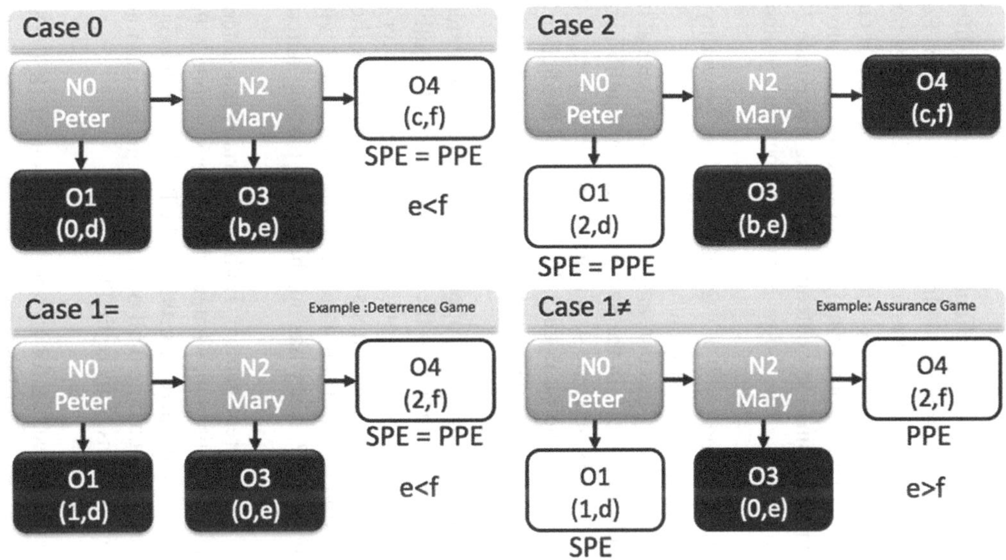

Figure 14.11 Biped games: the four cases

In our framework, only the order relation (preferences) between the outcomes for each player is relevant, so that without loss of generality we can assume that the payoffs are 0, 1 and 2 for each player. If we label the payoffs (*a*, *d*), (*b*, *e*) and (*c*, *f*), we have $\frac{3!.3!}{2}=18$ different games. (We divide by two because exchanging (*b*, *e*) and (*c*, *f*) does not change the game). Among these 18 games, we can distinguish four cases.

- Case 0 ($a = 0$, assuming $e < f$ without loss of generality – 6 different games). Both equilibria reach outcome 4. In the Subgame Perfect Equilibrium, if Mary plays at node 2, she will prefer outcome 4 which gives her f, and Peter will get c. Since $c > 0$ (no indifference), Peter at node 0 will choose node 2. In the Perfect Prediction Equilibrium, Peter cannot preempt anything but outcome 1 (with node 2, since any outcome stemming from node 2 is better than outcome 1) so that Mary can choose her favorite outcome: outcome 4. This is the PPE.
- Case 1 ($a = 1$, assuming $b = 0$, $c = 2$ without loss of generality – 6 different games). This case splits into two subcases:
- Case 1= ($e < f$, i.e., Mary has the same preferences as Peter at node 2). Both equilibria reach outcome 4. In the Subgame Perfect Equilibrium, Mary playing at node 2 chooses outcome 4. She gets f and Peter gets 2. Peter playing at node 0 will hence choose node 2. In the Perfect Prediction Equilibrium, Peter preempts outcome 3 with outcome 0 and then plays node 2. Mary has no choice but playing outcome 4.
- Case 1≠ ($e > f$, i.e., Mary has opposite preferences to Peter at node 2). The equilibria are different. In the Subgame Perfect Equilibrium, Mary playing at node 2 chooses outcome 2. She gets e and Peter gets 0. Peter playing at node 0 will hence choose outcome 1, which is the SPE. In the Perfect Prediction Equilibrium, Peter preempts outcome 3 with outcome 0 and then plays node 2. Mary has no choice but playing outcome 4, which is the PPE.
- Case 2 ($a = 2$–6 different games). Both equilibria reach outcome 1. In the Subgame Perfect Equilibrium, whatever Mary plays at node 2, Peter at node 0 will choose outcome 0 where he gets 2. In the Perfect Prediction Equilibrium, Peter preempts with outcome 0 all outcomes stemming from node 2 so that only outcome 0 remains. This is the PPE.

Hence, it is interesting to see that for 15 biped games out of 18, the Subgame Perfect Equilibrium and the Perfect Prediction Equilibrium are the same. Only three games lead to different equilibria.

For one of these three games ($d = 0$, $e = 2$, $f = 1$), the Subgame Perfect Equilibrium encounters the Backward Induction Paradox (see Section "The Backward Induction Paradox"), which is solved by the Perfect Prediction Equilibrium. For the two other games ($d = 2$, $e = 1$, $f = 0$ and $d = 1$, $e = 2$, $f = 0$), Peter's preempting power is also stronger than Mary's propensity to deviate, leading though to a PPE whose payoff is worse for Mary than at the SPE (o_1).

Annex – the PPE as the solution of a first-order-logic equation system

In this section, we present how a first-order-logic equation system can be built for each game, so that the PPE is the unique solution to this system. This sets up an unambiguous formal basis for defining the PPE.

The equations described in Section "The system of equations" induce a graph on the powerset of the outcomes: each equation contributes an edge from a set of logically impossible outcomes to a bigger set of logically impossible outcomes. Only the equations indexed on a vertex in the connected component of the empty set (i.e., all sets of logically impossible outcomes that can appear at all in any step of a reasoning) are considered for the system. A reasoning can be seen as a walk in the powerset graph induced by the first-order-logics equations, starting at the empty set. There is a unique outcome which belongs to no set in the connected component of the empty set, and this outcome is the outcome of the PPE.

Framework

The framework is the same as in this paper. O is the set of all outcomes, N is the set of all nodes, $F(n)$ is the set of the children of node n. $D(n)$ is the set of the outcomes which are descendants of node n. $P(n)$ is the parent of node or outcome n. p_n is the player playing at node n. a_p^o is the payoff of player p at outcome o.

Reaction path of a tree (second principle)

For each tree T, we say that a path R = $(r_i)_{0 \leq i \leq l}$ starting at the root is a reaction path of T if it fulfills the following conditions:

- r_0 is the root
- For any $0 < i \leq l$, $r_i \in F(r_{i-1})$
- (Second principle) For any $0 < i \leq l$: all outcomes in $D(r_i)$ are better than all outcomes descending from the siblings of r_i for the player at r_{i-1}
- It is maximal (there is no longer reaction path).

A non-empty tree always has exactly one reaction path (possibly simply its root). This is denoted $T \rightarrow R$. Since a path is uniquely identified by its last node, we will also write $T \rightarrow r_l$. Note that r_l (the last node in R) is not necessarily an outcome.

Preempting reaction path of a tree to an outcome (first principle)

For each tree T and each one of its outcomes o, we say that a path R = $(r_i)_i$ starting at the root is a preempting reaction path of T to o if it fulfills the following conditions:

- $(r_i)_{i<l}$ is a reaction path of T
- $r_l \in F\left(r_{l-1}\right)$

- $o \notin / D(r_l)$
- (First principle) All outcomes in $D(r_l)$ are better than o for the player at r_{l-1}.

This is denoted $T \overset{o}{\rightsquigarrow} R$. Since a path is uniquely identified by its last node, we will also write $T \overset{o}{\rightsquigarrow} r_l$. Note that a preempting reaction path may not exist given a tree and an outcome.

Outcome powerset graph

More precisely, we can organize all sets of outcomes (subsets of O) in a graph as follows.

For each reaction path $T \setminus U \rightarrow r$, there is an edge from U to $U \cup (O \setminus D(r))$.

For each preempting reaction path $T \setminus U \overset{o}{\rightsquigarrow} r$, there is an edge from U to $U \cup \{o\}$.

The semantics of an edge is: if all outcomes on the left cannot be in the solution, then all outcomes on the right cannot be either.

We call $\mathcal{U}$ the connected component of this graph containing the empty set. This corresponds to the sets of eliminated outcomes actually reachable in a reasoning.

The system of equations

Given a tree T, the system of equation is built as follows. Its unknowns are the variables S_n for every node or outcome n in the tree. S_n is true if and only if n is on the equilibrium path.

The PPE is defined as the (unique) solution of the system of equations as follows.

$$((C_n)_{n \in (N \cup O)}, (P_e^1)_{e \in E_1}, (P_e^2)_{e \in E_2})$$

The causal bridge equations

First, the equations maintaining the causal bridge are the following, for any node or outcome n:

$$S_n \Rightarrow S_{P(n)} \wedge \bigwedge_{s \in F(P(n)) \setminus \{n\}} \overline{S}_s \qquad (C_n)$$

i.e., if a node or outcome is in the solution, then its parent should be as well, and none of its siblings should be. This forces the solution to be a path on the tree.

The second-principle equations

Secondly, the second-principle equations are indexed on indices (U, r) in the subset E_2 of $\mathcal{U} \times O$ corresponding to reaction paths $T \setminus U \rightarrow r$:

$$\bigwedge_{p \in U} \bar{S}_p \Rightarrow S_r \qquad (P^2_{U,R})$$

The first-principle (preempting) equations

Finally, the first-principle equations are indexed on indices (U, o, r) in the subset E_1 of $\mathcal{U} \times O \times O$ corresponding to preempting reaction paths $T \setminus U \overset{o}{\rightsquigarrow} r$:

$$(\bigwedge_{p \in U} \bar{S}_p) \wedge S_o \Rightarrow S_r \qquad (P^2_{U,o,R})$$

Example for the assurance game

There are five variables here: S_0 = [root ∈ S], S_1 = [(P, D) ∈ S], S_2 = [(P, C) ∈ S], S_3 = [(M, D) ∈ S], S_4 = [(M, C) ∈ S] (here we use edge labels to allow comparison with Dupuy's original equations).

The reaction paths (and the corresponding edges in the outcome powerset graph) are:

$$\begin{array}{rl} T \rightarrow n_0 & \text{contributing edge } \emptyset \rightarrow \emptyset \\ T \setminus \{o_1\} \rightarrow o_3 & \text{contributing edge } \{o_1\} \rightarrow \{o_1, o_4\} \\ T \setminus \{o_3\} \rightarrow o_4 & \text{contributing edge } \{o_3\} \rightarrow \{o_1, o_3\} \\ T \setminus \{o_4\} \rightarrow o_1 & \text{contributing edge } \{o_4\} \rightarrow \{o_3, o_4\} \\ T \setminus \{o_1, o_3\} \rightarrow o_4 & \text{contributing edge } \{o_1, o_3\} \rightarrow \{o_1, o_3\} \\ T \setminus \{o_1, o_4\} \rightarrow o_3 & \text{contributing edge } \{o_3, o_4\} \rightarrow \{o_3, o_4\} \\ T \setminus \{o_3, o_4\} \rightarrow o_1 & \text{contributing edge } \{o_3, o_4\} \rightarrow \{o_3, o_4\} \end{array} \qquad (6)$$

In this example, only one preempting reaction path can be found:

$$T \overset{o_3}{\rightsquigarrow} o_1 \text{ contributing edge } \emptyset \rightarrow \{o_3\} \qquad (7)$$

The edges in the connected component of the empty set are marked in red.

Hence, the equations are:

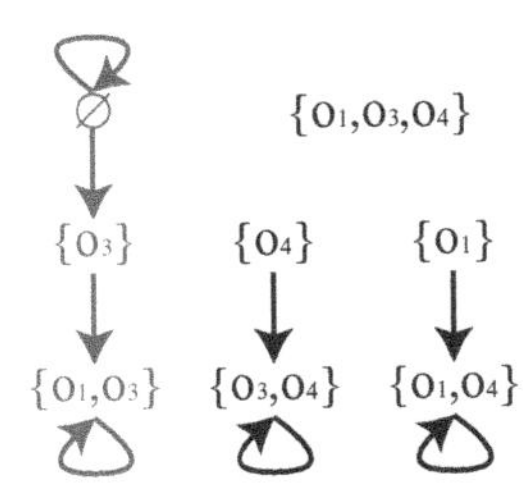

Figure 14.12 The Outcome Powerset Graph for the promise game

Causal bridge

$$
\begin{aligned}
S_0 &\Rightarrow true & (0 : C_0)\\
S_1 &\Rightarrow S_0 \wedge \overline{S}_2 & (1 : C_1)\\
S_2 &\Rightarrow S_0 \wedge \overline{S}_1 & (2 : C_2)\\
S_3 &\Rightarrow S_2 \wedge \overline{S}_4 & (3 : C_3)\\
S_4 &\Rightarrow S_2 \wedge \overline{S}_3 & (4 : C_4)
\end{aligned}
$$

First principle

$$S_3 \Rightarrow S_1 \qquad (5 : P^1_{\varnothing, o_3, o_1})$$

Second principle

$$
\begin{aligned}
\text{true} &\Rightarrow S_0 & (6 : P^2_{\varnothing, n_0})\\
\overline{S}_3 &\Rightarrow S_4 & (7 : P^2_{\{o_3\}, o_4})\\
\overline{S}_1 \wedge \overline{S}_3 &\Rightarrow S_4 & (8 : P^2_{\{o_1, o_3\}, o_4})
\end{aligned}
$$

Dupuy's equations correspond to (5) and (7), which imply S_0, $\overline{S}_1$, S_2, $\overline{S}_3$, S_4, i.e., root $\in S$, $(P, D) \notin S$, $(P, C) \in S$, $(M, D) \notin S$ and $(M, C) \in S$ (this is our equilibrium).

Let us show this again.

From (2) and (3), one can deduce $S_3 \Rightarrow \overline{S}_1$, so that because of (5), $\overline{S}_3$.

From (7) one deduces S_4, from (4) S_2 and from (2) or (6), S_0.

Is this a solution? With this assignment, the left part of (1), (3), (5) is false, making these implications all true, and in (0), (2), (4), (6), (7), (8), the left part is true, and the right part also, making the implications true as well.

Hence, it is proven that S_0, $\overline{S}_1$, S_2, $\overline{S}_3$, S_4 is the one and only solution of the system.

Annex – link with Newcombian States

At step i of the reasoning presented in Section "Construction of the Perfect Prediction Equilibrium", given the eliminated outcomes I_{i-1}, building a Newcombian State (η, p) corresponds to the following reasoning (we abuse notations by using a node for its number).

For the first principle (preempting an outcome o), using equation

$$P^1_{(O \setminus (I_{i-1}) \cup P_i\ (\text{discard}(p))), o, \eta}$$

and equation C_o leads for S_o to be false.

For the second principle (choosing η), using equation

$$P^2_{(O \setminus (I_{i-1}) \cup P_i\ (\text{discard};p)),\eta}$$

and equation C_η leads for S_η to be true and for S_o to be false for each sibling o of η.

Annex – the special case of invertible trees

The assurance game and take-or-leave game are special cases of games, which are called invertible trees in Dupuy (2000). They were the starting point for defining the PPE. Their trees detain a natural chronology: at each node, the outcome below the node is in the present, whereas the previous node on the left is in the past and the next one on the right is in the future.

For these games, the procedure is rather simple and we can give a simpler version of the algorithm (but it derives from the same procedure as in the general construction). At each node, starting from the root, the current player compares the present outcome with the outcomes in the future:

1 if the present outcome is better than all outcomes in the future, the procedure stops: the PPE outcome is the present one (the future outcomes are all preempted by the present Take-move)
2 if all outcomes in the future are better than the present one, then the player Leaves (the present outcome is preempted by the Leave-move)
3 if some outcomes in the future are worse and some better than the present outcome, then first all worse outcomes in the future are preempted by the present Take-move, and then the present outcome is discarded like in point 2.

15 Consumption externality and Pigovian taxation

A comparison between Rawls and Bentham

Herrade Igersheim and
Thi Kim Cuong Pham

Introduction

In November 2004, Philippe Mongin wrote in the French national newspaper *Les Echos* that:

> economists should give up treating value judgments as external parameters and make them the subject of explicit and argued assertions; in other words, they should fully take on the aim to construct a "normative science" of efficiency, justice and collective rationality.[1]

In order to elaborate a normative science, it is thus necessary to articulate explicitly some moral values and their axiomatic treatment. That is what modern theories of justice aim to do. According to Fleurbaey (1996), a theory of justice has to be developed in three stages: first, to select a philosophic theory of justice which advocates some moral values; second, to derive from it different axioms or formalized notions which reflect these values; finally, to study the consequences of the application of these axioms or notions to the problem at stake.

In line with this idea and following the lead of Sen (1974), the purpose of this paper is to apply two well-known welfare criteria – the Rawlsian maximin and the Benthamian utilitarianism – to a simple model with consumption externality. Then, employing a numerical example, we discuss our results in the light of the normative values encompassed by these two conceptions of justice.

In recent years, numerous empirical studies using a national household survey database shed light on the phenomenon of relative utility (Clark and Oswald, 1996; Ferrer-i-Carbonell, 2005; Clark, Frijters and Shields, 2008). Individual preferences are interdependent and the utility function of an individual depends partially on her relative consumption or wealth, often interpreted as her social status. This idea of relative utility is already present in Adam Smith's *Theory of Moral Sentiments*. Indeed, according to Smith, an individual can amass wealth not only to satisfy her basic material needs, but also to improve her relative position in society. This behavior is motivated by the desire to acquire a social status, which brings about social esteem, respect, admiration, etc. In the same line of ideas, Duesenberry

(1949) stresses that there is an effect of imitation in the consumption of individuals who belong to the same social categories. Sen (1992) mentions as well the relativity of well-being within his famous capability approach: being poor in a rich country implies a higher degree of social privation. Hence, the fact that individuals have a preference for social status leads to the sub-optimality of decentralized decisions for it gives rise to a negative externality. Indeed, social status is a relative notion: if one improves one's relative position, others see theirs as having deteriorated. This means that if one increases one's income, there is a loss of utility for others. Tax programs to restore the Pareto optimum are a subject of analysis for several papers (Wendner, 2003; Goméz, 2006; Turnovsky and Monteiro, 2007). But it is well-known that restoring the Pareto efficiency of the competitive equilibrium through public intervention is not sufficient *per se*: further investigations regarding the normative characteristics an equilibrium should satisfy are necessary.

In this specific setting and regarding the utilitarian case, we will come to the unsurprising conclusion that the strength of the social status motive influences the sum of transfers, but has no influence on the transfer distribution and hence on the welfare distribution. Conversely, in normal cases, a Rawlsian policy guarantees a real concern for the distribution of welfare. In particular, we will emphasize that the transfer distribution depends not only on the formal wage but on the real wage as well.[2] In other words, depending on how a society conceives the notion of labor disutility, the least-advantaged member of a society is not always the one with the lowest wage: other elements must be taken into account to characterize the *real* wage of an individual and thus her *real* opportunities. But in some extreme cases the Rawlsian policy leads to paradoxical results, since it recommends a higher transfer in favor of the most advantaged members of the society. Therefore, it could be concluded that the Rawlsian policy seems to be desirable in most cases but should be avoided in extreme ones.

Before going to the core of the paper, two matters should be made clear. First, we aim to develop new results at the collective level only. In other words, the Rawlsian and the utilitarian criteria are not used to frame questions at the individual level, i.e., the fact that individual well-being should be determined by a function based on utility (whether absolute or relative) or on primary goods is not discussed here. Second, our study belongs to a literature devoted to the comparison between these two criteria in different contexts. For example, Boskin and Sheshinski (1978) compare optimal income taxation in the presence of the social status motive. According to them, the optimal marginal tax rates in the utilitarian case are *more* sensitive to the variations of the social status motive than in the Rawlsian case. Besides, they show that one obtains substantial optimal redistribution taxation with either a utilitarian or a maximin social objective and thus claim that a utilitarian social objective is not necessarily "not egalitarian enough." Gary-Bobo (2006) compares the optimal allocations of education resulting from these two social welfare criteria and obtains two main results: first, when the information is symmetric, the optimal solution is the same whatever the type of the social planner (Rawlsian or utilitarian) and all the individuals obtain the same level of utility; second, asymmetric information gives rise to the paradox of the

Rawlsian optimum, i.e., the Rawlsian optimum increases the degree of inequality between the individual education levels. Their results contrast with ours with respect to two main points: in our study, the social status motive has more influence on the Rawlsian policy than on the utilitarian one and, for the former, gives rise to egalitarian concerns in most cases. But we accept Gary-Bobo's conclusions regarding one major issue: indeed, we show that the Rawlsian maximin can lead to paradoxical results.

The rest of our paper is organized as follows. In a second section, the normative implications of Rawlsian maximin and Benthamian utilitarianism are briefly reminded. The third section proposes a simple model with consumption externality and a numerical example. The fourth section concludes.

Rawls versus Bentham: two distinct optima

It is very well-known that the utilitarian rule is to maximize the sum of individual welfares, whereas the Rawlsian rule (through the difference principle) is to maximize the welfare level of the worst-off person. As a consequence, Rawls's maximin conception of justice and Bentham's utilitarianism lead to two distinct optima. But beyond these standard assessments, it could be worth emphasizing the normative implications of both rules. Let us on the one hand focus on utilitarianism. It corresponds to a teleological tradition since it derives the notion of rightness from the conception of the good. According to d'Aspremont (2011, p. 201), "the predominant example of the teleological approach is classical utilitarianism and the associated concept of utility". Utilitarianism, which proceeds from 18th century moral philosophy, is a social science which aims to make human beings happy. Initially developed by Hutcheson and Bentham, utilitarianism includes two levels: an individual level in which individual well-being is evaluated through the concept of utility and a collective level whose purpose is to aggregate all individual evaluations of social states and to deduce from this process the best social state for society. At the individual level, utility can be characterized in many different ways: for instance, while for Bentham utility relates to pleasure (hedonism), Sidgwick defines it as happiness (eudemonism). But, as stressed in the first section, our questioning in this paper concerns the collective level of utilitarianism. We know that the collective level of utilitarianism is obtained according to the famous Benthamian principle "the greatest happiness of the greatest number", in other words, the maximization of the sum of individual welfares or utilities.

On the other hand, the Rawlsian conception of justice gives priority to political and civic freedoms and shows a strong concern for equality. Indeed, Rawls's aim is to reconcile two rival traditions – Locke's related to freedom and Rousseau's connected with equality – and thus to develop a just and stable society in which individuals are free to pursue their own conception of the good (Rawls 1971, 1993). Hence, such a society must not only assure individuals that they will enjoy the formal freedom to live according to their aims, but also grant them the means thanks to which this formal freedom becomes real. As Rawls claims from the start, his objective is to elaborate a theory capable of competing with teleological doctrines, in particular utilitarianism. Like Kantian ethics, Rawls's justice as fairness is a deontological theory for which the right has priority over the good. Indeed, Rawls rejects utilitarianism and its sacrificial principle and sees individuals as ends and not as means. This objective becomes feasible in particular via the difference principle:[3] "all have equal basic liberties and the difference principle interprets the distinction between treating men as means only and treating them also as ends in themselves" (Rawls, 1971, p. 157). It should be noted that according to Rawls this statement is directly connected with the Kantian doctrine for his main aim is to consider each individual as an end, while he accuses utilitarianism of treating human beings as means for maximizing the collective sum of welfare.

Furthermore, the connection between the Rawlsian theory of justice and the maximin is suggested by Rawls himself. Indeed, he explicitly states that: "it is useful as a heuristic device to think of the two principles as the maximin solution to the problem of social justice. There is a relation between the two principles and the maximin rule for choice under uncertainty" (Rawls, 1971, p. 132). Thus, the well-known principle of maximin could be a way to formalize Rawls's theory, the difference principle in particular. But of course, one must keep in mind that Rawls's theory cannot be seen simply as the difference principle or the maximin. According to Edgren (1995, p. 332), "to take the difference principle as the essence of Rawls's work is an error". Let us recall too that the intense polemic between Rawls and some economists such as Arrow (1973), Musgrave (1974) or Harsanyi (1975, 1977) entertains some confusions and ambiguities on this issue. But beyond this polemic, many authors (see, among others, d'Aspremont and Gevers, 1977, 2002; d'Aspremont, 1985, 2011; Mongin and d'Aspremont, 1998 and Maniquet, 2004) propose to use the maximin or the leximin to deal with Rawls's theory in a welfarist framework.[4] Indeed, as utilitarianism, Rawls's theory can be defined by two levels: the individual one which proposes a non-welfarist evaluation of individual well-being (evaluation in terms of primary goods) and the collective one which aims to consider individuals as ends and not as means. It should be noted that these two Rawlsian levels differ in every respect from the utilitarian ones.

In a nutshell, the main normative distinction between the Rawlsian maximin and the utilitarian conceptions of justice relies in how both doctrines see individuals: either as ends or as means. Thanks to our simple model, we will show in the rest of our chapter how this normative difference occurs for the special case of Pigovian taxes with consumption externality.

A simple model with consumption externality

We consider a static economy where there are two groups of individuals distinguished by skills. The relative size is δ for the first group and 1- δ for the second, with $\delta \in (0,1)$. Individuals in each group are identical, so that there is a representative individual for each group. Each individual has a utility as follows:

$$u_i = (1-a)\ln c_i + a\ln s_i - b_i l_i \qquad (1)$$

where c_i, s_i, l_i are individual i's consumption, her social status and her labor time, respectively. s_i is supposed to be increasing with individual consumption c_i and decreasing with the average consumption in the society, $\overline{c}$. A simple manner to write this social status is: $s_i = c_i / \overline{c}$. Each individual is endowed with one unit of time that is divided between labor (l_i) and leisure ($1 - l_i$). Parameter a measures the strength of the social status motive, $a \in (0, 1)$. Note that the value of a is estimated at around 0.3 in Solnick and Hemenway (1998) and Johansson-Stenman, Carlsson and Daruvala (2002). Parameter b_i is the marginal disutility of labor or the marginal cost of effort in labor. Let us assume that group 2's skill is higher than group 1's skill so that if b_i is interpreted in terms of education years and training cost, one can suppose that $b_2 \geq b_1$ and $b_{1,}b_2 > 0$.

Competitive equilibrium

The competitive equilibrium of this economy is not efficient, because of the negative externality engendered by the individual quest for status. In this case, a Pigovian tax is established to reach an efficient competitive equilibrium. Consumption must be taxed to offset the incentive to overconsume in the quest for status. We assume that the government taxes individual i's consumption at the rate τ and distributes lump-sum transfers π_i so that the individual budget constraint is $(1 + \tau) = c_i = w_i l_i + \pi_i$. Transfers π_i are used to achieve a desirable distribution of welfare among individuals.

Considering a linear production function $f(L_1, L_2) = \gamma_1 L_1 + \gamma_2 L_2$ where γ_1 and γ_2 are marginal product of labor for agent 1 and 2. $\gamma_2 > \gamma_1$ and $L_1 = \delta\, l_1, L_2 = (1 - \delta) l_2$, competitive wages are $w_1 = \gamma_1$ and $w_2 = \gamma_2$. The government budget constraint is verified at the competitive equilibrium as individuals' budget constraints are balanced and the production function is homogeneous to degree 1:

$$\delta\pi_1 + (1-\delta)\pi_2 = \tau\left[\delta c_1 + (1-\delta)c_2\right] \tag{2}$$

At the competitive equilibrium, individual consumptions and labors are given by:

$$c_i = \frac{\gamma_i}{b_i(1+\tau)} \text{ and } l_i = \frac{1}{b_i} - \frac{\pi_i}{\gamma_i} \tag{3}$$

The social optimum and corrective taxation

Benthamian corrective taxation

A utilitarian optimal allocation, denoted, (c_i^u, l_i^u) is obtained if it solves the following problem:

$$\underset{(c_1, c_2, l_1, l_2)}{\text{Max}}\ \delta u_1(c_1, s_1, l_1) + (1-\delta)u_2(c_2, s_2, l_2)$$

$$\text{subject to} \begin{cases} \delta c_1 + (1-\delta)c_2 = f(L_1, L_2) \\ \overline{c} = \delta c_1 + (1-\delta)c_2 \end{cases}$$

Comparing the first-order conditions for a competitive equilibrium with that of the optimization problem above, it is straightforward to state that if each individual consumption is taxed at the rate:

$$\tau^u = \frac{a}{1-a} \tag{4}$$

and the following condition is verified:

$$\frac{\gamma_1}{b_1} = \frac{\gamma_2}{b_2} \tag{5}$$

then the competitive equilibrium is a utilitarian optimal allocation. It must be stressed that $d\tau^u/da > 0$, meaning that if the desire for social status increases, it implies an increase in the tax rate.[5]

At the utilitarian efficient competitive equilibrium, we obtain:

$$c_1 = c_2 = \frac{(1-a)\gamma_i}{b_i} \tag{6}$$

$$l_1 = \frac{1}{b_1} - \frac{\pi_1^u}{\gamma_1},\ l_2 = \frac{1}{b_2} - \frac{\pi_2^u}{\gamma_2} \tag{7}$$

$$u_1 = (1-a)\ln c_1 - 1 + \frac{b_1\pi_1^u}{\gamma_1},\ u_2 = (1-a)\ln c_2 - 1 + \frac{b_2\pi_2^u}{\gamma_2} \tag{8}$$

It should be noted further that only a competitive equilibrium with a similar distribution of marginal product of labor relative to marginal cost of labor, $\gamma_1 / b_1 = \gamma_2 / b_2$ is a utilitarian optimal allocation. In addition, the representative individual 1's utility may be higher or lower than the representative individual 2's utility, depending on the lump-sum transfers π_i^u , and the latter verify the government's balanced budget constraint (2). Then we observe that :

$$\pi_1^u \lesseqgtr \pi_1^u \rightarrow u_1 \lesseqgtr u_2 \tag{9}$$

Rawlsian corrective taxation

In the present model, the Rawlsian optimal allocation is the optimal solution of the following optimization problem:

$$\underset{(c_1,c_2,l_1,l_2)}{\text{Max}}\ u_1(c_1,s_1,l_1)$$

$$\text{subject to} \begin{cases} u_2(c_2,s_2,l_2) \geq u_1(c_1,s_1,l_1) \\ \delta c_1 + (1-\delta)c_2 = f(L_1,L_2) \\ \bar{c} = \delta c_1 + (1-\delta)c_2 \end{cases}$$

The first constraint, called the compatibility constraint, ensures that the Rawlsian optimal allocation will satisfy the maximin principle: individuals of kind 1's utility is maximized only if individuals of kind 1 are not better off than individuals of kind 2.

An important difference between the Rawlsian and the utilitarian policies is that condition (5) is not required for a competitive equilibrium to achieve the Rawlsian optimal allocation. In other words, individual wages relative to marginal costs of labor (γ_i/b_i) are not necessarily similar at the Rawlsian efficient competitive equilibrium. However, as the compatibility constraint is binding, since the Lagrange multiplier associated with this constraint is positive, then[6]

$$u_1 = u_2 \tag{10}$$

Concerning the tax rate, it is similar to the utilitarian one because of the specific form of our utility function. As a consequence, the difference between the two policies lies in the welfare distribution and in the transfer policies.

At the Rawlsian efficient competitive equilibrium, we have:

$$c_1 = \frac{(1-a)\gamma_1}{b_1},\ c_2 = \frac{(1-a)\gamma_2}{b_2} \tag{11}$$

$$l_1 = \frac{1}{b_1} - \frac{\pi_1^m}{\gamma_1},\ l_2 = \frac{1}{b_2} - \frac{\pi_2^m}{\gamma_2} \tag{12}$$

$$u_1 = \ln c_1 - a \ln \bar{c} - 1 + \frac{b_1 \pi_1^m}{\gamma_1},\ u_2 = \ln c_2 - a \ln \bar{c} - 1 + \frac{b_2 \pi_2^m}{\gamma_2} \tag{13}$$

Unlike the utilitarian criterion, the Rawlsian criterion requires that there is only one transfer distribution under which the competitive equilibrium is Pareto efficient. This transfer distribution must be such that $u_1 = u_2$ and the condition (2) is verified. Algebraic manipulation gives:

$$\pi_1^m = a\frac{\gamma_1}{b_1} + \frac{(1-\delta)(\gamma_1/b_1)(\gamma_2/b_2)}{\delta(\gamma_1/b_1)+(1-\delta)(\gamma_2/b_2)} \ln\frac{(\gamma_2/b_2)}{(\gamma_1/b_1)} \tag{14}$$

$$\pi_2^m = a\frac{\gamma_2}{b_2} + \frac{\delta(\gamma_1/b_1)(\gamma_2/b_2)}{\delta(\gamma_1/b_1)+(1-\delta)(\gamma_2/b_2)} \ln\frac{(\gamma_2/b_2)}{(\gamma_1/b_1)} \tag{15}$$

Following the values of marginal product of labor relative to marginal cost of labor, γ_i/b_i, the transfer for individuals of kind 1 may be more or less important than the transfer for individuals of group 2, even if group 1 is *a priori* less well off than group 2 in terms of the wage rate, the latter being equal to the marginal product of labor. We will develop this issue in the next section.

A numerical example

To illustrate the above results, the following parameters need to be defined: a, γ_1, γ_2, b_1, b_2 and δ. First, we fix a =0.3 as do Brekke and Howarth (2002), which corresponds to empirical findings. Based on 2010 French statistics examined by

Landais, Piketty and Saez (2011, chap. 1), we fix $\delta = 0.9$, $w_2 = 4.3$ and $w_1 = 1$. For a linear production function $f(L_1,L_2) = \gamma_1 L_1 + \gamma_2 L_2$, these wage rates mean that the marginal product of skilled labor, γ_2, is equal to $w_2 = 4.3$, while the one of unskilled labor, γ_1, is equal to $w_1 = 1$. Further, we normalize b_1 at unity while b_2 will be assumed to vary in $[1,+\infty[$.

Let us turn first to the analysis of the Rawlsian optimal allocation. Figure 15.1 illustrates how the ratios π_2^m / π_1^m vary according to the labor disutility of individuals of group 2, b_2. Three transfer profiles can be distinguished: a) $\pi_2^m < \pi_1^m$ and $w_2 / b_2 > w_1 / b_1$ (for low values of b_2); b) $\pi_2^m > \pi_1^m$ and $w_2 / b_2 < w_1 / b_1$ (for middle values of b_2); c) $\pi_2^m < \pi_1^m$ and $w_2 / b_2 < w_1 / b_1$ (for high values of b_2).

Let us begin with profile 1. Transfer profile 1 corroborates the intuition of the maximin criterion in every respect since it recommends a higher transfer in favor of individuals of group 1 for they are poorer ($w_1 < w_2$) and relatively poorer – namely, the wage rate relative to the marginal cost of labor of individuals of group 2 is higher ($w_2 / b_2 > w_1 / b_1$). It must be noted further that for some rather weak values of b_2, the transfer in favor of individuals of group 2 is even negative, which then corresponds to a second tax for them. Indeed, when b_2 is weak, individuals of group 2 can work a great deal without an important level of effort and thus consume a great deal. In order to compensate individuals of group 1's loss of utility due to a high c_2, the government taxes group 2.

Transfer profile 2 could at first sight seem contrary to intuition since $\pi_2^m > \pi_1^m$ even though w_1 is weaker than w_2. But one also needs to consider the impact of

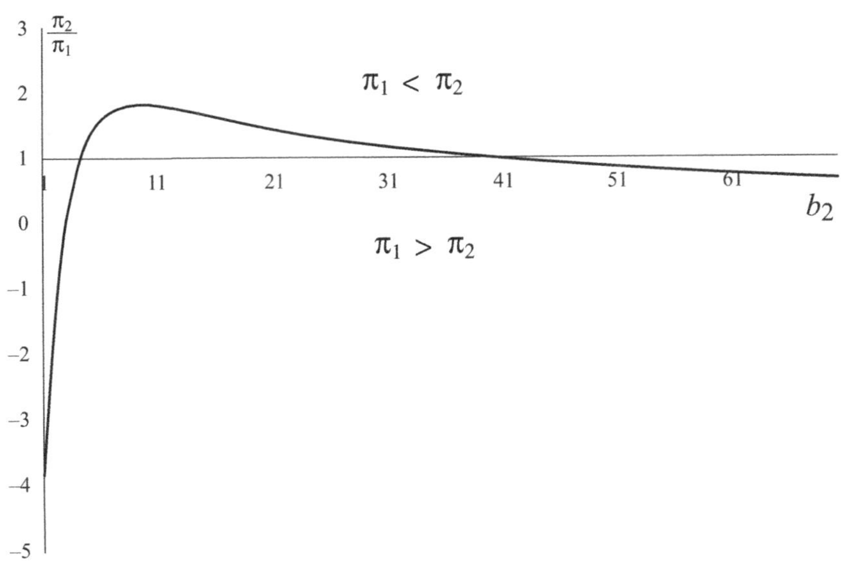

Figure 15.1 The Rawlsian maximin

the increasing disutility of labor of individuals of group 2, b_2. Indeed, for profile 2, one observes that $w_2 / b_2 < w_1 / b_1$. Thus, individuals of group 2 can be seen now as the least advantaged members regarding this ratio: we could say that they are relatively poorer than individuals of group 1.

Regarding the interpretations of profiles 1 and 2, it can be claimed that this model points out the phenomenon of the formal vs. the real wage. Indeed, the prescription in terms of transfers is consistent with the *formal wage* when b_2 is weak (profile 1), but this is no longer the case when b_2 increases. Then, the accent is put on the *real wage* (profile 2). When individuals of group 1 are richer than individuals of group 2 in terms of the real wage, i.e. $w_2 / b_2 < w_1 / b_1$, individuals of group 2 benefit from a higher amount of transfer.

Let us turn to transfer profile 3. Its recommendations contradict all preceding comments regarding the difference between the *formal wage* w_1 and *real wage* w_i/b_i and can be seen as paradoxical. As stated above, profile 3 arises with high values of b_2 (for instance, for $a = 0.3$, profile 3 occurs only when b_2 is superior to 40). As b_2 is very high, individuals of group 2 have to make more significant efforts to work. Then they work less. Thus l_2 and c_2 are low. Since social status matters in society, individuals of group 2 begin to suffer from the high value of c_1 regarding their own consumption. A first solution is to implement a high transfer in favor of individuals of group 2 as in transfer profile 2, but if this is not sufficient because b_2 is too high, a second solution is to implement a high transfer in favor of individuals of group 1 in order to curb l_2 and c_1 for $\partial l_i/\partial \pi_i < 0$: this second solution, which corresponds to transfer profile 3, is paradoxical since it amounts to decreasing the transfers in favor of the least advantaged group (i.e. individuals of group 2 with b_2 very high) and discouraging individuals of group 1 from working. This paradoxical result can be explained by the implications of the Rawlsian criterion: to equalize u_1 and u_1 in every circumstance. This echoes Gary-Bobo's Rawlsian paradox in terms of education (2006).

Let us now consider the utilitarian case. We stressed above that the competitive equilibrium is the utilitarian optimal allocation if $w_2 / b_2 = w_1 / b_1$, meaning here that b_2 / b_1 should be equal to 4.3. Let us admit that $b_1 = 1$ and $b_2 = 4.3$. We know that $\pi_1^u \lesseqgtr \pi_2^u \rightarrow u_1 \lesseqgtr u_2$ where $\delta\pi_1^u + (1-\delta)\pi_2^u = aw_i / b_i = a$ since here $w_i/b_i = 1$. Hence, for a weak preference for social status (such as $a = 0.3$ in our example), the sum of transfers is 0.3. The sum of transfers is increasing with the desire for social status: this result is logical and fully compatible with the tax rate which increases with a. Moreover, in this case, the utilitarian and Rawlsian sum of transfers are equal since $\delta\pi_1^m + (1-\delta)\pi_2^m = a(\delta w_1 / b_1 + (1-\delta) w_2 / b_2) = a$. Hence, no comparison between utilitarian and maximin transfer policies can proceed from the sum of transfers. However, it is possible to stress very important differences between the utilitarian optimal allocation and the Rawlsian optimal allocation on the basis of the transfer and welfare distributions. For the Rawlsian optimal allocation, when $b_2 = 4.3$ and $b_1 = 1$, the transfers π_1^m and π_2^m are identical: $\pi_1^m = \pi_2^m = a$. On the contrary, for the utilitarian optimal allocation, any distribution of transfers is possible, provided $\delta\pi_1^u + (1-\delta)\pi_2^u = a$. The same remark applies to the welfare distributions since the Rawlsian optimal allocation leads to $u_1 = u_2$ whereas the utilitarian optimal allocation makes no recommendation on these issues.

Concluding remarks

The aim of this paper was to apply the Rawlsian maximin conception of justice and the Benthamian utilitarianism to a model with consumption externality. The first step of our investigation was to recall the normative values of these two traditions, in particular the fact that they correspond to radically opposite theories: respectively, a deontological theory which conceives human beings as ends and a teleological one which sees them as means. Then, the second step consisted in applying these two doctrines to our model with consumption externality: two corrective policies were thus analyzed and compared.

The link between these doctrines and our results is rather straightforward. Specifically, the utilities of every individual must be equal so that the Rawlsian optimal allocation can be obtained, and the interpretation of the Rawlsian optimal allocation transfer profiles places the emphasis on the distinction between the formal and real wages for most cases. In other words, each individual is seen as an end since, first, no individual utility is favored over some others and, second, the *real* individual situations are assessed via the ratio w_i/b_i. But, for extreme cases (i.e. when b_2 is very high), the Rawlsian imperative to equalize u_1 and u_2 leads to a paradox since a higher transfer is made in favor of the most advantaged members of the society.

When considering a utilitarian social conception, we point out that there is no recommendation of transfer distribution to achieve utilitarian optimal allocation in a competitive economy with social status externality. This therefore means that one can obtain the utilitarian optimal allocation even if the transfer distribution systematically favors the richer group (whatever it is). This remark leads to the following statement: utilitarian optimal allocation policy does not take into account individuals *per se*, it just uses them as means in order to reach its objective. Thus, the interpretations of utilitarian and Rawlsian policies in the context of social status externality corroborate to some extent the normative values harbored by the Rawlsian theory of justice and Benthamian classical utilitarianism: human beings as means or as ends. But the paradoxical result we obtained in extreme cases sheds light on the limits of the implementation of Rawls's theory.

Notes

1 On this subject, see as well Mongin (2006).
2 It must be stressed that the notions of "real wage" and "formal wage" developed here refer to the Marxian distinction between real and formal freedom.
3 The difference principle is the second part of the second principle of justice and is defined as follows: "social and economic inequalities are to satisfy two conditions. First, . . . and second, they must be to the greatest benefit of the least advantaged members of society" (Rawls, 1993, p. 291).

4 In our model which includes two types of individuals only, maximin and leximin allocations lead to the same result.
5 On this issue, see also Brekke and Howarth (2002), Wendner (2003).
6 Spiegel (1993) obtained the same kind of results in another context.

Bibliography

Arrow, K.J. (1973), "Some ordinalist-utilitarian notes on Rawls's theory of justice", *The Journal of Philosophy*, 70, pp. 245–63.

Aspremont, C.D'. (1985), "Axioms for social welfare orderings", in L. Hurwicz, D. Schmeidler and H. Sonnenschein (eds), *Social Goals and Social Organizations: Essays in Memory of Elisha Pazner*, Cambridge University Press, Cambridge, pp. 19–76.

Aspremont, C.D.' (2011), "Interpersonal comparison with or without formal welfarism", in R. Ege and H. Igersheim (eds), *Freedom and Happiness in Economic Thought and Philosophy: From Clash to Reconciliation*, Routledge, London, pp. 201–11.

Aspremont, C.D.' and L. Gevers (1977), "Equity and the informational basis of collective choice", *Review of Economic Studies*, 44, pp. 199–210.

Aspremont, C.D.' and L. Gevers (2002), "Social welfare functionals and interpersonal comparability", in K.J. Arrow, A.K. Sen and K. Suzumura (eds), *Handbook of Social Choice and Welfare*, vol. 1, Elsevier Science, Amsterdam, pp. 459–541.

Boskin, M. and E. Sheshinski (1978), "Optimal redistributive taxation when individual welfare depends upon relative income", *Quartely Journal of Economics*, 92, pp. 589–601.

Brekke, K. and R.B. Howarth (2002), *Status, Growth and the Environment*, Edward Elgar, Northampton.

Clark, A.E., P. Frijters and M. Shields (2008), "Relative income, happiness and utility: An explanations for easterlin paradox and other puzzles", *Journal of Economic Literature*, 46, pp. 95–144.

Clark, A.E. and A.J. Oswald (1996), "Satisfaction and comparison income", *Journal of Public Economics*, 61, pp. 359–81.

Duesenberry, J.S. (1949), *Income, Saving and the Theory of Consumer Behaviour*, Harvard University Press, Cambridge, MA.

Edgren, J.A. (1995), "On the relevance of John Rawls's theory of justice to welfare economics", *Review of Social Economy*, 53, pp. 332–49.

Ferrer-i-Carbonell, A. (2005), "Income and well-being : An empirical analysis of the comparison income effect", *Journal of Public Economics*, 89, pp. 997–1019.

Fisher, W.H. and F.X. Hof (2000), "Relative consumption, economic growth and taxation", *Journal of Economics (Zeitschrift für Nationalökonomie)*, 73, pp. 241–62.

Fleurbaey, M. (1996), *Théories Economiques de la Justice*, Economica, Paris.

Gary-Bobo, R. (2006), "Éducation, Efficacité Économique et Justice Sociale: Une Approche Rawlsienne", *Revue d'Économie Politique*, 116, pp. 199–228.

Goméz, M. (2006), "Optimal consumption taxation in a model of endogenous growth with external habit formation", *Economics Letters*, 93, pp. 427–35.

Harsanyi, J.C. (1975), "Can the maximin principle serve as a basis for morality? A critique of John Rawls's theory", *American Political Science Review*, 69, pp. 594–606.

Harsanyi, J.C. (1977), "Morality and the theory of rational behaviour", in A.K. Sen and B. Williams (eds), *Utilitarianism and beyond*, Cambridge University Press, Cambridge, 1982, pp. 39–62.

Johansson-Stenman, O., F. Carlsson and D. Daruvala (2002), "Measuring hypothetical grandparents, preferences for equality and relative standing", *Economic Journal*, 112, pp. 362–83.

Landais, C., T. Piketty and E. Saez (2011), *Pour une révolution fiscale*, Seuil, Paris.

Lombardo, V. (2013), "Relative consumption and human capital accumulation", *Economics Bulletin*, 33(2), pp. 1091–1100.

Maniquet, F. (2004), "On the equivalence between welfarism and equality of opportunity", *Social Choice and Welfare*, 23, pp. 1–21.

Mongin, P. (2006), "A concept of progress for normative economics", *Economics and Philosophy*, 22, pp. 19–54.

Mongin, P. and C.D.' Aspremont (1998), "Utility theory and Ethics", in S. Barbera, P.J. Hammond and C. Seidl (eds), *Handbook of Utility Theory*, vol. 1: *Principles*, Kluwer, Dordrecht, pp. 371–481.

Musgrave, R.A. (1974), "Maximin, uncertainty, and the leisure trade-off", *Quarterly Journal of Economics*, 88, pp. 625–32.

Rawls, J. (1971), *A Theory of Justice*, Oxford University Press, Oxford, 1999.

Rawls, J. (1993), *Political Liberalism*, Columbia University Press, New York.

Rawls, J. (2000), *Lectures on the History of Moral Philosophy*, Harvard University Press, Cambridge, MA.

Sen, A.K. (1974), "Rawls versus Bentham: An axiomatic examination of the pure distribution problem", *Theory and Decision*, 4, pp. 301–9.

Sen, A.K. (1992), *Inequality Reexamined*, Clarendon Press, Oxford.

Solnick, S.J. and D. Hemenway (1998), "Is more always better? A survey on positional concerns", *Journal of Economic Behavior and Organization*, 37, pp. 373–83.

Spiegel, Y. (1993), " Rawlsian optimal population size", *Journal of Population Economics*, 3, pp. 363–73.

Turnovsky, S.J. and G. Monteiro (2007), "Consumption externalities, production externalities and efficient capital accumulation under time non-separable preferences", *European Economics Review*, 51, pp. 479–504.

Wendner, R. (2003), "Status, environmental externality, and optimal tax programs", *Economics Bulletin*, 5, pp. 1–10.

16 David Hume and rationality in decision-making

A case study on the economic reading of a philosopher

*André Lapidus**

Introduction

This paper is an unintentional product of an interrogation on the reasons why, as economists, we burden ourselves with the reading of past philosophers, whereas we already have a hard job in dealing with acknowledged economists of the past. The question might seem a bit rude and, for most of us, answering it would be superfluous: as economists, we do not need to answer it to go on working on philosophers. Rude though, this question is raised hereafter concerning the works of David Hume, as a special case study. It gave rise to four typical answers, which have in common to investigate alternative ways of borrowing something from a philosopher – here, from Hume. Something that we can use as economists:

1 A transposition of a way of reasoning, which had historically made sense for economists – and sometimes, still makes sense.
2 A direct contribution to economic ideas of his time.
3 An influence on acknowledged economists.
4 A challenge to contemporary economics.

Obviously, these four issues refer to possible approaches of the works of philosophers like Hume. Recalling their content should help emphasizing the last of them, which is retained in the following of the paper.

1 *A transposition of a way of reasoning.* The first issue echoes Karl Pribram's understanding of the history of economic reasoning, as applications of principles of reasoning elaborated elsewhere, namely in philosophy (Pribram 1983). This led him to stress the use of a nominalist method of reasoning, or of associationism, in Hume's criticism of Baconian economics (using Pribram's words) and in his contribution to the rise of utilitarianism. In the same way, Hume's careful attention to practical matters concerning economic life, his interest in the figure of the merchant, as emphasized, for instance, by M. Schabas and C. Wennerlind (2011), can be viewed as an effect of an empiricist approach to economic matters.

2 *A direct contribution to economic ideas of their time*. The second issue echoes J.A. Schumpeter's position, when he claimed that "[Hume's] economics has nothing whatever to do with either his psychology or his philosophy" (Schumpeter 1954: 474n.). This means that we would not be misleading when arguing that although a philosopher, we have good reasons to move away from Hume's *Treatise of Human Nature* (1739–40) and consider Hume to be an economist, when he deals, in some of the short texts introduced in his *Political Discourses* since 1752 onwards to be finally published as parts of the *Essays Political, Moral, and Literary* (1777), with such questions as interest, public expenditure, money and the balance of payment. It is in this way, for instance, that J.A. Frenkel and H.G. Johnson (1976) drew on Hume's price-specie flow mechanism in order to introduce historically the monetary approach to the balance of payments, or that M. Friedman (1987) opened his review article on the quantity theory of money.

3 *An influence on economists*. Typical of this issue is the attention paid to, say, the respective influence of Hegel and Kant on Marx and Walras. Such influence might be either complex, like in the case of Marx, when considering the transformations of the Hegelian concept of alienation into the Marxian concept of exploitation, or limited to a mere transposition, like for Walras who, drawing on a popularized knowledge of Kant, uses the distinction between phenomenon and noumenon in order to view exchange as a natural fact which constitutes the object of pure economics. Obviously, this issue is also involved in the discussion of Hume's influence on Adam Smith when, for instance, looking for the roots of the latter's moral philosophy or philosophy of knowledge, we are induced to go back from Smith's *Theory of Moral Sentiments* (1759) to books II or III of Hume's *Treatise* (1739–40), to his second *Enquiry* (1751) and to the 'Dissertation' (1757), or (with fewer textual evidence) from Smith's *History of Astronomy* to Hume's book I of the *Treatise* and to his first *Enquiry* (1748). Notably, such perspective focuses on a philosopher's work only insofar as it sheds special light on the work of the possibly influenced economist, which constitutes the determining stake.

4 *A challenge to contemporary economics*. The question is no more this of knowing how a philosopher – again, David Hume – did contribute to the shaping of the economic knowledge of his time, but how he might contribute to the shaping of the economic knowledge of our time. This means that when Hume writes as a philosopher, explicitly on those questions which Schumpeter, in the above quoted passage, regarded as irrelevant from an economic point of view, he challenges what we know in economics, analytically and methodologically. This claim was at least indirectly supported by such authors like Ken Binmore through the specific part he granted to David Hume in the history of ideas. Since the 1980s, he tried to explain various passages from the *Treatise on Human Nature*, book III, like the one about the "[t]wo men, who pull the oars of a boat, [and] do it by an agreement or convention, though they have never given promises to one another" (Hume 1739–40: 3.2.2.10;[1] see also 3.2.5.9). The same ideas are repeated, more than ten years

> later, in the second *Enquiry* (see Hume 1751: App. 3.8.) and provide a solution to some well-known difficulties in game theory concerning such topics like the selection of an equilibrium, or the implementation of a sustainable cooperation as equilibrium in repeated games (see Binmore 1994: 27–34; 2005: 4). Whatever our doubts about the question of knowing whether Hume did, or did not, have a firm enough intuition of a line of answers to these difficulties, I'd like to focus on the fact that Binmore's argument rests on the idea that Hume considered differently the relation between the self and the other, and that he aimed at investigating the consequences of such difference upon the interaction between individuals. From a methodological viewpoint, this paper might be considered in line with Binmore's approach to Hume. But analytically, it focuses not on interactions between individuals, but on decision-making in relation to rationality. Relying chiefly on books I and II of Hume's *Treatise*, it will be shown that he induces us to view rationality of both preferences and choices not as embedded in the axiomatic basis of decision-making, but as a possible outcome of a decision process.

This will proceed in the following way. The first step consists in recalling the characteristics of what can be regarded as a canonical understanding of rationality in decision-making – i.e., rationality of preferences and rationality of choice ('A canonical approach: rationality assumed' section). This allows, in a second time, to assess the type of modifications of this canonical view, which comes along with a Humean approach of decision-making, as modifications regarding the premises and properties of preferences and choice, giving birth to rationality as a possible outcome ('A Humean perspective: rationality as a possible outcome' section). Keeping this objective in mind explains that in the following, emphasis is laid on the consequences of a specific reading of Hume, rather than on the way such consequences are obtained (see, on this issue Diaye and Lapidus 2005a). The conclusion allows showing the precise scope of Hume's challenge to the canonical theory of decision – a challenge which regards the way we address the issue as economists, and our philosophical implicit assumptions.

A canonical approach: rationality assumed

The canonical way of considering rationality in the simplest framework of decision (that is, leaving aside time, risk or uncertainty) follows a representation of the tastes of a decision-maker through a *preference relation* and a *choice function* which respectively satisfy some meaningful properties. The preference-oriented side is now quite common, and rests on comparisons within pairs of alternatives, whereas the choice-function side is a bit less familiar, and amounts to the selection of one or some alternatives among subsets of the set of choices. Preference and choice might be viewed as either simultaneous or mutually exclusive primitives in the canonical approach. But in each case, the relations between the conditions of rationality of preferences and of choice (comparatively, the second might be viewed as the looser) constitutes a crucial issue.

Rational preferences

The preference side of the canonical representation was introduced in economic literature through successive attempts to identify the axiomatic basis which allows a binary relation of preference to be represented by a utility function – what G. Debreu achieved in 1954. Such was the case for R. Frisch (1926, 1933), F. Alt (1936, 1937) and H. Wold (1943). Though N. Georgescu-Roegen (1954: 119) traced back to Frisch's first published paper what he called the "modern" (i.e. post-Paretian) approach to choice, as distinct from preferences, he seems to have been more interested in the expression of preferences and of their relative intensity in order to build a function of utility. Frisch gave them the presumably first axiomatization (see Bjerkholt and Dupont-Kieffer 2007, and Dupont-Kieffer 2013: 27–35), consisting in completeness (Frisch's "axiome de choix"), transitivity ("axiome de coordination") and in an axiom on the effect of infinitesimal variations ("axiome d'addition"). This allowed him to accomplish what he called "le rêve de Jevons" (the dream of Jevons) (Frisch 1926: 79), that is, presenting a formal statement of the representation of preferences and of their intensities by a utility (cardinal) function. Yet, the influence of Frisch's paper, written in French in 1923 during a stay in Paris and published in a Norwegian journal, was rather poor. Although more available to the scientific community at the end of the 1950s thanks to its republishing in *Metroeconomica* (1957), it was not translated into English before 1971, together with the translation from German of the paper of his continuator Franz Alt (1936).[2] Frisch seems to have revisited this topic only once, again in Paris, for the Poincaré Lectures he gave in 1933 – that is, for an audience mostly composed with mathematicians or physicists, not with economists – where he proposed an extension of the axiomatic basis from 1926. Again, these lectures weren't translated into English before their recent publication by O. Bjerkholt and A. Dupont-Kieffer in 2009. The second of the three-parts study that H. Wold devoted to the theory of demand in 1943–44 also contained an axiomatization of preferences which consisted in completeness, transitivity, monotony, continuity and some other axioms, with the objective of building a utility function which represents preferences (Wold 1943). Since its recognition by Debreu as "the only rigorous one" in the topic (Debreu 1954: 159), Wold's paper is today widely acknowledged for providing a proof of a representation theorem. Nonetheless, though written in English, it was published in a Scandinavian actuarial journal and its immediate influence, again, seems to have been limited.

Two decades separate Frisch's first attempt and the more familiar representations of, now, both preferences and choice by K. Arrow. Concerning the preference side, Arrow seems to have been quasi-ignorant of his above-mentioned predecessors, with (like for Debreu) the exception of Wold's contribution, which he discovered when returning to Columbia after World War II. He rendered justice to Wold's 1943 paper on the occasion of an interview published in *Social Choice and Welfare* (Kelly 1987: 46). However, his concern with preference as a binary relation which could be a substitute for utility was far more anterior. It can be traced back to his undergraduate studies. K. Arrow attended the lectures given by

Alfred Tarski in 1940, at the department of philosophy of City College of New York, and became the proofreader of Olaf Helmer's translation into English of his *Introduction to Logic* (Kelly 1987: 44). So that, as Arrow put it, "whenever I saw a *U* for a utility function I translated to a preference ordering" (Kelly 1987: 46). The consequence was a most impressive Rand Corporation's working paper (Arrow 1948), presented at the December 1948 meeting of the Econometric Society in Cleveland: this paper introduced not only a first exposition of the impossibility theorem, but also the main ideas of the canonical approach to decision-making (Arrow 1948: 3–9) – a binary relation of preference with the properties of a complete preorder, and a choice function which satisfies consistency requirements, like already in the revealed preference approach pioneered by P.A. Samuelson in 1938. It therefore announced Arrow's following works: his article (Arrow 1950: 331–3) and his book (Arrow 1951: 11–7) on social choice and, some years later, his article on individual choice and preferences (Arrow 1959).

Rationality of preferences fits Arrow's early statement of the preference relation as a complete preorder.[3] It first depends on a double premise, this of the definition of the set of objects to which preferences are applied (the set of reference of choice), and after that, this of the relation of preference itself, expressed by a binary relation over the set of reference of choice:

$$X \text{ (set of reference of choice)} \quad [1]$$

$$R \subseteq X^2 \left(\textit{relation of preference}\right). \quad [2]$$

According to [2], preference of x on y is noted $(x,y) \in R$. The alternative and more commonly used notation is xRy, which reads "x is preferred to y" (which does not exclude the possibility that yRx, in which case x and y are said "indifferent"). In the canonical approach, the double premise [1] and [2] characterizes an individual, from a decision theory point of view. It concerns this part of the external world, pre-existing to him or to her, potentially subjected to his or her tastes, and these tastes, embodied in a given structure of preference.[4] At this point, nothing has been said about the properties of the preference relation, except that it exists, at least for some, if not all, x and y belonging to X.

Rationality comes along with the two following properties of the relation of preference, which make it a complete preorder and constitute the well-known axiomatic basis of the standard theory of consumer behaviour:

$$\forall x, y \in X, (x,y) \in R \text{ or } (y,x) \in R \text{ (completeness)} \quad [3]$$

$$\forall x, y, z \in X, (x,y) \in R \text{ and } (y,z) \in R \Rightarrow (x,z) \in R \text{ (transitivity)} \quad [4]$$

Our preferences are said "rational" when R is a complete preorder, that is, when they satisfy [3] and [4]. Both completeness and transitivity provide possible and not exclusive interpretations for rationality. On the one hand, completeness [3] refers to some kind of cognitive ability, in the sense where the comparability between any elements of X is independent of its dimension. This seems rather demanding, since it dismisses any answer of the kind: "Well, I really don't know. If I were indifferent, it would mean that I could toss a coin to decide. But here, it's not that I don't mind having x or y. I really don't know how to compare x and y. I just can't answer. . .".[5] Lack of completeness thus appears less as non-rationality than as a limitation to rationality, as what H. Simon called "bounded rationality" – which amounts to regard "mind as the scarce resource" (Simon 1978: 9). On the other hand, transitivity [4] refers to a consistency requirement, at least when strict preferences are at issue. When such is not the case, we can easily adhere to the idea that, because of an insufficient ability to discriminate between close elements of X, non-transitivity might occur when indifference is involved. Such restriction amounts to substitute quasi-transitivity for transitivity in [4], so that R becomes what R.D. Luce (1956) called a "semi-order". At least quasi-transitivity therefore expresses this necessity of the mind, which can hardly be ruled out since it contains the core of the idea of the rationality of preferences.

Rational choice

Understanding the rationality of preferences nonetheless allows bypassing an external feature of the characterization of the individual, this of the subset of the set of reference of choice, illustrated by the budget in the theory of consumer behaviour, over which some elements can be chosen. Now, focusing on choices over alternative non-empty subsets of the set of reference of choice, named "contexts of choice" (or "opportunity set", or "budget" or "menus", according to alternative terminologies), rather than on preferences on a set of reference of choice, continues an intuition drawn from Samuelson's path-breaking article on revealed preferences (Samuelson 1938), systematized by Arrow as soon as 1948 (Arrow 1948: 4–5; 1951: 15–17; 1959: 122–3). In this approach, the primitive of decision moves from the binary relation of preferences over X (what Sen 1987 called "binariness") to the function of choice. Here again, the analysis rests on given premises – the identification of the set of reference of choice, the set of alternative contexts (the "domain of choice") which are made available to the individual, and this of the choice function which is defined over it:

$$X \text{ (set of reference of choice)} \quad [1]$$

$$F \subseteq \mathrm{P}(X) \setminus \varnothing \text{ (domain of choice)} \quad [5]$$

$$C : F \to \mathrm{P}(X), S \mapsto C(S) \text{ (choice function)} \quad [6]$$

Like in the preference approach, the set of reference of choice X is given by [1]. Denoting $\mathrm{P}(X)$ the power set of X, [5] makes explicit the possible restrictions on the various contexts of choice S on which a choice can be made. When all non-empty parts of X are possible contexts – that is, when $\mathrm{F} = \mathrm{P}(X)\setminus\varnothing$ – the domain of choice F is said to be "abstract" or "non-restricted". Otherwise, when $\mathrm{F} \subset \mathrm{P}(X)\setminus\varnothing$, the domain F is "restricted". Note, for instance, that assuming that choices are submitted to an income constraint, like in elementary consumer theory, means that the domain of choice is restricted to the set of well-known triangles representing the expenses possibilities of the consumer. According to [6], {x}=*C*(*S*) reads "*x* is chosen over *S*". Note that this is a quite general formulation since, instead of the singleton $\{x\}$, we may have, for instance, $\{x,y\}$ or even, if *C* is non-selective, Ø. In the same way as in a preference-oriented approach, the choice-oriented approach acknowledges as its starting point something given in order to characterize an individual: the way external objects are made available to him or to her, and his or her possible choice among these alternative sets of objects. And here again, the question of the rationality of choices is raised when adding supplementary properties to the function of choice so simply defined as in [6].

On first view, these properties can be introduced without explicit reference to pre-existent preferences. Such was the case since Arrow (1948), with H. Uzawa (1956), and with Arrow (1959), who defined a rational choice function by choice-consistency conditions.

Reference to choice-consistency conditions deserves special attention. In his contribution from 1959, Arrow set out five alternative "definitions" of a rational choice function, labelled from C1 to C5, and explored their logical relations, showing the equivalence between C2 and C3, between C1, C4 and C5, and the implication of the first group of equivalent definitions by the second. This puts an end to an elaboration which started in 1948, when he gave one single definition of a rational choice function, which amounted to C4 (later known as Arrow's axiom), and continued with Uzawa (1959) who gave two definitions which amounted to C1 and C2. All these definitions regarded choice (and not preferences) as a primitive, so that whereas the way a rational choice was defined might have been different, it always amounted to internal consistency. Yet, the vocabulary in use concerning the definition of rational choice functions might be misleading. Again in Arrow (1959), definition C5 corresponds to the so-called Weak Axiom of Revealed Preferences (WARP) (Arrow 1959: 123), whose initial statement comes from Samuelson (1938). But in spite of its name, it didn't involve any pre-existent preferences (see Richter's reservation to Samuelson's terminology using the word "preference" [Richter 1971: 32, n. 4]). Its formulation in Arrow's article means that when I choose *x* on a context *S* where *y* was available and not chosen, there is no other context *T* in which *x* and *y* are available, and where *y* would be chosen. This amounts to the following statement, which clearly contains no reference to preferences:

$$\forall S \in F, \forall x, y \in S, x \in C(S) \text{ and } y \notin C(S) \Rightarrow \nexists T \in F : x, y \in T \text{ and } y \in C(T) \text{ (WARP)}$$

Yet, since M. Richter (1966, 1971), it has become difficult to make a so complete abstraction of preferences in the definition of a rational choice function, though the binary relation is now a property associated to the choice function, and not a representation of the tastes of an individual. We are indebted to Richter for a definition of the rationality of the choice function as the existence of a specific compatibility between our choices and a hypothetical underlying relation of preference – the *rationalizability* of a choice function by such hypothetical relation of preference (Richter 1971: 31). This does not imply any comeback from choice to preferences as a primitive; but it requires the introduction of the possibility of a preference relation as a criterion for rationality. A mere possibility: it does not mean that we do have preferences, but that this relation stands for those that we could have. And if such was the case, our choices on each context *S*, when rational, would have been in accordance with our preferences on this context. Following Richter, rationalizability hence amounts to:

$$\exists R \subseteq X^2 : \forall S \in F, C(S) = \{x \in S : \forall y \in S, (x, y) \in R\} \text{ (rationalizability)} \qquad [7]$$

According to [7], a choice function *C* defined on *F* is said rational when we can imagine a preference relation *R* with support *X* such that on each context of choice *S*, what is chosen over this context is also what would have been preferred, according to *R*. Numerous examples illustrate cases where a consistency condition is unsatisfied, so that no preference relation could, like in [7], rationalize the choice (see, for instance, A. Sen 1993: 500–3). But even when the choice is rational according to [7], it is clear that since nothing is said concerning the properties of the preferences *R* which rationalize the choice, they might be non-complete (not satisfying [3]) or non-transitive (not satisfying [4]), therefore non-rational.[6]

This explains that a significant part of the literature has been devoted to the search for conditions under which both choice and underlying preferences are rational. For instance, when the domain of choice is unrestricted (resp., restricted), the Weak Axiom of Revealed Preferences (resp., the Houthakker Axiom of Revealed Preferences) is a necessary and sufficient condition to the rationality of choice, the underlying preference relation being also rational. But generally speaking, rationality of choice is less demanding than rationality of preferences.

The canonical approach produced formal statements about both *rationality of preferences* and *rationality of choice*. Each of them is now as widely known as it is widely threatened, from about the middle of the twentieth century onward. Calling this approach "canonical" doesn't mean that it should be regarded as the most accepted to decision-making (see Zouboulakis 2014): it is "canonical" only because it conveys a reference against which alternative approaches can be, and use to be, assessed. In a sense, it plays the same role as, say, perfect competition, when the issue is the understanding of imperfect competition. In the following, it will therefore constitute the appropriate starting point to account for the importance of the challenge to which we are invited by the works of David Hume.

A Humean perspective: rationality as a possible outcome

Let us turn back to Hume. The decision process inferred from Hume's theory of passions, developed mainly in book II of the *Treatise* and in the *Dissertation*, has been formally described in Diaye and Lapidus (2005a). Whereas this paper does not conclude with the incompatibility between Hume's conception of a decision process and the rationality of preferences and choice (for an opposite view, see

Sugden 2005 and the answer of Diaye and Lapidus 2005b), it nonetheless challenges the canonical conception, in their premises ([1], [2], [5], [6]) and in the part played by rationality ([3], [4], [7]). This shows that a concern, as economists, about a possible change in our understanding of the individual as a decision-maker is far from being analytically neutral: such change, carried on by David Hume, comes along with a modification in the representation of decision-making.

Which premises for preferences and choices?

What David Hume called "passions" or "impressions of reflection" can be conveniently approached by what we would name today "emotions", but restricted to the modalities of – that is, to the ways to live – the sensations of pleasure and of pain. At the very beginning of book II of the *Treatise*, they are presented "as arising either from the original impressions [of pleasure and pain; A.L.] or from their ideas" (Hume 1739–40: 2.1.1.3). Round-trips between Hume's teaching on the passions and canonical decision theory allow showing the possible consequences of a Humean approach on the nature of the primitive for decision-making, on the stability of the preference structure and of the respective places of preferences and choice as well as this of the sets over which they are defined.

The nature of the primitive for decision-making

An often quoted passage from the *Treatise* emphasizes the asymmetry between reason and passions, presenting the first as the "slave" of the second (Hume 1739–40: 2.3.3.4). A result of this asymmetry is the picture of emotion-driven individuals (see Lapidus 2011), drawn all along Hume's philosophical works. The relevant emotions here belong to what he called the "direct" (by opposition to "indirect") passions, which "arise immediately from good or evil, from pain or pleasure" (Hume 1739–40: 2.1.1.4) and converge toward "desire" (or its opposite, "aversion") and "will" – the latter coming immediately before action (see part 3 of book 2 of Hume 1739–40, and section 1 of Hume 1757).[7] A comparison between this picture and the current one, drawn from canonical decision theory, rests on a transposition from Hume's desire and aversion to preferences, and from will to choice. Diaye and Lapidus (2005a: 94–6) give textual evidence which corroborates such transposition.

An immediate conclusion is that whereas canonical decision theory does not really settle the question of the primitive for decision-making – either preferences or choice – or even avoids asking it in such terms, the coexistence, within Hume's theory of passions, of both desire and will (though, as will be seen hereafter, Hume seems to hesitate counting the will among the passions), shows that both preferences (desire) and choice (will) can be regarded as the primitives for decision-making.

Nonetheless, it is obvious that this way of replacing desire and will in a decision theory framework overlooks a typical feature of Hume's explanation of action, the role of "belief", as a transitional device which gives to an idea a part of the "force and vivacity" (Hume 1739–40: 1.3.7.5) of the original impression of pleasure or pain, thus allowing desire or aversion. Yet, the relation between belief and desire and their respective parts in the determination of action constitute a classical philosophical issue. From a Humean viewpoint, this issue typically opposes those who, like M. Smith (1987) or E. Radcliffe (1999), claimed each in his or her own way that belief alone couldn't give rise to action because it has a mind to world direction-of-fit, and those who, like B. Stroud (1977), considered belief as somehow similar to a passion, thus liable to be at the origin of action; or like A. Baier (1991) for whom reason has some kind of access to the determination of action through belief; or like R. Cohon (2008: 30–62), who stressed the role of belief in expected pleasures, which cause motivating passions. I do not intend to underestimate the importance of this question (see Lapidus 2010; Diaye and Lapidus 2012), but whatever the answer, my purpose here is to focus on some of its consequences which might be taken up disregarding the explicit link to belief and pleasure. And indeed, it remains that desire is related to the will and to decision. It is only this limited aspect of Hume's contribution which constitutes the subject matter of the discussion favoured in this paper.

A changing structure of preferences

In contrast with the implicit assumptions of canonical decision theory, but in accordance with the intuitive view of any one who is not a professional decision-theorist or economist, a second difference between the canonical view on rational decision and Hume's conception is that for the latter, the individual is changing in his or her emotional state. Hume finds in the "rule of double relation" – relation of ideas, and relation of impressions (Hume 1739–40: 2.1.4; Hume 1757: 144–5) – the principle which explains such changes from one emotional state (one passion) to another, from one configuration of desire and choice to another. The "relation of ideas" leads from the object of the first passion to the object of the second. It follows the "natural relations" (resemblance, contiguity and causality; Hume 1739–40: 1.1.4.1–4) which Hume regarded as the elementary components which allow the working of our mind.[8] For instance, when discussing the case of pride associated to the organization of a feast, Hume draws on contiguity and causality in order to explain that the "feast" – the object of the initial direct passion of joy – is related to the "self" – the object of pride, the indirect passion which follows joy – for the one who is "the master of the feast" (Hume 1739–40: 2.1.6.2). The second element of the double relation is the "relation of impressions", based on the natural relation of resemblance. In the example of the feast, the pleasure which is at the origin of the direct passion of joy is associated to the one that arouses the indirect passion of pride: the pleasure which I feel in participating in a feast meets the one of organizing it. The working of the double relation is explicitly referred to when Hume tries to explain the transformation of our desire and will:

> [A] suit of fine cloaths produces pleasure from their beauty; and this pleasure produces the direct passions, or the impressions of volition and desire. Again,

when these cloaths are consider'd as belonging to ourself, the double relation conveys to us the sentiment of pride, which is an indirect passion; and the pleasure, which attends that passion, returns back to the direct affections, and gives new force to our desire or volition, joy or hope.

(Hume 1739–40: 2.3.9.4)

An individual, moved by this engine constituted by the double relation, can no more be represented both through given and unchanging preferences, and through a given and unchanging choice function, defined over a given and unchanging domain of choice. This does not lead to conclude that preferences [2] and choice [6] have become meaningless, but rather that they are fleeting, following the changes in our emotional state – which each of us already knows, especially if he or she has forgotten to be an economist or a decision-theorist.

The respective places of preferences and choice, and of the sets over which they are defined

The third difference between Hume's perspective and the canonical approach is less intuitive. In the latter, the set of reference of choice is given first; and then only a binary preference relation is defined, or a domain of choice and a choice function. Now, with Hume, this order (the set of reference first, then the primitives, preferences or choice) becomes irrelevant. In keeping with Hume, objects cannot be considered, in our minds, pre-existent data: rather, they are constructed by our desires and, more generally, by our emotions. So that the objects possibly submitted to our preferences and choice are not objects that would exist independently of our impressions, as pointed to us by our reason, but the only objects the existence of which we acknowledge through our emotions:

Where the objects themselves do not affect us, their connexion can never give them any influence; and 'tis plain, that as reason is nothing but the discovery of this connexion, it cannot be by its means that the objects are able to affect us.

(Hume 1739–40: 2.3.3.3)

Other objects could exist for other individuals or for an external observer, but for the agent who does not desire them, they simply do not exist. This is a way to say that what is given first is not something as general as a set of reference of choice, but a contextual preference relation R_S. And if so, the context of choice S can be easily identified as its support:[9]

$$S = \{x, y : (x, y) \in R_S \text{ or } (y, x) \in R_S\} \text{ (generation of the context of choice)} \qquad [8]$$

And as our desires change along with our emotional state, our contextual preferences also change, therefore changing the context of choice:

$$R_{S1}, R_{S2}, \ldots, R_{Si} \rightarrow S_1, S_2, \ldots, S_i \text{ (contextual preferences change)} \qquad [9]$$

As a result, when the context of choice changes according to [9], the general set of choice also changes, by union to the successive contexts:

$$X_i = X_{i-1} \cup S_i \text{ (set of reference of choice)} \qquad [10]$$

The result of this first investigation might seem a bit disappointing. The simple and elegant presentation of the canonical approach seems to have vanished: instead of a given set of reference of choice on which preferences and choice are built, we are facing the immediate emergence of contextual preferences, which come along with a corresponding context of choice and, therefore, with a revised set of reference of choice. But all that is constantly submitted to transformations due to emotional change, so that the provisional conclusion would be: we have preferences, but they are always moving; they are not submitted to any control, so that their greatest elements on the moving contexts of choice might be anything, and can be explained by no regularity depending on the properties of the preference relation.

Rationality as an outcome

Nonetheless, the picture of such an unstable individual, left as it is, would be most unfaithful to Hume's analysis. What we can understand from Hume's decision process shows three types of regulating devices, whose effect is to stabilize it into a resulting configuration of preferences and choice. These devices consist a) in a mental device which makes our contextual preferences complete, b) in a special link between preferences and choice and c) in a stabilizing property.

Completeness of contextual preferences

The above discussion of the "connexion" between objects (Hume 1739–40, 2.3.3.3) concluded an analysis developed in the *Treatise* of the possibility for reason, through the natural relation of causality, to make that some objects exist in our mind on its sole basis – which Hume denied. But the way the argument was developed before this conclusion is worth being quoted more extensively. Hume was talking about the aversion attached to an object:

> 'Tis also obvious, that this emotion rests not here, but making us cast our view on every side, comprehends whatever objects are connected with its original one by the relation of cause and effect. . . . Tis from the prospect of pain or pleasure that the aversion or propensity arises towards any object: And these emotions extend themselves to the causes and effects of that object, as they are pointed out to us by reason and experience.
>
> (Hume 1739–40: 2.3.3.3)

This amounts to saying that the contextual preferences R_S are connected (see Diaye and Lapidus 2005a: 96–7), in the sense that each element of S is linked to any other element through a chain of theses preferences, built by the natural relations of the mind.

Interestingly, this property of *connection* doesn't come alone. It takes place within an analysis of natural relations, introduced in book 1 of the *Treatise*, which provides also a rule of extension of the natural relation in the imagination and, therefore, of our desire or preferences:

> That we may understand the full extent of these relations, we must consider, that two objects are connected together in the imagination, not only when the one is immediately resembling, contiguous to, or the cause of the other, but also when there is interposed betwixt them a third object, which bears to both of them any of these relations.
>
> (Hume 1739–40: 1.1.4.3)

This is a way of saying that where three elements x, y and z of S are such that x and y, on the one hand, y and z, on the other hand, are related by contextual preferences R_S, x and z also are linked by R_S. Now (Diaye and Lapidus 2005: 97), it can be shown that when connection and extension both prevail as properties of the contextual preferences R_S, this means that they are also *complete*:

$$\forall x, y \in S, (x, y) \in R_S \text{ or } (y, x) \in R_S \text{ (contextual completeness)} \qquad [11]$$

Considering completeness, even when it is contextual, as the result of the natural working of the mind contrasts not only with canonical decision theory, but also with Simon's view, as recalled above: since our cognitive ability is supported by our emotions and their movements, claiming with H. Simon (1978) that the occurrence of completeness is prevented by the limits of this cognitive ability, would become meaningless.

Contextual compatibility between preferences and choice

The question of knowing whether the will is to be considered among direct passions is far from completely solved. On first view, some important textual evidence favours the idea that the will should be included among direct passions: this is explicitly the case at the end of the third part of book II of the *Treatise* on the will and the direct passions, in the section dedicated to the direct passions (Hume 1739–40: 2.3.9.2), as well as in that of the 'Dissertation' (Hume 1757: 139). On the contrary, other passages suggest that the will does not belong to the direct passions. It was included neither in the list which appears at the beginning of the first part of book II of the *Treatise* (Hume 1739–40: 2.1.1.4), nor at the beginning of its third part (Hume 1739–40: 2.3.1.1). Still more, in this last section, Hume writes that it is "not comprehended among the passions" (Hume 1739–40: 2.3.1.2).

Such seemingly contradictory statements require some explanation. The issue, for Hume, was highly polemical since it was this of free will, in which he supported a conception of freedom as "liberty of spontaneity" (that is, lack of violence in the determination of action), by contrast to the "liberty of indifference" (which implies that actions do not obey to necessity, that is, are independent from desires), which he rejected (Hume 1739–40: 2.3.2.1–2).[10] Suppose the will is excluded from the list of passions. It might therefore be understood as a faculty liable to determine action and to take precedence over the passions, allowing free will in the sense of the liberty of indifference. This clearly argues in favour of the opposite position, that is in the inclusion of the will within the list of passions. However, such inclusion is not fully satisficing, since it leaves open the possibility that the will is another determinant of action, with its own informational content. Now, Hume had explained at length how the determining role of pleasure and pain is distorted by belief in order to give rise to desire and aversion,[11] and there is no more room for a supplementary and hardly understandable distortion of desire which would give birth to different will. According to Hume, the will says nothing else than the desire already said – except that it is to be followed by action when it is not altered by a transformation of passions:

> DESIRE arises from good consider'd simply, and AVERSION is deriv'd from evil. The WILL exerts itself, when either the good or the absence of the evil may be attain'd by any action of the mind or body.
>
> (Hume 1739–40: 2.3.9.7)

In other words, the will only converts the prescriptions of desire into action. This is a sufficient ground to explain Hume's uneasiness facing the place of the will: there are good reasons to include it in the passions, but as such, it would add nothing to them – so that the basis of such inclusion is not that firmly established.

But leaving apart the question of knowing if the will is or is not a genuine passion, its characterization leads to the conclusion that from a Humean point of view, if we choose according to what we will in a context of choice, what has been chosen fits what we contextually prefer the most, according to our desire:

$$C(S) = \{x \in S : \forall y \in S, (x, y) \in R_S\} \text{ (contextual compatibility)} \qquad [12]$$

Such compatibility might be viewed as an attenuated kind of rational choice like in [7], but restricted to one context of choice and to contextual preferences.

Till the whole circle be completed: allowing free choice

Though contextual completeness [11] and compatibility [12] show an embryonic content in terms of rationality of preferences and of choice, the assumption of changing preferences seems far more important. This change means a revision of our general dispositions, which concerns more than isolated contextual preferences and the corresponding context of choice, as stated above in [9]. The story and the meticulous description of such changes is a typical exercise from Hume. In the second *Enquiry*, for instance, when he was discussing something apparently quite different (the "qualities useful to ourselves") he came to examine the comparative effects of close and distant agreeable objects. And he shows that when such object becomes nearer, this does not only mean that our desire for it increases, but also, in Hume's words, that our "general resolutions" have changed (Hume 1751: 6.15). The phrase is successful. It means that a change in specific desires (contextual preferences) R_{Si} gives birth to a change about which we have not that much information, except that it occurs and that it is general, thus involving general preferences R_{Xi} to such an extent that they can supersede the contextual preferences R_{Si} in case of conflict concerning the choices on S_i. This also leads to modifications of the domain of choice F_i, as described in Diaye and Lapidus (2005a: 101–2), as consequences of the effect on choices of the revised preferences. But generally speaking, whatever the precise characteristics of these modifications, they yield:

$$\left(R_{X_{i-1}}, F_{i-1}\right) \xrightarrow{R_{S_i}} \left(R_{X_i}, F_i\right) \text{ (general preferences, domain of choice)} \quad [13]$$

The revision procedures [9], [10] and [13] (which constitute a simplified version of the "UPDATE procedure" in Diaye and Lapidus 2005a) do not contain, by themselves, a regulating device which would take them to an end. It is when discussing the part played by the association of impressions in the mechanism of the double relation, that Hume suggests that there is a moment when the revision is completed:

> Grief and disappointment give rise to anger, anger to envy, envy to malice, and malice to grief again, till the whole circle be compleated.
>
> (Hume 1739–40: 2.1.4.3; see also Hume 1757: 145)

Till the whole circle be completed: Hume's expression suggests a cumulative process, in which grief, disappointment, anger, envy and malice – all the possible emotions linked by the natural relation of resemblance – follow one another again and again, till they do not change anything to our general resolutions, that is, to our desires and will. This amounts to saying that there exists a step, denoted n, after which the new contextual preferences which appear as in [9], preserve general preferences in [13]:

$$\exists n : \forall i \geq n, (x, y) \in R_{S_i} \Rightarrow (x, y) \in R_{X_i} \text{ (preference stabilization)} \quad [14]$$

Preference stabilization [14], jointly with contextual compatibility between preference and choice [12], show that there is a moment when the decision process is achieved, which means that decision is not prevented from occurring by emotional changes, and that it now respects stabilized preferences and choice. In other terms, it fulfils desire and will. Such fulfilment is obtained when the decision process is not interrupted by any external circumstance, and is left to its own evolution toward a stable configuration. This means that the described decision process leads to a *free choice*, in the precise sense of the already mentioned "liberty of spontaneity", which Hume had endorsed in the *Treatise*, by contrast with the "liberty of indifference". The first *Enquiry* is still more explicit than the *Treatise*:[12]

> By liberty, then, we can only mean *a power of acting or not acting, according to the determinations of the will*; that is, if we chuse to remain at rest, we may; if we chuse to move, we also may. Now this hypothetical liberty is universally allowed to belong to every one, who is not a prisoner and in chains.
>
> (Hume 1748: 8.23)

One aspect of the contrast between this liberty of spontaneity and the liberty of indifference, ruled out by Hume, should be stressed, when dealing with free choice resulting from Hume's decision process: the choice is free not according to an external observer like, for instance, from a libertarian viewpoint which would mean liberty of indifference, but only according to the feeling of the decision-maker himself or herself. With a different formalization, it has been shown in Diaye and Lapidus (2005a) that this decision process pictured by relations from [9] to [14] gives birth, when completed, to the two types of rationality in decision-making identified above, in the 'Canonical approach: rationality assumed' section:

1 *Rationality of choice*: when i is greater than or equal to n, the choice function $C(S)$ defined on F_i is rationalizable by the general preference relation R_{Xi}.
2 *Rationality of general preferences*: when i is greater than or equal to n, R_{xi} is a complete preorder, that is both complete and transitive.

This amounts to the claim that, in the specific meaning of the phrase in a Humean framework, a decision process leading to free choice makes this choice rational, along with the decision-maker general preferences.

Conclusion: from philosophy to economics

On first view, the rationality of choice and preferences seems to be a rather strong statement: in spite of a different treatment, the transposition of Hume's teaching in the words of decision theory brings about the same result as canonical theory does. But on second view, it becomes evident that such conclusion would be misleading. In canonical theory, rationality is assumed, as consistency hypotheses which come at the very beginning of the description of the properties of preference and choice: such is the case with rationality of preferences, insofar as completeness and transitivity are concerned; such is also the case with rationality of choice, which might be approached through various consistency assumptions, like the weak axiom of revealed preferences, or Houthakker's axiom of revealed preferences, or the so-called properties α or β. In all cases, rationality is embodied as consistency requirements of individual behaviour. On the opposite, Hume's initial statements do not recover such initial consistency requirements. It only expresses some disposition of our mind: a way to make the world inhabited by our emotions. See, for instance, what might have appeared as the first expression of minimal rationality content: contextual completeness [11]. It is not given as such, but it is a consequence of the working of our mind, when it appropriates the world through desires, going from one object to another, and relating two objects where they are linked by a third one. The same can be argued about the general conclusions on the rationality of preferences and choices. Such rationality was not presupposed at an initial stage. The only thing that we have to regard as granted is that our emotions are changing, among which our preferences, inducing us to revise them again and again; and since our mental world at last quiets down, after a certain point they do not need any more to be revised. If this point is reached, it means that we are in the conditions of a free choice. Then, rationality stands out, but now as a consequence of the working of our mind in the decision process, no more as its prerequisite.

As economists, this challenges directly the way we take up rationality in decision-making. It leads us to give up questioning its relevance as normative behavioural assumptions, and, conversely, we are prompted to question the effects of all the external or internal circumstances which might deviate or interrupt the functioning of the mental process which opens onto decision: instead of being alternative views of individual behaviour, rationality and irrationality become the outward signs of the absence or of the presence of a hindrance to the course of the decision process.

Yet, Hume's challenge is also more indirect, in that it concerns implicit but determining philosophical positions which govern the way we are presenting a problem as economists, like in the opposition made by Sugden in his seminal paper of 1991, between already Hume and Kant. Here, it compels us to question what usually remains to us out of reach, if not out of interest: our understanding of an individual whose description boils down to the specification of the part of the external world which constitutes his or her set of choice, and of his or her preferences. Such spontaneous understanding expresses a philosophical position. Hume obviously offers another one, in which the part of the external world on which choices are to be performed is constructed by our preferences. We may agree or disagree with this philosophical position. But after all, this is not the most important: what really matters is that as a by-product of an investigation on Hume, we acknowledge that we have a philosophical position, that the latter is responsible of what we do as economists and that, for this very reason, it has to be questioned.

Notes

* Phare, University Paris 1 Panthéon-Sorbonne – 106–12, boulevard de l'Hôpital – 75647 Paris Cedex 13 – France. E-mail: andre.lapidus@univ-paris1.fr.

1 Reference to Hume's works published by Oxford University Press are given according to the divisions of the edition: for the *Treatise*, book, part, section and paragraph numbers; for the 'Abstract', paragraph numbers; and for the two *Enquiries*, section and paragraph numbers.

2 Alt's paper in 1936 was directed against Oskar Lange's contribution from 1934, in which the latter established a link between what was to be later known as "cardinal utility" (the "determinateness" of the utility function, in the words of O. Lange), and the ranking of differences between allocations. The last paragraphs of Alt's paper, where he discussed solutions from his predecessors, shows that he was familiar with

Frisch's works, especially with his book from 1932 (where his previous axiomatic approach was only briefly recalled at the very beginning of the book; Frisch 1932: 2–3), but also with "some short articles by the same author" (einige kürzere Artikel desselben Verfassers) (Alt 1936: 167). On Alt's contribution, see T. Ellingsen (1994: pp. 121–2) and I. Moscati (2013: pp. 925–7).

3 A "weak ordering", in the terminology of Arrow (1948: 4; 1959: 122).

4 Though intuitive, the idea that X in [1] and in [2], as support of the preference relation, is typically constituted by goods or services, like in ordinary consumer theory, is not that obvious: underlying the notion of value function in D. Kahneman and A. Tversky (1979) for instance, and more generally in reference-dependent models, preferences are not defined on a state, figured by goods and services, but on a difference to a state of references, that is, on gains and losses. There is, of course, no objection to the representation of gains and losses by X.

5 In a paper rather critical on the rationality assumptions concerning preferences, H. Putnam (1996) illustrated the case of incomparability with the example of an individual, called Theresa, who is torn between an "ascetic" (y) and a "sensual" way of life but, in case she chooses the sensual way of life, who prefers as a lover x to z. Putnam showed that here, this lack of completeness would also violate negative transitivity $(\forall x, y, z \in X, (x, y) \notin R \text{ and } (y, z) \notin R \Rightarrow (x, z) \notin R)$, otherwise Theresa could not prefer x to z.

6 In his 1966 paper, Richter still held that R should be itself rational, that is, that preferences are complete and transitive. However, he noted in a footnote the possibility of a more general conception of rationality, where R would be non-complete and non-transitive (Richter 1966: 636, n. 4).

7 The direct passions presented in the *Treatise* and in the 'Dissertation' are joy and grief, hope and fear, desire and aversion, and volition or will. On Hume's theory of passions, P.S. Árdal's book from 1966 still remains an impassable introduction.

8 In the enthusiasm of the 'Abstract', Hume concludes that the natural relations "are really, to us, the cement of the universe, and all the operations of the mind must, in a great measure, depend on them" (Hume 1740: 35).

9 Rigorously speaking, regarding R_S as a binary relation would require the precondition of a universal set of objects on which it is defined (see Diaye and Lapidus 2005a: 97), so that it is by abuse of notation that we keep on using R_S to denote a binary relation defined on S.

10

> Few are capable of distinguishing betwixt the liberty of spontaneity, as it is called in the schools, and the liberty of indifference; betwixt that which is opposed to violence, and that which means a negation of necessity and causes. The first is even the most common sense of the word; and as it is only that species of liberty which it concerns us to preserve, our thoughts have been principally turned towards it, and have almost universally confounded it with the other.
>
> (Hume 1739–40: 2.3.2.1)

See the discussion of Hume's position on free will by N. Kemp Smith (1941: 439–41), P. Árdal (1966: 87–9), and P. Russell (2008: 225–38), who also replaces Hume's argument within the religious debates among his contemporaries.

11 On the place of Hume's beliefs in decision-making, see supra, p. 11.

12 As pointed out by P. Russell (2008: 375, n. 65), Hume's vocabulary has changed between the *Treatise* and the *Enquiry*. The "liberty . . . universally allowed" from the latter corresponds to the "liberty of spontaneity" in the former. From a strategic point of view, this change helped transforming an opposition between the supporters of different kinds of liberty, into an opposition between the supporters of a conjunction of liberty and necessity and those who deny it.

Bibliography

Alt, F. (1936) 'Über die Messbarkeit des Nutzens', *Zeitschrift für Nationalökonomie*, 7: 161–9; English translation: 'On the Measurability of Utility', in Chipman, J., Hurwicz, L., Richter, M. and Sonnenschein, H. (eds.) (1971) *Preferences, Utility and Demand*, New York: Harcourt Brace Jovanovich.

Árdal, P.S. (1966) *Passion and Value in Hume's Treatise*, Edinburgh: Edinburgh University Press.

Arrow, K.J. (1948) 'The Possibility of a Universal Social Welfare Function', *Rand Corporation*, [working paper], P-41, September 26.

Arrow, K.J. (1950) 'A Difficulty in the Concept of Social Welfare', *Journal of Political Economy*, 58(4): 328–46.

Arrow, K.J. (1951) *Social Choice and Individual Values*, 2nd edition (1963), New York: John Wiley and Sons.

Arrow, K.J. (1959) 'Rational Choice Functions and Orderings', *Economica*, 26: 121–7.

Baier, A.C. (1991) *A Progress of Sentiments – Reflections on Hume's Treatise*, Cambridge, MA and London: Harvard University Press.

Binmore, K. (1994) *Game Theory and the Social Contract*, Vol 1: Playing Fair, Cambridge, MA and London: MIT Press.

Binmore, K. (2005) *Natural Justice*, Oxford: Oxford University Press.

Bjerkholt, O. and Dupont-Kieffer, A. (2007) 'Ragnar Frisch's Axiomatic Approach in Econometrics', *12th European Conference on the History of Economics*, Sienna, October.

Cohon, R. (2008) *Hume's Morality – Feeling and Fabrication*, Oxford: Oxford University Press.

Debreu, G. (1954) 'Representation of a Preference Ordering by a Numerical Function', in R.M. Thrall, C.H. Coombs and R.L. Davis (eds.) *Decision Processes*, New York: John Wiley and Sons.

Diaye, M.-A. and Lapidus, A. (2005a) 'A Humean Theory of Choice of Which Rationality May Be One Consequence', *European Journal of the History of Economic Thought*, 12(1): 89–111.

Diaye, M.-A. and Lapidus, A. (2005b) 'Why Rationality May Be a Consequence of Hume's Theory of Choice', *European Journal of the History of Economic Thought*, 12(1): 119–26.

Diaye, M.-A. and Lapidus, A. (2012) 'Pleasure and Belief in Hume's Decision Process', *European Journal of the History of Economic Thought*, 19(3): 355–84.

Dupont-Kieffer, A. (2013) 'Mesure de l'utilité marginale et indice de prix chez Ragnar Frisch', *Oeconomia*, 3(1): 23–57.

Ellingsen, T. (1994) 'Cardinal Utility: A History of Hedonimetry', in M. Allais and O. Hagen (eds.) *Cardinalism*, Dordrecht: Kluwer Academic Publishers.

Frenkel, J.A. and Johnson, H.G. (1976) 'The Monetary Approach to the Balance of Payments – Essential Concepts and Historical Origins', in J.A. Frenkel and H.G. Johnson (eds.) *The Monetary Approach to The Balance of Payments*, Toronto: University of Toronto Press.

Friedman, M. (1987) 'The Quantity Theory of Money', in S.N. Durlauf and L.E. Blume (eds.) *The New Palgrave Dictionary of Economics*, 2nd ed., New York: Palgrave Macmillan, vol. 6: 793–815.

Frisch, R. (1926) 'Sur un Problème d'Economie Pure', *Norsk Matematisk Forening Skrifter*, Serie I, 16: 1–40; republished in *Metroeconomica*, 9(2), August 1957; English translation: 'On a Problem in Pure Economics', in J. Chipman, L. Hurwicz, M. Richter and H. Sonnenschein (eds.) *Preferences, Utility and Demand*, New York: Harcourt Brace Jovanovich, 1971.

Frisch, R. (1933) 'Poincaré Lectures', in O. Bjerkholt and A. Dupont-Kieffer (eds.) *Problems and Methods of Econometrics*, London and New York: Routledge.

Georgescu-Roegen, N. (1954) 'Choice and Revealed Preference', *Southern Economic Journal*, 21(2): 119–30.

Hume, D. (1739–1740) *A Treatise of Human Nature*, edited by D.F. Norton and M.J. Norton, Oxford: Oxford University Press, 2000.

Hume, D. (1740) 'An Abstract of a Treatise of Human Nature', in D.F. Norton and M.J. Norton (eds.) *A Treatise of Human Nature*, Oxford: Oxford University Press, 2000.

Hume, D. (1748) *An Enquiry Concerning Human Understanding*, edited by T.L. Beauchamp, Oxford: Oxford University Press, 1999.

Hume, D. (1751) *An Enquiry Concerning the Principles of Morals*, edited by T.L. Beauchamp, Oxford: Oxford University Press, 1998.

Hume, D. (1757) 'A Dissertation on the Passions', in T.H. Green and T.H. Grose (eds.) *The Philosophical Works of David Hume*, vol. IV, [London: 1882], Darmstadt: Scientia Verlag Aalen, 1964.

Hume, D. (1777) *Essays Political, Moral, and Literary*, edited by E.F. Miller, Indianapolis: Liberty Classics, 1987.

Kahneman, D. and Tversky, A. (1979) 'Prospect Theory: An Analysis of Decision under Risk', *Econometrica*, 47(2): 263–91.

Kelly, J.S. (1987) 'An Interview with Kenneth J. Arrow', *Social Choice and Welfare*, 4(1): 43–62.

Kemp Smith, N. (1941) *The Philosophy of David Hume – A Critical Study of Its Origins and Central Doctrines*, New York: Palgrave Macmillan, 2005.

Lange, O. (1934) 'The Determinateness of the Utility Function', *Review of Economic Studies*, 1(3): 218–25.

Lapidus, A. (2010) 'The Valuation of Decision and Individual Welfare: A Humean Approach', *European Journal of the History of Economic Thought*, 17(1): 1–28.

Lapidus, A. (2011) 'The Possibility of a Welfare Policy in a World of Emotion-Driven Individuals: A Humean Point of View', in R. Ege and H. Igersheim (eds.) *Freedom and Happiness in Economics and Philosophy*, London and New York: Routledge.

Luce, R.D. (1956) 'Semiorders and a Theory of Utility Discrimination', *Econometrica*, 24: 178–91.

Moscati, I. (2013) 'How Cardinal Utility Entered Economic Analysis, 1909–1944', *European Journal of the History of Economic Thought*, 20(5): 906–39.

Pribram, K. (1983) *A History of Economic Reasoning*, Baltimore: Johns Hopkins University Press.

Putnam, H. (1996) 'Über die Razionalitet von Praeferenzen', *Allgemeine Zeitschrift für Philosophie*, 21(3): 209–28; English translation: 'On the Rationality of Preferences', in H. Putnam (ed.) *The Collapse of the Fact/Value Controversy and Other Essays*, Cambridge, MA and London: Harvard University Press, 2002.

Radcliffe, E.S. (1999) 'Hume on the Generation of Motives: Why Beliefs Alone Never Motivate', *Hume Studies*, 25(1/2): 101–22.

Richter, M.K. (1966) 'Revealed Preference Theory', *Econometrica*, 34: 635–45.

Richter, M.K. (1971) 'Rational Choice', in J. Chipman, L. Hurwicz, M. Richter and H. Sonnenschein (eds.) *Preferences, Utility and Demand*, New York: Harcourt Brace Jovanovich.

Russell, P. (2008) *The Riddle of Hume's Treatise – Skepticism, Naturalism, and Irreligion*, New York: Oxford University Press.

Samuelson, P.A. (1938) 'A Note on the Pure Theory of Consumer's Behaviour', *Economica*, 5: 61–71.

Schabas, M. and Wennerlind, C. (2011) 'Hume on Money, Commerce, and the Science of Economics', *Journal of Economic Perspectives*, 25(3): 217–30.

Schumpeter, J.A. (1954) *History of Economic Analysis*, New York: Oxford University Press.

Sen, A. (1987) 'Rational Behaviour', in J. Eatwell, M. Milgate and P. Newman (eds.) *The New Palgrave Dictionary of Economics*, 1st ed., New-York: Palgrave Macmillan, vol. 4: 8452–70.

Sen, A. (1993) 'Internal Consistency of Choice', *Econometrica*, 61(3): 495–521.

Simon, H.A. (1978) 'Rationality as Process and as Product of Thought', *American Economic Review*, 68(2): 1–16.

Smith, M. (1987) 'The Humean Theory of Motivation', *Mind*, 96: 36–61.

Stroud, B. (1977) *Hume*, London: Routledge & Kegan Paul.

Sugden, R. (1991) 'Rational Choice: A Survey of Contributions from Economics and Philosophy', *Economic Journal*, 101: 751–85.

Sugden, R. (2005) 'Why Rationality Is Not a Consequence of Hume's Theory of Choice', *European Journal of the History of Economic Thought*, 12(1): 113–18.

Tarski, A. (1941) *Introduction to Logic and the Methodology of the Deductive Sciences*, New York: Oxford University Press.

Uzawa, H. (1956) 'Note on Preference and Axioms of Choice', *Annals of the Institute of Statistical Mathematics*, 8: 35–40.

Wold, H. (1943) 'A Synthesis of Pure Demand Analysis, Part II', *Skandinavisk Aktuarietidskrift*, 26: 220–63.

Zouboulakis, M.S. (2014) *The Varieties of Economic Rationality*, London and New York: Routledge.

17 The ontology of Schelling's "Theory of Interdependent Decisions"

Lauren Larrouy

Introduction

Schelling early advocated for a "reorientation of game theory" in order to understand, and then propose a "theory of interdependent decisions" (Schelling 1980[1960]: 83), first in strategic contexts and then in social contexts. I will therefore concentrate on the one hand on *The Strategy of Conflict* (1980[1960]) and on the other hand on his models of residential segregation (1969, 1971a, 1971b and 1972) and attempt to show how they can both participate of *a common conceptual innovation.*

His criticism of standard game theory (of von Neumann and Morgenstern 1944; and Nash 1950, 1951), underpins the new type of modeling he proposes in the dynamic models of residential segregation. I argue that the dynamic models of residential segregation – as the precursors of the agent-based models (e.g., Cohendet et al. 2003; Aydinonat 2005, 2007; Kirman 2011; Epstein and Axtell 1996; Epstein 2006) – are a methodological answer to some of the main constraints Schelling early identifies in standard game theory.

For Schelling, situations involving interdependence of individual choices are

> These situations, in which people's behavior or people's choices depend on the behavior or choices of other people, are the ones that usually don't permit any simple summation or extrapolation to the aggregates. To make that connection we usually have to look at the system of interaction between individuals and their environment, that is, between individuals and other individuals or between individuals and the collectivity. And sometimes the results are surprising. Sometimes they are not easily guessed. Sometimes the analysis is difficult. Sometimes it is inconclusive. But even inconclusive analysis can warn against jumping to conclusions about individual intentions from observations of aggregates, or jumping to conclusions about the behavior of aggregates from what one knows or can guess about individual intentions.
>
> (Schelling 2006[1978]: 14)

As I will show the methodological consequence, i.e. the impossibility of aggregation, is true both for strategic and social interactions. Such claim is hardly compatible with standard game theory and even with its contemporary development: the epistemic program.

Standard and epistemic game theory are mainly mathematical theories having for purpose to provide determined solutions for games, by specifying the set of players, the set of their strategies, their payoff function and eventually, in epistemic game theory, the set of players' beliefs, i.e. the information structure of the games.[1] Such mathematical and static specification of games, grounded on an aggregative mechanism, is therefore both normatively and positively inadequate regarding Schelling's account of interdependence. However, the agent-based modeling (ABM) is adequate. In this perspective, I will highlight the behavioral dimension involved in Schelling's vision of game theory more than the epistemic one; while acknowledging that – what is generally recognized as his main methodological contribution – the focal point conciliates those two dimensions. I will concentrate on the evolutionary, historical and path-dependent elements involved in work on game theory. However, contemporary ABM can encompass the epistemic and behavioral – or evolutionary – dimensions (Phan 2004). They can now account for individuals' reasoning processes while both standard and epistemic game theory cannot (see Larrouy and Lecouteux 2017).

To understand why I claim that Schelling's works in game theory and residential segregation participate of a common analytical innovation, I will point out the social ontology underlined by his conception of a "theory of interdependent decisions." Besides, revealing Schelling's ontological commitments can help to clarify some of the methodological debates with respect to his work on game theory. Schelling is indeed simultaneously perceived as a "dissent" (Latzko 1998) or an "errant" economist (Schelling 1984), and as a "pre-eminent pathfinder" (Colman 2006: 607).

In rough terms, social ontology deals with the mode of being of society, its structure and organization. Schelling does not aim to investigate, explain and define what are social facts, or what are the mode of existence of society, institutions and collective. Nevertheless, he makes very strong claims toward these social objects and their mode of existence.

> One prominent justification for the study of social ontology is that the social sciences have regularly imported methods of analysis from the natural sciences or mathematics without considering whether such methods are well suited to their object of study. A deeper analysis of that object has the potential to inform both methodological reflection and theory development within the social sciences.
>
> (Latsis 2013: 1)

Schelling adopts a critical point of view vis-à-vis standard microeconomics methods. He is against *a priori* and *deductive* methods in game theory. The new type both of *experimentation* and *modeling* in economics he proposes, the agent-based modeling (ABM), can be considered as a way, either to enrich contemporary game theory, or to build a distinctive theory of game.[2] Stressing Schelling's social ontology helps to clarify why he challenges the orthodoxy within economics. To my view, his very peculiar approach of game theory is merely explained by a specific social ontology. Therefore, revealing Schelling's ontological commitment helps to understand: a) why he challenges *standard methodological individualism* in game theory – and more generally in economics – and b) why I argue that the agent-based models are a formal tool that better suits his account of strategic interactions. Besides, investigating Schelling's epistemology through social ontology can be very useful for the ongoing questioning of methodologists or philosophers of game theory. Considering the current methodological turn in game theory, due to the rise of behavioral game theory, Schelling's epistemology is today more than ever the bearer of fertile thinking. In this perspective, the agent-based modeling can be used as an *exploring* "tool," a "*starting set*" in the refinement of our understanding of the fundaments of strategic interactions (Schelling 2006[1978]: 184).

The paper is structured as follows. The first part presents Schelling's vision of game theory and his main methodological innovations with respect to his account of strategic interdependence. The second part discusses the models of residential segregation and how, as the precursor of the ABM, they provide a promising tool to account for Schelling's conception of interdependence. The third part reveals the social ontology underlying Schelling's work. The last part stresses how Schelling challenges methodological individualism in game theory – at least in its strong version.

Reorienting game theory for building theory of interdependent decisions in strategic interactions

In *The strategy of Conflict* (1980[1960]), Schelling presents what should be game theory in order to be useful to solve practical decision problems. The key innovations that he introduces in this book are drawn on a) a specific conception of what involves strategic interdependence, b) an emergent account of equilibrium, and a dynamic conception of games and c) the concept of focal point and salience. From that prospect, Schelling (1980[1960]: 84) proposes to enrich game theory with two dimensions that impinge on players' reasoning: "the perceptual and suggestive" and "the structural elements" on which players may rely in their decision-making.[3] Accordingly, contrary to standard game – and even later to epistemic game theory (see Larrouy and Lecouteux 2017) – Schelling integrates players' reasoning process in games.[4]

First of all, for Schelling, game theory is straightforwardly an abstract representation of "gamelike" situations (e.g. Schelling 1984: 236) involving *interdependency*: the interdependency of agents' choices and actions. It means for Schelling that

> [t]here is no independently 'best' choice that one can make; it depends on what the others do. . . . Any 'solution' of a problem like this is necessarily a solution for both participants. Each must try to see the problem from the other's point of view, but when he does he sees himself trying to reach a

> decision. . . . Each must base a decision on his expectations. . . . Game theory is the formal study of the rational, consistent expectations that participants can have about each other's choices.
>
> (Schelling 1984: 214–15)

Schelling has a strong vision of *interdependency* in game theory since for him the resolution of a game is not an individual and independent decision process but more a kind of "*collective-decision process*" (ibid.: 236) – and this statement is reinforced in coordination games in which he claims that it "*is a 'team' situation*" (ibid.: 220). Such account of strategic interdependence means that in order to solve a game "the players must *together find* 'rules of the game' or suffer the consequences" (Schelling 1980[1960]: 107). Strategic interdependence requires coordination of individual perceptions, intentions, beliefs and choices. It is in the search for this coordination that intervene what Schelling identifies as "the perceptual and suggestive" and "the structural elements" (Schelling 1980[1960]). As I will expose such elements are manifold.

One of the prime methodological consequences is his rejection of zero-sum games (i.e. divergent interest games) both as the core of game theory and as an abstract representation of a "game-like" situation implying divergent interests. According to him, one of the mistakes made by game theorists in zero-sum games is to analyze players' decision-making through individual decision-making. For Schelling, any game – even of possibly divergent interests – implies the kind of interdependency he sees, i.e. coordination.

> In a zero-sum game the analyst is really dealing with only a single center of consciousness, a single source of decision. True, there are two players, each with his own consciousness; but minimax strategy converts the situation into one involving two essentially unilateral decisions. No spark of recognition needs to jump between the two players; no meeting of minds is required; no hints have to be conveyed; no impressions, images, or understandings have to be compared. No social perception is involved. But in the mixed-motive game, two or more centers of consciousness are dependent on each other in an essential way. Something has to be communicated; at least some spark of recognition must pass between the players. There is generally a necessity for some social activity, however rudimentary or tacit it may be; and both players are dependent to some degree on the success of their social perception and interaction. Even two completely isolated individuals, who play with each other in absolute silence and without knowing each other's identity, must tacitly reach some meeting of minds.
>
> (ibid.: 163)

As emphasized in the quotation such analysis of zero-sum games implies the neglect of individuals' interdependence.[5]

To solve a game, "[t]he players must *jointly discover* and mutually acquiesce in an outcome or in a mode of play that makes the outcome determinate" (ibid.: 107).

In this perspective, Schelling's starting point relies on the fact that in reality, the resolution of a "game-like" situation is mostly a dynamic process, constantly evolving and uncertain. The solution is therefore specific to each game, to the context of play and the set of players (ibid.: 57–8). For instance, the same game in the same conditions but played by different players will lead to different outcomes. In the same way, the same game with the same set of players but different conditions leads to different solutions. He blames game theorists for being "concerned with *outcomes*, not intermediate processes" (Schelling 1984: 239). The solution of games therefore emerges during the resolution process. This implies that in his account: a) there is no *a priori* predetermined equilibrium in games and b) there is no guarantee that any equilibrium results from joint maximization or possesses a character of optimality. A game is a *discovering* process.

Schelling (1980[1960]: 115) characterizes the equilibrium of a game in terms of convergent expectations (or stabilized convergent expectations). A game is solved when there is between players a "*meeting of minds*" which means "to read the same message in the common situation" (ibid.: 54), i.e. the coordination of individual perceptions, expectations and then behaviors. In the dynamic process leading to players' meeting of minds, at a certain point of time one of the numerous potential suggestive details surrounding and within the game will stand out. As Schelling argues:

> Most situations – perhaps every situation. . . – provide some clue for coordinating behavior, some focal point for each person's expectation of what the other expects him to expect to be expected to do. Finding the key, or rather finding *a* key – any key that is mutually recognized as the key become *the* key – may depend on imagination more than on logic.
>
> (ibid.: 57; original emphasis)

The solution of a game therefore primarily stems from the specific key that is found by the players, *together*, during the game. From that prospect, the context of the game strongly matters (see also Orléan 2004: 205). In the search for this key, players have to grasp all available pieces of information and such information stems from both their physical and socio-cultural environment.[6] In the former environment, Schelling asserts that players can pay attention to some "*objective details*" (Schelling 1980[1960]: 71). These objective details can be "natural boundaries," geography, etc. In the latter environment, players can rely on "precedents," "institutions," "conventions," "clichés" (ibid.: 84–5), etc. – everything that may involve *stable patterns of behavior*, i.e. rules of behavior.

This key leads to what Schelling calls a *focal point*, which makes one behavior salient. Salience and focal point can be understood either in a naturalistic way or in a social – i.e. *community-based* – way in Schelling's work (Hédoin 2014, 2016). In the former case salience is linked to "an objective and natural property of some entities (events, strategies, outcomes)" (Hédoin 2014: 366). This is for instance the case of the geographical elements, "precedent" that Schelling mentions or historical elements: "salience is essentially natural as far as it derives from cognitive mechanisms which are themselves the ultimate product of our evolutionary history" (Hédoin 2016: 3). In the latter case, "community membership is the basis for salience" (Hédoin 2014: 385). Salience becomes explained by the history of a specific community (Hédoin 2016: 3; Orléan 2004). Salience is therefore linked to what Schelling identifies as conventions, traditions and institutions, which form the identity of a community (see Orléan 2004).[7]

In each case, however, salience induces common understanding and then symmetric or common reasoning. "[C]ommon understanding . . . defines the set of events that have the properties to generate a common knowledge set of consistent expectations" (Hédoin 2014: 385). Common reasoning induces common inductive inferences (ibid.). Common understanding and reasoning both characterize what Schelling calls "the meeting of minds." A recurring practice, or behavior, that has led in the past to successful coordination has indeed every chance to work in the future; players can be confident on the fact that such practice or such behavior can make consensus. They become obvious and therefore salient. This generates common expectations towards the other behavior and a symmetric reasoning. In a similar way, regarding conventions and institutions, in a given community players will interpret such "social facts": a "shared institutional heritage . . . brings common understanding into a population" (Hédoin 2014: 383). When belonging to a common community, players "have confidence in the fact that they interpret the same institutional fact in a similar fashion" (ibid). This is what Hédoin (2016: 4) calls "community-based salience" and which is induced by "community-based reasoning." Community-based reasoning entails that the players believe that they are all members of the same community and it ultimately leads to a common belief among the players that everybody will follow the same pattern of behavior (ibid.: 16).

From that prospect, players have to pay attention to the others' behaviors during the resolution process of the game. These behaviors reveal their underlying value system. Schelling (1980[1960]: 139) claims that "[a]n important characteristic of any game is how much each side knows about the other's value system." Through their interactions players have therefore to discover each other's value system, they have to progressively understand each other in order "to discover patterns of individual behavior that make each player's actions predictable to the other" (ibid.: 84–5). In this process, players' social position – i.e. "[t]he concept of role in sociology" (ibid.: 92) – matters. Social positions are related to patterns of behaviors, i.e. to behavioral routines or to specific practices. These routines imply some way of doing and thinking that orient players' expectations and ultimately lead to the convergence of expectations. This is in this manner that for Schelling, players' behavior can be communicative. Therefore, players' behaviors evoke some *suggestive* details. The way players interact; the way they are responding to each other provides "clues" in the determination of a solution.

A focal point can therefore be given *exogenously*, by social conventions, institutions, "precedents," etc. if players perceive it as a reliable device of coordination in the conditions they face, i.e. if they belong or feel belonging to the same community; in other words, if they reason symmetrically and accordingly adopt a community-based reasoning. Or a focal point can be built *endogenously* through players' interactions and through *communicative* behaviors, i.e. through behaviors that can be identified as a stable pattern of behavior in a given community and inform the other player on what common grounding they can interact (again to ultimately lead to a common understanding and reasoning). When there is no exogenous and reliable pre-existent focal point, players determine, *together*, during their interaction process one prominent outcome as the solution. One pattern of behavior orienting toward the convergence of players' subjective beliefs may emerge through their interactive decisions or actions. This implies in particular that focal points have a dynamic and evolutionary content. In Schelling's words a focal point can be "inherently unstable" (ibid.: 112). In fact, focal points are extremely sensitive to the competitive suggestive details of games and their reliability at the moment players make decisions (ibid.: 111). These suggestive details depend on players' perceptions which are both context-dependent – and therefore specific to the interaction process and the context of play – and socio-culturally determined (see also Orléan 2004: 201).

The dynamic models of residential segregation: the creation of a new modeling for the theory of interdependent decisions

Schelling develops his models of residential segregation (and tipping)[8] in four contributions in 1969, 1971a, 1971b and 1972. As I will show, they constitute both a continuation and an extension of his work on game theory. Some of the underpinnings of Schelling's reorientation of game theory indeed permeate his conception of social interactions.[9]

The kind of interdependence involved in the segregation models is characterized by

> people responding to an environment that consists of people who are responding to each other. As people respond they change the environments of the people they associate with, and cause further responses. Everybody's presence affects, if only slightly, the environment of everybody else.
>
> (Schelling 2006[1978]: 169)

Interdependence in this kind of situation, like in "game-like" situations, implies that every individual's decision relies on the others' ones. It explains why the process of interactions is of such importance. Like for "games of strategy," what matters for Schelling is the *process* leading to residential segregation, i.e. the dynamic of interactions (ibid.: 142; 2006: 259). Obviously, the difference is that the epistemic dimension is not present. Besides, the latter are not "games of strategy" due to the fact that "strategic analysis typically involve a small number of interacting decision units" (Schelling 2006: 203). Players' intersubjective capacity no longer prevails: they do not have to see the problem through the others' eyes. Nevertheless, Schelling asserts that his dynamic models of residential segregation are n-players games: he says "I do appreciate that it is easily construed as multi-person game theory" (ibid.: 4).

The purpose of the models is to "see" how such interdependence of individual decisions instantiates a process that collectively led to an unintended pattern. While each agent is not individually in favor of residential segregation, the process of interactive decision-making leads to a segregated area. The models investigate how individuals' perception of their environment collectively enhance residential segregation (ibid.: 254).

The starting point of the models is a twofold population (e.g. blacks and whites, women and men, etc.). Schelling then confers to the agents a "mild segregationist preference." Each agent wants a certain ratio between these two populations in her neighborhood (Schelling 2006[1978]: 169). Two types of neighborhoods are simulated in order to see if the way a neighborhood is defined impacts on the result of the process: a) the "spatial proximity model" and b) the "bounded neighborhood model."[10] In the former, according to her location, everybody has her own subjective definition of her neighborhood (Schelling 2006: 260); while in the latter, there is one common objective neighborhood (Schelling 2006[1978]: 155; 2006: 284).

In both types of model, Schelling studies individuals' successive motions and stresses the impact of different initial conditions on the aggregate. In the "spatial proximity model" even with variations of the variables intervening in individuals' decision-making, the result is unambiguous: a segregated area appears. Clusters of "like-color" are a regular pattern.[11] Even if there are different final repartitions of the two populations, segregation is a strongly robust outcome of the dynamic of interactions. The same pattern is recorded in the "bounded neighborhood model." Again, Schelling compares the aggregate with different initial conditions.[12] And again, a general pattern appears: there are only two stable equilibria, one in which there is a full occupancy of blacks or to the contrary, of whites. Mixed equilibria are too unstable. In case of mixed occupancy some of the outsiders are attracted; this integration causes a dynamic of new entrances, and in turn new departures, which induce more departures, and so on.

Therefore, in these models, Schelling explains that residential segregation occurs from individuals' interdependent decisions – and then actions – but without their desire of such a result.[13] The fact that residential segregation is fairly robust over the different *tests* reveals for Schelling that this is predominantly the process of individuals' interactive decisions that explains the outcome, like he states in game theory.

When developing these models Schelling builds them as experiments. He numerously uses such terms to characterize his work on the models (Schelling 2006[1978]: 150–51, 156–57, 164). He experiments with some hypotheses, some mechanisms, explores potential explanations. He reasons inductively. He tests an intuition. He even advises his readers to test themselves the models with different initial conditions in order to see how the mechanism that leads to residential segregation operates: "If the reader reproduces the experiment himself, he will get a slightly different configuration, but the general pattern will not be much different" (Schelling 2006[1978]: 151). The cornerstone of Schelling's methodology is in fact experimentation (see also Innocenti 2007: 410). Schelling's use of experimental method begins early in his theory of games. By building an experiment (in Schelling 1980[1960]), he is one of the first to demonstrate the empirical evidence of the players' capacity to coordinate in situations characterized by pure coordination games – whereas standard game theory is trapped in the inescapable *indeterminacy* problem (Colman 2003, 2004, 2006; Sugden and Zamarrón 2006: 612–13). Besides, he writes an entire chapter in *The Strategy of Conflict* (1980[1960]) to propose experiments to build, and to discuss experimental protocols to test some of the propositions he made for a more realistic account of games. For Ayson (2004: 126), Schelling "believed that experimental games were often more useful than formal game theory since, in the latter, 'the constraints imposed by the quantitative structure of the game are insufficient to determine a solution.'"

From an experimental point view, the models constitute *a starting set* in the exploration and in turn the explanation of a phenomenon which is mostly explained by the dynamic of interaction. They are especially drawn to test different processes, different dynamics. They offer a new *theoretical apparatus* for economists to formalize *emergent* systems and to test the importance of individual interactive decisions on the macrostructure they build. As emphasized by Sugden (2000b: 9), "Schelling is making an important contribution [which] *is conceptual.*" This conceptual contribution is, according to me, to provide a new type of modeling suitable for most of the methodological innovations he proposes – comparing to standard game theory – in his conception of strategic interactions.

Schelling ascribes two purposes for modeling:

> [S]implified models of artificial situations can be offered for either of two purposes. One is ambitious: these are "basic models" – first approximations that can be elaborated to simulate with higher fidelity the real situations we want to examine. The second is modest: whether or not these models constitute a "starting set" on which better approximations can be built, they illustrate the kind of analysis that is needed, some of the phenomena to be anticipated, and some of the questions worth asking.
>
> (Schelling 2006[1978]: 183–4)

Schelling's dynamic models of residential segregation can be seen as *a starting set*. They constitute a *framework of analysis* in which Schelling offers a *conceptual contribution*, and to go further, a *conceptual exploration*. The first agent-based modeling he proposes in the dynamic models of segregation is *a first step* in economics to introduce complexity and emergence. Besides, Schelling considers both theories and models like tools: "a model is a tool; to be useful, it has to be adjustable or to consist of a set from which we can select the appropriate member" (ibid.: 90). The agent-based models (ABM) as both a type of theorizing and experimentation provide such a tool. They are adjustable and adaptable to the circumstances and phenomena under interest. To paraphrase Schelling: the dynamic models of residential segregation "illustrate the kind of analysis that is needed" to account for his conception interdependency in social interaction and for some parts of his conception of strategic interdependence. The dynamic models of residential segregation are indeed a very rudimentary form of ABM.

However contemporary ABM, with their spread and subsequently their improvements provide, in my opinion, the methodological tool suitable for Schelling's conception of interdependence both in strategic and social interaction.

Contemporary ABM can indeed conciliate the two perspectives that are developed in Schelling's account of game: the "epistemic" or "eductive" one and the "evolutionist" one (Phan 2004: 371). While the work of Schelling in game theory is generally analyzed through the lens of the eductive perspective (Bacharach 1993, 2006; Metha et al. 1994a, b; Sugden 1995; Bardsley et al. 2010; Hédoin 2014, 2015, 2017), the models of residential segregation correspond to the evolutionist approach. The epistemic program is grounded on players' reasoning process and analyzes the way individual perceptions, beliefs and behaviors may converge while the evolutionist program only involve simple rules of behavior. Even if it is mainly the evolutionist approach that is developed in the agent-based computational economics (ACE) a "learning dimension" is more and more integrated in a more complex way than a simple adaptive learning like generally in evolutionary game theory (Phan 2004: 372). In ACE, the eductive perspective which involves learning implies either "belief revision" or "eductive coordination in the case of rational agents playing a game with their nearest neighbourhood" (ibid.: 373). This is accordingly perfectly suitable for Schelling's conception of game theory.

ABM enable the introduction of complexity into economics. They can account for heterogeneity and emergence, and formalize the processes and dynamics of interactions. The agents peopling the ABM have limited cognitive ability, adapt to the others' behavior, and follow rules of behavior. This is why I claim that ABM provide an analytical tool to formalize some of Schelling's main methodological innovations, even in the early and rudimentary form he suggested.

Heterogeneity is for Innocenti (2007) for instance, the pillar of Schelling's methodology. In some way, in Schelling's vision of games, this is precisely because players are heterogeneous (in their identities, perceptions, ways of reasoning, etc.) that they can finally coordinate instead of being trapped in the indeterminacy problem of coordination games (see Innocenti, 2007). In that perspective, the rough critic addressed by Schelling of the concept of *symmetry* included in the concept of Nash's equilibrium and players' rationality can be mentioned (Schelling 1980[1960]: 278). As Schelling claims, in reality, "[t]he uncertainty that can be usually presumed to exist about each other's value systems also reduces the usefulness of the concept of mathematical *symmetry* as a normative or predictive principle (ibid.: 117–18).

The ABM formalize emergence and Schelling's models of segregation are considered as an example of "strong emergence" (Phan 2004: 382). The dynamic models of residential segregation exhibit those outcomes in interactional contexts, even enhanced by individuals' intentional decisions, "have no recognizable counterpart at the level of the individual" (Schelling 2006: 256). The outcomes do not characterize individuals' preferences; they are instead emergent. This is precisely why he offers a kind of modeling allowing paying attention to the dynamic of interactions. Moreover, they demonstrate that these outcomes do not necessarily possess any property of optimality. There is no way to define the result of agents' interaction process in the ABM before the occurrence of the process. There is in fact, a plurality of possible solutions. Again, we find the same methodological statements in Schelling's conception of games.

The ABM allow to account for individuals with limited cognitive abilities. According to Innocenti (2007) this is precisely because players have limited rationality that they can be successful in coordination games. In the ABM, the agents use simplistic forms of reasoning like rules of behaviors and generally adaptive behaviors. They are nevertheless able to learn in at least simplistic forms (see Phan 2004). We can argue that such simplistic learning could be present in Schelling's game theory like adaptive behavior since every form of learning is possible in his account of games. Players' reasoning relies to a large extent on the context of the game (Orléan 2004). Their behavior is determined by the objective and institutional environment surrounding the game and by the other's behavior. This is in this perspective that it can be argued that players have a form of adaptive behavior. Rules of behavior are also strongly present in Schelling's game theory. Such rules of behavior are identified when players follow patterns of behaviors associated with their social position, with norms, conventions and traditions, etc.

ABM can also formalize networks structure to account for the strength of interaction, e.g. their frequency. Such dimension in reality necessarily matters for the creation spread and persistence of norms and other institutional facts, which enter in Schelling's account of game theory. This could be an implicit dimension in Schelling's reorientation of game theory.

In other words, the ABM provide the formal tool to account for the richness of the methodological assumptions made by Schelling in his view of what should be game theory.

What social ontology is behind Schelling's conception of interdependency?

Schelling resorts to concepts – aside that of interdependence – like stability (i.e. stable pattern of behaviors), traditions, emergence, feedback, value systems, social role, etc. which are some of the fundaments of social reality. Some of the underpinnings of his work are topics that clearly refer to social ontology. Besides, he incorporates in his work a vision of society as a complex, multidimensional and dynamic system characterized by multileveled interactional systems among individuals, between individuals and collectives, and between individuals and their environment (cultural or physical) in which people create, modify and act on this environment in the same way as this environment acts on them through continuous and recursive feedbacks. As Schelling claims:

> What we typically deal with in economics, as much as in the social sciences, is a feedback system. And the feedback 'loop' is typically one of these relations that holds no matter how people behave. An output of one part of the system is an input to another part.
>
> (Schelling 2006[1978]: 50)

Schelling makes assessments both on the creation and the mode of existence of social phenomena – or social facts. The *Strategy of Conflict* and the dynamic models of residential segregation offer complementary ontological perspectives by relying on some different however complementary aspects of human interdependence in social reality. In each case however, social facts are created through and by human interactions. And in each case, such "macrostructure" created in turn intervene in and even shape players' decisions and behaviors. On the one hand, in the dynamic models of residential segregation, social facts correspond the social structures that *emerge* from individuals' interactive decisions and behaviors. They are described by a stable macrostructure involuntarily created by purposive individual without necessarily the awareness of such a result (Schelling 2006[1978]: 140). On the other hand they correspond to "institutional facts" (Searle 1995, 2010) through the concept of focal points, which leads to traditions, norms, conventions, etc. and which are this time voluntarily shaped by individuals through their strategic interactions.

Schelling defines institutional facts – and then institutions – as devices allowing individuals to coordinate (see also Hédoin 2014, 2017). They correspond to human artifacts. Humans create institutional facts in order to compensate either the uncertainty surrounding coordination (because of their heterogeneity, i.e. because of their different value system) or the possibly divergent interests among individuals or collectives (Schelling 2006[1978]: 127). Institutions, whether identified as conventions, traditions, social norms, etc. induce convergent and stable patterns of behaviors which ultimately allow the players' meeting of minds. They are accordingly associated with *rules of behaviors* which point toward consistent and convergent expectations (see Hédoin 2017: 49). Rule-following is defined by Hédoin as

> a behavioral event that finds its roots in expectations that are constitutive of a practice. More exactly, the persons' behavior corresponds to a practice that entails the knowledge or the belief that some rule holds and where the rule's meaning is defined by the very practice it is constitutive of.
>
> (ibid.: 50)

When players follow a rule, they know what they should do in the context in which the rule prevails and know or at least believe that every other individual will also reason in the same way. They infer the other's behavior from the knowledge that the rule prevails. "In the case of rule-following, the rule indicates something to be done to everyone, and there is a common reason to believe so because everyone reasons the same way on the basis of some mutually accessible event" (ibid.: 62–3).

Concerning focal points, Schelling asserts:

> The "incidental details" may facilitate the players' discovery of expressive behavior patterns; and the extent to which the *symbolic* contents of the game – the suggestions and connotations – suggest compromises, limits, and regulations should be expected to make a difference. . . . The fundamental psychic

> and intellectual process is that of participating in the creation of *traditions*; and the ingredients out of which traditions can be created, or the materials in which potential traditions can be perceived and jointly recognized, are not at all coincident with the mathematical contents of the game.
>
> (Schelling 1980[1960]: 106–7)

Therefore, from focal points "traditions" emerge. This implies that traditions, i.e. institutional facts, are emergent "objects." They are emergent objects in the sense that they do not correspond to any individual characteristics (there is no aggregative mechanism in Schelling's work and the solution of games do not correspond to joint maximization). They emanate from the process of interaction, i.e. from the transitory collective entity composed by the individuals who manage to coordinate. As detailed below, two kinds of institutions are compatible with this reading: the regulative and constitutive rules.

Focal points are first specific to a particular set of individuals, a particular time and a particular place; this is the first step or the creation *per se* of these institutional facts. In outline, and referring to Searle (1995, 2005, 2010), institutional facts are ontologically subjective and epistemologically objective. Focal points, as institutional facts, are ontologically subjective because they depend on players' subjective perceptions. But then, after a certain amount of time these institutional facts progressively acquire an autonomous status. They become anchored in individuals' social background – or social knowledge.[14] They are collectively accepted as devices of coordination as soon as they enter in individuals' social background. This is in this manner that they lead to the convergence of individual subjective expectations. For Schelling, institutions (and their associated patterns of behavior) exist as soon as they are perceived and understood in a common way even by different individuals; i.e. even by heterogeneous individuals who do not have the same value system, but belong to a common community in which exist, or which is constituted by, such institutions (see Orléan 2004). Institutions are therefore objective entities in the sense that they may be taken for granted by these individuals. They become objective facts taken abruptly as such, without the need of interpretation (see Hédoin 2014, 2016).

In some readings of Schelling's conception of focal points, it becomes an institutional fact if it recurrently serves as a successful coordination device. This explains why he asserts that focal points have a content that is inherently dynamic or evolutionary (see Schelling 1980[1960]: 111–12). The persistence of an institutional fact is dependent upon individuals' acceptance. Subsequently, Schelling's conception of emergence is diachronic. In order for institutional facts to act in turn on individuals' behavior by orienting toward some predetermined patterns of behavior, they have to be anchored in individuals' knowledge of the functioning of society. Focal points are conceived in a pragmatic way (Sugden and Zamarrón 2006). In other words, they have to recurrently allow successful coordination. These institutional facts are therefore reproduced through interactions by their practical dimension. In such reading salience is made by precedents. This is accordingly similar to Rawls's notion of "rules as summary view" and which echoes to Searle's account of institutions as "regulative rules." Such rules "emerge from the agents' actions but do not play any causal or functional role in the rise of these actions" (Hédoin 2015: 6). They "regulate an existing practice or activity" (ibid.: 4). They even "facilitate a social activity or even contribute to enhance its efficiency"; this is exactly the role that the focal points play: they facilitate coordination and eventually arbitrate between individual and collective divergent will. Salience and focal points as institutional objects in this case emanate from individual behavior but do not explain such behaviors: "given the history of past plays in a game, each agent is incentivized to reproduce the behavioral pattern, thus leading to a further reinforcement of the pattern" (Hédoin 2015: 6).

With another reading of Schelling, institutional facts like conventions, norms, etc. are associated with Searle's "constitutives rules" (Searle 1995, 2010). "Constitutive rules literally create a new institutional reality" (Searle 2010: 97). When players together decide that one suggestive detail, one key becomes the key, to paraphrase Schelling, making accordingly a focal point, they ascribe constitutive rules to such focal point. They decide that such focal point induces common reasoning and convergent expectation, i.e. serve as a coordination device. Focal points indeed create a "new institutional reality," as they are responsible for the creation of traditions or norms, conventions, etc. They establish new practices (see Hédoin 2015: 2). Such rules change the game that the players are playing, making such game a coordination game and possibly defining new strategies, new beliefs and preferences:

> to be constitutive, a rule must in one way or another define the game the players are actually playing . . . a constitutive rule is directly responsible for the game's structure (e.g., the players' strategy sets or payoff functions) and possibly for the players' beliefs and behavior.
>
> (ibid.)

Some focal points – as institutions – in Schelling's work indeed transform the game the players are playing, making a divergent interest game into a coordination game, change the set of strategies, preferences that initially defined the game, or modify players' beliefs.

It means that the structure of social reality, as well as the institutional system, shapes the resolution process of games. Schelling claims that "[t]he solution depends on some kind of social organization, whether that organization is contrived or spontaneous, permanent or ad-hoc, voluntary or disciplined" (Schelling 2006[1978]: 126). Accordingly, the institutions that shape such social organization causally affect individuals. They orient and condition individuals' decisions and actions. Subsequently, in Schelling's work, society is among others, constituted by a set of institutions.

> A good part of social organization – of what we call society – consists of institutional arrangements to overcome these divergences between perceived individual interest and some larger collective bargain.
>
> (Schelling 2006[1978]: 127)

Society is constituted by "institutional arrangements" facilitating and allowing the conciliation between both heterogeneous agents and collectives, since the aggregate is emergent and does not necessarily match with individuals' intentions. Society is an enduring entity grounded on stable institutional and organizational systems. In Schelling's view, there are enduring and pervasive patterns in the social world. This is true for institutions but not only, as it is emphasized in the segregation models. In these models, even considering perpetual ongoing processes at the micro level, there are stable patterns at the macro level. Micro variations exist; however they do not necessarily lead to social modifications. This is one of the conclusions that emerge from the dynamic models of residential segregation. Therefore, Schelling's account of both strategic and social interdependent decisions stands from open-systems (Lawson 2003). Schelling declares:

> Abstractly speaking, stable organization comes in at least two forms or 'systems', the first of which we might refer to as an environmentally closed, or equilibrium, system, and the second of which we can label an environmentally open, or far-from-equilibrium, . . . equilibrium systems are stable if there are no disturbances from the outside environment; far-from-equilibrium systems require perpetual inputs from the environment to endure and be stable.
>
> (Schelling 1984: 357)

Because micro variations exist constantly, the pervasiveness of social and institutional facts, when there is no legal enforcement, requires "perpetual inputs" or individuals' continuous acceptance of the underlined patterns of behavior.

Another aspect that appears in Schelling's work is that society is multileveled. Several interdependent types of collective (like ethnic, religious, socio-professional categories, etc.) constitute it. Each one possesses its own underlying value system. Innocenti (2007: 416) suggests for instance that Schelling, through observation, builds categories of individuals and that it constitutes the underpinning of his work. Therefore, different complementary types of collectives exist in Schelling's account of economic systems. First, there are collectives which correspond to social, cultural, ethnic, etc. categories. Those collectives enhance the identification of common characteristics; for instance, common perceptions and common way of reasoning, i.e. community-based reasoning, with respect to the rules that hold in these communities. Second, there are collectives which are formed by specific interactional contexts, i.e. strategic contexts. In the latter category, a collective is formed as soon as there is a strong interdependency between individuals, i.e. a situation involving a strategic interdependence. When players create a new institutional fact when making a focal point, they become a specific community, even transitory. As such focal point induces common reasoning, it is associated with rule-following which is mainly a "community-based practice" (Hédoin 2014, 2015, 2017). And all of these types of collectives participate to the construction of social reality.

In summary, the ontological commitments behind Schelling's theory of interdependency emphasize that he attempts to incorporate in economics a rich account of social reality. Through his vision of game theory and his dynamic models of residential segregation Schelling offers different but complementary aspects of the structure of interdependence in social life. In the *Strategy of Conflict* Schelling describes the way individuals are reasoning when they have to coordinate; their reasoning process is eductive. In the dynamic models of residential segregation, the process is evolutionary; it exhibits how are built and selected some patterns of behavior at the macro social level. They offer complementary aspects of social life. In some way, the latter can offer the basis of the selection of stable patterns of behavior that constitutes the raw material for the selection of focal points, as understood in terms of regulative rules, for strategic interactions. All of this necessarily impacts in a very significant way his epistemology and in particular the role he confers to methodological individualism.

Challenging methodological individualism in economics

The richness of the social ontology behind Schelling's theory of interdependence has important methodological consequences, especially regarding the role of *methodological individualism* within social sciences and *a fortiori* in economics. As Schelling stresses:

> A pervasive question for social phenomena is the role, or the exclusive role, of 'methodological individualism', the notion that the ultimate analysis is a rational, or at least a purposive, individual. Some believe that any social phenomenon that cannot be reduced to the behavior (choices) of individuals is a black box and therefore unsatisfactory.
>
> (Schelling 2006: 235)

This statement is obviously explained by Schelling's ontological commitments. In this regard, I will assess how Schelling challenges methodological individualism through his insight into both strategic and social interactions and his analysis of interdependence.

In the following quotation, Schelling draws a parallel between an ants' colony and human society:

> What I asked you to be amazed at . . . is simply the enormous complexity of the entire collective system of behavior, a system that the individuals who comprise the system needn't know anything about or even be aware of. If we see pattern and order and regularity, we should . . . inquire first of all what it is that the individuals who comprise the system seem to be doing and how it is that their actions, in the large, produce the patterns we see. Then we can try to evaluate whether, at least according to what the individuals are trying to do, the resulting pattern is in some way responsive to their intentions.
>
> (Schelling 2006[1978]: 22)

As stated in this quotation, while questioning, in some respect, the role of methodological individualism, he is embedded in this paradigm. However, as I explain in this section, he is more inclined to a loose version of methodological individualism than the standard rational choice theory (RCT) and standard rationality in game theory – which is a direct extension of the RCT (e.g. see Bacharach and Hurley 1991; Mariotti 1995).

Boudon (2004) identifies six postulates – among which three are characteristic of methodological individualism – underlying RCT. First, every social or economic analysis has for its purpose to understand the individual intentions, beliefs, decisions or behaviors that led to social or economic phenomena. Second, understanding the individual beliefs, decisions or behavior is to explain the meaning that they have for the individual. Third, they are reasons behind individual beliefs, decisions and actions, i.e. there is a rationality postulate behind those attitudes. The three other postulates characterize such rationality principle. First, the individual is concerned by the consequences of her decisions and actions; second, she is concerned by the consequence only for her; and third, the individual is a maximizer.

While, as the quotation above emphasized, Schelling ascribes to the first and second postulate, he deviates in some respects from the standard way that the other postulates are implemented in economics and game theory.

There is no maximization in Schelling's account of strategic interactions. Schelling does not believe in the optimality of games equilibrium, nor in the fact that individual self-serving behavior can lead to a social desirable state (demonstrating this statement was one of the purposes of his dynamic models of residential segregation). Players' rationality is limited (see also Innocenti 2007). Indeed, players are not necessarily able to draw complicated conclusions from a mathematical structure; they are not over-skilled computational entities. It means that economists and game theorists have to acknowledge that departures from perfect rationality – as defined in rational choice theory and standard game theory – are more current than the benchmark they have defined. In addition,

> The critical question is not whether a person is "rational" according to any particular definition, perfectionist or merely approximate, but whether his choice is determined in large part by the situation he is in and by what we can guess about his values.
>
> (Schelling 1984: 205)

Recall that it is the suggestive details of a game or surrounding a game that orient toward one solution among all of the possible ones. Players draw their reasoning, their expectations, both on the objective and the institutional environment surrounding the game. Players' reasons for acting are partly determined by this multidimensional environment; they are no longer intrinsic to the individuals. For instance, it can be more rational for an individual to rely on conventions than to follow what could be identified as her preferences, even if following these institutional devices will discriminate against her (see Schelling 1980[1960]: 100). Some behaviors consist in following rules; it is therefore difficult to resort to a peculiar concept of rationality. The stable patterns of behaviors, i.e. the rules of behaviors that Schelling mentions in game theory, which correspond to social role, traditions, institutions, conventions, etc., do not rely on rational principles. Besides, what is rational to do for players depends to a great extent on the others with whom they interact, on what they perceived about these others and their intentions, value systems, etc.

Therefore, strategic rationality cannot derive solely from axioms and exogenous preferences, but primarily from the way individuals perceive their decision problem. As soon as Schelling asserts that solving a game is a discovering process, constantly in evolution, there is no room for a deductive account of rationality.

> There is . . . no way that an analyst can reproduce the whole decision process either introspectively or by an axiomatic method. There is no way to build a model for the interaction of two or more decision units, with the behavior and expectations of those decision units being derived by purely formal deduction.
>
> (Schelling 1980[1960]: 163)

During the interaction, players commit themselves; some opportunities arise while some others disappear. Players' preferences are built during the decision process. They are defined and evolving during interactions. Unlike in standard game theory, players' preferences are therefore neither given exogenously nor determinately in Schelling's work. Recall that the players must find the rule of game while playing (i.e. the set of beliefs, preferences and payoffs). Since rule-following and its associated mode of reasoning, community-based reasoning, is constitutive of practices, i.e. has the power to change the game they are playing, the norms that are followed condition the players' preferences, utility functions and eventually, beliefs. The 'rules-as-normative-expectations' (Bicchieri 2005) – a specific form of rule-following – induce "a conditional preference for conformity entering directly into the agents' utility functions. As a consequence, their preferences are a function of their beliefs, and hence of the norms" (Hédoin 2015: 16). The other form of rule-following induced by 'rules-as-correlated-devices'

> set the stage for the fact that the agents have a common prior and lead them to behave in a particular way. In other words, the norm defines a specific epistemic game and a change in the norm would change not only the agents' behavior but also the whole characteristics of the epistemic game (starting with the agents' prior).
>
> (ibid.: 17)

It therefore defines the players' beliefs.

Accordingly, the rationale of a decision is judged a posteriori and by its success, i.e. by players' capacity to coordinate. There is no possibility to define a priori and deductively a rational decision in interactional systems. This is very far from any claim within the RCT and standard modern game theory.

Players have the faculty of reflexivity: they can "reflect on their mode of reasoning" (Hédoin 2014: 381). They can reflect on their beliefs and those of her co-player. For instance, as emphasized by Orléan (2004) players are able to distance from their 'personal' belief to ascribe to what they guess being the beliefs of the collective. He considers that in Schelling's work, the group beliefs are possibly disconnected from the beliefs that the individual inside those collective believe (Orléan 2004: 200): "Each individual can believe *P* and, at the same time, believe that the group believe *Q*" (ibid.: 199). Such account does not correspond to a strict methodological individualism as the group beliefs or collective beliefs are no longer the aggregate of the individual beliefs (ibid.: 211).

The meeting of minds, i.e. the convergence of players' modes of reasoning, and common understanding takes place inside a given community: "the basis for common understanding is community membership" (Hédoin 2014: 384). Players' reasoning is therefore determined by their collective identities and no longer intrinsic preferences, or beliefs. In the same way, rule-following is linked to the belonging of a given community (Hédoin 2017: 60–1). It therefore entails a "non-individualistic conception of salience" (Hédoin 2014: 366)[15] which contradicts methodological individualism.

Another aspect of Schelling's account of strategic interdependence is players' capacity of empathy, i.e. their ability to put themselves in the others' shoes (see Goldman 2006). "Each must try to see the problem from the other's point of view" (Schelling 1984: 214–15). This is explained to a large extent by the fact that players are heterogeneous. Unlike within standard game theory, to understand the others and their rationality, intentions, etc. players have progressively to discover and understand their value system, to ultimately see the decision problem from the others' place. Recall that by paying attention to others, their decisions, behaviors, etc. players have to guess and finally to have a picture of others' value systems and representations. Each player has to converge on a meeting of minds. This requires that, at least transitorily, players must abandon their own individuality to see the problem through the other's angle. They must therefore inhibit their own vision of the problem to attempt to be in the other's shoes (especially when considering that the other's behavior reveals that they possibly have a different value system).

This last statement can explain another main aspect underscored in Schelling's account of game theory: collective decision-making, i.e. collective rationality. Due to the strong interdependency of players in any type of games, coupled with players' capacity of empathy, the set of players become a collective entity. Players form a collective in the sense that they have a common purpose which is solving the game and this requires a certain proclivity for cooperative behavior. This is true that players do not become a team in a restrictive sense. They do not decide by a common agreement to become a "plural subject" in the logic of Gilbert (1989, 1996, 2003, 2013) or a "team" as conceptualized by Sugden (1993, 2000a, 2005, 2007) or Bacharach (1999, 2006) in game theory. They become a collective entity by virtue of the problem they have to solve. Players recognize that they face *together* a common problem and that they will be able to solve it only by their mutual acknowledgment of their strong interdependency. By virtue of the situation, players know that they will have to learn together in a very unique and specific way, how collectively they can manage to coordinate. This aspect tends to argue in favor of collective rationality. Players become a unique and transitory "team" during the time of the resolution process of the game, they adopt as a consequence, a distinctive mode of reasoning which is driven by the collective they form. It does not mean that players' purposes or 'preferences' are directly deduced from those of the collective like in Bacharach's or Sugden's approaches. It means that the way players decide and act is defined by their interaction and is specific to whom they are. In this sense, this is a collective form rationality.

Hédoin's approach can also be mentioned in the claim that Schelling's conception of interdependence induces a form of collective rationality. He indeed states "In some ways, community-based salience works along a form of collective intentionality" (Hédoin 2014: 391).

Conclusion

Schelling sees game theory as a "framework for analysis" more than an " 'instant theory' just waiting to be applied" (Schelling 1984: 241). Such framework of analysis relies on the interdependence of an individual's decision and not the abstract, mathematical and deductive account that standard game theory offers. From that prospect, and considering that interdependence for Schelling entails non-aggregative mechanisms, any form of game theory, being standard or epistemic cannot suit to his vision of game theory. However, a more malleable analytical tool like ABM can.

The continuity that is rarely stressed in Schelling's works (except for Ayson 2004, Innocenti 2007, and Aydinonat 2005, 2007) is therefore deeper than persistent concepts. Investigating Schelling's ontological commitments as well as his implicit social ontology highlights that both *The Strategy of Conflicts* and the dynamic models of residential segregation are complementary. The dynamic models of residential segregation even being very rudimentary and being mainly grounded on simplistic behavioral and not eductive or epistemic mechanisms, as the precursors of the ACE, opened a new framework that nowadays can couple both mechanisms and therefore account for Shelling's conception of game theory. Actually, what we have to keep in mind is the fact that models and theories are merely tools for Schelling (2006 [1978]: 90). Their purpose is ultimately to understand reality whatever the step to which our scientific knowledge of a socio-economic phenomenon has progressed. The need to focus his interest either on basic models or on more peculiar models depends on the existing amount of scientific knowledge. For instance, Schelling declares "after a certain amount of heuristic experiments with building blocks, it becomes more productive to identify the actual characteristics of the phenomena we want to study, rather than to explore general properties" (ibid.: 183–4). The dynamic models of residential segregation as the precursor of the agent-based models are the first 'building block' in the constitution of a new formal tool to refine or to build a distinctive theory of games.

Moreover, focusing on the social ontology behind Schelling's account of interdependent decisions explains the pluridisciplinary aspect of his work (again that is rarely stressed excepting in Ayson 2004; Colman 2006; Rivzi 2007). Economics cannot be conceived as a "closed-system" in Schelling's account. Conversely it is an "open-science" (e.g., Lawson 2003), i.e. a social science that can no longer be confined within strict boundaries but must be linked and crossed with the other social sciences. Understanding human behavior and human relationship with her social and cultural environment requires appealing to psychology, social psychology, sociology, information theory, organization theory, etc. (see Ayson 2004).

This concern is today very much at the core of the improvements that are needed in microeconomics. In fact, considering nowadays that microeconomics undergoes deep modifications, Schelling's insights into a "theory of interdependent decisions" are more than ever bearer of further new fertile thinking. Pointing out the social ontology that underlies his work can help to better circumscribe what scholars can pick up in his work and generalize and how they can manage it. As emphasized by Sugden and Zamarrón (2006: 620):

> [G]ame theorists have persisted in using their customary research tools; and they have been continually frustrated by their inability to create a theory of focal points. Schelling's 'vision', his proposal for the reorientation of game theory, remains unrealized. The process of realizing it has hardly begun.

Notes

1 For this statement regarding standard game theory see Sugden (2001) and for epistemic game theory see Larrouy and Lecouteux (2017).
2 Some scholars assert that the agent-based modeling is a new way of theorizing (e.g. see Epstein 2006) while others argue that it is a new form of experimentation (e.g. see Aydinonat 2007; Tesfatsion 2002). For epistemological and methodological thinking on agent-based modeling see Ferber (2007), Phan et al. (2007), Livet (2007), Livet et al. (2008) or Tubaro (2011).
3 Schelling (1980[1960]: 84) argues that the predominance of zero-sum games within game theory is responsible for the lacks of concern for these perceptual and structural elements.
4 See also Walliser (2004: 183) who claims that in classical economic theory the "substantive individual rationality" entails "no mental deliberation process leading to the chosen action." He however considers that epistemic game theory is an attempt to overcome such insufficiency.
5 See also Giocoli (2003: 265).
6 These claims are independent of a positive or normative account of game theory. Indeed,

> the influence that the suggestive details of a game may have on its outcome and the dependence of the players on what clues and signals the game provides are relevant not merely to the study of how players actually do behave in a nonzero-sum game. It is not being argued that players just do respond to the non-mathematical properties of the game but that they ought to take them into account, hence that even a normative theory – a theory of the strategy of games – must recognize that rational players may jointly take advantage of them.
>
> (Schelling 1980[1960]: 108; original emphasis)

7 For Orléan (2004: 200) the identity of a community is shaped by its "cultural and historical context."

8 Schelling defines tipping as follows: "'Tipping' is said to occur when a recognizable new minority enters a neighborhood in sufficient numbers to cause the earlier residents to begin evacuating" (Schelling 2006: 302).

9 The model of "dying seminar" (Schelling 2006[1978]) is another example of the kind of social interdependence involved in the dynamic model of residential segregation; I am however more interested by the simulation aspect of the latter and its presentation by the author in a more systematic way.

10 The bounded neighborhood model allows studying the tipping phenomenon. This phenomenon occurs when the entrance of a minority in a neighborhood (i.e. a bounded neighborhood) induces the departure of the occupant majority.

11 In the "spatial proximity model" he experiments with different initial: a) distributions area (in line or within a square) and configurations of the two populations (each time, Schelling positions them randomly), b) size of both populations, c) rules of motion, d) size of neighborhood, e) preference over the color ratio within the subjective neighborhood of each player (Schelling 2006: 265).

12 In the "bounded neighborhood model" Schelling tests different initial a) "cumulative frequency distributions of 'tolerance'" for each population (Schelling 2006[1978]: 157), b) occupancy ratios in the neighborhood and c) dynamic of motion.

13 The mechanism involved in the dying seminar, is the critical mass. If it can be identified in the bounded neighborhood model and tipping, this is not the case for the spatial proximity model.

14 Social or cultural knowledge is a knowledge "of which arrangements are salient or traditional in that culture and so provide coordination" (Bacharach and Hurley 1991: 3). It corresponds to a "shared institutional heritage that brings common understanding into a population" (Hédoin 2014: 383) or to the knowledge of the set of "historical and cultural points of reference that define the identity of the group" (Orléan 2004: 208).

15 This statement means that salience does not come from players' cognition as in Bacharach's (1993, 2006) framework for instance. More specifically, when players perceive a decision problem, a set of frames characterizing such decision problem comes to their mind and some of them are more salient than others. In matching games (i.e. games in which players must choose the same object), those frames can be the color, the shape, the size, etc. As an example, the frame color can be more salient than the frame size.

Bibliography

Aydinonat, N.E. (2005) 'An interview with Thomas C. Schelling: Interpretation of game theory and the checkerboard model', *Economics Bulletin*, 2: 1–17.

Aydinonat, N.E. (2007) 'Models, conjectures and exploration: An analysis of Schelling's checkerboard model of residential segregation', *Journal of Economic Methodology*, 14: 429–54.

Ayson, R. (2004) *Thomas Schelling and the nuclear age: Strategy as a social science*, London: Frank Cass.

Bacharach, M. (1993) 'Variable universe game', in K. Binmore, Al. Kirman and P. Tami (eds.) *Frontiers of game theory*, Cambridge, MA: MIT Press.

Bacharach, M. (1999) 'Interactive team reasoning: A contribution to the theory of cooperation', *Research in Economics*, 53: 117–47.

Bacharach, M. (2006) *Beyond individual Choice: Team and frame in game theory*, Gold N. and Sugden R. (eds.), Princeton, NJ: Princeton University Press.

Bacharach, M. and Hurley, S. (1991) 'Issues and advances in the foundations of decision theory', in M. Bacharach and S. Hurley (eds.) *Foundations of decision theory*, Oxford: Blackwell.

Bardsley, N., Mehta, J., Starmer, C. and Sugden, R. (2010) 'Explaining focal points: Cognitive hierarchy theory versus team reasoning', *Economic Journal*, 120: 40–79.

Bicchieri, C. (2005) *The grammar of society: The nature and dynamics of social norms*. Cambridge: Cambridge University Press.

Boudon, R. (2004) 'Théorie du choix rationnel ou individualisme méthodologique?' *Revue du MAUSS*, 24: 281–309.

Cohendet, P., Kirman, A. and Zimmermann, J.B. (2003) 'Émergence, formation et dynamique des réseaux: Modèles de la morphogenèse', *Revue d'Économie Industrielle*, 103: 15–42.

Colman, A.M. (2003) 'Cooperation, psychological game theory and limitations of rationality in social interaction', *Behavioral and Brain Science*, 26: 139–98.

Colman, A.M. (2004) 'Reasoning about strategic interaction: Solution concepts in game theory', in K. Manktelow and M. C. Chung (eds.), *Psychology of reasoning: Theoretical and historical perspectives*, London: Psychology Press.

Colman, A.M. (2006) 'Thomas C. Schelling's psychological decision theory: Introduction to a special issue', *Journal of Economic Psychology*, 27: 603–8.

Epstein, J.M. (2006) *Generative social science: Studies in agent-based computational modeling*, Princeton, NJ: Princeton University Press.

Epstein, J.M. and Axtell, R. (1996) *Growing artificial societies: Social science from the bottom up*, Washington, DC: Brookings Institution Press.

Ferber, J. (2007) 'Multi-agent concepts and methodologies', in A. Phan (eds.) *Agent based modeling and simulations in the human and social sciences*, Oxford: The Bardwell Press.

Gilbert, M. (1989) *On social facts*, London: Routledge.

Gilbert, M. (1996) *Living together: Rationality, sociality, and obligation*, Lanham, MD: Rowman & Littlefield.

Gilbert, M. (2003) 'The structure of the social atom: joint commitment as the foundation of human social behavior', in F.S. Frederick (ed.) *Socializing metaphysics*, Lanham, MD: Rowman & Littlefield.

Gilbert, M. (2013) *Joint commitment: How we make the social world*, New York: Oxford University Press.

Giocoli, N. (2003) *Modeling rational agents: From interwar economics to early modern game theory*, Cheltenham: Edward Elgar Publishing.

Goldman, A.I. (2006) *Simulating minds: The philosophy, psychology, and neuroscience of mindreading*, New York: Oxford University Press.

Hédoin, C. (2013) 'Collective rationality in economics: Making Searle's theory of institutional facts relevant for game theory', *Erasmus Journal for Philosophy and Economics*, 6: 1–27.

Hédoin, C. (2014) 'A framework for community-based salience: Common knowledge, common understanding and community membership', *Economics and philosophy*, 30: 365–95.

Hédoin, C. (2015) 'Accounting for constitutive rules in game theory', *Journal of Economic Methodology*, 22: 439–61.

Hédoin, C. (2016) 'Community-based reasoning in games: Salience, rule-following, and counterfactuals', *Games*, 7: 36.

Hédoin, C. (2017) 'Institutions, rule-following and game theory', *Economics and Philosophy*, 33: 43–72.

Innocenti, A. (2007) 'Player heterogeneity and empiricism in Schelling', *Journal of Economic Methodology*, 14: 409–28.

Kirman, A. (2011) *Complex economics: Individual and collective rationality*, London: Routledge.

Larrouy, L. and Lecouteux, G. (2017) 'Mindreading and endogenous beliefs in games', *Journal of Economic Methodology*, 24: 318–43.

Latsis, J. (2013) 'Social ontology', in J.D. Wright (ed.) *International encyclopedia of the social and behavioral sciences*, 2nd ed., Amsterdam: Elsevier.

Latzko, D. (1998) 'Thomas Schelling's dissent from the narrow scope of economics', in R.P.F. Holt and S. Pressman (eds.) *Economics and its discontents: Twentieth century dissenting economists*, Cheltenham: Edward Elgar Publishing.

Lawson, T. (2003) 'Theorizing ontology', *Feminist Economics*, 9: 161–69.

Livet, P. (2007) 'Towards an epistemology of multi-agent simulations in social sciences', in D. Phan and F. Amblard (eds.) *Agent based modeling and simulations in the human and social sciences*, Oxford: The Bardwell Press.

Livet, P., Phan, D. and Sanders, L. (2008) 'Why do we need ontology for agent-based models?' in K. Schredelseker and F. Hauser (eds.) *Complexity and artificial markets*, Berlin: Springer.

Mariotti, M. (1995) 'Is Bayesian rationality compatible with strategic rationality?' *The Economic Journal*, 105: 1099–109.

Mehta, J., Starmer, C. and Sugden, R. (1994a) 'The nature of salience: An experimental investigation of pure coordination games', *American Economic Review*, 84: 658–73.

Mehta, J., Starmer, C. and Sugden, R. (1994b) 'Focal points in pure coordination games: An experimental investigation', *Theory and Decision*, 36: 163–85.

Nash, J.F. (1950) 'The bargaining problem', *Econometrica*, 18: 155–62.

Nash, J.F. (1951) 'Equilibrium points in n-person games', *Proceedings of the National Academy of Sciences*, 36: 48–9.

Orléan, A. (2004) 'What is a collective belief?' in P. Bourgine and J. P. Nadal (eds.) *Cognitive economics: An interdisciplinary approach*, Berlin: Springer.

Phan, D. (2004) 'From agent-based computational economics to cognitive economics', in P. Bourgine and J. P. Nadal (eds.) *Cognitive economics: An interdisciplinary approach*, Berlin: Springer.

Phan, D., Schmid, A.F. and Varenne, F. (2007) 'Epistemology in a nutshell: Theory, model, simulation and experiment', in D. Phan and F. Amblard (eds.) *Agent based modeling and simulations in the human and social sciences*, Oxford: The Bardwell Press.

Rawls, J. (1955) 'Two concepts of rules', *Philosophical Review*, 64: 3–32.

Rivzi, S.A.T. (2007) 'Introduction: Thomas Schelling's distinctive approach', *Journal of Economic Methodology*, 14: 403–8.

Schelling, T.C. (1969) 'Models of segregation', *American Economic Review*, 59: 488–93.

Schelling, T.C. (1971a) 'Dynamic models of segregation', *Journal of Mathematical Sociology*, 1: 143–86.

Schelling, T.C. (1971b) 'On the ecology of micromotives', *The Public Interest*, 25: 61–98.

Schelling, T.C. (1972) 'The process of residential segregation: Neighborhood tipping', in A.H. Pascal (ed.) *Racial discrimination in economic life*, Lexington, MA: D.C. Heath.

Schelling, T.C. (1980[1960]) *The Strategy of Conflict*, Cambridge, MA: Harvard University Press.

Schelling, T.C. (1984) *Choice and consequence*, Cambridge, MA and London: Harvard University Press.

Schelling, T.C. (2006[1978]) *Micromotives and macrobehavior*, London and New York: W.W. Norton. Cambridge, MA: Harvard University Press.

Schelling, T.C. (2006) *Strategies of commitment and other essays*, London and New York: W.W. Norton. Cambridge, MA: Harvard University Press.
Searle, J.R. (1995) *The construction of social reality*. New York: Simon and Schuster.
Searle, J.R. (2005) 'What is institution?' *Journal of Institutional Economics*, 1: 1–22.
Searle, J.R. (2010) *Making the social world*, New York: Oxford University Press.
Sugden, R. (1993) 'Thinking as a team: Towards an explanation of non selfish behavior', *Social Philosophy and Policy*, 10: 69–89.
Sugden, R. (1995) 'A theory of focal points', *The Economic Journal*, 105: 533–50.
Sugden, R. (2000a) 'Team preferences', *Economics and Philosophy*, 16: 175–204.
Sugden, R. (2000b) 'Credible worlds: The status of theoretical models in economics', *Journal of Economic Methodology*, 7: 1–31.
Sugden, R. (2001) 'The evolutionary turn in game theory', *Journal of Economic Methodology*, 8: 113–30.
Sugden, R. (2005) 'The logic of team reasoning', in N. Gold (ed.) *Teamwork – multi-disciplinary perspectives*, Basingstoke and New York: Palgrave MacMillan.
Sugden, R. (2007) 'Collective intentions and team agency', *Journal of Philosophy*, 104: 109–37.
Sugden, R. and Zamarrón, I.E. (2006) 'Finding the key: The riddle of focal points', *Journal of Economic Psychology*, 27: 609–21.
Tesfatsion, L. (2002) 'Agent-based computational economics: Growing economies from the bottom up', *Artificial Life*, 8: 55–82.
Tubaro, P. (2011) 'Computational economics', in D. W. Hands and J. B. Davis (eds.) *The Elgar companion to recent economic methodology*, Cheltenham: Edward Elgar.
von Neumann, J. and Morgenstern, O. (1944) *The theory of games and economic behaviour*, Princeton, NJ: Princeton University Press.
Walliser, B. (2004) 'Topics of cognitive economics', in P. Bourgine and J. P. Nadal (eds.) *Cognitive economics: An interdisciplinary approach*, Berlin: Springer.

18 Instrumental rationality, prudence and communicative action

Deliberation in, and communication through, individual rational decision-making[1]

Jean Mercier Ythier

Introduction

Rational choice is usually defined, in economics, as preference maximization. It is generally interpreted, substantively, as agent's instrumental rationality. Specifically, the mode of agency that consists of selecting the best means (agent's choice of an act) for attaining certain given ends (the outcome of action that the agent prefers), whatever these ends may be. It coincides with the notion of rationality as preferential (reflective, deliberated) choice developed in the *Nicomachean Ethics* (1941), with a few additional precisions relative to the formal properties of agents' preference rankings (the so-called axioms of rational decision theory).

Prudence (*phronēsis*) is one of the basic virtues distinguished by the *Nicomachean Ethics* and by major ensuing ethical traditions. Aristotle (1941) characterizes prudence as the individual's ability of 'aiming in accordance with calculation at the best for man of things attainable in action' (6.7.1141b). It is, in other words, practical judgment at its best, exerted in the singular circumstances of action, whatever these circumstances may be.

Aristotle's contrasted accounts of rational decision-making in the *Nicomachean Ethics* as instrumental rationality in book 3 and prudence in book 6 are not easy to reconcile. One reads, for example, in Paul Ricoeur's *Soi-même comme un autre* (1990):

> Numerous commentators have seen a discordance between book 3 and book 6. Some hold it to be unsurmountable, others do not. The discordance consists in this: in book 3 . . . everything rests on the tie between preferential choice and deliberation. Now the same book proposes a model of deliberation that seems to exclude deliberation about ends. . . . This puzzlement, which later will supply us with food for thought, forces us to admit that the ends-means model does not cover the entire field of action but only that of *technē*. . . .
>
> Book 6. . . offers, however, a more complex model of deliberation. Here, deliberation is the path followed by *phronēsis*, practical wisdom (translated in

> Latin by *prudentia*), and, more precisely, the path that the man of *phronēsis* – the *phronimos* – follows to guide his life. The question posed here would seem to be the following: What counts as the specification best suited to the ultimate ends pursued? In this regard, the greatest lesson of book 6 concerns the close tie established by Aristotle between *phronēsis* and *phronimos*, a tie that becomes meaningful only if the man of wise judgment determines at the same time the rule and the case, by grasping the situation in its singularity.
>
> (pp. 173–5)[2]

The representation of choice-act as the maximization of a binary preference relation in a set of alternative courses of actions sets a norm of rational preferential choice. We develop an interpretation of this norm in terms of the individual's reflective, deliberated preferential choice, according to the two modalities sketched above, namely: a) instrumental rationality, where preference maximization proceeds from the individual's deliberation about the best *means* for achieving his singular ends in generic circumstances of choice; and b) prudence, where preference maximization follows from the deliberation of the wise individual about the appropriate *ends* of his action, conducted in the singular circumstances of action.

The notion of action that we consider in this paper is the *communicative* action of Habermas (1981, 1983), which is associated with, and flourishes from, valid intersubjective communication through and about the choice of courses of action. We argue that each of the two variants of rational preferential choice distinguished above supports a distinct set of practices of communicative action, namely: a) contracts, and notably the contracts of market exchange, which perform the integration of the singular ends of instrumentally rational individual agents into efficient interaction; and b) forms of prudential decision-making, such as jurisprudence, or the clinical practice of medicine, which perform the integration of the singular cases confronting "prudent" individual agents, under common rules for contextual action. These sets of practices provide a wide phenomenological basis both for rational preferential choice per se, and also for the distinction between instrumental rationality and prudence, as conceptually and practically distinct developments of the norm. We argue, finally, that the full flourishing of communicative action, as ethical norm and practice, calls for the development of both types of norms and practices (i.e. the instrumental and the prudential types), and supposes moreover that an appropriate balance be struck between them.

The paper is organized as follows: the second section develops the norm of instrumental rationality as reflective, deliberated preferential choice of means from singular preferences in generic circumstances of communicative action; the third section characterizes the norm of prudence as reflective, deliberated preferential choice of ends in singular circumstances of communicative action; and the last section recapitulates the whole analysis and puts it in general ethical and practical perspective.

Instrumental rationality as reflective, deliberated preferential choice of means from singular preferences in variable circumstances of communicative action

A characteristic example of instrumental rationality in the sense above is provided by the microeconomic theory of consumer's demand: the household chooses the demands and supplies of market commodities that maximize its (fixed) consumption preferences, subject to a budget constraint determined by its economic environment (market prices, principally). A core feature of rational consumer behavior is the behavioral pattern known as the law of demand. Namely, the rational consumer's demand (resp. supply) of any market commodity is decreasing (resp. increasing) in *ceteris paribus* variations in the commodity's market price.[3] The instrumental rationality of the consumer takes place in a wider process of social communication. That is, the communication of consumers and profit-maximizing firms about the allocation and use of scarce resources, by means of commercial contracts and market prices, or, simply put, market exchange. We argue below that the rational demand and supply of market commodities are forms of communicative action in the sense of Habermas (1983).[4] Competitive economic equilibrium achieves their integration into the Pareto-efficient allocation of market commodities. The liberal social contracts of Kolm (1985), Gauthier (1986) and Mercier Ythier (2011, 2013, 2018) extend the former to the activities of the public economy, namely, the redistribution of wealth, the regulation of externalities and the production of general public goods. These norms of allocation of scarce resources and the corresponding practices support instrumental rationality as the variant of rational preferential choice which fits best the field of economic activities.

We establish the link between the norm of the liberal social contract and Habermas's norms of communicative action in a small number of brief steps. We first recall the two principles which together define the norms of communicative action according to Habermas, namely, his principles of *universalization* (hereafter principle (U)) and of *discourse ethics* (principle (D)). We recall, next, a number of definitional features of the norm of the liberal social contract, and synthesize them into a notion of *communicative instrumental rationality*. We show, finally, that the latter verifies some of the main features of the norms of communicative action, that is, non-strategic interactions, unanimous agreement, truth, rightness and truthfulness, and also, in an appropriate sense, impartiality.

Habermas's (1983) two principles are formulated as follows:

> (U) For a norm to be valid, the consequences and side effects that its *general* observance can be expected to have for the satisfaction of the particular interests of *each* person affected must be such that *all* affected can accept them freely.
>
> (D) Every valid norm would meet with the approval of all concerned if they could take part in a practical discourse.
>
> (pp. 120–1)

We define now a notion of communicative instrumental rationality that captures the main features of the norms of the liberal social contract referred to above, and translates them into Habermas's vocabulary and concepts. It consists of a *shared definition of the situation and an induced Pareto-efficient allocation of resources that is unanimously preferred to some legitimate initial (i.e. pre-contractual) situation.*[5] We develop the definition below, beginning from the end.

The allocation of the *initial situation* is a hypothetical allocation of scarce resources that would both prevail in the absence of the activities (of consumption, production, or market or non-market transfers of resources) of the social contract, and proceed from a state of legitimate initial rights, specifically, from a state of rights verifying principle (D) (property rights, notably if not only).

An allocation of resources is the list of consumption and production plans of economic agents (individuals and firms). It is *attainable* if it verifies a number of conditions defined independently from the activities of the social contract, and notably the resource constraints in primary goods and labor and the technical production constraints. It is *Pareto-efficient* if it is attainable and there exists no other attainable allocation that is preferred by all individuals and strictly preferred by some of them. Below we denote by X the set of attainable allocations of a set (society), $N = \{1,\ldots,n\}$ of n individuals, and by R_i individual i 's reflexive, complete and transitive preferences on X.[6]

A shared definition of the situation consists, in the context of the liberal social contract, of a set of competitive market prices, levels of production of public goods, and lump-sum taxes on individuals' endowments of the initial situation. We denote them respectively by p (vector of market prices), z (vector of public good production), and τ (vector of lump-sum taxes), and let $s=(p,z,\tau)$. It determines, for each individual $i \in N$ and each firm $j \in F=\{1. . ., f\}$: a set of plans of action accessible to the agent in situation s, namely, a set $X_i(s)$ of consumption plans x_i accessible to individual i, and a set $Y_j(s)$ of production plans y_J accessible to firm j; and a (reflexive, complete and transitive) preference relation $R_i(s)$ (resp.$R_j(s)$) of the agent on her accessible consumption plans (resp. its accessible production plans).

Finally:

> **Communicative instrumental rationality**: A shared definition of the situation $s = (p,z,\tau)$ and attainable allocation $a = (x_1, \ldots, x_n, y_1, \ldots, y_f)$ set a norm of communicative instrumental rationality if: a) for all individual i, x_i maximizes $R_i(s)$ in $X_i(s)$; b) for all firm j, y_j maximizes $R_j(s)$ in $Y_j(s)$; and c) allocation a is Pareto-efficient and is (weakly) preferred to the allocation of the initial situation by all individuals.

This notion subsumes the norms of allocations of scarce resources evoked above. If, for example, the theme of the social contract reduces to market exchange, the situation s reduces to competitive market prices (i.e. it does not include public goods, and lump-sum taxes are set = 0). Communicative instrumental rationality coincides then with competitive equilibrium from legitimate initial endowments.

If the theme is extended to the redistribution of wealth in order to take into account individuals' concerns relative to the distribution of wealth, the situation includes the distribution of wealth z (viewed as a public good), the competitive market prices of p and the redistributive lump-sum taxes of τ. Communicative instrumental rationality coincides then with the distributive liberal social contract (Mercier Ythier, 2011). The notion can be further extended to the production and consumption of physical public goods by means of suitable adjustments in the definition of situations and allocations.[7]

Lastly, we finish by showing that communicative instrumental rationality is a form of communicative action in the sense of Habermas. We discuss, in particular, the relation of communicative instrumental rationality to principles (D) and (U) and to the norms of truth, rightness and truthfulness.

Principle (D) is designed to ensure that communication does not force agreement. It requires, notably, that the process of deliberation leaves enough room for the expression of individual preference and choice, without bias in favor of the particular interests of some of the participants. It is, in other words, a principle of procedural impartiality.[8] In the context of the liberal social contract, it reduces essentially to the following two features: *legitimate* initial endowments and *parametric* shared situation.

Initial endowments are legitimate if they satisfy the Lockean proviso,[9] that is notably: if they are acquired through non-coercive means; and if they allow for acceptable achievements of individuals within the social contract, in terms of personal wealth and welfare. We retain the following definite formulation of the proviso:

> (L) The endowments of the initial situation are freely accepted by all, and there exists an attainable allocation of resources that all individuals (strictly) prefer to the allocation of resources of the initial situation.

A shared situation s is parametric if the agents freely accept to take it as given when they determine their plans. That is, in other words, if agents accept to take part in the process of action/deliberation knowing that it is specified so as to preclude their manipulating prices, endowments or public good provision in pursuit of their particular ends.[10]

Communicative instrumental rationality verifies these two features of procedural impartiality. We formalize this statement below, through the specification of a variant of (D), adapted to the context of economic activities:

> (D') Every valid norm of allocation of scarce resources would meet with the approval of all concerned if they could take part in a practical discourse, that is, *if initial endowments verified the (L) proviso and if the shared definition of the situation was parametric.*

The initial situation defines a hypothetical point of reference for the evaluation of the alternatives considered in the elaboration of the social contract. If, for example, the theme of the contract is market exchange, the initial situation consists of individuals' consumption of their respective initial endowments. If the theme of the contract is the redistribution of private wealth and welfare and the provision of public goods through the relevant branches of public finance, the initial situation consists of the competitive equilibrium that would prevail in the absence of these activities of redistribution and public good provision. Communicative instrumental rationality requires that the allocation of the social contract be preferred by all individuals to the allocation of the initial situation. This yields the following variant of principle (U), where individuals' free acceptance follows from their comparison of the allocation of the norm with the initial situation:

> (U') For a norm of allocation of scarce resources to be valid, the consequences and side effects that its general observance can be expected to have for the satisfaction of the particular interests of each person affected must be such that all affected can accept them freely, that is, *that all affected (weakly) prefer the allocation of the norm to the allocation of the initial situation.*

Finally, truth and truthfulness follow from the agents' maximization of complete, transitive preferences in parametric situation. Notably: agents' choices reveal their preferences (as a consequence of Mas-Colell et al. [1995], propositions 1.D1 and 1.D.2: see endnote 6 above); and market prices coincide with agents' marginal valuation of market commodities. In particular, the market prices of the norm of communicative action are fair, in the sense that they are not manipulated, and they are true, in the sense that they mirror agents' true preferences relative to their alternative uses of scarce resources. In other words, communicative instrumental rationality entails the traditional notion of commutative justice. Rightness, to finish with, follows from the self-enforceability of the norm: Pareto-efficiency implies that the allocation of the norm cannot be improved, for the society considered as a whole; and individuals who freely participate in the process of action/deliberation of the norm freely choose the plans that implement the allocation of the norm.

Prudence as reflective, deliberated preferential choice of ends in singular circumstances of communicative action

The Aristotelian prudence somehow turns upside down the perspective of instrumental rationality. It refers to the agent's deliberation over the ends of her action in fixed circumstances of action. Prudence itself, also called practical wisdom, is the virtue that consists of the (somewhat mysterious) ability of deliberating properly over ends. Precisely, of selecting through deliberation the appropriate ends of action, and from this the appropriate action, in given circumstances: 'The man of wise judgment determines at the same time the rule and the case, by grasping the situation in its singularity' (Ricoeur, 1990, p. 175). The central focus of practical wisdom, in particular, is not so much choice per se, as choice conducing to action. The choice that it considers is a choice of ends (i.e. the choice of a decision *rule*), which determines the action in its context.

We propose below a formulation of practical wisdom using the conceptual apparatus of rational preferential choice. This is done first through the detailed analysis and interpretation of Sen's (1997) example of Dr. Chang. Next, we proceed to a brief discussion of the meaning of prudence as practical reason and of the scope of its application to some professional practices. We define then a general notion of communicative prudence, adapting Habermas's general notion of communicative action to teleological deliberation (that is, to rational deliberation over the ends of action). Finally, we illustrate the general notion through an application using Dr. Chang's example.

An Example: Dr. Chang faces two children who have both contracted the same fatal disease. He has only one unit of medicine, which can save only one child. The probability of cure, following medical treatment, is slightly higher for one child (say child *A*) than for the other (child *B*). Statistical studies of clinical trials yield recovery rates after treatment of 91% for children of the type of child *A*, and 90% for children of the type of child *B*. The difference between the two survival rates passes the tests of statistical significance. Dr. Chang can either choose the child who will receive the medicine, or transfer the decision of attribution of the medicine to an anonymous probabilistic mechanism.

Alternatives may be conveniently described as lotteries, that is, as probability distributions over the following three consequences: child *A* survives and child *B* dies (consequence c_1); child *A* dies and child *B* survives (consequence c_2); or both children die (consequence c_3). Giving the medicine to child *A* yields the probability distribution $p=(.91,0,.09)$ on $c=(c_1,c_2,c_3)$. Giving the medicine to child *B* yields the lottery $q=(0,.90,.10)$. A probabilistic mechanism attributing the medicine to child *A* with probability $\alpha \in \,]0,1[$ and to child *B* with probability $1-\alpha$ is represented by the compound lottery $\alpha p+(1-\alpha)q$. The set of alternatives of Dr. Chang is $X=\{\alpha p+(1-\alpha)q : \alpha \in [0,1]\}$. [11]

We develop now a deliberation on ends, conducing to a prudent decision of attribution of the medicine in this context. By prudent decision we mean Dr Chang's well-justified choice of, jointly: the procedure of attribution of the medicine (the "rule" of the case); and the beneficiary of attribution if applicable.

The deliberation goes through the examination of two lines of argument that we consider in turn.

The first line of argument emphasizes the maximization of survival expectation as the basic motive that should underlie choice in this context. The survival expectation associated with a policy of attribution of units of medicine in a population of patients of the type above is the total sum of the numbers of treated patients of each type, weighted by their respective probabilities of recovery, that is, $.91n_A+.90n_B$, where n_A (resp. n_B) denotes the number of treated children of type *A* (resp. *B*). Its integer part measures the number of lives saved by the policy. Applied to the context of Dr. Chang's decision problem, this criterion of evaluation yields the ranking of alternatives $pP\alpha p+(1-\alpha)qPq$ for all $\alpha \in \,]0,1[$, where P denotes strict preference.[12] The corresponding decision is the attribution, by Dr. Chang, of the unit of medicine to child *A*.

This first line of argument raises two problems at least. The first problem is the lack of meaning of expectation calculations applied to only *two* patients. The integer part of $.91n_A + .90n_B$ is 0 in this case, for all policies that Dr. Chang might consider. The policy attributing all units of medicine to children of type *A* saves one life more than the policy attributing all units of medicine to children of type *B* in a group made of 100 children of type *A* and 100 children of type *B*. In other words, the maximization of survival expectation makes sense, in terms of differences in the number of lives actually saved by different policies, only for large numbers of patients (groups of 200 children evenly distributed across types, for example). This observation leads us to the second issue raised by the first line of argument, namely, an issue of fairness. At societal level, a public health policy that gives a systematic priority to children of type *A* in the attribution of scarce medicines is an obvious case of discrimination, close to a form of eugenism. In other words, such a policy is a clear case of violation of the basic rule of justice that prescribes an equal treatment of equals.[13] Furthermore, at the micro-social level, suitable variants of the latter rule are also relevant as deontological rules of good medical practice that prescribe, essentially, to propose to all patients the best available treatment corresponding to their state of health. Considered in this light, Dr. Chang's decision problem becomes a problem of *choice of interpretation* of the rule (of equal treatment) in his context of action.

The remarks above introduce the second line of argument. The context makes it reasonable (but by no means implies) to view the two children as "equals" in the contextual interpretation of the rule. On the one hand, the only difference between the children, in terms of their medical status, is their slight difference in cure probabilities. This is not a difference in health states, and this difference corresponds to a practically relevant fact only for large populations of patients. On the other hand, the attribution of the unit of medicine to any one child entails the sure death of the other. Suppose, from there on, that Dr. Chang *decides*, on the basis of such considerations, to view the two children as equals (in terms of their health states). Let R^* denote the preference relation built through the second line of argument. A translation, in terms of R^*, of this first decision of Dr. Chang is: [non pR^*q] and [non qR^*p], alternatives p and q are not comparable relative to R^*, or, in policy terms, Dr. Chang does not want to choose the beneficiary of the treatment.[14] We have, here, a clear case of preference incompleteness, corresponding to a dilemma: Dr. Chang has a good reason to give the unit of medicine to child *A* (this would almost certainly save the child); he has an equally good reason to give the unit of medicine to child *B* (the same); and he does not want to decide between these conflicting reasons. It follows that, in terms of the choice of a procedure of attribution of the unit of medicine, Dr. Chang has opted for the anonymous probabilistic mechanisms. As a result, he must choose some alternative of the type $\alpha p + (1-\alpha)q$, $\alpha \in]0,1[$. Equal treatment of equals, combined with the former decision of considering the two children as equals, then clearly imposes the choice of $\frac{1}{2}p + \frac{1}{2}q$, that is, of the lottery that gives both children an equal chance of getting the medicine. In preferential terms, this translates as: $\left(\frac{1}{2}p+\frac{1}{2}q\right)P^{*}\left(\alpha p+(1-\alpha)q\right)$ for all $\alpha \neq \frac{1}{2}$, where P^{*} denotes the asymmetric factor of R^{*}. This concludes the second line of argument.[15]

The two lines of argument have produced two preference rankings (P and P^{*}), associated with two different decisions (p and $\frac{1}{2}p+\frac{1}{2}q$ respectively). Speaking in the name of Dr. Chang (and following the closely related discussion of Sen), I claim, from the deliberation above, that P^{*} and $\frac{1}{2}p+\frac{1}{2}q$ are the appropriate, prudent ranking and decision in this case.

It should be noted that this conclusion is by no means necessary, in the logical, mathematical sense of the word. It is derived by means of *sufficient reasons*. Some of them are logically determinate; namely, the translation of the ethical aim into a preference ordering, and the latter's maximization. But the most important ones are matters of choice. Specifically, this choice involves the selection of an ethically appropriate principle of decision (survival expectation maximization versus equal treatment of equals, in the deliberation above), and the choice of interpretation of the ethical rule in the context of action (the decision to view the two children as equals or not). It is not argued here that all agents would or should arrive at the same conclusion in appropriate conditions of deliberation about a similar case. On the contrary, in a large population of agents facing the case, some, I presume, would opt for p. Moreover, it cannot be excluded *a priori* that alternatives other than $\frac{1}{2}p+\frac{1}{2}q$ be persuasively defended as "the" prudent decision, for small variations in the circumstances of a similar case. In other words, the conclusion above entails no claim of objectivity, either in terms of the circumstances of action, or in terms of the unanimity of agents facing the case in appropriate conditions of deliberation.[16] It is construed as an expression of the (subjective, conscious) freedom of the agent, which stems from the consideration of persuasive sufficient reasons, elaborated through careful deliberation, in the singular situation of action. The core of this free act consists of, jointly, the choice of a rule of decision appropriate to the context and a choice of interpretation of the rule for its appropriate application to the case.

The exercise of prudence generally supposes, in the actual conditions of practice, the existence of a body of widely accepted rules of evaluation and decision. The person of wise judgment cleverly selects, in this body of existing rules, those that are applicable to the case, and adapts them to the latter by means of judicious choices of interpretation. Prudent decision-making is, in other words, a form of communicative action that involves a *creative* use of the rule, particularly at the level of its contextual interpretation. These creative acts are not considered "wise" (that is, they do not succeed as *communicative* actions) as long as they are not considered so by (a sufficient number of) disinterested observers (i.e. observers who were not involved in the treatment of the corresponding cases). This implies that the body of accepted rules that grounds the exercise of prudence is not only inherited, but also *evolves* by the collective acceptation of any of the creative acts (of interpretation or otherwise) that it inspires.[17] Jurisprudence and clinical practice are two characteristic applications of this general mode of elaboration of prudent practical reason, to the fields of law and medicine respectively.[18] They apply large bodies of rules of conventional origin (law) or of scientific origin (medicine) to cases that derive much of their singularity from the singularity of the persons involved as litigants or as patients.

Prudence so construed is a form of procedural rationality, albeit quite different from Herbert Simon's (1957, 1982) variant of the notion. We propose a formal definition of *communicative prudence* below, built from preferential choice and Habermas's principles (U) and (D). It transposes to teleological deliberation the pattern of instrumental deliberation of communicative instrumental rationality. It consists of a *shared definition of the situation and an induced Pareto-efficient decision rule that is unanimously preferred to some accepted default rule*. It may serve as an objective-normative support for actual prudential norms, when grounding them on the putative consent of affected persons makes sense. For example, in the case of the rules of allocation of scarce organ transplants to patients on a waiting list, or in the case of the rules governing the decision to administer or not a painful treatment to some severely ill patient when the chances of recovery are low.

The notion of situation used here is Habermas's general notion recalled above (see endnote 5).

A decision rule is defined as a binary preference relation that is reflexive and acyclic.[19]

A shared definition of the situation consists here of a list of common knowledge features defining both the circumstances of action and the set of rules applicable to the case. Formally, situation s defines the following shared features: a (finite) set of alternative courses of action $S(s)$ (the circumstances of action); and a set $\mathfrak{R}(s)$ of reflexive, acyclic, preference relations over $S(s)$ (the rules applicable to the case).

We denote by $N = \{1, \ldots, n\}$ the set of individuals affected by actions taken in $S(s)$, and by $R_i(s)$ individual i 's *true* preference relation over $S(s)$ (assumed binary, reflexive and acyclic). We suppose that the rules of $\mathfrak{R}(s)$ each have a single maximal element in $S(s)$.[20] We say that a rule $R \in \mathfrak{R}(s)$, with maximal element $a \in S(s)$, is *Pareto-efficient* if there exists no alternative course of action $a' \in S(s)$ that all individuals prefer and some individuals strictly prefer to a, that is, no $a' \in S(s)$ such that $a' \in R_i(s)a$ for all $i \in N$ and $a' P_i(s) a$ for some $i \in N$. Likewise, we say that individual i (contextually) prefers rule $R \in \mathfrak{R}(s)$ with maximal element $a \in S(s)$ to rule $R' \in \mathfrak{R}(s)$ with maximal element $a' \in S(s)$ if $aR_i(s)a'$.

The default rule is a single element R^0 of $\mathfrak{R}(s)$, which serves as a hypothetical point of reference for the definition of (unanimous) agreement. It is the decision rule that is adopted if no other admissible rule is (truly) preferred by all. It also defines, equivalently, an individual right of veto in the process of action/deliberation of the norm. An individual who reports convincingly that s/he truly (strictly) prefers the default rule to some other rule vetoes the latter by the same token. S/he excludes it from agreement, albeit *not* from deliberation. The specific role of the default rule in the framing of the deliberation process must be well understood and *accepted* by all participants in practical discourse, as a basic application of principle (D) to the notion of communicative action developed here.

From these premises, the formal definition of communicative prudence reads as follows:

> **Communicative prudence**: A shared definition of the situation s, *accepted* default rule $R^0 \in \mathfrak{R}(s)$, decision rule $R \in \mathfrak{R}(s)$, and action $a \in S(s)$ set a norm of communicative prudence if: a) a is the maximal element of R in $S(s)$; b) R is Pareto-efficient relative to individuals' *true* preference relations $R_i(s)$; and c) R is preferred to R^0 by all individuals.

We previously suggested (see endnote 16) that communicative prudence defines a form of reflective equilibrium, albeit quite different from Rawls's. Rawls's (1971) reflective equilibrium consists of the unanimous agreement of individuals considering *general* circumstances of justice under the conditions of *substantive* impartiality defined by the veil of ignorance. By contrast, the reflective equilibrium of communicative prudence consists of the unanimous agreement of concerned individuals considering the *singular* circumstances of the case under the conditions of *procedural* impartiality defined by principle (D). In particular, individuals' approval of the norm follows from the consideration by each person of 'the consequences and side effects that its general observance can be expected to have for the satisfaction of his/her *particular* interests' (principle (U); my emphasis). We design below the variants of principles (U) and (D) that appear suitable for prudential decision-making. They are built on the same basic pattern as (U') and (D'), which are transposed to teleological deliberation in the natural way, by shifting emphasis from means to ends in the design of practical discourse.

We first transfer to prudential decision-making the notions of legitimate initial situation and parametric shared situation making up (D'). In order to satisfy principle (D), the default rule must satisfy the following two conditions: first, it must be applicable to the case and, second, its specific role in shaping deliberation, as a basic point of reference for the construction of general agreement, must be well understood and accepted by all. We summarize these requirements in the following variant of the (L) proviso, adapting the latter to prudential decision-making:

> (L') The default rule is applicable to the case, and its role in shaping practical discourse is freely accepted by all.[21]

Likewise, we say that the situation is parametric if the participants in deliberation freely renounce any strategic manipulation of it, that is: a) if common knowledge features s unambiguously define both the (common) circumstances of the case $S(s)$ and the (common) set of decision rules $\mathfrak{R}(s)$ applicable to it; and b) if the individuals freely accept to report their *true* preferences $R_i(s)$ in the comparisons of the decision rules of $\mathfrak{R}(s)$ that they perform in deliberation.[22]

The variant of principle (D) built in the definition of communicative prudence reads therefore:

> (D") Every valid norm of prudential rationality would meet with the approval of all concerned if they could take part in a practical discourse, that is, *if the default rule verified the (L') proviso and if the situation was parametric.*

Likewise, communicative prudence verifies the following variant of principle (U):

> (U") For a norm of prudential rationality to be valid, the consequences and side effects that its general observance can be expected to have for the satisfaction of the particular interests of each person affected must be such that all affected can accept them freely, that is, *that all affected (weakly) prefer the decision rule of the norm to the default rule.*

Finally, truth and truthfulness are implied by the condition of parametric situation of (D"). And rightness follows from the self-enforceability of the norm: Pareto-efficiency implies that the decision rule cannot be improved by unanimous consent; and individuals who freely participate in the process of action/deliberation of the norm freely choose the decision rule of the norm.

We conclude this section by applying the norm of communicative prudence to the example of Dr. Chang for illustration purposes.

The type of situation confronting Dr. Chang may be described in the following generic terms. There are n units of medicine, to be distributed in a population of ill children of two types A and B, namely: n_A children of type A, whose survival probability is p_A=*.91* if they receive one unit of medicine, and =0 if they are not treated; and n_B children of type B, whose survival probability is p_B=*.90* if they receive one unit of medicine, and =0 if they are not treated. There is a severe shortage in medicine, that is, $n \leq \min\{n_A, n_B\}$, so that no child may receive more than one unit of medicine in any case. Children are designated by an index i running in $N=\{1,\ldots,n_A+n_B\}$. We denote by N_A (resp. N_B) the subset of children of type A (resp. B). A probabilistic *distribution* rule $\delta = (\delta_1,\ldots,\delta_{n_A+n_B}) \in \mathbb{R}_+^{n_A+n_B}$ attributes to any child i a probability δ_i of receiving one unit of medicine. We denote by $\Delta(s)$ the set *admissible* probabilistic distribution rules of the situation, that is, the set of distribution rules that can be considered for deliberation and choice. Any distribution rule $\delta \in \Delta(s)$ determines a unique distribution of survival probabilities $\pi(\delta)$ in the population N of ill children, namely, distribution $\pi(\delta) = (\pi_1(\delta),\ldots,\pi_{n_A+n_B}(\delta)) \in \mathbb{R}^{n_A+n_B}$ such that: $\pi_i(\delta)=.91\times\delta_i$ if $i \in N_A$; and $\pi_i(\delta)=.90\times\delta_i$ if $i \in N_B$.

There is a general agreement, in Dr. Chang's society, that any decision rule applicable to this type of situation should respect a principle of equal treatment of equals. But, within this context, individuals differ in their interpretation of this *ethical* rule.

Some consider that the difference in survival probabilities actually matters, and justifies giving priority to type A in treatment. They argue that such policy could save more lives, on average, than fully equal distribution. They favor, consequently, a probabilistic distribution rule giving all children of type A the same probability $\delta_i = \frac{1}{n_A}$ of getting one unit of medicine. Precisely, this probabilistic distribution rule (and this one only) maximizes life expectancy $\sum_{i \in N} \pi_i(\delta)$ in the set of feasible probabilistic distribution rules compatible with their contextual interpretation of the ethical rule, that is, in $\{\delta \in \Delta(s) : \exists (d,d') \in \mathbb{R}^2 \text{ such that } \delta_i = d > d' = \delta_j \ \forall (i,j) \in N_A \times N_B\}$. We denote it by δ^{LE}, where superscript LE stands for "life expectancy". The (simplest) decision rule supported by this argument is the reflexive, acyclic binary relation R^{LE} defined on $\Delta(s)$ by: $\delta I^{LE} \delta$ for all δ and $\delta^{LE} P^{LE} \delta$ for all $\delta \neq \delta^{LE}$ (where, as above, I^{LE} and P^{LE} denote, respectively, the symmetric and asymmetric factors of R^{LE}).

Others consider that the difference in survival probabilities is out of proportion with the consequences that the priority above would impose on children of type B. They support the distribution rule that gives all children the same probability $\delta_i = \frac{1}{n_A + n_B}$ of getting one unit of medicine. We denote it by δ^{EO}, where the superscript stands for "equality of opportunity". The contextual interpretation of the ethical rule imposes here, in other words, the choice of δ^{EO}, as single compatible distribution rule. The decision rule supported by this argument is the reflexive, acyclic binary relation R^{EO} defined on $\Delta(s)$ by: $\delta I^{EO} \delta$ for all δ and $\delta^{EO} P^{EO} \delta$ for all $\delta \neq \delta^{EO}$.

Many agree that distribution cannot be properly organized if it does not conform to a valid norm. That is, the absence of agreement about the norm would create a situation of unbearable disorder in the health system. This includes large uncertainties about the legal foundations of distribution, making it very difficult or altogether impossible for physicians to perform medical treatment. Equal treatment of equals would then imply $\delta = 0$, that is, no medicine could be ("normally") distributed. We let δ^{ND}, where the superscript ND stands for "non distribution". The decision rule supported by this argument is the reflexive, acyclic binary relation R^{ND} defined on $\Delta(s)$ by: $\delta I^{ND} \delta$ for all δ and $\delta^{ND} P^{ND} \delta$ for all $\delta \neq \delta^{ND}$. Its adoption as the default rule of the case means that all concerned individuals understand that some agreement must be met in order to make valid distribution possible.

We may, at this point, summarize the shared features of the situation as follows: the common knowledge features of $s=(n,n_A,n_B,p_A,p_B)$ define the circumstances of action $S(s)=\{\delta^{LE},\delta^{EO},\delta^{ND}\}$ and the set of decision rules applicable to the case $\Re(s) = \{R^{LE},R^{EO},R^{ND}\}$, where R^{ND} is the default rule.

We still have to derive individual preferences that appear plausible in this context. Concerned individuals are the persons affected by the decision, that is, children of both types and their relatives. We denote by M_A (resp. M_B) the set of children of type A (resp. B) and their relatives. Plausible preferences for members of M_A are simply $\delta^{LE} P_i \delta^{EO} P_i \delta^{ND}$, $i \in M_A$, corresponding to a ranking of the alternatives of $S(s)$ according to their consequences in terms of survival probabilities of the children of type A. Guessing individual preferences of members of M_B appears a little bit more complex. One may reasonably suppose $\delta^{EO}P_i\delta^{LE}$ for all of them, but their preference ranking over the pair (δ^{LE},δ^{ND}) does not appear so clear. One may imagine, for example, that the dismal prospect of sure death simply crushes any preference, either because it entails radical subjective disinterestedness (i.e. incomplete preference) or because it entails a radical albeit considered indifference between the terms of the alternative: "why *should I* care since I am (or my cherished child is) to die?". One can imagine also that some concerned relatives adopt a decentered, reactive attitude, which may then take on one of the following two positions: either preference $\delta^{LE}P_i\delta^{ND}$, on the basis of the (contextually implausible, albeit possible) altruistic motive that "saving some lives is better than saving no life at all"; or preference $\delta^{ND}P_i\delta^{LE}$, on the basis of the (contextually highly plausible) motive that "policy δ^{LE} entails unbearable unjust discrimination against the children of type *B*". We suppose that some members of M_B (one of them at least) do have the latter preference, that is, they credibly oppose policy δ^{LE} by spending scarce resources on fighting it by all legal means available, such as alerting the medias, suing in court or lobbying the political system. In other words, they credibly oppose their veto to policy δ^{LE} in practical discourse: they want it at no price, and fight it at all cost.

We conclude that the situation described above verifies (D''), including the (L') proviso, and it also verifies (U''). It yields a single norm of communicative prudence for the case, namely, decision rule R^{EO} and associate policy δ^{EO}. This prudential reflective equilibrium provides (some kind of) putative objective support for Dr. Chang's contextual decision.[23]

Rational decision-making and communicative action as moral norms and facts

In this last section of the paper, we first return to the contrast, briefly evoked above, between the notions of communicative rationality developed here and Herbert Simon's notions of substantive and procedural rationality. We show that the main differences follow from the *moral* structure of communicative action as *agreement*. Finally, we discuss the relation between the instrumental and prudential variants of communicative rationality that we distinguish, and the parallel distinction between the *agent*'s and *patient*'s perspectives on action.

Simon's substantive rationality consists of the maximization of stable, complete, transitive preferences, under conditions of complete information, by an agent endowed with the corresponding computational abilities. Simon argues that, in many actual circumstances of action, agents lack (some of) the computational skills or the information required to behave rationally in the substantive sense. Actual rational behavior is *bounded*, in other words, by the cognitive (i.e. informational and computational) limitations of the agent. Simon's procedural rationality refers to the systematic rules or procedures of decision-making developed by the agents in response to such cognitive limitations, as proxies or substitutes for inaccessible substantive rationality.

The perspective adopted in the present paper is quite different from Simon's, albeit to some extent compatible with it. Rational decision-making is construed as reflective, deliberated action. Deliberation can be internal or external to the agent. External deliberation is successful if it results in agreement. The norms of communicative action consider two dimensions of agreement: procedural, bearing on the normative features of practical discourse (principle (D)); and substantive, bearing on the consequences of action for the individuals affected by action (principle (U)). They are ethical norms, giving practical sense to such moral concepts as true or truthful intention or commitment, to the extent of their influence on actual behaviors or conducts.[24]

This basic conception is further developed by introducing the distinction between two abstract types of circumstances of action, namely: a) circumstances where the persons affected by action are the agents themselves (the decision makers); and b) circumstances where the persons affected are not those who decide (they are "patients", not agents, in the circumstances of action).

In the first type of circumstances, the agents' ends (their "preferences") set the decision rule of communicative action. This is what is ordinarily meant by "contract", that is, an agreement freely consented by autonomous decision makers. The corresponding norm of communicative action simply sets the procedural features of *valid contracting*. This task is performed through our notion of communicative instrumental rationality. The corresponding form of deliberation is a deliberation over the choice of means for achieving the definite ends of the agents, that is: at the individual level, the maximization of agents' definite, complete, transitive preferences; at stakeholders' level, bargaining in the conditions of impartiality of discourse ethics.

In the second type of circumstances, communicative action submits the decision rule of the agent to the patients' ends. It defines then, in other words, a *norm of regulated power*. This is the object of our notion of communicative prudence. The corresponding form of deliberation is a deliberation over the choice of ends for decision in definite circumstances of action, which implies, in our version of the norm: at the individual level, the maximization of patients' reflexive, acyclic (possibly incomplete) preferences; at stakeholders' level, some form of (democratic) political control, under the conditions of impartiality of discourse ethics.

The agent's and patient's perspectives are abstract in the sense that any individual person is bound to experience the both of them in roughly equal proportions over his/her lifetime. The development of communication ethics requires, consequently, the development, both, of norms of valid contracting, and of rules of *good practice*. It requires also, still more importantly perhaps, an appropriate balance between both types of norms, that is, as far as communicative action is concerned, an appropriate balance between the perspective of exchange (contract) and the perspective of power (good practice). We illustrate this point, to finish with, through a brief discussion of Locke's account of the normative structure of liberal democracy, such as anticipated by him in his *Second Treatise*.

In the terms of the present article, the citizens of a democracy are both agents, as individual members of the sovereign people, and patients, as individual subjects of the sovereign people. Accordingly, the political society of a liberal democracy proceeds, in Locke's conception, from the unanimous consent of its individual members in a putative social contract. Moreover, that good government supposes notably, according to Locke, a division of labor between the legislative power setting the rules of political action by majority voting, and the executive power adapting them to the singular circumstances of action.[25]

Locke's social contract is a clear case of application of the norm of communicative action. However, his pragmatic account of the good government of a *representative* democracy (majority decision-making of the legislative power, and the prerogative of the executive power, in particular) falls substantially short of it, and also, it may be argued, of important aspects of the political practice of contemporary liberal democracies such as the existence and determinant political influence of public opinion and the medias (including internet, naturally). The achievements of communicative action in *deliberative* democracy, if any, suppose *unanimous* agreement from both the active and the passive perspectives of the concerned citizens, that is, shared conviction supporting good government practice.

Notes

1 An extended version of this article was first presented at the second international conference of economic philosophy of Strasbourg, October 9th and 10th, 2014. It benefitted from the comments of attendants to the conference, and also from the advices of the editors of the present volume. I gratefully acknowledge the both of them. All errors are mine, if any, naturally.

2 Deliberated preferential choice plays a central role in Ricoeur's ethics. One reads for instance in Ethique et Morale (1991):

> Ce qui est fondamentalement estimable en soi-même, ce sont deux choses : d'abord la capacité de choisir pour des raisons, de préférer ceci à cela, bref, la capacité d'agir intentionnellement; c'est ensuite la capacité d'introduire des changements dans le cours des choses, de commencer quelque chose dans le monde, bref, la capacité d'initiative. En ce sens, l'estime de soi est le moment réflexif de la praxis : c'est en appréciant nos actions que nous nous apprécions nous-mêmes comme en étant l'auteur, et donc comme étant autre chose que de simples forces de la nature ou de simples instruments.
>
> (p. 259)

3 See for instance Mas-Colell et al. (1995), chapters 1 through 3, and notably sections 2.F and 3.J. The main expression of preference maximization in demand behavior is the negative semi-definiteness of Slutsky's matrix, which implies the law of demand in the sense above.

4 'I call interactions communicative when the participants coordinate their plans of action consensually, with the agreement reached at any point being evaluated in terms of the intersubjective recognition of validity claims' (p. 58).

5 According to Habermas (1983): 'A situation denotes a segment of lifeworld that has been delimited in terms of a specific theme. A theme arises in connection with the interests and objectives of actors. It defines the range of matters that are relevant and can be thematically focused on' (p. 135).

6 In more general terms, let X denote the set of alternatives of an individual agent, that is, a set of (at least two distinct) "plans" or courses of action imagined by him. A binary preference relation R of the agent over his set of alternatives is a subset E of the Cartesian product $X \times X = \{(x, y) : x \in X, y \in X\}$. xRy means $(x, y) \in E$ and reads "alternative x is preferred or indifferent to alternative y for the agent". R is: reflexive if xRx for all $x \in X$ (reading: "any alternative is preferred or indifferent to itself

in X"); complete if "xRy or yRx" for all distinct $x, y \in X$ (reading: "any pair of distinct alternatives is such that one of them is preferred or indifferent to the other"); transitive if [[xRy and yRz] implies xRz] for all $x, y, z \in X$ (reading: "if x is preferred or indifferent to y and y is preferred and indifferent to z, then x must be is preferred or indifferent to z"). These three properties of the preference relation, taken jointly, are necessary and sufficient for choice to reveal, in an appropriate sense, preferences in any finite set of alternatives, as a consequence of Mas-Colell et al. (1995), propositions 1.D.1 and 1.D.2. They are also sufficient (and the first two of them are necessary) for the existence of a maximum of R in any finite subset of X. A maximum of R in $S \subset X$ is an alternative $x \in S$ such that xRy for all $y \in S$, that is, an alternative preferred or indifferent to all others in S.

7 This extension is performed in Mercier Ythier (2018). The latter develops a notion of liberal social contract that covers the whole field of economic activities, that is, the production, market exchange and consumption of private commodities, the redistribution of private wealth, and the production and consumption of public commodities.

8 'Discourse ethics . . . establishes a procedure based on presuppositions and designed to guarantee the impartiality of the process of judging. Practical discourse is a procedure for testing the validity of hypothetical norms, not for producing justified norms' (Habermas, 1983, p. 122).

9 The proviso is specified as follows in Locke's *Second Treatise of Government* (1690): 'Nor was this appropriation of any parcel of land, by improving it, any prejudice to any other man, since there was still enough and as good left, and more than the yet unprovided could use' (§ 32); and also

> though men had a right to appropriate by their labor, each one to himself, as much of the things of nature that he could use, yet this could not be much, nor to the prejudice of others, where the same plenty was still left, to those who would use the same industry.
>
> (§ 37)

10 The cases of strategic manipulation most frequently considered in economic theory are: firms' manipulation of market prices in conditions of imperfect competition; endowment manipulations in relation to the transfer paradox; and the manipulation of public good provision in conditions of imperfect information.

11 This set is infinite, but only one compound lottery will emerge as an interesting practical alternative to p and q in the deliberation below, namely, lottery $\frac{1}{2}p + \frac{1}{2}q$. That is, the set of practically relevant alternatives reduces, actually, to the triple $\left\{p, q, \frac{1}{2}p + \frac{1}{2}q\right\}$ in this case.

12 From a preference relation R on X, one defines: a strict preference relation P by xPy if "xRy and [not yRx]" (reading: x is strictly preferred to y if x is preferred or indifferent to y and y is not preferred or indifferent to x); an indifference relation I by xIy if "xRy and yRx" (reading: x is indifferent to y if x is preferred or indifferent to y and y is preferred or indifferent to x). The binary relations P and I are referred to, respectively, as the asymmetric and symmetric factors of R.

13 It may be said here that the maximization of survival expectation, as a rule of conduct, fails the test of universalization prescribed by Kant's (1964) categorical imperative: 'Act only on that maxim through which you can at the same time will that it should become a universal law' (p. 88). It also fails the test of universalization of Habermas, as shown at the end of this section.

14 This essential feature of the example is realistic enough. The French procedure for assigning scarce organ transplants to patients, for example, is almost entirely automated. Assignment is performed nationwide by means of a dedicated software,

appropriately named Cristal. Whenever Cristal assigns an organ to a patient, the team in charge of the transplantation has a short delay to accept or refuse it. The latter decision is taken on the basis of the team's evaluation of the chances of success of the transplantation for their patient(s) at the time when the organ is proposed. If the team refuses, that is, if none of its patients can be successfully transplanted, Cristal reassigns the organ to some other patient and team. See Philippe Steiner (2010, pp. 223–7).

15 Note that P^*, while a very partial ordering, suffices here, as far as decision-making is concerned. By contrast, survival expectation, as an aim, yields a preference ordering over X that satisfies all the standard axioms of rational choice under uncertainty, including completeness and independence.

16 The construction of the prudent decision of this example may be viewed as a case of reflective equilibrium in the sense of Rawls (1971, p. 20). Rawls's own reflective equilibrium, that is, his theory of justice, differs, nevertheless, from the reflective equilibrium of our example in two essential respects (letting aside the obvious difference in scope): it is supposed to apply to general circumstances of justice; and to be unanimously agreed upon by all individuals placed in appropriate conditions of deliberation (that is, placed behind Rawls's veil of ignorance). Rawls's theory of justice is construed, in other words, by his author as objective in these two senses. We develop below a notion of reflective equilibrium that provides another form of objective support to Dr. Chang's particular solution, by grounding it on Habermas's principles (U) and (D).

17 This refers to one of the basic topics of Ricoeur's philosophy: The meaning of a text includes all of its subsequent interpretations, and evolves therefore with any addition to them.

18 One may add casuistry, as an application to moral problems.

19 Let R be a binary relation on X, and let P denote its asymmetric factor (see endnote 12). A cycle of P is a sequence $(x_k)_{k\in\{1,\ldots,n\}}$ of distinct elements of X, $n \geq 2$, such that $x_k P x_{k+1}$ for all $k < n$ and $x_n P x_1$. R is acyclic if P has no cycle. Transitivity implies acyclicity, whereas the converse is not true. Reflexivity and acyclicity, taken together, are necessary and sufficient for the existence of a maximal element of R in any finite subset of X, as a consequence of Sen (1997), Theorem 5.2. A maximal element of R in $S \subset X$ is an alternative $x \in S$ such that there exists no $y \in S$ such that yPx, that is, an alternative of S that has no strictly preferred alternative in S. A maximum is a maximal element, whereas the converse need not be true. Generic existence is much less demanding for maximal elements than for maxima, in terms of the properties of the underlying preference relation: the former (i.e. the generic existence of maximal elements) does not require complete preferences, whereas the latter (the generic existence of maxima) does require it. Nevertheless, if preferences are complete the two notions (maximal element and maximum) are equivalent, as a consequence of Sen (1997), Theorem 5.3.

20 They must have some by the Theorem 5.2 of Sen (1997), but they could have several due to preference incompleteness or to indifference. The completeness of preferences seems unnecessarily demanding for prudential decision-making. What is really at stake in this decision mode is the determination of a definite course of action in the definite circumstances of the case. Preference completeness does not imply definite choice, due to the possibility of indifference; and definite choice does not require preference completeness (see the example above: Dr. Chang's prudent ranking is very incomplete and nevertheless yields a definite choice of action). Preferences are instrumental to action, so to speak, in prudential decision-making; they are preferences for action. Our assumption that decision rules (i.e. elements of $\Re(s)$) have definite maximal elements in the context of decision is meant to capture this characteristic feature.

21 Note that acceptance subsumes understanding here and in the definition of communicative prudence above. That is, acceptance is considered acceptance, based on an appropriate understanding of the specific role of the default rule in deliberation.

22 The cases of strategic manipulation most frequently considered in social choice theory are the manipulations of voting procedures by individuals who report false preferences for strategic purposes in a voting game.

23 Note that Rawls's reflective equilibrium, that is, his maximin criterion of distributive justice, cannot be applied to the distribution issue of the case, for a simple reason of basic logical consistency, namely, the worst off of the case are precisely those who do not receive any unit of medicine. That is, any distribution policy produces worst-off individuals (children dying because of the lack of treatment), so that all policies are indifferent from the standpoint of Rawls's criterion here, including the "non distribution" one. The leximin criterion does not substantially improve the matter: it rules out non distribution, but it implies indifference between any distribution making use of the whole stock of medicine units.

24 Simon's substantive rationality is also a norm, although not an ethical one. Bounded rationality is defined by difference, as a gap between the actual conditions of decision-making and the ideal conditions of substantive rationality. The notion of incomplete information supposes the existence and influence of an imaginary state of complete information in the agent's mind: "I lack some significant information and I would possibly change my plans if I happened to get it".

25 Locke (1690), chapters 8 through 14. Notably § 156:

> The power of assembling and dismissing the legislative, placed in the executive, gives not the executive a superiority over it, but is a *fiduciary trust* [my emphasis] placed in him for the safety of the people in a case where the uncertainty and variableness of human affairs could not bear a steady fixed rule. For it not being possible that the first framers of the government should by any foresight be such masters of future events as to be able to prefix so just periods of return and duration to the assemblies and the legislative, in all times to come, that might exactly answer all the exigencies of the commonwealth, the best remedy could be found for this defect was to trust this to the *prudence* [my emphasis] of one who was able to be present, and whose business it was to watch over the public good.

And also § 160:

> This power to act according to discretion for the public good, without the prescription of the law and sometimes even against it, is that which is called prerogative; for since in some governments the law-making power is not always in being and is usually too numerous, and so too slow for the dispatch requisite to execution, and because, also, it is impossible to foresee and so by laws to provide for all accidents and necessities that may concern the public, or make such laws as will do no harm, if they are executed with an inflexible rigour on all occasions and upon all persons that may come in their way, therefore there is a latitude left to the executive power to do manythings of choice which the laws do not prescribe.

Bibliography

Aristotle. 1941. Ethica Nichomachea. In: McKeon, R. ed. *The basic works of Aristotle*. New York: Random House.

Gauthier, D. 1986. *Morals by agreement*. New York: Oxford University Press.

Habermas, J. 1981. *Theorie des kommunikativen handelns*. Frankfurt am Main: Suhrkamp Verlag.

Habermas, J. 1983. *Moral consciousness and communicative action*. Translated from German by C. Lenhardt and S. W. Nicholsen, 1990. Cambridge, MA: MIT Press.

Kant, I. 1785. *Groundwork of the metaphysics of morals*. Translated from German by H.J. Paton, 1964. New York: Harper and Row.

Kolm, S. 1985. *Le contrat social libéral*. Paris: Presses Universitaires de France.
Locke, J. 1690. *Second treatise of government*. Reprint 1960. Cambridge: Cambridge University Press.
Mas-Colell, A., M.D. Whinston and J.R. Green. 1995. *Microeconomic theory*. New York: Oxford University Press.
Mercier Ythier, J. 2011. Optimal redistribution in the distributive liberal social contract. In: Fleurbaey, M., Salles, M. and Weymark, J.A. eds. *Social ethics and normative economics: Essays in honor of Serge-Christophe Kolm*. Berlin and Heidelberg: Springer-Verlag, pp. 303–26.
Mercier Ythier, J. 2013. Distributive justice and benevolence: The welfare state as practical distributive liberal social contract. *Revue d'Economie Politique*, 123(5), pp. 737–61.
Mercier Ythier, J. 2018. Non-paternalistic benevolence, consumption externalities and the liberal social contract. *Revue d'Economie Politique*, 128(2), pp. 267–96.
Rawls, J. 1971. *A theory of justice*. Cambridge, MA: Harvard University Press.
Ricoeur, P. 1990. *Oneself as another*. Translated from French by K. Blamey, 1992. Chicago: University of Chicago Press.
Ricoeur, P. 1991. Ethique et morale. In: *Lectures 1 : Autour du politique*. Paris: Seuil.
Sen, A. 1997. Maximization and the act of choice. *Econometrica*, 65, pp. 745–79.
Simon, H. 1957. *Models of man*. New York: Wiley-Blackwell.
Simon, H. 1982. *Models of bounded rationality*. Cambridge, MA: MIT Press.
Steiner, P. 2010. *La transplantation d'organes: Un commerce nouveau entre les êtres humains*. Paris: Gallimard.

19 Conflicts between liberty and social welfare in historical perspective

Iona Tarrant and Jonathan Perraton

Introduction: Sen's result and logical resolutions

Sen (1970) first formalized the result that 'in a very basic sense, liberal values conflict with the Pareto principle.' Implicit in the acceptance of Pareto optimality as an objective is acceptance of Paretian value judgements: whatever gives an individual utility is good and individual preferences are accepted as brute facts. Thus, in pursuing Pareto optimality as a policy objective, economists typically accept Paretianism as a value judgement.

In the Paretian liberal paradox, Sen shows that it is logically inconsistent to be committed to all of the following ideas:

1 Acceptance of Paretian value judgements (condition P)
2 Some minimal commitment to individual liberty (condition L*)
3 Acceptance of any possible configuration of individual preferences (condition U)
4 Acceptance of a social welfare function (SWF) as representative of the social good.

Sen (1970) showed that it was not possible to derive an acyclical set of preferences for society from the preferences of individuals via a SWF where the conditions reflected both liberal and Paretian value judgements. Intuitively, Sen's paradox can be thought of as the impossibility of social judgements reflecting a commitment to individual liberty as well as to Paretianism. More specifically, Sen asks the question as to how liberty might fit into the SWF, together with Paretianism. Sen's paradox is often linked with Arrow's impossibility theorem because Sen was interested in constructing a SWF of the same type (i.e. one that produces a ranking of social outcomes representative of social welfare). The key difference lies in the axioms imposed.[1] Sen was concerned that the SWF reflects the idea that it is better that individuals be allowed to decide certain private matters for themselves irrespective of the views of others (condition L*). He also retains two of the axioms imposed by Arrow (1963) – conditions U and P. Condition U reflects the value judgement that individuals should be allowed to hold *any* preferences they want over alternatives (the only constraint is that they be rational) and condition

P reflects the value judgement that a unanimous preference over any given pair of alternatives should be reflected in the social ranking. Condition U is central here; assuming this condition with the SWF leads to the potential for 'invasive' preferences that lead to conflicts with commitments to liberty and impossibility results.

Point three above constitutes a third value judgement, but this is often overlooked. This leads inevitably to an interpretation of Sen's results as a conflict between just two value judgements, Paretianism and liberalism *per se*. Yet, provided one rejects the idea of a SWF, there is no necessary conflict between these ideas. It is the attempt to incorporate liberty into a Paretian SWF which precipitates the impossibility result. Sen has presented us with a particular view of liberty and social welfare which appears to be logically inconsistent. The paradox thus poses the question: What views of liberty and social welfare are logically consistent?

Three answers are suggested immediately from inspection of Sen's result itself. One can accept any two of the value judgements, provided one lets go of the third. This implies the following logically consistent positions on liberty and social welfare:

1 Commitment to a Paretian SWF, but abandonment of some minimal commitment to individual liberty
2 Commitment to Paretian value judgements *and* the desirability of individual liberty, but rejection of the concept of social welfare as something which can be represented by a SWF
3 Commitment to the desirability of individual liberty and the concept of a SWF, but rejection of Paretian value judgements.

Elsewhere Sen (1976) sees Condition P as the main problem and some subsequent contributions relax Paretian assumptions following (3).

The rest of this paper is structured as follows: the second section sets out the rationale for taking a historical perspective on the liberty versus social welfare problem, with particular reference to the thought of Jean-Jacques Rousseau. An interpretation of Rousseau's thought in microeconomic terms, and identification of a dual utility analytical device that resolves conflict, is presented. The third section discusses how the liberty-welfare conflict might be resolved. The fourth section outlines the dual utility device and relates this to resolving the liberty-welfare conflict. The fifth section concludes.

A historical perspective on Sen's paradox

Historically, political philosophers have been concerned with social welfare and the importance of individual liberty. There are a number of reasons why a historical approach to these issues may be useful.

Much of the economics work in the field after the original contributions of (in particular) Sen and Arrow has been formidably technical; nevertheless, in a virtually unparalleled response, by the 1980s significant numbers of economists were sceptical that further progress could be made by continued formal modelling and core journals ceased to accept papers in this field.[2]

If there is a genuine conflict between liberty and social welfare, it would be surprising if earlier writers were not aware of this conflict in some sense, even if they did not formalize it. This paper focuses on the thought of Rousseau. Rousseau did not adopt a utilitarian approach to social welfare; instead, all issues are to be subordinate to the general will which is representative of the common interest. Rousseau's thought can be characterized by the following points:

1 There is a concept of the common interest which is analytically distinct from the private wants of individuals.
2 It is this concept of common interest which should form the basis for governing society.
3 Individual liberty is valued.

The above three points also describe a situation where the SWF is accepted as representative of social welfare and thus used to determine all aspects of the social state, but there is also a desire to incorporate a commitment to individual liberty within this approach to social welfare. It is in this sense that the problem which Rousseau set himself has key points of similarity with the problem set out by Sen. Rousseau was committed to the idea that there exists some distinct concept of social good, the general will, which is analytically distinct from the private wants of individuals. Further, he was of the view that this general will should form the basis for governing society:

> the general will alone can direct the forces of the state in accordance with the purpose for which it was created, namely, the common good. It is exclusively on the basis of this common interest that society must be governed.
>
> (Rousseau 1953: 25)

This is why Rousseau can be thought of as reflecting a view of social welfare which could be described as 'social welfare function dominant': Rousseau's view that all issues in society should be determined exclusively by the general will is analogous to the idea that all aspects of the social state are to be determined by a SWF. In other words, Sen's SWF serves the same role as Rousseau's general will. Rousseau's concept of the general will implies that he would be committed to the idea that a SWF exists which is representative of the social good, but there is also a clear commitment to individual liberty in that Rousseau wanted all rights to be subordinate to the general will, whilst individuals remained 'as free as before':

> To find a form of association . . . where each, while joining with all the rest, still obeys no one but himself, and remains as free as before. This is the fundamental problem to which the social contract provides the answer.
>
> (Rousseau 1953: 14–15)

As Riley (2001: 148) notes, 'had Rousseau not been centrally concerned with freedom – above all with the voluntariness of morally legitimate human actions – he would never have made "the general will" the core idea of his political philosophy.' The complexities of the 'Social Contract' reflect, in part, Rousseau's attempt to reconcile the general will with liberty through a social contract. His account has been influential for conceptions of a social contract from Kant through to post-war theorists, notably both Arrow and Rawls.

Sen (1970) established the result that a SWF may not exist when we attempt to incorporate some minimal commitment to individual liberty into it. In the light of Sen's result, one can ask whether Rousseau had in mind some form of analytical device which resolved the conflict between dominance of the general will (which effectively serves the same role as Sen's SWF) and individual liberty. This paper argues that dual utility can serve as such a device and that this is consistent with Rousseau's work.

Rousseau refers to two types of will of society: the general will and the will of all. These are derived from two types of will of individuals: the belief of the general will and the private will. We interpret the two types of individual will as two sets of individual preferences. This implies that Rousseau was essentially working within a dual, rather than a mono, utility framework in that there are two sets of preferences attributed to each person. Instead of individuals having a single ranking of alternatives from which a single ranking for society is derived, individuals have two rankings of alternatives and there are thus *two* possible rankings of alternatives for society. The general will is established by individuals expressing their beliefs of it. It is the general will, and not the will of all, that represents the common interest of society. In other words, the general will is the analogue of the SWF insofar as its role of determining the common good is concerned.

Although Rousseau stresses the common interest of individuals, and the role that individuals play in promoting that public good, he also acknowledges that individuals are, by nature, physically separate and, as such, have a notion of themselves as individuals. It is the individual's consideration of himself as a private individual with personal interests that explains his having a private will:

> Each individual may, as a man, have a private will contrary to, or divergent from, the general will he has as a citizen. His particular interest may speak to him quite differently from the common interest; his existence, being naturally absolute and independent.
>
> (Rousseau 1953: 18–19)

The above also clearly indicates that each individual has a dual role in society: as a citizen and a private individual. As a citizen, the individual is motivated by the utility of the collective, whereas as a private individual the individual is motivated by personal utility. *A single utility function is incapable of capturing the different motivations behind these two roles.* Two utility functions are required to correspond to the two roles and these are the private will and the belief of the general will. An individual's private will is interpreted as the individual utility function conventionally used by economists.

The general will, by contrast, is the common interest of society. It represents the idea that there is a common interest of society separate from the private wants of individuals: 'the general will is always right and always tends to the public good' (Rousseau 1953: 28–9). The general will is something that does not alter, irrespective of the behaviour of the individual; it is 'always constant, unalterable and pure' (Rousseau 1953: 114). There must, in theory, be some ordering of social states consistent with this notion of good. It is the welfare function of each individual, but could be different from any single individual's belief of the general will prior to its establishment, given the fallibility of individuals.

The general will is established separately for specific issues by asking members of society to vote on the issue in question. In the act of voting, each individual is supposed to be acting as a *citizen* rather than a private individual in that he is expressing his opinion of the common good rather than his individual private good. Each individual should be motivated by his preferences that represent his belief of the general will as opposed to his private will. Given this motivation, the view of the majority will express the general will.

Owing to the presumption that there is only one general will, any single individual can only have an opinion, a belief about his general will prior to its establishment. This enables Rousseau to justify subjecting all members of society to the majority view, since this is the means by which the general will is discovered whereas any single individual could be wrong. However, the general will is not *axiomatically* the majority view, since individuals could be expressing private wills or could be wrong in their belief of the general will. The method of majority decision is merely the most likely means of discovering the true general will. Rousseau is making an empirical assumption that the view of the majority will result in expression of the general will. Such conceptions led to subsequent work in late eighteenth/early nineteenth-century social choice theory on the efficacy of majority voting, notably Condorcet's Jury Theorem (Grofman and Feld 1988; McLean 1995).[3] Rousseau acknowledges that he cannot guarantee that the majority will result in the expression of the general will:

> This assumes, to be sure, that all the characteristics of the general will continue to be found in the majority. When this ceases to be true, whatever action is taken there is no more liberty.
>
> (Rousseau 1953: 118)

In the language of welfare economics, individuals are expressing opinions of the SWF (rather than privately motivated preferences) in voting. Once the actual SWF is established by the majority view, each individual accepts this as his own SWF, irrespective of whether it agrees with the opinion he expressed in his vote. This is because each individual member of society has already accepted the majority view, rather than his individual view, as representative of the general will in entering society: 'Except for the original contract, the majority always binds the minority; this is a consequence of the contract itself' (Rousseau 1953: 117).

The will of all is of no use as a guide to the desirability or otherwise of social states. But it replaces the general will when individuals subordinate their general will to their own private will when voting. Referring to this situation, where individuals express their private rather than their general wills when voting, Rousseau comments:

> the general will falls silent; guided by secret motives, no one thinks as a citizen any more than as if the state had never existed; and under the guise of laws are enacted iniquitous decrees whose only purpose is to further private interests.
>
> (Rousseau 1953: 114)

The difference between the will of all and the general will stems solely from the difference in the *motivation* behind the individual preferences from which they are derived. Thus, to follow Rousseau, we would need to be sure that the preferences expressed are motivated by consideration of the public, and not the private interest:

> Each individual may, as a man, have a private will contrary to, or divergent from the general will he has as a citizen. His particular interest may speak to him quite differently from the common interest; his existence being naturally absolute and independent.
>
> (Rousseau 1953: 18–19)

There is a clear parallel here with Rawls's idea of a sense of justice. The parallel lies in Rawls's argument for the individual cultivation of a sense of justice with reference to the social, rather than the individual, good:

> It can even happen that there are many who do not find a sense of justice for their own good. . . . Yet none of this nullifies the collective rationality of the principles of justice; it is still to the advantage of each that everyone else should honour them.
>
> (Rawls 1971: 576)

Similarly, according to Rousseau, individuals should act (or vote) according to their general will. Thus, there is clearly some form of SWF implicit in Rawls's analysis. One could argue that it is consistent with the general will that individuals have a sense of justice. This aspect of Rawls's theory means that he has more in common with Rousseau than with other post-war contractarians for whom the idea of a SWF is absent or viewed as meaningless.[4]

There are two types of freedom in Rousseau's 'Social Contract,' corresponding to whether one is ruled by one's private or one's general will. Rousseau refers to these two types as 'natural liberty' and 'civil liberty' respectively. That the general will is 'always right' and 'always tends to the public good,' whereas the private will is not necessarily in the interest of the individual, implies that the utility framework is hierarchical. The private will is subordinate to the general will and therefore civil liberty, where individuals are ruled by the general will, is better for them than natural liberty. This explains why individuals agree to the social contract in first place. In entering the social contract, individuals are trading their natural liberty for civil liberty that makes them better off:

> Although in this [civil] state he [man] loses many of his natural advantages, he gains so many in return, his faculties are exercised and developed, his ideas are broadened, his sentiments ennobled and his whole soul elevated to such an extent that if the abuses of his new condition did not degrade him beneath his former state, he ought unceasingly to bless the happy moment which wrested him forever from it, and turned him from a stupid and limited animal into an intelligent being and a man.
>
> (Rousseau 1953: 20)

Entering society does not preclude the possibility of individuals being able to exercise their private wills, but such a sphere of choice is dependent on the general will allowing it: 'the rights which are taken for parts of sovereignty are all subordinate to it, and always presuppose the existence of a supreme will which these rights merely put into execution' (ibid.: 27). There cannot be absolute rights to a private sphere of choice, i.e. rights that are independent of the general will, because if there were such rights then they could conflict with the general will. In cases of such conflict, these absolute rights would make society worse off. The private will is subordinate to the general will, thus any private sphere of choice is subordinate to the general will:

> If the individuals retained certain rights, each would be his own judge in certain matters, and would soon claim to be in all; the state of nature would continue, and the association would necessarily become tyrannical and meaningless.
>
> (Rousseau 1953: 15)

There is a clear moral element to the general will. The notion of reason is important; it is a considered judgement: 'along with the civil state, man acquires moral liberty, which alone makes him truly master of himself; for impulse of mere appetite is slavery, and obedience to self-imposed law is liberty' (ibid.: 15). Nevertheless, there remains a commitment to individual liberty and Rousseau appears to allow for individuals to have a private sphere of choice outside of the general will. In a statement that could almost have come from the pages of Mill's *On Liberty*, Rousseau (1953: 152) argues. '"In the republic", says the Marquis d'Argenson, "everyone is perfectly free to do anything that does not harm others" This is the invariable boundary-line; it cannot be more accurately defined.'

Resolution of liberty/welfare conflict

The axioms of Arrow's and Sen's theorems represent basic value judgements which are often deemed to be desirable. In 'The Social Contract,' however, there is some general will which is 'out there' to be discovered; all we need to do is to bring about the conditions which are most likely to discover it. In other words, if the SWF were merely a means of discovering the general will, we would be looking for axioms which were most likely to make that general will known. On this view, one could interpret the Paretian liberal paradox as follows: The conditions P, L* and U may not enable us to discover the general will and thus are not appropriate axioms to impose on a SWF. The social choice theorist, however, concludes that the value judgements are not consistent with each other.

Rousseau states that the general will is found by the majority view, and he suggests that the larger the majority, the surer we can be that we have found the general will. There is a clear link between unanimity and Sen's condition P, given that the latter is an equivalence between a unanimous preference over a given pair of alternatives and society's ranking of these two alternatives. But a unanimous preference is just one aspect of Paretian value judgements. Rowley and Peacock (1975: 7–9) identify two others:

1 Each individual is considered to be the best judge of his own welfare.
2 Social welfare is solely dependent on the welfare of individual members of that society.

Rousseau's idea of an infallible general will which is 'always right' and should, therefore, govern society runs contrary to the Paretian value assumptions (1) and (2) that Rowley and Peacock propose. This is not only because it questions the judgement of the individual, but also in its suggestion of a less straightforward link between individual and social welfare. The fundamental point is that the only link between Sen's condition P and the general will lies in the fact that unanimity is a process by which the general will may be discovered. The link does not apply to Paretian value judgements *per se*.

However, it is the similarity between the SWF and the general will which is the underlying theme of this paper. Sen requires that the ranking of alternatives generated by the SWF be acyclical, i.e. 'R [the social preference relation] should generate a "choice function", that is, in every subset of alternatives there must be a "best" alternative' (Sen 1970: 152–53).[5] The similarity between the general will and the SWF lies in the fact that the latter identifies an outcome which is socially 'best.' The difference lies in the interpretation of the two, discussed above. But if one accepts the idea that one can derive a ranking of alternatives which is representative of society's good, to which all issues are subordinate, then there is a sense in which one is accepting the idea of the SWF as *analogous* to the general will. To be more specific, the Sen paradox may be interpreted as stemming from giving the SWF the *status* of the general will, i.e. of accepting that all issues, including basic rights and liberties, are to be subject to the SWF.

The analogy applies to the *role* and status of the general will, as the device which represents the social good and determines *all* issues within society. Acceptance of the idea that there is some general will which exists prior to the process of preference aggregation, which this process is designed to discover, is not necessary for the acceptance of this analogy. One has to accept interpretation of one of the SWF set out in the introduction, that the SWF is generally accepted as a device which identifies the best social state, together with the further value judgement that the function should actually be *used* to determine the complete social state.

Only the general will is representative of the public good. Therefore, 'society' is a better judge of its welfare than the individual. The link with a Paretian SWF should now be clear. The Paretian SWF represents the view of 'society' because it reflects the unanimously held view. Provided the individual preferences are motivated by the common interest, the Paretian SWF is representative of the general will. Given the argument that any individual private sphere is contingent on the general will, liberalism is subordinate to Paretianism. Thus one 'Rousseauist' resolution to the Paretian liberal conflict is the following: Condition P has priority, provided that the motivation underlying the individual preferences is the common interest rather than the individual's private interest.

Sen has established the result that if we attempt to construct a SWF that satisfies both conditions P and L*, then such a function may not exist. If one is to interpret the exercise as an attempt to discover the general will of society, then one is committed to responding by dropping either of the conditions P or L*. This is because the general will always exists by definition, so there must exist some SWF that is representative of it (in other words, one is committed to the concept of a SWF). There can be no absolute right to a sphere of private choice, given Rousseau's view that all rights depend for their existence on the general will. However, Rousseau clearly viewed such a private sphere as important:

> In addition to the public person, we have also to consider the private persons who compose it, and whose life and liberty are naturally independent of it. The problem is, therefore, to distinguish clearly between the respective rights of the citizens and of the sovereign; and between the duties the former must fulfil in their capacity as subjects, and the natural rights they must enjoy in their capacity as men.
>
> (Rousseau 1953: 118)

This could provide a rationale for imposing Sen's conception L* upon the SWF in addition to condition P. However, given Rousseau's view that unanimity is the best means of discovering the general will, if P and L* were to come into conflict then it would be L* that would be abandoned. Condition L* would go, but with no loss of individual liberty on the basis that the SWF established is a welfare function of each individual. Thus, it is this idea of dual utility, that each individual has two sets of preferences corresponding respectively to private common interests which could resolve the conflict between liberty and social welfare.

However, the success of this dual utility device in resolving conflict between liberty and social welfare rests upon whether or not individuals express their general, as opposed to their private, will. A key problem for Rousseau here is that he can provide us with no way of knowing that the SWF is representative of the general will rather than the will of all.

In the light of Sen's result, one possibility suggests itself: where conditions P and L* come into conflict it might be interpreted as indicating that individuals are actually expressing preferences which reflect their private wills, not views of the general will. If Rousseau had been unambiguously clear that some minimal natural rights were an aspect of the general will, then this would be a possible interpretation: failure of the SWF to satisfy L* could indicate that individuals are failing to 'see' the general will. On this view, the dual utility device implies that there will always exist an SWF satisfying conditions P and L*, provided that individuals are motivated by the common interest.

However, given the ambiguity in Rousseau's discussion of a private sphere of choice and Rousseau's insistence that unanimity is the best way of discovering the general will, the preceding paragraph is not an accurate reflection of his view. Rousseau's view actually appears to be more straightforward: he acknowledges the problem that individuals might express private as opposed to general wills when voting, but provides no solution. Instead he simply assumes that the will of the majority does reflect the general will. Thus, one can think of a SWF which is based upon condition P as representative of the general will. Such a welfare function may or may not allow a private sphere of choice for individuals, but where it does not, this is not important because the SWF is the true welfare function of each individual. Rousseau is often associated with the idea of being 'forced to be free': 'anyone who refuses to obey the general will shall be forced to do so by the whole body; which means nothing more or less than that he will be forced to be free' (Rousseau 1953: 19). It is this idea of being forced to be free that is fundamental to the way that Rousseau attempts to resolve conflict between liberty and social welfare.

Numerous possible solutions to Sen's paradox have been proposed and space precludes a full survey. Many writers in the social choice literature are not prepared to abandon the idea that there is a Paretian SWF that represents the social good. What is interesting about most of these writers is that the Paretian SWF appears to be assigned the status of the general will whilst other issues, including the idea of a private sphere of choice, are merely subordinate to it. However, unlike Rousseau for these writers there is no evidence of any dual utility device being invoked. This implies that these writers are not able to resolve the conflict, but effectively choose social welfare over liberty. For example, Blau (1975) accepts unanimity as a test of social welfare and, therefore, it is liberalism that must be relaxed to resolve the paradox. Blau (1975) notes that Sen's result stems from each individual's utility being more affected by the private choice of the other than it is by his own private choice, and thus deems these individuals to have 'meddlesome' preferences. This makes it somewhat ironic that he opts for allowing these 'meddlesome' preferences to be representative of condition P. His concern at the 'meddlesome' nature of preferences would constitute a reason for retaining L* so that individuals were not subject to meddlesome intervention in their private choices, not weakening it.

This literature has not systematically invoked a dual utility device to resolve Sen's paradox. Sen (1974) provides a discussion of choices and preferences which seems to indicate acceptance of the dual preference idea of private and general will, but does not go on to use this to resolve conflict between liberty and social welfare. Fine (1975) proposes a resolution of the conflict using what is essentially a dual utility device. He initially separates the individual's commitment to liberalism from his preference over outcomes. There is a dual utility device being used here as we can identify two sets of preferences over outcomes: one ranking that incorporates the liberal sentiment, and another that reflects the individual's private preferences over the outcomes. The liberal sentiment is a preference about how much individual freedom the state should allow its citizens, i.e. it is a preference that relates to society as a whole. For Fine, if each *individual* accepts the liberal value judgement, and acceptance of this is reflected in his preferences, then there will be no conflict between liberalism and Paretianism at the *social* level (the ranking of alternatives when conditions L* and P are imposed on the SWF will be acyclical). This is because each individual will, firstly, prefer that other individuals have their own preferences reflected in issues which are personal to them because of his commitment to individual liberty. Any preferences which he may have over the *outcomes* of such private decisions are subordinate to his commitment to liberty. One could separate this individual commitment to liberalism from individual preferences over social outcomes, in which case the liberal value judgement would create a divergence between preference and choice: the commitment to liberty would stop individuals from acting on some preferences. This is the dual utility idea: the individual has a set of actual preferences over outcomes, but this is not necessarily the set he would want to act upon because he also has a sense of justice. The set of preferences that underlies his choices is his preferences considered in the light of his desire for liberty. Such a resolution works at the social level in that condition U is no longer imposed on the SWF, thus making P and L* consistent with one another. Restricting individual preference profiles to be liberal is tantamount to restricting the domain of the SWF, i.e. abandoning condition U.

Alternatively, following Sen (1976), other studies have attempted to resolve his paradox through weakening condition P – position (3) from the introduction. Space precludes a detailed examination of such studies.[6] Weakening condition P opens up new possibility results; this can lead to liberal collective choice rules that preserve a protected private sphere for individual rights. Igersheim (2013) provides a recent extension of such results.

The dual utility device

Sen's Paretian liberal paradox is formulated within a mono-utility framework. The term mono-utility refers to the number of utility functions (or sets of preferences) attributed to each *individual*. This paper has argued that Rousseau's notions of the private will, the general will and the will of all necessarily require a multiple, as opposed to a mono, utility framework. This means that it requires us to attribute more than a single utility function to each individual. This paper therefore interprets the two types of will which Rousseau attributes to individuals as two distinct *individual* utility functions. If one then aggregates individual preferences using majority voting to make a collective decision, then it follows that there will be two corresponding social rankings of alternatives, only one of which will be representative of the true SWF (general will). Indeed, Brennan (1989) notes that the dual utility concept can be traced back to Rousseau, although he does not develop the point in detail.

Goodin (1986) notes that the mono-utility framework is mathematically tractable and has allowed rigorous results to be derived in social choice theory, but argues that this has been at the expense of a broader understanding of human motivation. In a closely related paper, Sen himself noted the limitations of this conception and criticized the notion of a single preference ordering as being representative of all possible interests of a person (Sen 1977).

Margolis (1981, 1982) formulated a model of rational choice in which the individual was conceived of as having two different motivations: selfish and unselfish; he argues that 'the notion of a distinction between a person's motivation as a private individual and as a citizen goes all the way back to Plato' (Margolis 1981: 266). Margolis views the individual as allocating his resources between selfish and unselfish interests rather as an individual allocates his income between alternative goods, i.e. the individual behaves as a utility maximizer but has more than one utility function. The multiple utility framework has been developed further.[7] Etzioni (1986: 177) takes the view that ethical considerations require a different utility function because what gives one pleasure and what is right may well be mutually exclusive: 'due to moral factors, choices do not reflect simple, one-dimensional, preferences but are multifaceted.' This dual utility approach can be seen in the wider context of broader conceptions of the individual agent beyond maximizing a mono-utility function and incorporating wider motivation from morality, altruism and other social preferences (see: Hodgson 2013; Davis 2003).

Conclusions

In the Paretian liberal paradox, Sen has presented us with a result which indicates that it is logically inconsistent to be committed simultaneously to an acceptance of Paretian value judgements, individual liberty and a social welfare function as representative of the social good. All three conditions, though, are commonly maintained in welfare economics.

Sen's Paretian liberal paradox was formulated within a mono-utility framework. Given this analytical framework there are a limited number of logically consistent positions on liberty and social welfare implied by Sen's result. Many subsequent authors have either maintained a commitment to a Paretian SWF, but retreated from a commitment to individual liberty or, alternatively, maintained a commitment to individual liberty, but rejected the concept of social welfare as something that can be represented by a SWF. Others have relaxed the commitment to Paretianism in various ways.

However, the ways out of the Sen paradox could be increased if we were to modify this analytical framework. This paper has argued that it is the modified analytical framework implicit in the thought of Rousseau (each individual has a social, as well as a private, utility function) which enabled him to argue for both individual liberty *and* the social good. In the light of the discussion of Rousseau presented here, we can identify an alternative route out of the liberty-social welfare conflict through a commitment to a Paretian SWF and commitment to individual liberty, but a rejection of the mono-utility conception.

Some more general observations may also be made on the approach here. The axiomatic method of post-war social choice theory provided a means of formalizing and clarifying conceptions of collective decision-making and highlighted, amongst other things, a generic conflict between social welfare and liberty. One argument here is that historically political philosophers and economists, including Rousseau and John Stuart Mill amongst others, had an intuitive grasp of such problems. A historical approach to these issues may still be of value, not least in the enduring influence of such thinkers on contemporary political philosophy. The account here indicates that a key limitation in attempting to resolve these issues lies in the narrow conception of an agent's preference function in conventional microeconomics.

Elsewhere Sen argues for the consideration of moral factors as well as self-interested ones. However, Sen adopts the mono-utility framework for the Paretian liberal paradox. Here we have outlined a dual utility approach to move beyond some of these problems to incorporate preference formation in the context of social decision-making. Recently various authors have attempted to broaden the economic conception of agents' social decision-making and behaviour and dual utility offers one possible approach to this. Dual utility is increasingly being used to explain behaviour in a variety of contexts. This is reinforced by recent work arguing that an individual's collective preferences may well be just as important as their private preferences and that this should also be used to model individual choice. Given the increased importance and application of the dual utility framework, it is interesting to note its application to potentially resolving the liberty-social welfare conflict (cf. Igersheim 2007).

Notes

1 Strictly speaking Sen was concerned with establishing the existence of a social decision function, whilst Arrow was concerned to establish a social welfare function. A social welfare function should generate a social ranking of alternatives R that is transitive. A social decision function implies the weaker requirement that the social ranking of alternatives generated, R, be acyclical. In this paper the term social welfare function is used because it emphasizes the normative interpretation of R.

2 See, further, Igersheim (2017), Salles (2005, 2014).

3 This has spawned a vast literature; List and Pettit (2002) show that impossibility results may apply here, too.

4 There are similarities in our interpretation of Rousseau here with Brooke (2007).
5 Strictly this is a social decision function – see endnote 1.
6 See, further, Igersheim (2013), Suzumura (2010) and the references therein.
7 See in particular: Etzioni (1986), Lutz (1993), Gilbert (2001) and Sugden (2000), but see also the criticisms in Brennan (1989, 1993).

Bibliography

Arrow, K.J. (1963) *Social Choice and Individual Values*, 2nd edn. New Haven, NJ: Yale University Press.

Blau, J.H. (1975) 'Liberal values and interdependence', *Review of Economic Studies*, 42: 395–402.

Brennan, T. (1989) 'A methodological assessment of multiple utility frameworks', *Economics and Philosophy*, 5: 189–208.

Brennan, T. (1993) 'The futility of multiple utility', *Economics and Philosophy*, 9: 155–64.

Brooke, C. (2007) 'Aux limites de la Volonté Générale: silence, exil, ruse et désobéissance dans la pensée politique de Rousseau', *Les Études philosophiques*, 83: 425–44.

Davis, J.B. (2003) *The Theory of the Individual in Economics*, London: Routledge.

Etzioni, A. (1986) 'The case for a multiple utility conception', *Economics and Philosophy*, 2: 159–83.

Fine, B. (1975) 'Individual liberalism in a Paretian society', *Journal of Political Economy*, 83: 1277–82.

Gilbert, M. (2001) 'Collective preferences, obligations and rational choice', *Economics and Philosophy*, 17: 109–19.

Goodin, R.E. (1986) 'Laundering preferences', in J. Elster and A. Hylland (eds.), *Foundations of Social Choice Theory*, Cambridge: Cambridge University Press.

Grofman, B. and Feld, S. (1988) 'Rousseau's general will: A Condorcetian perspective', *American Political Science Review*, 82: 167–76.

Hodgson, G.H. (2013) *From Pleasure Machines to Moral Communities: An Evolutionary Economics without Homo Economicus*, Chicago: University of Chicago Press.

Igersheim, H. (2007) 'Du paradoxe libéral-parétian à un concept de métaclassment des préférences', *Recherches économiques de Louvain*, 73: 173–92.

Igersheim, H. (2013) 'Invoking a Cartesian product structure on social states: New resolutions of Sen's and Gibbard's impossibility theorems', *Theory and Decision*, 74: 463–77.

Igersheim, H. (2017) 'The death of welfare economics: History of a controversy', CHOPE Working Paper No. 2017–03, Duke University Press, Durham.

List, C. and Pettit, P. (2002) 'Aggregating sets of judgments: An impossibility result', *Economics and Philosophy*, 18: 89–110.

Lutz, M. (1993) 'The utility of multiple utility: A comment on Brennan', *Economics and Philosophy*, 9: 143–54.

Margolis, H. (1981) 'A new model of rational chaoice', *Ethics*, 91: 265–79.

Margolis, H. (1982) *Selfishness, Altruism and Rationality: A Theory of Social Choice*, Cambridge: Cambridge University Press.

McLean, I. (1995) 'The first golden age of social choice, 1784–1803', in W. Barnett (ed.), *Social Choice, Welfare and Ethics*, Cambridge: Cambridge University Press.

Rawls, J. (1971) *A Theory of Justice*, Oxford: Oxford University Press.

Riley, P. (2001) 'Rousseau's general will', in P. Riley (ed.), *The Cambridge Companion to Rousseau*, Cambridge: Cambridge University Press.

Rousseau, J.-J. (1953 [1762]) 'The social contract', in *Political Writings*, trans F. Watkins, Edinburgh: Nelson.

Rowley, C.K. and Peacock, A.T. (1975) *Welfare Economics: A Liberal Restatement*, Oxford: Martin Robertson.

Salles, M. (2005) 'The launching of "Social Choice and Welfare" and the creation of the Society for Social Choice and Welfare', *Social Choice and Welfare*, 25: 557–64.

Salles, M. (2014) '"Social Choice and Welfare" at 30: Its role in the development of social choice theory and welfare economics', *Social Choice and Welfare*, 42: 1–16.

Sen, A.K. (1970) 'The impossibility of a Paretian liberal', *Journal of Political Economy*, 78: 152–57.

Sen, A.K. (1974) 'Choice, orderings and morality'; reprinted in *Choice, Welfare and Measurement* (1982), Oxford: Basil Blackwell.

Sen, A.K. (1976) 'Liberty, unanimity and rights', *Economica*, 43: 217–45.

Sen, A.K. (1977) 'Rational fools: A critique of the behavioural foundations of economic theory', *Philosophy and Public Affairs*, 6: 317–44.

Sugden, R. (2000) 'Team preferences', *Economics and Philosophy*, 16: 175–204.

Suzumura, K. (2010) 'Welfarism, individual rights and procedural fairness', in K. Arrow et al. (eds), *Handbook of Social Choice and Welfare: Volume Two*, Amsterdam: Elsevier.

20 Oneself, the other and both in bargaining models

Fabrice Tricou

Introduction

The field of bargaining models is well suited to investigate the diversity of links between "oneself and the other" as it involves several conceptions of the individual(s); it shows many ways one considers the other and it displays a wide range of representations of their relation.

To begin with, the bargaining setting questions the assumption of *individual rationality*, as the prevalence or explicit recognition of this standard assumption in strategic models contrasts with its absence or subsidiarity in axiomatic models. From the perspective of "rational choice theory", this dual situation especially expresses the oddity of axiomatic models, and more broadly of cooperative game theory. But the singularity is too big to be ignored (one can't neglect the Nash solution . . .) and then calls for a normalization treatment called "Nash program", that endeavors to bring the lost sheep of cooperative game theory back to the mainstream flock of non-cooperative game theory.

Subsequently, oneself and the other are differently conceived in non-cooperative models and in cooperative ones. In strategic models, prior to the question of interindividual equilibrium, the operation of *one's rationality requires some objectification of the other*, typically reduced to her/his given action, through the substantial scheme *à la* Cournot; or to her/his rule of reaction, through the procedural scheme *à la* Stackelberg. Some cognitive capture of the other is thus operated in non-cooperative models. In axiomatic models, oneself and the other are both and together *axiom makers and takers*, every specific set of unanimously chosen principles determining one proper bargaining solution. Some cooperation with the other is thus achieved in cooperative models.

Finally, the bargaining setting displays neither the full peace of the pure convergence of interests, nor the strict war of the pure divergence of interests. More subtly, the bargaining problem precisely stems from a "*conflicting coordination*" issue, with converging interests to cooperate but diverging interests about the terms of cooperation. Formally expressed by the multiplicity of Pareto optima, this problem of mixed interests appears as the duality of opposite efficient Nash equilibria in the "battle of the sexes" and as the non-uniqueness of the core in the Edgeworth box.

In the bargaining context represented by the one shot hawk-dove game, the achievement of a good solution, as a unique efficient equilibrium, is difficult to obtain on the basis of the postulate of rationality (first section). The suggested explanation of this cooperation failure is that rational agents are *independent* individuals without *autonomous* abilities. This central proposition is explained and defended in the three following sections.

First, individual independence or "negative liberty" essentially means independent determination of the individual choice, while autonomy or "positive liberty" is the ability of a free entity to obey the rules the entity chose for self-direction and self-government. Such a notion of autonomy is relevant for the economic field when one wonders about the institution of the rules of a structured interaction, and also when one considers the joint decision sealing the agreement in an unstructured "one-to-one" relation (second section).

Second, strategic bargaining models *à la* Rubinstein (1982) show that a good solution of the problem can be obtained through an adequate interaction of rational agents. But this is no real objection to our main proposition, as poorly resourceful independent players slightly contribute to the success of their coordination: the solution is aimed at by the shrewd and powerful model designer whose mind determines and whose hand institutes the relevant rules of the game that structure the play. *The capacity of autonomy is here taken by the model designer from the agents who are denied as rule makers of the non-cooperative game* (third section).

Third, axiomatic bargaining models *à la* Nash (1950) also deliver a good solution to the problem, with the display of a synthetic cooperation rule derived from a set of reasonable axioms. And this confirms our main proposition, as the model maker no longer intervenes as a manipulating puppeteer, but instead as a counseling representative to autonomous beings. *The capacity of autonomy is here borrowed by the model designer from the agents who are hidden as axiom selectors of the cooperative game* (fourth section).

Such a view may lead to a critical appraisal of the Nash program, understood as the general attempt to found cooperative game theory on non-cooperative game theory: if the interaction of independent players rests on common rules that are at least unanimously accepted and at most socially chosen, then one may envision cooperative foundations of non-cooperative equilibria (conclusion).

In a nutshell, the bargaining problem can only be solved if participants are channeled or channel themselves in the pursuit of their individual interests, which is accomplished either when one externally imposes rules of the game instituting the non-cooperative interaction between *independent* individuals; or when one assumes an internal capability of *autonomous* persons to cooperate acknowledging the other not as a thing to be managed but as another respectable being.

The bargaining situation as a challenge for mechanically rational individuals

a) In bargaining models, the basic data are the set of feasible utilities $\{(u_i; u_j)\}$ and the disagreement point of guaranteed utilities $\boldsymbol{D} = (\underline{u}_i; \underline{u}_j)$. Any particular concept of solution operates as a specific way to determine an agreement $\boldsymbol{S} = (u_i^*; u_j^*)$. If the consideration of utilities is put aside,[1] a simple example of the bargaining problem is given by the splitting of a pie (of size 1) between two individuals receiving the respective parts α for i and β for j (α and β being greater than 0 and smaller than 1) if such a splitting is decided on or emerge, and nothing (α = β = 0) if no agreement is reached.

Basically, the plain notion of individual rationality determines any move as a betterment for each: $u_i^* > \underline{u}_i$ and $u_j^* > \underline{u}_j$ in the general case; or α > 0 and β > 0 in the simplified case (Pareto improvement). And the simple notion of interindividual rationality determines the final settlement as a point of social exhaustion, a state of full exploitation of mutual opportunities: $(u_i^*; u_j^*)$ is a Pareto optimum in the general case; or α + β = 1 in the simplified case (Pareto optimization).[2] As the indetermination on the terms of the agreement is thus reduced but persisting, the notion of rationality has to be refined, beyond the primitive conception of an exhausting mutual improvement. The stakes are high, as the achievement of some deal requires its complete determination.[3]

Individual rationality is commonly developed as some maximization under constraint, the basic constraint stemming from physical feasibility. Under this sole constraint, maximizers i and j claim the best possible result for each of them (α = β = 1), causing a strong general disagreement. Under the simple assumption of a common and blind *maximalist rationality*, both individuals will stick to their highest claim and will eventually get nothing. So the simple and strong form of rationality is self-defeating when it is unanimously operated: two hawkish individuals seeking too big "a slice of the pie" end up in a lose-lose situation, experiencing a frozen and frustrating symmetric failure.

Let's now equip i and j with a more sophisticated form of rationality and see if it can solve the problem: can *strategic rationality* expel the bad scenario of a general failure? More precisely, a simple idea would be to consider that each individual may play it tough, like a Hawk, or play it cool like a Dove. As a simultaneous game due to Maynard Smith and Price (1973), the strategic interaction is accurately represented in the normal or strategic form:[4]

HH is a bloody war; DD is a 50–50 fair peace; HD and DH are domination scenarios. There are three Nash equilibria: HH, DH and HD. The DH and HD polarized and symmetrical equilibria echo the configuration of a chicken game, or a structure of dual leadership expressing two possible dominations of one on the other. The HH equilibrium echoes the configuration of a prisoner's dilemma, or a structure of "cooperation failure" that underlines the diabolical absurdity of a

Table 20.1 The basic Hawk-Dove Game

i's strategies/j's strategies	*Hawk (H)*	*Dove (D)*
Hawk (H)	(0; 0)	(1; 0)
Dove (D)	(0; 1)	(½; ½)

social situation which is a suboptimal equilibrium, that is to say a bad and sticky situation. And DD, the 50–50 split, is not an equilibrium, even if it is fair (as opposed to DH and HD), and optimal (as opposed to HH).

b) So the basic Hawk-Dove Game (henceforth HDG) leads to a deceiving conclusion mixing "cooperation failure" (HH vis-à-vis DD) and "conflicting coordination" (DH versus HD). Let us consider variants of the basic HDG to investigate on the robustness of the socially bad results obtained in this simple version. Six remarks may be suggested.

First and foremost, the repetition of the HDG is explicitly put aside, be it played a definite or indefinite number of times, as the selected framework is the one shot bargaining problem. It is well known that cooperation may arise from repetition;[5] but the issue of cooperation also deserves to be treated for one shot games.

Second, the sequentialization of the HDG can lead to the domination of the first mover, who tries to exploits his/her advantageous position to give rise to the asymmetric equilibrium he/she prefers (HD). But it can also lead to the unanimously bad situation (HH), the second mover being indifferent between HD and HH since he/she gets 0 in both cases. In any case, mutual cooperation (DD) does not arise.

Third, the introduction of an intermediate strategy in the HDG (see table 20.2) does not undo the sticky bad conclusions: if such a "Sparrow" strategy is added in the game, there is no real change as we have more chicken game equilibria (SH, DH, HS, HD) and still one prisoner's dilemma equilibrium (HH). This suboptimal equilibrium remains the more likely one, as playing Hawk is still a weakly dominant strategy for i and for j.

Fourth, the consideration of cautious strategies does not justify cooperation. Playing H, i or j would at least get 0; and playing H, i or j would at least get 0. So there is no obvious minimax strategy justifying the choice of D for each, and consequently the emergence of DD.

Fifth, the consideration of probabilistic strategies does not generate cooperation. Let's denote by p_{ji} the probability that j plays H according to i, and p_{ij} the probability that i plays H according to j. It follows that i's expected utility when playing H is $E_i(H) = p_{ji} \times 0 + (1\text{-}p_{ji}) \times 1 = 1\text{-}p_{ji}$; and that i's expected utility when playing D is $E_i(D) = p_{ji} \times 0 + (1\text{-}p_{ji}) \times ½ = (1\text{-}p_{ji})/2$. As $E_i(H) \geq E_i(D)$, i decides to play H and so does j, leading to the bad and sad emergence of HH as the social result.[8]

Sixth, some more substantial strategic restructuring of the HDG (see table 20.3) does not produce better cooperative results. If the basic game is modified thanks

Table 20.2 The Hawk-Sparrow-Dove Game

i's choices/j's choices	*Hawk*	*Sparrow*	*Dove*
Hawk	(0; 0)	(1; 0)	(1; 0)
Sparrow	(0; 1)	(0; 0)[6] or (½; ½)[7]	(1; 0)
Dove	(0; 1)	(0; 1)	(½; ½)

Table 20.3 The basic Hawk-Dove Game as a claim game

i/j	*1*	*¾*	*½*	*¼*	*0*
1	(0; 0)	(0; 0)	(0; 0)	(0; 0)	(1; 0)
¾	(0; 0)	(0; 0)	(0; 0)	(¾; ¼)	(¾; 0)
½	(0; 0)	(0; 0)	(½; ½)	(½; ¼)	(½; 0)
¼	(0; 0)	(¼; ¾)	(¼; ½)	(¼; ¼)	(¼; 0)
0	(0; 1)	(0; ¾)	(0; ½)	(0; ¼)	(0; 0)

to the idea that each individual expresses a claim (as a number of quarters in the game below), then one can clearly distinguish the upper triangle of disagreements (0; 0), the diagonal line of optimal agreements ($\alpha + \beta = 1$) and the lower triangle of suboptimal agreements ($\alpha + \beta < 1$). Nash equilibria are on diagonal line of optimal agreements and "11". Any optimal division of the pie is here obtained as an equilibrium, but which one will could or should be selected? The "11" or HH situation is no longer an equilibrium in dominant strategies, but still is a Nash equilibrium. So one can assert that this other game does not make the HDG obsolete, as it changes the terms of the cooperation problem but does not solve it: it does not eliminate the persisting disagreement and it does not generate one single efficient equilibrium.

So we have to conclude that, despite various modifications of the basic HDG, the achievement of cooperation in a bargaining setting still appears as difficult and unjustified. In the HDG framework, cooperation would make sense, as a fair way to elect and sustain one optimal equilibrium. But the postulate of rationality does not easily back or rationalize the common choice of cooperation, the failure of mutual cooperation coming from the unanimous interest for domination.

c) The inability of rational behavior to lead to good results in the bargaining situation may be expressed by three specific statements that all raise questions. Firstly, the maximalist attitude is self-defeating, even though it is backed by the postulate of strategic rationality, as shown by the emergence of a suboptimal equilibrium (in weakly dominant strategies) in the Hawk-Dove Game. This is true only if such an inflexible behavior is universal, but for which rational reason would one give up and let the other have her/his way? Secondly, the scenario of an unbalanced split is backed by the postulate of strategic rationality with two polarized Nash equilibria in the Hawk-Dove Game. But is there any rational endogenous reason to explain the selection of one of the two equilibria? Thirdly, no rational justification can be provided in this framework in favor of the emergence of the balanced peaceful solution of a 50–50 split, which is an optimum but not an equilibrium. Why is the standard rational behavior so far away from the reasonable attitude leading to a fair division?

As rational choice theory is challenged in the setting of bargaining situations, let us, for a moment, put aside the postulate of individual rationality and even suspend the principle of individual independence, switching from open strategies to given determined behaviors. Typically, under an exogenous "strength relation"[9] establishing some hierarchy between i and j,[10] an asymmetric solution follows. The big one – landlord or dictator or leader – seizes everything or most of the pie and the small one – peasant, subject or follower – receives nothing or just leftovers. Alternatively, the happy scenario of fifty-fifty division could indeed be implemented, if i and j are two doves "by nature" or if a social rule of equality prevails. Be it asymmetric with the strong-weak relation or symmetric with the equality principle, the arisen solution does not appear as an equilibrium between independent individuals,[11] or even an agreement between autonomous persons: it is objectively determined, naturally given or socially imposed.

The principle of an exogenous force of some kind leads to interesting and effective results. But it overshadows abstract rationality: one would like to obtain the maximum but actually gets what is assigned to her/him by some psychological or sociological determination. It also oversteps Modern forms of liberty, individualistic independence or humanistic autonomy. And as we stated the problem of coordination in Modern terms, we have to consider solutions developed within the framework of Modernity. So we will first go back to the line of rationality with a more adapted or successful model of strategic bargaining, echoing Modern independence, before tackling the alternative line of axiomatic bargaining, echoing Modern autonomy. Before that, we have to develop the conceptual opposition between independence and autonomy, a relevant distinction proposed by Renaut (1989).

Independent individuals and autonomous persons as two depictions of human beings

a) A key notion for Modern social philosophy, individual independence has been especially developed by economic theory, both ontologically and methodologically. The point can be illustrated by the usual opposition between the depiction of the *homo oeconomicus*, consciously pulled by his/her own interest or oriented by the prospect of private advantages, and the portrayal of the *homo sociologicus*, unconsciously pushed or determined by "social forces" (Heap *et al.*, 1992, chapter 5).

To clarify the notion of "independence" and assess its importance from an economic point of view, let us first distinguish three economic concepts of individual independence and then see how these abstract elements are actualized in three basic economic models.

Individual independence essentially means independent determination of the individual choice (level 2); but this definition of the free choice relies on the independent setting of the individual goals (level 1) and leads to the full accomplishment of the individual action (level 3).

Level 1: the condition of individual independence. An independent individual freely defines his/her objectives or ends, formally represented by a preference relation on attainable situations, with no influence or injunction from the others or from the whole society. The independent individual turns into a rational decision maker if her/his preference relation is complete and transitive; but these constraints of totality and of consistency are formal logical requirements and not substantial social impositions. About the individualistic goal setting, one could speak of value independence.

Level 2: the core of individual independence. An independent individual freely chooses his/her action. *Lato sensu* – this means that the agent is not *hardly forced* to make a certain choice by another one: free individual decisions are non-coerced choices and free social relations are voluntary exchanges. *Stricto sensu* – this means that the choice of the agent is not *softly influenced* by the choice of another one. About independent decision determination, one could differentiate *weak* choice independence, i.e. without coercion, and of *strong* choice independence, i.e. without influence.

Level 3: the completion of individual independence. The action of an independent individual leads to the expected result. In doctrinal terms, one here moves from basic individualism to economic liberalism, adding the faith in social order to the principle of individual freedom thanks to market self-regulation. In theoretical terms, one here jumps from individual rationality to interindividual equilibrium, defined as a social situation of mutual compatibility between individual choices, or as a social state of general fulfillment of individual projects. About the individualistic action accomplishment, one could speak of independence achievement.

Basic models developed by modern and contemporary economics can be interpreted through this conceptual framework of individual independence. Indeed, the one individual economy, the Walrasian economy and non-cooperative games all include value independence as a given structural element (level 1) and independence accomplishment through the closing assumption of interindividual equilibrium (level 3). But the property of choice independence (level 2) is diversely displayed in the mentioned basic models of the economic society.

The one individual economy, also known as the Robinson Crusoe economy (Mas-Colell *et al.*, 1995, pp. 525–9), presents by definition a view of *absolute independence*, as the individual and social realities here perfectly coincide. There is no other one and no overhanging society to force or to influence Robinson's goals, decisions and achievements; there are only objective constraints of production and of time, weighing on his solipsistic utility maximization or rational decision-making.

The Walrasian economy displays price-taking individuals, a situation often based on, or justified by, the assumption of absence of market power for each of the agents (Berta *et al.*, 2012). The mediation of prices ensures the independence of each agent, through the strong and equal dependence of all agents on objective parameters given by the benevolent institution of the "auctioneer". The domination of A on B is then excluded, as far as it is substituted for the common imposition of prices on A and B. Finally, under a general normative interpretation (Rebeyrol, 1999), perfect competition may appear as an artificial construction aiming at a utopian society of independent Robinsons.

Expelled by perfect competition for all agents, strategic rationality prevails for all players in non-cooperative games and for at least one agent in imperfect competition. Two strategic behavioral patterns may be distinguished. The player *à la* Cournot takes the action of the other as a given element and then plays his/her best reply. Such a player is a follower, as his/her behavior is reactive and his/her action literally depends on the other's choice. The player *à la* Stackelberg catches the choice of the other as the reaction to his/her own action, which is structurally correct if the other plays as a follower. Such a player is a leader, as his/her behavior is pro-active and he/she operates a manipulation of the other. The leader-leader setting displays a disequilibrium (level 3) and the leader-follower setting presents a weak independence of the dominated player (level 2), but the follower-follower setting exhibits an equilibrium and a symmetric relation. So the game permitting the deepest independence (levels 1–2–3) for all players is the Cournot one, while the Bowley setting ends up in a "lose-lose" open war and while the Stackelberg setting institutes a definite domination.

Robinson's independence is obvious because of his loneliness, but individual independence is challenged in a society made of at least two individuals. Then the natural paradise is lost, but it may be artificially rebuilt following two structural lines. In the Walrasian framework, A's action s_A and B's action s_B are independent because they all depend on an external parameter P: $s_A = s_A(P)$ and $s_B = s_B(P)$. This is independence for each without any individual power: A and B depend on given prices. In the Cournotian framework, A's strategy and B's strategy are objectively interdependent; and mutual influences may cancel each other out: $s_A = s_A(s_B)$ and $s_B = s_B(s_A)$. That is independence for each through a balance of individual powers: A depends on B and B depends on A.

b) If the notion of independence has especially been developed by economic theory, the notion of autonomy has been promoted by other intellectual fields. One has to mention *social autonomy*, which is relevant for sociology and underlines that the social matter or whole is not reducible to its individual elements or components (Durkheim), echoing the "no bridge" statement of disjunction between the micro and the macro levels revealed by fallacies of composition in economics.[12] But one will here focus on *moral* and/or *political autonomy*, which is crucial for ethics and for politics, to name this ability of a free being (Kant) or of a free society (Rousseau) to obey the rules the entity chose for self-direction and self-government.

To show that the notion of autonomy should be acknowledged by economic theory, let us first show that autonomy is different from independence; and then argue that the structure of economic models and/or the solution of economic problems rely on some notion of autonomy.

It is possible to start considering that independence and autonomy are two different but close terms expressing the same idea of self-determination, as oppositely dependence and heteronomy both mean the operation of some external leverage. On one side, beyond self-determination, the notion of independence expands on the logical requirements of completeness and transitivity: an independent individual defines what he/she wants, entirely knows what he/she wants and is consistent about it. And on the other side, beyond self-determination, the notion of autonomy enlarges on the operation of an internal imposition: the entity as a sovereign, or rule maker, imposes the law on the entity as a subject, or rule taker. In other terms, while economic independence underlines formal *consistency*, moral or political autonomy highlights substantive *reflexivity* (Heap *et al.*, 1992, chapter 6). An independent individual, a rational being, defines and is defined by a proper preference relation; while an autonomous entity imposes its own law on itself.

The difference between autonomy and independence may furthermore be elaborated thanks to the classical distinction between two forms of freedom due to Berlin (1969). On one side, in the line of Constant or Stuart Mill, "negative liberty" means the absence of leverage by others and corresponds to individualistic independence, whose domain is defined by the question: "What is the area within which the subject . . . is or should be left to do or be what he is able to do or be, without interference by other persons?". On the other side, in the line of Rousseau or Hegel, "positive liberty" means the presence of self-mastery and is correlated with humanistic autonomy, whose operation is determined by the question: "What, or who, is the source of control . . . that can determine someone to do, or be, this rather than that?" (pp. 121–2).[13] Humanistic autonomy and individualistic independence are brought closer but also distinguished by Renaut (1989) as two Modern capacities. More precisely, the Modern swing is not monistic but dualistic: first theocratic societies of transcendent heteronomy are turned into democratic societies of human autonomy; then hierarchic societies of personal dependence are transformed into equal societies of individual independence.

So autonomy and independence are not two redundant notions. But why would not the notion of independence be sufficient to deal with economic issues? Why should the notion of autonomy be acknowledged in the economic field? Two justifications can be advanced.

Beyond the Robinson Crusoe economy, in a multiple agent economy such as the Walrasian society or as a non-cooperative game, basic elements of the model are not only preferences and technologies, but also rules of social interaction. The Walrasian *tâtonnement* is densely organized as an iterative process going from given prices to exchange plans and from market demand to price movements, under the major rule forbidding disequilibrium trading. Non-cooperative games are not defined by the sets of possible strategies for each player, the strategic interaction unfolding under the crucial rules establishing if agents play simultaneously or sequentially and if the game is one shot or repeated. Economic modeling focuses on individual action and on social equilibrium in these given social frameworks, but the *instituting* rules are also *instituted* rules. The obvious rule maker is the model designer, who can be considered either as a divine puppeteer if agents are denied the ability to make the common rules; or as a representative, a delegate of the body of agents/citizens making the ultimate and prior decision on the common rules, according to a capacity of political autonomy that would precede the economic interaction.

The notion of autonomy thus lies in the structure of multiple agent economic models; but it is also relevant to transcend some limitations of the rational behavior of the independent individual, who knows external or objective constraints but is not capable of self-restriction and of intersubjective action. Such a rational individual is able to make an independent choice in the non-cooperative framework where the social situation r_{ij} is the emerging result of independent actions: $r_{ij} = f(s_i; s_j)$.

But this independent agent is not equipped to conclude with the other a joint choice in the cooperative framework where the social situation r_{ij} is the expression of a common agreement: $r_{ij} = a_{ij}$. The making of such a joint decision requires the ability of self-restriction of each individualistic interest and an openness to the other an independent is unable to. Moral autonomy is needed to oblige oneself not to be a blind maximizer or a "rational fool" (Sen); and political autonomy is required for the notion of common interest or of public good to prevail as the general will.

Strategic models of bargaining: independent individuals may generate an equilibrium

In the field of bargaining theory, Rubinstein's works in the 1980s are definitely noteworthy. In his 1982 seminal paper, he proposes a proper strategic game that displays a "relevant" equilibrium, identified to an agreement, for the bargaining problem. This is a first hit: taking up the challenge of accurately dealing with bargaining situations under the assumption of non-cooperative rationality, strategic models rise as legitimate alternatives to pre-existing axiomatic models. And in his 1986 paper, co-authored with Binmore and Wolinsky, the coincidence between the Rubinstein equilibrium and the Nash solution is obtained, when players are patient. That is a second hit: strategic models claim the ability to "found" or to justify axiomatic models, achieving the essential objective of the Nash program.[14]

Let's quickly describe the game. First round ($t = 0$): i proposes (x_0; $1\text{-}x_0$) as a division of the pie. Then j has two options: if (s)he accepts it, there is an agreement, the game is over and the deal is implemented; if (s)he refuses it, there is no agreement and the game goes on. Second round ($t = 1$): that is now j's turn to make an alternative offer (x_1; $1\text{-}x_1$) that i can accept or refuse. Moreover, time passing, there is a discount factor λ so if i accepts the offer (s)he would get λx_1 and j would get $\lambda(1\text{-}x_1)$. If i refuses j's offer, the game goes on with a new proposition made by i, (x_2; $1\text{-}x_2$), that would give $\lambda^2 x_2$ to i and $\lambda^2(1\text{-}x_2)$ to j if j accepts it, and so on. . . . The number of possible rounds is not limited. If i and j never agree, the pie vanishes so the shares are (0; 0).

Such a sequential game of alternate offers is accurately represented in extensive form (by a tree). Information is complete and perfect. The horizon is infinite and payoffs are discounted. Solved by backwards induction, the Rubinstein game displays ($1/(1+\lambda)$; $\lambda/(1+\lambda)$) as the strategic equilibrium, obtained from the first round. If the discount rate vanishes ($\lambda \rightarrow 1$), then the 50–50 split emerges as the limit equilibrium of the game!

The assumption of complete and perfect information may be justified for the study of the ideal case[15] but it basically expresses (and also appeases) a general tension (and a possible contradiction) between the operation of one's rationality and the independence of the other. On the one side, one's rationality requires some transparency, as one needs to know the result of each of her/his options to define her/his optimal decision. But such a result also depends on the other's choice in a strategic one-to-one relation. On the other side, the recognition of the other's freedom should imply her/his opacity for oneself: your independence is a source of uncertainty for me and that could blur the determination of my rational decision.

Under the assumption of strategic rationality, the other is not treated as another person by oneself, but as a means or an obstacle that has to be controlled, not by force (it is independent) but by prediction (its choice has to be grasped by anticipation).[16] The only way to respect the other as a decision maker (the other acknowledged as a subject) and to make one's rational operation possible (the other taken as an object) is to give both players all information required, and that means "a lot of" knowledge, about the structure of the game and about the type of behavior of the other. Generally speaking, the taming of uncertainty is founded in non-cooperative game theory on the assumption of common knowledge, which postulates that everybody is rational and that everybody knows this about everybody else, and so on. . . .

But this abstract strategic rationality has to be made explicit by the specific way each agent seizes or captures the other's behavior. As the type of conjecture about the other depends on the structure of the game, the determination of these specific conjectures is framed by (and has to be consistent with) the rules of the considered game. Indeed, the *objectification* of the other may be operated through the *substantive capture* of her/his action (conjecture *à la* Cournot in a simultaneous game or for a follower in a sequential game) or through the *procedural capture* of her/his reactive rule of decision (conjecture *à la* Stackelberg for a leader in a sequential game).[17] In the case of the Rubinstein (alternate and transparent) game, the solution is found thanks to a backwards induction procedure which is here a reverse cascade of alternatively anticipated best replies: I can guess what would be your optimal move at the last step n (and you know it) so I can decide on my optimal move at the last but one step n-1 (and you can guess it) so I can guess what would be your optimal move at step n-2 (and you know it), and so on till the first step. . . .

Rational players interact under structural rules of the game that are given to them. There is no prior game justifying or explaining the prevalence of the set of rules at work based on some previous strategic interaction, otherwise an infinite regression would be triggered. The rules of the game, and thus also the related types of rational behavior and therefore finally the obtained equilibria, are decided by the model designer. The players are granted with full strategic abilities but denied any capacity of "political autonomy", as the rules of the game are given to them, as *heteronomous* subjects or "law takers", by the sovereign model maker. And it is impossible to say that the model designer "represents" the agents, as the capability to decide on common rules is very different from the capability to make independent choices. So the model maker is not the passive observer of the story or the faithful representative of the protagonists: setting the scene in such a way that both rational agents may operate and that a nice equilibrium would rise, (s)he is rather an active puppeteer. . . .

First, under the strong assumption of complete and perfect information (already commented), the smartly built model enables the smooth operation of complex rational computations *à la* Stackelberg that are organized by and consistent with the sequential structure of the game.

Second, the assumption of an infinite horizon, even if questionable,[18] enables to avoid the arbitrariness tied to the equilibrium obtained in finite horizons, which too strongly depends on the exogenous number of steps and on the given identity of the player making the last move.

Third, the assumption of a discount factor, which may be defensible for appropriateness reasons,[19] prompts impatient players to quickly agree and enable the getting of a balanced equilibrium,[20] which has later been proven as asymptotically similar to the Nash solution.

So the accomplished "tour de force" in Rubinstein's path-breaking paper is not due to resourceful players at work, but to a shrewd theorist who proved his ability to design a game structure determining a relevant solution as an equilibrium emerging from the strategic interaction of non-cooperative rational agents embedded in a structure given to them: he is the rule maker and they are the rule takers. . . .

Axiomatic models of bargaining: autonomous persons reach an agreement

In strategic models, non-cooperative players are independent decision makers under rules respected by them and chosen by the model designer. In axiomatic models, the status of players is not as clear and may be clarified through the way the model maker operates. In his 1950 ground-breaking paper, Nash picks a set of axioms and mathematically determines the only solution respecting all these assumptions.

How can the individuals be related to the story? What could i's and j's parts be in the play? Two different answers are possible. . . .

The usual interpretation develops the operation of the Nash program and echoes the working of the second theorem of welfare economics.[21] It states that Nash's solution expresses some ideal social solution first developed as a thought experiment by a theorist. If this vision of the social good is submitted to a legislator that adheres to this ideal, this law maker would subsequently wonder how to implement it in a society of individualistic agents. Here the support of coinciding strategic models would be absolutely necessary, to reveal which rules the social planner should establish to let rational agents generate this ideal situation as an emerging strategic equilibrium under these rules of the game.

An alternative interpretation is possible. Nash's solution is the synthetic solution deriving from "reasonable" principles chosen by a theorist who can be seen as the representative of a set of citizens or cooperative agents who would (s)elect the same reasonable principles and consequently adhere to the same synthetic solution. Here the support of coinciding strategic models is not necessary, as it would make sense for autonomous persons to respect and apply the rules they freely chose, and even to enforce them by force if some individualistic free rider tries to evade these laws.

This duality of interpretations is not proper to the specific class of bargaining models, as it corresponds to a general divide between two visions of cooperative game theory (henceforth: CGT) and of the way it is related to non-cooperative game theory (henceforth: NCGT).

Following Harsanyi's definitions,[22] there is no binding agreement in NCGT, so contracts need to be self-enforceable to be fulfilled; while there are binding agreements in CGT, so contracts can be enforced by a superior agency. Here no explicit difference between non-cooperative players and cooperative players is put forward to differentiate the two kinds of games.

Following Moulin's views,[23] the difference between NCGT and CGT could be rooted in two alternative conceptions of the players. In NCGT, players are independent through the strategic freedom granted to each of them. But this freedom of *independence* for the other causes the situation of uncertainty for the one, and vice versa. So there may be a mutual interest for the players to equally renounce their individual freedom, signing a binding agreement canceling the mutual uncertainty and promoting their common interest.[24] Such CGT players basically exercise a capacity, and a freedom, of *autonomy*.

In some way, CGT displays binding agreements in both the Harsanyi line and the Moulin line, but agreements are respected (and contracts are fulfilled) because of an exogenous enforcement agency policing rational players in the first case and, in the second case, thanks to an endogenous enforcement by cooperative players following their commitments and fulfilling their duties.

What could this alternative interpretation in terms of autonomous players reveal in the specific case of the axiomatic models of bargaining? If the jump is assumed from rational agents to reasonable persons, these cooperative players agree to some conditions their "social contract" should respect, the set of chosen axioms defining a solution that determines the content of the common *autonomous* choice made by the partners. Substituting strategic interdependence for some form of *intersubjectivity* or *social association*, it is possible to display several forms of (vertical or horizontal) associations depending on the specific content of each solution.

In the vertical mode of association, both agents decide to together constitute a community. Here the agreement is found thanks to the pursuit of some superior interest.[25] This social good is defined by the Utilitarian sum, the addition u_i+u_j, when interpersonal comparisons of utilities are allowed; or alternatively by the Nash product, the multiplication $(u_i - \underline{u}_i)(u_j - \underline{u}_j)$, when such comparisons are excluded. In the case of the Utilitarian solution, the conversion of the strategic player to the Utilitarian good goes deep, as far as the prevalence of the superior interest over each individual concern may legitimize an individual sacrifice. In the case of the Nash solution, the positivity of the Nash product ensures that i and j gain[26] together; and the notion of social good is not as substantial since the notion (to be maximized) of "social utility" is replaced by the notion of mutual improvement area or consensus territory.

In the horizontal mode of association, the social compact implies a mutual recognition without establishing some transcendent community. Here the agreement is found thanks to the resort to some notion of commutative justice. The demand for justice may be high, if any element of bargaining power is put aside for an unconditional notion of equality to prevail, as for the Egalitarian solution: $u_i - \underline{u}_i = u_j - \underline{u}_j$. But the content of reciprocity may also be low, if some balance of power is acknowledged to determine a conditional equitable deal, as for the Kalai-Smorodinsky solution (what one obtains relative to the maximum she/he can claim is equal to what the other obtains relative to the maximum she/he can claim): $(u_i - \underline{u}_i)/(u_{imax} - \underline{u}_i) = (u_j - \underline{u}_j)/(u_{jmax} - \underline{u}_j)$.

The vertical mode of association displays the working of a *cooperation* of some sort, as oneself and the other are the equal citizens of the community they decide to build. The horizontal mode of association shows the operation of a *coordination* of some sort, as oneself and the other stay separate but find a reasonable way to work out their disagreement through a mutual recognition, one accepting that the other is another subject with rights and claims as legitimate as one's rights and claims.

Conclusion

In the example of the pie to be shared, the 50–50 split emerges as one of the ways to maximize the aggregate utility (one Utilitarian optimum), as the way to maximize the area of consensus (the Nash solution), as the highest equal utility gain for each (the Egalitarian solution) and as the Pareto optimum respecting the acknowledged proportionate balance of power (the Kalai-Smorodinsky solution). This striking and confusing merging may suggest that dividing a pie is more than getting to a division of it. Against the consequentialist view typical of mainstream economics,[27] it may be asserted that the result is not what only matters. The way the solution is obtained counts: in particular, the mere fact of agreeing makes sense. When peace is made, one certainly gets the objective advantages of the agreement, but peace making also transforms the vision of the other, from the portrayal of an opponent into the picture of a partner.

This reflection may also concern the coincidence between strategic equilibria and cooperative solutions or agreements.[28] Comparing quantitative results is certainly legitimate and possibly fruitful, but the qualitative specificities of each model, expressed by the types of behavior and the kinds of interaction, cannot be underestimated or overshadowed. Getting an identification of results between a cooperative solution and a non-cooperative equilibrium may condition but does not ensure the success of an "implementation" of the cooperative solution and, moreover, does not mean that it is "founded", even if it could be said that it is "sustained", by the non-cooperative equilibrium. Two different stories leading to the same end are definitely not the same story. . . .

Notes

1 This case is utility free but actually corresponds to the situation of transferable utility.
2 An agreement may be Pareto-optimal ($\alpha + \beta = 1$) or not ($\alpha + \beta < 1$); and there is no agreement if $\alpha + \beta > 1$.
3 There is no such thing as an agreement without definite terms: an indeterminate deal is no deal at all.

4 The Appendix justifies the choice of the Hawk-Dove Game, and not of the Battle of the Sexes Game, as the relevant framework displaying the bargaining problem. It also reminds that the Chicken Game and the Prisoner's Dilemma Game are two possible versions of the Hawk-Dove Game.
5 As Osborne (2000) puts it (p. 389): "a player may be deterred from exploiting her short-term advantage by the 'threat' of 'punishment' that reduces her long-term payoff". The emergence of cooperation is often studied in the repeated Prisoner's Dilemma Game: see Kreps et al. (1982). For models of the repeated HDG, applied to contests between animals, see Houston and McNamara (1991).
6 In case of hawkish sparrows.
7 In case of dovish sparrows.
8 The failure of cooperation does not stem from the uncertainty about the other's behavior: if one (i) is absolutely convinced that the other (j) plays D ($p_{ji} = 0$), then one rationally decides to play H: a cooperative gesture from the other is not seen as a chance to reciprocate fairness, but as an opportunity to exploit naivety.
9 See Piccione and Rubinstein (2007).
10 Because of psychological reasons: one is bad-tempered and the other is good-natured; or because of sociological reasons: one is socially higher than the other.
11 The sequential version of the Hawk-Dove Game cannot properly represent objective domination, as the strategic advantage of the first player (i) does not annihilate the strategic independence of the second one (j). Actually i definitely plays H (i would get 0 playing D as j would reply by H), but then j's reply is indeterminate as (s)he obtains 0 playing H or D; so i hopes to get 1 but may obtain 0. Strategic manipulation is not social control.
12 Major examples include the Smithian invisible hand, the Marxian tendency of the rate of profit to fall and the Keynesian Kaldor-Kalecki principle.
13 See Carter (2016) for a full presentation of "positive and negative liberty".
14 The so called "Nash program" (Rubinstein), aiming at "founding" cooperative solutions as non-cooperative equilibria, was opened in Nash's demand game (1953).
15 See Guerrien (1993, pp. 21–2).
16 The only difference between playing against nature and playing against the other is that the state of nature does not depend on my action, while the other's strategy is based on her/his expectation about my strategy.
17 The objectification of nature takes the typical form of a probabilistic capture.
18 When would a possible disagreement be recorded in an endless model? See Giraud (2000, pp, 202–3).
19 A persisting strike is indeed costly to employees and employers.
20 If the introduction of different discount factors ($\lambda_i \neq \lambda_j$) is analytically manageable, the removal or neutralization of any discount factor ($\lambda_i = \lambda_j = 1$) raises serious analytical difficulties.
21 In the Edgeworth box, let A be the Pareto optimum the planner wants to achieve. The competitive (i.e. non-strategic) implementation of A rests on the definition of the line tangent to i's and j's indifference curves going through A as the equilibrium budget line. Thus the initial endowment location has to be shifted somewhere on this line. Through such an appropriate restructuring of initial endowments (state intervention), followed by the play of perfect competition (market procedure), A would be generated as a Walrasian equilibrium.
22 Harsanyi (1966). See also Aumann (1987).
23 Moulin (1981). See also Lengaigne (2004).
24 The prisoner's dilemma provides a crystal clear illustration of this social pattern. It is often said that this suboptimal equilibrium profile displays a "cooperation failure"; but it is alternatively possible to argue that it displays a failure of the strategic paradigm that can be overcome thanks to cooperation by commitment.

25 The maximization of this social good (the Utilitarian sum or the Nash product) also determines its optimal distribution (u_i* and u_j*). So the making of the agreement involves some form of distributive justice.
26 Or lose together. But that case is economically irrelevant.
27 The operation of rational choice (the optimal option leads to the best possible result), the argument of the invisible hand (the self-interested behaviors lead to the social good) and the instrumentalist methodology (the best hypotheses lead to the realistic conclusions) all display a consequentialist structure.
28 As pursued with the "Nash program", but also with game theoretic "foundations" of competitive equilibria à la Walras thanks to the core à la Edgeworth or to imperfectly competitive equilibria à la Cournot. See Mas Colell *et al.* (1995, chapter 18).

Bibliography

Aumann, R. (1987) 'Game theory', in J. Eatwell, M. Milgate and P. Newman (eds.) *The New Palgrave*, London: Palgrave Macmillan, 460–82.

Berlin, I. (1969) 'Two concepts of liberty', in *Four Essays on Liberty*, London: Oxford University Press, 118–72. Reprinted in H. Hardy (ed.) (2002) *Liberty*, Oxford: Oxford University Press.

Berta, N., Julien, L.A. and Tricou, F. (2012) 'On perfect competition: Definitions, usages and foundations', *Cahiers d'Economie Politique/Papers in Political Economy*, 63: 7–24.

Binmore, K., Rubinstein, A. and Wolinsky, A. (1986) 'The Nash bargaining solution and economic modeling', *Rand Journal of Economics*, 17: 176–88.

Carter, I. (2016) 'Positive and negative liberty', *The Stanford Encyclopedia of Philosophy* (Fall 2016 Edition), Edward N. Zalta (ed.), URL = <https://plato.stanford.edu/archives/fall2016/entries/liberty-positive-negative/>.

Giraud, G. (2000) *La théorie des jeux*, Paris: Champs Université, Flammarion.

Guerrien, B. (1993) *La théorie des jeux*, Paris: Economie Poche, Economica.

Harsanyi, J.C. (1966) 'A general theory of rational behavior in game situations', *Econometrica*, 34(3): 613–34.

Heap, S.H., Hollis, M., Lyons, B., Sugden, R. and Weale A. (1992) *The theory of choice: A critical guide*, Oxford and Cambridge: Wiley-Blackwell.

Houston, A.I. and McNamara, J.M. (1991) 'Evolutionarily stable strategies in the repeated hawk-dove game', *Behavioral Ecology*, 2(3): 219–27.

Kalai, E. (1977) 'Proportional solutions to bargaining situations: Interpersonal utility comparisons', *Econometrica*, 45: 1623–30.

Kalai, E. and Smorodinsky, M. (1975) 'Other solutions to Nash's bargaining problem', *Econometrica*, 43: 513–18.

Kreps, D.M., Milgrom, P., Roberts, J. and Wilson, R. (1982) 'Rational cooperation in the finitely repeated prisoners' dilemma', *Journal of Economic Theory*, 27(2): 245–52.

Lengaigne, B. (2004) 'Nash: changement de programme?' *Revue d'économie politique*, 114(5): 637–62.

Mas-Colell, A., Whinston, M.D. and Green, J.R. (1995) *Microeconomic theory*, New York and Oxford: Oxford Student Edition.

Maynard Smith, J. and Price, G.R. (1973) 'The logic of animal conflict', *Nature*, 246: 15–18.

Moulin, H. (1981) *Théorie des jeux pour l'économie et la politique*, Paris: Hermann. Trans. (1986) *Game theory for the social sciences*, New York: New York University Press.

Nash, J.F. (1950) 'The bargaining problem', *Econometrica*, 18: 155–62.

Nash, J.F. (1953) 'Two person cooperative games', *Econometrica*, 21: 128–40.
Osborne, M.J. (2000) *An introduction to game theory*, Oxford: Oxford University Press.
Piccione, M. and Rubinstein, A. (2007) 'Equilibrium in the jungle', *The Economic Journal*, 117: 883–96.
Rebeyrol, A. (1999) *La pensée économique de Walras*, Paris: Théories économiques, Dunod.
Renaut, A. (1989) *L'ère de l'individu*, Paris: Bibliothèque des idées, NRF, Gallimard. Trans. (1997) *The era of the individual*, Princeton, NJ: Princeton University Press.
Rubinstein, A. (1982) 'Perfect equilibrium in a bargaining model', *Econometrica*, 50: 97–109.

Appendix

Cooperation in the Hawk-Dove Game and related strategic settings

a) The bargaining setting, the Hawk-Dove Game (HDG) and the Battle of the Sexes Game (BSG).

As mentioned in the introduction, the bargaining setting rests on a situation of mixed interests that displays an issue of "*conflicting (interest) coordination*" formally expressed by the multiplicity of Pareto optima, a problem illustrated by the duality of opposite Pareto Nash equilibria in the BSG. So why not select that generic game, instead of the HDG, as the relevant simple version of the bargaining problem? To answer this question, let's compare the two games (Tables 20.4 and 20.5):

Considering the HDG, it obviously appears that, for i and for j, H is the aggressive or non-cooperative strategy and D is the peaceful or cooperative strategy. Similar qualifications may be applied to the BSG, stating that the aggressive strategies are F for h and O for w and that the peaceful strategies are and O for h and F for w.

As a consequence, trying to match these types of games with the bargaining setting, it clearly appears firstly that the disagreement points are FO and HH,

Table 20.4 The basic Battle of the Sexes Game

h's strategies/w's strategies	*Opera*	*Football*
Football	(1; 1)	(3; 2)
Opera	(2; 3)	(0; 0)

Table 20.5 The basic Hawk-Dove Game

i's strategies/j's strategies	*Hawk*	*Dove*
Hawk	(0; 0)	(1; 0)
Dove	(0; 1)	(½; ½)

secondly that the unbalanced agreement points are OO plus FF and DH plus HD. But if DD can be seen as a balanced agreement point, OF is a dramatic general failure, even worse than FO.

So the HDG actually displays a simple but somehow rich structure of the bargaining problem, with a (suboptimal) disagreement point and three optimal conceivable agreement points: there are two polar and one intermediate or fair possible settlements. On the contrary, the BSG just allows two opposite agreement points and no balanced possible settlement (such as the 50–50 split).

Effective cooperation, understood as a reasonable (fair and optimal) situation for all, is abstractly possible in the HDG, but simply inconceivable in the BS one shot Game. Playing cooperative (D) is risky but meaningful in the HDG: it leads to exploitation (DH) if the other is opportunistic, but to mutual cooperation (DD) if the other also is cooperative: cooperation as a fair deal, a semi-win/semi-win situation (like a medium price agreed on in an isolated bilateral exchange) is accessible. But playing cooperative (F for w and O for h) does not make any sense in the BSG: it leads either to accepted submissiveness or "voluntary servitude" if the other is opportunistic, or to a common disaster if the other also is cooperative: mutual cooperation is downgraded to a lose-lose situation.

In a nutshell, the HDG is preferable to the BSG as a simple game displaying the structure of the bargaining problem, since it includes an optimal and fair situation that may be implemented or rationalized as the reasonable solution. The selection of such a game does not of course ensure that cooperation will be effective, but simply makes it meaningful.

Moreover, while the achievement of cooperation is facilitated as one makes it a reasonable option, the easiness of its emergence with time is here excluded as one does not consider and lean on the repetition of the game, which allows a reasonable solution in the BSG with alternate mutual choices such as h and w together enjoy opera this week and football next week.

b) The Hawk-Dove Game (HDG), the Chicken Game (CG) and the Prisoner's Dilemma Game (PDG).

Proposed by Maynard Smith and Price (1973) to explain the "logic of animal conflict", the HDG involves two parameters: the value of the contested resource (V) and the cost of an escalated fight (C). The structure of the game follows:

When C > V, the HDG turns into the CG, with DH and HD as the two opposite Nash equilibria: the HDG here comes closer to the BSG with its two domination

Table 20.6 The original Hawk-Dove Game

i's strategies/j's strategies	*Hawk*	*Dove*
Hawk	((V-C)/2; (V-C)/2)	(V; 0)
Dove	(0; V)	(V/2; V/2)

optimal equilibria; but a major difference remains, as a meaningful cooperative situation is displayed (DD is here Pareto-optimal).

When C < V, the HDG turns into the PDG, with HH as the suboptimal equilibrium, as the cooperative situation DD here dominates the equilibrium point HH.

When C = V, the HDG generates three equilibria: HH, DH and HD. The selection of this specification (with V = C = 1 in the simplest version) is relevant, as it is intermediate and actually displays a complete synthesis of the two types of anticoordination patterns here at stake: "conflicting (interest) coordination" with DH and HD as opposite equilibria and "cooperation failure" with HH as a bad equilibrium.

Index

For Product Safety Concerns and Information please contact our
EU representative GPSR@taylorandfrancis.com Taylor & Francis
Verlag GmbH, Kaufingerstraße 24, 80331 München, Germany